JOHN OF GAUNT

JOHN OF GAUNT

The Exercise of Princely Power in Fourteenth-Century Europe

Anthony Goodman

Longman

Longman Group UK Limited,
Longman House, Burnt Mill,
Harlow, Essex CM20 2JE, England
and Associated Companies throughout the world.

First published 1992

British Library Cataloguing-in-Publication Data

A catalogue record for this book is available from the British Library

Cased ISBN 0 582 50218 7
Paper ISBN 0 582 09813 0

Transferred to digital print on demand, 2002
Printed & Bound by Antony Rowe Ltd, Eastbourne

Contents

List of Maps and
Genealogical Tables

Maps

Tables

List of Abbreviations

A.C.	Galbraith, V.H., ed. (1970) *The Anonimalle Chronicle 1333 to 1381*, Manchester University Press
A.C.A.	*Archivo de la Corona de Aragon*, Barcelona
A.N.	*Archives Nationales*, Paris
Annales	Riley, H.T., ed. (1866) *Johannis de Trokelowe . . . Chronica et Annales*, Rolls ser., London
B.I.H.R.	*Bulletin of the Institute of Historical Research*
B.J.R.L.	*Bulletin of the John Rylands Library*
B.L.	British Library
B.R.U.C.	Emden, A.B., ed. (1963) *A Biographical Register of the University of Cambridge to 1500*, Cambridge
B.R.U.O.	Emden, A.B., ed.(1957–9) *A Biographical Register of the University of Oxford to 1500*, 3 vols, Oxford
C.A.	Thompson, E.M., ed. (1874) *Chronicon Angliae*, Rolls ser., London
C.C.C.	Corpus Christi College, Oxford
C.C.R.	Calendar of Close Rolls
C.E.P.R.	Bliss, W.H. *et al.* (eds) *Calendar of Entries in the Papal Registers relating to Great Britain and Ireland*, H.M.S.O., London. 1896: *Petitions to the Pope*, Vol. 1, 1342–1419; 1897: *Papal Letters*, Vol. 3, 1342–1362; 1902: ibid., Vol. 4, 1362–1404; 1904: ibid., Vol. 5, 1396–1404
C.F.R.	*Calendar of Fine Rolls*

C.H.K.	Lumby, J.R., ed. (1895) *Chronicon Henrici Knighton*, Vol. 2, Rolls ser., London
C.I.P.M.	*Calendars of Inquisitions Post Mortem*, 1970–4, Vols 15–16. H.M.S.O., London
C.P.	C[okayne], G.E., new edn Gibbs, V. *et al.* (1910–59) *The Complete Peerage of England, Scotland, Ireland and Great Britain and the United Kingdom*, 13 vols, London
C.P.R.	*Calendar of Patent Rolls*
C.Q.P.V.	Luce, S., ed. (1892) *Chronique des quatre premiers Valois (1327–1393)*, Société de l'histoire de France, Paris
C.R.C.	Cayetano Rosell, D., ed. (1919) *Crónicas de los reyes de Castilla*, Vols 1 and 2, Biblioteca de Autores Españoles, Madrid
D.C.	Perroy, E., ed. (1933) *The Diplomatic Correspondence of Richard II*, Camden 3rd series, Vol. 48, London
E.H.R.	*English Historical Review*
Eulogium	Haydon, F.S., ed. (1863) *Eulogium historiarum sive temporis*, Vol. 3, Rolls series, London
Foedera	*Foedera, conventiones, litterae* . . . [1101–1654] ed. T. Rymer (1704–35), 20 vols, London; [1069–1383] ed. A. Clarke, F. Holbrooke and J. Caley (1816–69), 4 vols in 7 parts, London
F.Z.	Shirley, W.W.H., ed. (1858) *Fasciculi Zizaniorum*, Rolls series, London
G.A.	Riley, H.T., ed. (1867–8) *Gesta Abbatum Monasterii Sancti Albani*, 3 vols, Rolls series, London
H.A.	Walsingham, T., ed. H.T. Riley (1863–4) *Historia Anglicana*, 2 vols, Rolls series, London
H.M.C.	Historical Manuscripts Commission
J.B.S.	*Journal of British Studies*
J.G.R. 1372–6	Armitage-Smith, S., ed. (1911) *John of Gaunt's Register*, 2 vols, Camden 3rd series, Vols xx–xxi, London
J.G.R. 1379–1383	Lodge, E. C. and Somerville, R., eds (1937) *John of Gaunt's Register, 1379–1383*, Camden 3rd series, Vols lvi–lvii, London
J.M.H.	*Journal of Medieval History*
L.B.	Barckhausen, H., ed. (1867) *Livre des Bouillons*, Archives municipales de Bordeaux, Vol 1, Bordeaux
P.R.O.	Public Record Office

R.P.	*Rotuli Parliamentorum*, 1783, 4 vols, London
R.S.	(1819) Rotuli Scotiae, 2 vols, London
St Denys	Bellaguet, M.L., ed. (1839–40) *Chronique du religieux de Saint-Denys*, 2 vols, Paris
Test. Ebor.	*Testamenta Eboracensia*, Vol. 1, Surtees Society, 1836
V.C.H.	*The Victoria History of the Counties of England*
V.R.S.	Stow, G.B., ed. (1977) *Historia Vitae et Regni Ricardi Secundi*, University of Pennsylvania Press
W.C.	Hector, L.C. and Harvey, B.F., eds (1982) *The Westminster Chronicle 1381–1394*, Clarendon Press, Oxford

Preface

The spur to my interest in trying to discover the historic John of Gaunt was a normal one – his speech in *King Richard II* which has become one of the best-loved in the English language, 'Methinks I am a prophet new inspir'd . . .'. When I was an undergraduate I was privileged to sight the real Gaunt, when reading the old Oxford Special Subject on Richard II under the eagle eye of the late Bruce McFarlane. Each week he would hand out opaque passages from the chronicles of Thomas Walsingham for David Morgan or myself to comment on, and when we had done so he would reveal exciting glimpses of the political world obfuscated by that tiresome monk.

In writing this book, I owe thanks to the help and encouragement of many friends and colleagues. Jackie Goodman, my wife, did most of the research on which Chapter Two is based, when she was a reader in the Huntington Library, San Marino, California. References were given to me by Dr Michael Bennett, Professor Al Brown, Dr Alan Cameron, Professor Jim Gillespie, Dr Chris Given-Wilson, Dr Jeremy Goldberg, Dr Gerald Harriss, Professor Michael Jones, Dr Michael R. Jones, Ms Ann Kettle, Dr P. Lindley, Professor José Enrique López de Coca, Dr Alison McHardy, Dr Philip Morgan, Professor Nick Orme, Dr John Palmer, Mrs Elizabeth Peel, Dr Brian Powell, Dr Peter Rycraft, Dr Nigel Saul, Dr Peter Symms and Dr Simon Walker.

I owe particular thanks to Michael Bennett for drawing my attention to the Gaunt references in the Selby Abbey Cartulary; to Chris Given-Wilson for allowing me to use his calendar of the

Charter Rolls; to Professor Ralph Griffiths for giving me transcripts of a document in the Folger Library, Washington, and of one in the Somerset Record Office; to Dr Richard Rose for his transcript of a royal Privy Seal letter in Bishop Appleby of Carlisle's Register, and for helping to decipher some inadequate photocopies of Glynde Place MSS; to Professor González Jiménez for his illuminating transcripts from the Archivo Municipal of Carmona; to Simon Walker for alerting me to the Sherley indenture. The late James Sherborne, from whom I anticipated pithy comments on this book, generously shared his ideas about the financing of the 1386 expedition.

I have benefited from the stimulating comments (and, in some cases, bibliographical advice) of Professor Barrie Dobson, Professor Ken Fowler, Professor Angus MacKay, Professor George Stow, Dr John Thomson, Professor Anthony Tuck and Dr Selby Whittingham, who generously allowed me to read his mother's fascinating paper on early portraits of Gaunt. Ken Fowler, Chris Given-Wilson, Michael Jones, Angus MacKay and John Thomson undertook the chore of each reading a chapter draft.

I am unable to record individually the many debts I owe to archivists and librarians; I am grateful to Dr David Smith, director of the Borthwick Institute, York, for a particular favour. I have been helped by the staff of Edinburgh University Library, the National Library of Scotland, the Public Record Office, the British Library and the Institute of Historical Research. I was admitted without demur to the Archives Nationales and made to feel at home at the Archivo de la Corona de Aragon. The grant of a Fletcher Jones Fellowship by the Huntington Library gave me access to some unexpected Lancastrian material. The staff of various county record offices have cheerfully dealt with my enquiries and requests – at Cheshire, Cumbria, Lancashire, Leicestershire, Lincolnshire, Norfolk, Northumberland and Nottinghamshire Record Offices and at the Archives Department of Leeds City Council.

As an aspiring biographer of Gaunt, I have worked in the shadow of Sydney Armitage-Smith's *John of Gaunt* (1904); over the years my admiration for his deep knowledge and good sense has increased. I am conscious of the topics I have failed to cover fully. Proper consideration of the Lancastrian estates in itself would require more than one dissertation. I abandoned much of the material I had accumulated on Gaunt's affinity on hearing that Simon Walker was devoting a thesis to the subject; his *The Lancastrian Affinity* (Oxford, 1990) came out too late for me to make use of it.

A few technical points need to be made. I have assumed throughout that Gaunt was at the places on the dates given in his charters and letters. This was not always the case, but it was generally so. I have not given references to Gaunt's will: I have used the text printed in volume one of *Testamenta Eboracensia* and have consulted this text in Bishop Buckingham's Register. The references given to citations from Froissart's *Chronicles* are throughout to Kervyn de Lettenhove's edition. Where quotations from the *Chronicles* are made in the text in translation, they are taken, unreferenced, and sometimes with minor amendments, from Thomas Johnes's vigorous nineteenth-century version.

Finally, I owe thanks to Ms Rachel Hawkes for typing early chapter drafts and to Mrs Gloria Ketchin for undertaking two chapters; the bulk of the manuscript was typed with great skill and patience by Mrs Doris Williamson. This book would not have been completed without my wife's help: she urged me on whenever I was discouraged and coped stoically with the often overbearing presence of Gaunt in our lives. My daughter Emma came to my rescue in the final stages, when I was feeling ill.

For my daughter Emma

Chapter One

The Inheritance of Edward III and Richard II

Edward III (reigned 1327–77) was, for several centuries, as David Morgan has pointed out, regarded as one of the greatest, if not the greatest, of England's medieval kings. Recent works have gone some way to resuscitating this high reputation.[1] Edward's achievements and failures need to be put in the context of his family's (the Plantagenets) rule and their aims, methods and problems back to the later twelfth century. Like the other English kings of the fourteenth century, Edward was a direct descendant of Henry Plantagenet (d. 1189), who, already count of Anjou and duke of both Normandy and Aquitaine, inherited the kingdom of England in 1154. Henry II notably extended royal power in the British Isles. He received oaths of homage from Welsh princes (not unprecedently), as well as the customary ones from Norman lords whose rule was established in the Marches of Wales. Invading Ireland in 1171, he compelled Irish kings, and the Anglo-Norman lords who had recently carved out lordships, to acknowledge his overlordship. He also reserved areas for direct royal rule. In 1174 William the Lion, king of Scots, captured in battle, assented to Henry's feudal superiority over himself and his kingdom. Henry's lordships and claims to overlordship made up the most powerful entity in Christendom, 'the Angevin empire', including principalities stretching from the Cheviot Hills to the Pyrenees over which Henry tried to impose his own rule.

In this 'empire' England occupied a crucial role, if not, in some respects, the central role. Though it gave Henry his most exalted title, England was one among several of his great principalities. Normandy

1

was geographically the centre of empire: the speech and lifestyle of his court and barons were predominantly Norman; they and the higher clergy shared the religious and secular culture of northern France. Henry and his sons were often to be found in France.

However, the kingdom of England was the hinge on which the Plantagenet family's hegemony in the British Isles turned. Its resources sustained their rule in France. Rapidly expanding English agrarian wealth was augmented by the production of high-grade wool, large amounts of which were exported to the looms of Flanders: a situation which in turn served to stimulate the rise of commercial native cloth production. These developments were factors in the growing dominance of a wealthy London mercantile elite and in the growth of London, whose population of 30,000–40,000 by 1300 far outstripped that of any of the burgeoning urban centres in the British Isles.

The first Plantagenet kings, Henry and his sons Richard I (d.1199) and John (d.1216) elaborated ways of tapping the wealth of England on the foundations laid by their Anglo-Saxon and Norman predecessors. There was the vast royal demesne, scattered through England, which William the Conqueror had gained. There were ways of exploiting financially the feudal superiority which William had imposed on the persons and estates of a newly constituted baronage and Church hierarchy. There were profits to be made from the development of royal justice to a pitch with which no baronial jurisdiction could compete, and from the grant of privileges to subjects, for example, corporative governing rights to urban elites.

Kings of England were able to carry out such exploitation since their powers had been exalted from before the Norman Conquest. They were sacred persons, possessed of a specific miraculous healing power, lauded and propped up by a normally subservient and immensely wealthy Church hierarchy. Subjects generally accepted public obligations to submit to royal justice, and to render military service and pay taxes in national emergencies. Royal rights were enforced by the king's officers in the shires and in many of their subdivisions, the hundreds or wapentakes. Some forms of public obligation withered after the Conquest, partly because of the rise of baronial jurisdictions and the prevalence of the concept of personal obligations mutually owed by kings and tenants-in-chief. Henry II, in particular, tried to ensure that such jurisdictions did not generally absorb or overshadow the shire system. Lesser nobles (predecessors of the gentry) were obliged to cooperate with sheriffs and the king's judges in operating the expanding system of royal administration. The knightly fee-holder, beholden to his baronial overlord, might also be the sheriff or a royal commissioner, an agent of the Crown. Through much of England, the magnate (bishop and abbot, earl and baron) had to compete with the Crown for the service of gentle-folk, whose goodwill he needed to safeguard his property rights. The need for magnates to develop patronage systems was increased by the decline of hereditary feudal bonds from the later thirteenth century onwards, which facilitated the luring away of 'their' knights by rival noble patrons. In order to maintain their hereditary power-bases and to consolidate dominance over local societies, magnates needed the supplements of royal goodwill and favour. Their stock among neighbouring gentlefolk depended not only on the benefits they could dispense from their own resources, but on the additional access they could provide to the king's personal benevolence. For the magnate's maintenance of his family's interest and honour, a harmonious, familial personal relationship with the king was crucial.

In the thirteenth century, though royal control of the realm had been enhanced by the elaboration of a sophisticated bureaucracy, based partly in the royal household and partly in Westminster Palace, kings faced dire crises. The Angevin empire became politically convulsed. It emerged drastically reshaped and transformed into England and its satellites, a collection of proto-colonial fiefdoms attached in various ways to the English Crown. As England became the centre of Plantagenet power, kings placed more emphasis on their sovereign claims over the British Isles. As a corollary to this painful transformation, within England politically involved individuals and communities grew more militant – baronially led protest movements about Crown policy gained in respectability and political sophistication. In 1327 opinion even tolerated or applauded the deposition of Edward II, after an invasion disreputably headed by his foreign queen, Isabella, and her lover, Roger Mortimer, earl of March. Edward was then probably murdered. This precedent of deposition – the first since before the Norman Conquest – added to the problems of Edward's successors.

An examination of certain aspects of changing Plantagenet fortunes in the century or so before 1327, when Edward III, aged fourteen, succeeded his father in such dismal circumstances, will help to set the fourteenth-century scene, starting with the fate of the Angevin empire. Philip Augustus, a French king with a greatly strengthened power-base, in 1204 wrested Normandy and most of the other former continental possessions of Henry II from King John, whom Philip, as his overlord, had condemned to their forfeiture as a disloyal vassal. The expensive efforts by John and his son Henry III (reigned 1216–72) to regain the lost provinces all ultimately failed. Henry was left only with some slivers of Normandy (the Channel Islands) and the duchy of Gascony (or Guienne), a fragment of Aquitaine. Gascony had become by 1300 a vital English interest, through mutual trading links: it was a lucrative source of customs revenue derived from Anglo-Gascon trade based on the export of wine from Bordeaux and the supply of the duchy with a variety of commodities by English merchants. The royal administration in Gascony, headed by a lieutenant and centred on Bordeaux, had to take care not to encroach on the governmental privileges of communes and *seigneurs*. In 1254 Henry III declared Gascony to be a lordship annexed permanently to the English Crown, as the lordship of Ireland had been since his father's reign. In 1259 Henry made a peace treaty with Louis IX of France, renouncing Plantagenet claims on the lost provinces and receiving Louis' recognition of his right to Gascony, to be held by him and his successors as a fief of the French Crown. The status accorded to Gascony was to cause prolonged diplomatic wrangling and, eventually, warfare. From the late thirteenth century onwards French attempts to play a judicial role in Gascon affairs came into conflict with English kings' concept of their sovereignty in their dominions. In 1294 Philip IV of France confiscated Gascony from Edward I; in 1324 Philip's son Charles IV confiscated it from Edward I's son Edward II. Edward III, after he had seized power from his mother and the earl of March in 1330, was confronted with a seemingly insoluble Gascon problem, the duchy having once more been restored. The death of Charles IV in 1328, with no direct male heir, had further complicated Edward's relations with the French Crown. His own claim to the succession, as grandson of Philip IV (d.1314), through his mother, had been rejected in favour of a more distant collateral, Philip of Valois (d.1350), who as Philip VI proved an able and ambitious ruler.

Edward III also inherited confrontational problems in the British Isles, where the imperial ambitions of his recent forbears, frustrated in France, had become concentrated. In Ireland there had developed a royal administration under a lieutenant, with institutions based on English ones radiating from Dublin, directly controlling the ports and their hinterlands. The fact that the Dublin administration came to have a surplus of revenue in the thirteenth century attests its vigour, and the expansion of Irish agriculture and overseas trade, stimulated by Anglo-Norman settlers. A byproduct of the Scottish Wars of Independence was Robert I's brother Edward Bruce's invasion of Ireland in 1315; the Scots campaigned there till 1318, wrecking the English administration. The Anglo-Irish lords were unable to regain the initiative from Irish kings, whose encroachments also threatened the Dublin administration's enclaves. It now lacked an adequate power-base: Edward III inherited a lordship of Ireland in political decay, vulnerable to external threat.

In Wales, in the thirteenth century, the position of the Marcher lords and, indeed, the security of adjacent English shires, had been threatened by the hegemony over other Welsh principalities achieved by Llewelyn the Great (d.1240) and his grandson Llewelyn ap Gruffudd (d.1282), princes of Gwynedd. In 1267 Henry III recognised the latter's position and his title to be prince of Wales. The new principality was destroyed by Edward I's campaigns, culminating in the annexation of Gwynedd in 1282–4. Edward founded his own principality of Wales, composed of two separate blocs, Gwynedd, and the older Crown lordships in south Wales. The principality was given a superstructure of English institutions; Gwynedd was ringed by imposing new castles and adjacent boroughs peopled by English folk. Both in the principality and the Marches the Edwardian conquest and settlement inaugurated the era of what Professor Rees Davies has termed 'colonial Wales',[2] whose higher offices in Church and secular administration were mainly filled by Englishmen. The system reflected distrust of the Welsh, and left the aspirations for office, honour and profit of the descendants of the native elites difficult to fulfil.

In Scotland the English Crown had had to come to terms with the parallel rise of a more formidable princely power, also a potential threat to the security of parts of England. By the time of Alexander III's death (1286), the Scottish Crown had established itself as the undisputed sovereign over the Scottish mainland. Through its feudal control of the new baronial and burgess elites in lowland regions, the Crown was able to impress its will in ancient earldoms. Awareness of the newly developed wealth and power of the Scottish realm strengthened Edward I's determination to impose recognition of his feudal superiority over it on the competitors for its throne who sought his adjudication in 1290, and his determination to inflict an unprecedentedly meddlesome sovereignty over the successful competitor, John Balliol. Balliol's eventual defiance led to his deposition and Edward's occupation of Scotland (1296). Edward subsequently failed to define Scotland's kingless status, ruling it through Englishmen as a lordship of the English Crown, with its own separate institutions. The aged Edward's death in 1307 and the succession of the unmilitary Edward II enabled the Scottish resistance to destroy English power in Scotland by 1314. The collapse exposed the north of England to devastating raids and ransomings. In 1328 the minor Edward III's mother and the earl of March made on his behalf what was regarded in England as a shameful peace with Robert Bruce, recognising his independent kingship. Edward inherited intractable Scottish as well as English problems. The seemingly lack-lustre hegemony over Scotland had been paraded as a jewel of the English

Crown; the north of England lacked security. The Scots exposed a structural weakness in the English polity. Dr R. S. Schofield's analysis of the geographical distribution of wealth based on the assessments of movables for the 1334 lay subsidy demonstrates that seven of the nine poorest shires lay north of a line from the Severn to Flamborough Head.[3] Richer regions to the east and south had to prop up the defences of geographically vulnerable, sparsely inhabited and unproductive border regions – devastated Cumberland, Westmorland and Northumberland were all exempted from the 1334 subsidy.

To support their external pretensions, from the later thirteenth century onwards the Plantagenet kings needed to commit the military and financial resources of these richer shires recurrently on a large scale in Scotland and on the continent. For the great royal demesne bequeathed by William the Conqueror had drastically shrunk, scarcely covering the ordinary expenses of government, notably the increasing costs of the royal household. The Crown's feudal rights over the Church and baronage could no longer be exploited by kings with the same zest as in the twelfth century. In 1215 King John, defeated in France, had been compelled to accept Magna Carta, the first attempt of lasting significance to define, in unprecedented detail, the ways in which the king ought to exercise his judicial powers. Magna Carta also contained a clumsy and ephemeral conciliar mechanism for coercing the king if he failed to adhere to its terms – nevertheless, a precedent for a series of baronial protest movements aimed at forcing John's successors to remedy the particular grievances of magnates and sometimes those of a wider political community, and at devising institutional means of making their reforms stick. A tradition of popular support for baronial heroes (however self-serving) is reflected in the unofficial canonisation of Henry III's opponent Simon de Montfort, killed in battle against the king's supporters, and of Edward II's cousin and long-term critic, Thomas earl of Lancaster, executed in 1322 after rebelling. Rebels could now become holy, not just kings. A royal commission was appointed in 1323 to enquire into and punish those who had published at Bristol 'idolatrous tales' about miracles performed at the place where the bodies of the rebels Henry de Montfort and Henry de Wylyngton were hanged, in order 'to alienate the affection of the people from the king'.[4]

In this climate of opinion, the development of parliament provided a necessary means for kings to seek consent and cooperation from a lively and quite widely defined 'community of the realm'. By the start of Edward III's reign it was customary for elected 'knights of the shire', citizens and burgesses, to be summoned to meetings of parliaments, in which kings sought the counsel of their principal tenants-in-chief and considered petitions. In his reign the shire and urban representatives came to sit as one assembly (the Commons) and he enhanced their status by giving them the leading role in the grant of lay taxation. These developments tended to undercut baronial leadership of protest movements. Moreover, Edward 'tamed the magnates' by his sensitivity to their family interests and ambitions, by his chivalrous camaraderie with them and his congenial addiction to warfare.

How did Edward fare in handling the problems of empire? For the most part, he left the lordship of Ireland to decay, though he strongly backed the lieutenancy of his son Lionel duke of Clarence (1361–4). He had created his eldest son Edward – known to posterity as the Black Prince – as prince of Wales. The prince led adventurous Welshmen to seek their fortunes in his military retinues in France. As holder of the royal earldom of Chester, he took off many Cheshiremen too. The earldom was 'palatine' – it had a separate government, headed by a justiciar, its status similar to that of the 'private' governments of the lordships in the Marches of Wales. In Wales, tensions fostered by 'colonial' government erupted only in 1400, with the start of Owain Glyn Dŵr's revolt. Fear of Welsh revolt in governing circles in the 1370s is revealed by the king's council's reactions to the activities of Owain Lawgoch, who claimed to be rightful prince of Wales. A professional soldier in France, he switched allegiances and planned invasions of Wales with French and Spanish assistance. Welsh discontents still posed a threat to Plantagenet and Marcher rule there and to the English midlands.

By the 1370s, the north of England was again seriously threatened by the Scots. In 1333 Edward had repudiated the 1328 peace, intervening in Scotland to support the precarious rule of John Balliol's son Edward, who recognised English overlordship. Faced with English occupation, the majority of Scots adhered to the cause of Robert I's infant son David II, but with the start of the Anglo-French war (1337), Edward III switched his main effort to the continent. The capture of David, invading England in 1346, enabled Edward to contain the Scots by occupying Scottish border shires and committing the defence of the English borders to local lords, holding office as wardens of the Marches. This was an expensive policy for the Crown, necessitating its subsidising of garrisons and military retinues on either side of the frontier. After Robert II (the first Stewart king) succeeded David in 1371, the continued English occupation and claims over the Scottish Crown led to deteriorating Anglo-Scottish relations.

Edward's boldest innovations in foreign relations concerned French problems. After Philip VI formally confiscated Gascony in 1337, Edward threw the weight of English resources into its defence, with the ultimate aim of forcing the French Crown to recognise his sovereignty there. In 1340 he assumed the title of king of France. Edward strenuously sought recognition of his title within France and received it for a time from Flemish burgesses, dependent on English wool exports, and from supporters of the claim of the infant John de Montfort to the duchy of Brittany.

Edward had some early success in making alliances against Philip VI with princes in the Low Countries and Rhineland (within the Holy Roman Empire); his marriage in 1328 to Philippa, daughter of the count of Hainault, and future mother of John of Gaunt, was a help here. However, the Empire had a francophile ruler from 1347: Charles IV (d.1378), of the House of Luxembourg, whose rule in the Empire was strengthened by his kingship of Bohemia. Richard II's first queen was to be his daughter Anne. Edward had no hope of a papal alliance. The papacy, resident at Avignon in Provence (then part of the Empire) was occupied by subjects of the French Crown, often suspected in England of pro-French leanings. Popes in fact worked strenuously for an Anglo-French settlement, in order to restore the peace of Christendom, and as the main hope of effectively relaunching the crusade to free Jerusalem. However, papal policy was completely reversed by the outbreak in 1378 of the Great Schism, which lasted till 1419. Gregory IX, who had taken the papal court back to Rome, died soon afterwards; the French cardinals who reluctantly elected an Italian as his successor (Urban VI) fled from Rome, repelled by his reformist zeal and determination to stay there rather than return to Avignon. They denounced the election and elected one of their number, 'Clement VII'. The king of France recognised him as true pope, as did his Scottish ally. The English, not surprisingly, adhered to Urban; the antipope set up business at Avignon. In the 1380s Urban cheerfully supported English attacks on the French and Castilians as crusades against schismatics.

Edward III's great military successes stemmed from the efforts of his own subjects rather than his allies: the most notable were the victory he had over Philip VI at Crécy (1346) and that of an Anglo-Gascon army commanded by the Black Prince at Poitiers (1356), which led to the capture of Philip's son and successor John II (d.1364). Victory at Crécy facilitated Edward's capture of Calais (1347), which he turned into an English port ('Calice'), to be lost only in 1558. The port and its hinterland, the 'March of Calais', of immense strategic value, were heavily and permanently garrisoned.

The capture of John II eventually led to an Anglo-French peace, agreed on at Brétigny (1359), by which John II granted the English Crown an extensive duchy of Aquitaine in full sovereignty, and Edward agreed to renounce his claim to the French throne. Much

English diplomatic effort in Richard II's reign was to be devoted to trying to get the lines of the 1359–60 settlement, a high point of English achievement, restored. For John's son and successor, Charles V, (d. 1380) was determined to re-assert the rights of his Crown. By accepting judicial appeals made to his court in 1368 by Gascon lords against the government of the Black Prince (whom Edward had granted the duchy of Aquitaine), Charles effectively repudiated Brétigny. The consequent war of 1369–75 was a disaster for the English in south-west France: their control was mostly reduced to a coastal strip of Gascony, from the Bordeaux region south to Bayonne.

Something needs to be said about Iberian affairs, since peninsular involvements were a feature of Edward's later years and loomed large in John of Gaunt's career. There were five Iberian kingdoms. The minor ones were Portugal, the Islamic kingdom of Granada to the south of Castile (a perennial objective for English crusading enthusiasts) and Navarre in the north-west. Navarre was important in English policy partly because its king, Carlos II (d. 1387) was a Norman magnate too. His relations with Edward were complicated by the fact that he was a great-grandson of Philip IV of France and had a claim to the French throne. His kingdom was of strategic importance to the English because it commanded the main Pyrenean route from Gascony to Spain.

As potential allies for the English Crown, Castile and Aragon held the most attraction. Aragon was made up of three principalities – Valencia and Catalonia, as well as Aragon proper, which all had strong traditions of constitutional government. One royal preoccupation was the defence of an extensive Mediterranean empire. But Aragonese kings were mindful of the affairs of the largest, the central Iberian kingdom, Castile, with which Aragon and Valencia had extensive frontiers. From 1336 to 1387 Aragon was ruled by the astute Pere III, whose prolonged conflicts with Castile and uneasiness about French ambitions led him into alliances with England. However, domestic constraints and his cautious approach restrained him from wholehearted commitment to the English cause. The English, to their surprise, eventually found a stauncher ally in Portugal, which in the mid-1380s was engaged in an epic struggle to repudiate Castilian rule. The Treaty of Windsor (1386) between João (John) of Portugal and Richard II has proved significant down to the twentieth century.

The great Iberian prize for which the French and English competed strenuously was the alliance of Castile, a kingdom with a tradition of strong kingship, a warlike nobility and a powerful royal galley-fleet, capable of summer operations in northern waters. In England Castile's rulers had long been referred to as kings of Spain; as a result of an Anglo-Castilian alliance of 1254, Edward III had a

Spanish grandmother, Eleanor, wife of Edward I and daughter of the crusading hero Fernando III. In the 1360s there was civil war in Castile between the chillingly tyrannical Pedro I and his illegitimate half-brother Enrique of Trastamara. The Black Prince restored Pedro to his throne in 1367 – he backed the wrong horse. In 1369 Enrique killed the captured Pedro; well into the fifteenth century he and his successors made the French alliance a pillar of their now royal House of Trastamara's diplomacy. In the 1370s Enrique II allied offensively with the French Crown, assaulting the English and Gascons by sea and land. Hence the role allotted by the declining Edward III and ailing Black Prince to John of Gaunt – to compass the downfall of the Spanish usurper.

To sum up Edward III's achievements abroad: he brought off some of the most resounding military and diplomatic successes of any English medieval king, but when he died in 1377 there were few remaining territorial prizes – just some vulnerable and expensive bases and strips of territory in France and Scotland. In order to wage repeated warfare against the vastly superior resources of the French Crown, Edward had to take 'the community of the realm', through the medium of frequent parliaments, into partnership, persuading magnates and others that his wars were just, to their profit, necessary for defence. Royal propaganda fostered the concept of an English nation – a nation whose resources must be devoted to maintaining defences and raising armies, to sustaining an imperial role, because it was surrounded by a ring of implacably hostile nations – notably the Scots, the French and, latterly, the Spaniards. By 1377 the English were more aware of themselves as a national community – one whose southern heartlands of power were as badly menaced as was its weaker northern periphery. They now expected kings not just to maintain the tenets of Magna Carta, but to use the vast sums granted to them in subsidies to win a final peace which would give England security. Under Richard II this proved a much more difficult task for government to perform than the grudging grant of domestic liberties by earlier kings. It produced crises of confidence, in John of Gaunt and then in Richard himself. The evolution of parliament in Edward's reign, and in particular the Commons in parliament, provided powerful means for the expression of this lack of confidence as well as of support for the Crown. Edward III bequeathed his grandson Richard a tame nobility and ways of raising armies for service abroad on a grand scale, but there were potentially threatening features in the legacies which the ten-year-old boy received in 1377.

Richard II inherited a realm gripped by several sorts of social crisis, besides that over the defence of the Plantagenet empire. The elites in society felt that their divinely instituted hierarchical control was under threat, notably from what they considered to be a contagion of wicked and disordered aspirations spreading among husbandmen and all sorts of common labourers, erupting most horribly in the violence and radicalism of the Peasants' Revolt (1381). A new, specifically English heresy was abroad, questioning the justification of ecclesiastical powers and privileges; this had lay sympathisers in courtly circles. Disagreement over religion was a minor fissure compared to other splits that came to divide the Ricardian nobility. The operations of the patronage system which was part of their bonding became controversial. Richard, wilful and divisive, developed the conviction that critics were damaging royal prerogative. His remedies seemed to some magnates and gentlefolk to threaten their interests and liberties.

It is not the place here to enquire into the origins of fissive Ricardian trends, but to note that they produced a widespread sense of unease – a sense that old certainties were crumbling, that old values needed to be either reasserted or modified. The considerable evidence for John of Gaunt's experience of and reactions to these problems makes his career an interesting and colourful prism through which to view fourteenth-century society. He reflected an age of doubt and upheaval in a more profound sense than, say, Thomas of Lancaster in the early fourteenth century or Warwick the Kingmaker in the fifteenth century.

What was the nature of these destabilising factors? Since the first of the plague pandemics (1348–50), there had been drastic fluctuations in population size, which threatened landowners' systems of estate exploitation and their agrarian profits. They were securely trapped in the last decades of the century in the scissors of falling demand for their demesne produce and the rising cost of labour. It became difficult for their estate officials to extract customary works and other obligations owed by those tenants who were villeins by birth and others who rented servile tenements. Where stewards were unable to enforce heavy work services, more reliance than hitherto had to be placed on the hire of labour, at a time when labourers tended to be mobile and negotiated toughly for high wages and short contracts. Commissions of justices of labourers, appointed to enforce wage maxima prescribed by statute, provided occasional hope of relief for less competitive employers. Such punitive government attempts to rig the labour market – and, besides, the assistance which the Crown provided for landowners intent on recapturing absconded villeins – intensified tensions between elites and commons. A lack of real sympathy with the latter's problems is reflected in the readiness of the Commons in the Northampton parliament (1380) to shift the burden of financing the war in France on to the shoulders of their social inferiors. They accepted the option the Lords presented of a poll tax at a flat rate, imposing it on all above the age of fifteen, with no statutory provision for relief from what would be a crushing burden to the poor. This tax was one of the triggers of the Peasants' Revolt.

Richard's reign witnessed the emergence of the first English heresy: its instigator was the celebrated Oxford theologian John Wycliffe (d. 1384), the 'morning star of the Reformation'. In his sermons and treatises he developed a fundamental Biblical critique of the Church which dismissed the spiritual and secular pretensions of clerks and lambasted in particular the behaviour of its hierarchy, from the pope downwards. In Edward III's last years Wycliffe started to be employed by the Crown; in government circles his anti-papal and anti-clerical rhetoric had political uses. His advocacy of a devout and simple life, focussed on faith in Christ, was appreciated in the university, among the friars and in princely households. However, support wavered when the unorthodox radicalism of his views on the ministry, on good works and the sacraments became more fully understood. This was particularly so in the early 1380s, when a vigorous new archbishop of Canterbury, William Courtenay, exposed the heretical nature of Wycliffe's views and determinedly prosecuted his leading clerical disciples. Wycliffism ebbed in high places, but at some humble levels of society 'proto-Protestant' doctrines flowed from his teaching, mostly hidden, until they merged with the Reformation.

By Richard II's reign the feudal system of relations between nobles based on the tenure of territorial baronies and knight's fees had, during the previous hundred or so years, lost much of its vigour. A statute of Edward I (1290) had halted the creation of hereditary territorial fees. Instead, nobles gave rewards for a variety of services in the form of annual retaining sums to knights, esquires and other gentlefolk. Often associated with these money grants were the right to free board in the noble's household (*bouche de court*) and provision of clothing in the lord's heraldic colours. In the later fourteenth century the giving of emblematic badges and collars became popular retaining devices; the Commons in parliament voiced particular concern about the widespread distribution of suchlike tokens, particularly when given to men of lower status who were not their patron's household servants or other ministers, but attached casually to a noble or gentle affinity.[5] The Commons in parliament (among whom were habitually numbered many lords' retainers) repeatedly expressed fears about the spread of crime and abuses of the law coloured by the protection afforded by such tokens; they wanted a remedy for the abuses of the patronage system. This was an issue that vitally concerned John of Gaunt, as he possessed the largest retinue of any subject.

Finally, it is necessary to give a brief narrative of the central political crisis of Richard's reign (1386–8), as it is frequently alluded to below, but not analysed, since Gaunt was – crucially – abroad for most of these years. In the parliament of October 1386 the Commons set out to impeach the chancellor, Michael de la Pole, earl of Suffolk. Richard, then aged nineteen, was coerced by threats into acquiescing in the impeachment and the appointment in parliament of a council to supervise aspects of government for a year. Leading lights on this council were two of his principal critics – his uncle Thomas of Woodstock, duke of Gloucester (Gaunt's younger brother) and Thomas Arundel, bishop of Ely (the earl of Arundel's younger brother). The violence and extremism of opposition in parliament had been prompted by the failure of Richard's ministers to pursue what the Commons felt were financially prudent prescriptions or to take adequate measures against a menacing (though abortive) French invasion threat. In 1387 Richard tried to evade conciliar control and to arrange a peace conference with the French. He secretly procured rulings from royal judges asserting that some of the measures taken in the recent parliament were against the royal prerogative and either treasonable in intent or acts of treason. The judgements leaked out, precipitating an armed rising in November led by Woodstock and the earls of Arundel and Warwick, who launched an appeal of treason against five of Richard's favourites and councillors. They alleged that the accused had misled the king, then of tender age; unprepared for a show of strength, Richard promised that the appeal would be heard by the Lords in parliament. However, his most obnoxious favourite and bosom companion, Robert de Vere, duke of Ireland, raised an army in the king's defence, principally from the earldom of Chester. The lords appellant were now joined in their appeal, and in arms, by Gaunt's son and heir Henry of Bolingbroke (the future Henry IV, about Richard's age) and Thomas Mowbray, earl of Nottingham. They defeated Vere, who fled abroad (as did two other appellees, Michael de la Pole and Alexander Neville, archbishop of York). Richard had to admit the appellants to the Tower of London, where they remained closeted with him over New Year, 1388; threats of deposition were apparently bandied about. In the subsequent Merciless Parliament, the Appeal of Treason was found proved; the two appellees who had been arrested, Robert Tresilian, chief justice of the King's Bench, and Nicholas Brembre, former mayor of London, were executed. The Commons impeached a number of the servants of the king's chamber. They were found guilty of treason and promptly executed – among them, to Richard's grief, Sir Simon Burley, a supervisor of his education. The control of the lords appellant over government soon weakened; there were divisions among them, and support for their control and their subsequent measures soon ebbed. In August the English suffered their worst military defeat since Edward II's reign – at the hands of the Scots, at Otterburn in Northumberland. The

13

appellants appeared to have left the north of England at their mercy. In May 1389 Richard successfully asserted his control over government. A cowed young man, he displayed a new caution, and he urgently recalled Gaunt from abroad.

If Gaunt had not sailed away to Spain in the summer of 1386, it is likely that the domestic political crisis would not have evolved in such a damagingly confrontational way. Those events cast a sombre shadow on English political life till exorcised by the deposition of Richard in 1399, a crisis which was to have even more dire long-term consequences. How far Gaunt knew about and was involved in the events of 1386–8 remains an enigma. One thesis of this book is that they ran, for the most part, entirely against the model which he tried to present of ideal conduct for nobles, an ideal which his own beloved son Henry of Bolingbroke further undermined by usurping Richard's throne in 1399.

Notes and References

1 I refer to a lecture given by DAL Morgan to the Anglo-American Conference of Historians in 1989. The recent studies of the reign are by WM Ormrod (1990) and Scott L Waugh (1991).
2 Davies RR 1978.
3 Schofield RS 1965.
4 *C.P.R. 1321–4*, p. 578. I owe thanks for this reference to Dr Richard Rose.
5 Saul N 1990.

Chapter Two

Gaunt in History

The historical reputation of John of Gaunt has, on the whole, been poor; his shortcomings and failures have been well remembered. This low repute sprang from the events of 1398–9 and from the policies of his descendants the Lancastrian kings, and was reinforced by the strictures of contemporary chroniclers, notably those of the monk of St Albans, Thomas Walsingham. The usurpation of 1399 highlighted Gaunt's failure to restrain Richard II or to protect the Lancastrian inheritance from him, and it negated the loyalist principles to which Gaunt had always adhered. Henry V's invasion of France finally destroyed the fruits of the peace policies which Gaunt had doggedly pursued, and replaced the primacy of Aquitaine in English policy in France, which he had reinforced. For the Lancastrian kings and their subjects, Gaunt's concerns and policies rapidly appeared anachronistic or irrelevant, and this was reflected in the slight or perfunctory references to him in fifteenth-century chronicles. Henry IV's servant John Gower, in his 'Tripartite Chronicle', a panegyric on his master and justification of his usurpation, pointedly neglected his master's father.[1] John Strecche, canon of Kenilworth (a house which had been in Gaunt's patronage), found nothing positive to say about him.[2] Hostile memories persisted. One early fifteenth-century chronicler gives an unfavourable account of Gaunt's policies in 1376–7 (ultimately derived from Walsingham).[3] The Oxford academic Thomas Gascoigne, writing in the 1440s, told a scurrilous story alleging that Gaunt became ravaged by mortal disease as a consequence of his promiscuity (see p. 167). This perhaps echoes the scandalous reputation the duke had acquired in the 1370s (evident in Walsingham's denunciations) as a result of his liaison with Catherine Swynford (see p. 357). It was only from the milieu of his grandchildren of the House of Avis that a glowing account of Gaunt emerged: in the Portuguese historian Fernão Lopes's *Crónica de D. João I*, Gaunt is shown as dignified and pious, in adverse as well as happy circumstances (see pp. 124–5). In the Spanish kingdoms as well as in Portugal he was to be remembered as an honourable progenitor; in Castile, as in Portugal, his alliance had helped to confirm the rule of a usurping dynasty.

More positive views of Gaunt survived in England outside the chronicle tradition. A possible echo of his patronage of Wycliffe, and an indication that his authority was considered prestigious in obscure circles, is found in a Lollard tract alleging that he had advocated the use of the Gospels in English.[4] A Lancastrian civil servant, the poet Thomas Hoccleve, recalled the duke as 'a noble prince' in *The Regement of Princes,* holding him up as an example to the future Henry V.[5] The Lancastrian and Beaufort families as well as Iberian princes had incentives to present Gaunt as a revered ancestor. The Lancastrian kings must have appreciated that he had augmented their landed inheritance (principally with lands of the Bohun earls) and had drawn into Lancastrian service and raised the fortunes of families on whose riches and loyalty their rule heavily relied. He had procured for his Beaufort children much of the material (as well as the legal) basis of their advancement. The Lancastrian image of Gaunt as a worthy ancestor who had connected his house prestigiously with the Iberian principalities is seen in the portrait of him in stained glass in the chapel of All Souls College, Oxford. Here he is shown crowned apparently as king of Castile and León, a grave hierarchical figure whose royal blood and status prefigured the dynasty's regal apotheosis.

The Yorkist dynasty had no reason to honour Gaunt. 'Jon of Gaunt gate Harry wich unryzthfully entretid Kyng Richard' stated one pro-Yorkist chronicler.[6] Allegedly Gaunt had asserted Bolingbroke's claim to the succession in parliament in the 1390s, on the grounds that Edmund Crouchback was Henry III's eldest son, a claim made by Bolingbroke himself in 1399.[7] Gaunt procured the legitimation of the Beauforts, facilitating the eventual aspirations to the succession which were to make them deadly rivals of the Yorkists. Edward IV, in the early years of his reign, made some play with his claim to the Crown of Castile, through his descent from Gaunt's brother Edmund of Langley and his wife Isabella of Castile. The research instituted by Edward's father Richard duke of York had made his family circle aware that in the Treaty of Bayonne (1388) Gaunt had let his brother's claim go by default.[8] Addressing Edward

IV in *The Governance of England,* Sir John Fortescue alluded to Gaunt's Spanish involvement, in the course of presenting him as the archetypal 'overmighty subject' – though not one to whom he explicitly attributed domestic turmoils, a moderation which probably sprang from his background of Lancastrian service.[9]

The succession of Henry VII enhanced Gaunt's standing, since it was through his Beaufort descent from Gaunt that Henry claimed the throne. In his reign a new inscription was placed on Gaunt's tomb in St Paul's Cathedral: this emphasised the distinguished descendants from his three marriages, including Henry himself.[10] In his seminal *Anglica Historia,* whose writing was encouraged by Henry, Polydore Vergil gave Gaunt an honourable character, using Froissart to emphasise his unflagging military career.[11] The Spanish alliance and dynastic connection promoted by Henry VII provided another reason for recalling Gaunt, one alluded to in the new inscription on his tomb: through the issue of his second marriage 'ab Henrico [Enrique III of Castile] reges Hispaniae sunt propagati'. In the pageants for the reception of Catherine of Aragon in London in 1501, allusion was made to her descent and that of her bridegroom Prince Arthur from Gaunt. For the reception there in 1522 of Henry VIII and the Emperor Charles V, one of the pageants took the form of a genealogical tree stemming from Gaunt and culminating in the two monarchs.[12] The stem image of Gaunt appeared again in Grafton's 1550 edition of Edward Hall's *Chronicle,* whose frontispiece depicts the two genealogical trees of Lancaster and York originating in Gaunt and his brother Edmund of Langley.

Publication of medieval chronicles made information about Gaunt accessible to early modern historians, notably the publication of Berners' translation of Jean Froissart's *Chronicles* (1523–5) and the publication by Matthew Parker (1574) and William Camden (1603) of a large part of the text of Walsingham's *Historia Anglicana,* a text in which the chronicler had diluted his earlier virulent criticisms of Gaunt. Two Tudor popularising historians, Grafton and Holinshed, give occasional anecdotes about Gaunt, not amounting to a clear picture. They were both interested in the animus of the rebels against him in 1381, with Holinshed providing a vivid cameo of the destruction of his house between London and Westminster, The Savoy. The episode was calculated to arouse sympathy for Gaunt. Holinshed commented on his behaviour in several episodes during the reign: prudently dissembling during his negotiations with the Scots in 1381, hastening back from Gascony in 1389 in order to effect peace between the king and his opponents and, after Gloucester's death, determined (with Langley) 'to cover the stings of their griefes for a time and if the king would amend his maners to forgete also the injuries past'.[13] Froissart's account of the brothers' reactions to Gloucester's death was to retain particular interest for historians writing in the humanist tradition; the brothers' situation provided good examples of the dilemma confronting a noble when the demands of family loyalties and of the state came into conflict. This episode also demonstrated Gaunt's inability to restrain Richard's fatally headstrong courses. Holinshed's occasional remarks about Gaunt, especially here, provided Shakespeare with components for his portrait of the duke as a worthy but ineffective elder statesman.

Interest in Gaunt may have been quickened not only by the themes highlighted in Grafton's and Holinshed's 'best-sellers', but by his continuing relevance to burning dynastic issues. In 1594 the Jesuit Robert Parsons published anonymously *A Conference about the next succession to the Crowne of Ingland*.[14] He argued that the legitimation in 1396–7 of the Beauforts (through whom the Tudors claimed the throne) did not extinguish the prior right of the kings of Portugal to both the duchy of Lancaster and the English Crown, derived from the marriage of João I to Gaunt's daughter Philippa in 1387. Philip II of Spain (himself descended from Gaunt's daughter Catherine) was as king of Portugal 'the chief titler of that house unto England . . . he ioyneth the inheritance of both the two daughters of John of Gaunt, in one'.[15] One reaction to Parsons's arguments is found in a letter from Robert Beale to Sir Robert Sidney (25 September 1595), asking him to procure a copy of the book, whose author derived 'a strange Pretence from John of Gaunt Duke of Lancaster, uppon the King of Spaine, which he mindethe shortlye to challenge'.[16]

The characterisation given to Gaunt by Elizabethan authors remained variable, reflecting the gamut of attitudes to him in contemporary chronicles. The author of the play *Woodstock* (generally assigned to the period 1590–5), a historically muddled piece, portrays Gaunt as a rumbustious and ineffective critic of Richard, in contrast to his calm and tragic brother Thomas of Woodstock.[17] A more hostile picture of Gaunt was given by Samuel Daniel in *The First Fowre Bookes of the ciuile wars between the two houses of Lancaster and Yorke* (London, 1595). Here Gaunt is an ambitious, sinister but ultimately ineffective figure:

> Too great a subiecte growne, for such a state
> The title of a king and what h'had done
> In great exploits his mind did eleuate

Above proportion kingdomes stand vpon,
Which made him push at what his issue
[i.e. Henry IV] gate. . .[18]

Shakespeare's *King Richard II* (published in 1597) provides a characterisation of Gaunt which is new and in sharp contrast with those of the author of *Woodstock* and Daniel. By opening the play with the events of 1398, Shakespeare brushed aside the criticisms of Gaunt which other authors derived from chroniclers of the early years of the reign. In his rehabilitation of Gaunt, Shakespeare even invented a scene in which he rejected the duchess of Gloucester's plea for him to wreak vengeance on Richard for his brother's death, having the duke state instead, in Lily B. Campbell's words, 'the accepted Tudor philosophy of kingship which his son is later to deny in becoming Henry IV'.[19] In giving Gaunt the deathbed peroration chiding his royal nephew's follies, Shakespeare makes him the play's voice of reason, at once speaking for the true and common interests of both Crown and commonwealth, not just as the transmissory agent of the claim to the throne that was to help, in the eyes of Shakespeare's contemporaries, to undermine the power of the one and the tranquillity of the other in the fifteenth century. One reason why Shakespeare apotheosised Gaunt in this way may have been his awareness (and that of his audience) that Gaunt was the progenitor of the queen's paternal family, whereas she had no descent from the controversially rebellious Bolingbroke. Her ancestor, in describing how Richard's behaviour was undermining the commonwealth, was signalling to the audience how the queen was worthily maintaining an ideal articulated long ago in her family.

A favourable view of Gaunt (perhaps derived from that in the play) is found in John Hayward's *The First Part of the Life and Raigne of King Henrie the IIII* (London, 1599). Here the themes of Gaunt as a worthy but politically unsuccessful figure, implicit in his casual dismissal in earlier historiography and projected on the stage, are for the first time discussed in a work of historical analysis. Gaunt, says Hayward, 'was a man of high and hardie spirit, but his fortune was many times not answerable, either to his force or to his forecast'.[20] He is shown as trying to act dutifully and honourably in difficult circumstances. In 1384–5 he prepares his defences against the king at Pontefract but is reconciled 'with respect of his duty and faith' and partly by the entreaty of the king's mother.[21] After the 1397 arrests, he and his brother Langley rise against the king, but when Richard tells them that the arrests were made for new offences and gives them further assurances, 'the Dukes dissembled their feares

19

and dissolved their forces'.[22] Hayward next comments on Gaunt when describing his death and burial and provides an elaborate epitaph:

> hee was a man aduised and warie in his passages of life, liking better safe courses with reason than happy by chaunce: of his owne glory, he was neither negligent, nor ambitiously careful: towards the King he caried himselfe in tearms honourable inough for a moderat prince, and yet not so plausible as a vaine man would desire; whereby there neuer happened to him any extraordinary matter, either in preiudice, or preferment.[23]

One of the first histories dealing with aspects of Gaunt's career which was based on the more scientific seventeenth-century appreciation of documents and chronicles was Joshua Barnes's *The History of that Most Victorious Monarch Edward III* (Cambridge, 1688). Barnes, catering for the tastes of James II, to whom he injudiciously dedicated the volume, concentrated on war and diplomacy in Edward's last years, emphasising the importance of Gaunt's role. Barnes's Gaunt was ambitious and (rather like Barnes's patron) 'of too Rough and Martial a Temper to please the People'.[24] In his account of domestic affairs, based heavily on Walsingham, Barnes was the first historian to reject Walsingham's animus against the duke. Eighteenth-century historians were less original. Paul de Rapin-Thoyras, in *The History of England*,[25] gave a full account of Gaunt's part in political affairs, based carefully on contemporary chronicles and leaning heavily on their judgements. Speaking of the start of Richard's reign, he opines that

> It was not without reason, that the Duke of Lancaster was hindered from having the sole Management of Affairs. This Prince was of a proud and haughty Temper, which suffered him not to have much regard for his Inferiors, particularly in Affairs where his Interest was concerned.[26]

David Hume, whose survey of Gaunt's role in affairs was sloppy and perfunctory compared to that of Rapin-Thoyras, offered these thoughts on his standing and behaviour at the start of Richard II's reign:

> his age and experience, and authority under the late king, gave him an ascendant among them [the royal uncles], though his integrity seemed not proof against great temptations, [he] was neither of an enterprising spirit, nor of a popular and engaging temper.[27]

Nineteenth-century historians also applied narrowly political judgements to Gaunt, and found him wanting. The Flemish historian Wallon, in his life of Richard II (Paris, 1864) commented exasperatedly on him. According to Wallon, Gaunt was primarily responsible for the reverses in the renewed conflicts with France and its allies after 1369. He reproduces hostile chronicle accounts of his part in politics in the 1370s, though hesitating to accuse him of designs on the throne (as did some French commentators at the time). He frequently stresses Gaunt's unpopularity, though admitting that he had much to contend with. Wallon was incensed, though, at what he saw as the folly of the 1386–7 Iberian invasion.[28]

The English constitutional historians of the later nineteenth century had pointed and influential views on Gaunt, above all about the significance of his policies at the end of his father's reign and the start of Richard II's. To William Stubbs, Gaunt appeared to exercise remarkably untrammelled power after the Good Parliament of 1376, and was then the central figure in government and politics (if an incompetent one). He was 'an unscrupulous politician' who exploited the politically naive Wycliffe; the duke 'was a vicious man, and chose his spiritual advisers from among the friars'. However, as a result of his experience of the Peasants' Revolt, Gaunt became a politically reformed character, directing his ambitions abroad.[29] To John Richard Green too, Gaunt was notable in 1376 as a force opposed to the progress of constitutional liberty. Green made the telling point that the duke 'had no taste for the policy of the Lancastrian house or for acting as leader of the barons in any constitutional opposition to the Crown'.[30] Green used Walsingham's 'Scandalous History' as evidence of his contempt for members of parliament and his 'unscrupulous tampering' with shire elections.[31] But the historians' stance in reproving Gaunt's actions was not always tamely accepted. Other Victorian intellectuals discerned in him a sympathetic patron of men of letters who encouraged the flowering of literary and religious trends which was seen as the springtime of modern English nationhood. This view of Gaunt is projected in the carefully researched paintings of Ford Madox Brown. In his *John Wycliffe reading his Translation of the Bible to John of Gaunt* of *c.* 1847 (Bradford Art Galleries and Museum), the reports by Walsingham, Knighton and in the Carmelite file on Lollardy (*Fasciculi Zizaniorum*) of Gaunt's sympathy for Wycliffe and some of his supporters form the launchpad of a leap of artistic licence. The painter turned again to a related theme in his *Wickliffe on Trial* of 1886 (City of Glasgow Art Collections). Here he chose an actual historical scene – the confrontation between Gaunt, supported by Henry Lord Percy, and Bishop Courtenay of London in St Paul's Cathedral. This painting is executed in a painstakingly academic way, though again the artist takes licence by including (with no historical warrant) the Duchess Constance and Geoffrey Chaucer! The latter's intrusion may well have reflected an awareness of the personal links between the duke and the poet. Ford Madox Brown created a romantic image of the duke, one which was echoed (though probably not consciously) in Anya Seton's *Katherine* (1954), a finely conceived romance based on the enigmatic facts known about Gaunt's long-lasting liaison with Catherine Swynford.

Such sympathetic views of Gaunt were not regarded as worthy of consideration in academic circles; proliferating record studies from the later nineteenth century onwards failed to establish a revisionist view. Instead, G. M. Trevelyan's analysis projected Gaunt's establishment in the government of Edward III's last years of a dominant Lancastrian party: Edward's death ended Gaunt's tyranny.[32] Trevelyan seems to have been concerned to flesh out Stubbs's remarks about Gaunt's role in 1376–7. But he did demonstrate the decline of Gaunt's power in Richard's early years, though not explaining why the duke faded to a shadow of his former malignant self.[33] The Stubbsian Gaunt, an 'unscrupulous son' in 1376–7, was once more wheeled out by Tout in his general history, published in 1905.[34]

Trevelyan, in the preface to his 1909 edition, listed Sydney Armitage-Smith's *John of Gaunt* (1904). This still indispensable work put the study of Gaunt on a new foundation and provides a model, in its breadth of interests and disciplining of a wide range of sources, of how the biography of a medieval prince ought to be tackled. Armitage-Smith gave a coherent and solidly based account of his subject's policies and milieu, opening up a range of subjects. But his conclusions on Gaunt were an exercise in timidity:

> For safety, as usual, a middle path must be chosen midway between the grotesque caricature of the Monk of St. Albans and the uncritical encomium of Chandos Herald.[35]

Not surprisingly, Armitage-Smith's view of Gaunt was uninfluential. A rude riposte came from Sir James Ramsay (*Genesis of Lancaster*, ii, 1913), who delighted in hurling abusive epithets at Gaunt. Ramsay apostrophises his behaviour and policies as preposterous, foolish, vindictive, unscrupulous, infatuated and (ultimately) grovelling.[36]

Twentieth-century academics have on the whole been more cautious in assessing Gaunt's character and policies than their robust Victorian predecessors. However, in a paper read in 1928, Maude Clarke boldly claimed that Gaunt organised and headed a 'Lancastrian party' which was an important element in politics in the decade from 1376.[37] Richard II's biographer, Anthony Steel (Cambridge,

1941) accepted this and, indeed, revived the party's existence from Gaunt's return to England in 1389 as the 'moderate middle party'.[38] His implicit explanation of why the Lancastrian party figures so little in the policies of the reign was that Gaunt was a poor party leader. Echoing Armitage-Smith, Steel declared that Gaunt had 'been alternately blackened and whitewashed to a ludicrous extent, first by contemporaries . . . and (less excusably) by most modern historians'. He preferred the view that Gaunt was 'an, on the whole, amiable nonentity of no special attainments – a man neither good nor bad within the conventions of his age, yet always forced to fill a role too big for him'.[39] Some other twentieth-century historians have provided similarly unenthusiastic judgements, when discussing Gaunt in a variety of contexts. K. B. McFarlane, in his lectures on Lancastrian kings, remarked in his steely way that Gaunt showed signs of premature senility after his return to England in 1389.[40] Professor Peter Russell reacted to Gaunt in the way that Latins did to less sympathetic members of the British officer corps in the Mediterranean in the 1940s.[41] Russell's Gaunt is rather like the duke of Wellington as portrayed in a recent Spanish television series – aloof, more concerned with the social niceties than with the realities of the struggle.

More recently, historians have examined and sought to understand Gaunt's policy aims with more sympathy – above all, the works of John Palmer and George Holmes have illuminated them.[42] Gaunt's historical reputation has risen after long being in a trough – this, curiously, has brought academic opinion at last more into line with popular historical traditions.

For besides the historiography of Gaunt found in the literary and academic mainstreams, there are the local traditions, often long of oral provenance, associated with place-names, buildings and his former lordships. Where these traditions reflect on Gaunt's role and personality, they project him as a powerful and, sometimes, benign lord. In some cases these traditions may genuinely reflect memories of the rule and progresses of the last of the earls and dukes of Lancaster to rule and patronise their dependants independently of the Crown. In other cases traditions may have been manufactured by local antiquaries wishing to associate their localities with the awesome and patriotic figure of Shakespeare's play. The Shakespearian image of Gaunt was clearly more widely persuasive than the more ambiguous constructions of scholars.

One characteristic of such traditions is that they occur in many parts of England, reflecting the wide spread of Lancastrian lordship. In Lancaster itself the centre of Penny Street and Market Street crossing is marked by a horseshoe fixed in the pavement and periodically renewed: 'As to its origin one story says that when John of Gaunt visited the town his horse dropped a shoe there, and the townsmen fixed it on the spot to commemorate the visit.'[43] Such a visit may well have been memorable, for it is likely to have been a rare occurrence. However, there was good reason for him to be long remembered in the town, where his statue was put up over the main gate of the castle in 1822; for it was at his request in 1362 that a royal charter favourable to the judicial privileges of the borough was granted, which the townsmen 'jealously guarded . . . down to the last century'.[44] A less likely personal association of the duke with his castle at Halton, Cheshire, was preserved by a local antiquarian in a book published in 1873:

> The popular voice ascribes to John of Gaunt the name of the neighbouring Fiddlers' Ferry, in Cuerdley, which it is said was given to it after he had once passed over it with a party of stringed musicians, probably to examine the ancient earthworks of the adjoining marsh.[45]

Traditions about Gaunt are still preserved in the Leeds region which, though they may in themselves be spurious, do in fact tally with his genuine interest in hunting in the environs, in contrast to his lack of enthusiasm for Lancaster or Halton. According to Jean Collins, in the vestry of Holy Trinity Church, Rothwell (Yorks., West Riding) there are the remains of a padded leather surcoat reputedly worn by Gaunt when he killed the last wild boar in England nearby above Styebank, where now stands John O'Gaunt's Hotel in an area called 'Johnnie Gants'.[46]

Staffordshire too has been rich, and deservedly so, in Gaunt associations. An early seventeenth-century antiquary reconstructed the vanished interior magnificence of the ruinous castle of Newcastle-under-Lyme, and attributed the lifestyle there, and its attendant benefits for local folk, to Gaunt:

> there be manie that need be tould what John of Gaunt his Newcastle was, and will sore lament it now is not, to give the needy sojourner largess of bread, beef, beer. Our grandames doe say that their grandames did delight to tell what it had been, and how well it was counted off before theire days.[47]

From the seventeenth century onwards antiquarians elaborated and debated over a variety of stories connected with Gaunt's tenure of Tutbury Castle, with such themes as his rebuilding of the castle and magnificent lifestyle there, his patronage of the gild of the minstrels, grants of distinctive tenures and his wife Constance's introduction of the Tutbury bull-running (a matter of past scholarly dispute).[48] The legend of Gaunt's Tutbury was summarised by Stebbing Shaw in the volume of his county history published in 1798: 'during his residence at this castle, where he had vast power, and lived with almost as much splendour and attendance as the king himself, to please the people and gain their affection, he instituted several odd customs and tenures.'[49]

Gaunt was hereditary constable of Lincoln Castle, but it is not the castle but other buildings in the city which have been associated with him. There are John of Gaunt's Stables, ruins which have been dated to *c.* 1160, and which were later in the possession of a civic gild, that of St Mary. There was a house in the city associated with him (with equal lack of warrant); from this house the exquisite oriel window now in the castle, near the present main entrance, was removed in the nineteenth century.[50]

Such recollections, or pseudo-recollections of Gaunt, are to be found mainly in the north, where his lordships were concentrated. But there are also scattered memories of him in the south. In present-day Leicester, *caput* of his most important southern honour, he is commemorated at race meetings by the John O'Gaunt Novices Chase. The site of his hunting-lodge in Leicester Forest was remembered in the nineteenth century as John O'Gaunt's Summer House.[51] An elaborate story of his grant of parcels of land in Enderby had him alighting from his horse on a journey from Market Bosworth to Leicester when he observed merry-making at the hay harvest at Ratby, and joining in the fun and games.[52] At his manor of Daventry (Northants.) there was the John O'Gaunt Motel; near Mundesley (Norfolk), of which he held the advowson, is a house named after him.[53] At the ducal manor of Hungerford (Wilts.), the town crier still signals Hocktide by blowing Gaunt's horn at the Corn Exchange.[54] At another ducal manor, Canford Magna (Dorset), there is the so-called 'John of Gaunt's Kitchen'.[55]

These widespread associations of customs and buildings with Gaunt may derive in part from oral history going back to the fourteenth century about the lord, his household and administration, but to a large extent such associations are probably the constructions of later ages. They reflect the coagulation of a number of strands of ideas in addition to any genuine historical memories. There was the desire of common folk to hold up mythical models of the past power – power used benevolently – of a 'great man'. The antiquarians, seeking to enhance the fame of their locality, were ready to identify the great man as Gaunt, especially where their documentary researches pointed to a genuine historical association with him. Because of his Shakespearian associations, Gaunt was particularly welcome as a supposed past builder, merry-maker, or patron. The 'Old John O' Gaunt' of popular imagination is comparable as a romantic construct to 'Bluff King Hal' and 'Good Queen Bess'. However large a heap of chaff this construct is, one must watch out for the grain of truth. Literary and academic history have produced a mess of potage. Nowhere has such history turned up the possibility that Gaunt may have been judged differently in his lordships than in the chronicles. We cannot entirely reject the idea that, beneath the layers of popular and antiquarian fancies, we are glimpsing traces of a great lord among his dependants which the sources used by Stubbs or Tout were incapable of revealing.

Notes and References

1   Stockton E W 1962, p. 289ff.
2   Strecche's chronicle is contained in B.L., Add. MS 35,295. Strecche was a canon at Kenilworth in the first quarter of the fifteenth century; his history of England went down to the death of Henry V (Gransden A 1982, Vol. 2, pp. 405–8).
3   San Marino, Huntington Library, HM 19960 f 155d (and ff). The chronicler favoured Gaunt's opponent of 1376–7, Bishop Wykeham and presents a verse eulogy on him (f 150d and ff).
4   Cited in Colman J 1981, p. 321.
5   Hoccleve T 1897, Vol. 3, pp. 19, 20, 121.
6   Gairdner J 1880, p. 170.
7   *Eulogium,* Vol. 3, pp. 369–70. The chronicler's dating is muddled.
8   The text of the Treaty of Bayonne was secured by three of Richard duke of York's councillors in 1444 (Goodman A, Morgan D 1985, p. 64).
9   Fortescue J; Plummer C ed. 1885, p. 130.
10   Inscription given by Baines E 1836, p. 153.
11   Vergil P 1556, ff. 392ff, 415–16, 424.
12   Anglo S 1969, pp. 61, 189, 194–5.
13   Holinshed R 1807, pp. 751, 800, 838.
14   '. . . published by R. Doleman. Imprinted at N. with Licence.'
15   Ibid., pp. 161–6.
16   Cited in Campbell L B 1947, p. 179. Parsons' book also provoked a reply by 'Dickson', existing in a late sixteenth-century hand (National Library of Scotland, Adv. MS 31.4.8).
17   Rossiter A P 1946.
18   Daniel S 1595, pp. 5d–7d, 10r–10d. He maintained his critical view of Gaunt in a later, more historically minded work (Daniel S 1621, pp. 216–20).
19   See discussion in Campbell L B 1947, pp. 195–9.
20   Hayward J 1599, p. 3.
21   Ibid., p. 7.
22   Ibid., p. 39.
23   Ibid., p. 52.
24   Barnes J 1688, p. 896.
25   Rapin-Thoyras P de 1732, Vol. 1.
26   Ibid., p. 454a.

27 Hume D 1834, p. 2.
28 For example, Wallon H 1864, Vol. 1, pp. 3–4, 117, 224–5; Vol. 2, p. 10.
29 Stubbs W 1875, Vol. 2, pp. 436–7, 445, 463.
30 Green J R 1875.
31 Ibid., p. 288.
32 Trevelyan G M 1899, pp. 9, 17–18, 31–2, 35–7, 41, 68, 257.
33 Ibid., pp. 408–9.
34 Tout T F 1905, p. 438.
35 Armitage-Smith 1904, pp. 408–9.
36 Ramsay J H 1913, Vol. 2, pp. 18, 21, 47.
37 Clarke M V 1937, ch. 2.
38 Steel A 1941, p. 178n.
39 Ibid., p. 21.
40 McFarlane K B 1972, p. 37.
41 Russell P E 1955, pp. 466–7, 479.
42 Holmes G 1975; Palmer J J N 1972.
43 *V.C.H. Lancashire* 1914, Vol. 8, p. 34. Other stories connect the horseshoe with the Young Pretender and the horse fair.
44 Ibid., pp. 10, 43 and n. For a turret at Lancaster Castle known as John O'Gaunt's Chair, ibid., p. 8.
45 Beaumont W A 1873, p. 66.
46 *Dalesman Magazine,* June 1983.
47 Passage quoted from Pape T 1928, pp. 124–5.
48 In *The Natural History of Staffordshire* (Oxford 1686), Robert Plot had a long description of the Tutbury minstrels' court and bull-running (pp. 435–50). He was apparently the first to suggest that Gaunt introduced the bull-running to make Constance feel at home (p. 440), a suggestion denied by Samuel Pegge in a paper read before the Society of Antiquaries, 14 Feb. 1765 (Mosley O. 1832, p. 84 and n). Mosley agreed with Plot, as have some twentieth-century writers, but Norman Edwards, in *Medieval Tutbury* (Lichfield 1949) rejected the Spanish origin; the Tutbury custom was simply a form of English bull-baiting (p. 128). I owe thanks for this information to Ms A. Kettle.
49 Shaw S 1798, Vol. 1, p. 42.
50 Beaumont W 1873, pp. 66–7; Hamilton Thompson A 1935, pp. 3, 6.
51 Fox L and Russell P 1948, p. 34.
52 Thompson J 1849, pp. 172–3.
53 I owe thanks for information about the Mundesley house to Dr Peter Symms.
54 *Sunday Express Colour Supplement,* 22 August 1982.
55 Wood M 1981, p. 250.

Chapter Three

The Education of a Prince (1340–61)

In March 1340 Edward III, king of England, was experiencing mixed fortunes. For nearly three years he had been at war with his kinsman Philip VI, king of France, who in 1337 had declared Edward to be a disloyal vassal and confiscated his lands in France – principally the duchy of Gascony. In the autumn of 1339 Edward invaded north-east France, but his campaign had little to show for it except huge debts. When Edward met his English subjects in parliament in March 1340, lords and commons were prepared to help him generously with war subsidies in return for a favourable hearing of petitions dealing with fiscal and administrative grievances against the Crown.[1] The difficulties of financing war with France and combatting discontent with royal policy were to be recurring, often interlinked preoccupations of the adult John of Gaunt. He was to embrace the soaring international aspirations of his family and likewise to plummet in esteem because of the inability or reluctance of the community of the realm to sustain them.

But in 1340 Edward had had a moment of triumph. At Ghent in January he assumed the title of king of France and received the homage as such of his allies among the Flemish burgesses. His claim to the French throne had been a factor exacerbating his relations with Philip VI; his assumption of the title introduced a lasting dimension to the issues dividing the two Crowns.[2] Edward's new dignity did little to alleviate his daunting political problems, but in March he had a cause of rejoicing: his wife Philippa of Hainault then gave birth to a son in Ghent, probably at the abbey of St Bavo.[3] The news that he had another son was brought to Edward, harassed in parliament, not by a royal messenger, but by three of the queen's maids, Amicia de Gloucestria, Alice de Betyngfeld and Margery de Semor. He rewarded them handsomely with a gift of £200.[4]

French and Flemish sources say that the baby was held at the font by Jacques van Artevelde, architect of the bourgeois alliance with Edward. The chronicler Jean Froissart – himself from Hainault, but only a small child at the time – says that Gaunt's godfather, after whom he was named, was Edward's powerful vassal, John duke of Brabant.[5] If Artevelde was one of Gaunt's godfathers as well, this English prince had an intriguing spiritual relationship with a leading burgess family of Ghent – a family whose name continued to be linked with the cause of bourgeois revolt against princely rule. The adult Gaunt is unlikely to have valued highly such an embarrassing kinship link, but he cherished those he had with the French-speaking princely families of the Low Countries and was always ready to acknowledge that he was of the comital family of Hainault.

In November 1340 Gaunt went to England with his parents and his brother Lionel, aged two. A wardrobe account for Edward III's children (August 1340 to April 1341) details the provision of brightly coloured bedding (green and red) for the infant John, and of clothing for him, including a silken robe. His individual servants were listed – his nurse and female cradle-rocker, three *domicelli*, two esquires of the body and six male chamber servants.[6] Little is known of Gaunt's early years. According to Professor Nicholas Orme, medieval educational theorists distinguished the first stage of childhood, *infancia*, as lasting from birth to the age of seven. Aristocratic infants of the period were commonly brought up, once they had left their wet-nurses, under the care of women.[7] Gaunt was probably in the nursery with his elder sisters Isabella and Joan, and his brothers Lionel and Edmund of Langley (born 1341). In 1389, many years after Joan's death, Gaunt was to endow an obit for her in the cathedral of St André at Bordeaux, where her body lay buried in the choir.[8] Because of Edward III's intense involvement in the war in France, Queen Philippa may have been particularly concerned in overseeing the running of the royal nursery. The adult Gaunt's affection for his mother was to be remarked on.[9] Philippa was robust, sensible and kindly; she achieved the unusual feat, for a foreign queen, of pleasing the touchy English, despite her favours to her fellow countrymen from Hainault. Doubtless her production of sturdy and congenial boys boosted her reputation.

In 1342 Edward sailed with an army to Brittany to support John de Montfort's claim to the duchy: the rival claimant, Charles of Blois, was recognised as duke by Philip VI. The succession crisis in Brittany had arisen as a result of the death of the childless John III. In 1341 Edward appointed the queen as custodian of his former English lands and fees: he stipulated that £1,000 of the income from these estates was to go to the upkeep of Lionel, John, Edmund and their sisters.[10] The following year Philippa was granted the guardianship of the children and of the ducal inheritance in England, which comprised the earldom of Richmond: the earldom was granted to Gaunt.[11] Within a few years Edward was casting around for a marriage for his son. In 1345 he wrote to Maria queen of Castile, soliciting her support for a match between John and one of her sisters, daughters of Alfonso IV of Portugal; nothing came of this.[12]

The infant earl of Richmond can be glimpsed in 1343 at a pious family gathering in Lincoln Cathedral. The cathedral chapter then admitted him to the confraternity together with his father, his elder brothers Edward (the Black Prince) and Lionel, and the aged, blind Earl Henry of Lancaster. This was the start of Gaunt's lifelong attachment to the cathedral and its chapter.[13] In 1349 he formed a connection with another rich and prestigious religious community; he was then, according to contemporary theory, in the stage of *puericia,* when boys were educated separately from girls, under male tutelage.[14] He and his brothers Lionel and Edmund visited St Mary's Abbey, York, where in chapter 'at their own demand and request' they were admitted to prayers and fraternity of the house.[15] What may have given the ceremony especial poignancy was that it took place during what was to be the most terrible universal occurrence in their childhood, the first plague pandemic, to which their sister Joan had succumbed the previous year, now taking a hideous toll in York.[16] Presumably with slender hope of survival into *adolescentia,* Gaunt and his brothers grasped spiritual benefit at a house dedicated – like Lincoln Cathedral – to the Virgin Mary, for whom he was to have a special devotion later in his life (see below, p. 246). By the end of the year the intensity of the Black Death was declining.

When he visited York, Gaunt may already have been put in the tutelage of his eldest brother the Black Prince, a relationship which led to lifelong affection. The Black Prince had established a dazzling youthful reputation for chivalry at the battle of Crécy in 1346 and had crowned it by his victory and capture of John II of France at the battle of Poitiers ten years later. The Black Prince, handsome, brave and athletic like his father, was one of those unfortunate individuals whom the gods shower with gifts in their youth, but who is soured by ill-health and failures in middle age. Gaunt's basic steadfastness and decency are shown by his loyalty in those darkening years to the haughty and querulous invalid who had shone as the mentor and paragon of his youth. Gaunt was probably a member of his brother's household at least between 1 March 1350 and 20 May 1355, because between these dates Lambekyn, saddler of Cologne supplied the Black Prince with saddles and other tack for both himself and his young brother.[17] In March 1351 the prince ordered his receiver-general to provide complete sets of clothes for Wolfard Gistels, child of Gaunt's chamber, Nicholas, the prince's henchman and Maak, Gaunt's henchman. Material was to be provided for clothes for Sigo and Nakok, the 'Saracen' children.[18] In June 1352 it was said that the prince and Gaunt planned to stay a great deal at Byfleet (Surrey).[19]

In 1350 Gaunt had had the excitement of witnessing the Black Prince and their father in battle. Exceptionally for an English nobleman, Gaunt's first experience of war was at sea, and with Spaniards as opponents, not Frenchmen or Scots. The saturnine Pedro I of Castile had allied with the French Crown; Edward wished to destroy the threat of Castilian naval support for the latter. He embarked in the Narrow Seas in order to intercept a Castilian fleet bound home from Flanders. The English won, but only after a hard fight. Froissart says that John of Gaunt was with his father, 'too young to bear arms, but he had him with him in his ship, because he much loved him'.[20] The anonymous writer, known as Chandos Herald, of a poem (*c.* 1385) about the Black Prince's heroic life says that Gaunt was knighted on this occasion.[21] Though the herald's master Sir John Chandos entertained the king on shipboard before the action (demonstrating a new German dance), the herald was writing three decades later, long after Sir John's death. He may have confused this expedition with the one in the Downs in 1355, when, according to the well-informed Leicester canon Henry Knighton, Gaunt and his brother Lionel were knighted with noblemen's sons.[22]

After the victory over 'Les Espagnols sur Mer', in which the rash attacks of Gaunt's father and of his brother the Black Prince are likely to have given Gaunt a terrifying introduction to the horrors and hazards of war, the fleet docked at Rye and Winchelsea. The queen was relieved to greet Edward and her sons. Since it had been a clear day, she had been able to watch the engagement from the shore, and had been in agony over the outcome. That night the king and his companions – perhaps including the young Gaunt – passed the time 'in revelry with the ladies, conversing of arms and matters of love'.[23]

In 1351 Edward demonstrated his favour to his son by confirming the grant of the earldom of Richmond.[24] Four years later Gaunt took part in his first military expedition to France. Despite Edward's military and diplomatic successes in the 1340s – the defence of Gascony, the recognition of his title to the Crown of France by many of its subjects, his defeat of Philip VI at Crécy and his capture of Calais – he had been unable to bring the war to a satisfactory conclusion. In the early 1350s negotiations with Philip's successor, his vigorous son John II, petered out. In 1355 Edward hoped to exploit the quarrel between John and his slippery vassal Carlos II, king of the small Pyrenean kingdom of Navarre, whose fiefs in Normandy John was determined to confiscate. In July Edward embarked in London with his sons Lionel, John and probably Edmund and cruised off Normandy. Carlos landed at Cherbourg the following month, but quickly came to terms with John II.[25] Edward, frustrated, adapted his military plans. Having returned to England, he crossed with his forces – and with Lionel and John – to Calais about the beginning of November. To counter this threat, John II raised his standard at Amiens, and strongly garrisoned St Omer and other places near Calais.[26] The English advanced southwards from their base, pillaging and burning as far as the Hesdin region. But John prudently refrained from challenging Edward in the field. Rigorous removal of victuals to garrisoned places soon forced Edward to retreat, plundering as he went through the *comté* of Boulogne.[27] At Calais he received bad news: a Franco-Scottish force had captured the town of Berwick, though the castle still held out.[28]

Despite his recent campaign and a harsh winter, Edward was soon riding northwards. Lionel and John went too. Advancing from Newcastle, the king relieved Berwick Castle and hemmed in the Scots in the town. They surrendered on 13 January 1356. After the frustration of Edward's attempts to negotiate a peace with his captive David II, and this annoying resurgence of Scottish belligerence, it looked as though Anglo-Scottish relations were moving in Edward's favour. The candidate whom he had once strongly supported for the Scottish Crown, Edward Balliol, came to meet him at Roxburgh and there on 20 January sulkily gave up his claim to the throne and vested it in the English king. Lionel and John headed the secular witnesses to Balliol's written instruments. Armed with these, Edward III fished for the allegiances of Scottish nobles and, to induce their compliance, crossed the Lammermuir Hills to Haddington and pillaged Lothian. But he was unable to maintain his army in Lothian since the Scots, as was usual during English invasions, kept victuals out of his way, and his supply fleet was scattered in stormy weather. According to Knighton, 'the English had nothing to drink for a whole fortnight except rainwater, and so they retreated'. The Scots grew bold in attacking stragglers. Edward withdrew ingloriously from Melrose Abbey and returned to England.[29] The campaign was an instructive lesson for Gaunt about England's Scottish problem, whose significance he was never to underrate as an adult.

In 1357, probably because Gaunt had shown mettle on his apprentice campaigns, Edward granted him the reversion of the castle and lordship of Liddel in Cumberland, highly vulnerable to Scottish raids.[30] He intended his son, fittingly for a northern magnate, to invest his profits in the defence of the West March. The following year Gaunt celebrated Christmas and then New Year 1359 in Yorkshire at Hatfield, probably in the company of his sister-in-law Elizabeth countess of Ulster, Lionel's wife, and of other members of the royal family.[31] The young Geoffrey Chaucer was there in the countess's service. Gaunt's father was soon to secure for him, if he had not already done so, what turned out to be the most rewarding prize he was ever to win – the marriage of Blanche, younger daughter and co-heir of Henry of Grosmont, duke of Lancaster. The duke was one of Edward's closest friends, for years a chief executor of his diplomatic and military policies, known to Gaunt doubtless from infancy.[32] The talented Duke Henry, tall and elegant, was a man of great charm, the sort of companion dear to Edward. He was self-indulgent but capable of self-criticism – vain of his person and eager to show off, a gourmet and lover of fine wines, an ardent player in the game of courtly love who also enjoyed the frank responses of common women to his kisses.

By his marriage to Blanche Gaunt stood to obtain half of the largest inheritance in England after the Crown. The marriage strengthened Gaunt's ties with his mother's family, for Blanche's sister, Maud, was married to William of Hainault, count of Holland and Zealand. Since Maud lived abroad, on succeeding to Blanche's half of the inheritance Gaunt might hope to wield the principal share of Lancastrian influence in England.[33] Then there was the youthful Blanche herself. Chaucer and Froissart were both to mourn her in the conventional terms used to describe the heroines of romances – but nevertheless perhaps with heartfelt grief. In *The Boke of the Duchesse*, Chaucer dreams that he meets an eloquent mourner in a forest:

> A wonder wel-faringe knight –
> By the maner me thoughte so –
> Of good mochel, and yong therto . . .
> Upon his berde but litel heer,
> And he was clothed al in blakke.

The man in black (i.e. Gaunt) said that from an early age he had taken Love as his craft:

> For that tyme Youthe, my maistresse,
> Governed me in ydelnesse;
> For hit was in my firste youthe,
> And tho ful litel good I couthe,
> For al my werkes were flittinge,

> And al my thoghtes varyinge.
> Al were to me y-liche good,
> That I knew tho; but thus hit stood.

But when he first saw Blanche in a company of ladies, he was utterly captivated by her charms of personality and physique:

> And gode faire WHYTE she hete,
> That was my lady name right.
> She was bothe fair and bright,
> She hadde not hire name wrong.
> Right faire shuldres, and body long
> She hadde, and armes, every lith
> Fattish, flesshy, not greet therewith;
> Right whyte handes, and nayles rede,
> Rounde brestes; and of good brede
> Hir hippes were, a streight flat bak.

Whatever the real Blanche was like, it did not appear ludicrous in Lancastrian circles to recall her in such superlative terms. Froissart's brief evocation of Blanche in *Le Joli Buisson de Jonece*[34] is more affecting than Chaucer's sometimes laboured lament:

> Ossi sa fille de Lancastre,
> Haro! mettés moi un emplastre
> Sur le coer! Car quant m'en souvient,
> Certes souspirer me couvient,
> Tant sui plains de merancolie.
> Elee morut jone et jolie,
> Environ de XXII ans,
> Gaie, lie, frisce, esbatans,
> Douce, simple, d'umle samblance,
> La tres bonne dame eut nom Blanche.

Also her daughter of Lancaster [Queen Philippa's daughter-in-law] / Help! Put a plaster / On my heart! For when I remember about it, / To be sure, I am overwhelmed by sighs, / I am so full of melancholy. / She was young and pretty when she died, / About twenty-two years old, / Gay, joyous, frolicsome, frisky / Sweet, simple, modest of mien, / The excellent lady was called Blanche.

The wedding had taken place at Reading on 20 May 1359, the ceremony being performed by Thomas de Chynham, clerk of the queen's chapel. Gaunt's immediate kinsfolk made gifts of plate and jewellery to the bride costing £670 5s., his father's present alone costing £389 11s. 6d. Gaunt gave Blanche a jewel – a great balas surrounded by large pearls set in gold – and a gold ring with a diamond.[35] Jousts were held in honour of the 'new Diana', the first ones at Reading. The couple set out for London, Gaunt holding jousts on the way to entertain his knights. Another tournament was held in London to honour Blanche, an intriguingly planned event which was also intended to demonstrate and cement good relations between the king and the citizens of London. The mayor, sheriffs and aldermen announced a tournament, undertaking – mysteriously for men of unknightly avocations – to hold a field in person against all comers on the three Rogation Days (27–29 May). When the time came they expertly defended the city's honour in lists set up in Smithfield, the horse market outside Aldersgate. On disarming they revealed themselves to be in fact the king, his sons Edward, Lionel, John and Edmund and a group of nobles. The tournament was probably jocularly referred to at court as 'the merchants' fair' (*feer marchaunt*); it is so described in the allowance made on the treasurer of the household's account for wax, spicery, napery, etc., for the feast held in his lodgings afterwards.[36] The king showed his delight in his new daughter-in-law by granting her £100 *p.a.* in August towards the expenses of her chamber. His affection for Blanche is also revealed in a Privy Seal letter of 1360 or 1361, in which he said that the countess of Richmond was 'heavily pregnant' and that 'because of the concern that we feel for her condition' he wished her to stay with the queen for the month or two before her delivery.[37]

Soon the court's attention was to be focussed again on the business of war. The French Estates, meeting in Paris, rejected the terms of the treaty which Edward had negotiated for the release of his prisoner John II of France, spectacularly captured by the Black Prince at the battle of Poitiers in 1356. During August and September 1359 preparations were under way to gather a large army for the invasion of France. Near the end of October, Edward, accompanied by the prince, Lionel and Gaunt, landed at Calais with the main force. Gaunt was in the 'battle' commanded by the prince, one of the three into which the army was divided; probably for the first time, he captained his own substantial retinue.[38] The Black Prince's division advanced independently south-eastwards to cross the Somme: the army linked up to besiege Reims, where Edward hoped to be crowned. According to a French chronicler, Gaunt was joint commander of one of three 'battles' which made an unsuccessful assault on the city. But Edward seems to have pinned his main hope of surrender on blockade. Gaunt and his retainers meanwhile took part in raiding expeditions in the region. For instance, after dusk on 29 December he set out from camp with a party including his father-in-law Lancaster, the earl of March and the renowned Sir John Chandos. Next day they surprised the defences of Cernay-en-Dormois, accepted the surrender of its castle and set the township ablaze. Gaunt was probably with Duke Henry of Lancaster when he went on to ravage the deserted townships of Autry sur Aisne and Meuran, returning with forces unscathed.[39]

Having failed to capture Reims after a siege of over five weeks, Edward decamped early in January 1360. The army moved through Champagne and Burgundy, turning northwards to menace Paris at Easter. Frustrated by the determination of John II's son, the future Charles V, not to give battle, Edward withdrew south-west from Paris, moving towards the Loire valley. But his army, suffering from shortage of victuals and the foul weather, was now showing signs of strain. His campaign petered out as a result of negotiations begun near the end of April, which led to the conclusion of the Treaty of Brétigny on 8 May. Edward's failure to win a victory had led him to revert to the less onerous conditions for peace which he had considered in 1358. In return for giving up the style of king of France, he was to receive a duchy of Aquitaine, in which Gascony was just one component, in full sovereignty, and to accept a reduced ransom for John II.[40] After the conclusion of the treaty, Edward and his army moved to Normandy, staying at Le Neubourg. He and his sons embarked for England from Honfleur on 18 May.[41] Two days after this, perhaps as a token of his appreciation of Gaunt's conduct on campaign, Edward granted him a fitting residence within easy reach of London – Hertford Castle.[42] Gaunt had another reason for pleasure on his return, or soon afterwards: his first child by Blanche, a daughter, was born in 1360. She was christened Philippa, with the queen presumably as godmother.[43]

On 24 August Gaunt left London with his father and the prince for Calais, where peace terms were ratified and John II was released. The members of the English court returned to England between 22 October and 6 November.[44] A few months later an event occurred which transformed Gaunt's status and fortunes. On 23 March 1361 Duke Henry of Lancaster died of plague – in the second pandemic – at Leicester. Gaunt was probably present when the duke was buried in the collegiate church in the Newarke at Leicester which he had founded, on 14 April. In his will he had requested that the Black Prince and his brothers should attend the funeral.[45] Gaunt was then in temporary control of all the duke's estates. whose custody the king had granted him two days after the duke's death;[46] he had just then come of age.

How had his education equipped him for such high responsibilities? Gaunt had doubtless been formally schooled in the traditional noble codes of chivalry and courtesy, as his lifelong delight in the finer points of jousting and his courtly manners suggest (see pp. 356, 360). There is no absolute evidence that he was *litteratus*, able to read Latin, or literate in French or English, or numerate. But the fact that the Carmelite friar Nicholas of Lynn dedicated his Latin *Kalendarium* to Gaunt in 1386 suggests that the duke was *litteratus*, and able to grasp astronomical formulae.[47] Froissart (whose evidence in such matters is not wholly reliable) depicts him as able to read French with ease. Gaunt probably received some instruction in the liberal arts, the equivalent of, at least in part, a university education or one at the budding inns of court. For chroniclers remarked on his skill in rhetoric and logic. The Anonimalle Chronicler described him as putting a case in the Lords 'advisedly and in good form, as if he was a man of law'[48] and the Westminster Chronicler frequently complimented his forensic skill.[49]

Gaunt's literary interests can be used only tenuously as evidence for his education, since the evidence as to what, if any, they were is inconclusive. Remarkably little is known about the books he possessed. No library catalogue survives, like the one of his brother Thomas of Woodstock's remarkable book collection at Pleshey.[50] No surviving volumes have been positively identified as belonging to Gaunt. Apart from service books from his chapel, the only books which he bequeathed in his will of 1399 were his missal and prayer book (*portheus*), doubtless especially dear to him since they had belonged to the Black Prince. There is no firm evidence that Gaunt commissioned a literary work or rewarded an author for his writings. The poet John Gower looked to his son Henry of Bolingbroke as a literary patron.[51] Sir Othon de Graunson, one of Gaunt's retainers, was a voluminous writer of courtly verse in his native French. But there is no evidence that any of his poems were written for the duke.[52]

Gaunt was a patron of the two most remarkable English writers of his time, Geoffrey Chaucer and John Wycliffe, but there is no secure evidence that he rewarded them for their writings. Chaucer was receiving an annual fee from the duke at the end of Edward's reign. His wife Philippa was a well-established member of the ducal household, being the sister of the duke's mistress Catherine Swynford, whom he married in 1396. Chaucer may have been rewarded by the duke because of these links and his business services. But there is some evidence that Chaucer was appreciated as a poet by the Lancastrian family, including Gaunt. Speght's edition of his works (1602) has a heading to the *A.B.C.*: 'made, as some say, at the request of Blanch,

Duchesse of Lancaster, as a praier for her priuat vse, being a woman in her religion very deuout.'[53] If *The Boke of the Duchesse* was written to console the duke, it is surprising that no dedication to him survives. It is likely that it was made for him rather than, say, just Blanche's *domicellae*. For however formal and derivative its elegiac sentiments are, they are intensely personal. Nevertheless, the fact that Chaucer wrote in English rather than French – which the duke understood perfectly well – suggests that the poem was intended to be read as well by members of his household whose French was 'after the scole of Stratford atte Bowe'.

The Boke is a telling piece of evidence about learning and literary taste in Gaunt's household in the 1360s. Helen Phillips has written that 'of all his [Chaucer's] major original works this is the one which is closest to French courtly poetry in form, style and spirit'.[54] It would have been appreciated by a reader familiar with the classic courtly allegory, the *Roman de la Rose* and with contemporary French poets. Chaucer assumes the reader's acquaintance with and enthusiasm for classical mythology. The poem relates the Lancastrian household to the proto-Renaissance of the later fourteenth century. In view of Gaunt's deep involvement in French affairs, it is not surprising to find this most French of Chaucer's poems originating there.

Some of his other poems have Lancastrian links. The ballad *Fortune* is addressed to princes 'three . . . or tweyne': the most familiar princely trinity in Ricardian England consisted of Gaunt and his younger brothers. *The Compleynt of Mars*, according to a fifteenth-century writer, was composed at Gaunt's request.[55] The eulogy of his father-in-law Pedro I of Castile in *The Monkes Tale* clearly reflects the feelings about the king of the Duchess Constance and a version of his death current in the Lancastrian household.

Gaunt certainly patronised Wycliffe – notoriously so; he liked to have learned clerics as confessors (see pp. 247–8). The scraps of evidence which survive about his attainments and literary interests suggest, it may be concluded, that he received a formal education which was scholarly as well as knightly. He probably learnt to read Latin as well as French and English and absorbed a great deal of classical as well as devotional lore. He had an aptitude for rhetoric and the application of logic, which he put to practical use in later life. He developed a sophisticated taste for courtly literature. He revelled too in knightly skills, though he was to disclaim any merit as a jouster (see p. 360).

His father had been schooled besides in worldly adversities. Edward expected his sons to play a part in public affairs long before they attained their majorities. Gaunt was taught from his early teens by experience how princes should conduct themselves in war and diplomacy. He was present at a bloody naval battle at the age of ten. By the time he was sixteen he had experienced the problems of campaigning in the Channel and in France and Scotland, and had witnessed a treaty concerned with the intractable problem of Anglo-Scottish relations. By the time he was twenty-one, he had campaigned extensively in France and had experienced the fundamental problems encountered there by the English invading armies throughout his life. He must have known a great deal about the making of the Treaty of Brétigny, which was to remain a principal point of reference in Anglo-French diplomacy.

Perhaps the best testimony to the character and abilities of the young Gaunt is that those two shrewd politicians and seasoned men of action, Edward III and Henry duke of Lancaster, were prepared to entrust him with the major controlling influence over the greatest English magnate inheritance, that of the House of Lancaster. Sooner, and more fully than they expected, he was to become the embodiment and custodian of the duchy's tradition of military and diplomatic service to the Crown. But there was also a more controversial and menacing Lancastrian tradition – that of Thomas of Lancaster's rebellion and 'martyrdom' in 1322 as Edward II's opponent. Pilgrims came to pray at his tomb in Pontefract Priory. There in 1359, the year of Gaunt's joyous marriage and exciting campaigning in France, there was a reminder of the other Lancastrian tradition which Gaunt was now heir to. Blood ominously flowed from Thomas of Lancaster's tomb.[56] Was Gaunt fated to be caught up in a revival of his opposition to the king?

Notes and References

1   McKisack M 1959, pp. 162–3.
2   Lucas HS 1929, p. 365.
3   Armitage-Smith J 1904, pp. 1–3.
4   *C.C.R. 1341–3*, p. 467.
5   Armitage-Smith J 1904, p. 3 and n; Lucas HS 1929, pp. 354, 376–7 and 377n.
6   Armitage-Smith J 1904, p. 4; P.R.O. E101/389/9.
7   Orme N 1983, p. 69; Orme N 1984, ch. 1. Gaunt's nurse Isolda Neweman was granted a royal annuity of £10 in 1346 (*C.P.R. 1345–8*, p. 55).
8   A.N. *Inventaire Sommaire Gironde* 1892 sér. G, C317. Joan died at Bordeaux on her way to marry the future Pedro I of Castile.
9   Froissart J 1869, Vol. 7, p. 429.
10 Jones M 1970, ch. 1; *C.P.R. 1340–3*, pp. 197–8, 236.
11 Ibid., p. 569; *C.P.R. 1343–5*, pp. 4–5, 42–3; Armitage-Smith 1904, pp. 4–5.
12 *Foedera* 1825, Vol. 3. pt 1, pp. 46–7.
13 Crow MM and Olson CC 1966, p. 92.

14   Orme N 1983, pp. 69–70.
15   *A.C.*, pp. 30, 162.
16   *Foedera* 1825, Vol. 3, pt 1, p. 171; Le Baker G 1889, p. 97.
17   *Register of Edward the Black Prince*, Vol. 2, p. 35; Vol. 4, pp. 54, 90, 164. In Nov. 1352 cloth for housings was to be delivered for the prince's palfreys and three of Gaunt's (ibid., p. 66).
18   Ibid., p. 10.
19   Ibid., p. 54.
20   Suarez Fernandez L 1958 pp. 13–14; Froissart J 1868, Vol. 5, p. 258. Sir Thomas Reresby remarked many years later that Edward had three sons with him – Lionel and Edmund as well as John (Nicolas NH 1832, Vol. 2, p. 307).
21   Pope MK and Lodge EC 1910, p. 139.
22   *C.H.K.*, Vol. 2, pp. 81–4.
23   Froissart J 1868, Vol. 5, pp. 264–5.
24   Armitage-Smith 1904, p. 5n.
25   *C.H.K.*, Vol. 2, p. 80.
26   le Bel J 1863, Vol. 2, p. 180; Reading J de 1914, p. 121.
27   Ibid., pp. 180–3; *C.H.K.*, Vol. 2, pp. 83–4.
28   Reading J de 1914, pp. 121–2.
29   *Foedera* 1708, Vol. 5, pp. 832–43; *C.H.K.*, Vol. 2, pp. 84–6; *C.A.*, p. 34; Nicholson R 1974, pp. 160–2.
30   *C.P.R. 1354–8*, pp. 543, 562; Somerville R 1953, p. 53.
31   Household account of countess of Ulster, B.L. Add. MS 18632 (printed Crow MM and Olson CC 1966, p. 15). Hatfield was in the custody of the queen as guardian of her son Edmund.
32   Fowler K 1969.
33   Gaunt and Blanche, related in the third and fourth degrees, needed a papal dispensation to marry, granted Jan. 1359 (*C.E.P.R. Papal Letters*, Vol. 3, p. 605).
34   Froissart J 1975, p. 55 (ll. 241–50).
35   Devon F 1837, Vol. 1, p. 170; P.R.O. E101/393/10; Armitage-Smith J 1904, pp. 14–15 and 15n. The keeper of the great wardrobe received an allowance on his account for purveyances for the marriage at Reading (*C.C.R. 1360–4*, p. 36). According to the fifteenth-century writer John Capgrave, the couple were blessed by Robert (Wyvil), bishop of Salisbury (Capgrave J 1858, p. 164).
36   Reading J de 1914, p. 131; *C.A.*, p. 39; *C.C.R. 1360–4*, p. 36–7. For the Black Prince's gift of a shield to Sir Bartholomew Burghersh at these jousts, see his Register, Vol. 4, p. 324.
37   *C.P.R. 1358–61*, p. 265; P.R.O. SCI/50/124.
38   le Bel J 1863, Vol. 2, p. 254; *A.C.*, p. 44; Fowler K 1969, pp. 197ff.
39   Ibid., pp. 201ff; *C.Q.P.V.*, pp. 105–6; *C.H.K.*, Vol. 2, pp. 107–9.
40   Fowler K 1969, pp. 204ff.
41   *A.C.*, p. 49.
42   Somerville R 1953, p. 54; *C.P.R. 1358–61*, pp. 375, 428.
43   Armitage-Smith J 1904, p. 94.
44   Crow MM and Olson CC 1966, p. 20.
45   Fowler K 1969, pp. 216–18; Nicolas NH 1826, Vol. 1, p. 65.
46   Somerville R 1953, p. 48.
47   Eisner S and MacEoin G 1980, pp. 58ff.
48   *A.C.*, pp. 154–5.

49   *W.C.*, pp. 66–9, 490–1.
50   Goodman A 1971, p. 80. I owe thanks to Dr Jeremy J. Smith and Professor Derek Pearsall for advice about Gaunt's possession of books and relations with Chaucer.
51   Fisher JH 1965, pp. 68, 124. One can be more confident than Fisher in concluding that the heraldic evidence in Huntington MS E1 26 A17 (*Confessio Amantis*) indicates that it was a pre-1399 presentation copy for Bolingbroke.
52   Braddy H 1947.
53   Chaucer G 1974, p. 855.
54   Phillips H 1982, p. 3.
55   Cowling GH 1926, pp. 405ff.
56   *C.A.*, p. 41.

Chapter Four

Rise to Power (1361–77)

In July 1361 directions were issued for the division of the late duke Henry of Lancaster's inheritance. Gaunt's portion was mainly north of the River Trent, including the earldoms of Lancaster and Derby: he became the principal magnate in northern England, consolidating and extending his influence there as earl of Richmond. His enhanced status was reflected in his new style – 'John son of the King of England, earl of Lancaster, Richmond, Derby and Lincoln and High Steward of England'.[1]

The winter of 1361–2 was a time of both joys and sorrows for Gaunt and his family. In October he was at a family gathering at Windsor Castle, witnessing the marriage of his beloved elder brother the Black Prince to Joan, 'the fair maid of Kent' whose first husband, the valiant Sir Thomas Holand, grizzled and one-eyed, had recently died.[2] A grand-daughter of Edward I, and sister of the earl of Kent, Joan had an exciting marital past and was one of the most remarkable personalities in English court circles. Froissart described the future mother of Richard II as 'the most beautiful lady in the whole realm of England and the most amorous'. Her courtship by the Black Prince and their marriage could plausibly be described in the period in the conventions of courtly love. In maturity, during her son's minority Joan showed herself as a calming political influence and a good friend of Gaunt.

Early in 1362 the Black Prince and his bride were to leave for Aquitaine, granted by Edward III to the prince. However, Gaunt's younger sister Mary duchess of Brittany died before 13 September

1361 and his younger sister Margaret countess of Pembroke died later that year. Both may have been victims of the current plague pandemic; soon the death of another kinswoman dramatically transformed Gaunt's fortunes. On 10 April 1362 Gaunt's sister-in-law Maud countess of Leicester died unexpectedly. As she was childless, Gaunt gained her portion of the Lancastrian inheritance in right of his wife Blanche. In a session of parliament at Westminster on 13 November, the king girded a sword on Gaunt, placed a furred cap on his head, and, over it, a circlet of gold and pearls, and named him duke of Lancaster. He presented his son with a charter of title.[3]

As an exceedingly rich young knight who had worthily served his military apprenticeship, Gaunt might have been expected in the 1360s to go crusading, as the earl of Hereford did in Prussia in 1363–4 and in Egypt in 1365, or to join his brother the prince in Aquitaine.[4] He was probably kept in England by the business of consolidating his control over the Lancastrian estates.[5] It was expedient for him to visit some of his new possessions. At Leicester, for instance, where he was first received as lord, with Blanche in his company, probably in June 1362, it was rumoured that Maud had been poisoned in order to reunite the inheritance.[6] At the start of the following month he was at his Staffordshire castle of Tutbury and in August at his Derbyshire manor of Ravensdale, probably enjoying hunting the game in his fine northern chases.[7] The pattern of a tour in the summer and early autumn of his principal midland and Yorkshire estates was to be one which he often repeated.

Gaunt's brothers had either acquired or seemed likely to acquire territorial interests abroad: the prince held Aquitaine, Lionel duke of Clarence's wife had brought him the earldom of Ulster, and it seemed probable that Edmund of Langley would gain a principality in the Low Countries. In 1363 David II of Scotland was promoting an earlier scheme for Gaunt to be his successor (see p. 177): David's tenacious willingness to contemplate this role for Gaunt suggests that he thought highly of the young man. The king's judgement is worthy of respect, for he was proud and canny, and would only have been prepared to contemplate Gaunt as a future king of Scots if he discerned marked qualities of mind, spirit and accomplishments in him. As a result of the absence in the 1360s of Gaunt's elder brothers governing south-west France and Ireland, while he dreamed of the Scottish Crown, he grew prominent in his father's counsels. He was closely involved in the attempt to provide Edmund of Langley with a foreign inheritance and to extend English influence in the Low Countries at the expense of the French. Margaret, daughter of Louis de Male, count of Flanders, a wily politician, was prospective heir not only to her father's possessions, but to the counties of Artois and Burgundy, and the duchy of Brabant. In 1362 Edward proposed to Louis that Edmund should marry the recently widowed Margaret; agreement for alliance was reached by 1364.[8] That September Gaunt set out on embassy to the count at Bruges and probably returned to England escorting him to meet the king at Dover Castle. There Edward sat up late feasting his guest. Negotiations ensued for three days, followed by a pilgrimage to the shrine of St Thomas at Canterbury. On 19 October Gaunt and the highly respected earl of Arundel swore to treaty terms on Edward's behalf at Dover Castle. According to these, the marriage was to take place at Bruges the following February. The king agreed to grant Edmund and his issue by Margaret, besides the reversion of English properties, Ponthieu and the March of Calais, to be held of the English Crown. Edward would concede to Edmund all right which he had through his queen in Hainault, Holland, Zealand and Friesland. He and his sons were to assist Louis in the conquest of territories to which he and his family had a right, such as Brabant.[9] The help Gaunt was prepared to give his younger brother in these affairs typified his strong sense of family solidarity. It was, indeed, to be frequently reciprocated over many years by the genial Edmund; in Richard's reign he tended to follow doggedly Gaunt's political leads. Brave and dependable in warfare, Edmund of Langley was otherwise the least able of Edward's sons. He was the mild one of a forceful brood, lacking in political weight, preferring private pleasures. As ruler of Flanders (a task which taxed the able Count Louis) he promised to be a disaster.

The creation of a great new principality in the Low Countries and north-east France, ruled by an English prince holding the French parts from the English Crown, was an alarming prospect for Charles V of France. More immediately, the Anglo-Flemish alliance threatened the control of his brother Philip over the imperial county of Burgundy. Charles V's diplomacy was to prove more than a match for the English. Slight of build, bookish, deeply imbued with belief in the divine sanctions of his kingship, Charles lacked the chivalrous flamboyance of his father John II; as regent during his father's captivity in England, he had as a youth learnt politics the hard way. In the 1360s and 1370s his calculating political and military strategies outsmarted the tired manoeuvres of Edward III and his sons. Charles managed to prevail on Pope Urban V to refuse the dispensation necessary for the marriage of Edmund and Margaret. Agreements between Edward and Louis to postpone the wedding, and Edward's preparations in 1365 to help him secure towns and castles in the county of Burgundy and elsewhere, show that the parties were for some time optimistic that the legal obstacle would be overcome – wrongly so, as it turned out.[10]

In 1364–5 Gaunt is likely to have been deep in his father's and brother Edmund's counsels over Flemish affairs and prepared to bring the Lancastrian retinue to the count of Flanders' aid in fulfilment of his father's obligations.[11] With the failure to implement the Flemish alliance, the focus of English diplomacy was shifting to Spain, where, as in Flanders and Brittany, rivalry continued between the English and French Crowns. In 1362 Edward had secured the alliance of the strongest peninsular power, the kingdom of Castile. Its tyrannical ruler, Pedro I, was locked in bitter struggles with his wily neighbour Pere III of Aragon and with his own illegitimate half-brother Enrique of Trastamara, rival for his throne, a hard man like himself. In 1366, backed by Pere and Charles V, a force partly composed of the companies, mercenary bands used to fighting in France, invaded Castile under the command of Bertrand du Guesclin. This scion of a minor Breton noble family had established himself over the past ten years as a tough and reliable fighter and leader of mercenaries, doing sterling service to uphold French royal interests. Charles V was to elevate him to the constableship of France, and he was to be honoured by burial with French kings in the abbey of St Denys, where his effigy has a blunt, soldierly appearance. This plain and thickset man of camps rather than courts was to be on occasion a worthy opponent of Gaunt. Du Guesclin and his companions revealed the vulnerability of Castile in 1366 by putting Enrique on the throne. Pedro fled to the protection of the Black Prince in Gascony: the prince rashly promised to restore him. That summer a decision was taken by Edward and Gaunt that the latter should lead a retinue to assist the Black Prince in his proposed invasion of Castile.[12] In order to finance his expedition, Gaunt received loans from the Crown which may have totalled 5,000 marks. As security for repayment he pledged various properties, which were put in the hands of a rising clerical minister of the Crown, William Wykeham, and a group of Lancastrian retainers.[13]

In September Gaunt attended the provincial chapter of the Benedictines at Northampton and was received into their confraternity; their prayers were particularly needful in view of the hazards of his undertaking.[14] On the 16th royal orders were issued to raise contingents of archers for his retinue; military preparations for his expedition continued into November.[15] Gaunt's departure was delayed by a serious dispute, involving property, with the Gloucestershire landowner Edward Lord Despenser. They were both summoned to the royal council, which mediated successfully between them.[16] On 14 November Gaunt dated a warrant at his manor of Kingston Lacy (Dorset); this suggests that he was en route to a west-country embarkation port – possibly Plymouth, with which he was to become familiar on his travels.[17] He sailed to the Cotentin in Normandy, avoiding the long sea route, and passed through Brittany (where he was entertained by the duke) and Poitou. At Bordeaux he met his sister-in-law Princess Joan, who had recently given birth to the future Richard II (5 January 1367). He hastened on for a joyful reunion with his brother the Black Prince at Dax.[18] But their joy was clouded by uncertainty over the intentions of Carlos II of Navarre, whose Pyrenean kingdom was strategically crucial to their campaign; Gaunt had experienced the effects of his desertion of the English in northern France in 1355. In January 1367 Carlos allied with Enrique of Trastamara and closed the Pyrenean passes to the Black Prince. At the end of January the latter sent Gaunt to meet Carlos at St Jean Pied de Port and to escort him to a conference with the prince and Pedro at Peyrehorade. There the king once more changed sides and the terms for an alliance were reaffirmed.[19] Setting out in mid-February, the army struggled through snow-covered passes till they reached the shelter of Roncesvalles. Remembrance of relief received at the hospice there may have prompted Gaunt's favour many years later to the hospice's cell near The Savoy (see p. 253). Gaunt, commanding the vanguard, took a conspicuous part in the Castilian campaign and in the decisive victory of Najera (see p. 228). Soon after Enrique's defeat, the duke was at Burgos with his brother the Black Prince, lodging in the suburban monastery of San Pablo. On 2 May they rode through the city to the cathedral of Santa Maria, where before the high altar Gaunt witnessed the restored Pedro's affirmation of his promises to the prince; in August the English withdrew to Gascony. The Castilian venture had turned sour for the brothers. The Black Prince's health had deteriorated and he was soon plotting to seize Pedro's throne himself, since his ally had failed to provide him with the promised lordships in Castile.[20] Gaunt hastened back from Gascony to England before the weather broke. Doubtless he was anxious to view his infant son and heir Henry of Bolingbroke; in June and July Edward III had rewarded bearers of the tidings of the birth of the future Henry IV. Gaunt witnessed a royal charter dated at Westminster on 8 October; he probably had the task of reporting to his father on the Black Prince's new plans for intervention in Castile.[21]

The Black Prince was diverted in 1368 from further Spanish adventures by growing Anglo-French tension, precipitated by his own bad relations with Gascon nobles and communities. Charles V's acceptance of appeals against the prince's government challenged the basis of the peace. But for Gaunt the prospect of war was probably eclipsed by personal tragedies: Dr John Palmer has proved that it was on 12 September in this year that the Duchess Blanche died.[22] According to Armitage-Smith, she was aged twenty-six or twenty-seven, and had borne Gaunt five children in nine years, including two sons who died in infancy, the last of them born possibly in 1368. Perhaps she died as a result of childbirth.[23] The following month Gaunt's vigorous brother Clarence, who had recently married Violanta Visconti, died in Piedmont.[24]

To win an advantage for his family over the French Crown, Gaunt was ready to contemplate remarriage soon after his bereavement. In December he was proposed to the count of Flanders as bridegroom for that elusive widow, his daughter Margaret. The count turned down the offer. In June 1369 the Valois family won the prize at last, by her marriage to Charles V's brother Philip duke of Burgundy.[25] That month war broke out between the English and the French Crowns. Preparations had been under way for Gaunt to reinforce the Black Prince in Aquitaine: on 12 April orders were issued for the array of archers for Gaunt's retinue, to be ready to embark at Southampton by the beginning of June.[26] However, it was decided that Gaunt's force should constitute the vanguard of an army which Edward intended to take to Calais. On 11–12 June Gaunt contracted to serve with his retinue for six months and was appointed lieutenant in the March of Calais; he had crossed there by 16 July.[27] On 7 August Edward ordered the rest of the army to assemble at Sandwich in ten days' time. But on the 14th the assembly date was postponed till 3 September: James Sherborne suggested that the delay was caused by the queen's illness – she died on 15 August. Edward gave up command of the whole expedition to Gaunt; the royal retinue crossed to join the duke towards mid-September.[28] Gaunt's conduct of the campaign was the first major setback to his military reputation (see pp. 229–32 for the campaign).

By 18 December he was back home at The Savoy: he then wrote to his warrener at Aldbourne (Wilts.) ordering him to have thirty pairs of rabbits caught and delivered to the king's house at Langley (Herts.), where he intended to spend Christmas with his father. The rabbits were to be delivered on Christmas Eve and they were to be fresh, seasonable and of the best quality.[29] After festivities probably muted by the queen's death, father and son were to have another shock: Sir John Chandos, foremost among English soldiers, was mortally wounded in a skirmish on New Year's Eve.[30]

In 1370, since the main French threat was now to Aquitaine, it was decided that Gaunt should reinforce the Black Prince there, as had been originally planned in 1369. On 18 April he issued mandates for the purchase of horses and other necessities 'against our next journey to Gascony' and (28th) for payment of letters dispatched that month from London to his Lancashire retainers.[31] By the end of June Gaunt was at Plymouth with his soldiers; on 1 July the king granted him full powers to act in concert with the Black Prince to re-establish peace in Aquitaine.[32] These powers may have been conferred with the prince's chronic illness in mind. When Gaunt met the prince and their younger brother Edmund of Langley at Cognac, after his voyage to Bordeaux, he was doubtless shocked to find that his brother could no longer sit astride a horse. He had to be carried in a litter to besiege Limoges.[33] But the effort made the Black Prince worse. Before the campaign was over, he handed over command to Gaunt and soon afterwards, intending to return to England to recuperate, made Gaunt his lieutenant in Aquitaine (see p. 189). The prince and princess embarked in December, delayed probably by the illness and death of their son Edward, the future Richard II's elder brother. The prince's sorry state is reflected in his failure to stay for his son's funeral: Gaunt arranged this in the cathedral of St André at Bordeaux.[34]

Gaunt gave up his lieutenancy in Aquitaine on 21 July 1371. His most significant action during his stay in the duchy happened afterwards: he remarried. The failure of the Black Prince's Castilian policies had facilitated the expansion of French influence. This culminated in Enrique of Trastamara's capture and assassination of his half-brother Pedro at Montiel in 1369, and seizure of his throne. Enrique failed to secure Pedro's daughter and heir Constance and her sister Isabel: they fled to Bayonne. Early in September Gaunt married Constance at Roquefort near Mont-de-Marsan.[35] He was anxious to return to England: after staying briefly at Bordeaux for celebrations with his bride, he arrived at La Rochelle by 25 September. The young queen's voyage to her prince's home was apparently made in a salt ship: Gaunt requisitioned a ship at anchor, the *Gaynpayn*, obliging her master John Payn to discharge a cargo of Bay salt. Constance presumably embarked with the duke in the *Gaynpayn*, with the presents she had recently received, including one from him – a gold cup 'fashioned in the manner of a double rose with pedestal and lid with a white dove on the lid'.[36] They landed at Fowey by 4 November and six days later were, it seems, staying at Plympton Priory.[37] They were so short of cash that Constance had to pawn cloth of gold and a chalice to some Dartmouth men. On their progress to London the duke and duchess visited Exeter Cathedral, where they could afford to make an offering of 20s.[38] Gaunt travelled, probably via Salisbury, to London and was installed at The Savoy towards the end of the month.[39] His young children, Philippa (the eldest, aged ten), Elizabeth and Henry of Bolingbroke probably had the exciting experience of going to greet their father: on his return to England their transfer from Ware (Herts.) to Deeping (Lincs.), planned by their mistress Lady Wake, was cancelled. Gaunt appears to have gone down to Kingston Lacy (Dorset) to celebrate Christmas and the New Year. Possibly he had left Constance there to rest after the voyage and accustom herself to unfamiliar surroundings. During Christmas at Kingston he probably rewarded a mariner for service on the voyage, a certain Cok Wille, and possibly then gave a Christmas present to the countess of Salisbury, a daughter of his particular friend Lady Mohun.[40]

In January 1372, according to the Anonimalle Chronicler 'by the common counsel of England the name and arms of the duke of Lancaster were changed and he was called king of Castile and León, and took the arms of Spain, quarterly with a label'. For the next sixteen years Gaunt was in the unusual position for an English magnate of claiming to be king of one of the principal realms of Christendom, conducting himself around England as befitted a king of Spain as well as the son of the king of England and the duke of Lancaster. He was not to find it easy to wear such a bewildering collection of dazzling hats; some of the domestic suspicion of him which gathered force in the 1370s grew in reaction to his assumption of alien aspirations and royal *hauteur*. English folk often expressed disgust at foreigners; the desire of an English magnate to become one puzzled them.

On 10 February following Constance was publicly received in London by the Black Prince, by many lords and knights, and the mayor and commonalty who escorted her through the city 'and in Cheapside there were many people and ladies and girls viewing the beauty of the said young lady'. The party rode out to The Savoy, where Gaunt greeted his wife.[41] At the end of April he was showing solicitude that she should be fittingly arrayed as a queen. The clerk of the duke's wardrobe was ordered to deliver to Alyne Gerberge, *demoiselle* of Constance's chamber, all manner of things needful for her headgear, 1,808 pearls of the largest kind and 2,000 of the second best (presumably for sewing into her dresses); a little circlet of gold bejewelled with emeralds and balas rubies; a string (*filet d'or*) with four balas rubies and twenty-one pearls set in gold. The clerk was also to deliver to Constance a gift from her husband, a reliquary shaped like a barrel, trimmed with gold and precious stones.[42] Relics may have been among the prized possessions which this serious and devout young lady had clung to on her flight from Spain. That year the king gave her a golden crown ornamented with balas diamonds and pearls. The Black Prince gave her a golden jewel depicting St George ornamented with balas sapphires, diamonds and pearls. She did not like the silver enamelled cup with the figure of a minstrel on the cover presented to her by Bishop Sudbury of London, for she soon gave it away.[43]

On a personal level, the marriage of Gaunt and Constance was not a whole-hearted success. A wary mutual respect did, indeed, develop. Constance was deeply passionate, devoted to the memory of her astoundingly ferocious father Pedro and consumed with hatred for his slayer and the persecutor of her family, her uncle Enrique II. Living as a refugee among the prickly and self-righteous English, in their often cheerless and sodden landscapes, she cherished flickering hopes of returning gloriously to Spain to right wrongs. Valuing the company of her fellow countrymen and women, she wrung respect from the English for her dignity and piety and from her husband for her judgements on Iberian affairs. What lay between them like a sword was his settled course of adultery with Catherine Swynford. In the 1370s, in the springtime of Gaunt's marriage with Constance, Catherine produced a whole handful of healthy babies whose paternity he acknowledged and to whom he gave the surname Beaufort, possibly in allusion to their infant appearance. Gaunt's lengthy liaison with Catherine, conducted without discretion, scandalised some English contemporaries and probably worsened his reputation in Richard's minority. The affair is a prime example of Gaunt's princely wilfulness, sometimes pursued to the detriment of other objectives. Though one monastic chronicler described Catherine Swynford as a she-devil, she seems to have been eminently suited to be a prince's paramour, unlike the tottering Edward's scratchy bedfellow Alice Perrers, who drove Thomas Walsingham, apoplectic, to cast unmonastic aspersions on her deficiencies of complexion and figure. Catherine was the daughter of one of Queen Philippa's knightly followers from Hainault, the widow of a Lancastrian knight and a former *domicella* of Gaunt's first wife, the Duchess Blanche. In later life Catherine was shown great respect by Gaunt's son and heir Bolingbroke and, after she married Gaunt, she was a worthy duchess of Lancaster.

Constance appears to have been expected to give birth just nine months after her wedding. In a ducal warrant dated 6 June 1372 at The Savoy, Gaunt ordered the receiver of Leicester to have 'Ilote the wise woman' sent to Constance at Hertford 'with all the haste that in any manner you can'. She had attended the Duchess Blanche and is elsewhere referred to in the ducal *Register* as 'our well-beloved Elyot the midwife of Leycestre'.[44] The expected baby was probably their one surviving child, Catherine (Catalina), the future queen of Castile.[45] Gaunt does not seem to have anticipated being on hand about the time of his wife's confinement: on 6 and 7 June he gave orders for the laying in of stocks of good wine at Kenilworth Priory and Tutbury Castle for the visits which he intended to make there soon. It is not certain that he carried out the intention: ducal warrants suggest that from May till mid-August he was mostly at The Savoy.[46] He probably made a visit to Reigate Castle (Surrey), one of the residences of his ageing financial benefactor the earl of Arundel, on 7 July. He is likely to have been at Wallingford (Berks.) on the 11th for the marriage of his exceedingly dull brother Edmund to Constance's too lively sister Isabel. On her wedding day Gaunt gave her a 'triper', a three-legged, vessel, silver-gilt and shaped like a monster, with three buttresses, and figures of 'sergeants de macz' (mace-bearing sergeants?) on a green ground. There were also a matching cup and ewer enamelled with crowned roses and 'babewyns' – grotesque figures, not necessarily monkeys. These amusing conceits were appropriate for Isabel, who was to acquire a reputation for light-heartedness, in contrast to her intense sister Constance.[47] At the end of the month Gaunt may have fitted in a quick hunting expedition, staying at his lodge, Bird's Nest, in Leicester Forest.[48]

Besides being in the south during his wife's confinement and his brother's marriage, there were good reasons for Gaunt to stay there in the summer of 1372 and to forgo the pleasures of visiting midland and northern estates. He was heavily involved in diplomatic and military preparations which required consultation with the king and royal council. A strenuous diplomatic campaign was under way to win Iberian allies for his claim to Castile (see p. 113). But Gaunt accepted that he should give his family's interest in France priority. On 24–5 February numerous indentures had been drafted for service on an expedition to be led by the rapidly ageing king. The Black Prince was probably too weak to participate, but by 3 March Gaunt was preparing to do so.[49] Plans for this expedition may have been modified by the naval disaster which occurred in June. The new lieutenant going out to Aquitaine, the fierce young earl of Pembroke, was defeated and captured off La Rochelle by the Castilian galley-fleet. After this, the English gave priority to challenging this fleet: in the indentures for military service which Gaunt sealed on 1 July, he undertook to serve for a year 'on and over the sea'. Among the contingencies envisaged were operations in Aquitaine and Gaunt's diversion with his retinue, after six months' service, to Spain. But in the letters of summons which Gaunt issued ten days later, ordering his retinue to assemble on 8 August, he said that the service was to be at sea and without horses. The embarkation port, Sandwich, was ideally situated for a cruise in the Channel rather than the Bay of Biscay.[50]

To support his father's cause in 1372, Gaunt not only sacrificed his hopes of going to Spain, but gave up his oldest title of nobility. In the winter of 1371–2 Edward had started negotiations for an alliance with the duke of Brittany, who visited him in February 1372. Duke John, by upbringing and successive marriages, was very much a younger member of Edward III's family. However, he was a calculating politician who had to put his often precarious dynastic interests first. He pitched his terms high: he wanted his ancestral earldom of Richmond back. Edward agreed to this in July. Gaunt was compensated for his loss of the earldom by royal grants of the Yorkshire lordships of Tickhill and Knaresborough, among other properties (see pp. 309, 330–1).

The lengthy negotiations for the Brittany alliance, probably complicated by the Richmond issue, may have delayed the start of the royal expedition. Gaunt was at Sandwich on 18 August and stayed at the nearby Premonstratensian abbey of Langdon almost till the end of the month, when he probably moved on shipboard in Sandwich harbour.[51] On the 30th, in the king's stateroom (*aula*) on board *la Grace de Dieu*, he was present at about nine o'clock when the chancellor, Sir John Knyvet, delivered the great seal to Edward and received another seal from him. Next day the fleet weighed anchor. But what was to be Edward's last expedition turned out a fiasco. The ships tried in vain to beat their way down the Channel against a strong westerly, then returned to port. Gaunt was back in London by 12 September, when he witnessed a royal charter dated at Westminster.[52] He was probably at The Savoy for most of the rest of the year, making brief visits to Hertford.[53] On 19 November he may have been enjoying Bishop Wykeham's hospitality at Winchester; he made plans to spend Christmas and the New Year at Hertford.[54]

The experience which Gaunt acquired in military command in the years 1367–72, his sense of loyalty to Edward III and the Black Prince, and their relative debility, made him the natural choice to lead the main expedition to France in 1373. For the first six months of the year he seems to have been based mainly at The Savoy, preoccupied with the planning of the expedition. Probably on 11 January he attended the obit of Eleanor countess of Arundel, a sister of Duke Henry of Lancaster who had died the previous year. Perhaps this was held in Archbishop Whittlesey's chapel in his palace at Lambeth; afterwards Gaunt hired bargemen at Lambeth to row him across the Thames to The Savoy. He probably celebrated the feast of the Purification of the Blessed Virgin (2 February) at Hertford; he rewarded a friar, John Parys, with 6*s*. 8*d*. for preaching at the castle on that day.[55]

On 11 May the king granted Gaunt the privilege that his executors might hold his lands for one year after his death, to settle his debts. They were headed by distinguished friends, Bishops Wykeham and Sudbury and the earls of Arundel and Hereford. In the event of the duke's death, William Lord Latimer and Guy Lord Brian, both skilful men of business, were to be among the administrators of the lands.[56] Gaunt arranged for coal and wood to be taken to Tutbury Castle, where Constance was to stay during his absence.[57] His headquarters before he left, from the end of June to mid-July were at Northbourne (Kent), a grange of St Augustine's Abbey, Canterbury, situated between Sandwich and Dover.[58] He was to be in France for over nine months: as in 1369, his campaigning was a disappointment to his fellow countrymen (see p. 233). He returned from Bordeaux to England in April 1374, landing at Dartmouth, where ducal warrants were dated on the 26th.[59] From May to early July he was apparently much of the time at The Savoy.[60] This probably enabled him to participate in the council's discussions about the proposed expedition to Brittany in aid of the duke, and in meetings with Pope Gregory IX's envoy Pileo de Prata, archbishop of Ravenna. He was in England in June and July to prepare for the Anglo-French negotiations which the pope was promoting.[61]

Though Gaunt's brother Edmund of Langley was to contract to lead a retinue on the Breton expedition on 1 August, Gaunt was conspicuous by his absence. This was unlikely to have been the result of his quarrel with John of Brittany in 1373 (see p. 186) or of a failure to realise the strategic worth of the duchy. The Crown had accumulated massive debts to Gaunt for war services over the past few years (see p. 220): he may have decided it would be financially draining on his resources to lead another military retinue until he could recoup. Moreover, his experiences had made him realise as much as anyone the debilitating territorial and financial losses suffered by the English Crown since 1370 and the problems of reversing them. His failure to do so by military means on the 1373 expedition probably convinced him of the wisdom of trying to make peace.

For the past few years war and diplomacy are likely to have prevented Gaunt from touring his estates as much as he would have liked: Chaucer's image of him as a 'sylvan knight' had apparently soon become anachronistic. In the summer of 1374 he determined to cast aside international cares. He was at Leicester early in August; thence he moved to Tutbury and Ravensdale.[62] He stayed in Yorkshire for the first half of September, visiting his castle at Pontefract, his hunting lodge at Rothwell, his newly acquired castle at Knaresborough and his manor of Cowick.[63] Later that month he visited another of his recent acquisitions, Gringley (Notts.) and after a visit to Lincoln came south via Stamford.[64] He seems to have spent most of the rest of the year at The Savoy[65] and was there in January and February 1375.[66] On 8–9 March he was at Dover, preparing to embark as leader of the delegation to the peace conference at Bruges. He arrived there on the 24th; between the end of the month and the end of June there were three rounds of talks. Gaunt may have made one or more trips to England during the conference to consult his father and the royal council. No peace agreement was reached, only one for a year's truce. Gaunt had been criticised for his conduct of the 1369 and 1373 expeditions: the Bruges negotiations probably made him widely unpopular for the first time. In arranging the details of the truce, he apparently failed to consult the leaders of the expedition then in Brittany or take account of their objectives. The date set at Bruges for the cessation of hostilities robbed them of a promising opportunity to capture both Quimperlé and many of Duke John of Brittany's principal opponents.[67] Moreover, the expectation of peace in England was disappointed. By Gaunt's assent and counsel, the Anonimalle Chronicler remarked sarcastically, the negotiators accepted 'a marvellous truce'. His stay at Bruges had contributed to 'excessive costs with no profit', and he had made there 'great expenses and great disport' with Charles V's brother Louis duke of Anjou, recently an opposing commander in Aquitaine, with whom he went revelling and dancing each day.[68]

Gaunt returned to England by 15 July, and soon withdrew to his midland estates, spending much of August at Leicester and moving on to Kenilworth.[69] Thence he apparently went on a tour of the west country in September: warrants were dated at Cirencester (Gloucs.) on the 8th and at his favourite manor of Kingston Lacy (Dorset) on the 10th, 17th and 19th.[70] He was back in harness at The Savoy by the end of the month and during October, preparing for another round of Anglo-French negotiations, with which his presence at Dover in October may have been connected.[71] He was at Bruges on 7 December and till at least 20 January 1376; a ducal warrant was dated at The Savoy again on 16 February. The only achievement of this Bruges conference was the making of a truce to last till 1 April 1377.[72]

In 1374–5 Gaunt had emerged as a leading proponent of peace negotiations under papal auspices with the French Crown, a policy closely linked, as Professor Holmes has shown, to a settlement of Anglo-papal disputes with Pope Gregory XI.[73] It is not clear whether Gaunt had been so closely involved in English domestic politics before 1374 as he was to be from then till the end of the reign. Since he was a principal commander for much of the war (1369–74), he is likely to have had great influence on diplomatic as well as strategic decisions. But his absences abroad and his absorption in continental affairs certainly detached him to some extent from the politics of court and parliaments. The decline in Edward III's energy and attention to business and the Crown's need for administrative expertise and financial backing, especially when at war, enhanced the influence of favoured household officials, notably William Lord Latimer, and of syndicates of London financiers with court connections. Moreover, Edward indulged the greed for rewards and political influence of his widely disliked mistress Alice Perrers. In the first parliaments of the 1370s the Commons displayed a collective disquiet which heralded the explosion of 1376. But as yet it was not targeted at individual courtiers and merchants. The Commons, labouring under the burden of high war taxation, expressed discontent instead at the clergy's wealth and influence and at papal mulcting of the English Church. In the parliament of February 1371 the Commons petitioned for the replacement of the king's chief clerical ministers by laymen. In April Convocation was summoned to The Savoy (during Gaunt's absence in Aquitaine): there the Black Prince and other lay lords browbeat the clergy into making a large grant of subsidy. In the 1373 parliament (held when Gaunt was campaigning in France) the Commons complained about papal taxation. Their attempt to pressurise the clergy ran into difficulties. A firm protest was made by William Courtenay, the young and highly principled bishop of Hereford whom a few years later Gaunt was to find a formidable opponent. [74]

In the early 1370s Gaunt had retainers and friends who were near the centre of government. One of his most trusted retainers, Sir John Ypres, was controller of the royal household from 1368 to 1376. [75] Another, John Lord Neville, was steward of the household from 1371 to 1376; its chamberlain in this period, Lord Latimer, was Neville's father-in-law, a man respected by Gaunt. The duke's retainer Richard Lord Scrope was treasurer from 1371 to 1375. [76] The presence of these powerful and able northerners at court in the early 1370s was doubtless useful to Gaunt as a way of maintaining his interest there, especially during his absences abroad and in the north. But there is no evidence that he controlled government through them: the protests of 1376 were not against the domination of government by a Lancastrian caucus, but against individuals and coteries suspected of exploiting Edward's cantankerous but still forceful reliance on them.

In the parliament which assembled at Westminster on 28 April 1376 Gaunt's role was described by one contemporary as 'lieutenant of the king to hold parliament'. [77] For the king was too ill to attend and preside over parliament and the Black Prince apparently managed to attend only the opening session before retiring in sickness across the Thames to his house at Kennington. [78] On 29 April the chancellor, Sir John Knyvet, gave the Commons their 'charge', requesting a subsidy, but the Commons' prolonged and excited debates made clear that the request would not have plain sailing. On 9 May Gaunt was presiding over the Lords when a Commons delegation arrived with an answer. According to the Anonimalle Chronicler of St Mary's Abbey, York (apparently incorporating an eyewitness account into his chronicle), the duke appeared apprehensive – 'he started to speak very uneasily:

"which of you has the task of setting out what you have decided among yourselves?"' The Commons spokesman was the eloquent and redoubtable knight of the shire for Herefordshire, Sir Peter de la Mare, steward of Edmund Mortimer, earl of March. The earl, aged twenty-four, lacked experience, but had great potential, not just because of his vast spread of lordships in England, Wales and Ireland, but because he was the husband of Gaunt's niece Philippa, sole daughter and heir of his brother Lionel of Clarence (d. 1368). It was a moot point as to whether Philippa (or through her, her little son Roger) or Gaunt had a higher place in the succession to the Crown. It was clearly important for domestic peace that the Mortimer and Lancaster interests should not be at odds. The confrontations between March's steward Sir Peter and Gaunt threatened harmony among the royal kin, though good sense eventually prevailed. Sir Peter de la Mare on this occasion boldly outfaced the duke by refusing to report till all the Commons were present. Royal assent was given to their request to 'intercommune' with a committee of Lords. In a session of parliament on 12 May, after the intercommuning, Sir Peter on the Commons' behalf denounced men close to government as profiteers at the Crown's expense. Gaunt 'marvelled and said "How is that and who are they who have profited?".' Sir Peter made detailed charges. When Gaunt tried to rebut one against Latimer and the Londoner Richard Lyons, the shire knight countered with precise assertions. According to the St Albans Abbey chronicler Walsingham, Gaunt one evening in conference with his servants (his council?), denounced the shire knights – 'they think they are kings or princes of this realm'. He intended to awe them into submission. But one of his esquires warned him of the dangers of opposing them, pointing out that they had the support of the Lords, the Black Prince, the Londoners and the common people. Gaunt was duly impressed; he adopted a benign attitude to the shire knights which the hostile Walsingham considered hypocritical.[79] On 19 May parliament heard evidence about recent royal finances. As a former treasurer, Gaunt's friend and retainer Scrope gave evidence and so did a London merchant with whom Gaunt had connections, John Pyel: their evidence was to help convict Latimer and Richard Lyons.[80]

But Gaunt's cooperation did not appease the Commons: he was very annoyed that he was not among the councillors appointed in response to their petition for new ones. The vicious stories repeated by Walsingham show how his honourable attempt to defend his father's interest had made him suddenly hateful to a wide spectrum of public opinion. For instance, he was alleged to have delayed parliamentary condemnations for pecuniary gain and to have bribed a former captain of Latimer's Norman castle. St Sauveur-le-Vicomte, to withhold evidence.[81] There was worse. After the Black Prince's death on 8 June, the Commons petitioned that his nine-year-old son Richard should be brought before them, which was done on the 25th; they asked that he should be granted the principality of Wales in the same manner as his father. Their concern may have been intensified by rumours that Gaunt was plotting to succeed to the Crown – rumours circulating abroad too.[82]

Parliament – the longest yet held – ended on 10 July. To mark the occasion, the shire knights held a splendid feast. The king sent two barrels of red wine and eight deer; the Lords contributed a great sum of money to the costs, as well as giving wine. The bishops were present at the banquet; so were Gaunt's brothers Edmund of Langley, Thomas of Woodstock and the earls of March, Warwick, Suffolk and Salisbury, many barons, the mayor of London, and citizens and burgesses from London and elsewhere. Gaunt was conspicuous by his absence from this celebratory gathering of the political elites.

Edward himself could not be present; after a harrowing leave-taking of his dying son the Black Prince at Kennington, he was conveyed back to a country retreat, his house at Havering (Essex). Soon afterwards his health deteriorated so badly that the physicians despaired of his life – it was only about 3 February 1377, when 'a great impostume' burst, that he gradually responded to treatment. But, despite the attacks in the Good Parliament on the way royal authority was exercised, it continued to be vigorously so in the last year of Edward's life. According to the Anonimalle Chronicle, 'the ordinance of the said parliament [of 1376] was defeated the next day'. Walsingham had no doubt who was in charge of government and the prime mover in overturning the Good Parliament's achievements: the king, he said, put government wholly into Gaunt's hands.[83] The death of the Black Prince, the rapid deterioration of the king's health and the attacks on government in the Good Parliament made way for a Lancastrian ascendancy. The king put his trust above all in his eldest surviving son, whom he named first among his executors in the will he made on 7 October.[84] Gaunt's two younger brothers were to show political solidarity with him in the next few years. The lords appointed as councillors during the Good Parliament were not habitual opponents of the court nor of Gaunt; among them, Archbishop Sudbury of Canterbury was probably a particular friend of Gaunt's, and his kinsman Henry Lord Percy, associated with him in war, was soon to show himself a close political ally. Though his retainer Lord Neville and Neville's father-in-law Latimer had had to relinquish their respective offices as steward and chamberlain of the royal household, his retainer Ypres was moved to the stewardship in Neville's place.

Gaunt's influence on government soon after the end of the Good Parliament is reflected in royal orders made on his information on 22 July, and in a royal grant made with his assent on the 31st. He presided as royal lieutenant at the great council which met in October, in which Bishop Wykeham of Winchester, who had conspicuously abetted the prosecution of Latimer, was accused of malversations committed when he was keeper of the Privy Seal and chancellor and, predictably, found guilty. Allegedly Gaunt and his supporters wanted Wykeham to be imprisoned, but the bishops present opposed this, and he was deprived of his temporalities.[85] The following month Gaunt picked off another parliamentary adversary: Sir Peter de la Mare was arbitrarily imprisoned.[86]

It was easy for Gaunt's opponents to portray these punishments and the reversal of the Good Parliament's achievements as the fruits of his vindictive malevolence. Even if there was truth in this, his hostile feelings were intermixed with the principled and filial desire to uphold the Crown's dignity and win his father's blessing. Moreover, policy was affected by Edward's will and by the influence of courtiers on it, however sporadic. Illness may have made the king capricious and dictatorial, increasing his son's odium. On 8 October, at Havering, Edward 'with his own hand' gave a petition for Latimer's pardon to the chancellor and ordered that it should be granted, Gaunt being among those present – and probably promoting the petition.[87] It is unlikely that he supported the pardon granted to Edward's grasping mistress Alice Perrers a fortnight or so later or her assertions of influence over royal policy. Her treatment of his knight John Swinton shows how hollow the courtesies were between them. Swinton was unable to recover from her the jewels, valued at £400, which she had allegedly taken from the effects of Swinton's wife when she died. She had seized them in 1374 while he was campaigning in Brittany under Edmund of Langley, 'through the great power which she had at that time', against which his royal letters of protection were of no avail. Swinton petitioned Richard II and his council over the matter; so his master Gaunt's influence had not helped him in 1376–7.[88] In her trial in Richard's first parliament, Gaunt's testimony was designed to show how he had distanced himself from her interventions in policy and had been unable to nullify them. He had not, he alleged, supported her agitation for the revocation of Sir Nicholas Dagworth's commission to enquire into her husband Sir William Windsor's government in Ireland (October/November 1376). He said that when he had gone one day to Havering, Alice and Sir Roger Beauchamp showed him a bill about the matter. Soon afterwards it came up when he was talking to the king (clearly at a council meeting): Edward said that it did not seem reasonable to him that one enemy (Dagworth) should judge another (Windsor). Gaunt replied, 'such enmity between them is not yet proved; but it is certain that the said Sir Nichol is to be sent there for the good of the Land and of the whole Realm'. The councillors decided that both parties should be summoned before the council, so that Windsor could have a chance to prove Dagworth's bias, in which case his commission would be revoked. The king agreed. As soon as Gaunt came out of the chamber, he was accosted by Alice, who prayed him 'cherement' to stop Dagworth from going to Ireland at all costs. His rejection of her was brusque – 'he would do nothing other than what was decided in the King's presence'. Alice, seeing his determination, left him. Next day Gaunt went to take leave of his father, lying in bed; Edward charged him 'on his blessing' not to allow Dagworth to go; so he was countermanded. Asked about Richard Lyons's pardon (20 April 1377) Gaunt alleged that Alice was 'principale promotrice' of it and that he was not present when it was made.[89] In fact a ducal warrant is dated The Savoy that day.[90]

Gaunt's testimony must be seen in the context of the political backlash after Edward's death, which became concentrated on Alice. At least his testimony tells us that he wished to present himself as a proponent of orderly, not petticoat, government and as a dutiful son. If, at the same time, he was exposing his father's shame just to protect himself politically, he would have seemed transparently hypocritical. More probably, he painfully recounted these scenes, humiliating to both his father's memory and to himself, in order to denounce an evil court influence which had poisoned policy in the last phase of Edward's rule.

It may be that Gaunt's revelations about the limitations on his influence astonished many; at the time it had seemed so powerful as to be sinister. In December 1376 Charles V of France was speculating that Gaunt's 'rigour' betokened his desire to crush opposition to his designs on the throne.[91] In the new year Gaunt was anxious to emphasise the status of his ten-year-old nephew Prince Richard and hence his own loyal intentions. He was keen to rally support in case of renewed war. On 25 January the Londoners laid on a 'great entertainment and solemnity', a carnivalesque entertainment for Richard. A company of 130 vizored mummers rode from Newgate through Cheapside and across London Bridge to his house at Kennington. They were in groups tricked out as squires, knights, an emperor and pope with their retinues, cardinals and papal legates. The legates were cast as the villains of the piece, with horrible masks. The mummers came in the dark, with a great din and blazing torches. The prince, attended by his mother Princess Joan, Gaunt, Langley and Woodstock, the earls of Warwick and Suffolk with other lords, walked 'out of the chamber into the hall' to meet the dismounted mummers. They presented

Richard – so poignantly like his handsome father – with a set of loaded dice, with which he won three gold objects from them; his companions received gold rings. Richard had wine brought and drank joyfully. Then he called on the minstrels to play: 'they commenced to play trumpets, nakers and pipes'. He and the lords danced on one side and the mummers on the other.[92]

Thus Gaunt, absent from the banquet celebrating the end of the Good Parliament, danced harmoniously with the Londoners in honour of the heir to the throne. In the parliament which met two days later he and his nephew both acted as its presidents. Gaunt showed that he was prepared to play the populist politician: the treasurer Sir Robert Ashton attacked the papacy in parliament, a theme foreshadowed by the 'diabolic' legates in the Londoners' mumming. Though Walsingham's claim that Gaunt 'packed' the Commons with his retainers appears to be baseless, tight control was kept over them. A leading Lancastrian retainer, Sir Thomas Hungerford, was elected Speaker: the composition of the Lords' section of the intercommuning committee was pro-Gaunt. A large experimental subsidy – a graded poll tax – was granted. Pardons were issued to those impeached in the Good Parliament, but not to Wykeham or De la Mare.[93]

But the degree of unity Gaunt secured for his aims was now marred; the anticlericalism he was fostering got out of hand, provoking adverse reactions. The inclusion of the clergy in the poll tax stirred up the bishops; in Convocation they refused to grant a tax till they were joined by Wykeham. Gaunt gave way.[94] But he proceeded to display an intransigent crassness which is hard to parallel in his career, and whose motivation is in part mysterious. He succeeded in uniting the Londoners against him in defence of their liberties as well as the Church's. On 19 February, according to Walsingham, he proposed that the mayor of London should be replaced by a captain.[95] The same day John Wycliffe, royal protégé and stern critic of the justification for clerical wealth, appeared in St Paul's, on summons by Archbishop Sudbury to answer charges of unorthodoxy. When Wycliffe appeared, he was impressively escorted through the crowd by Gaunt, Lord Percy and a friar from each of the four orders. Gaunt furiously protested to Bishop Courtenay of London against the episcopal bench's arraignment of Wycliffe, 'saying that he was more worthy of sitting there than any of them'. Percy was carrying his baton as marshal of the realm. Gaunt's attempt to get Percy to arrest Wycliffe's prosecutors produced a strong rejoinder from Courtenay: he denied Percy's right of jurisdiction, protesting the liberties of Holy Church, and threatened excommunication. Gaunt's baffled, enraged reply was of the stupid sort for which his nephew Richard was to become notorious in the 1380s – he threatened to drag the bishop from his see by the hair. Gaunt and his companions left, consumed by anger, the duke retiring to The Savoy.[96]

Rumours spread among the Londoners that Gaunt had either threatened or beheaded their bishop; there was a surge from around Cheapside and St Paul's – the crowd aimed to kill the duke. When Courtenay heard this, he rushed after the rioters, catching up with them in Fleet Street, and managed to persuade them to return to the city. But Gaunt was not out of danger. London opinion was further aroused against him and Percy by the presentation of bills in parliament aiming to curb the city's liberties – the explosion of anger in St Paul's against the two of them had probably been augmented by the suggestion that Percy should exercise the marshal's jurisdiction within the city. According to Walsingham, on the 20th the city government met to debate how their liberties could best be defended. The meeting was interrupted by the arrival of two peers, Lords FitzWalter and Brian. FitzWalter was a youngish knight, a cousin of Percy, who was eventually to die abroad in Gaunt's service (see p. 292). Brian was a mature lord who had served Edward III with distinction and had been involved in Gaunt's business affairs (see pp. 292–3). It is a measure of how high feelings were running that lords with such connections now behaved in an inflammatory way which might have cost Gaunt and Percy their lives. They told the Londoners that, contrary to the city's liberties, Percy had arrested and was holding a man who had uttered derogatory remarks about the duke and himself. A mob promptly rushed to Percy's house, broke in and released the prisoner. They found out that Percy was dining with the duke at the house of the latter's retainer Ypres. The diners were eating oysters when news was brought of the approaching rioters. Gaunt got up so quickly that he barked his shins on the table. He was rowed across the Thames to take refuge at Kennington with Princess Joan and Prince Richard. It was no longer safe to reveal oneself as a Lancastrian retainer or sympathiser in London. The Londoners proclaimed the duke to be a traitor to knighthood by fixing his arms reversed on the doors of St Paul's Cathedral and Westminster Hall, together with bills saying that he was not the son of Edward III and Queen Philippa, but of a butcher of Ghent, substituted for a dead royal infant. This horribly scandalous accusation was 'graunt noys et graunte clamour' through the city and, indeed, throughout the kingdom.[97]

The Londoners were immediately summoned to appear before the king at Sheen. Only a small number of leading citizens dared to come. Gaunt, consumed with mortified fury, addressed them. What had been done, he said, was an insult to the king and to his sons and lineage. It was reasonable to punish them for it so severely that it would be an example for the whole of England. The mayor and citizens, distracted, fell to their knees and begged for mercy. The duke 'en sa ferocite' laid down conditions for his pardon. They must erect a marble pillar with his arms on it in the middle of Cheapside and go in procession with a wax candle to be offered at St Paul's. Mayor, sheriffs and aldermen must be replaced and those responsible for reversing the ducal arms condemned to death, subject to the duke's mercy. These demands met with a mixed reception next day at the Guildhall. The commons agreed only to the change of officials. They did not participate in the expiatory procession. Gaunt had to rest content with a qualified apology.[98]

Gaunt's fury with the London delegation is in some ways reminiscent of his father's behaviour to the submissive burgesses of Calais in 1347, as described by Froissart. Fellow nobles may have felt that Gaunt had just cause for outrage. But he had rashly provoked insult and humiliation in the last days of a parliament intended to restore respect for himself and the Crown. He now needed a salve for his dignity. But those responsible for reversing his arms remained unpunished; his rift with the Londoners was only patched over.

Gaunt continued to receive royal favours. On 28 February he received the signal one of a grant of palatine rights for life in Lancashire (see p. 315). On 5 and 6 March royal commands were issued on his information[99] and on the 18th he was granted the wardship of the baronial Strange family's heiress (see p. 280). External threats to the realm strengthened his hand against court coteries and his critics outside the court, by promoting the need for cooperation between the Lancastrian interest and the magnates. The approaching termination of the truces in June stimulated nervousness in governing circles about the enemy's intentions. Among the causes of summons pronounced to parliament by the chancellor, Bishop Houghton of St David's (doubtless sensitive to rumours of impending invasion of his diocese) was the need for advice on how to meet the threat from the French Crown and its Spanish and Scottish allies. Overseas intelligence had revealed that the French were making great military and especially naval preparations. The Commons showed responsiveness by their subsidy grant.[100]

Fears had arisen that Enrique II of Castile was planning an invasion of Wales. On 7 February Sir Thomas Felton, the lieutenant in Aquitaine, wrote to his deputies and to the citizens of Bayonne that Enrique had concentrated an unprecedented amount of shipping in Castile, and that his certain intention was to land at M(ilford Haven?), with Owain Lawgoch, an anglophobe, adventurous soldier who claimed the principality of Wales, in his company. An official of the princess of Wales, who had been shown a copy of this letter when touring Wales, informed her of its contents in March. There were fears, he indicated, that the Castilians anticipated gaining support in the principality; Felton's report received confirmation daily from merchants arriving from Gascony, 'so that rumour of it is exceedingly great and notable'. The officials and vassals of Princess Joan and her son Prince Richard advised them and her council to represent the necessity to the king and his council of sending a force of 200 to South Wales as soon as possible, and by 15 May at the latest, to garrison in equal portions the castles of P(embroke?) and K(Carmarthen?).[101] Felton's information may have been related to the capture at Pamplona in Navarre of a renegade English knight, John Menstreworth. He had become a liege of Charles V; 'he promised to bring the Spanish fleet to his support for the invasion of England'.[102] The royal council took these rumours of an imminent invasion of Wales seriously and instituted defence measures of the kind advocated by Princess Joan's officials. On 22 April the gallant, anglophile Sir Degory Sais was said to have been sent to Wales with 30 men-at-arms and 30 archers in his retinue for the safeguard of those parts; he took command of Pembroke, Tenby and Cilgerran Castles. Sir Rhys ap Gruffydd took over the defence of Milford Haven.[103] A royal sergeant-at-arms was sent with Privy Seal letters to Wales to order the earls of March, Warwick and Stafford, the countess of Norfolk and Lord Despenser to safeguard their estates there against the king's enemies.[104] Suspected local sympathisers with the enemy were arrested, notably the alien prior of Pembroke, whom the royal council ordered to be arrested and brought before it.[105] The special garrisons in south-west Wales were maintained into Richard's reign; worries about pre-emptive strikes against England before the expiry of the truces were reflected in orders in May and early June for defence measures in the Isle of Wight, the west country and Suffolk.[106]

An expedition against the French was planned too. Final plans may have been concerted at a great council summoned to meet on 9 April, which Gaunt probably attended (soon after spending Easter at Hertford Castle), and to which Archbishop Sudbury, Bishops Erghum of Salisbury and Buckingham of Lincoln, Edmund of Langley, the earls of March, Warwick and Stafford, and Lords Basset and FitzWalter were summoned.[107] At a Garter ceremony at Windsor on 23 April – for which the king was rowed up the river from Sheen – Prince Richard was knighted by his grandfather, as were Thomas of Woodstock, Bolingbroke and other young noble heirs, probably as a prelude to their participation in the coming expedition.[108]

From the end of May naval preparations intensified for the expedition. By 20 June seventy ships were gathered in the port of London: royal chancery clerks were pressed into service to write many letters under Gaunt's seal ordering the knights and esquires of his retinue to be present in London on 13 July, well arrayed to serve in his company at sea. Contracts were made in June for the service of 3,940 soldiers: the retinue leaders were Prince Richard, Gaunt, the duke of Brittany, the earl of Warwick, Lord Latimer, Guy Lord Brian, Thomas of Woodstock, Sir Michael de la Pole and (jointly) Sir Richard Stury and Sir Philip la Vache.[109] Thus the leadership of Prince Richard and Thomas of Woodstock in war was promoted for the first time. The captaincies also demonstrate how foreign threats drew together in arms recent political opponents. The earl of Warwick had been a member of the Lords' 'intercommuning' committee with the Commons which had encouraged their attacks on Latimer and the court in 1376. Guy Brian had recently assisted the Londoners in defence of their liberties. Stury and la Vache were knights of the royal chamber, the former of whom had incurred the Commons' wrath in 1376.

There is no clear indication of the aims of the expedition. The Kent ports were the usual bases for expeditions through Calais to northern France; Southampton and the west country ports for Normandy, Brittany and Aquitaine. The port of London was more convenient for a naval sweep in the Narrow Seas and down the Channel, perhaps with the aims of attacking enemy trade with Flanders (and putting pressure on its count), spoiling any naval concentration and, if opportunity arose, seizing a port. There may have been a non-strategic reason for the choice of London as a base port. This was most convenient for Gaunt; if he was at The Savoy, he could more easily keep in touch with the tricky situation at court than he could have if he were making military preparations on the southern coast. On 17 and 20 June payments were made at the Exchequer for his retinue's wages.[110] The next day Edward III died at Sheen; because of this, the expedition was cancelled. Gaunt consequently lost an opportunity to redeem his military reputation, prove his loyalty to Richard, reassert his leadership among the magnates and force the French back to the negotiating table in a more conciliatory frame of mind. Success on this expedition might have created political conditions in which Gaunt could have successfully claimed the regency during Richard's minority.

However, as things turned out, Gaunt's uneasy and controversial role in domestic politics from 1376 to 1377 – an episode not typical of his past career – heavily influenced his role in the minority. In the 1376 parliament he became for the first time a leading political figure, thrust into the limelight to represent the Crown just when discontent peaked. Faced with a crisis in which the Commons displayed novel critical vigour, he tried to defend the interests of his family and friends. This quickly gave him an evil reputation, which was reinforced by the measures which he promoted after the parliament, during the last year of his father's life, when he was generally regarded as the most powerful force in government. Thus Edward's reign ended with a brief and controversial Lancastrian ascendancy. Gaunt's retainer Ypres was steward of the household; his political ally Lord Percy replaced the earl of March as marshal of the realm; in January 1377 his close friend Bishop Houghton of St David's became chancellor. But his ascendancy was not total; Alice Perrers reasserted an influence whose aims were sometimes opposed to his own. Office in the royal household was not dominated by Lancastrian servants; from the Good Parliament to his father's death, Gaunt stayed mostly at The Savoy, occasionally and briefly visiting his father's country retreats. It is instructive of Gaunt's mentality and aims that he did not stage a palace coup with the aid of the magnates with whom he had become closely associated in war. He did not instal in court and council a 'Lancastrian party' to carry off the spoils of patronage. Instead, he used his power to undermine the achivements of the Good Parliament, in so doing alienating elements in the political community whose interests he handled clumsily. He also used his power to strengthen the position of Prince Richard, for which he was not given credit. Unfortunately, no *apologia* for his conduct in 1376–7 exists; accounts of it are hostile. Even so, they unwittingly reveal Gaunt as a stern and principled defender of royal authority, and one who, though at times vindictive and crass, never fell into the delusion of identifying royal interests wholly with his own aggrandisement as a magnate.

Notes and References

1 Somerville R 1953, pp. 49–50; *C.P.R. 1361–4*, pp. 171, 202–3.
2 *Foedera* 1830, vol. 3, pt 2, pp. 626–7. Four days previously, on 6 Oct., Gaunt issued letters patent dated Hertford Castle (*C.P.R. 1361–4*, p. 171).
3 Jones M 1970, p. 17 and n5; Reading J de 1914, pp. 150, 292–3; Somerville R 1953, p. 50; *R.P.*, Vol. 3, p. 273. Both sisters had only been recently married, Margaret in 1359 to the earl of Pembroke. I owe thanks to Professor M. Jones for information about the sisters. Maud was in England in 1361 (*Foedera* 1830, Vol. 3, pt 2, p. 262; Quicke F 1947, p. 79n.).
4 There had been preparations for Gaunt to go to Aquitaine in July 1361 (*Foedera* 1830, Vol. 3, pt 2, p. 622).
5 Somerville R 1953, pp. 50–1.
6 Bateson M 1901, Vol. 2, p. 131; *C.H.K.*, Vol. 2, p. 116.
7 Ducal letters were dated Tutbury Castle 1 July 1362 and Ravensdale 5 Aug. (*J.G.R. 1372–6*, 255, 748).
8 Quicke F 1947, p. 75: Delachenal R 1916, Vol. 3, pp. 399–400; Vaughan R 1962, pp. 4–5. In 1363 Gaunt dated documents at Aldermaston

(Berks.) 15 Jan. (*C.P.R. 1361–4*, p. 397), The Savoy 8 May (*C.P.R. 1367–70*), p. 380), Leicester Castle 13 July (*C.P.R. 1361–4*, p. 517) and Bolingbroke Castle 12 Dec. (*J.G.R. 1372–6*, no. 1810).

9 *Foedera* 1830, Vol. 3, pt 2, pp. 750–1. Gaunt left for Bruges on 24 Sept. and returned to Dover on 12 Oct. (P.R.O. E101/314/32; Mirot L and Déprez E 1899, p. 181).

10 *Foedera* 1830, Vol. 3, pt 2, pp. 758, 777; Reading J de 1914, pp. 220–1; *Eulogium*, Vol. 3, pp. 235, 237; Armitage-Smith 1904, pp. 29–31; Delachenal R 1916, Vol. 3, pp. 499ff; Vaughan R 1962, pp. 4–5.

11 Gaunt dated letters at Bolingbroke Castle on 18 April 1365 (*J.G.R. 1372–6*, no. 748), at The Savoy on 4 June, at Leicester Castle on the 12th, at The Savoy on 14th, 24th and on 1 Dec. (Oxford, C.C.C. 495). The 'boys of the Lord Duke' were given sixpence-worth of white bread by Leicester corporation on their way to Bolingbroke in 1365 or 1366 (Bateson M 1901, Vol. 2, p. 241).

12 Russell PE 1955, pp. 63, 79–80.

13 *C.P.R. 1364–7*, pp. 333–4, 415; Delpit J 1847, no. CC11.

14 Pantin WA 1937, pp. 56–60; cf Worcestre W 1969, pp. 224–5. Gaunt dated letters patent at Leicester 1 June (*C.P.R. 1367–70*, p. 297).

15 *Foedera* 1830, Vol. 3, pt 2, pp. 799, 810, 812. Gaunt's name is listed amongst the witnesses to the agreements between Pedro and the Black Prince dated Libourne in Gascony, 23 Sept. (*ibid.*, pp. 802ff). Armitage-Smith concluded that Gaunt visited Gascony that month (1904 pp. 41, 43). This is unlikely. A ducal warrant is dated The Savoy, 1 Oct. (*J.G.R. 1372–6*, no. 748).

16 Reading J de 1914, pp. 174–5; *Eulogium*, Vol. 3, p. 241.

17 C.C.C., 495 f16.

18 Pope MK and Lodge EC 1910, p. 153; Froissart J 1869, Vol. 7, pp. 147–8; Armitage-Smith S 1904, pp. 43–4.

19 Russell PE 1955, pp. 75–9.

20 *C.R.C.*, Vol. 1, pp. 563ff; Russell PE 1955, chs 5 and 6; *Foedera* 1830, Vol. 3, pt 2, p. 825.

21 P.R.O. E403/431/13, 19; C53/150 m2. Ducal letters were dated The Savoy 8 and 22 Nov.; Gaunt was party to an indenture dated Hertford Castle 8 Dec. (*C.P.R. 1370–4*, p. 351; *J.G.R. 1372–6*, no. 748; Lewis NB 1964, no. 1).

22 Palmer J 1973–4: 253ff. Palmer's conclusion is supported by the defective text of a letter from Gaunt to his receiver-general, dated 17 Aug. 1369, in which he referred to Blanche as deceased and which is apparently concerned with her obit (C.C.C., 495 f15). Other corroborative evidence is in Bishop Wykeham's Register (Kirby TF 1899, vol. 2, pp. 71–2) and a Wigmore chronicle (Taylor J 1987, pp. 294–5).

23 Armitage-Smith S 1904, pp. 21, 94.

24 *C.P.*, Vol. 3, p. 358. Gaunt's movements in 1368 are particularly obscure. He witnessed deeds dated Westminster 21 Feb. and 'Hasilwode' 12 May (*C.C.R. 1364–8*, p. 465; *C.C.R. 1369–74*, p. 93).

25 Palmer JJN 1973–4: 253–5.

26 *Foedera* 1830, Vol. 3, pt 2, p. 864. Gaunt dated letters at The Savoy 7–9 May (*C.P.R. 1367–70*, p. 432; *J.G.R. 1372–6*, nos 317, 1811).

27 C.C.C., 495 f.15.

28 Sherborne JW 1986, pp. 41ff.

29 C.C.C., 495 f.15.

30 Froissart J 1869, Vol. 7, pp. 443–50. Gaunt took Chandos's clerk Guyon into his service (*J.G.R. 1372–6*, no. 783).
31 C.C.C., 495 f.15. Gaunt dated an indenture at The Savoy on 24 March, and warrants there in April and May, the latest 14 May (Lewis NB 1964, no. 2; C.C.C., 495 f.15).
32 Armitage-Smith S 1904, pp. 79–80 and 79n; Champollion-Figeac M 1847, Vol. 2, no. xcviii; Delpit J 1847, no. ccxvii.
33 Froissart J 1869, Vol. 8, pp. 13–14, 29–30.
34 Ibid., pp. 60–1.
35 Russell PE 1955, pp. 147–8, 165–8.
36 *J.G.R. 1372–6*, nos 5, 215, 786, 1090.
37 Ducal letters were dated 'Fenwyc'/'Fouwyk' 4 Nov. and Plympton on 12th and 14th (ibid., nos 210, 215, 381, 878, 892).
38 *J.G.R. 1372–6*, no. 931; Exeter Cathedral, D and C archives, obit accounts, 3767 (no foliation) records *sub* Michaelmas term (i.e. Mich.–Christmas) – 'oblat' per ducem lancastr' et ducessa lancastr', 20s.' I owe this reference to Professor N Orme. Gaunt dated a letter at Exeter, 16 Nov. 1372 (*J.G.R. 1372–6*, no. 83).
39 Ibid., nos 8, 211–12, 214, 879, 940.
40 Ibid., nos 940, 973, 1090. The reference to the countess of Salisbury is dated 20 Jan. 46 Edward III – a mistake? Ducal letters were dated Kingston 2, 3, 7 and 9 Jan. 1372 (ibid., nos 7, 282, 382, 782) and Hertford Castle 3 and 10 Jan. (ibid., nos 64–5).
41 A.C., p. 69. Gaunt dated warrants at The Savoy from 22 Jan. onwards (*J.G.R. 1372–6*, nos 85, 184–5, 386, 388, 753, 789, 792–3) and throughout Feb.; including five on 10 Feb. (ibid., nos 86–7, 217–18, 794).
42 Ibid., nos 1123–4.
43 Ibid., nos 1124, 1133.
44 Ibid., nos 983, 1728. 'Elene midwyf' was receiving an annuity from Leicester honour in 1377–8 (P.R.O. DL29/212/3247).
45 For Edward III's reward to Catherine Swynford for announcing the birth of a daughter to Constance, dated 31 March 1373, Devon F 1837, p. 195.
46 *J.G.R. 1372–6*, nos 983–4. Ducal letters were dated Hertford Castle 2 May and 20 July (ibid., no. 250) and The Savoy 2 May (ibid., nos 255, 739).
47 Ibid., nos 162, 1124; Russell PE 1955, pp. 175–6.
48 *J.G.R. 1372–6*, nos 445, 1019, 1024, 1026.
49 Sherborne JW 1964: 725; *J.G.R. 1372–6*, nos 221–4.
50 Ibid., nos 51, 63; Sherborne JW 1964: 725.
51 *J.G.R. 1372–6*, nos 260, 453, 492, 494.
52 *Foedera* 1830, Vol. 3, pt 2, p. 962; Armitage-Smith S 1904, pp. 98–9; Holmes G 1975, pp. 22–3; P.R.O. C53/153/4. The king remained on shipboard till 14 Oct. (Tout TF 1928, Vol. 3, p. 283).
53 Ducal warrants were dated The Savoy 1, 10, 26 May; 8, 12, 13 and 20 June; 1, 7–9 July, and at Hertford Castle 20 May (*J.G.R. 1372–6, passim*).
54 Ibid., nos 752, 1126.
55 Ibid., no. 1242.
56 *C.P.R. 1370–4*, p. 279.
57 *J.G.R. 1372–6*, no. 1369.
58 Forty-seven ducal warrants were dated at Northbourne between 27 June and 16 July (ibid., *passim*).

59 Ibid., nos 667–8. Gaunt freighted a ship from Marcelline Albertson for the voyage and paid Henry Brem 'lodesman' for navigating 'la nief de nostre sale' from the Downs to London (ibid., no. 1430).

60 Ducal warrants were dated at The Savoy 1, 10, 26 May; 8, 12, 13, 20 June; 1, 7–9 July and at Hertford Castle 20 May (ibid., *passim*).

61 Holmes G 1975, pp. 33–4, 37ff.

62 *J.G.R. 1372–6*, nos 1450–1, 1454–82, 1486.

63 Ibid., nos 1483–5, 1487–9, 1491–1512.

64 He dated warrants at Gringley on 22–4 Sept. (ibid., nos 1522, 1525–6, 1528–9, 1531), at Lincoln on 25th (ibid., no. 1532) and at Stamford on 29th (ibid., no. 1542). On 22nd he had also dated them at his newly acquired castle of Tickhill (ibid., nos 1520–1, 1523).

65 Ibid., nos 1543–5, 1547–90. Christmas and the New Year were spent at Hertford Castle (ibid., nos 1591, 1593–8).

66 Ibid., nos 1608 and ff. Gaunt apparently celebrated the New Year with his father at Eltham Palace (ibid., no. 1661).

67 Ibid., no 1759; Perroy E 1952, pp. 8n, 9; Holmes G 1975, p. 45.

68 *A.C.*, p. 79. In Feb. 1375 Gaunt ordered his clerk of the wardrobe to pay the treasurer of the household 1,000 *m*. 'pur noz despences vers Flaunders' (*J.G.R. 1372–6*, no. 1675).

69 Ibid., *passim*.

70 Ibid., nos 375, 378, 717, 1765.

71 Ibid., nos 1788–9.

72 Ibid., no. 1794; Perroy E 1952, p. 36n.

73 Ibid., pp. xvii–xix; Holmes G 1975, ch. 3.

74 Tout TF 1928, Vol. 3, pp. 266ff; Holmes G 1975, pp. 16–19.

75 Tout TF 1928, Vol. 3, p. 307.

76 Holmes G 1975, pp. 64–7; Tout TF 1928, Vol. 3, pp. 276–7.

77 This account is based, except when stated otherwise, on *A.C.*, pp. 83–94.

78 *C.A.*, pp. 74–6.

79 Ibid., pp. 79, 81–2.

80 Holmes G 1975, p. 113.

81 *C.A.*, pp. 102–3, 107; cf ibid., pp. 86–7, 93–4.

82 Holmes G 1975, pp. 51–2, 52n. Walsingham says that Gaunt tried to get parliament to recognise the Lancastrian line as having precedence in the royal succession over the earl of March's, a move likely to have fuelled malign rumours about his alleged designs on the Crown (*C.A.*, pp. 92–3). Richard was formally invested with the principality of Wales on 20 Nov. 1376 (Tout TF 1928, Vol. 3, p. 312).

83 *C.A.*, pp. 102–3.

84 Nicolas NH 1826, Vol. 1, pp. 10–12.

85 *C.P.R. 1374–7*, pp. 299, 306; *A.C.*, pp. 95–9; *C.A.*, pp. 106–7; Tout TF 1928, Vol. 3, pp. 309ff. For chronological gaps in the evidence, Holmes G 1975, pp. 178–9 and 179n.

86 Ibid., p. 183.

87 Ibid., p. 160.

88 P.R.O. SC8/139/6910; text printed by Swinton GSC 1919: 266. The petition is undated; I have been unable to read the endorsement.

89 *R.P.*, Vol. 3, p. 13; Clarke MV 1937, p. 160.

90 P.R.O. DL28/3/1.

91 Perroy E 1952, p. 60.

92 *A.C.*, pp. 102–3.

93   *C.A.*, pp. 111–12; Holmes G 1975, pp. 184ff. The shire knights were not wholly subservient; they tried to get De la Mare released.

94   *C.A.*, pp. 113–14.

95   Holmes G 1975, p. 189.

96   *A.C.*, pp. 103–4; *C.A.*, pp. 118–21; Tout TF 1928, Vol. 3, p. 319. For Gaunt's relations with the Londoners, Holmes G 1975, pp. 188–90, 192–3.

97   *C.A.*, pp. 121–6; *A.C.*, pp. 104–5; Tout TF 1928, Vol. 3, pp. 319–20.

98   *A.C.*, pp. 105–6. For an account of more protracted negotiations between Gaunt and the Londoners, involving the king and Princess Joan, *C.A.*, pp. 126–9, 131–4.

99   *C.P.R. 1374–7*, pp. 434, 438.

100   *R.P.*, Vol. 2, pp. 362, 364.

101   Legge MD 1941, no. 138.

102   *H.A.*, Vol. 1, p. 326.

103   P.R.O. E403/462/3–4.

104   P.R.O. E403/462/5; *C.C.R. 1374–7*, p. 487.

105   P.R.O. E403/462/3; *C.C.R. 1374–7*, p. 506.

106   Ibid., pp. 496–8. For payments made in July 1377 for the service of Sais and Gruffydd, P.R.O. E403/464/2, 4. Gruffydd's account for the service of his retinue at Milford 9 Aug. to 18 Sept. 1377 is in P.R.O. E101/37/5.

107   P.R.O. E403/462/1, 2.

108   *A.C.*, p. 106.

109   Alexander AF 1933, pp. 40–4, 388; P.R.O. DL28/3/1 m8. According to Walsingham (*C.A.*, p. 138), the 'whole fleet' was gathered by Gaunt at London about Easter (29 March).

110   P.R.O. E403/462/15, 19.

Chapter Five

From Dominance to Exile (1377–81)

As it became clear that Edward III's death was imminent, there was worried speculation about the future. On the day he died (21 June) a delegation of Londoners asked Richard to end the quarrel between Gaunt and the city. Next day, prompted by Richard's envoys, a group of citizens went to Sheen where they found the new king, his mother and uncles gathered at the royal palace where Edward's body lay. On their arrival the business of reconciliation was put in hand. Gaunt, kneeling before Richard, agreed to royal arbitration, showing his goodwill by his plea that his imprisoned opponents should be released and pardoned. He then forgave the citizens and received them into his grace, swearing to give them friendship and to protect their interests. He gave the delegates the kiss of peace. Walsingham regarded his changed behaviour as a miracle of St Alban, whose feast day it was.[1] But, once the shock of Edward's death had worn off, the old enmity was to reappear.[2]

Early in July Gaunt appeared before the king and council to claim the right to perform ceremonial tasks at the coronation – the office of steward, as earl of Leicester; the right to carry the king's principal sword, *Curtana*, as duke of Lancaster, and to carve before him at the coronation banquet, as earl of Lincoln. These claims were allowed. He fulfilled the office of steward in person; in this capacity he held a court of claims in the White Hall at Westminster. He gave his son Henry of Bolingbroke (aged about eleven) the task of carrying *Curtana* during the ceremony from the mass after the coronation onwards, and the earl of Stafford that of cutting the king's bread and meat at

70

table in Westminster Hall. On 15 July, the day before the coronation, Gaunt and the marshal, Lord Percy, riding exceptionally large and fine horses, together with their retinues made a way through the London crowds, so that Richard could ride along the processional way from the Tower through Cheapside and along Fleet Street to Westminster. The skill and courtesy with which Gaunt and Percy carried out the task made a favourable impression.[3]

Some foreign observers thought that Gaunt took control of government during Richard's minority.[4] Walsingham was more aware of the complexities of the situation and of the diminution of Gaunt's influence over government consequent on his father's death. The chronicler says that Gaunt, realising that there was now a new situation, and that he was liable to be blamed for any disasters which might occur, a few days after the coronation obtained royal licence to retire to his estates, promising to come to Richard's aid in an emergency. But before he left for Kenilworth Castle, the appointment of councillors and the form of government were settled to suit his interest. The influence of councillors likely to fall in with his plans – his former chancellor Bishop Erghum of Salisbury and his friend Lord Latimer (see p. 289) – was, Walsingham says, camouflaged by the appointment of others unlikely to oppose them, such as Bishop Courtenay. Yet Courtenay is an unlikely example of timid acquiescence. Gaunt was in fact prudently prepared to moderate the exercise of his influence within a variously composed council. But, as Walsingham's comments show, so great a prince, and one so recently unpopular, was bound to be blamed for public ills and to be accused of secret manipulation of the government.[5]

That summer Gaunt, far from court, indulging in sports and hunting in the north, did not escape criticism. Walsingham accused him of leaving his castle at Pevensey on the Sussex coast undefended in face of the danger of enemy raids. When his men asked him to appoint a guardian, in case the castle was occupied by the French, he replied, 'If they destroy it to the foundations, I have the power to rebuild it a second time.' He may have considered that the costly garrisoning of this antique Romano-Norman fortress was no real defence against Franco-Castilian raids. What was needed was naval action, which the fleet commanded by his youngest brother Thomas of Woodstock (newly created earl of Buckingham) was intended to provide.[6]

On 14 October Gaunt was present in the Painted Chamber of Westminster Palace for the start of Richard's first parliament.[7] The Commons petitioned for him to lead the committee of lords whom they wished to consult about their 'charge', to which the king agreed. Gaunt's reaction reflects his angry awareness of continuing slanders.

Kneeling before the king, he declared himself unwilling to accept the task until he was exonerated from the evil which the Commons spoke about him, tantamount to a charge of treason. None of his ancestors, he said, was a traitor and it would be amazing if he deviated from them, as it would be unnatural and he had more to lose than anyone else in the realm. He was ready to defend himself in combat against anyone who accused him of treason or any form of disloyalty. Both Lords and Commons responded by unanimously and emphatically reassuring him. But the duke was not completely mollified. He said that since such talk had for long spread through the realm, he marvelled that anyone could renew or continue it. The instigator of this, by provoking discord between lords which might endanger the realm, was the real traitor. He wanted measures to be taken in parliament against future slanderers and pardoned past offenders against himself.[8]

Gaunt demonstrated his goodwill to the Commons' aims and eagerness to dissociate himself from the unpopular acts of his father's last years by participating in the trial of Edward's former mistress Alice Perrers. He headed the parliamentary committee which examined witnesses and himself appeared as one, denigrating her past influence, doubtless to exculpate himself from any association with it.[9]

Gaunt and his two brothers were given a special jurisdiction by parliament over cases involving maintenance of quarrels by any of the councillors then appointed 'to be continually resident in the council for the needs of the realm'. Groups of these 'continual councillors' received appointments and met frequently from July 1377 till the discharge of the final group in the parliament of January 1380. The fact that the royal uncles do not figure among them does not imply that they were excluded from influence or preferred to stay away from court: their omission probably reflects the assumption that their nearness in blood to the king gave them a natural right and indeed duty to counsel. It is unlikely that they were expected to sit frequently, in contrast to the 'continual councillors'.[10]

The belief of foreigners that Gaunt controlled government in Richard's minority is not surprising in view of his friends' tenure of key positions in royal government, and of the central roles which he soon came to play in war, diplomacy and political controversy. His friend Adam Houghton, bishop of St David's was chancellor till October 1378, to be replaced by one of the most trustworthy Lancastrian retainers, Richard Lord Scrope, who held office till January 1380.[11] The steward of the royal household was Sir Hugh Segrave, who had been steward of Gaunt's household in Gascony.[12] Gaunt's ostentatious withdrawal to Kenilworth was probably seen in noble circles as one of several gestures intended to confound detractors, like the reconciliation with the Londoners and the protestation of loyalty in parliament. Gaunt was soon being customarily treated as the greatest subject in the realm. At an Anglo-Scottish conference in September 1377, negotiators headed by the earls of Northumberland and Douglas agreed that Gaunt and Robert II's eldest son, John earl of Carrick (the future Robert III) should attend a 'March Day' to settle unresolved border grievances.[13] Apparently, at a great council early in 1378, the duke sought control of the subsidy, affirming that he would use it to defend the realm and for other national priorities for one year. Walsingham, the source for this, says that the lords agreed to this reluctantly, as they were pessimistic about his chances of success, but that they were unwilling to oppose him.[14] On 18 January 1378 Gaunt met Carrick for the March Day – the start of a deep involvement in Anglo-Scottish negotiations over the next few years.[15] Walsingham denounced Gaunt for not taking part in the naval expedition which embarked in April, saying that he delayed his arrival at the embarkation port for several months through fear of the enemy's fleet, and went touring with his mistress Catherine Swynford, scandalous conduct which aroused indignation against him, as did the plundering of his troops and an English defeat at sea.[16]

The duke had worthier motives for delay than fear and lust. More shipping had to be concentrated for his retinues.[17] He was heavily involved in government business. Privy Seal letters summoning him to the king's council in London were taken to the north and to Leicester probably in March.[18] He attended a council meeting at Westminster on 29 April specially concerned with the secret affairs of the king and realm. together with the chancellor (Houghton), the treasurer (Bishop Brantingham of Exeter), Bishops Erghum of Salisbury and Appleby of Carlisle, the earl of March and other magnates.[19] He was summoned to another meeting on 1 June. When staying at Southampton preparatory to embarkation, he received communications from the earls of March and Northumberland and others assigned to hold a March Day on the Anglo-Scottish frontier, and from the lords of the council.[20]

Gaunt and his fleet weighed anchor in July. His naval operations were inconclusive and his siege of St Malo (August–September) was a failure (see pp. 226–7). On his return to England, he immediately became involved in the aftermath of a scandal which had blown up in his absence over the issues of ecclesiastical liberties and excommunications. Two royal officers, his friend Sir Alan Buxhill and Sir Ralph Ferrers,[21] had led an attempt to arrest two fugitive squires, Robert Hawley and John Shakell, who had taken refuge in Westminster Abbey. During a scuffle in the abbey church, a sacristan was mortally wounded and Hawley was killed.[22] Walsingham says that Gaunt attended a council at Windsor at which he angrily denounced Bishop Courtenay for having published sentence of excommunication against those who had participated in or consented to the outrage, despite royal requests to the bishop not to do so. He also denounced Courtenay for his failure to attend the council and offered to bring him along forcibly, in despite of the Londoners whom he termed 'ribalds'. He asserted that all that had been done at Westminster was done by his order and with his support. Walsingham says that it was at the duke's instigation that parliament was held (commencing late in October) at Gloucester: he thought that the bishops, commons and Londoners would be less able to withstand him there. It was rumoured that he planned heavy taxation, and spoliation of the Church's possessions. But Archbishop Sudbury of Canterbury and the episcopal bench were firm. Gaunt, realising that he could not make headway, dropped his proposals: 'he transformed himself into an angel of light'.[23]

For over two years after the Gloucester parliament, Gaunt managed to avoid major confrontations – though the 1381 revolt was to show how strong popular animus against him remained, particularly in London. He had the support of the king's council for initiatives against Castile. But it was necessary to secure the realm against neighbouring enemies in order to persuade the wider political community that it was in their interest to back his Spanish schemes. Gaunt hoped to ensure security for the north and good opinions generally by assuming a lieutenancy over the Marches towards Scotland in February 1379, an appointment which was to be renewed in 1380 and to last till 1384.[24] However, he was to fail in his attempt to clear the way for an expedition against Castile by appeasing Scottish belligerence.

Gaunt celebrated New Year in 1380 in Kenilworth.[25] That year he was on occasion in the king's company, and helped to launch energetic efforts to reverse the tide of French success by revamping old alliances and seeking new ones. Expenditure by the community on overseas expeditions might be more acceptable when they were led by his brothers, while he toiled virtuously at the difficult task of preserving and extending the truces with the Scots. In January the duke of Brittany accredited envoys to both Richard and Gaunt – the minstrels of one of them, Sir Robert Beaumanoir, performed before Gaunt at The Savoy. On 1 March an Anglo-Breton alliance was drafted, which the king confirmed a fortnight later.[26] This facilitated the reception of an English army in Brittany later in the year, led by Gaunt's twenty-five-year-old brother Thomas of Woodstock, and his attempt to seize Nantes, possibly to create another overseas 'barbican' with an English garrison, like Brest (leased in 1377) and Cherbourg (leased in 1378). Woodstock's invasion of France from Calais in 1380, ending up in Brittany, was the only major English one in Richard's reign; it was Woodstock's first great land command. In later life he apparently looked back on this dismal episode (with its echoes of Gaunt's failure in 1373) with nostalgia as his finest military hour. Woodstock was well educated, perhaps the most learned of the brothers, whose devotion to chivalrous pastimes he shared. In some ways he resembled Gaunt: he was intelligent, ambitious, forceful in speech and intimidating to many. He may well have developed, as he grew older, a festering sense of grievance that current policy trends and failures denied him the opportunities to seek honour and profit in war enjoyed by his elder brothers in Edward's reign. Unlike them, he gained a rapport with the gentry over their anxieties and grievances, which he articulated against royal policies and councillors with devastating success in 1386–8. Woodstock, along with his conspicuous piety, had a streak of ruthless brutality, which he amply demonstrated then, entirely lacking in the sometimes threatening but generally merciful Gaunt. In the late 1390s Froissart came to see Woodstock as a deeply unattractive and essentially unchivalrous figure, standing for a narrow English nationalism against the attempt to revive the unity of Christendom on a basis of Anglo–French courtly culture.

On 1 April 1380 Gaunt was at Windsor to attend the marriage of the king's half-sister Maud Courtenay (née Holand) to Waleran count of St Pol, a wedding celebrated 'with a great concourse of trumpeters and entertainers', which had important diplomatic implications.[27] On 7 June Gaunt was present with the king and other lords for an occasion with more sinister undertones. A vast crowd assembled at Westminster to watch a judicial duel between Sir Hugh Annesley and Thomas Catterton. The issue between them was a charge of treason which Annesley had originally made against Catterton in the 1376 parliament. His prosecution had then been thwarted, it was widely assumed, because of court influence. But on this occasion, according to Walsingham, Gaunt showed no inclination to protect Catterton, whose prevarications he brusquely brushed aside. The duke swore that, since Catterton was a defendant, he would be hanged forthwith unless he accepted the challenge. This remark was generally approved – many doubtless were impatient to see a good fight. It was a hard one with a popular result: Annesley won and Catterton expired next day.[28] The popular rejoicing doubtless impressed on Gaunt how deep a mark the controversies of the Good Parliament had made.

At The Savoy, the day after the duel, Gaunt received a knight of Wenzel, king of the Romans (and Bohemia), in England in connection with the negotiations for the marriage of Wenzel's sister Anne to Richard. The alliance was a blow for the French Crown, with which the imperial Luxembourg family had long been allied.[29]

On 18 June Richard was probably again in his uncle's company at Hertford: Gaunt then made gifts of money to royal esquires, valets and pages.[30] The following month, through his domination of his family and of royal policy, he had a striking diplomatic success. A delegation from Fernando I of Portugal, which had been in England since early in the year, agreed terms for the marriage of Edmund of Langley's son Edward to the king's daughter Beatriz, and for Fernando's cooperation with Edmund in the invasion of Castile (see pp. 113–14).

Eager to stabilise Anglo-Scottish relations so that he could join Edmund, Gaunt prepared to lead an expedition to the borders. In the first half of August, while at Tutbury Castle, he appointed John Norfolk as treasurer of his household for the expedition and ordered the summons of bachelors and esquires of his retinue in the duchy and Yorkshire to serve on it.[31] Later in the month, when at Leicester Castle, he sent out orders for them to assemble arrayed for war at Newcastle by 28 September.[32] From mid-September to mid-October, however, he was in the north, mainly on his estates at Ravensdale, Pontefract and Knaresborough.[33] On 6 September he had been formally reappointed as lieutenant in the Marches, with extensive powers to make truces and to enforce them, and to supervise defences.[34] He wrote urgently from Ravensdale (Derbyshire) a few days later arranging a new date for Yorkshire retainers to meet him in York; he stayed there at the end of the month. He was at Newcastle on 18 October, nearly three weeks after he had planned for his retinue to be assembled there.[35] The delay may have arisen because of the need to supply and organise his retinue and those of the nobles who were to accompany him – Archbishop Neville of York, the earls of Warwick, Stafford and Northumberland and Robert Hales, prior of the Order of St John.[36] On 27 and 28 October he was far north on the Northumberland coast, at the royal castle of Bamburgh. There he issued a safe-conduct for the Scottish envoys – including the earls of Douglas and March and Sir Archibald Douglas – to come to Berwick within the next few days:[37] he made an indenture with them on 1 November confirming a truce to last till 9 June 1381.[38] The unruly behaviour of Gaunt's retinue had not impeded agreement. Companies amounting to over 400 men, drawn wholly or partly from the duchy, committed outrages against the earl of Douglas and his tenants; the earls of Northumberland and Warwick guaranteed payment of compensation.[39] English borderers suffered too from the depredations of Gaunt's army, whose behaviour they compared irritably with that of Scottish raiders. If the weather was as bad as it was then in the east midlands, it doubtless contributed to the friction between hungry and shelterless soldiers and suspicious inhabitants.[40] Gaunt's forceful exercise of his lieutenancy induced mixed local feelings.

After the conclusion of the truce, Gaunt seems to have been in no hurry to return south, despite his obligation to attend the parliament summoned to meet at Northampton. He stayed probably because he still had lieutenancy business to dispatch; perhaps travelling conditions were bad. He was back at Bamburgh Castle on 4 and 5 November. There he ordered the dispatch of a barrel of wine to the earl of Northumberland, probably in return for hospitality recently received at Alnwick or Warkworth.[41] On the 8th, at Newcastle, the duke ordered the wardens of the West March, headed by Lords Clifford and Dacre, to hold a March Day to redress cross-border offences with Sir Archibald Douglas and to settle matters at issue between him and the earl of Northumberland.[42] Gaunt stayed at Durham on the 10th and 11th.[43]

The unusual location of the 1380 parliament, at Northampton, like that of 1378 at Gloucester, was said by Walsingham to be at Gaunt's instigation, but contrary to the wishes and without the assent of other magnates. The chronicler attributes a similar motive to Gaunt on both occasions – a desire to avoid pressure from hostile Londoners. In 1380, Walsingham says, he was determined that one of them, John Kirkeby, should be convicted in parliament for the murder of a Genoese, and feared the reaction if Kirkeby was executed in the city's vicinity, particularly in view of the 'inveterate hatred' between Londoners and himself.[44] At the adjourned opening session of parliament on 8 November it was announced that Gaunt with 'great part of the Earls and Barons of the Realm' in his company had not yet departed from the Marches: it is not clear when he arrived at Northampton.[45] In parliament the grant was made of the subsequently notorious ungraded poll tax, principally for the purpose of financing a campaign in France in the spring of 1381, by Thomas of Woodstock's army, currently wintering in Brittany. The unhappy determination of the Commons to provide adequate war finance at high cost to the common people was doubtless spurred by the year's vigorous diplomatic and military activities, and not least by the manner in which Gaunt had subordinated the fulfilment of his Spanish ambitions to the safeguard of the northern border.

Gaunt probably celebrated Christmas joyfully at Leicester Castle.[46] He may have felt that opportunities had now been created for his family and himself once more to eclipse the Valois princes of France and outshine them and their allies in Christendom: such expectations were to be disappointed. Thomas of Woodstock was soon to withdraw from Brittany in humiliating circumstances and in 1382 Edmund of Langley was to have a similar experience in Portugal.

Gaunt's plans to invade Spain from Gascony did not materialise. The king's marriage into the imperial family, a splendid diplomatic coup, brought no long-term political gains. Worst of all for Gaunt, within six months of Christmas he was to be an exile, his family in hiding and his great palace outside the walls of London reduced to a blackened ruin.

Gaunt took leave of his brother Edmund prior to his departure for Portugal before 6 March 1381, though that did not occur till June. Gaunt gave him as a leave-taking present a covered cup (*hanap*) of gold.[47] On 3 April Gaunt gave a banquet at The Savoy for the cardinal of Ravenna, Pileo de Prata (an old colleague from the Bruges negotiations) and the envoys of Wenzel, king of the Romans, headed by the duke of Teschen. They were all in England to conclude the royal marriage treaty. This was one of the last occasions on which The Savoy was the setting for a glittering occasion. The treaty was concluded by the negotiators and the cardinal-legate, in the presence of the king, leading prelates, Gaunt and the earls of Arundel, Stafford, Salisbury and Suffolk.[48] Commissions Gaunt received about this time confirmed his key role in keeping the northern borders settled. He was reappointed lieutenant in the Marches and given powers, together with Bishop Gilbert of Hereford and the earl of Stafford, to meet the Scots for a 'day of the March'. On 10 May the envoys' officials received Exchequer payments for the purpose, as did others who were to accompany them – Sir Nicholas Sharnsfield, Sir Robert Rous, Sir Roger Fulthorpe and Master John Coddeford.[49]

The day after the renewal of Gaunt's lieutenancy was issued, he had ordered the receiver's lieutenant at Pontefract and the duchy receiver to forward with all possible haste letters addressed to certain knights and esquires – presumably requiring them to assemble for another expedition to the borders.[50] Gaunt was at Knaresborough by the end of the month and set out for the Marches after Whitsun (2 June). Sir Robert Rous had set out from London on 14 May; he joined up with Gaunt at Beverley (Yorks.).[51]

While Gaunt was in Yorkshire, popular disturbances broke out in Essex which sparked off the Peasants' Revolt. The zenith of the rising in the south-east was the rebels' domination of London from 13 to 15 June.[52] From early on in the revolt, rebels in southern parts displayed boiling hostility to Gaunt. In Kent they forced pilgrims travelling to Canterbury to swear that they would have no king called John – in allusion to Gaunt's Castilian title.[53] He was the first-named on the list of those for whose execution the rebels petitioned the king when encamped at Blackheath.[54] The ferocious hatred of the Essex and Kent rebels in London for Gaunt is seen in their erection of his 'jack' (a jerkin reinforced with defensive padding) on a lance to use for target practice. Then they smashed it up with their weapons.[55]

Anyone associated with Gaunt was a likely target too. The Kentish properties of the controller of his household, Thomas Haselden, were sacked and a vain search was made for Haselden, in order to execute him. His manor of Little Chesterford (Essex) was attacked and looted.[56] When on 14 June Richard left the Tower of London to meet the rebels at Mile End and they entered the Tower, among those seized was a celebrated physician and surgeon, the Franciscan friar William Appleton. He was executed on Tower Hill simply because he had served Gaunt.[57] On the same day in London a certain John Wiltshyre of Little Burstead (Essex) cut off the head of Gaunt's squire Grenefeld.[58] Gaunt's son, Henry, left in the Tower by Richard − presumably so that he could attempt to escape, as Archbishop Sudbury attempted to do − believed that he owed his life when the rebels entered to a certain John Ferrour of Southwark, who hid him.[59] Gaunt's mistress Catherine Swynford vanished into hiding.[60] The Duchess Constance fled to her husband's castle of Pontefract, whose keeper was so distracted, according to the chronicler Knighton, that he refused to admit her. Constance perforce carried on northwards towards another ducal castle, Knaresborough, travelling by night guided by a lantern. She was honourably received by the keeper of the castle, Richard Brennand, who gave her refuge till the emergency was over and did his best to console her.[61]

The panic among those with Lancastrian connections appears vividly in Knighton's recollections of events in Leicester. The mayor, fearing that the rebels would come and ransack the duke's property there, called out the town militia to man the defences. The keeper of the duke's wardrobe hastened up from London to safeguard his master's goods in Leicester Castle. Fearing that the rebels would destroy everything that they found there, he speedily had its contents loaded up for safe-keeping in Leicester Abbey. But Abbot Kereby's nerve failed: he refused to receive them, frightened that their reception would provoke the abbey's destruction. So the carts moved on and were left loaded in the yard of the church of St Mary de Castro within the castle precinct.[62]

There is not much evidence that Gaunt's properties were plundered by the rebels or that many of his tenants rebelled. His manor court rolls were destroyed in some places.[63] Gaunt's most spectacular loss was the destruction of The Savoy, the great symbol of his wealth and status. Chroniclers' accounts of how it was burnt down suggest that, for many contemporaries, this was the most shocking destruction of property in 1381. The manner in which his precious jewels and plate were destroyed rather than looted shows the indignation which animated the rioters. On the day the rebels entered London, they broke down the gates of The Savoy. Entering the wardrobe, they lit the torches they found there and burnt valuable beds and bed furnishings. Napery and other goods were piled up in the great hall for a bonfire. Gold and silver vessels were hacked to pieces with axes and thrown into the Thames at the bottom of the garden or into the sewers. Precious cloths and hangings were shredded and trampled underfoot. Rings and jewellery were ground up in mortars. Some rebels broke into the cellar and grew merry on sweet wine. The great hall, private apartments and other buildings of the palace were set alight. Allegedly, the hall blazed more fiercely after the rebels threw in three barrels which they thought contained gold and silver, but which in fact were full of gunpowder. The cellar was blocked by fire and debris; the partygoers there eventually perished. Subsequently there were to be allegations that the Londoners, Gaunt's old enemies, had instigated or carried out the destruction of the residence Walsingham described as 'unrivalled in splendour and nobility within England'. The fact that Gaunt never rebuilt his famous palace reflected not only the extent of its destruction, but his own anger and chagrin. He may have wished the ruins to remain as a memorial to the mad fury of the rustics and their London sympathisers and to the fragility of worldly splendour.[64]

On the days when the commons were lording it over London (13–15 June), Gaunt was based on Berwick with his fellow envoys.[65] According to Knighton, rumours of the revolt had reached him when negotiations were nearly complete, but he kept a calm and cheerful countenance, hastening their conclusion.[66] Warrants which he issued on 17 June, dated at Berwick, suggest that he decided to make provision to stay on his estates in the north until the situation further south became clear. He informed the receiver of Leicester that by advice of his council the household was to stay at Pontefract and ordered him to arrange for the carriage thither of the stuff of the great wardrobe and chapel and of wine stocks. Knighton's account implies that the receiver, if this order reached him, was unable to carry it out fully in the atmosphere of panic gripping Leicester. Other ducal warrants for the transport of wood and wine suggest that the duke intended to visit Lancashire as well as Yorkshire.[67]

On 18 June Gaunt met Robert II's son Carrick at Ebchester near Ayton (Berwickshire), then an area in the English allegiance, to seal the indentures for the truce that had been concluded in Ayton kirk. To the Scots' regret, their spies brought news of the revolt only after the conclusion of the truces. They promptly offered to join Gaunt with 20,000 soldiers to fight the rebels. He spiritedly refused, predicting that even if the whole power of Scotland came, they would have a stiff fight on their hands before they reached York.

He boasted of the numbers and bravery of the English and asserted that, if the Scots made such an attempt, they would be reduced to a laughing-stock. The Scottish lords probably had their doubts: it was to be exceptional when, in 1388, one of their raiding forces penetrated south of the Tyne. Despite his bravura, Gaunt was a supplicant. He apparently applied before his return to England for a safe-conduct in order to take refuge in Scotland, presumably at this stage as a precaution. Considered by David II as worthy to be king of Scots, he had cultivated good relations with the Stewarts and Douglasses, especially through his part in border affairs in recent years.[68]

Gaunt's alarm is reflected in orders of 18 and 19 June, dated Berwick, for the garrisoning and victualling of his decrepit castles in Monmouthshire and of two of his northern castles, Tutbury and Tickhill.[69] Soon afterwards he was back in England, at the imposing royal castle of Bamburgh on the Northumberland coast, probably (with Berwick) a supply base for his expedition.[70] He expected that his dear kinsman, fellow veteran and frequent political ally the earl of Northumberland would aid him and he set store by the invitation he received from the earl to dine and stay the night at Alnwick Castle. It came as a rude shock when (according to the Anonimalle Chronicler) on his arrival at Alnwick, perhaps at the presently standing barbican of the castle, Sir John Hotham and Thomas Motherby esquire met him and, on the earl's behalf, asked him – the greatest prince in the realm and the king's lieutenant – to go away, as the earl dared not receive him 'for doubt of his lord' (the king). Moreover, these envoys allegedly made it clear that Northumberland would not permit the duke to enter any royal castle or manor in his custody until he knew whether the duke had the royal goodwill.[71]

New light on the motives of Northumberland and the circumstances in which he rebuffed Gaunt is provided by the letter which Hotham and Motherby produced on the earl's behalf when they met the duke on his way to Alnwick Castle. This is headed 'The credence related to the duke of Lancaster by Sir John de Hotham and Motherby is this'. The text is as follows:

My lord the lords of Hereford Stafford and Northumberland recommend themselves to you and send to you that having regard both to the letters of privy seal directed to the Earl of Northumberland and to the news related to him by one of his valets being among the Commons at London the day of Corpus Christi and the following day until the hour of None, their counsel is without better advice from your knights and Esquires that you stay in the Castle of Bamburgh and reside there for the time being until you are well informed about the estate of the King and the business of the Commons.[72]

The letter modifies chronicle information about Gaunt's and Percy's behaviour. It makes clear that Gaunt's fellow envoys Bishop Gilbert of Hereford and the earl of Stafford (presumably both staying at Alnwick) conjointly with Percy sent unwelcome advice – an action which (unlike in Percy's case) did not impair the duke's close relations with Gilbert or embroil him with Stafford. These lords were, ostensibly, not attempting to precipitate Gaunt's flight abroad, but offering the sound advice that he should lie low.

This advice was based partly on reliable information about events in London – unfortunately for the principals, information which had speedily become out of date. The earl of Northumberland had had a spy in the ranks of the rebellious commons on 13 June, the day they entered London and burnt The Savoy, and until the late afternoon of the 14th, the day on which the king agreed to their petitions at Mile End and on which 'traitors' were executed on Tower Hill. It is implicit in the letters of credence that the Privy Seal letters Percy had received had implications for Gaunt: these may have been the four such letters which Percy was to produce in parliament in his defence. They may have been related to Richard's assent to Wat Tyler's petition that the commons might arrest 'traitors'. The commons must have been very exercised over their failure to capture Gaunt; perhaps letters were sent on the subject to the northern lords at their request. Clearly, the content of the letters and the report of the Percy spy were so grave that they precipitated hasty action by Gaunt and his friends and colleagues in the north, unaware that the crisis of the revolt had passed.

Gaunt retraced his steps to Bamburgh; he rejected the advice in the letter, having preparations made for immediate flight to the Scots, for which Carrick and Robert II were to issue the promised safe-conducts. Gaunt dismissed his retinue; Knighton declared that nearly all of them departed 'like the disciples from Christ'. Sir John Marmion and Sir Walter Urswick remained for good or ill.[73] The servants loaded up wine and 200 loaves for the journey and the company took a difficult and circuitous route, avoiding Berwick (of which the earl of Northumberland was keeper) and entering Robert II's land from the English-held enclave at Roxburgh, probably on 23 June – ironically the day on which Richard issued orders for his uncle's protection.[74]

According to Froissart, the Scots met Gaunt with an honourable escort of spears en route between Roxburgh and Melrose Abbey and amicably escorted him towards Edinburgh.[75] The Scottish chronicler Wyntoun says that he arrived there next morning, having stayed the night at Haddington. He lodged in Edinburgh at Holyrood Abbey. The earl of Douglas was attentive to see that he did not lack victuals.[76]

He may have arranged for messengers from Gaunt to go to and from the English West March, where Gaunt's friend and retainer Lord Scrope had been warden since February. On 25 June, soon after his arrival in Edinburgh, Gaunt wrote to the receiver of Lancaster, strictly charging him to send all the money which he had in hand and all that he could borrow by any means as speedily as possible to Carlisle to be delivered to Sir James Pickering; the latter was presumably to bring or forward it to Edinburgh.[77]

Whilst in Scotland, Gaunt paid out in Scottish money the equivalent of £64 4d. in English coin. He took a considerable quantity of wine to Scotland and bought there for his consumption wax, 'gingibre', 'poudre', saffron and other spices.[78] By warrant dated Edinburgh 10 July, he ordered his treasurer of the household to deliver gifts of plate to Scottish nobles – presumably those who specially favoured and succoured him. They were the earl of Carrick, Lord Lindsay and the earl of Douglas's son 'Master Douglas', who succeeded his father in 1384 and died at the battle of Otterburn. The latter received the most splendid gift – 'a golden salt-cellar made in the shape of a dove with a white turtle-dove on the lid and various letters of our arms on the foot'.[79]

Within a few days of Gaunt's arrival in Edinburgh he had recovered his nerve, buoyed up doubtless by the splendid hospitality he received. As was proper, his first objective seems to have been to rescue the Duchess Constance, whom he believed was still languishing in Knaresborough Castle, with its leaky roofs above her, and below this decrepit eyrie, a forest teaming with peasants with a tradition of ill-will towards ducal government. The warrants he dispatched on 29 June apparently related to a projected rescue attempt. Particular northern retainers were to array 558 men-at-arms and archers, rendezvous with him at Berwick on 13 July and ride to Knaresborough.[80] However, he soon received a letter from Richard which filled him with joy: the king ordered him to return to London and denied rumours that he was in disfavour. If his household was not large enough, he was to augment his escort with contingents provided on the way.[81] With their customary courtesy, the Scottish lords escorted Gaunt to Berwick with a retinue of over 800 spears; he probably arrived there on the date he had originally intended, but in more auspicious circumstances.[82]

The Great Revolt was undoubtedly a terrifying and humiliating experience for Gaunt, threatening, even if he survived it, to destroy the eminence he had enjoyed in the realm. For four years he had been the most influential person in England; the rebels were right to pin responsibility for policy above all on him. During those years he had used his military and diplomatic weight to defend his nephew's possessions and his domestic power to stabilise rule. He did not attempt to exercise semi-regal control as his grandson Humphrey of Gloucester was to try to do in Henry VI's minority, fomenting political tensions in the process: his attacks on his enemies were verbal. The respect which the rebels of 1381 showed to Richard was in part inspired by an abstract awe for kingship, in part by consideration for his youthful innocence. Yet the fact that they could view Richard as a figure radiating power rather than as a plaything of faction or a symbol of defeat by the French was in no small measure due to Gaunt's dogged restraint and determination to defend Richard's interests, as he had those of Richard's father and grandfather.

Notes and References

1   *C.A.*, pp. 146–9. Richard also reconciled Gaunt and Bishop Wykeham, and released and pardoned Sir Peter de la Mare (ibid., p. 150).
2   Ibid., pp. 154–5; *A.C.*, pp. 107ff.
3   Wickham Legg LG 1901, pp. 130ff; Vernon Harcourt LW 1907, pp. 177, 182; *C.A.*, pp. 161–2. Gaunt summoned his retainers to London for the coronation (P.R.O. DL28/3/1 m8).
4   *C.Q.P.V.*, p. 262; cf. *Eulogium*, Vol. 3, p. 340.
5   *C.A.*, pp. 163–4; cf Tuck A 1973, pp. 36–7.
6   *C.A.*, pp. 168–9; Jones M 1970, pp. 83–4. For expenditure on the fabric of Pevensey Castle, see below, p. 323 n. 34. A ducal warrant was dated Pontefract 1 Aug. 1377 (P.R.O. DL28/3/1 m10).
7   *R.P.*, Vol. 3, p. 3. Ducal letters patent were dated Leicester Castle 8 Oct. (*C.P.R. 1396–9*, p. 518). In parliament Gaunt headed the triers of petitions for England, Wales and Scotland, as he did (and usually for Ireland too) in subsequent parliaments (*R.P.*, Vol. 3, pp. 4, 34, 56, 72, 89).
8   Ibid., p. 5. The slanders he referred to were probably about his alleged designs on the throne.
9   Ibid., p. 12.
10 Ibid., p. 6; Tuck A 1973, pp. 38, 40–1; Lewis NB 1926: 246–8 and 248n.
11 Tout TF 1928, Vol. 3, pp. 332, 342.
12 Ibid., pp. 328–9, 344.
13 *R.S.*, Vol. 2, p. 3; Bain J 1888, Vol. 4, no. 242; *C.A.*, pp. 194–5.
14 Ibid., p. 194.
15 *R.S.*, Vol. 2, p. 3.
16 *C.A.*, p. 201. Ducal warrants were dated The Savoy 7 and 26 Feb. 1378 (P.R.O. PL3/1/33; *C.P.R. 1396–9*, p. 547).
17 Appointments of commissioners to arrest ships and mariners were made in May (*Foedera*, 1869, Vol. 4, pp. 40–1).
18 P.R.O. E403/465/17, 18. Ducal warrants were dated The Savoy 11 and 22 May (P.R.O. PL3/1/130, 169).
19 P.R.O. E403/468/1.
20 Ibid., 4, 8. Commissioners were appointed to hold musters of Gaunt's retinues on 25 June (*Foedera*, 1869, Vol. 4, p. 45). Ducal warrants were dated The Savoy 4 July and Southampton 7th (*J.G.R. 1379–83*, no. 88; P.R.O. PL3/1/128).

21 For Gaunt and Buxhill, *J.G.R. 1372–6*, nos 893, 1342, 1377; *J.G.R. 1379–83*, no. 491.

22 *A.C.*, pp. 121–3; *C.A.*, pp. 206–10.

23 Ibid., pp. 210–11. Ducal documents were dated Leicester Castle 4 Oct. (*J.G.R. 1379–83*, no. 1070), Gloucester 1 Nov. (H.M.C.; Rawdon Hastings R 1928, Vol. 1, p. 30) and The Savoy 9 Nov. (P.R.O. PL3/1/134).

24 *R.S.*, Vol. 2, p. 14.

25 *J.G.R. 1379–83*, no. 327. A ducal warrant was dated Leicester Castle 8 Aug. 1379 (P.R.O. PL3/1/121).

26 Jones M 1970, p. 89 and n; *J.G.R. 1379–83*, nos 463, 1200; cf below, p. 186.

27 Froissart J 1869, Vol. 9, pp. 131–2; cf below, p. 182. For gifts given to Maud Courtenay by Gaunt and Bolingbroke on her wedding day, *J.G.R. 1379–83*, no. 463 (p. 152).

28 *C.A.*, pp. 261ff.

29 *J.G.R. 1379–83*, no. 463 (pp. 152–3); Perroy E 1933, p. 145 and n; see below, p. 182.

30 *J.G.R. 1379–83*, no. 463 (p. 153).

31 Ibid., nos 526–7, 1100. On 1 Aug. a ducal warrant was dated Ightenhill, one of the Lancs. hunting preserves (P.R.O. PL3/1/118).

32 *J.G.R. 1379–83*, nos 357–9. For orders for preparations for the expedition issued at Leicester Castle 4 and 5 Sept., ibid., nos 366, 370.

33 Ibid., *passim*. Gaunt was at York on 28 Sept. (P.R.O. PL3/1/98, 100).

34 *R.S.*, Vol. 2, pp. 27–9.

35 *J.G.R. 1379–83*, nos 377, 1080; *A.C.*, p. 132.

36 Storey RL 1957: 595.

37 *J.G.R. 1379–83*, nos 1185, 1209.

38 *R.S.*, Vol. 2, pp. 29–30; Bain J 1888, Vol. 4, no. 296; *A.C.*, p. 132.

39 *J.G.R. 1379–83*, no. 439 and n.

40 Otterbourne T 1732, pp. 153–4; *R.P.*, Vol. 3, p. 88.

41 *J.G.R. 1379–83*, nos 415, 417.

42 Ibid., no. 1206.

43 Ibid., nos 440, 968.

44 *C.A.*, pp. 280–1; Bird 1949, p. 50. For a ducal warrant of 2 Oct., ordering preparations for Gaunt's stay at Northampton, *J.G.R. 1379–83*, no. 404.

45 *R.P.*, Vol. 3, p. 88. Gaunt was at Northampton 29–30 Nov. and 1–6, 8 Dec. (*J.G.R. 1379–83, passim*).

46 Ibid., no. 556.

47 Ibid.; Russell PE 1955, pp. 302ff.

48 Perroy E 1933, pp. 149–50 and 150n, 151 and n.

49 *R.S.*, Vol. 2, pp. 35–7; P.R.O. E403/485/2.

50 *J.G.R. 1379–83*, nos 500–1.

51 Ibid., no. 547; *A.C.*, p. 133; P.R.O. E101/318/31.

52 *A.C.*, pp. 133ff, 193.

53 *C.A.*, p. 286.

54 *A.C.*, p. 139.

55 *C.A.*, p. 289.

56 *A.C.*, p. 138.

57 Ibid., p. 145; *C.A.*, p. 294; *C.H.K.*, Vol. 2, p. 133. Gaunt retained friar Appleton, 'phisicien et surgein' in 1373 to serve him in peace and war

for 40 marks *p.a.*, in consideration of past and future services (*J.G.R. 1372–6*, no. 836; *J.G.R. 1379–83*, no. 72). In 1381 Gaunt gave him a New Year's present (ibid., no. 557).

58   Liddell WH, Wood RGE 1982, p. 88. This work also contains documentary references to a band which attacked Hertford Castle and to Gaunt's prosecutions of a large number for the burning of The Savoy (ibid., pp. 44–5, 57, 60, 89, 91).

59   Kirby J L 1970, p. 19.

60   *A.C.*, p. 153.

61   *C.H.K.*, Vol. 2, p. 144; *A.C.*, p. 153. According to the Anonimalle Chronicler, Constance stayed a while at Pontefract Castle before fleeing to Knaresborough.

62   *C.H.K.*, Vol. 2, pp. 142–3; Somerville R 1953, p. 365; cf below, p. 316.

63   *J.G.R. 1379–83*, pp. xiv–xv; cf below, p. 339.

64   *A.C.*, pp. 141–2; *C.H.K.*, Vol. 2, pp. 134–5; *C.A.*, pp. 288–9.

65   Gaunt dated warrants Berwick 11, 15, 17–19 June (ibid., nos 530–6, 541, 548–51, 1096, 1188).

66   *C.H.K.*, Vol. 2, pp. 144–5.

67   *J.G.R. 1379–83*, nos 541, 548–51.

68   Wyntoun A 1879, Vol. 3, pp. 16–17. Gaunt had addressed a petition on behalf of Robert II's younger son the earl of Fife to Sir John Knyvet as chancellor, dated Nuneaton (Warwicks.) 7 Aug. (P.R.O. SC1/63/244). This probably dates from the period 1372–6.

69   *J.G.R. 1379–83*, nos 530–6.

70   Ibid., nos 537–9.

71   *A.C.*, p. 152; cf. *C.A.*, p. 328; *C.H.K.*, Vol. 2, pp. 145–6.

72   P.R.O. C49/F12/11.

73   *C.H.K.*, Vol. 2, p. 145. Gaunt dated a warrant Bamburgh Castle 21 June; Carrick as lieutenant of the Marches dated a safe-conduct for him and 100 companions to come to Edinburgh, the following day and on 28th Robert II dated one for him at Scone (*J.G.R. 1379–83*, nos 1097, 1186–7).

74   *J.G.R. 1379–83* nos 537–9; ibid., no. 643 confirms that Gaunt travelled from Bamburgh to Roxburgh. This warrant mentions payments for a stay of 21 days in Scotland which makes it possible that he was there from 22 June.

75   Froissart J 1869, Vol. 9, pp. 420–1.

76   Wyntoun A 1879, Vol. 3, pp. 116–17; *C.H.K.*, Vol. 2, p. 147.

77   *J.G.R. 1379–83*, no. 559. Gaunt also dispatched warrants from Edinburgh to his Yorks. receiver and the treasurer of his household (ibid., nos 560–1, 563–4).

78   Ibid., no. 643.

79   Ibid., no. 564. For his gifts of wine to the earl of Carrick and Sir John Edmanston and of a golden goblet to the earl of Douglas, ibid., no. 643.

80   Ibid., nos 561–2.

81   Froissart J 1869, Vol. 9, p. 424; *C.H.K.*, Vol. 2, p. 148; *C.A.*, p. 329.

82   Wyntoun A 1879, Vol. 3, pp. 17–18. Gaunt dated warrants Berwick 13 and Bamburgh 14 July (*J.G.R. 1379–83*, nos 1189–90; P.R.O. PL3/1/91).

Chapter Six

Gaunt and Richard II (1381–6)

Was the revolt of 1381 a turning-point in Gaunt's life? The chroniclers of St Mary's Abbey, York and of Leicester Abbey thought he saw it as such at the time, repenting in misfortune of his immoral behaviour and resolving to reform it. Walsingham's increasingly mellow view of his political role after 1381 presumably reflects a wider opinion than that of the cloister at St Albans.

From Gaunt's return to England in 1381 until his departure in 1386 he often appeared as dominant in council and parliament and in defending the realm and negotiating with foreign powers as hitherto. Especially in the years 1381–3 he aroused opposition in familiar quarters, among citizens of London, members of the Commons and leading ecclesiastics. But this appearance of dominance was to some extent deceptive. After his isolation and apparent rejection by king and community of the realm in the Great Revolt, Gaunt pursued his own interest more forcefully than in the first years of the reign, rather than subordinating it to the interest of the Crown. He precipitated a crisis over his quarrel with the earl of Northumberland and he campaigned vigorously to harness the war effort to his Iberian ambitions. In 1384–5 he had to defend himself against the intrigues of hostile factions at court. Richard II, increasingly assertive after 1381, often appears to have regarded his uncle's influence as a constraint rather than a support. Uncle and nephew found a solution to their problem in 1385 in the promotion of Gaunt's Iberian ambitions. Nevertheless, the underlying situation remained that, for the first time since 1330, the Crown and the House of Lancaster were not in close alliance: in these circumstances the king was unable to resist the constraints put on his authority in the 1386 parliament, and by rebellion in 1387.

It was not unusual for medieval kings who succeeded as minors to resent the authority of the regent or councillors who had hitherto exercised power in their name, and to assert their fledgling regality by kicking out at hated mentors. Thus Richard's treatment of Gaunt reflects a fairly common pattern; Richard when more mature showed he was perfectly capable of getting on with his uncle. The rising tension between them in the early 1380s reveals much about their characters. Gaunt behaved in the face of provocation at court more circumspectly than he had in response to the earl of Northumberland's less malevolent behaviour. Richard, aged fourteen in 1381, handsome, athletic in build, acted towards his uncle petulantly, indifferent to kinship obligations. Generally he was influenced by knights high in his service and by young noble friends. One might have expected mature knights such as Simon Burley and Michael de la Pole to have instilled in him respect for Gaunt. However, they did not wish to offend their volatile master: they were intent on feathering their nests. Some callow young nobles were as determined as Richard to cut Gaunt down to size, seeing the diminution of his influence (mistakenly, as it turned out) as the key to deflating the role of the royal uncles. Prominent among the anti-Lancastrian nobles were Robert de Vere, earl of Oxford and Thomas Mowbray, earl of Nottingham, neither of them heirs to distinguished earldoms nor marked out by the performance of chivalrous deeds. Richard's willingness to favour them and tolerate their hostility to Gaunt did him no honour.

On 13 July 1381 the duke's retinue probably met him at Berwick on his return from Scotland. Escorted also by Northumberland gentlefolk, he rode via Bamburgh and Newcastle to Durham, where he apparently enjoyed Prior Berrington's hospitality.[1] He had courteously but pointedly refused the offer of personal protection which the king had ordered the earl of Northumberland to give him.[2] The ducal retainer Lord Neville accompanied him southwards to the bishopric of Durham's manor of Northallerton. There Gaunt had an affecting public encounter and reconciliation on the highway with Constance and the ducal company relaxed before setting out next day for Boroughbridge. On the way, in the fields of Kirby Moorside, they were met by Neville's brother Alexander, archbishop of York, with an armed retinue. The day afterwards it was the civic governors and citizens of York who met them with a guard, arrayed on a pleasant hill near Wetherby. The ducal party was to rest at Pontefract Castle for several days.[3] Gaunt then resumed his journey southwards through Nottingham and Leicester, escorted in a

triumphal procession by armed companies in each shire. He eventually
met the king at Reading, where a great council had been summoned
to meet on 4 August.[4]

It was probably at this council that Gaunt's appointment to hear and
determine as sole justice all crimes connected with the insurrection
was decided upon.[5] More dramatically, at the council he accused
the earl of Northumberland in Richard's presence of having acted
disobediently and faithlessly.[6] Froissart says that at a feast which
Richard held at Westminster on 15 August the two lords quarrelled
violently. He represents the duke as persisting haughtily in face of
the earl's respectful excuses. The essence of Gaunt's complaint was,
he says, that the earl had 'much wronged my honour, in thus giving
credit to reports in circulation that I wished to commit treason with
the Scots, by shutting against me on my return the king my lord's
towns, and in particular that in which my provision and stores were'.
Gaunt then challenged the earl by throwing down his glove. The king
intervened to excuse the earl and asked his uncle to abate his anger.
The earls of Arundel, Salisbury, Suffolk, Stafford and Devon went on
their knees before Gaunt in support of the royal request. The duke was
still inflamed with anger, but after a while spoke more courteously to
the lords, a prelude to reconciliation.[7]

In September Gaunt was in York, presiding with fellow justices
over the investigation of 'various treasons, insurrections and other
evils' in Yorkshire.[8] On 9 October he was at another royal council
at Berkhampsted (Herts.), at which the issues between him and the
earl of Northumberland were once again aired. The quarrel was longer
drawn out than Froissart thought – perhaps his uncharacteristically
hostile account of Gaunt's conduct was a garbled version of what
transpired at Berkhampsted, a piece of anti-Lancastrian propaganda
in which his and the earl's roles were reversed. At Berkhampsted,
the earl, in defiance of the king's command, replied to the duke's
accusations with insults 'in the manner of his people', exclaimed
the southerner Walsingham. It sounds as if the earl may have
given way to the border habit of 'bauchling' (public villification).
His later apology to Gaunt shows that he caused grave offence on
this occasion to the king and duke by replying to the latter's charges in
disrespectful terms and by throwing down his gage. Gaunt's charges
were that he had acted disobediently to the king and himself, and
unnaturally towards himself. The earl was arrested for *lèse-majesté*,
but released on the sureties of the earls of Warwick and Suffolk
for his appearance in the parliament which was due to meet the
following month.[9] Thus the earl of Northumberland's later apology,
and the account of Walsingham, so often hostile to Gaunt, show that
at Berkhampsted it was the former, not the latter, who reacted

unreasonably in public. Moreover, the English sources make clear that the confrontation at the council intensified the crisis. As retinues arrived in London for parliament, the recently restored peace in the realm was again threatened. Northumberland had a large company of armed northerners: the Londoners, expressing their hatred of the duke, welcomed him vociferously; citizenship was conferred on him. When Gaunt appeared with an impressive retinue, also armed, the gates were guarded to prevent their entrance. He apparently stayed outside the city in the bishop of London's house at Fulham. Conflict was daily expected. The common people, according to Walsingham, did not care which lord they supported, but saw the quarrel as an opportunity to revenge the recent executions for rebellion.[10] The Parliament Roll confirms that such fears were felt by king and council. In hopes of settling the dispute, parliament was adjourned for several days: there was 'great rumour' among the people – a phrase like ones sometimes used to describe the Peasants' Revolt.[11]

The dispute went before parliament early in November. The fullest account of its resolution is given by the Anonimalle Chronicler. On the third day of the session, as on the day before, the duke rode to the parliament house with a large company. Seated in the presence of king, lords and commons, he rehearsed his grievances. The earl started to reply, but Richard ordered him to have his answer ready for the next day. When parliament reconvened then, Richard told his uncle not to move or to say anything during Northumberland's speech. To justify his behaviour, the latter exhibited four royal letters which he had received. The following day Gaunt spoke, bringing in at some length new matters of accusation. Northumberland, the Anonimalle Chronicler thought, made a good reply. Richard then took the quarrel into his own hands in order to make an accord. At Gaunt's suit and 'in ease of his heart' the envoys whom the earl had sent to him in June were imprisoned in the Tower for exceeding their instructions. One of them, Motherby, had produced in parliament the letter he and Hotham had carried from the earl to Gaunt in June, as his justification, according to an endorsement on it in a contemporary hand. If the Anonimalle Chronicler's account of that interview is accurate, their verbal message was, indeed, a considerable elaboration of their credence. Next day, the earl on his knees begged for the king's and duke's pardons and for the latter's good lordship 'which I desire wholeheartedly'. At the request of the chancellor, Courtenay, speaking on the king's behalf, Gaunt and the earl exchanged the kiss of peace before the assembled parliament.[12]

Doubtless, after his recent abasements, it was gratifying for Gaunt to have Northumberland acknowledge him in parliament as 'the greatest lord and the most exalted person in the realm after my liege lord the king'. King and council had handled a dangerous dispute between two leading subjects judiciously. The sources give no indication as to how Richard regarded his uncle's persistence in the matter. Before the duke's return to England, king and council had hoped that the duke and earl would soon link up and that Gaunt's bruised honour would be healed by the elaborate receptions laid on for a regal progress to court. But Gaunt's attitude had stiffened from exiled abjectness to princely haughtiness. His suit and Northumberland's angry reactions to it may have come as an irritating shock at court. The issue threatened the fragile domestic peace and the security of the borders. Richard by his own efforts had helped to secure his throne from rebels animated partly by hatred of Gaunt. Now Gaunt's behaviour was precipitating a new crisis. There is no indication that fellow magnates approved of his intransigence. His insistence on his dignity may have isolated him from them and alienated Richard, however much the latter was growing up as the stickler for his dignity who gazes proudly at us from the Westminster Abbey portrait.

The reconciliation between Gaunt and Northumberland reduced tension in London. On 11 November the duke set out from his Fulham lodgings and was admitted with a large retinue to the city. He was met by the mayor and aldermen who accompanied him to St Paul's to attend mass for the soul of Duchess Blanche. Yet again duke and city governors were formally reconciled and they cordially escorted him from London.[13] His restored pre-eminence was apparent. He headed the committee of the lords appointed in parliament to survey the estate and government of the royal household.[14] He revealed his opinion of the sincerity of Northumberland's apology, and a vindictive determination to deny the earl the 'good lordship' for which he had begged, by replacing him in December as warden of the East March and keeper of Berwick. The Lancastrian retainer Lord Neville received the wardenship, another retainer Sir Thomas Ilderton the keeping of the town, together with Sir John Heron.[15]

When parliament was adjourned because of the imminent arrival of Richard's bride Anne of Bohemia, it was Gaunt who went to meet her shortly after 20 December on her landing at Dover. He escorted her to celebrate Christmas at the royal castle of Leeds, near Maidstone, and he probably went with her to the court at Eltham – where he dated a warrant on 16 January 1382 – and to her official reception by the Londoners two days later, when she was escorted to Westminster. Gaunt gave his daughter Elizabeth a velvet saddle embroidered with lions for her attendance at the royal wedding, which took place on the 20th, followed by Anne's coronation on the 22nd. On the queen's wedding day Gaunt gave the bride a silver enamelled ewer on a little stand. He was present at the magnificent jousts held to celebrate the wedding at Smithfield – so recently the scene of the king's triumph over the rebels. Bolingbroke took part in the jousts; Gaunt gave presents to the heralds and minstrels there.[16] Henry of Bolingbroke, Gaunt's son and heir, on whom he had bestowed the title of earl of Derby, was the apple of his father's eye. Aged about fifteen, he was a robust and short boy, affable and shrewd, developing strong literary interests, but emerging as one of the keenest jousters of his generation. Gaunt was doubtless proud to see him in the lists at Smithfield, perhaps in part because he recognised a burgeoning skill superior to his own. The royal dynastic union celebrated at Smithfield turned out, surprisingly, to be a love match. Richard was to behave inconsolably after Anne's untimely death in 1394. This wisp of a girl had given no offence to the English, though in the early 1380s some of her Bohemian servants caused irritation. The marriage was unfortunately childless. Did Richard believe that God withheld this supreme blessing because of his failures in upholding his divinely bestowed regality?

On 27 January parliament reconvened. The debates in it, and the feelings which they provoked, show how the Great Revolt had changed the political atmosphere in ways liable to constrict Gaunt's initiatives abroad, though he seems at first not to have appreciated this. His assertive attempts to win the backing of parliaments for his Iberian schemes aroused misgivings in a political community wary of imposing heavy taxation or sending forces out of the realm and uncertain as to the best strategy to adopt in the war.

Parliament had for its consideration, left over from the previous session, Gaunt's offer to lead an expedition to Spain in return for a subsidy. His recent experience of vicissitudes may have given him an unaccustomed eagerness to live in Castile. But, in the aftermath of revolt, the restoration of his power militated against rather than in favour of this scheme. Lancastrian power was needed as a bulwark against domestic as well as foreign threats. There was 'great dispute and altercation' over his proffer. The Parliament Roll reveals that it provoked lengthy debate in the Lords. Some argued that it would profit the realm as a means of rescuing Edmund of Langley's army, in dire straits. Others asserted that if Gaunt took abroad the forces that he wanted, royal power would be impaired. If 'riot' – or worse – broke out, the absence of Gaunt and other lords would be perilous.[17]

This new controversy provoked by Gaunt speedily revived hostility to him in London. On 23 February about 600 citizens, headed by civic and gild officials, visited the king at Kennington to receive a confirmation of the city's liberties and privileges. The Westminster Chronicler heard that they had asked to have only one king and to be ruled by him alone. This sounds similar in tone to the oath administered by the Kentishmen in 1381 against having a king called John and suggests that the Londoners were incensed by Gaunt's renewed assertiveness. Mercantile interests may have been concerned lest an expedition to Spain divert resources which they considered would be better employed in protecting Anglo–Flemish trade, by supporting Ghent in its rebellion against the pro-Valois count of Flanders, Louis de Male. Gaunt was alarmed by the Londoners' hostility, fearing that it presaged another attack on him. He sought royal licence to withdraw, leaving London in haste about noon on the day after the Londoners' visit to Kennington. He probably remained for much of March at Hertford Castle, returning for a prolonged stay in or near London only when another parliament met in May. Young Bolingbroke, Gaunt's son, eager to win honour, took part in jousts at Hertford held to celebrate May Day.[18]

Gaunt's desire to win support for his Spanish strategy was probably among the factors that led him that summer to avoid an opportunity for confrontation with the bishops. On 16 June, when he was at his manor of Tottenhall (Middlesex), Wycliffe's Oxford disciples Nicholas Hereford and Philip Repingdon visited him, appealing against suspension by the university. The duke rejected the plea and ordered them to submit to Archbishop Courtenay: he would no longer extend his 'good lordship' to critics of the ecclesiastical hierarchy, when they supported propositions defined as heresy (see p. 242). The duke was then preparing to go northwards for a congenial tour of his estates. His presence was unnecessary in the south, since plans for the king to lead a summer campaign in France had been dropped as a result of the unwillingness of the Commons in the recent parliament to finance it.[19] Gaunt was probably in London for much of June,[20] but at his castle of Higham Ferrers (Northants) on the 24th and 25th, on his way to Lincoln.[21] Again demonstrating his religious orthodoxy, he was present in the chapter house of Lincoln Cathedral on 11 July with Bolingbroke to hear Bishop Buckingham sentence the reconciled Leicester heretic William Swinderby, to whose eccentric evangelism Gaunt had given encouragement (see p. 243). On 28 and 29 July and early in August he was at Leicester Castle and by 16 August had once again moved northwards, as far as Pontefract.[22] He seems to have spent most of September in Yorkshire, staying at Pontefract and Pickering Castles and in York, and he returned to London early in October for parliament.[23] It was a time of mourning for him: his sister Isabella countess of Bedford died on 5 October.[24]

About the time Gaunt was in Lincoln, Richard II was exercising his personal authority in a manner doubtless uncongenial to Gaunt – he dismissed the latter's friend Lord Scrope from the chancellorship, incensed by his opposition to the royal will over the distribution of patronage.[25] But king and council still backed Gaunt's plans to invade Spain. In August Richard wrote to Pere III of Aragon that his uncle would take an expedition there through Aquitaine in the spring of 1383.[26] In parliament royal ministers advocated this. When the estates assembled in October in the Painted Chamber at Westminster, the new chancellor Bishop Braybrooke of London (a cleric probably particularly close to Gaunt) listed among the causes of summons the need to aid the English nobles in Portugal, who he said were in great peril. In fact this was not the case, because hostilities between the Portuguese and Castilians had ended in August. Three days later, in a speech in the White Chamber, the treasurer Bishop Gilbert of Hereford implied that the Anglo-Portuguese alliance was functioning well militarily. There were, he said, two strategic alternatives or, as he phrased it, two 'noble ways' – that of the Flemings and that in Portugal. The latter, he asserted, presently gave the best chance of victory. If Gaunt joined the forces in Portugal with sufficient backing, within six months he would either be king of Spain or have a decisive battle. His success would end the wars. After these controversial propositions, Gilbert outlined the terms of the duke's proffer. In order to deflect the opposition of the pro-Flemish lobby, he suggested that the voyages to Spain and Flanders might both be given financial backing. But opinion in the Commons in favour of parsimony and the 'way of Flanders' triumphed. Humiliatingly for Gaunt, a clerk made a military proffer which appeared more attractive to the knights and burgesses than his own – a bishop who had a frustrated military vocation and who had daringly attacked and routed peasant rebels the previous year, while Gaunt was sheltering from them among the Scots. The Commons petitioned the king to approve Bishop Despenser of Norwich's proffer to lead an expedition to Flanders hallowed as a crusade against schismatic opponents of Pope Urban VI, for which Despenser had procured bulls from Urban. The Commons failed to provide a sufficient subsidy for either a Flemish or Portuguese expedition: they hoped that the fiery Despenser's crusade would go ahead, financed partly by pious donations.[27]

But the invasion of Flanders by a French royal army precipitated plans for a speedier military intervention than Despenser could have mustered. Once more Gaunt recognised that his first duty lay in north-west Europe. On 20 November he dispatched letters to the bachelors and esquires of his retinue; this was the day before Ypres surrendered to Charles VI. On the 27th his army won a crushing victory over the Gantois at Roosebeke. His uncle Philip of Burgundy (heir by marriage to Flanders), hoping to put pressure on Ghent by disrupting its cloth industry, embargoed wool imports through Bruges, further disrupting the main artery of English overseas trade.[28]

On 12 December Gaunt ordered the receiver of Kenilworth to supply a cart for the carriage of armour thence to London, 'the duke needing it for his journey to France'. At a great council the king was advised to lead an expedition there – presumably spurred by the example set by the young Charles VI in Flanders.[29] The contrast with Richard's failure to head an army (except against fleeing peasants in 1381) was glaring. He and Charles had much in common; by the mid-1380s, Richard may have shrewdly realised that they had some identity of interest. They were both well set-up teenagers, of average intelligence, under the often irksome thumbs of powerful uncles. Both were excitable and obtuse and possessed an idealistic streak. Charles had apparently not yet exhibited symptoms of the mental instability which was to have such tragic political consequences, eventually enabling Gaunt's grandson Henry V to negate his and Richard's pacific ideals by launching new invasions of battered France. However, 1382 was Charles's moment of triumph, the longed-for revenge of the French nobility on the Flemish 'artisans' whose ancestors had humiliated theirs at the battle of Coutrai in 1302. Why, one wonders, had not Gaunt promoted his nephew's leadership abroad of an army in the early years of the reign, as had been planned in the last months of Edward III's? Instead, from 1377 to 1380 the council had preferred to rotate military and naval commands among members of a few noble families. Consequently, Richard, unlike his father and grandfather, was denied the opportunity to display youthful prowess. If he had behaved steadily on expedition in his early teens, he would have been better placed politically in the testing 1380s. He might have acquired a taste for campaigning, an enhancement to his reputation, as he seems to have done belatedly in Ireland in 1394–5.

A royal expedition for the speedy rescue of Ghent was the scheme proposed by Braybrooke as chancellor in the parliament which met in February 1383. Another proposal was that Gaunt or one of his brothers should lead an expedition to France. But the speaker of the Commons, Sir James Pickering – a Westmorland man reflecting northern opinion to which Gaunt was doubtless sensitive – argued that, since there was a danger of war with Scotland, it would be preferable for the king's uncles to stay in the realm until the March was secure. Pickering probably promoted the common petition for the safe-keeping of the March, to which the king replied that he had appointed Gaunt (the lieutenant in the Marches) and other lords to negotiate with the Scots.[30]

Pickering's argument about the Scottish danger was among those he used to justify the Commons' objections to alternative strategies to Despenser's proffer. It was agreed in parliament that his operations should have priority: there was the sop for Gaunt that, thereafter, the episcopal army should join up with forces to be led by him to Gascony for an invasion of Spain.[31] However, Gaunt is likely to have been annoyed and humiliated by the Commons' drift, despite Pickering's tactful explanations. He was certainly angered by the support given to Despenser by two royal retainers, Archbishop Courtenay's brothers Sir Philip and Sir Peter. Some injudicious remarks which he allegedly made about them fanned hostility to him in London: with a few companions he mounted horse and fled.[32]

Richard's reactions to developments in parliament are unknown. One might expect him to have been upset by the Commons' failure to support his personal resolution. Perhaps his feelings towards Gaunt were ones of growing irritation. The uncle who was so insistent on his status and dignity was unable to promote the royal interest or his own in parliament. At times the duke did not feel it was safe to sleep in London. Were his precipitate departures a matter for mirth and scorn among Richard and his cronies?

For much of April Gaunt stayed at Kenilworth Castle.[33] On May Day, when Despenser was preparing to embark his crusaders, the duke held a tournament at Hertford:[34] on 8 June he was at St Edmund's Abbey in Suffolk with the king and queen, at the shrine of the royal saint to whom they shared a devotion.[35] Soon afterwards Gaunt set out northwards to discharge his obligations to make the Marches secure, so as to be ready to link up in Gascony with the crusaders, once they had finished campaigning in Flanders. He was probably at Bawtry (Yorks.) on 17 June, at Durham on the 25th and Morpeth (Northumberland) on the 28th and 29th.[36] His arrival in the Marches was opportune: that month the Scots sacked Sir John Montague's castle of Wark-on-Tweed and English squires raided across the border in reprisal. On 12 July, at Muirhouselaw in Teviotdale, Gaunt made terms with the Scots headed by Carrick. They agreed on a truce to last till 2 February 1384 and on reparations. But Gaunt had difficulty in enforcing the terms: the English esquires who had raided took refuge in the Cheviots rather than be handed over to the Scots in accordance with what the Westminster Chronicler thought were Gaunt's unjust orders. The sack of Wark and the behaviour of the local gentry demonstrated to Gaunt how difficult it was to rule the borders without the full cooperation of the Percies.[37]

Gaunt left the frontier region before 20 July, when he was at Durham: he moved on to Yorkshire, where he stayed at his castles of Knaresborough and Pontefract. Towards the end of the month he also visited his castles of Tutbury (Staffs.) and Melbourne (Derbys.).[38] But events in Flanders were soon to wrench him from his tour of his estates. About 8 August Despenser withdrew his increasingly indisciplined forces from the siege of Ypres, moving them to garrison the places he had captured earlier. On 22 August Gaunt wrote to his receiver in the duchy, sending him letters addressed to the bachelors and esquires of his retinue to be forwarded in haste – presumably to summon them for an expedition to rescue the crusaders in Flanders or to defend Calais against Charles VI's army.[39] About two days later Gaunt and Thomas of Woodstock, having heard that Charles was threatening English-held territory, wrote warning the king, and themselves set out for the Kent coast. There they may have maintained their retinues arrayed throughout September: according to an account for the payment of Gaunt's men-at-arms and archers, he waited in the Isle of Thanet for his passage to Flanders to rescue the crusaders.[40] Richard wrote to Despenser saying that he had appointed Gaunt to come quickly to his relief. But soon after Charles VI arrived at Bourbourg on 12 September, the bishop negotiated the withdrawal of his forces to Calais and the surrender of Bourbourg and the port of Gravelines. There were no longer English forces for Gaunt to rescue in Flanders. The royal council showed good sense in restraining Richard's chivalrous inclination to hasten across the Channel.[41] Though Gaunt probably derived some satisfaction from the bishop's failure, it was not in his own interest, since as a result of the disintegration of the crusading army and French success in Flanders, plans for a campaign against Castile had to be dropped.[42] However, there was the consolation for Gaunt that the débâcle boosted his prestige and influence. His opponents had failed and reliance was placed on his military power and diplomatic expertise to limit the damage. On 8 and 12 September he received powers to negotiate with the French and to exercise a lieutenancy in Flanders and France in place of the bishop.[43]

However, ducal influence was soon to receive a domestic reverse. At the mayoral election in London on 13 October, Sir Nicholas Brembre was elected to replace John Northampton, who had been elected for the previous two years. Brembre was a grocer who represented the interests of the rich merchants and victuallers. Northampton was the leader of a political movement challenging their control of city government, a movement supported by less wealthy masters in a variety of non-victualling trades. Gaunt was the patron of Northampton: perhaps he hoped by making this connection with the 'popular' party in the city to lessen his unpopularity there, though this does not seem to have been the effect up to 1383.[44] On the day of Brembre's election, Northampton and his supporters decided to try and overturn it. A delegation went to see Gaunt at La Neyte, the abbot of Westminster's house near the abbey. They complained to the duke that the election had been carried out by force and asked for a royal writ to hold a new one. But the maintenance which Gaunt was prepared to give Northampton was limited: he would not be drawn so controversially into London politics. He brusquely replied, 'Nay, certes, writ shul ye non haue, auise yow amonges yewr selue.'[45] The consequent downfall of Northampton and his party was for long to be a dent in Gaunt's prestige (see pp. 101, 106, 147).

Parliament met on 26 October. In his opening speech the new chancellor Sir Michael de la Pole (a former retainer of Gaunt) referred to the latter's negotiations with the Scots. He said that a principal cause of summons was the need to settle Anglo-Scottish relations. The priority given to this may have been a reflection of Gaunt's influence in the royal council – he was probably eager to divest himself of the toilsome northern lieutenancy, so that he could concentrate either on peace negotiations with the French Crown or the invasion of Spain. When a serious Scottish breach of truce occurred during parliament, the council entrusted frontier defence to local lords, not to the duke.[46] One cause of satisfaction for Gaunt during parliament was the impeachment and conviction of Despenser for his conduct of the Flemish expedition. The charges alluded to ways in which he had frustrated Gaunt's efforts to lead forces to France. The latter was present at the trial, but over a fortnight before parliament ended on 26 November, he set out to negotiate with the French. Among his fellow envoys were Bolingbroke, gaining his first experience of major negotiations at about the same age as Gaunt had in Scotland in 1356, and Richard II's half-brother Sir John Holand, a future son-in-law of Gaunt. Holand was one of the sons of Princess Joan by her first marriage. Like Bolingbroke, he was to gain a reputation for jousting. He clearly had great charm and considerable ability, but he was violent, ruthless and self-seeking. His elder brother Sir Thomas, who was to inherit the earldom of Kent, was more amenable; John had the impatient acquisitiveness of a younger son on the make. He was soon to distinguish himself by seducing Gaunt's married teenage daughter Elizabeth countess of Pembroke, and by killing the earl of Stafford's son and heir in a brawl, an incident which earned him deserved execration in noble circles. Gaunt, however, seems to have had a soft spot for John Holand and rehabilitated his fortunes; Holand was, after all, a kinsman, the son of Princess Joan and beloved of his daughter.

The negotiations were held at Leulighen between Calais and Boulogne. The French envoys included the duke of Berry, one of Charles VI's uncles, and the duke of Brittany and the count of Flanders. The latter, like Gaunt, had had to flee abjectly from rebels. The count entertained him and his fellows in 'the great tent of Bruges'. On 26 January 1384 a truce was concluded to last till 1 October following: peace proposals were to be referred to principals. Gaunt returned to report to the king at Eltham at the start of February. [47]

Soon after his return, there occurred the most serious Scottish incursion since the start of Gaunt's lieutenancies. The earls of Douglas and March captured Lochmaben Castle, the last English-held outpost in Annandale. The council promptly appointed Gaunt and Thomas of Woodstock to lead a retaliatory expedition. For most of March and April Gaunt was occupied with preparations for and the execution of a campaign in the eastern lowlands of Scotland. This expedition failed to force the Scottish border lords to observe the truce and refrain from attacking the remaining enclaves held in their regions by the English. [48] Anxious to relinquish the lieutenancy, Gaunt recognised that in order to provide sounder defences he needed to extend to the earl of Northumberland the good lordship which he had been reluctant to give him since 1381. At Durham on 23 April 1384, after his return from Scotland, Gaunt made an agreement with the earl. The latter was to remain in the Marches to defend them from 1 May till 11 June and was to receive the custody of Carlisle Castle and the town of Berwick, powers to array the lieges of the border shires and to invade Scotland, and £40,000 for his expenses. [49]

When parliament met at Salisbury on 29 April, Gaunt was still in the Marches. He did not arrive till after 9 May; in his absence the chancellor de la Pole's advocacy of the proposals for peace made at Leulighen elicited non-commital responses. [50] The chroniclers, especially the more reliable anonymous 'Monk of Westminster', show how in this parliament tensions in the political community, particularly at court, produced bitter criticisms and conflict. For the first time the sources reveal clearly Richard's attitude to his uncle – one of hostility, even hatred. This may have been intensified by Gaunt's assertion of control over war and diplomacy as a result of the Despenser débâcle.

An incident during parliament demonstrated Gaunt's pre-eminent influence and Richard's youthful intemperance. Richard earl of Arundel was its instigator. Aged thirty-eight, he had succeeded his aged and distinguished father, a close friend of Edward III, in 1376. Arundel had failed as yet to make the military reputation he craved – Bishop Despenser had rejected him as lieutenant on his crusade. Arundel seems to have been an awkward and abrasive man, in contrast to his emollient, talented brother Thomas Arundel, then bishop of Ely. Richard and Gaunt were to conceive a deep personal antipathy for the earl, which was probably heartily reciprocated. When Arundel made a speech bluntly criticising government in the 1384 parliament, the king with a furious expression retorted that if the earl blamed him 'you lie in your face: go to the devil'. Gaunt broke the ensuing tense silence with a tactful explanation of Arundel's remarks.[51] More serious and more widely reported was the mysterious affair of the obscure Carmelite friar, John Latimer. He had the task of saying mass in the king's presence – perhaps significantly, in the chamber of the latter's bosom friend Robert de Vere, earl of Oxford. Latimer obtained permission to address the king and then spectacularly and insistently accused Gaunt of plotting Richard's death. Richard promptly ordered his uncle to be executed! The lords present protested the duke's right of trial and the king at once relented. Gaunt, when he heard about the accusation, came to Richard and exculpated himself. Latimer never revealed his sources of information, nor were his motives explained: within days he died in custody, as a result of being horribly tortured by knightly courtiers, including ones apparently acting in Gaunt's interest – an interesting glimpse of the seamy side of Ricardian court culture, so admired by twentieth-century commentators for its characteristic sophistication and delicacy of sentiment.[52] A possible explanation of Latimer's conduct is that he was one of those naive eccentrics occasionally drawn to make dangerous remarks to kings, and that he could not reveal his sources under extreme pressure because he had none. He may have conceived a grudge against Gaunt because the latter favoured rivals within the Carmelite Order, or because he patronised heretics (see p. 241ff).

The Latimer affair soon subsided. Its one significant effect may have been to demonstrate to the king's close friends such as Oxford how dearly he longed for his uncle to go to the devil. Moreover, Gaunt's unfavourable response to agitation by the Commons demonstrated the apparently widespread unpopularity of his overweening power. The Commons complained about the prevalence of oppressions and of the maintenance of disputes, caused by the abuses of livery tokens distributed by lords. They petitioned for a statute to curb the activities of such oppressors. This was of particular concern to Gaunt, since he had a larger retinue than any other lord. His livery collar of linked esses was famous, perhaps the first such collar to be widely used (see p. 217). The Commons petition may have appeared to be aimed particularly at restricting Lancastrian influence: it was Gaunt who spoke against the proposal. He argued that more specific complaints should be brought forward, since lords were competent to punish their dependents:

> in temporal matters and worldly power, he said, he himself, after the king, surpassed the rest of the lords of the realm, and if any of the people in any way dependent on him should be found guilty or chargeable in this respect and it should happen to come to his knowledge, the offender would suffer such punishment as

would strike into the hearts of the rest a terror of committing similar misdeeds.

He promised the same on behalf of his brothers. The Commons, sensing that no legal remedy was going to be provided, kept silent.[53] Gaunt probably gained the goodwill of fellow peers for his staunch defence of their liberties, which was to stand him in good stead in his troubles with Richard the following year.

On 27 May, the last day of parliament, Gaunt and Woodstock were appointed to lead the embassy for peace negotiations with the French Crown.[54] On 1 June Gaunt was at Newbury (Berks.), probably on his way from the Salisbury parliament to London or the Kent coast.[55] He and his fellow envoys crossed the Channel during the month. Their meetings at Leulighen with Charles VI's able uncles, the dukes of Berry and Burgundy, failed to make progress towards peace. Philip of Burgundy, now count of Flanders, was determined to end the revolt of Ghent; the English were resolved to support it. On 14 September a truce was concluded to last only till 1 May 1385. Gaunt and his colleagues returned to England early in October; he and his brother reported to Richard and his council that the French were more inclined to war than to peace.[56]

During Gaunt's absence in France, the prestige of his lordship had received a further setback over London affairs. The king publicly displayed irritation with the Lancastrian interest and a lack of concern to protect it. John Northampton's London opponents engineered his arrest and that of his leading supporters on charges of plotting to overthrow the city's form of government. Northampton was brought to trial at a royal council held at Reading in August. He imprudently expressed the hope that Richard would not proceed to judgement in his uncle's absence: when he heard this the king flared up and asserted that he was competent to sit in judgement on Northampton and on the duke of Lancaster as well. Northampton was condemned to death – a sentence later commuted to life imprisonment. His clumsy attempt to procure his lord's maintenance had exposed its limitations and produced another point of tension between Richard and Gaunt.[57]

Gaunt attended the parliament which met at Westminster from 12 November to 14 December.[58] He was probably at court in November: on the 19th with the king, Archbishop Courtenay and other lords, he was at Westminster to hear the arguments of a Franciscan, William Buxton, in favour of the antipope Clement VII.[59] On the 30th he was present at the lists there to watch a judicial combat with the king and was among those who rewarded the victor.[60] But behind the show of unity, tensions between uncle and nephew were coming to a head. They were precipitated by the new strategic dilemma posed by Gaunt's failure to make peace in 1383–4. He now appears to have been preoccupied not with advocating priority for war with Castile, but with combatting the danger to England posed by Burgundy's determination to control Flanders. At a council session probably in February 1385, Gaunt argued that it would be best to forestall a French invasion of England by launching a royal expedition to France. But some councillors vigorously repudiated this expedient; they asserted that it was sounder to defend the realm from attack. Gaunt said that he was unwilling to provide his support or his men's unless the king determined to go to France. He and his brothers indignantly withdrew from the council chamber.[61]

Gaunt probably feared that unless aggressive action was taken, Ghent would capitulate. In January he was upset by the agreement which the duke of Burgundy made for the marriages of William of Bavaria, heir to Hainault, Holland and Zealand, and of his sister to Philip of Burgundy's children.[62] Gaunt's behaviour in council was ill-considered and provocative: apparently some lords wanted to frame charges against him after his withdrawal from council, but were deterred by fear of his power and political skill. So they plotted his assassination instead, the Westminster Chronicler says. On 13–14 February the king held jousts apparently inside the wide space of Westminster Hall. There was a plot to kill the duke on the second night, which some said the king approved. Gaunt, forewarned, secretly fled with a few companions.[63] The Monk of Westminster's assertions are corroborated by Walsingham. He says that there was grave dissension between the king and his uncle, instigated by young men brought up with the former who plotted his uncle's death. Gaunt fled to Pontefract Castle, which he stocked with arms and victuals. The young men probably included Robert de Vere, earl of Oxford and Thomas Mowbray, earl of Nottingham, with whom Gaunt had a formal reconciliation later that year.[64] Robert de Vere seems to have been a lightweight youth, pleasure-seeking, acquisitive and commendable only in his devotion to the king. Thomas Mowbray had inherited his titles after the recent untimely death of his brother, John, who had been Gaunt's ward; their grandmother, the countess of Norfolk, was to remain a close personal friend of Gaunt. Mowbray, an ambitious and tricky young man with a good conceit of himself, married to the earl of Arundel's daughter, never seems to have liked Gaunt. Eventually his strained relations with the House of Lancaster produced the mutual downfall of 1398.

The sequel to the plot, according to the Westminster Chronicler, was that on the night of 24 February Gaunt went with an armed force to the riverside opposite the king's house at Sheen (now Richmond) with the intention of confronting his nephew. Gaunt crossed the Thames;

leaving soldiers to guard his barge and the palace gates, he entered the royal presence wearing a breastplate, with a few companions. He spoke bitterly and harshly to Richard, advising him to replace evil councillors. He upbraided the king for acting shamefully and lawlessly and for letting down his office by countenancing vengeance by murder. Richard replied quietly and ingratiatingly: he admitted injustices and promised reform. The duke then excused himself from his customary attendance on the king, on the grounds that there were those at court who wished to kill him. He left Sheen and recrossed the Thames, spending the night at Tottenham. Thence he went to Hertford Castle, where he stayed with his retainers. The king's mother, Princess Joan, shocked by the rift, tried to bridge it. At her persuasion Richard came to Westminster on 6 March; she visited Gaunt and persuaded him to accompany her for a formal reconciliation with her son.[65] However, the crisis was not over: it had produced wider repercussions among the higher nobility. Lords were alarmed by the plot to assassinate Gaunt. Their spokesman at a council held at Westminster immediately after the reconciliation was Archbishop Courtenay, often hitherto an opponent of Gaunt. He complained about the evil precedent set by councillors who had induced the king to agree to his uncle's death, a precedent which could throw the realm into turmoil. The patience Richard had demonstrated at Sheen was exhausted: he responded with angry threats, compounded afterwards by physical menaces to Courtenay, whom unfortunately he encountered on the Thames coming to court under Woodstock's safe conduct.[66]

Apart from the French and Scottish threats, Gaunt's reverence for kingship probably prevented rebellion from breaking out in 1385 rather than 1387. Despite his withdrawals from court, dramatised by the chroniclers, he continued to cooperate in government. On or soon after 19 February the royal council sent a Privy Seal clerk to Leicester to confer about indentures to be made between him and the king concerning the latter's proposed expedition either to France or Scotland.[67] Gaunt witnessed royal charters on 8 April and 1 and 13 May.[68] On 19 April payment of wages to a royal sergeant was recorded, for his journey to the north with instructions for Gaunt, Archbishop Neville, Bishop Fordham of Durham, the earl of Northumberland, Lords Neville and Clifford and other lords in those parts, about the safeguard of the Marches.[69]

The decision was agreed in a council at Reading early in June that the king should lead an expedition to Scotland. The large scale of the expedition was doubtless planned not only to overwhelm the enemy, but to burnish Richard's prestige, which his ill-considered assertions of will had tarnished. It was to be hoped that on campaign magnates would display heartfelt obedience and cooperation.[70] On 19 June Gaunt received the first instalment of wages for himself and his military retinue for service on the king's expedition.[71]

The process of reconciliation continued as the expedition got under way. When, on 20 July, the army was at Durham, Gaunt was reconciled at the king's insistence to Nottingham, Oxford and Salisbury. On 6 August at Hoselaw Loch, near Sprouston (Roxburghshire), Gaunt witnessed the creation of his brothers Edmund and Thomas as, respectively, dukes of York and Gloucester and of the chancellor Sir Michael de la Pole as earl of Suffolk.[72] But recent tensions were near the surface. Gaunt, a military veteran well-versed in Scottish campaigning, and well-acquainted with Scottish magnates, had a huge retinue.[73] By contrast, Richard's knowledge of soldiering and Scotland was minimal. He seems to have been fearful lest his uncle exact vengeance on him in Scotland for the plot: perhaps news of the death (on 8 August) of his mother, who had protected him against Gaunt's wrath, made him overwrought. When, according to the Westminster Chronicler, Gaunt advised him to extend the campaign north of the Firth of Forth, Richard rejected this course on the probably reasonable logistic grounds that victuals were scarce and it was likely to lead to starvation among the common soldiers. Richard also said that his uncle's advice sprang not from loyal zeal but from treachery – and added many shameful things about the duke.[74]

Froissart's version of the quarrel differed from that of the Westminster Chronicler. He says that the three royal uncles (with other leaders) advised that the army should move south-west into Cumberland, in order to cut off the Franco-Scottish army invading England. The king ordered this plan to be adopted. But the earl of Oxford privately dissuaded him from it, accusing Gaunt of promoting a hazardous mountain crossing in order to procure Richard's death so that he could succeed to the Crown. Next morning Richard told Gaunt that, if he wanted to go south-west, he would be on his own. The duke protested his loyalty. Before they returned to England, uncle and nephew were once more reconciled.[75] After Richard's return to England, Gaunt remained in the north, necessitating much traffic of messengers and letters between him and the king and council on affairs of state. In the latter part of September Gaunt was at Lancaster and other places in Lancashire: on 5 October, just over a fortnight before the opening of parliament, he was at his hunting lodge of Rothwell (Yorks.).[76] His sojourn in the north after the Scottish expedition may have been intended, besides the pursuit of private business and pleasure, to keep a watch on the enforcement of the new truce: it helped to ensure that, in the light of his new scheme to invade Spain, he could not be accused of abandoning the frontier when its defences were in turmoil.

The recurrence of tensions on the expedition suggests that another personal crisis between Richard and Gaunt might well eventually have arisen, if circumstances had not unexpectedly combined to favour an expedition to Castile. In the autumn, England appeared to be more secure from invasion threats. In July the capture of Damme by the Gantois had demonstrated the continued vigour of their revolt, necessitating postponement of current French plans to invade England from Flanders.[77] After Richard's invasion of Scotland, the Scots had been prepared to make a truce. In September news arrived that João I of Portugal had defeated Juan I of Castile's invading army at Aljubarrota the previous month, an event which Froissart credibly depicts as electrifying Gaunt.[78] Juan had succeeded his father Enrique II in 1379; though prone to melancholy and self-doubt, he inherited something of the formidable Enrique's determination and acquisitiveness. In 1383 Juan married the ailing Fernando of Portugal's daughter and heiress Beatriz. Soon after Fernando's death, Juan shrugged off his undertakings not to rule Portugal as king in right of his wife. This provoked revolt, centred in Lisbon, which threw up a worthy leader in the person of Fernando's illegitimate half-brother João (d.1433), master of the crusading Order of Avis. In an epic resistance movement, João – elevated as king of Portugal – reasserted Portuguese independence against the Castilians. The House of Avis was to rule Portugal till the later sixteenth century; it was João's descendants who were responsible for founding the first European overseas empire.

Parliament met from 20 October to 6 December. On 9 November the king invested Gaunt's brothers and other newly elevated peers with their dignities. Gaunt gave a splendid banquet for them and other peers, and for the king and queen. In parliament he made his proffer to lead an expedition to Castile to the king and lords, arguing the benefits that would accrue from it to the realm. He took care to persuade the Commons too. At long last his proposals received a modicum of financial support. The hostility and indifference with which his Spanish schemes had been greeted in 1382–3 had subsided.[79]

In parliament Gaunt demonstrated how usefully he could support the Crown in the face of unwelcome Commons agitation. The Commons petitioned for a resumption of Crown revenues from grants which they considered had been made extravagantly – a line of criticism likely to incense Richard. Gaunt argued that it would not be fair if the king could resume grants which he had made for the term of his life. Gaunt's opposition defeated the petition. However, as John Palmer has demonstrated, 'all the king's more recent grants came under attack, and some may have been withdrawn to placate the Commons'. The Commons won substantial concessions over the ways in which the king used his revenues and over their own control of supply. Palmer surmises that Gaunt's petition to have his palatine rights in the duchy of Lancaster made hereditary, and the grant of the earldom of Cumberland to his friend and retainer Lord Neville (for both of which we have only chronicle evidence) fell victim to the Commons opposition in parliament.[80] As in 1376, there is no evidence that Gaunt showed any sympathy with attempts by the Commons to reform government, but in 1385 his opposition may have been more limited and circumspect, not only because of his enmity with some of the court beneficiaries of Richard's largesse, but also because of his need for parliamentary support for his Spanish venture. In 1386 and 1388 Thomas of Woodstock and the Arundel brothers were to take a line diametrically opposed to Gaunt's over the continuing Commons agitation, abetted at least tacitly at first and eventually actively by Henry of Bolingbroke. If Gaunt had not been abroad from 1386 to 1389, it seems unlikely that such a terrible domestic crisis would have arisen.

At the end of parliament Gaunt obtained as a royal favour the release of his protégé the Londoner John Northampton and his associates, though they were not allowed to come near London. Concomitant with this was Gaunt's reconciliation on 5 December with Northampton's opponent Nicholas Brembre, mayor of London. That night Brembre supped with the duke; also present were the king and queen. However, subsequently Northampton's opponents in London had the concessions made to him revoked.[81]

Gaunt celebrated Christmas and the New Year at Leicester Castle.[82] Soon after Twelfth Night, he was back in London, among the nobles present with the king for the consecration of Walter Skirlaw as bishop of Coventry and Lichfield in Westminster Abbey.[83] He was present in the chapter house of Lincoln Cathedral for the reception of his sons Bolingbroke and Sir John Beaufort (Catherine Swynford's son), among others with Lancastrian connections, into the confraternity on 19 February.[84] Gaunt was back at court, in Westminster, on 8 March, when Richard declared in council that he was the true heir of Spain, and on the 22nd, when, with the Duchess Constance, he took leave of the king in anticipation of his expedition. Gaunt went on a tour of shrines, doubtless to pray and have prayers said for the welfare of his soul and of his crusade. It was early in 1386 that the duchess, intending to go to Spain with him, was received with her retinue into the confraternity of St Alban. On 1 April the abbot and convent of Barlings (Lincs.) added Gaunt to their obit list. On 25 March he had set out for the west country where he visited more

shrines before arriving at Plymouth, his embarkation port.[85] He
stayed thereabouts for several months, conducting a great deal of
diplomatic business, especially connected with the Anglo-Portuguese
alliance, as well as making military preparations for the expedition.[86]
There is a glimpse of him and Bolingbroke on 14 June, being examined
by commissioners in the *Scrope v. Grosvenor* case in the Court of
Chivalry, convened in the refectory of the Plymouth Carmelites.[87]
On 30 June the galleys and transports which he had requested from
João I of Portugal put into port: all was now ready for departure.
On 9 July Gaunt and Bolingbroke were supping on shipboard. A
strong and favourable wind at last sprang up, the sails were hoist;
father and son made their farewells, and Bolingbroke and his men
disembarked. That night the fleet put out under full sail. With Gaunt
went his wife, his daughters Philippa and Catherine and 'the youth
of the realm'.[85] But neither Gaunt nor Constance were youthful, as
they had been as newlyweds in 1372, when he had thought a crown
was within his grasp, and she that she would soon see her father's
tragic death avenged, and take his bones to lay them in his beloved
Seville. Over the next year these middle-aged adventurers were to
experience Iberian triumphs and tragedies. It was to be over three
years after leaving Plymouth before Gaunt returned to England, a
failure as a soldier, no longer the pretender to a crown. However,
he did achieve an important settlement, which significantly altered
the general diplomatic scene (see p. 127ff). He returned to a realm
where the memory of his quarrels with Richard had been blotted out
by intense political and constitutional conflict, by magnate rebellion,
by condemnations for treason and the executions of royal councillors
and courtiers, even probably by threats of Richard's deposition. When
Gaunt stepped ashore in England in 1389, the political scene bore the
marks of an upheaval which was to prove more ominous than those
of 1376–7 or 1381.

Notes and References

1 *J.G.R. 1379–83*, nos 565–6, 643; A.C., p. 154.
2 *C.H.K.*, Vol. 2, pp. 148–9.
3 A.C., p. 154; cf. *J.G.R. 1379–83*, no. 643. Ducal warrants were dated
   Boroughbridge 21 July and Pontefract 21–5 July (ibid., nos 553, 567–78).
   On 23rd he was exercising authority as lieutenant of the Marches (no.
   573). Knighton says he passed through York.
4 *C.H.K.*, Vol. 2, p. 149; *W.C.*, pp. 18–21; P.R.O. E403/485/11. Ducal
   warrants were dated Leicester on 1 and 3 Aug. and Sonning (Berks.) on
   7 and 8 Aug. (*J.G.R. 1379–83*, nos 80–3, 579, 583). Gaunt witnessed a
   royal charter dated Reading 11 Aug. (C53/159/1).

5   *Foedera*, 1709, Vol. 7, p. 323.
6   Armitage-Smith S 1904, p. 255.
7   Froissart 1869, Vol. 9, pp. 425–7. Ducal warrants dated Southam (Warwicks.) 13 Aug. and Brackley (Northants.) 18 Aug. throw doubt on Gaunt's presence at Westminster on 15 Aug. (*J.G.R. 1379–83*, nos 1103, 1113).
8   *C.P.R. 1381–5*, pp. 35, 77. Warrants were dated Rothwell (Yorks.) 17 and 25 Sept. (*J.G.R. 1379–83*, nos 1104, 1178).
9   *C.A.*, pp. 329–30; *W.C.*, pp. 20–1; *J.G.R. 1379–83*, no. 1243. Summonses had been sent in Sept. for Gaunt, Northumberland, the earl of Warwick and Bishops Buckingham of Lincoln and Erghum of Salisbury to attend a council at Berkhampsted on 7 Oct. (P.R.O. E403/485/14).
10 *C.A.*, p. 330; *W.C.*, pp. 20–3. Ducal warrants were dated Fulham 1, 18, 24, 26, 28–30 Nov. and 1–5, 7–10, 12–14 Dec.: London 15 Dec. (*J.G.R. 1379–83, passim; C.P.R. 1396–9*, p. 492).
11 *R.P.*, Vol. 3, p. 98; cf. *A.C.*, p. 155.
12 Ibid., pp. 154–6; *C.A.*, p. 330; C49/12/11. For the text of Northumberland's petition for the duke's pardon, *J.G.R. 1379–83*, no. 1243.
13 *A.C.*, p. 156.
14 *R.P.*, Vol. 3, p. 101; Tout TF 1928, Vol. 4, pp. 380–1. Gaunt was appointed on the committee of Lords with whom the Commons wished to 'intercommune' (*R.P.*, Vol. 3, p. 100).
15 *R.S.*, Vol. 2, pp. 33, 40.
16 *W.C.*, pp. 22–3; *C.A.*, pp. 332–3; *J.G.R. 1379–83*, no. 714.
17 *R.P.*, Vol. 3, p. 114. The Commons, in their grant of the wool subsidy for the defence of the realm, specified that it was not intended to finance the war in Spain.
18 *W.C.*, pp. 24–5; *C.A.*, pp. 345–7, 349; Palmer JJN 1972, pp. 44–5; Vaughan R 1962, pp. 23–4. Warrants were dated Hertford 15 and 26 Feb., 2, 3, 8, 20, 31 March and 2 and 6 April (*J.G.R. 1379–83, passim*).
19 *R.P.*, Vol. 3, pp. 122–3.
20 Gaunt witnessed royal charters dated Westminster 4, 11, 18, 25 June (P.R.O. C53/159/2).
21 Ibid., nos 718, 998.
22 Ibid., nos 716–17, 719, 729, 733–4.
23 Ibid., *passim*.
24 *W.C.*, pp. 28–9 and 28n.
25 *C.A.*, pp. 353–4.
26 *D.C.*, no. 32.
27 *R.P.*, Vol. 3, pp. 132–4, 140; Russell PE 1955, pp. 336ff. Edmund of Langley returned to England, after the failure of his expedition, on 24 Nov. (ibid., p. 343n). Convocation, meeting at Oxford 18 Nov., probably referred to this débâcle when alleging that tenths previously granted had been more useful to enemies than to the realm (*W.C.*, pp. 28–9 and 28n).
28 *J.G.R. 1379–83*, nos 775–80; Vaughan R 1962, pp. 25–8.
29 *J.G.R. 1379–83*, no. 786; Aston M 1965: 138–9 and 139n.
30 *R.P.*, Vol. 3, pp. 144–6; Tuck A 1973, p. 40.
31 *W.C.*, pp. 33–5; *R.P.*, Vol. 3, pp. 144–5; Aston M 1965: 139–40, 143–4; Russell PE 1955, pp. 347–50.
32 *W.C.*, pp. 34–7.
33 Ducal warrants were dated Kenilworth 6–10, 13, 14, 18 and 19 April

(*J.G.R. 1379–83, passim*). Gaunt visited Windsor Castle for the Garter feast on 23 April (ibid., no. 803).

34   Ibid. Despenser landed at Calais on 17 May (*W.C.*, pp. 38–9 and 39n).

35   Arnold T 1896, Vol. 3, p. 133. When Gaunt was at Kenilworth on 6 May he was making preparations for his journey to the Marches (*J.G.R. 1379–83*, no. 915).

36   Ibid., nos 891–2, 897, 1041–3.

37   *W.C.*, pp. 41–3 and 42n; Bain J 1888, Vol. 4, no. 318; Storey RL 1957: 597. On 7 May a prest was delivered at the Exchequer of £1,000 for Gaunt's wages to hold a day of the March on 1 July (P.R.O. E101/89/29). Ducal warrants were dated Roxburgh 7, 8 and 11 July (*J.G.R. 1379–83*, nos 893–4, 1195).

38   Ducal warrants were dated Knaresborough 23 and 24 June, Pontefract 24th, Tutbury 26th and Melbourne 31st (ibid., *passim*).

39   *W.C.*, pp. 44–5 and 44n; *C.H.K.*, Vol. 2, p. 199; Vaughan R 1962, pp. 29–30; *J.G.R. 1379–83*, no. 909.

40   *W.C.*, pp. 48–9; *C.A.*, pp. 356–7; *C.H.K.*, Vol. 2, pp. 199–20; Vaughan R 1962, p. 30; P.R.O. E101/39/29.

41   *W.C.*, pp. 44–9; Aston M 1965: 130.

42   Froissart J 1870, Vol. 10, p. 272.

43   *Foedera*, 1709, Vol. 7, pp. 407–8, 412–18; *W.C.*, pp. 48–9 and 48n; Aston M 1965: 146–7. For payments to Gaunt for the costs of his diplomatic expedition to Calais, P.R.O. E101/39/29.

44   Bird R 1949, 81–2 and 81 n5.

45   Chambers RW and Daunt M 1931, pp. 28, 30–1.

46   *R.P.*, Vol. 3, p. 149; *W.C.*, pp. 48–51 and 50n.

47   *R.P.*, Vol. 3, p. 153; *W.C.*, pp. 50–1 and 50n; Froissart J 1870, Vol. 10, pp. 273–5; *St Denys*, Vol. 1, pp. 298–9; Palmer JJN 1972, p. 50; Vaughan R 1962, p. 32.

48   Wyntoun A 1879, Vol. 3, p. 22; *W.C.*, pp. 58–9; Tuck A 1973, p. 43.

49   *W.C.*, pp. 66–7; Storey RL 1957: 598–9; Tuck A 1973, p. 42. The agreement between Gaunt and Percy was confirmed by the Crown.

50   *R.P.*, Vol. 3, pp. 166–7; Palmer JJN 1972, pp. 50–1. Gaunt was present at the royal palace of Clarendon (Wilts.) on 19 May when he received the duke of Brittany's envoy (Morice H 1744, Vol. 2, p. 450) and next day dated a warrant at Wilton (P.R.O. PL3/1/74).

51   *W.C.*, pp. 68–9.

52   Ibid., pp. 70ff; cf Tuck A 1973, pp. 92–3.

53   *W.C.*, pp. 80–3.

54   *Foedera*, 1709, Vol. 7, pp. 428–31.

55   Oxford, Magdalen College MS 84, ducal privy seal letter.

56   *W.C.*, pp. 88–9; Palmer JJN 1972, pp. 50ff; Armitage-Smith S 1904, p. 287n.

57   *W.C.*, pp. 90ff; Bird R 1949, pp. 82–3.

58   *R.P.*, Vol. 3, p. 185; *W.C.*, pp. 102–7. Gaunt displayed animus in parliament against the earl of Northumberland for his failure to safeguard Berwick Castle (ibid., pp. 104–5). The duke dated a warrant Westminster 24 Nov. (P.R.O. PL3/1/71) and an indenture on 10 Dec. (Lewis N B 1964, no. 6).

59   Perroy E 1933, pp. 70–1.

60   *C.H.K.*, Vol. 2, p. 204; *W.C.*, pp. 104–7; *C.A.*, p. 361.

61   *W.C.*, pp. 110–13.

62 Froissart J 1870, Vol. 10, pp. 312–14.

63 *W.C.*, pp. 110ff.

64 *C.A.*, p. 364; *W.C.*, pp. 112–15. Gaunt dated a warrant Westminster 9 Feb. 1385 (P.R.O. PL3/1/68).

65 *W.C.*, pp. 112ff.

66 Ibid., pp. 114–17 and 116n. Gaunt witnessed royal charters dated Westminster 8 April, Easthampstead 1 and 13 May (P.R.O. C53/160/4–5).

67 P.R.O. E403/508/2.

68 Ibid., C53/160/4, 5.

69 Ibid., E403/508/2.

70 Lewis NB 1958; *W.C.*, pp. 120–1.

71 P.R.O. E403/508/12.

72 *W.C.*, pp. 120ff; P.R.O. C53/160/5; *R.P.*, Vol. 3, pp. 205–7. On 7 July the king and queen had visited Leicester and presumably enjoyed ducal hospitality there, though it is not known whether the duke was present (*C.H.K.*, Vol. 2, pp. 149–50).

73 Lewis NB 1958: 17.

74 *W.C.*, pp. 128ff.

75 Froissart J 1870, Vol. 10, pp. 395–7; *W.C.*, pp. 130–1. Gaunt witnessed royal charters dated Newcastle 19 and 20 Aug. (P.R.O. C53/161/1).

76 Ducal warrants were dated in Lancs. 20, 23, 25, 27 Sept. (P.R.O. PL3/1/43, 48, 53, 56–7, 60–1); for Rothwell. ibid., 52.

77 *W.C.*, pp. 124–5; Palmer JJN 1972, p. 60. The French recaptured Damme in Aug. (*W.C.*, pp. 132–3 and 132n).

78 Froissart J 1870, Vol. 11, pp. 270–2; *W.C.*, pp. 140–3.

79 *R.P.*, Vol. 3, pp. 203ff; *W.C.*, pp. 138–45.

80 *W.C.*, p. 146; Palmer JJN 1971, pp. 477–90.

81 *W.C.*, pp. 148–51; Bird R 1949, pp. 83–4.

82 P.R.O. PL3/1/51; Nottinghamshire R.O., Foljambe of Osberton MSS, i, 787. Gaunt had dated a warrant Westminster 20 Nov. (P.R.O. PL3/1/63).

83 *W.C.*, pp. 154–7.

84 Lincolnshire R.O., D and C archives, Chapter Acts 1384–94, A.2.27, f13r; extract printed in Crow MM and Olson CC 1966, pp. 91–2.

85 *W.C.*, pp. 164–5; *C.H.K.*, Vol. 2, p. 207; B.L. Cotton Nero D vii, Liber Benefactorum f132d; London, Guildhall Muniments, St Paul's D and C archives, A74 no. 1944. Ducal warrants were dated London 20 Feb. and 10 March (P.R.O. PL3/1/54–5, 64).

86 Russell PE 1955, pp. 414ff. Ducal warrants were dated Plympton 20 May (P.R.O. PL3/1/49) and Plymouth 25 June (B.L. Add. Ch. 13, 190); ducal letters patent under privy seal Plymouth 18 June (Norfolk R.O., Norwich, Le Strange NA 44).

87 Nicolas NH 1832, Vol. 2, pp. 45, 49–50.

88 *C.H.K.*, Vol. 2, pp. 207–8; *Eulogium*, Vol. 3, p. 358; *V.R.S.*, p. 95; Froissart J 1870, Vol. 11, pp. 325–7; Russell PE 1955, pp. 416–17.

Chapter Seven

Gaunt and Iberian Affairs

It was the Black Prince, ruling the duchy of Aquitaine ceded in 1360 in full sovereignty to the English Crown, who (doubtless in consultation with his father) first involved Gaunt in Iberian affairs, in order to bring the weight of Lancastrian wealth and military expertise to bear on them. In 1366 the prince resolved to intervene in the civil war in Castile between Pedro I and his half-brother Enrique of Trastamara, rival claimant to the throne, in order to sustain the English alliance of 1362 with Pedro, an alliance for which Edward had long sought patiently. Castilian support gave the hope of powerful protection, by sea as well as land, to the enlarged duchy over which the prince as yet precariously ruled.[1] Gaunt's first formal involvement in Anglo-Castilian relations as an adult was the appearance of his name in the witness lists to the agreements which Pedro I, Carlos II of Navarre and the prince made at Libourne in Gascony (23 September 1366). These laid down the terms on which Carlos and the Black Prince intended to restore Pedro to his throne. Pedro granted Carlos and the prince lordships as well as financial compensation, but Gaunt received no specific promise of reward.[2] He was currently pursuing the Lancastrian claim to Provence, perhaps with the expectation of the prince's support with an Anglo-Gascon army, once the issue of Castile was settled (see p. 177).

Gaunt's experience of campaigning in Castile in 1367 did not deter him from fuller involvement in its affairs after Enrique's capture and assassination of Pedro in 1369. Gaunt's marriage in 1371 to Pedro's daughter and heiress Constance and Edward III's recognition of him as king of Castile in 1372 had the aims of honouring him with a crown and countering the threat posed to the English Crown by Enrique's alliance with Charles V (1368–9), particularly the threat to its beleaguered possessions in Aquitaine.[3] Gaunt was to prove no more indissolubly united to his Castilian claim than his father had been to his French one: both of them probably hoped that Gaunt could use the claim either as a bargaining counter to win the House of Trastamara from the French alliance or to assist invasion in the cause of legitimacy, as in 1367. But hopes of destroying the Franco-Castilian axis by negotiation for long remained unfulfilled. Enrique II (d.1379) was immovable and his son Juan I (d.1390) was strongly inclined to stick to his father's francophile policies. In the early 1370s Carlos II of Navarre conveyed peace proposals from Edward III and the Black Prince to Enrique: they were prepared to give up their support for the claims of Pedro's daughters and have amity with Enrique (as was Gaunt), on condition that Enrique gave up the French alliance. This he refused to consider.[4] Early in Richard's reign, when Gaunt had considerable influence over the conduct of foreign policy, there were efforts to make peace with Castile. In 1378 Sir John Blount was dispatched to Castile, 'to negotiate with the ambassadors of the king's kinsman, the king of Castile and León' – a notable English recognition of Enrique's title, and his kinship with Richard (stemming from the Anglo-Castilian royal marriage of 1254).[5] In 1380–1 Pere III of Aragon, with the encouragement of Richard's government, urged Juan to accept his mediation with the English, including negotiation on the legitimist claim. In April 1383 Richard granted powers to negotiate peace and alliance on behalf of himself and his uncles with Juan to a group consisting of Gaunt's retainers and of men whom Gaunt was to use again on diplomatic missions – Juan Gutiérrez, the Gascon Florimond lord of Lesparre, Sir Robert Rous, the Gascon jurist Raymond Guillem and Robert Waldby, clerk. Some progress was achieved in this negotiation – Juan made a peace offer, which included financial compensation to Richard. In the light of Carlos II's earlier mission, and Gaunt's readiness to compromise his claim in 1386, it is likely that the 1383 negotiations broke down principally on the unwillingness of the House of Trastamara to abandon a French alliance for an English one, rather than (as Russell supposed) as a result of intransigence on Gaunt's part.[6]

In the 1370s, in default of a compromise with Enrique, Gaunt concerted with his father policies of trying to intimidate or eject Enrique, by seeking Iberian alliances against him; a harmonious working pattern between royal and Lancastrian councillors and diplomats was apparently established in the concurrent pursuit of both Gaunt's personal aims in the peninsula and wider English objectives. In 1372 his envoys made an alliance with the volatile Fernando I of Portugal, by which the king undertook to attack Castile once a Lancastrian army had entered Navarre on its way to invade Castile. As a consequence Fernando was faced with a Castilian invasion and had to make a peace and alliance with Enrique (1373). This did not deter him from proceeding with a contradictory alliance with Edward III; however, Fernando's promises were clearly not to be relied on.[7]

Gaunt's need to postpone intended invasions of Castile, because of combinations of the English Crown's financial penury and of the emergencies it faced in France, prevented attempts to make an alliance with Aragon in the 1370s from being implemented. In 1373–4 negotiations for such an alliance against Castile went well, but were dashed by Gaunt's return from Gascony to England in 1374. The following year Pere made peace with Enrique.[8]

Because of Charles V's successes in the war of 1369–75, Gaunt's claim to Castile, instead of being a central asset to English strategy, turned out to be more of a liability. This remained the situation in the first decade of Richard's reign, except that the pressures on English foreign policy made it more difficult to justify and pursue the specifically Lancastrian interest in the peninsula. Though widespread English indignation was aroused by the Franco-Castilian attacks on the southern English coasts which commenced with the renewal of the war in 1377, public opinion persisted in regarding the French and Scots as the most threatening opponents. Walsingham and the Anonimalle Chronicler fail to mention the role of the Castilians in the landings in southern England in 1377. During the royal minority, broadly based opinions on the conduct of the war were vociferous and not easy to dismiss; Gaunt recognised this and appreciated the reasons for demands that he and his resources should be available to defend the realm. He repeatedly put the need to contain the French or Scots first. But his strong conciliar influence enabled him to get backing for Iberian diplomatic initiatives. In 1377 negotiations commenced with Navarre and Aragon which led to alliances, but a Castilian invasion of Navarre induced Carlos II to make peace in 1379; Pere III would not stir till the English committed an army to the peninsula. This they found impossible to do, because of the more pressing need to concentrate resources elsewhere.[9]

However, an English force did actually reach the Castilian frontier in 1382. In 1379, according to the later Portuguese chronicler Fernão Lopes, a Castilian exile high in favour with Gaunt and his brother Langley, Juán Fernández Andeiro was prompted by Fernando I to broach to them the question of a renewed alliance with Portugal.

Andeiro was dispatched as Richard's envoy to Fernando's court. In 1380 the Anglo-Portuguese alliance of 1373 was reaffirmed. Fernando agreed to receive an army led by Edmund of Langley; when Edmund and his army arrived, Fernando would wage war against Castile in pursuit of Gaunt's claim. Moreover, a marriage agreement was reached which was intended to give the Plantagenet family the prospect of another Iberian throne: Fernando's daughter and heiress Beatriz was to marry Langley's son Edward.[10]

Warfare broke out on the Portuguese-Castilian frontiers in May 1381; in July Edmund, his family and army docked at Lisbon. His force had a strongly Lancastrian complexion; it included Gaunt's leading Castilian councillor, Juan Gutiérrez, and notable ducal knights, such as Sir Thomas FitzSimond (the duke's standard-bearer), Sir Matthew Gournay, marshal of the army, Sir Thomas Fichet, Sir Mauburney de Linières and Sir John Falconer.[11] The betrothal of Edmund of Langley's son and Fernando's daughter was duly carried out, but the expedition turned out to be a fiasco. There were problems over pay and over the procuring of mounts and victuals in Portugal: indiscipline and deteriorating relations with the inhabitants were apparently compounded by poor leadership. Some of Langley's troops did manage to raid across the frontier in 1382, but Fernando and Juan I were both reluctant to commit themselves to battle and in August made peace without consulting the English. The angry Edmund and his forces were shipped home in Castilian ships. Obloquy has been heaped on him by historians. Doubtless he failed to make the most of difficult circumstances, but he had much to contend with – an ineffectively equipped and financed army and, in Fernando, a volatile ally, embroiled in a domestic political crisis. Had Gaunt appeared with an army in Gascony, Edmund's inactivity would not have been decisive.[12] But the internal and international situation made it impossible for Gaunt to procure the community's support in parliament in 1382 for the commitment of further resources to the Iberian wars (see pp. 92, 94). In the following years (1383–4) Gaunt's diplomatic and military energies became focussed on the confrontations with the French in Flanders and with their allies the Scots. A new crisis in relations between Castile and Portugal was to concentrate his attention once more on Iberian affairs. In 1383 Queen Leonor of Portugal and Andeiro (her lover) took advantage of Fernando I's deteriorating health to make a treaty with Juan I, whereby he was to marry Beatriz, heiress to Portugal. The wedding took place in May; the bride's father Fernando died in September. Juan soon showed disregard for the terms of regency which he had agreed to in the event of Beatriz's minority: he intended to rule Portugal as king. His attempts to occupy the realm provoked revolt in Lisbon, supported by other ports whose prosperity depended heavily on trade with England and on the Flemish trade, vulnerable to English attack. Fernando's illegitimate brother João, master of the Order of Avis, was elevated by the rebels as regent. In 1384 his envoys to Richard eventually obtained permission to recruit soldiers in England. That summer Lisbon was successfully defended against a Castilian siege and in April 1385 João was proclaimed king of Portugal. He now sought a formal English alliance. But Richard and Gaunt were preoccupied with a political crisis and with threats of invasion from Flanders and Scotland. They may not have been impressed by João's claim to the throne, with its similarities to the Trastamaran claim to Castile. The stunning victory which he won over Juan at Aljubarrota in August transformed his prospects: God had blessed his cause. Moreover, in the autumn England's international and domestic situation appeared to be transformed too. The invasion threats had receded and the tension between Richard and Gaunt had subsided. Their recent quarrels had probably made both of them – and magnates generally – newly receptive to the plan that Gaunt should go abroad to pursue his claim. The royal council and Gaunt took up the Portuguese offers. In the parliament which met in October 1385 Gaunt advocated intervention in a speech to the king and Lords. He argued that he would damp down Scottish hostility by recruiting Scots, and would make Gascony more secure by recruiting the count of Armagnac and the lord of Albret. He undertook that, if he conquered Castile, he would make a perpetual peace between it and England. He assiduously canvassed the Commons; with some success, for part of the subsidy which they granted was earmarked for his proposed expedition. The aid was, however, grudging, for the subsidy was also intended to provide for the keeping of the sea and the Marches towards Scotland and for aid to Ghent. In Convocation on 18 November the clergy stipulated that their subsidy was for defence and a royal expedition to France.[13]

In fact the amount of the parliamentary subsidy which he was promised, *c*.£13,300, was, on earlier calculations made by him and his councillors, hopelessly inadequate for an invasion of Spain. In the 1381–2 parliament he had proffered to serve in the peninsula for six months with 2,000 men-at-arms and 2,000 archers in return for a subsidy of £60,000, to cover wages and 'regard'.[14] In October 1382 he lowered the amount, for the same service, to £43,000.[15] He was probably envisaging the subsiding of service in 1386 too of 2,000 men-at-arms and 2,000 archers for six months. It was for six months' service that Sir Thomas Percy sealed an indenture with him on 15 February 1386, with a retinue of 80 men-at-arms and 160 archers, and that Hugh de Sherley esquire retained two archers in his company in London on 14 March to serve Gaunt.[16]

How could the Commons have realistically expected Gaunt to mount an expedition with such small financial aid, and how could Gaunt have accepted this and carried on with his military plans? He may, indeed, have recognised that, after the recent invasion scares, it was reasonable for the community to allocate resources to meet the threat of an emergency such as did, indeed, arise in 1386. Moreover, both he and the Commons may have anticipated that he would receive profits from his crusading indulgence. It is not clear whether they were substantial. Walsingham says they were not, because people were disillusioned with such crusades against supporters of the anti-pope, but the continuator of the *Eulogium* asserts that a great deal of money was collected.[17] There was probably the anticipation, too, that Gaunt's private wealth would enable him to raise substantial loans as security, as he had done for previous expeditions abroad. A ducal privy seal warrant dated Westminster, 10 February 1387 ordered the Yorkshire receiver to pay Catherine Swynford £100, in part payment of £500 marks which she had recently lent Gaunt in his great necessity, according to the agreed terms.[18] In fact the Crown came to his rescue: on 7 February 1386 Richard and Gaunt were parties to an indenture by which the former was to lend him c.£13,300, an identical sum to the subsidy.[19] Payment of the moneys promised to Gaunt was slow: his officials do not appear to have received any of the parliamentary subsidy until 26 July, a fortnight or so after he had sailed.[20] The Crown probably had difficulty in paying the loan. On 22 May two Italian bankers, Matteo Cennini and Gualtero Bardi, received bonds acknowledging, respectively, loans to the Crown of £2.700 and £2,733 in aid of naval expenses and Gaunt's expedition. Cennini, in fact, was acting for Catalan and Aragonese merchants – so funds from Aragon helped to launch Gaunt.[21] Since, as the indenture he made with Percy in February shows, he was committed to paying six weeks' wages to the retinues when the indentures were sealed and six weeks' wages at the embarkation port, he must have been considerably out of pocket before he set sail.

The amounts Gaunt was due to receive from the Crown and from the lay subsidy for the expedition totalled only just over £26,000, well below the minimum £40,000 he had requested in order to pay 4,000 soldiers in 1382. Walsingham, however, said that his army was large, and Knighton, usually well informed about Lancastrian affairs, and citing a roll of the army's marshal, gave the figures of 2,000 men-at-arms and 8,000 archers.[22] Fernão Lopes was to give more realistically 2,000 men-at-arms and 3,000 archers.[23] Contemporary foreign estimates were lower:

	men-at-arms	archers	'varlets'
Juan I	1,600	2,000	
Ayala	1,500	800	
Froissart	1,000+	2,000	1,000

The low number of archers given by Ayala is contrary to the higher proportion normally found in English armies of the period. Juan's estimate – made in July 1386 – looks the most plausible. It is probable that Gaunt landed with an army comparable in size to the force of 3,000 which his brother led to Portugal in 1381.

Froissart says that remarks were made at Juan's court about the absence of the great captains of the past from Gaunt's army.[24] Famed knights such as Calveley and Knolles were probably mentioned there, and the late John Chandos. But there were highly reputed veterans who did enrol – men such as Lords Talbot and FitzWalter, Sir Baldwin Freville, Sir Thomas Percy, Sir Thomas Morieux (master of the king's horse), Sir Richard Burley, Sir Mauburney de Linières, Sir John Falconer and Sir John Dabridgecourt.[25] No magnates served on the expedition, nor, apart from two Percies, did any members of leading northern noble families who had close Lancastrian links. Barons came from other parts of England, and so did adventurous young gentlefolk – 'the flower of . . . youthful chivalry', as the chronicler Adam Usk was to put it.[26] Examples of young bloods were Lords Poynings and Scales, the northerner Sir Thomas Percy the younger (who all died on the expedition), and Gaunt's son-in-law Sir John Holand. Had Gaunt's expedition been a notable military success, he would have emerged as the idol of young English knights. The absence of leading nobles adversely affected the expedition: their eminence and control of long-term retainers were usually helpful to discipline. Nobles may have held off (especially northerners) because of concern about the defence of the realm. There were probably well-founded doubts about the financial basis of the expedition. Gaunt's recognition of the problem of inducement is reflected in letters under his privy seal which he issued to Sir Thomas Percy, undertaking that Percy should not have to pay expenses for himself and the men of his household from the time he reached the embarkation port, but would commence his contracted six months' service then. Moreover, Gaunt waived his share of any profits of war made by Percy and his men, except in the case of important prisoners. Gaunt would pay 10,000 francs for Juan I, or one of his brothers, or sons or lieutenants taken on the field of battle, the constable or marshal of his host, etc.[27] On this expedition Gaunt had to rely heavily for counsel, command and diplomacy on his family circle and on intimate retainers. The expedition was markedly Lancastrian in complexion and, apparently, markedly English, with few foreigners, even Spaniards, participating.[28] Castilian exiles had been a significant element in some English expeditions early in Richard's reign. For example, there was the retinue mustered in 1378 by Fernán Rodriguez and Juan Alfonso, of 13 knights, almost all Castilian, and 66 esquires, mostly Castilian.[29] But many exiles had drifted away from Gaunt, in some cases back to the Iberian Peninsula. The faithful Juan Gutiérrez, bishop of Dax, was prominent among those who accompanied him. Lope Pérez, knight of Spain, received royal licence to go on the expedition, and an Exchequer payment to help cover his debts in London and to recompense him for sums which the king had promised him when he was in royal service.[30]

What were the objectives of Gaunt's expedition? His professed aims were to rescue Castile from schism and to make good his claim to the kingdom. Palmer has argued that his 'real concern was to sell his dynastic claims as dearly as he was able'.[31] The possibility that he would succeed in winning Castile was certainly taken seriously by Richard and Gaunt. On 8 April 1386 they appointed procurators to implement the treaty of perpetual alliance between them and their heirs as kings of England and Castile.[32] It seems that Gaunt had hitherto only been accorded precedence in council and royal household as a duke: Richard now treated him as a royal equal. At a great council on 8 March the king confirmed that Gaunt was the true heir of Spain and caused him to be seated at the council table next to himself, above the archbishops, for the first time.[33] On Easter Day (22 April), according to Knighton, Richard presented golden crowns to Gaunt and Constance, and ordered that Gaunt be addressed as king of Spain and given all royal honours.[34] The crown which Richard gave Gaunt was probably the one he took to Castile for his intended coronation and gave to Juan I in 1388.[35]

After landing in Spain, Gaunt continued to act as its lawful king. He sent a herald to Juan to assert his right and to offer battle if it was denied.[36] Froissart attests the fervour with which he continued to hope for a battle whilst in Spain – his mind presumably dwelling on the momentous outcome of victory at Najera.[37] The decision to take his wife and three daughters (a highly unusual one) does not clearly signal his intent. It might have signified either that he wished to make marriage alliances against the House of Trastamara and set up permanent court in Spain, or that he wished to compromise his claim with Juan by a marriage alliance.

The latter course may have seemed to him a more likely means to peace, in view of the habitual reluctance of Juan's French allies to risk battle, and the crushing defeat he had recently suffered at Aljubarrota.

There is one piece of evidence suggesting that Gaunt anticipated being back in England and based there soon after the expiry of the stipulated six months' military service, rather than installed as king in Castile. The Carmelite Nicholas of Lynn, a member of an order with private access to Gaunt's intentions (see pp.244–5), in the prologue of his almanac, says that he composed it in 1386 at Gaunt's 'petition and pleasure'. The *Kalendarium* commenced with the last part of an existing almanac; the new part running from 1 January 1387 is made for the longitude and latitude of Oxford and was useless in the Iberian Peninsula.[38]

The indenture to which Richard and Gaunt were parties dated 7 February 1386 reveals that, before the public occasions on which Gaunt's *regalitas* was projected, he and the king's council had considered the implications for the English Crown of an agreement between Juan and Gaunt.[39] The latter promised not to recognise Juan as king unless he was prepared to grant Richard a satisfactory sum for the damages done by his subjects to the realm and its shipping and unless he made a perpetual alliance with Richard. Key elements in a settlement between Juan and his adversaries had probably already been the subject of negotiation. Juan had offered compensation of 200,000 *doblas* to Richard; it is unlikely that the proposal made to Gaunt at Orense in autumn 1386 by Juan's envoy Juan Serrano, prior of Guadalupe – that Gaunt's daughter Catalina should marry Juan's son Enrique – was new.[40]

What strategy did the Lancastrians intend on the 1386 campaign? Prior diplomacy gives few clues. We may accept that, as Lopes and Froissart assert, Portuguese overtures were well received by Richard and Gaunt from the autumn of 1385 onwards. Agreement was reached for the escort of Gaunt's fleet of transports by Portuguese galleys. The terms of the celebrated Treaty of Windsor, the Anglo-Portuguese alliance with its mutual defence obligations, were agreed to in Gaunt's absence on 9 May; he adhered to it on the 21st, and it was formally ratified in 1387, after Gaunt's expeditions in Castile. Gaunt avoided making a formal military agreement with João for joint action in Castile. The duke probably set more store by an Aragonese alliance, and in March and April 1386 may have been trying to revive earlier plans for an invasion of Castile from Gascony in conjunction with Aragon. This would have taken Gaunt and his veterans into Old Castile, where they had campaigned in 1367, and would have set him on the best course for a coronation at Burgos. But the aged Pere III, inclined to neutrality, was now interested only in promoting settlements of the Anglo-Castilian and Anglo-French dynastic disputes. His son and heir Joan headed a francophile faction opposed to any English alliance.[41]

Official references (in the Issue Rolls of the Exchequer) to Gaunt's expedition before its embarkation in 1386 refer to it as going 'to the parts of Spain'; the indenture sealed by Gaunt with one of his captains, Sir Thomas Percy, in February, obliged Percy 'to work with him whenever it pleases the said King and Duke'. In March Hugh de Sherley was uncertain as to where the duke might lead him; he made his archers promise 'to work with him in whatever parts please the said Hugh'. Service in Brittany too may already have been under consideration. Froissart appears to have thought that the original decision was to sail to Portugal, but that this was overturned at a council of war after the relief of the English garrison at Brest, on the grounds that it was more honourable and threatening to land on the enemy's coast.[42] It may well be that a landing in Portugal was discussed – but if Gaunt had sailed there, he would have been heavily jeopardising his chances. For when his fleet sailed from Plymouth on 9 July, the campaigning season was well advanced; the landing in Brittany imposed a short further delay. Since he had no military agreement with João, it was doubtful whether an Anglo-Portuguese offensive could be launched in 1386 before the funds provided for the expedition ran out.

So the Lancastrian army landed in and more or less conquered Galicia. The province had the advantages of proximity to Portugal and a history of legitimist sentiment; its coast was well known to the English as pilgrims. Gaunt may have believed that Santiago's rescue from schism would win the saint's favour and strongly influence Iberian sentiment. The fleet put in at La Coruña on the saint's day (25 July) – which had the practical advantage that the defending fleet, celebrating the feast, was unprepared. The garrison of the well-fortified port showed no disposition to surrender until after Gaunt had decamped and received the surrender of more weakly defended Compostela. Its citizens had agreed to receive Gaunt and Constance as king and queen for as long as they remained in the city and garrisoned it strongly. Gaunt ceremonially received the keys and went in procession with his wife and daughters to the shrine of Santiago. A proclamation in favour of Urban VI was made in the cathedral, and an Urbanist bishop was installed there. La Coruña and other Galician communities, sometimes after a show of resistance, submitted to Gaunt's rule on similar terms to those made by the citizens of Compostela.[43] According to Froissart, the Breton garrison in Orense put up a tough resistance to his siege; its capture was important for ease of communications both with the Castilian heartlands and with Portugal. After the fall of Orense, Gaunt held court there in the autumn and winter of 1386.[44]

The conquest of Galicia was a considerable achievement. Froissart has preserved anecdotes illustrating how Gaunt's son-in-law Sir Thomas Morieux led a force to secure the submission of communities which the English knights regarded as uncouth and savage, and urbanely succeeded through a mixture of tact and intimidation.[45] Key factors in gaining submissions were probably Gaunt's lenient treatment of the inhabitants and strict enforcement of his ordinances of war (courses which his grandson Henry V was to follow in his conquest of Normandy). Lopes says that the peasants brought in provisions and horses for sale in his army, which his troops – on pain of capital punishment – purchased at the vendors' prices.[46]

The attitudes of the Galicians were also swayed by Juan's failure to challenge the English, a matter doubtless intensely disappointing to the Lancastrian command. Juan made his negative response clear in a newsletter he wrote to the officials and councillors of Seville within a week of Gaunt's landing. He attempted to minimise Gaunt's threat to his kingdom, stressing the lateness of his arrival in the campaigning season, his landing in 'such a mountainous and craggy land, like a gorge enclosed by mountains on every side' and the smallness of his forces.[47]

In fact the letter reflects credit on Gaunt's achievement in occupying a rugged province with limited numbers; that achievement brought Juan to the negotiating table. But, in effect, Gaunt had shot his bow without vitally challenging the Crown – for which he needed to advance on Burgos in Old Castile. Why did he expend most of the slender resources at his command in Galicia? Part of the answer may be that he and some of his senior commanders remembered painfully the Black Prince's reverse at Vitoria after his invasion of Castile in 1367, resulting from his failure to secure an adequate base and a line of communications to friendly territory. Gaunt's desire to avoid these pitfalls, and to establish his rule securely on Castilian soil, defeated his prime strategic objective. This might have been attained if he had landed in Old Castile to threaten Burgos directly, or even secured Asturias and mounted an attack on the city of León. But Englishmen's perception of Galicia (so different from Juan's) may have given them an inflated idea of its symbolic and strategic worth – they may, indeed, have underestimated its distance and isolation from Old Castile. As we have seen, Gaunt seems to have had few eminent Castilian knights available in his company to give him strategic advice.

Juan's failure to make a treaty with Gaunt reflected a perception that the latter's position was weakening. Charles VI's impressive preparations in the summer to invade England were well known at the Aragonese court – and were therefore presumably reported to the Castilians.[48] These preparations made it unlikely that Gaunt would receive reinforcements in the near future. His thinly stretched forces were being depleted. As food stocks diminished, relations between the occupation forces and the inhabitants deteriorated; peasants attacked English foragers.[49] Epidemics broke out in the army whose ravages were much more effective than the enemy's. Walsingham says that ninety famous knights died of sickness on the 1386–7 campaigns.[50] The Castilian command, on the other hand, was buoyed up by the prospect of major French reinforcements to provide a field army balancing its native forces and the foreign mercenaries now tied up in garrisons.

As the end of the year approached, Gaunt was confronted with a major dilemma. His military contracts would soon run out; no parliamentary provision had been made to 'refresh' his army, such as the Northampton parliament had made in 1380 for his brother Woodstock's army in Brittany. The logical course for Gaunt would have been to return to England, as he had done from Bordeaux, abandoning Iberian plans, when his army's pay had run out in 1374. But it would have been to his dishonour in 1386 if he had abandoned his rule of Galicia, giving it over with no peace treaty to the 'schismatic' and 'illegal' rule of Juan. He gambled on mounting a new campaign in 1387 with Portuguese assistance.

Presumably he made new contracts with his captains. But how did he finance their service? Some resources from his estates may have been available after the Michaelmas payments to his receivers. Communities and individuals in Galicia could be asked for levies and loans, especially as they were anxious for the goodwill of their new king and his protection from depredations by his troops. The problem of financing his army was to some extent alleviated by its dwindling size and by the necessity of leaving garrisons in Galicia, who were probably given licence to 'ransom' the districts which they protected, a familiar device of English occupying forces in Brittany and other parts of France. However, it is clear from privy seal letters issued by the duke at Coimbra and directed to his councillors in England in July 1387 that he was unable to pay some of his soldiers and was heavily dependent on the goodwill of his permanent retainers to finance their retinues even for part of the first six months' service. He ordered his councillors to assign to his deceased chamberlain Sir John Marmion's attorney over £342 owed to him for his own and his retinue's wages for this term. He also ordered assignments to be made to pay over £1,675 owed to his bachelor Sir Thomas Fog for himself and his retinue on the present expedition.[51] The councillors were to make out letters of assignment to the soldiers whom he lacked the cash to pay in Portugal, on their presentation of bills made out under the seals of Sir Richard Abberbury, Thomas Tutbury and J. Noke.

Payments of parts of sums still owing are recorded in the receiver-general's account for 1392–3 to Sir Robert Rokeley, Robert Preston, valet, Rodriguez Alfonso, esquire, William Walton, valet and Arnold son of Sir John Palays of Cologne.[52] Inadequate financing probably rendered Gaunt's control over his soldiers much less effective on the 1387 campaign than it had been in 1386, and may in part have accounted for the desertions which occurred in 1387, and which he condoned, after only a few weeks in the field.

In effect, Gaunt's failure to force a decision over his claim in 1386 left him wholly dependent on the intentions of João I, who speedily exploited the opportunity, sending envoys to Gaunt with proposals for a conference. They met on 1 November on the frontier between Galicia and Portugal, João and his entourage honouring Gaunt by crossing the River Minho at Ponte do Mouro to greet him.[53] Amidst cordial junketings, agreements were reached and ratified by Gaunt and Constance on 11 November. João pledged himself to take the field in 1387 with a force of 5,000 and to maintain it in arms for eight months. He and Gaunt would conduct a joint campaign in Castile. João undertook not to make a separate peace while Gaunt was in the peninsula attempting conquest. Gaunt bound himself to help defend Portugal. The potentially burdensome price he was prepared to pay for João's help was the cession to the Portuguese Crown of the western borderlands of Castile. João was to marry Gaunt's daughter Philippa, a marriage concluded in February 1387.[54]

The precise strategic objectives of the Anglo-Portuguese invasion of the kingdom of León in 1387 are unclear. The terms of the Treaty of Ponte do Mouro suggest that the allies hoped to force Juan to take refuge in a city or fortress or to meet them in battle. The line of advance taken was probably in part dictated by its convenience for the conjunction of the allied forces. Russell surmises that the English arrived at the Portuguese frontier city of Braganca in mid-March and that the English army was only about 1,500 strong – Ayala estimates it at 600 lances and 800 archers – and so dwarfed by the Portuguese force of 9,000.[55] Gaunt's contribution to the new invasion of Castile was little more than a token one: the campaign was overwhelmingly a Portuguese undertaking and therefore, from a military viewpoint, its failure was a Portuguese failure, to which inexperience of such large-scale offensive operations probably contributed. The very capable constable of Portugal, Nun' Alvares, held the vital command of the vanguard, though João had been inclined to allow it to Gaunt. João's embarrassed failure to honour his father-in-law in this way brought home to the latter and, indeed to everyone else, the insignificance of Lancastrian power.[56]

The frontier was crossed late in March; the army headed towards

Zamora, but at Alcañices swung northwards towards Benavente de Campos, reached on 2 April.[57] Juan had anticipated invasion of this region: its defences and those of the city of León were carefully prepared.[58] Benavente was strongly garrisoned by native troops and foreign mercenaries. The allies stayed there for eight days, jousting and skirmishing with some of the garrison. João refrained from launching an assault, as he lacked the requisite siege equipment – though he had a siege-tower (belfry) and a 'crane' (probably a *trebuchet*).[59] From Benavente the army moved eastwards across the River Esla; a Portuguese force was detached to ride northwards towards Valencia de Don Juan (over half way to León from Benavente). One objective was to gather supplies, scarce around Benavente; another, possibly, to probe defences on the approach to León, whose capture may have been the ultimate objective. The search for victuals was probably now of more immediate importance. This was one factor which drew the army into a siege of a 'soft' target, Valderas, whose garrison surrendered on threat of assault. Tension between the Portuguese and English troops came to a head when João, punctilious in deferring to his father-in-law, allowed the English to enter and sack Valderas first: the stern João moved quickly to quell the resulting affrays.[60]

After staying fifteen days at Valderas, the army moved early in May southwards to Villalobos, a town with good defences, which was invested. This was a retreat, albeit a short one, presumably dictated by shortage of supplies and the hope of augmenting them from the resources of Villalobos. Hay was acutely needed; attempts to forage were hampered by vigorous Castilian attacks. Juan's council correctly foresaw that the invaders would soon have to withdraw through lack of supplies. But at Villalobos Gaunt enjoyed a minor triumph. Despite the inadequacy of João's siege equipment, in face of Portuguese persistence the garrison proposed terms. These were negotiated with Gaunt: the townsmen were to do him homage and he was to take formal possession. As in Galicia, the townsmen's goods were protected and they agreed to sell supplies to the army.[61] But now, according to Lopes, though it was still only May, João proposed to Gaunt that the campaign should be abandoned, and Gaunt agreed amicably. João was disappointed that townsmen were disinclined to welcome Gaunt; the weak towns which the allies were able to take, so far in in the interior, they could not hold. The attempt to conquer the land piecemeal seemed impossible to João, especially in view of Juan's increasing foreign support and the allies' inadequate forces. João said that Gaunt's force was 'now so small for such a task, that it was dishonourable for such a great lord as he was'. João suggested that the duke might either return to England to raise reinforcements or seek a settlement with Juan. Gaunt agreed with these arguments and indicated that he thought an honourable settlement was now feasible, and that he was amenable to it:

> He was of this mind also on account of his men who were very sick, so that there were some who had already sent to the King of Castile for letters of safe-conduct in order to pass through his country, for they felt that such an agreement with him was now inevitable. The [Portuguese] King was astonished at this statement and at such behaviour.

The leaders agreed to retreat, but returning to Portugal by a different route.[62] The discreet Lopes only hints at disagreement between king and duke (his work was commissioned by Duarte I, the king's son and the duke's grandson). But the uninhibited Walsingham recounts a sharp exchange between the two, shaming to the duke. João pointed out to him that his men were deserting to the enemy; he proposed to go and have them killed. Gaunt urged him not to do so, insisting that they had been driven to this by necessity and not through treason. Slumped over his horse, he wept bitterly.[63]

The decision, after only about six weeks on Castilian soil, to abandon the campaign is at first sight a surprising one, and its consequences were fraught with danger for both Portuguese and English. Perhaps there had been more friction between the allies on campaign than Lopes reveals. His account suggests that the Lancastrian force reached the point of disintegration and that its leadership was demoralised. Walsingham says that desertion was on a large scale, a necessity resulting from food shortages, sickness and mortality. Froissart portrays Gaunt in León as dispirited, sick, made listless by the heat (memories of whose intensity surface in Lopes's account).[64] Already, at the siege of Valderas, Lopes says, Gaunt's forces were 'in disarray, and poorly equipped . . . sorely depleted and the worse for wear'.[65] Froissart is explicit about the disillusionment with Gaunt's leadership – as in Gascony in 1374, he had asked his men to endure the unendurable.[66] The loss through illness of some of Gaunt's finest retainers must have been demoralising for him and his army – for instance, the death in León in May of one of its marshals, Burley, whose personal closeness to the duke was reflected in his recent testamentary dispositions that he should be buried in the wall of St Paul's Cathedral, opposite Gaunt's intended grave, and have a chantry at Gaunt's own altar.[67] The effectiveness of the Lancastrian army even before the invasion of León had been reduced by the deaths of leading knights – Lord FitzWalter (September 1386), Sir Hugh Hastings (November), Lord Scales (December) and Sir John

Marmion (March 1387).[68] The duke's military drive was perhaps constricted by the need to transport his wife and daughters Catherine and Elizabeth, and their *domicellae*, who were with the army in León, and by the fear that they might succumb to privations or epidemics. Apart from personal considerations, the deaths of Constance and her daughter would have adversely affected his ability to make terms of settlement with Juan.[69] Though the assertion of the Chronicler of St Denys that Constance was pregnant when she went to Spain is nowhere corroborated, it should not be entirely discounted.[70] It may well be that, despite past rifts, Gaunt and Constance strenuously and piously cohabited in the months leading up to the expedition, aware of the possible political benefits. The hope of having a son born on Spanish soil (such as did in fact occur, according to St Denys) would help to explain why Constance went to Spain, why the landing was in Galicia, and why negotiations with Juan for long produced no results.

In 1387 João, besides disillusionment with his ally, may have had a more urgent reason for ending the campaign. A large-scale invasion of Castile was probably straining Portuguese military capacity, and producing tensions over his leadership among his followers, which he, as a recent usurper, could ill afford. Ayala's and Lopes's accounts of the campaign indicate that the Portuguese did not have an adequate commissariat, but were crucially dependent on the scarce Castilian stocks. The harsh punishments which João meted out to the disobedient suggest that discipline was hard to maintain.

The impasse into which he and Gaunt ran is above all attributable to Juan's effective strategy. Did Gaunt anticipate that Juan might successfully apply against him in León the kind of measures with which Charles V had countered his invasion of France in 1373? Perhaps the duke underestimated his opponents' will to resist and was overconfident about the inhabitants' willingness to accept his rule, especially in the light of his Galician experience. It is, however, more likely that he entered on the León campaign in a pessimistic frame of mind, feeling that he had no alternative but to persevere, hoping that the nuisance he caused would bring his opponent back to the conference table in a more amenable frame of mind. Even that hope probably faded as his army disintegrated, in Juan's full knowledge. To Gaunt's amazement he found, when it seemed too late to succeed, that he had succeeded. Russell has exclaimed at the 'nonchalance with which Lancaster seemed now to treat the humiliating collapse of the pretensions about which so much had been heard for the previous fifteen years'.[71] This judgement ignores the willingness Gaunt had repeatedly – and recently – shown to compromise his claim, and the pressure he was now under to do so from some of his followers as well as from his ally.[72] By invading León in difficult circumstances he had satisfied honour, but it cannot but have been galling that his attempts to unravel the Schism and force peace on the French by victory in Spain had failed so lamentably. And, indeed, Walsingham's account strongly attests his reduction by the débâcle to a pitiful state of despair.

The allies withdrew southwards towards Salamanca: João was perhaps hoping to gain territory west of the city ceded to him by Gaunt. But the frontier towns proved too strongly garrisoned and the forces there inclined to sally out boldly against an allied army depleted, short of supplies and afflicted by sickness. The allies first moved south from Valderas to Villalpando; thence in mid-May they continued on the same route. On the 15th the River Duero was forded without interference from the nearby garrison at Zamora. The army went on to Salamanca, crossing the River Tormes and remaining in the city's vicinity for about a week. A threat from the garrison was repulsed by an attack led by Nun' Alvarez Pereira. By 26 May the march appears to have resumed, at first westwards towards Ledesma, and then to Cuidad Rodrigo, to the south, approached on the 31st. Its garrison troops, reinforced from other garrisons, attempted a confrontation. While the allies were encamped there, Sir John Holand, his wife Elizabeth (Gaunt's daughter) and other English knights left the army, setting off through Castile under Juan's safe-conduct. The next day the allies crossed into Portugal near Val-de-la-Mula, and the day afterwards the Portuguese moved to the fortress of Almeida prior to disbandment (4 June).[73] This was a time of great danger for the allies: Juan was soon to be reinforced by 2,000 French lances. Many of his commanders, including some of the French ones, urged him to invade Portugal, though others were doubtful of the availability of victuals. Juan was anxious to dismiss his burdensome and expensive foreign mercenaries and to exploit the opportunity to reach a settlement with Gaunt. His subjects were impoverished by the costs of defence and burdens of warfare. Gaunt still occupied Galicia; João in adversity in 1384–5 had proved a formidable opponent.[74]

A settlement between Juan and Gaunt was drafted and agreed on in negotiations carried out in a few weeks in June and July 1387 at Trancoso, where Juan's envoys caught up with Gaunt as he was on his way to visit his daughter Queen Philippa at Coimbra.[75] Gaunt's letters of procuration for his negotiators Sir Thomas Percy and Sir John Trailly are dated 10 June, and his oath to observe the first version of the accord (Trancoso 1) was made two days later. Three versions of the agreements have been published by John Palmer and Brian Powell, which they date respectively as 10–12 June, 29 June or soon after, and early July.[76] The speed with which agreement was reached on the main issues and much of the 'fine print' is notable; the ground had presumably been well worked over in negotiations in 1386 and earlier, whose lost draft proposals are likely to have been utilised. According to Trancoso 1, Juan and Gaunt were to swear to work:

> for the unity of Holy Mother Church, in all ways that may be licit and fitting, so that there may be one sheepfold and one shepherd.[77]

They would both work for the making of a peace or long truce between England and France and Castile, and (with Constance) for a marriage between Juan's son and heir Enrique and Catherine of Lancaster.[78] Juan committed himself to the grant of certain lordships to sustain the marriage, and to sustain Catherine, if she were widowed. He or his successors were to pay in instalments to Gaunt and Constance the sum of 600,000 francs, and 40,000 francs *p.a.* for their lives.[79] They were to renounce their rights in the Castilian Crown in favour of Juan and his successors.[80] Juan was to give naval support to France as obliged by treaty.[81] He was to free certain kinsfolk of Pedro I, pardon those who adhered to Gaunt's allegiance up to the entry into Galicia, and the communities there and individuals who had accepted it.[82] Gaunt and Constance agreed to hand over the places they held in Galicia and release their inhabitants from oaths and allegiance.[83] The contracting parties insisted that they intended to make an alliance as well as a peace.[84]

Certain important modifications were made to the previous drafts in Trancoso 3, for example, about the obligations of Juan's hostages, the methods of payment of the indemnities and Juan's naval obligations to the French. His second son Fernando was to marry Catherine if Enrique died young. Juan granted lordships to Constance.[85] The terms agreed at Trancoso were not ratified as a binding treaty: this did not occur till almost exactly a year later, when, with few modifications, Trancoso 3 was confirmed in what has become known as the Treaty of Bayonne.[86]

Why was there such a long delay? Palmer and Powell have suggested that it was caused by Juan's inability to meet the deadlines for payment of instalments of the indemnity and his need to renegotiate the relevant clauses.[87] Moreover, Juan had to reassure his French allies (no easy task) and Gaunt had to seek royal approval for making terms with Juan which did not have as a necessary corollary the Anglo-Castilian agreements stipulated in his indenture with Richard II of February 1386. Late in 1387 or early in 1388 Gaunt dispatched to England Sir Thomas Percy, his chief negotiator with Juan.[88]

Some modern commentators (but not Palmer and Powell) have denigrated Gaunt's settlement as a betrayal of his English and Portuguese obligations. Contemporary English chroniclers were mild in their comments – partly, probably, because they, like the king and political elites. were preoccupied with domestic crises in 1386–8, and partly because they found it difficult to get information about Gaunt's campaigns and settlement. Knighton had heard about the capture of La Coruña and Santiago – 'Now I will be silent about the pious duke until I hear more news.' The next news he heard was about the settlement – in particular the huge size of Gaunt's indemnity.[89] The Westminster Chronicler says that rumours about Gaunt's activities in Spain were circulating near the end of June 1387. Most of Galicia had been conquered by 'vigorous operations' but, with the coming of summer, the expedition had suffered heavy losses 'so some say, owing to the unfortunate weather, which induced deadly plague'.[90] News reached the chronicler in October 1388 about the match between Catherine and Juan's son. He sensibly remarked that it was impossible to establish peace between England and Castile without French goodwill, as Juan was so firmly leagued with France – a view he perhaps picked up from neighbouring royal officials.[91] The continuator of the *Eulogium*, who had a good account of Juan's strategy, gave a plausible reason for his willingness to make peace with Gaunt – Juan believed the story the duke spread abroad that he had sent to England for reinforcements.[92] This was a credible rumour after the failure of Charles VI's attempted invasion of England. In June 1388 Sir Thomas Percy brought reinforcements from England to Gaunt in Gascony, though these were not intended for use in Spain (see p.193). Walsingham had almost no information about Gaunt's Spanish campaigns, except that his army suffered heavy losses from food shortages and dysentery. He did not condemn Gaunt for the débâcle and regarded his peace settlement as favourable, since it was made as a result of Gaunt's prayers and was a sign of divine favour.[93] The heavy mortality, especially from sickness, was what impressed folk in England about the campaigns. A Somerset legal document noted how Sir Thomas Fichet died shortly after his arrival in Spain, and his esquire John Catecote immediately afterwards: 'and they were buried with a large number of lords, knights and esquires at the time in the company of John duke of Lancaster who claimed the Crown of Spain in right of his wife'.[94] This baneful revelation of the divine will justified Gaunt's abandonment of his claim in the eyes of public opinion. English chroniclers tended to regard the Lancastrian settlement as realistic. Doubtless the king and his councillors were disappointed that Gaunt had made peace without the immediate prospect of Juan settling with the English Crown. But both they and Gaunt may have anticipated that he would, subsequent to the Treaty of Bayonne, be able to move Juan to make such a settlement. For this purpose he was granted powers by Richard on 1 June 1388 to make a peace, truce, or alliance with Castile on Richard's behalf.[95] As we shall see, he was then taking seriously (and continued to do so) the pledges drafted at Trancoso a year before to work for peace between England and Castile – and, as well, for an end to the Schism.

There remains the charge that Gaunt abandoned the cause of his Portuguese son-in-law. Lopes is at pains to stress their amicable relations in León and Portugal in 1387; his account of João's suggestion that Gaunt might seek an honourable settlement with Juan implies a willingness to discharge him from treaty obligations. But Lopes's account of unclouded relations between João and Gaunt strains credulity; commissioned by João's son Duarte I, he was writing at a time when the House of Avis had a high regard for its links with the Lancastrian kings. João is likely to have been bitterly disappointed with Gaunt, but prepared to countenance his settlement because he saw clearly that the legitimist cause was hopeless and that his own crucial interest lay in the Anglo-Portuguese alliance, which Gaunt's goodwill would be useful in oiling. Before João left for León in 1387 he had tokens of English concern to implement the Treaty of Windsor: Sir William Elmham and Sir William Faringdon arrived in Portugal to request the dispatch of galleys to English ports under its terms.[96] After João's return to Portugal, at Coimbra on 12 August, he confirmed the treaty: Faringdon was a witness.[97] Gaunt continued to value his Portuguese connection; this is likely to have been one factor in mind in the stipulation made at Trancoso (and confirmed at Bayonne) that the intended alliance between Juan and himself was not to prejudice his existing alliances.[98]

Gaunt stayed four months in Portugal before sailing at the end of September 1387 for Bayonne with a fleet of fourteen Portuguese galleys – a contrast to the impressive armada with which he had sailed from Plymouth the previous year.[99] There were a number of reasons for his long stay in Portugal – for recuperation, the settlement of business with João and for conviviality with Queen Philippa, now pregnant. The vicissitudes experienced by João and Philippa may have imposed further delays. João fell desperately ill on his way to join Philippa and Gaunt at Coimbra. His life was despaired of, and Philippa miscarried. They both recovered and went with Gaunt to Coimbra; there a plot by a Castilian knight to poison the duke was uncovered. From Coimbra Gaunt went to Oporto, where he spent some time before embarking with Constance.[100]

Early in 1388 a Castilian embassy arrived at Bayonne to finalise the terms agreed at Trancoso.[101] Gaunt ratified the treaty there on 8

July; among the witnesses were his chamberlain Sir Thomas Percy, his steward Sir John Imcourt, his under-chamberlain Sir Richard Abberbury and two Castilian knights. Juan ratified the treaty on 17 July, Gaunt's envoys Master Raymond Guillem and Sir John Trailly being among those present.[102]

According to Ayala, after the conclusion of the Treaty of Bayonne Juan and Gaunt agreed and ordained that the titles of prince and princess of Asturias should be bestowed on Enrique and Catalina.[103] The text of the creation of the principality of Asturias apparently does not survive, but in a letter dated 22 August 1388 Joan I of Aragon referred to Enrique as prince of Asturias, duke of Soria and lord of Molina[104] – titles which have a certain symmetry with those of the Black Prince and, in 1376–7, his son Richard – prince of Wales, duke of Cornwall and earl of Chester. It is possible that the creation of the Asturian principality for Enrique was to honour him in imitation of Gaunt's late brother, who had always been referred to by Ayala as 'principe de Gales', and therefore was probably commonly known as such in Castilian court circles. It also satisfied Gaunt that his son-in-law was fittingly endowed.

In endorsing and perhaps promoting the elevation of his prospective son-in-law, Gaunt may have been copying developments associated with the Anglo-Castilian treaty of 1254, for long the foundation of relations between the two dynasties, whose importance continued to be stressed in English diplomatic circles. Alfonso X had then renounced his claim to Gascony, and married his half-sister Eleanor (Leonor) to Henry III's son and heir Edward, to whom his father had granted the duchy (1249), the lordship of Ireland and extensive lands in Wales and England (1254). Alfonso, in return for his renunciation, gained among other benefits a paternal relationship with a powerful young prince; Gaunt may have hoped to do so too in reverse.[105]

The creation of the principality was not the subject of a clause in the Treaties of Trancoso and Bayonne, which refer only to the proposed grant to Enrique and Catalina of Soria, Almanzán, Atienza and Molina, intended to constitute Catalina's dower.[106] Yet it would be surprising if such a notable creation had not been a subject of negotiation before the making of the Treaty of Bayonne, perhaps at Trancoso. Why then, considering that it was a subject of joint agreement, did it not appear in the treaties? A possible reason may be deduced from one of Froissart's characteristic mistakes. He says that, after Constance had reached Castile in 1388, Juan and Gaunt ratified an agreement that Enrique and Catalina should receive all the revenues of Galicia, and that Enrique should be styled 'prince of Galicia'.[107] According to the terms of the Treaty of Bayonne, Gaunt had agreed to hand over Galicia to Juan and release communities and individuals there from their oaths of obedience.[108] Gaunt was to show a concern that English pilgrims should be able to visit Santiago, despite the Schism. It would have been particularly appropriate and face-saving for him if the rule of his former Castilian subjects had been transferred to his son-in-law, who might feel obliged to allow access to the schismatic English at Gaunt's petition. But the perpetuation of a link between Galicia and Gaunt is likely to have been uncongenial to Juan and his council. Froissart's mistake, therefore, may have sprung from rumours he had picked up about a proposal from Gaunt for the creation of a principality of Galicia for Enrique, the subject possibly of disagreement and protracted negotiation with Juan. The creation of the principality of Asturias, though demonstrating Gaunt's influence in Castilian affairs, may in fact signify a limitation put upon it.

It appears that in 1388, in accordance with his agreements with Juan, Gaunt was attempting to convene a conference to try to end the Schism; Richard II declared his willingness to participate.[109] Ayala remarks on the love which had grown up between Gaunt and Juan; through their correspondence and conversations with each other's *familiares* they may have discovered their common intensity of devotion to the Virgin Mary and to the solution of the ills universally oppressing Holy Church.[110] In October Constance met Juan and put to him her husband's proposal for a meeting with the Spanish kings, one purpose of which would be to discuss ways of ending the Schism. Juan was receptive: he agreed to meet Gaunt on the Castilian frontier at Logroño on 2 February 1389. But Carlos III of Navarre and Joan I of Aragon refused to attend the conference. Juan's enthusiasm waned: he sent the bishop of Osma, Ayala (the chronicler) and his confessor Fray Ferrando Illescas (involved in the 1386 negotiations with Gaunt) to the duke at Bayonne to plead his illness as an excuse to cancel the meeting.[111] On this occasion Gaunt's well-known diplomatic smoothness deserted him; the eyewitness Ayala shows him as unable to conceal his vexation and disappointment. The duke proceeded to argue in favour of an Anglo-Castilian peace, as he had intended to do with Juan. He asserted that there was no cause of war between England and Castile now that he had given up the claim; it was against conscience for war to continue. The envoys clearly had no instructions to move on this issue; they rehearsed the causes of the war and the French alliance, and took their stand on the Treaty of Bayonne. Juan favoured an Anglo-French peace and would work for it. Gaunt reiterated his desire for an Anglo-Castilian alliance, which would be in the service of God and to the benefit of both realms. Their merchants and pilgrims would be able to travel securely by land and sea, especially the pilgrims going to Santiago.[112] It is likely that the pilgrimage had started up again during Gaunt's occupation of Galicia, for in 1389 writs were directed to the keepers of English ports ordering them to ban pilgrims from going on it.[113]

The failure of the negotiations in 1389 – soon to be followed by Juan's death – marked the end of Gaunt's major involvement in Castilian affairs and in Iberian affairs generally. This was partly because his Iberian diplomatic experience in 1388–9 convinced him that negotiations with the French Crown provided the best means to bring about general peace and an end to the Schism. But his absorption in Anglo-French negotiations in the early 1390s, as well as his paternal relationship to Enrique III (d. 1406) and João I (d.1434) made him sensitive to Iberian issues – the continued mutual hostility of Castile and Portugal might upset the general peace process as well as damaging his daughters' interests. Moreover, as duke of Aquitaine from 1390, Gaunt had a vital interest in good relations with Navarre, Castile and Aragon. This continuing interest in Iberian affairs, and the unrivalled expertise in them he possessed, ensured that he and his retainers continued to play leading roles in Anglo-Iberian relations. In March 1392, for instance, the royal council responded to Aragonese envoys 'in the way that the duke of Guyenne [Gaunt] replied to them in the King's presence at Eltham'.[114] Castilian and Portuguese visitors still paid visits to the ducal court, as a series of payments he made in 1392 illustrates. That year ducal payment was warranted for wine purchased from an Italian merchant and sent to Philippa of Portugal.[115] In 1394 Bolingbroke gave a jewel to a Portuguese knight. Lancastrian family ties remained strong.[116]

Gaunt's influence may not always have fostered English interests in this period. His past wars and diplomacy had probably left legacies of distrust in Castile and Aragon, revived by his new family interests in the peninsula and novel proximity as the duke of Aquitaine. Concern about possible Lancastrian infiltration had been shown in Clause 4 of Trancoso 3, stipulating that Catalina of Lancaster, if she was widowed, should not place in her allocated estates 'judges and officials except those born in the kingdom of Castile'. The same proviso was made as regards the towns granted to Constance (clause 24).[117] Enrique's governing council pointedly failed to notify Gaunt about his father's death and about the present government. In instructions drafted in Gaunt's name for Gutiérrez and the other envoys appointed to go to the Castilian court on Richard's and his own behalf in 1391, they were told to express how he 'greatly marvelled' at these omissions, since he believed that because of the ties between him and the Castilians they ought to have informed him. He wished them to do so speedily 'for he had a great desire to hear and learn about it and it would give him very great pleasure and ease of heart'. As in 1389, Gaunt went on to propose an Anglo-Castilian alliance, arguing that Constance's claim had been the reason for the Castilian alliance with France and that there was now no reason for Castile to be at war with England. The envoys were to recall the past alliances and marriages between the houses of England and Castile and were to exhibit copies of the alliances. They were to emphasise the obstacle that a state of war continued to place to the commerce at sea of the two realms. Richard's instructions to the envoys ran on similar lines. The English council considered that, since the general truces of 1389, the Castilians might be more amenable to a separate peace – in itself a useful means of putting pressure on the French Crown to the same end. The envoys were instructed to try to make a peace and a perpetual alliance; if this was not possible, they were to propose a truce of thirty or forty years.[118]

The response to the proposals for peace and alliance was negative, as it was to be in 1393 when similar proposals were made on Richard's and the duke's behalf by the Lancastrian knights Walter Blount and William Par. The duke complained about the non-payment of his annuity for two years and more. At last the Castilian government showed willingness to remedy this; Gaunt renounced the debt.[119] Despite this moderate gesture, his pressure in favour of peace and for the payment of his annuity may have aroused hostility in governing circles which was vented on his daughter, Queen Catalina. She was induced to abandon the Roman papal allegiance through the machinations of Enrique's uncle, Fadrique duke of Benavente. The story is found in Walsingham, who is likely to have derived it from a member of the Lancastrian household. Thus the conformity forced on Gaunt's daughter was an insult to him known in England, and one likely to be especially galling to him as a leading proponent of compromise in the Schism.[120]

Consequently, he may have concluded that, as long as Castile was ruled by a suspicious and conservative-minded minority government determined to keep in step with the French, it did not provide a key to peace. There is more evidence for Gaunt's contacts with Aragon and Navarre in the 1390s than with Castile; this may not be entirely a distorted impression resulting from accidents of documentary survival.[121] In 1395 Gaunt sent Guillem Petri to Joan I of Aragon to negotiate concerning the Schism.[122] But relations with Joan (who had never been a friend to Lancastrian interests) were clouded by Gaunt's involvement in another issue. In September 1395 he wrote stiffly to Joan to press the claims of Sir Matthew Gournay (then serving under him in Gascony) and the late Sir Hugh Calveley – a total debt of 300,000 francs from the Crown of Aragon. The issue had exacerbated Anglo-Aragonese relations for several years. Gaunt was trying to obviate reprisals.[123] But there were continued suspicions at the Aragonese court that he was scheming to intervene in

Iberian affairs, not always in congenial ways. In May 1395 a report was received that he was raising an army with which to invade Granada – a scheme which may have had sinister secular overtones for those who remembered the intended crusade of the companies in 1366, and was clearly a distortion of Gaunt's plans for a crusade against the Turk.[124] In April and May 1397 there were rumours at the Aragonese court that he was giving financial support to the attempt of Matheu of Castelbon, count of Foix to gain the crown.[125] But in December these were countered by Henry Bowet's arrival with a proposal that Bolingbroke should marry into the Aragonese royal family.[126]

Gaunt's relations with Navarre in the 1390s had similarities with his relations with Britanny; alliances with both helped to secure his rule in Aquitaine. Carlos III probably valued Gaunt's good offices in procuring the surrender to him by the English Crown of his port of Cherbourg, just as John IV of Brittany hoped he would help to secure the return of Brest and Richmond. In 1390, as duke of Aquitaine, Gaunt granted Gascon lordships for life to Carlos's servant Charlot de Beaumont, who was involved in the negotiations for the return of Cherbourg.[127] In 1394 Gaunt wrote to Richard asking for instructions about this grant,[128] and he had close contacts with the court of Navarre in 1395 and 1397.[129]

Why did Gaunt fail in his ambitions to win the Castilian Crown, or at least to pose so formidable a threat to the House of Trastamara that it would perforce renew the old Castilian alliance with the English Crown? Gaunt never gained sufficient Iberian support nor was he able to concentrate the requisite English resources. These aims were hampered because he remained too Anglo-French in outlook and interests to rally a majority of Castilians to the legitimist cause. Generally, he put the interests of his family's house above those of Pedro I's.

P.E. Russell has shown how Gaunt as king of Castile used the appropriate seals and had a Castilian chancery which employed the correct forms; he had Castilian coins minted.[130] Exiles gravitated towards him and some received financial aid, particularly in the year he assumed the Castilian Crown. In 1372 he gave New Year's gifts of cups to three Castilian knights, including a knight of the crusading Order of Santiago, and in March was paying the expenses of thirteen Spaniards in his household.[131] In the early years of Richard's reign, Gaunt's Castilian subjects were prominent in the war; their expertise in combatting galleys may have been particularly valued by the English. The cleric Juan Gutiérrez (d. 1393) became one of his most valued councillors, staying high in his service after the Castilian claim had been relinquished. Sir Juan Fernández became one of his bachelors, and he had a soft spot for Sancha García, who married his knight

Walter Blount, and to whom he gave a New Year's present in 1380.[132] But the ducal household remained essentially Anglo-French in its composition and culture – a culture which influenced the Duchess Constance, who had in the late 1370s a jester called by the Welsh (or Arthurian or Breton) name of 'Yevan';[133] who became a devotee of the fashionable English cult of St Alban,[134] and who enjoyed a popular theme of Anglo-French courtly entertainment – that of the *wodewose* ('wild man').[135] Gaunt did not, it appears, start his own chapter of a Spanish military order, such as that of the Banda, to revive crusading enthusiasm, tarnished and neglected in English eyes both by the unchivalrous Pedro I and the schismatic House of Trastamara.[136] Like many of his fellow countrymen, Gaunt seems to have been a devotee of Santiago[137] – as was Bolingbroke, who planned to make the pilgrimage in 1398–9.[138] If Froissart is to be believed, in other respects Gaunt showed little sympathy for Spanish culture. His councillors anticipated his agreement when they said 'Castilians are the falsest and most ambiguous people in the world'.[139] In 1374, when Gaunt's daughter Catherine (Catalina), prospective heiress to Castile, was aged about two, Gaunt had appointed a Spaniard, Johan Martyns, to look after her, but in 1380 he sent her to Lady Mohun to receive an English education.[140] According to Froissart, Gaunt could not entirely follow an oration in Spanish made by Juan I's confessor in 1388.[141] Such a situation reflects an essentially foreign attitude to Spain. Had Gaunt tried to behave like a Spaniard and become involved in Castilian domestic politics, he might have had a solid basis of support in Castile in 1386–7. There is some slight evidence that he may have been trying to build up support in Murcia in 1372, but he was to make the legitimist cause an essentially exiled and alien one.[142]

Gaunt's apparently cool view, for the most part, of Spain and its inhabitants probably stemmed from his own and the Black Prince's experiences of Pedro I in 1366–7, and their hatred and contempt for Enrique of Trastamara. Such feelings are reflected in Chandos Herald's panegyric on the Black Prince (*c.*1385), which, John Palmer has suggested, is a Lancastrian tract.[143] Gaunt's Spanish experiences may have reinforced in his mind contemporary English noble concern that Spain was no longer the great Christian power it had been at the time when Duke Henry had taken part (in 1344) in Alfonso XI's siege of the Moors in Algeciras, a siege recalled by Chaucer. Perhaps Gaunt dreamed that as king of Castile he might revive the crusade against Granada, an ambition later attributed to him at the court of Aragon, and, according to Froissart, suggested to Bolingbroke by English nobles in 1398.[144]

Gaunt's apparent distaste for most things Spanish may, indeed, have masked a traditional family respect for the Crown of Castile which helped to induce him and two of his brothers to expend English energies on Iberian interventions. Gaunt can never have forgotten that he was the great-grandson of the Castilian princess, Leonor, whose marriage to Edward I had been part of the foundation of the amity between the two dynasties, which his own father had striven so assiduously to revive. A short distance from his house, The Savoy, was Charing Cross, one of those crosses set up by Edward I to commemorate her funeral procession, a unique iconographical reminder of the Anglo-Castilian alliance. Was Gaunt aware that his great-great-grandfather, Fernando III, was a saint and a hero of the Reconquista? The memory of Castile as the great crusading power had long persisted in English noble circles; the House of Lancaster associated itself with the revival of this reputation by Alfonso XI in the 1340s. Gaunt's descent, Plantagenet policy and English noble traditions may all have led him (together with his father and the Black Prince) to put a high estimate (as did the French) on the political importance of Castile, which in fact was being polarised by that noble factionalism which flourished there in the first half of the fifteenth century and reduced the Castilian Crown's international effectiveness. Since the 1340s Castile had ceased to be in the forefront of crusading powers; except in the war in Biscay and the Channel in the 1370s, Castile never became a crucial factor in French offensives. It would be easy to conclude that Gaunt, in his persistence in pursuing castles in Spain, was blinded for long to realities by the scales of traditional perception. However, one must remember that, in foreign relations, received ideas are potent influences. French councillors too attached great importance to the Castilian alliance and regarded Gaunt's threats to it as more dangerous to their Crown's interests than did the run of English shire knights, sceptical for parochial reasons. Gaunt, the sophisticated internationalist, was less shrewd in his estimate than these blinkered nationalists, but in the fantasy world of international diplomacy his treatment of Castile as a queen and not a pawn was effective play.

Gaunt's Spanish policies must not be dismissed as signs of a self-regarding and idiosyncratic obsession; in pursuing them he was attempting to further the interests of the Plantagenet dynasty. He did not neglect the dynasty's other foreign-policy interests; to him Spain was part of a general picture, in which the French Crown and principalities were central and the Empire, Netherlandish principalities and Scotland played roles which he recognised as more important at times than Spain to the fortunes of his dynasty.

Though he failed to make an Anglo-Castilian peace and alliance (objectives not attained till 1467), Gaunt did have, from the English viewpoint, some positive achievements in his Iberian involvements. His interventionist policies were factors in the 1380s in diverting the Castilian war effort from English possessions; the French Crown had to prop up its ally in 1386–7. The Treaty of Bayonne cleared the way for the French and English to make a serious attempt to achieve a lasting peace. Incidentally, in 1386–7 Gaunt assisted in laying foundations of amity between the Houses of Lancaster and Avis. In Fernão Lopes's reconstruction, João I and Gaunt were presented as the founding fathers of the Anglo-Portuguese alliance. The chronicler infused a warmth into the relationship between the illegitimate usurper and the stern legitimist which is probably a reflection of the feelings of their descendants in his own day.

Notes and References

1   Russell PE 1955, ch.1.
2   Ibid., pp.63–7.
3   Ibid., pp.167–75.
4   *C.R.C.*, Vol.1, p.18; Daumet G 1898, p.36; Russell PE 1955, p.222 and n.
5   Mirot L and Déprez E 1899, p.199.
6   *Foedera*, 1869, Vol.4, pp.165–6; Russell PE 1955, pp.288–92, 345–9. In a letter of credence issued to Pere's *familiaris* Guilhem Marques, dated Feb. 1381 by Perroy, Richard stated his willingness to enter into peace negotiations with Juan (*D.C.*, no.23).
7   *Foedera*, 1709, Vol.8, pp.19–22; Lopes F 1988, pp.36–57; Russell PE 1955, pp.87–9, 191–202.
8   Ibid., pp.206–17, 221–2.
9   Ibid., pp.252–61, 283–5. Carlos II apparently toyed with a match between his second son Pedro and a daughter of Gaunt (*C.Q.P.V.* p.265).
10 Lopes F 1988, pp.58–65; *Foedera*, 1709, Vol.8, pp.253–4; Russell PE 1955, pp.296–300. Gaunt apparently hoped to link the English royal family dynastically with the three Iberian realms; Richard's letter to Pere (fn.6 above) mentions the proposal for his marriage to Pere's daughter Isabel (*D.C.*, no.23).
11 *Foedera*, 1869, Vol.4, pp.93–5; Lopes F 1988, pp.64–7, 124–5. By indenture, dated London, 8 March 1381, Raulyn de Glanton and Watkyn Batheley esquires undertook to provide Sir Matthew Gournay with ten men-at-arms and ten mounted (*sic*) archers, themselves included, to follow him to war to Portugal, Spain, or anywhere else he might go for one year (H.M.C. Rutland, Vol.4, p.86, no.10). For payment of royal war wages to Gutiérrez, to Lancastrian knights (including Gournay), Sir Juan Fernandez, two 'barons of Spain' and other retinue leaders for service on the expedition, P.R.O. E403/485/1; ibid., 486/1, 15–16. For the campaign and its background, Lopes F 1988, pp.66–151; Russell PE 1955, Ch.14.

12 Richard II, in a letter to Pere dated 26 Aug. (1382) referred to Gaunt's invasion of Castile as imminent (*D.C.*, no.32). This was a fortnight after Fernando had given formal assent to peace terms with Castile (Russell PE 1955, pp.336–7).

13 Lopes F 1988, pp.161–89; *W.C.*, pp.142–3; Russell PE 1955, chs.16, 17; *R.P.*, Vol.3, p.204; Wilkins D 1737, Vol.3, 193–4.

14 *R.P.*, Vol.3, p.114.

15 Ibid., p.133.

16 P.R.O. E101/68/10; Leicestershire R.O., Shirley MSS, 26D53/2543. I owe thanks to Dr S Walker for this reference.

17 *H.A.*, Vol.2, p.143; *Eulogium*, Vol.3, p.358.

18 Nottinghamshire R.O., Foljambe of Obserton deeds, IX, i, 787.

19 *Foedera*, 1709, Vol.7, pp.679–80; Russell PE 1955, pp.408–9.

20 Perroy E 1933, p.234 and n6.

21 *C.P.R.*, 1385–9, p.147.

22 *H.A.*, Vol.2, p.143; *C.H.K.*, Vol.2, p.207.

23 Lopes F, 1988, pp.194–5.

24 Froissart J 1871, Vol.12, p.133ff.

25 Ibid., 1870, Vol.11, pp.326–7; *C.R.C.*, Vol.2, p.115. Protections for some of those intending to serve with Gaunt are recorded in *Foedera*, 1709, Vol.8, pp.490, 497, 501. They included Sir John Deincourt, steward of his household and William de Assheton, his chancellor. A Privy Seal letter (Westminster, 19 June, 9 Richard II) authorised provision of robes for Baldwin Bereford 'holding the office of master of the horse in the absence of our faithful knight Thomas Moreaux going to parts of Spain in the company of [Gaunt]' (P.R.O. E101/401/10 no.5). I owe thanks for this reference to Professor JL Gillespie.

26 Usk A de 1904, p.147; cf *Eulogium*, Vol.3, p.359.

27 P.R.O. SC1/51/26. Parts of the document (including the dating clause) are badly faded.

28 For an example of a Spaniard who served, see p.123 below. Sir John Palays of Cologne served with a retinue of 25 men-at-arms and four archers (P.R.O. DL28/3/2).

29 P.R.O. E101/38/10; cf Russell PE 1955, pp.180–1 and 181n.

30 P.R.O. E403/513/2 (10 May); cf Russell PE 1955, p.414 n.3.

31 Palmer JJN 1972, pp.68–70.

32 *Foedera*, 1709, Vol.7, pp.510–15.

33 *W.C.*, pp.164–5.

34 *C.H.K.*, Vol.2, p.207.

35 *C.R.C.*, Vol.2, p.121.

36 Ibid., p.111.

37 Froissart J 1871, Vol.12, p.200.

38 MacEoin G and Eisner S 1980; Eisner S 1976, pp.1ff.

39 *Foedera*, 1709, Vol.7, pp.679–80.

40 Ibid., Vol.8, pp.515–26, 561–2.

41 Russell PE 1955, pp.422–5; cf A.C.A., Cartas Reales y Diplomáticas, C 7146–7 for Gaunt's attempts to seek support for his invasion in 1386 from Pere III.

42 P.R.O. E403/513/1; ibid., E101/68/10; Leicestershire R.O., Shirley MSS, 26D53/2543; Froissart J 1870, Vol.11, pp.325, 338.

43 Lopes F 1988, pp.194–5, 212–13; Russell PE 1955, pp.422–5.

44 Froissart J 1871, Vol.12, pp.185ff; Russell PE 1955, pp.432, 436ff. For

a ducal indenture dated Orense, 4 Dec. 1386, *C.P.R.* 1396–9, p.489.

45 Froissart J 1870, Vol.11, pp.338ff, 377ff, 410ff.
46 Lopes F 1988, pp.212–13.
47 Archivo Municipal de Carmona, Privilegios y cartas reales, siglos XIII y XIV. The letter is dated Zamora, July 1385 (sic). I owe thanks for a transcript to Professor González Jiménez. For Juan's presence in Zamora in July 1386, Suarez Fernandez L 1977, Vol.1, p.407.
48 A.C.A., Cartas Reales y Diplomáticas, C 7030, C 7169 reflect the Aragonese Crown's interest in the French plans to invade England in 1385–6. Charles VI's instructions to his envoys to Juan, dated Amiens, 11 Sept. 1386, show anticipation that Juan would make peace with Gaunt and preparedness to countenance this if the French Crown was made party to the agreements (Doüet-D'Arcq L 1863, Vol.1, pp.74–6, no.xxxviii).
49 Lopes F 1988, pp.242–3.
50 *C.R.C.*, Vol.2, p.110; Usk A de 1904, p.147; Lopes F 1988, p.243; *H.A.*, Vol.2, p.193.
51 *J.G.R. 1379–83*, nos 1235–6, 1539.
52 P.R.O. DL28/3/2. The Hertford receiver's account for 1389–90 records payment to Robert Malmesbury (ibid., DL29/58/1081).
53 Lopes F 1988, pp.216–19; Russell PE 1955, p.438.
54 Ibid., pp.439ff.
55 *C.R.C.*, Vol.2, p.115; Lopes F 1988, pp.242–3; Russell PE 1955, pp.454, 456. A reconstruction of João's itinerary throws light on the allies' movements before and during the invasion of León (Baquero Moreno H 1988, pp.31–2, 241–2). For a Castilian report on their movements and intentions, AM Carmona, Varios, siglo XIV (15 Feb. 1387). I owe thanks to Professor González Jiménez for a transcript.
56 Lopes F 1988, pp.242–3.
57 Ibid., pp.242–5. For the invasion strategy, Russell PE 1955, pp.463–5.
58 For orders from the Castilian chancellor for the strengthening of the city of León's defences, 26 Aug. 1386 and 15 April 1387, Martin Fuertes JA and Alvarez Alvarez C 1982, nos 242–3; Lopes F 1988, pp.244–5. For defences in Andalucia, A.M. Carmona, Varios, siglo XIV (15 Feb. 1387).
59 *C.R.C.*, Vol.2, p.115; Lopes F 1988, pp.244–53; Russell PE 1955, pp.466–8.
60 *C.R.C.*, Vol.2, p.115; Lopes F 1988, pp.252–9; Russell PE 1955, pp.469–75. Before the investment of Valderas, Roales, defended by peasants, had been taken.
61 Lopes F 1988, pp.261–71; Russell PE 1955, pp.475–6.
62 Lopes F 1988, pp.270–3.
63 *H.A.*, Vol.2, p.193. Sir John Holand's withdrawal through Castile was to evoke João's 'astonishment' (Lopes F 1988, pp.282–3).
64 Froissart J 1871, Vol.12, pp.308ff; *H.A.*, Vol.2, p.193.
65 Lopes F 1988, pp.258–9.
66 Froissart J 1871, Vol.12, pp.311–12.
67 Parry JH 1915, pp.109–10. Burley was buried in St Paul's adjacent to the north aisle wall; his tomb has been mistakenly identified as Sir Simon Burley's (see plan in Benham W 1902, facing p.16).
68 *C.R.C.*, Vol.2, p.115; *C.I.P.M.*, Vol.16, nos 377, 406, 414, 482.
69 Sir John Holand took his wife Elizabeth and some of the duchess's ladies

through Castile on their way home before Gaunt re-entered Portugal (Lopes F 1988, pp.282–3).

70 *St Denys*, Vol.1, pp.448–9.
71 Russell PE 1955, p.479.
72 Lopes F 1988, pp.270–1.
73 Ibid., pp.274–83; Russell PE 1955, pp.481–6; Baquero Moreno H 1988, pp.32, 242.
74 *C.R.C.*, Vol.2, p.116; Lopes F 1988, pp.283–5.
75 Lopes F 1988, pp.286–7.
76 Palmer J and Powell B 1988.
77 Ibid., p.7, (cl.1).
78 Ibid., pp.7–8 (cl.2, 3).
79 Ibid., pp.8–10 (cl.4, 6, 7).
80 Ibid., pp.10, 12–13, (cl.8, 13–15).
81 Ibid., p.11 (cl.9).
82 Ibid., pp.11–12 (cl.11, 12).
83 Ibid., p.14 (cl.16, 17).
84 Ibid., pp.14–15 (cl. 22, 23).
85 Ibid., pp.xv, 35ff.
86 Ibid., pp.xiv, 49ff.
87 Ibid., p.xiv.
88 *W.C.*, pp.194–5, 344–5; Perroy E 1933, p.254–5; Palmer JJN 1972, p.126.
89 *C.H.K.*, Vol.2, pp.207–8, 210. Knighton had spoken to a member of the duke's household who had been with him in Spain; his lack of further information about the expedition may have resulted from the absorbing interest of the domestic crises of 1386–8.
90 *W.C.*, pp.190–3.
91 Ibid., pp.194–5, 344–5, 370–1.
92 *Eulogium*, Vol.3, pp.358–9.
93 *H.A.*, Vol.2, pp.193–4.
94 Dunning RW 1968, p.158.
95 *Foedera*, 1709, Vol.8, pp.587–8.
96 *D.C.*, no.73; Mirot L and Déprez E 1899, p.208. Faringdon's account for his mission covers the period 28 Jan. to 12 Nov. 1387.
97 *Foedera*, 1709, Vol.7, pp.561–2; Chaplais P 1971, pp.32–3; Russell PE 1955, pp.515–6, 518.
98 Palmer J and Powell B 1988, pp.15 (cl.23), 59 (cl.22). It is noteworthy that João was at Trancoso 8–11 June, when negotiations for the first treaty between Gaunt and the Castilians were being concluded (Baquero Moreno H 1988, pp.32, 242).
99 Russell PE 1955, pp.492–3.
100 Lopes F 1988, pp.286–97; Baquero Moreno H 1988, pp.32, 242. Gaunt dated letters at Coimbra on 23 and 24 July (*J.G.R. 1379–83*, nos 1236–7, 1239). João apparently took leave of his father-in-law some time before the latter embarked, for he was at Oporto on 9 and 10 Sept., but at Braga on the 11th (Baquero Moreno H 1988).
101 Russell PE 1955, p.501.
102 Palmer J and Powell B 1988, pp.62–4.
103 *C.R.C.*, Vol.2, p.120.
104 Russell PE 1955, p.508n.
105 Prestwich M 1988, pp.7, 9–11; Goodman A 1989, pp.43–4. In Feb. 1392

chancery clerks were paid for their continuous labour and diligence for two whole days in writing charters and instruments concerning the truces between Henry III and Alfonso X (P.R.O. E403/532/16). B.L. Cotton MS Nero D VI, a compilation of 1386–99, contains the text of their 1254 treaty (f. 56v).

106 Palmer J and Powell B 1988.
107 Froissart J 1871, Vol.13, pp.303–4.
108 Palmer J and Powell B 1988, pp.56–7 (chs.16, 17).
109 Palmer JJN 1968 : 516–17.
110 Russell PE 1955, p.519.
111 Ibid., pp.518–22.
112 *C.R.C.*, Vol.2, pp.123–4.
113 P.R.O. E403/524/6.
114 Baldwin JF 1913, pp.499–50.
115 P.R.O. DL28/3/2.
116 DL28., 1/4.
117 Palmer J and Powell B 1988, pp.37, 46–7.
118 B.L. Vespasian CXII ff.118, 120–1; *Foedera*, 1709, Vol.8, p.680; Russell PE 1955, pp.532–6.
119 *Foedera*, 1709, Vol.8, pp.681–2; Russell PE 1955, pp.538–9.
120 *Annales*, pp.162–4. However, relations between Enrique and his father-in-law probably improved. Allusion was made in the receiver-general's account for 1396–7 to Enrique's payment of expenses to Gaunt's envoy Sir Thomas Dale (P.R.O. DL28/3/5).
121 For a reference to messengers and letters from Gaunt to Catalina, *Annales*, p.162.
122 A.C.A., reg.1969, f27v (Joan's acknowledgment). I owe thanks for this reference and the ones from the chancery registers in notes 124–6 to Dr Peter Rycraft.
123 A.C.A., Cartas Reales y Diplomáticas, no.839 (22 Sept. 1395); *D.C.*, nos 149, 173, 200 and pp.244–6.
124 A.C.A., reg.2352, ff.21, 24.
125 Ibid., reg.2239, ff.98–110.
126 Ibid., reg. 1968, f.26v.
127 *D.C.*, nos 221–2.
128 Legge MD 1941, no.19.
129 Castro JR 1958, Vol.21, nos 278, 288, 314, 492; Vol.22, nos 91, 696.
130 Russell PE 1955, pp.176–85. For Gaunt's minting of coins in Spain and Portugal, Lopes F 1988, pp.214–17.
131 *J.G.R. 1372–6*, nos 915, 928; cf ibid., nos 533–4, 936. In 1376–7 payment of ducal annuities was recorded to Sir Juan Fernández, Juan Gutiérrez and Gonsalvo 'fferandus' (P.R.O. DL28/3/1 m5).
132 *J.G.R. 1379–83*, nos 296, 327, 337, 463; Russell PE 1955, p.179, n1.
133 Bateson M 1901, Vol.2, p.170.
134 Constance was received into the confraternity of St Alban in 1386. Six of the eleven companions received with her were English, the others probably Castilian (B.L. MS Cotton Nero D VII 'Liber Benefactorum' f132v).
135 This is deduced from the presence among her attendants at Pamplona in 1388, of 'un caballero sauvage' (Castro JR 1956, Vol.17, no.398).
136 Goodman A 1987a, p.76.
137 *C.R.C.*, Vol.2, p.124. Gaunt gave as a New Year's present to Princess

Joan in 1382 'un tablet dor et de perry ove une ymage de cokile' (*J.G.R. 1379–83*, no.715).
138   Vale MGA 1970, pp.33–4.
139   Goodman A 1987b, pp.76–7.
140   *J.G.R. 1372–6*, no.1597; *J.G.R. 1379–83*, no.56.
141   Froissart J 1871, Vol.13, p.134.
142   Pascal Martínez L 1983, pp.143–4 (no.97; 12 Aug. 1372).
143   Pope MK and Lodge EC 1910, pp.166–7; Palmer JJN 1982.
144   Froissart J 1872, Vol.16, pp.107–8.

Chapter Eight

From Dominance to Crisis (1389–99)

Returning from France after an absence abroad of over three years, the duke landed at Plymouth in good health on 19 November 1389. His ships' cargoes may have included the twenty tuns of Gascon wine which he gave to the royal household some time between November 1389 and July 1390. He soon set out with a large retinue for Reading, where he had been summoned to attend a royal council on 9 December. About 2 miles from the town he was met by the king – a signal honour. Richard and his companions gave Gaunt the kiss of peace. On this occasion or soon afterwards Richard demonstrated the relationship he now wished to have with his uncle by taking the latter's livery collar from around his neck and putting it on himself. He said that he wished to wear the collar to signify 'the good love heartfully felt between them' (*de bon amour d'entier coer entre eux*). Both of them were keen that Gaunt should be the supreme conciliator in domestic affairs for which his pre-eminent estate and his absence during the recent troubles uniquely qualified him. The duke's desire to emphasise his closeness to Richard in the 1390s is reflected in his heraldic devices, such as the white harts enclosed in collars of esses on the two copes presented to St Paul's Cathedral by the leading ducal servant Robert Whitby. Thomas of Woodstock was anxious to renew his old friendship with his brother: soon after his return, he presented him with something to appeal to his decorative taste – a particularly fine tapestry (*drap d'arras*).[1]

The Westminster Chronicler hinted that the peace which the king had made with Woodstock and his allies had frayed and that Gaunt's

144

renewal of it at the start of the Reading council was timely. Care was taken to remove any lingering threat to Gaunt's conciliatory role. At Richard's insistence he remitted his former enmity towards the earl of Northumberland, providing, the Westminster Chronicler thought, an excellent example of public accord. But Richard had to pay a price for conciliation, amounting to an at least nominal diminution of his authority and a concomitant increase of his uncles' influence over government. An ordinance was passed that no grants lessening royal income were to be made without the advice of the council and the assent of his uncles and the chancellor (Wykeham), or two of them. This second stipulation is bound to have offended Richard's authoritarian susceptibilities.[2] He probably viewed it as a necessary device to reassure public opinion, to flatter Gaunt and to split Woodstock from his more intransigent allies, notably the earl of Arundel. For Gaunt, the aftermath of the conflict between Richard and the lords appellant appeared rosy. At Reading he basked on a pinnacle of influence, unclouded by the threats to it which he had endured earlier in the reign. But after his return from France six years later, in 1395, his influence seemed to decline. He was unable to avert the death and forfeiture of his brother Woodstock or the exile of his son Bolingbroke. Before his death the House of Lancaster started to plunge into its biggest crisis since the execution of Earl Thomas in 1322. Why was there such a great change in Lancastrian fortunes? And how far was Gaunt responsible?

After the Reading council there was another public demonstration that Gaunt's quarrels prior to his departure to Spain were now ended; he was honoured by his old opponents the Londoners and by the hitherto unenthusiastic monks of Westminster. He went to London for a semi-regal reception. At Westminster he was welcomed by the mayor and the aldermen: the abbot and monks processed with him into the abbey church chanting the response *Honor virtus*. After the abbot had prayed, the duke gave alms and rode through the city to St Paul's, then went to his house.[3] He celebrated Christmas and New Year at Hertford Castle,[4] but was back at Westminster for the parliament which commenced on 17 January 1390, staying during the session at La Neyte, the abbot of Westminster's house.[5] In this parliament Richard's moderation, his harmony with the nobles and Gaunt's pre-eminence were displayed. On the king's behalf Gaunt received the Commons' assurance that they had no complaints against leading royal officers or the lords of the council (21 January). These were then reappointed with the addition of Gaunt and Woodstock as councillors.[6]

As the price of support for Richard, Gaunt strenuously extracted favours from the Crown to augment the Lancastrian interest, as he had done during previous brief periods of ascendancy at court – in the last months of his father's reign and after his reconciliation with Richard in the summer of 1385. On 16 February 1390 he was granted the duchy of Lancaster as a palatinate entailed on his heir male – a much more substantial diminution of the Crown's rights than the grant to him of palatinate powers in it for life in 1377.[7] On the last day of the parliamentary session (2 March), with the assent of the estates, he was created duke of Aquitaine for life – rendering nothing to the Crown for the duchy, as the Westminster Chronicler sourly noted. For Richard this reduction of authority had the advantage of reinforcing Gaunt's interest in making peace with the French Crown.

But the grant of the duchy turned out to be an over-extension of Lancastrian influence. Persistent Gascon opposition hampered the full establishment of Gaunt's authority, necessitating his visit to Gascony in 1394 to quell defiance. In 1390 he was presumably reluctant to resume his travels far away or for long, preferring to enjoy the company of his sons, his daughter Joan and of Catherine Swynford, to inspect his estates and sample their sport, to consolidate his new influence at court and promote peace. The Gascon grant ultimately harmed Gaunt's interests: it was a failure and, as Froissart observed at a great council in 1395, few in England wished to support it (see p. 197).

The entail of the palatinate which Gaunt secured in 1390, so favourable to Bolingbroke's future interests, and his subsequent favours to Bolingbroke indicate that father and son soon resumed their habitual good relations after Gaunt's return from France. As a former lord appellant, uncertain of the king's true feelings about his behaviour in 1387–8, Bolingbroke had reason to welcome his father's protection. Gaunt indulged his son's politic willingness to seek chivalrous adventures abroad. In November 1389 Jean de Boucicaut and two other distinguished French knights sent out challenges announcing that they would joust in March 1390 against all comers for the honour of France, at St Inglevert, between Calais and Boulogne. Gaunt wrote to Boucicaut on Bolingbroke's behalf asking him if he would joust with his son and allow him ten lance strokes instead of the five specified in the challenge, so that he might learn from the masterly Boucicaut. According to the Monk of St Denys, the three champions jousted with Bolingbroke and his company on the last day of the challenge, early in April. Among the thirty members of the Lancastrian contingent whom he listed were Bolingbroke's half-brother John Beaufort and Beaufort's half-brother Thomas Swynford; also the renowned borderer 'Hotspur' – Sir Henry Percy, the earl of Northumberland's son and heir.[8]

Talk of chivalrous projects with French knights at St Inglevert probably fired Bolingbroke's enthusiasm to seek adventure farther afield. He obtained his father's and the king's licence to join the crusade which the duke of Bourbon proposed to lead to Tunis. On 4 May he took leave of them and departed for Calais: there he waited for a safe-conduct to travel through France, which his herald set out to seek from Charles VI with Gaunt's financial assistance. Failing to get one, he returned to England, but, determined to go on crusade somewhere, probably on 19 July set sail from Boston (Lincs.) for Prussia, where he was to gain, like Chaucer's Knight, a great reputation crusading with the Teutonic Knights against the Lithuanians, his expedition heavily underpinned financially by his father.[9]

Soon after Bolingbroke set out, his father was enjoying his first summer of English country sports for several years, intermixed with some politicking to further his interests. Gaunt welcomed guests to a magnificent hunting party at Leicester (24 July 1390). Among them were the king and queen, the duke's brothers, his son-in-law Huntingdon and Archbishop Arundel. A council was held at which Gaunt requested, as he had vainly done in 1385, that John Northampton and his associates might be permitted to return to London and have their rights as citizens restored. The king now said that he thought that it was not presently in his power to grant this. Richard's recent visit to the tomb at Gloucester of Edward II (whom he regarded as a martyr) suggests his preoccupation with the evils of restraints to kings. Gaunt's rejoinder must have been music in the royal ears: 'On the contrary . . . you could do that and more. God forbid that your power should be so cramped that you could not extend grace to your liege subjects when circumstances call for such action.' Richard's reaction showed his resentment at the exile endured by some of his former councillors: 'If I can do what you say, there are others who have suffered great hardship; so that I know what to do for my own friends who are now overseas.'[10] But only Gaunt's friend benefited. The king granted Northampton leave to travel to London and elsewhere in the realm, and restored some of his forfeited goods. He was fully pardoned in parliament the following December.[11] Four days after the king's arrival at Leicester, he moved on to Nottingham.[12] In the autumn Gaunt was probably in the south, consulting with king and council about the growing threat of a renewal of warfare with the French Crown. Anglo-French tension developed as a result of Charles VI's plans to invade Italy in 1391, with the objective of driving Pope Boniface IX from Rome and replacing his princely adherents in Italy with Valois kinsmen and allies. The threat receded in February 1391, when Charles cancelled his expedition, scheduled to assemble the following month, and agreed to meet Richard. Gaunt had been heavily involved in the diplomatic and military measures taken in case war broke out.[13] He was present at the international tournament which Richard held for three days at Smithfield commencing on 10 October 1390, on the first day of which the king himself carried off the honours. Among the foreign guests were the count of St Pol and Gaunt's kinsman William count of Ostrevant. Gaunt held a lavish banquet for them. The entertainments were opportunities for anti-Valois lobbying.[14]

Little is known about Gaunt's activities in 1391. He may have been at Lincoln on 5 March, for a copy of a letter survives dated there (but with the year missing), which he wrote to Vladyslav II of Poland-Lithuania, eloquently pleading that the king might release from captivity two of Bolingbroke's knights, Sir Thomas Rempston and Sir John Clifton.[15] If Gaunt was in Lincoln so early in the year, it may have been to communicate more speedily with Vladyslav and with Bolingbroke in Prussia, and to greet the latter promptly on his return. Perhaps too Gaunt anticipated the dearth which was prevalent from mid-March, driving grain prices notably high in London: he may have thought it easier to victual his household from local stocks and Prussian imports in Lincolnshire.[16] At the end of April Bolingbroke disembarked at Hull; his crusading success doubtless delighted his father.[17] That summer Gaunt may have refrained from his customary visit to his northern estates;[18] he was probably concerned to confer with the papal envoy Damian de Cataneis, who arrived at the royal court at Sheen on 24 June and stayed in England till November.[19] Moreover, plague was prevalent in the north, being particularly virulent in York.[20] Gaunt was apparently at Hertford Castle in August, the month in which the king held a council at Canterbury, where Woodstock obtained leave to go to Prussia on crusade.[21] Woodstock's herald Croyslett had been on Bolingbroke's recent expedition there and a number of English nobles were currently in Prussia – Lords Despenser, FitzWalter, Beaumont, Clifford and Bourchier.[22] Since the Anglo-French truce of 1389, as after the Anglo-French peace of 1360, the thoughts of many English nobles had turned to a high traditional ambition of knights – to go on crusade. In the next few years their commitment to this ideal was to be powerfully reinforced by the verbal and literary eloquence of a group of propagandising idealists headed by Philippe de Mézières. They argued that it was necessary to end Anglo-French conflict and the papal Schism in order to unite Christendom against its enemies – principally the Turks. These propagandists stood for a revival of the medieval ideal of Christian unity at a time when a sense of nationality was threatening it, particularly among the English.

Woodstock's departure for his voyage near the end of September and embarkation at Orwell (Suffolk) in October were probably a relief all round. His absence excused him from a reluctant and possibly obstructive participation in peace negotiations with the French Crown, and enhanced the prospects of domestic tranquillity. However, his crusade never materialised – his fleet was scattered in a storm and he returned ignominiously to England before Christmas.[23]

Gaunt was present in the parliament which met from 3 November to 2 December[24] where the continuation of the peace negotiations and the elevation of Gaunt to head them received the stamp of the estates' approval. The Commons compliantly petitioned that if negotiations were to be held, Gaunt might participate 'because he is the most suitable [*le plus sufficeant*] person in the Realm'. Richard said that he was very willing for Gaunt to do so if he wished. This was the duke's cue to declare that 'he wished most heartily [*de tres bon coer*] to work at and do things which might turn to the honour and profit of the King and the Realm'.[25] Gaunt probably celebrated Christmas and New Year at Hertford with his son Bolingbroke. The latter had made preparations to take part in jousts there at Christmas and on 1 January rewarded his father's minstrels.[26]

More specific evidence than usual of Gaunt's participation in government is provided for 1392 by a journal kept by the clerk of the council. This reveals Gaunt's activity in attending meetings in February of that year, not long before he set off to meet Charles VI at Amiens.[27] He was present from 12–16 February at the sessions of a great council. The session on the 15th was notable for the reaffirmation made of domestic peace and the repudiation by those present of the violence associated with unlawful maintenance. The king's uncles (including Woodstock, delivered from the terrors of the deep) were among the lords who assured Richard of their future loyalty. All renounced the use of force on their men's as well as their own behalf against him or other lords, or in oppression of the people. They promised to join the king in coercing any contrariant. Richard for his part promised not to inflict punishments for any past misdemeanours which he might have cause to resent and not to restore any of those condemned in parliament.

What prompted recollection of the painful events of 1386–8? The implication is that they were a cause of tension not far below the surface. Perhaps it was rumoured that Richard planned to arrest Woodstock, the earl of Arundel and other former opponents and to reverse their achievements. The prospect of Gaunt spending his time away negotiating in France may have aroused fears of another domestic confrontation. Controversy at the council over the proposed peace terms recalled the accusations against Richard's

149

favourites in 1387–8 for allegedly planning a treasonable capitulation to the French. On 16 February Woodstock agreed that, if it was absolutely necessary, the concession should be made that Calais be held of the French Crown. The other lords present had already agreed to this.

The momentum to make peace, which had developed from the autumn of 1391 onwards, thus revived the scarcely dormant tensions of 1386–8, a revival which was to be one of the precipitants of the crisis of 1397. For unpopular aspects of a peace policy made Richard and his councillors once more vulnerable to criticism. Moreover, in these circumstances his sense of insecurity was likely to be aroused. A crisis did not arise in the early 1390s, because Gaunt was wholeheartedly in favour of the peace policy. He probably sympathised with the king over some of his experiences in 1388; in 1392 he contributed £10 to the costs of a tomb for Sir Simon Burley, whose execution had so upset Richard.[28] Woodstock, in view of his brother's determination, was not prepared to oppose the king. He was dependent on Gaunt's patronage to promote his dynastic interests abroad, to help him financially and to speak for him on occasion in council. At a council meeting on 24 February, when Gaunt and Bolingbroke were the only secular magnates present, Gaunt's advice was asked 'touching the rescue of the land of Ireland'. His reply was concerned with arrangements for Woodstock's proposed lieutenancy there.[29]

Preparations were under way early in 1392 for the peace embassy headed by Gaunt which was to meet Charles VI at Amiens. On 28 February the London customs collectors were ordered to refrain from making levies on wine, victuals, and so on, loaded by Gaunt in a ship docked in the port of London, the *Seinte Marie* of Calais.[30] He landed at Calais on 11 March with a large retinue, and was met on the way to Amiens by Charles VI's brother, Louis duke of Touraine, and the dukes of Berry, Burgundy and Bourbon.[31] According to Froissart, it was a joyful occasion. Berry and Burgundy rode either side of Gaunt to the gates of Amiens. He courteously refused to go to his lodgings, insisting on first paying his respects to the king. Charles prepared to receive him enthroned in the bishop's palace, attended by a throng of nobles eager to view the duke and his courtesies (*curialitates ejus*). According to the Monk of St Denys, he did not disappoint them, kneeling three times on his advance to the foot of the throne, to be warmly greeted by Charles.[32] Knighton boasted that the king hailed him as the most revered knight in Christendom, kings alone excepted.[33] Charles and his councillors were at pains to be hospitable to the English, taking precautions against disturbances in the city and defraying their expenses. The day after their arrival he held a banquet at which Gaunt and Bishop Skirlaw of Durham had the places of honour and the dukes of Touraine and Bourbon were among the servers. After dinner the king talked affably to the Lancastrian knights and esquires present and rewarded them, the French dukes following suit.[34]

Such careful and lavish stage management helped to create a friendly atmosphere. What was notable about the Amiens negotiations was that, though they ended in deadlock, the principals parted convinced of each other's good faith and optimistic about the chances of peace. An extension of the existing truce was confirmed on 5 May.[35] Gaunt was present at the great council held at Stamford on the 25th, where the terms which the French were prepared to accept received a critical reception from the large number of gentlefolk present. A central feature of the terms was a proposal to aggrandise Gaunt and his heirs: he was to hold a duchy of Aquitaine considerably enlarged from the present area of English domination – and hold it of the French Crown. The general feeling at the council was that this was far too high a concession by Richard in Gaunt's favour.[36]

Soon after the Stamford council, domestic tension blew up over an entirely different issue. At the end of May a mandate was issued for the trial of leading civic officials of London, and the Exchequer was ordered to open its session in York instead of at Westminster. The Westminster Chronicler blamed the royal explosion of malevolence against the citizens on Crown officials whose servants had been maltreated in London. He said that these officials had the support in their complaints of Gaunt and his son-in-law John Holand, earl of Huntingdon (a recent fellow envoy at Amiens). Gaunt was probably happy to give discreet encouragement to a quarrel between Richard and the citizens, as a means of lowering their pretensions, and of enabling Richard to assert his authority without provoking the higher nobility. On 25 June the mayor, sheriffs, aldermen and leading citizens were convicted by the king and council of defaults, at Nottingham; the liberties of the city were suspended, and the mayor and sheriffs were relieved of office and imprisoned until they paid fine and ransom at the king's pleasure. Gaunt seems to have wisely avoided playing too conspicuous a role in the Londoners' humiliation. He was omitted from the commission of 28 June, headed by his brothers, which was appointed to enquire into notorious defaults in the city's government.[37] Perhaps he excused himself from participation on the grounds that he was involved in Bolingbroke's preparations for another expedition to Prussia. On 2 and 3 July, at Leicester Castle, Gaunt granted annuities to three of his son's esquires, one of them his master cook.[38] On the 22nd he was at Windsor when the commissioners pronounced their predictably unfavourable verdict before a large assembly of London citizens. He was present too when the chancellor announced the appointment of a warden to govern the city.[39] Soon afterwards he may have withdrawn northwards. On 15 August he was probably at Kirkstall Abbey, a Cistercian house of his patronage not far from his hunting lodge at Rothwell (Yorks.).[40] This was a few days before the Londoners publicly launched the costly process of reconciliation with the king. On 21–2 August they gave him a lavish reception. The following month they received individual and corporate pardons, and their liberties were restored during good behaviour. Walsingham says that Gaunt and Woodstock interceded for them. But the dukes may not have played the most significant role in doing so. The Londoners certainly made much of Gaunt and his brothers that autumn. On 22 October, according to a contemporary correspondent, the three of them visited the king at S(heen) and accompanied him on the Thames to P(utney?). His uncles disembarked there and rode to Gaunt's house in Holborn: the king was rowed to Westminster. The city fathers had wished to meet the dukes *en route*, but they would not hear of it. So the citizens came to Gaunt's house and presented each of them with a gilt basin and a large sum of money.[41]

The king and Gaunt were eager to resume peace negotiations with Charles VI. On 20 August Richard had written to him saying that Gaunt and Woodstock would be at the usual place (Leulighen) to negotiate the following February. Woodstock's temporary involvement with the Irish lieutenancy had probably precluded his participation at the Amiens conference: royal councillors may now have considered it urgent to bring him into the negotiations in order to weaken the hostility to peace proposals which had been expressed at Stamford. But the first of what were to be Charles VI's recurrent breakdowns threw new doubts on the prospects of peace: Gaunt grew pessimistic. However, the frailty of Charles's health was only to slow down the impetus for peace.[42]

Parliament met at Winchester from 20 January to 10 February 1393 and granted a subsidy for the expenses of Gaunt and his fellow envoys. Gaunt was still in London on 4 March, but had reached Dover by the 8th and was in Calais on the 19th.[43] The conference was adjourned for a month on 29 April; renewed negotiations resulted in the sealing by the envoys of a draft treaty on 16 June.[44] Gaunt and Woodstock promptly returned to England: they were present in Westminster Abbey when their father's obit was commemorated on the 21st. Bolingbroke, returning through France after his extraordinary travels both to Prussia and Jerusalem, missed his father at Calais; he crossed to Dover probably on the 29th.[45] A crisis faced the returning nobles; a revolt had broken out mainly in the king's county palatine of Chester, with some support in the neighbouring duchy of Lancaster. Military veterans such as the Cheshire knight Thomas Talbot and the Lancashire knight Nicholas Clifton headed the movement. Walsingham says that it was caused by the belief of the Cheshiremen that Gaunt, Woodstock and Bolingbroke intended to surrender Richard's claim to the French Crown. They also feared that the liberties enjoyed by the palatinate were threatened with abolition. The rebels proclaimed their intention of killing the three magnates and other kinsmen of the king whom they suspected of harbouring treasonable designs. The first notice of the rebellion is a set of instructions under the Privy Seal given to the earl of Huntingdon and Sir John Stanley, who were sent to Cheshire and Lancashire. They were to tell the inhabitants that the king had heard of their inclination to rise up, and were to threaten them with forfeiture if there were risings. Huntingdon and Stanley were to assure them that if royal officers or anyone else took measures against them, they would have redress. A similar assurance was given on Gaunt's behalf as regards his ministers. This attempt to defuse the troubles failed. On 3 May writs were issued to Woodstock (justice of Chester), Gaunt and several sheriffs ordering them to suppress the insurgents. Gaunt took the lead in doing so, according to Walsingham. Rebels were apparently still active in Cheshire in mid-September, but Gaunt was able to force their submission there and in the duchy without resorting to attack, except on one occasion. Talbot was captured and confessed in Woodstock's and Bolingbroke's presence.[46] The finalisation of the peace treaty was postponed till 1394. A recurrence of Charles VI's illness would have necessitated this anyway, even if the Cheshire rising had not.[47] Gaunt was with his family for Christmas and the New Year at Hertford. Bolingbroke purchased a great quantity of arms and armour before Christmas and had them transported to Hertford for the use of himself and his half-brother Thomas Beaufort at the jousts to be held there. Probably during these festivities Bolingbroke rewarded a jester of Charles VI at Hertford; after he had left for London in January, he had a hamper of oysters, mussels and sprats sent thence to Hertford for his pregnant wife Mary.[48]

The parliament which met at Westminster in January 1394 witnessed the first public cracks in the harmony laboriously maintained between magnates since 1389. Controversy was stimulated by the peace proposals and intensified by the Cheshire rebellion. Gaunt accused the earl of Arundel of disloyalty, a charge presumably based on the accusations made to him and Woodstock during the Cheshire rebellion that the earl was in collusion with the rebels. The earl riposted by attacking Gaunt's policies and influence in council: Richard refuted his points, supported by the lords. Arundel, like Northumberland in 1381, had to seek the duke's pardon in public.[49]

Arundel's accusations, besides being a counter-attack against Gaunt's, were probably aimed at undermining the peace treaty, by destroying the credit and influence at court of the king's chief councillor. The proposals revolved around the considerable concession that Richard should hold Aquitaine of the French Crown by liege homage. Feeling was running high in the Lords and Commons against the treaty terms, according to the Westminster Chronicler, who himself considered them treasonable. He says that Woodstock would not join the opposition: it was rumoured that Gaunt had bought him off by a promise of territorial gain. Near the end of March, the two brothers travelled again to Leulighen, to tell Berry and Burgundy, 'the final will of the English'. There they remained in conference till the end of May or early in June; the truce was extended for four years, but the peace treaty was not ratified.[50]

The reason why peace was not made in 1394 is unclear. It may have seemed to Richard that the risks involved in ratification outweighed those involved in postponement. The risk of war breaking out was now reduced as a result of the close rapport which Richard had achieved with Charles VI. The risk of peace provoking domestic trouble had been increased by the Cheshire rebellion, the opposition to the treaty in parliament and Arundel's attack on Gaunt's influence. Richard is likely to have been alarmed lest a treaty further alienated the Cheshiremen, practically his only faithful supporters in 1387. The fate of Talbot suggests his anxiety to appease them. He had contrived to escape from prison before the 1394 parliament, in which Gaunt and Woodstock petitioned that his offence might be declared and judgement given against him. The royal response was a declaration that it was high treason. Talbot surrendered on 16 May, when Gaunt and Woodstock were across the Channel. But he was not brought to trial. In the first 1397 parliament Gaunt vainly petitioned that he should be: later that year Talbot received a large royal annuity, 100 marks.[51] In 1394 Richard saw as his priority the need to restore domestic tranquillity, threatened in England as well as by rebellion in Ireland and Gascony.

The royal and Lancastrian households were plunged into mourning in the spring and summer of 1394 by the deaths of princesses. The Duchess Constance died on 24 or 25 March, probably while Gaunt was in France. Her death does not seem to have interrupted his attendance at the peace conference. She may have died unexpectedly after a short illness, for the previous July she had gone to Bishop Braybrooke of London's house at Much Hadham (Herts.) for a hunting party. Three of the king's minstrels and one of Bishop Skirlaw's had provided entertainment.[52]

The queen, Anne of Bohemia, died too in 1394. In his grief Richard ordered a summerhouse which had been their favourite residence to be demolished. It is not certain that Gaunt returned to England for the queen's funeral service in Westminster Abbey on 9 June. But he travelled to Leicester for Constance's magnificent exequies (5 July): she was buried in Newarke College, far from Gaunt's intended place of burial. In death, as in life, there was to be a distance between them. Bolingbroke had also become a widower, at about the same age when his father had first become one. The day after Constance, young Mary de Bohun, the future Henry V's mother, was buried in the same church. She had died in childbirth.[53]

In August the duke went north. On the evening of the 24th he arrived at Pontefract Castle where his guests were gathered – his two brothers and his nephew, Edmund of Langley's elder son Edward earl of Rutland. This may have been a family meeting to console Gaunt for his bereavements and to say farewell before he left on an expedition to enforce his ducal authority in Gascony, and before Woodstock and Rutland joined the king for his expedition to Ireland. The next day Gaunt wrote an effusive letter to Richard thanking him for warranting a grant and emphasising his own and his guests' goodwill towards the king. He said that a certain person 'of low standing, I don't know who he is', had entered the royal household and uttered remarks against his honour touching the royal estate. Gaunt protested, 'I believe and truly hope, my lord, that you have always had such proof [of my loyalty] by experience of all my dealings with you, that you would not be inclined to believe any such utterances tending to contradict my said dealings'.[54] This was, surely, a heartfelt statement, with an implicit contrast between Gaunt and those (including, indeed, his own son Bolingbroke) who had challenged and coerced the king during Gaunt's absence abroad in 1386–8. There is no reason to doubt that Richard accepted the protestation as sincere. However, the letter suggests a certain apprehensiveness on Gaunt's part, an awareness that there were those at court who would like to see him plucked down, and that his volatile nephew was inclined to be oversensitive in his reactions to accusations against his kin.

As Gaunt intended to be in Aquitaine for a year,[55] he may with reason have wondered whether the support which he had given Richard since his return in 1389 had secured him sufficient royal affection and favour to survive a prolonged absence. A deeper cause of disquiet than this accusation in the royal household may have been that Talbot, who had accused him of treason, still went unpunished – he was in fact to be removed from custody in the Tower at the end of the following month to the more congenial surroundings of Windsor Castle.[56]

On 24 August Sir Matthew Gournay contracted for Simon Raly to serve with an archer in his retinue on Gaunt's expedition; before 13 September the royal council had ordered the requisition from northern ports of ships for the duke's passage.[57] The assembly date for the retinues of his army was 26 September, but Gaunt appears to have been at Leicester Castle on that day. He sailed from Plymouth early the following month. His decision to take the long sea voyage at an unseasonable time of year was a measure of the urgency with which he regarded the situation in Gascony. In fact he had a troublesome voyage. Contrary winds hampered his progress around the coasts of Brittany and he put in at the Breton port of Blavet, where he wrote on shipboard to Richard (7 November) that he and his company were in good order and waiting for a favourable wind. Eventually he sailed into the Bay of Biscay and landed at Libourne on the Dordogne.[58] He stayed in the duchy for a little under a year, making on his way back a more congenial land journey through Brittany and Normandy. He had only limited success in getting the Gascons to accept his authority, but at least avoided military conflict (see pp.196–7).

Gaunt arrived back in England soon after Christmas 1395. He probably made a pilgrimage to Canterbury to thank St Thomas for his safe return – Bolingbroke had 19 ells of velvet motley delivered to him there as a New Year's gift.[59] One of Gaunt's first visits was to pay his respects to the king at Langley. Richard received him with fitting honour, but, some said (according to Walsingham), 'without love'. The king licensed his withdrawal from court and he set out for Lincoln, where, not long after 13 February he married his ageing mistress Catherine Swynford – to universal amazement, Walsingham says.[60] He was probably with her at Pontefract Castle on 23 February and 10 March and at Rothwell soon afterwards.[61] Perhaps they were touring his estates so that Catherine might first be received as duchess by his provincial retainers and tenants, likely to be more gracious to her than censorious kinsfolk, backbiting royal courtiers and rude Londoners.

Froissart grew garrulous about the scandal of the duke's marriage to a woman of low lineage, who had been his mistress. He says that high-born ladies such as Woodstock's wife Eleanor de Bohun and the countess of Arundel (a Hastings) declared that Gaunt had sadly disgraced himself by marrying his mistress and that their hearts would burst with grief if they had to allow her precedence. So they resolved to avoid the new duchess. Woodstock and Eleanor were specially outraged. In fact that year the indignant ladies had to swallow their pride, since Catherine was necessarily prominent at the king's wedding celebrations. Very reasonably, Froissart attributed

Gaunt's eccentric marriage to his affection for his children by her, the Beauforts, and his desire to get them legitimised.[62]

Richard was to show himself willing to humour his uncle's dynastic ambitions for his Beaufort family. The king continued to acknowledge him as duke of Aquitaine and in June 1396 granted him an important charter of liberties for the duchy of Lancaster. Nevertheless, it is likely that Richard greeted Gaunt in 1395 less wholeheartedly than on his previous return from Aquitaine. Gaunt never regained the unique influence in council that he had exercised from 1389 to 1394. This was due to a number of factors. Richard's successful Irish expedition had made him more reliant on a younger generation of nobles such as his half-brother John Holand, earl of Huntingdon; his favourite of the early 1380s, Thomas Mowbray, earl of Nottingham and Edmund of Langley's son and heir Edward earl of Rutland (d.1415). Rutland, unlike his father, was forceful and devious; he got on well with Gaunt. He was to translate into English *Le Livre de la chasse* written by Gaunt's friend the count of Foix. During the hectic political events of 1399–1400, Rutland earned a perhaps unfair reputation for treachery. He may in fact have had a strong but frustrated sense of loyalty to Richard. He and Mowbray negotiated in 1396 with the French : Richard and Charles VI then inclined to a dynastic marriage as a means of alliance. Richard may have come to doubt Gaunt's ability to restrain Woodstock's misgivings over a policy of peace. Woodstock, according to Froissart, was violently opposed to the king's French marriage and continued to agitate against the francophile policy until the time of his arrest in 1397.[63] This suggests that Gaunt was less effective than hitherto in promoting political stability. Though he was still very active physically, one reason may have been that his health was declining, and that he had a recurrent malady which made travelling difficult (see p.355).

Gaunt certainly continued to be closely associated with royal policies, but no longer as their principal instigator or executor. In March 1396, when he was in Yorkshire or about to arrive there, Rutland and Mowbray concluded in Paris a truce of twenty-eight years and the agreement for Richard to marry Charles's daughter Isabella.[64] Gaunt was not entirely left out of the negotiations: Rutland wrote at least two letters from France to him about his mission's progress. A herald of the duke and his treasurer apparently accompanied the envoys to the French court and were sent back to report to Gaunt by Rutland.[65] On 1 May the three royal uncles were among Richard's kinsmen who sealed an undertaking at Windsor for the return of Isabella to France in the event of Richard's death.[66] Richard promoted Lancastrian dynastic interests in connection with his marriage – but not apparently Woodstock's. In June Richard proposed to Charles

VI the marriage of Bolingbroke's eldest son (the future Henry V) to Charles' youngest daughter Michelle.[67]

Gaunt had recently solicited the king's sympathetic aid in his family affairs. Tension had arisen between him and Bolingbroke, according to Froissart, because Bolingbroke was keen to join his kinsmen the counts of Hainault and Ostrevant in an expedition against the rebels in Friesland. Gaunt held many conversations with the duke of Guelders, then visiting England, about the proposed expedition and was so worried by Guelders' descriptions of the hazards of campaigning in Friesland that he forbade his son to go and persuaded the king to add his prohibition.[68] Yet a few years before, Bolingbroke had undertaken far-flung and perilous journeys, even beyond the bounds of Christendom, with his father's blessing and support. If Froissart is right about Gaunt's motives for opposing the Friesland expedition, it may be an indication of a changed mental attitude, perhaps an onset of anxiety resulting from physical deterioration. Gaunt may have been afflicted with worry lest as a result of the hazards of his son's adventurous life, he would die soon without an adult male heir. Fear of his own imminent death probably also spurred on his determination to promote the interests of his Beaufort children.

Gaunt had a suitably honourable part in the conferences and festivities surrounding the king's wedding in November. He probably crossed in Richard's party from Dover to Calais on 7 August for a preliminary meeting with the duke of Burgundy.[69] He was probably at Hertford on 7 October, but at the end of the month was back in Calais for the royal wedding. He was present on 27 and 28 October for the first meetings of Richard and Charles, between Calais and Ardres; on 4 November for the marriage ceremony in St Nicholas's Church, Calais, and by the town walls the next day, with Woodstock and Rutland, to witness Richard's accord with Berry and Burgundy, committing him to help solve the papal Schism by following 'the way of cession'.[70]

In the parliament which met in January 1397 Gaunt once more appeared as a staunch upholder of his nephew's regality and was the recipient of dynastic favour. Richard was grievously offended by the Commons' complaint about aspects of government, expostulating to the Lords that some of the articles which the Commons had submitted were 'greatly against his regality and royal estate and liberty', especially the one requesting the reduction of household expenses. He ordered Gaunt to find out from the Commons Speaker who had presented the original bill of complaint. On 7 February the culprit, a certain Thomas Haxey, clerk, was brought to the White Chamber at Westminster, questioned by the duke and, in accordance with the Lords' declaration, condemned as a traitor.[71]

The chancellor, Archbishop Arundel, declared in parliament how the pope had legitimised John Beaufort, his brothers and sister, and recited the charter in which Richard confirmed the legitimisation at Gaunt's request. Sir John appeared in parliament and was created earl of Somerset.[72] Soon after parliament, Gaunt went northwards; early in July Richard had Woodstock, Arundel and Warwick arrested. On 15 July, by writs dated at Windsor, Richard ordered the sheriffs and Gaunt or his chancellor in the duchy of Lancaster to have proclamations issued asserting that leading nobles, including Gaunt, Langley and Bolingbroke, had given assent to the arrests.[73] Gaunt and Bolingbroke were probably present with the king at Nottingham Castle in August when a group of lords appealed Woodstock, Arundel and Warwick of treasonable acts in 1386–8. Bolingbroke had a force of men-at-arms and archers stationed not far off at Dale Abbey (Derbyshire) during the king's stay at Nottingham, to help guard him.[74] The weight of Lancastrian power and influence appeared to be firmly behind the king and arrayed against those who had once so grievously infringed his prerogatives. Among the new lords appellant were Gaunt's son John Beaufort, earl of Somerset, his son-in-law John Holand, earl of Huntingdon, and his leading councillor and administrator Sir William Scrope.

There are no reliable contemporary accounts of what led to Richard's decision to turn on his old opponents in 1397. Froissart says that Woodstock was stirring up opinion then against the king, who told Gaunt and Edmund of Langley that their brother and the earl of Arundel were plotting to seize him and deprive him of the exercise of authority. Gaunt and Edmund replied that Woodstock would not succeed in this; not wishing to take sides, they withdrew from court with their families and went deer-hunting. Froissart says that they were to regret this decision, for by it they lost the chance of moderating Richard's actions.[75] The French author of the *Chronique de la Traison et Mort de Richard Deux*, a piece of Ricardian hagiography, says that the arrests were made in response to a plot which Woodstock instigated in the summer of 1397. Bolingbroke, Mowbray and Archbishop Arundel were among those who agreed with him to seize the king, Gaunt and Edmund, to imprison them for life and execute the other lords of the council. This plot was betrayed by Thomas Mowbray. The implausibilities in the account have been pointed out by Palmer and Tuck.[76]

It seems impossible to ascertain how much prior knowledge, if any, Gaunt had of Richard's intention to make the arrests and what he thought Richard's ultimate aim was. Gaunt is unlikely to have been concerned about the fate of the earl of Arundel, whom he probably considered to have been as malignant in disrupting their kinship bonds as the earl of Northumberland in 1381. Gaunt's accusation then of 'unnatural' conduct against the latter (the son of his first wife's aunt) showed the high regard which he held for such bonds (see p.89). One deduction from this regard is that in 1397 Gaunt felt strongly obliged to protect his brother Woodstock, with whom he and Bolingbroke had maintained a variety of ties, of a cordial as well as a business nature, in the 1390s. But for Gaunt fraternal obligation conflicted with his strong sense of the sacredness of royal authority and his corresponding abhorrence of assaults on it such as his brother had perpetrated. Woodstock's arrest and the formulation of charges of treason against him and his principal allies of 1386–8 posed cruel dilemmas for Gaunt. Bolingbroke's vulnerability as a political supporter of Woodstock in 1387–8 probably influenced Gaunt in his apparently unfraternal conduct – for instance, in permitting his son, John Beaufort to participate in the accusations against Woodstock and his allies.

Though Richard's revenge was doubtless long premeditated, the reasons why he unleashed it in 1397 are unclear. Maybe calculations about the future of the House of Lancaster influenced the timing. Gaunt was nearing the age of sixty; if his health was variable (see p.355), Richard may have decided that it would be safer to reverse the policies of 1386–8 while he was still active, rather than face the reactions of the vigorous, unpredictable and popular Bolingbroke as head of the House of Lancaster. At the moment Bolingbroke was very much at his father's command, as the matter of the Friesland expedition showed. Gaunt, Bolingbroke and Langley were licensed to bring armed retinues to the parliament which met at Westminster on 17 September, as were the lords who were to bring an Appeal of Treason against the arrested lords.[77]

In parliament the earl of Arundel was the first of the accused to be brought to answer the charges (21 September). Gaunt conducted proceedings in his capacity as high steward of the realm. The pro-Lancastrian and pro-Arundel Walsingham described prosecutor and accused as arguing the case with dignity, and Gaunt as displaying forensic skill to refute the earl's appeals to his revoked pardons. On Richard's order, the duke pronounced sentence. The earl was executed the same day. But the less inhibited chronicler Adam Usk portrays a different scene, with venomous exchanges between the duke and earl, the duke soon denouncing Arundel as a traitor, and Bolingbroke joining in to recall treasonable words uttered by him in 1387. Three days later Mowbray, who as captain of Calais was responsible for holding Woodstock in custody, announced in parliament that he could not produce the duke to answer the Appeal of Treason, since he was dead.

Circumstantial details were to be made public after Henry IV's accession about the assassination of Woodstock at Calais on Richard's orders, under Mowbray's direction. However, it is possible that he died of natural causes; he was sick when arrested, and the shock of this and his imprisonment may have produced a fatal, but, from Richard's viewpoint, extraordinarily timely deterioration. It is not clear whether it was Gaunt who publicly pronounced the sentences of treason on his brother or on Warwick, whose lachrymose confession of his guilt in parliament reduced Richard and Gaunt to tears (perhaps, in the former's case, tears of happiness). The proceedings brought some gratification for Gaunt. His sons Bolingbroke and John Beaufort, earl of Somerset, were elevated respectively as duke of Hereford and marquis of Dorset. On 29 September the parliamentary session was adjourned till the New Year.[78]

Within a few days of the adjournments, Gaunt performed a macabre supplementary task for Richard. With other nobles he went to the church of the Austin Friars in London, to disinter Arundel's body under cover of night: to Richard's annoyance, the tomb was becoming the centre of a cult of political martyrdom.[79] A fortnight later (14 October), Gaunt received a royal grant of forfeited Arundel property in Norfolk, a reward for his services in dealing with the earl, troublesome in death as in life.[80] About this time Gaunt went with the king to visit the earl's more congenial brother Archbishop Arundel, to insist that he should go into exile in accordance with his sentence in parliament and to comfort him.[81] Early in November Gaunt and Bolingbroke were probably together at Hertford Castle; on 18 December and on Christmas Day Gaunt was at Leicester. He was making preparations to negotiate with the Scots; a warrant informed John Wynter, the receiver in Norfolk and Suffolk, that he was sending the butler John Curteys to the region to buy wine, which Wynter was to ship to Hull for Gaunt's anticipated journey northwards.[82]

How are we to judge Gaunt's failure to protect his brother's life or to insist that the circumstances of his death be investigated, as they were as soon as his son became king? Though it is possible that Woodstock died of natural causes, the circumstantial evidence produced in the 1399 parliament suggests that he was assassinated at Calais. Perhaps Gaunt failed to press for or secure clemency because, like other well-informed people, he was deceived into thinking that Woodstock was dead a month or more before he actually was. After Woodstock's official demise Gaunt may have kept quiet out of fear (again, especially for Bolingbroke) and in return for the royal favours heaped on his kinsmen and friends.[83]

No contemporary chronicler blames Gaunt for failing to protect or defend his brother, or to protest about his demise in suspicious

161

circumstances. But one would not expect them to do so, since they were nearly all pro-Ricardian or pro-Lancastrian. It is significant that Froissart, who generally favoured Gaunt and was a punctilious judge of aristocratic behaviour, saw a need to explain his and his brother Langley's passivity. Froissart says that when they heard about Woodstock's death, they angrily blamed the king for it and agreed to meet in London. Its citizens, also outraged, defied a royal ban on receiving Gaunt. But their anger cooled and they offered to mediate. The king made peace with his uncle and agreed to be guided by him – a promise which he failed to keep. But there is no corroborative evidence for Froissart's story and it does not fit in easily with the known chronology of events between the arrest and condemnation of Gloucester.[84]

However, it is possible that the new political crisis of 1398, which had such grave consequences for both Richard and the House of Lancaster, had as one of its roots Gaunt's desire to avenge his brother's death. This crisis blew up from a stray meeting in December 1397 between Bolingbroke (now duke of Hereford) and his fellow lord appellant of 1388, Mowbray (now duke of Norfolk). They met on the road between Brentford (Middlesex) and London, both probably returning from court. Shortly before parliament resumed, at Shrewsbury, on 27 January 1398, Bolingbroke appeared on summons in the royal presence. Richard said that reportedly he himself had been slandered by Mowbray in Bolingbroke's presence. At Richard's command Bolingbroke wrote an account of this conversation on the road, which was read when he appeared before Richard in parliament on 30 January. Allegedly, Mowbray had said that the two of them were about to be punished for their part in the 1387 rising. A plot had been laid by certain nobles to kill Gaunt and Bolingbroke: the plotters intended to destroy other magnates whom he named (closely related to the House of Lancaster) as well as Mowbray himself. This supposed plot (like the supposed plot against Richard and Gaunt in the summer of 1397) is full of implausibilities. It is most unlikely that Thomas Holand, duke of Surrey, wanted to encompass the ruin of his uncle John Holand, duke of Exeter, or that Gaunt's friend William Scrope, earl of Wiltshire (whom he continued to hold in trust and affection), had similar designs against him. Such allegations suggest that Mowbray's remarks were either crass in the extreme or maliciously distorted by Bolingbroke so as to make him appear as a troublemaker intent on sowing discord. One reason for Mowbray's outraged bitterness over the charge was probably that it impugned his family honour just as he was attempting to raise it to a new height – an elevation, religious in character, in which Bolingbroke had participated, just as he had in the recent movement to exalt the Crown. Dr Anthony Luttrell has discovered and commented on a letter dated 10 November 1396 from Jacobus the Vicar and the brethren of the Dominican convent at Pera or Galata. It stated that an envoy from Mowbray had been in Galata and had told the brethren that he wanted to have the body of his father (killed by Saracens in 1368); he had promised and in part paid them alms of 150 ducats. The Dominicans had privately collected the bones and handed them over in a jar in the presence of John Mowbray *heraldus* and a Hospitaller knight, John Ingilby. The friars requested that the remains be buried in a convent of their order. This letter is recited in a notarial copy dated London, 15 March 1397. It is prefaced by a statement recording that Mowbray had recovered his father's 'bones or relics' and that he had unhappily been slain by treacherous Saracens in a battle between them and Christians. His father is described as 'catholicus', 'as if', Luttrell remarks, 'he were the object of some cult'. Thomas Mowbray did not have the remains reburied in a Dominican church, but in the Carmelite house in Fleet Street, London, where his own elder brother was buried. This was a house particularly reverenced by the Lancastrian family (see p.245). In 1397 Bolingbroke made an offering at Whitefriars 'on the tomb of the late lord de Mowbray father of the Duke of Norfolk whose bones were brought from Rhodes'. It may have been on this occasion that Bolingbroke dined in the Whitefriars *hospitium* with the king and queen and purchased rich hangings to adorn the canopies of the chairs provided for the royal couple, brightening the austere conventual setting. Mowbray could have reasonably regarded Bolingbroke's participation in his father's cult as strengthening their personal relations – if the times had not been out of joint.[85]

There is evidence suggesting that Mowbray was practically in a state of private war with the House of Lancaster from about the time that Bolingbroke made his accusation public. According to the chronicler Usk, before parliament met at Shrewsbury, Mowbray

> laid snares of death against the duke of Lancaster as he came thither; which thing raised heavy storms of trouble. But the duke, forewarned by others, escaped the snare.[86]

Some time after the end of parliament, on 1 and 3 March, Sir William Bagot of Baginton (Warwicks.) entered into a series of recognisances perhaps related to the plot outlined by Usk. Bagot was a long-standing Mowbray retainer; he also received a fee from Bolingbroke. He pledged himself not to procure the disinheritance of Gaunt, his wife or any of his children; he was to be executed without further judgement if he killed them. Could it be that Bagot's Lancastrian connection prompted him to confess his knowledge of, or intended participation in, a Mowbray plot aimed at Gaunt?[87]

The surmise is, then, that Mowbray reacted violently against Gaunt in response to Bolingbroke's accusation, because he rightly believed that it was inspired by the former to revenge Woodstock's death. If these were Mowbray's forebodings they cannot have been allayed by the composition of the parliamentary commission appointed on 31 January to terminate petitions after the dissolution of the session and to settle matters arising from Bolingbroke's complaint. The commission was headed by Gaunt, and included his brother Langley, his nephew Aumale (Langley's son), his son-in-law Exeter, his son Dorset (John Beaufort) and his close friends the earls of Wiltshire (William Scrope) and Worcester (Thomas Percy).[88]

However, Gaunt had business in Scotland likely to restrict his participation in the commission's activities. In August 1397 it had been planned that he should take control of negotiations with the Scots, and on 2 October an agreement was reached with them that he should meet Robert III's son the earl of Carrick on the border in the East Marches on 11 March 1398.[89] On 5 February he and his fellow negotiators (who included the earls of Wiltshire and Worcester) had been empowered to redress violations of the general truces and seek to obtain the oaths of the king and nobles of Scotland to adhere to them.[90] On 20 February Gaunt was at Pontefract Castle, on his way to the border, and three days later a royal payment of £566 13*s* 4*d* was made at the Exchequer for his expedition to the Marches with a retinue of 200 men-at-arms (including 20 knights) and 400 archers.[91] On the appointed day the commissioners met the Scots at Howden Stank in the barony of Sprouston (Roxburghshire), near Kelso. Five days later they sealed an indenture by which they agreed to prolong the truce till Michaelmas and appointed conservators who would enforce appropriate local measures.[92]

Just over three weeks before this agreement, Mowbray and Bolingbroke had appeared before the king at Oswestry (23 February); there Mowbray denied the accusations. They appeared before the king and parliamentary commission at Bristol on 19 March, presumably in the absence of Gaunt, Wiltshire and Worcester. At Bristol it was decided that the quarrel should be tried by battle.[93] The matter is likely to have speeded Gaunt's return from Scotland; a letter-writer referred to his arrival at Westminster with Bolingbroke and other nobles from Windsor possibly on the evening of 25 March.[94] On 14 April he was at Leicester Castle, and presumably at Windsor on 28–9 April to attend the great council before which the disputing dukes appeared. It was almost certainly at this council that one of Bolingbroke's knights made new accusations against Mowbray on his master's behalf, including one that 'by his false counsel [he] caused to be put to death my dear and beloved uncle the Duke of Gloucester [Thomas of Woodstock]'. The author of the *Traison* says that Mowbray did not reply to this charge. According to the official record of the process, at Windsor Mowbray admitted certain less heinous offences in the appeal. Since there were no definite proofs of his guilt, the council agreed to trial by battle, to be held at Coventry on 16 September.[95] Perhaps Bolingbroke had hoped from the start for this outcome – fundamentally, to satisfy his own and his father's honour over Woodstock's death. Gaunt, a keen connoisseur of jousting, who had encouraged his son's enthusiastic tourneying and had often watched him perform, may have been convinced of his ability to beat Mowbray in a good cause and eager to see his son avenge the terrible deed. Father and son may have recalled how on previous occasions Gaunt had received what some contemporaries considered to be miraculous marks of divine favour. That summer they both prudently retired north; Gaunt was at Pontefract on 9 June and 14 July, Bolingbroke being with him on the previous occasion. On 17 July Gaunt was at his lodge at Rothwell to hunt.[96] At the start of the month the king had confirmed the extension of Lancastrian influence in the north by renewing his commission as lieutenant in the Marches for the duration of the truces.[97]

Gaunt was present on 16 September at Coventry for the duel. Crowds had flocked to see it from all parts of England. Bolingbroke had been practising his skills strenuously and was equipped with the choicest Milanese armour, provided by Giangaleazzo Visconti, duke of Milan. Mowbray had relied on German armourers. When the protagonists appeared in the lists and were ready to fight, the king, sitting in his tent in royal state, girded with a sword, intervened to forbid the fight and take the issue into his own hands. Richard ordered his judgement to be proclaimed – Bolingbroke was to go into exile for ten years and Mowbray for life; the king attached blame to both of them. At his uncle's pleading he reduced Bolingbroke's term of exile to six years. Gaunt may have had hopes of further clemency; it was indicative of Richard's cordial mien, despite the sentence, that a few days later he apparently stayed at Gaunt's borough of Leicester – letters patent were dated Leicester 20–4 September, and the belated royal ratification of the truce made at Howden Stank in March was made there on the 22nd.[98] According to Froissart, Bolingbroke inclined to visit Hainault, seeking the company of his kinsman the count of Ostrevant (*persona grata* to Richard). But he accepted his father's shrewd advice to go instead straight to Paris and attend on Charles VI and the Valois princes.[99] Perhaps Gaunt was thinking that he and his son might enlist the support of Valois circles which he knew so well in order to persuade Richard to mitigate the sentence further. Gaunt was present at the royal palace of Eltham (Kent) when his son took leave of the king before going into exile. Dr Kirby thinks that the latter probably set out from London for Dover on 13 October. In Paris Bolingbroke soon grew restless and planned to go on crusade with Marshal Boucicaut, his old jousting adversary of 1390. But he first sent a knight for his father's advice, whom Gaunt received in Hertford Castle. Once more Gaunt showed keener political sense than his adventure-seeking son. His advice was that Bolingbroke should visit the Castilian and Portuguese courts, where his sisters reigned. Bolingbroke's knight reported back that Gaunt's physicians said that he had such a dangerous disease that he could not live for long. His son sensibly gave up plans for further travels.[100] Yet, at the royal court, it had been anticipated in October that Gaunt's health would continue to be adequate for business and travel: he had apparently soon recovered from the fever which had led him to retire with the Duchess Catherine to Lilleshall Abbey at the end of the Shrewsbury parliament. On 3 October Richard had alluded to the intention that outstanding Anglo-Scottish problems would be settled by the dukes of Lancaster and Rothesay (i.e. Carrick) at their proposed meeting in 1399.[101] So it is possible that Gaunt's health collapsed suddenly in the autumn and that his fatal illness was only diagnosed then.

The earliest extended account of Gaunt's final illness and deathbed appears in a text written about twenty years later, in a foreign chronicle, that of Andrew Wyntoun, prior of Loch Leven (Fife). He says that Gaunt

> In til a suddane langure fele,
> Bath for eld [old age], and hevynes
> That his son tretit wes
> In til his chawbir [chamber] bede held he,
> Travalit in that infirmité.
> Quhile that he yalde in that langure
> His spirite til his Creature.

Wyntoun was the first writer to mention Richard's alleged visit to his uncle on his deathbed. The king spoke to him

> rycht curtasly,
> And gaive hym consale of dysporte
> Wyth plesand wordis of comforte.

Nevertheless, the 'prevé billis' which the king left on his uncle's bed did nothing to ameliorate his 'langure'. Soon after they were read to him, he expired.[102] What did Wyntoun believe they contained?

The story of a royal visit crops up again in Thomas Gascoigne's *Loci e Libro Veritatum*, written in the 1440s. He tells a very different story. Gaunt showed the king how his genitals and other parts of his body had putrefied, because of 'the exercise of carnal intercourse with women'. Gascoigne gives this example to illustrate his point that sexual intercourse frequently has this effect on men. It is a typical clerical canard: Gaunt's deserved reputation as what Gascoigne termed 'a great fornicator' made him an obvious subject for an exemplary tale. Armitage-Smith, who commented on Gascoigne's story in Latin so as not to offend his readers' modesty, indignantly rejected the story. Can it be taken seriously as evidence of Gaunt's physical condition or of the causes of his death? A window in York Minister may provide a clue. The St Cuthbert window occupies a bay of the south choir aisle. In the lowest row are figures of donors and their associates grouped in attitudes of devotion around a figure of St Cuthbert. An inscription below the figure of Thomas Langley, bishop of Durham (d.1437), who had been dean of York 1401–6, records that the window was his gift. It has usually been dated to the mid 1440s, though it has recently been suggested on stylistic grounds that it may be as early as *c.*1430.[103]

In the 1390s Langley was in Gaunt's service; he owed his early preferment above all to the duke's benevolence (see p.251). Therefore it is not surprising that Gaunt (in his life a devotee of St Cuthbert) figures in the window, correctly labelled, as at the time of his death, 'Johannes dux acquitannie et lancastrie'. He kneels, looking upwards, with hands joined, wearing a crown, pink robe, ermine-bordered mantle and white girdle. The full face is smooth, middle-aged, with a neatly cropped beard and a haggard, agonised expression. The duke is at a desk, on which lies an open book, inscribed: 'Domine ne in furore tuo arguas me neque in ira tua corripias me. Miserere me(i) domine quum infi(r)mus sum saua me dom. . . .' The first sentence is from the first verse of Psalm 38: 'O Lord, rebuke me not in thy wrath: neither chasten me in thy hot displeasure.' It continues:

2 For thine arrows stick fast in me, and thy hand presseth me sore.

3 There is no soundness in my flesh because of thine anger; neither is there any rest in my bones because of my sin. . . .

5 My wounds stink and are corrupt because of my foolishness. . . .

7 For my loins are filled with a loathsome disease: and there is no soundness in my flesh.

8   I am feeble and sore broken: I have roared by reason of the disquietness of my heart.

10   My heart panteth, my strength faileth me: as for the light of mine eyes, it also is gone from me.

11   My lovers and my friends stand aloof from my sore: and my kinsmen stand afar off.

12   They also that seek after my life lay snares for me: and they that seek my hurt speak mischievous things, and imagine deceits all day long. . . .

18   For I will declare mine iniquity; I will be sorry for my sin.

19   But mine enemies are lively, and they are strong: and they that hate me wrongfully are multiplied.[104]

One can read into the psalm parallels to genital disease and the sort of family and political distress which might have compounded the dying Gaunt's agonies. Might it be that Langley chose this verse with painful memories of how he had observed his late master's deathbed, and in the conviction that Gaunt's repentance and faith, with the aid of St Cuthbert, would heal his soul?

Gaunt spent his last days at Leicester Castle. He was there on 2 January 1399 and made the final version of his will and died on 3 February, as Dr J.B. Post has shown.[105] It is inherently probable that Richard visited him on his deathbed, the natural course of kinship and Christian charity. The king was in the midlands in January. It is very likely that Gaunt was inconsolable, not only because of his son's exile, but because of well-founded fears that the king might withhold the Lancastrian inheritance from him.[106] Over the previous eighteen months Richard had revealed an ability to dissemble, a ruthlessness, unpredictability and political inventiveness which may have shocked his uncle. But Gaunt went out of his way in his will to demonstrate fondness for Richard, appealing to the ties of natural affection. Among his bequests to Richard were his best gold cup, recently given to him at New Year by the Duchess Catherine, his best jewel, and a gold dish engraved with the Garter motif and having a dove carved on the cover.

Chroniclers' obituaries were brief: general interest in Gaunt was soon overshadowed by the dramatic events after his death. The anonymous continuator of the *Eulogium Historiarum* hinted that his death presaged political upheavals, noting that shortly beforehand there had been an earth tremor under St Paul's Cathedral – the duke's intended place of burial.[107] The poet, John Gower, Hereford's retainer, wrote with remarkable perfunctoriness that 'death resolved everything for . . . [Bolingbroke's] father, whom God absolved'.[108] Froissart said that all the duke's friends grieved greatly, but that Richard seemed little affected, writing an account of his uncle's demise to Charles VI 'with a sort of joy'.[109] In Paris Bolingbroke and his attendants went into mourning. The king and his brother the duke of Orleans and his uncles the dukes of Berry and Burgundy were among those present at a requiem mass.[110]

According to the provisions of Gaunt's will, his body was to remain unburied at the place of his death for forty days and was not to be embalmed during that period. Dr Post has shown that this interval was adhered to and that Gaunt was probably buried in St Paul's Cathedral on Passion Sunday (16 March).[111] The cortège had come southwards on its way from Leicester to London through Dunstable, St Albans, where the corpse lay in the abbey church overnight to be prayed over by the monks, and through Barnet, where it lay in the abbey's chapel of St John overnight. Duchess Catherine, her son Bishop Beaufort of Lincoln, and Gaunt's old acquaintance Bishop Braybrooke of London, accompanied the procession all or part of the way.[112] Presumably it went, when it arrived in London, to the Carmelites' church in Fleet Street for the night, as Gaunt's will directed, before a further night of exequies and interment next day in St Paul's. The executors had been directed to summon the duke's 'cousins and friends' to attend the funeral. There was to be no 'solempnitie ne feste', except that the poor were to receive alms for prayers. Nevertheless, the funeral was appropriately magnificent. Walsingham says that Richard attended.[113]

At the funeral the king's mind may have been absorbed by the fate of his uncle's inheritance as much as by the fate of his soul. On 18 March the parliamentary committee set up at Shrewsbury announced that Bolingbroke's sentence was made into perpetual banishment, that the licence granted to his attorneys to receive the inheritance was revoked and that it was forfeit to the Crown. These decisions were to set in motion the sequence of events leading to his usurpation and the foundation of the Lancastrian royal dynasty.

When Adam Usk wrote that the plot against Gaunt in 1398 caused 'heavy storms of trouble', did he have these events in mind? The most likely reason why Mowbray plotted the duke's death was his perception that the latter was determined to ruin him. The death of Woodstock dramatically marked the decline of Gaunt's influence over political affairs since his return from France in 1395. But in the winter of 1397–8, with Bolingbroke's accusations against Mowbray, the power of Lancaster was reasserted in a way most unwelcome to Richard. The Lancastrian accusation of treason against Mowbray was a more subtle version of the accusations of treason against Richard's favourites which the lords appellant had made in 1387–8. In a veiled fashion, the king's policies were being attacked through the attempt

169

to discredit one of their principal agents, Mowbray. Richard was able to blunt the Lancastrian threat only by exiling Mowbray, one of his staunchest supporters in the last few years. In 1398 Gaunt, true to his royalist principles, did not emulate the rebelliousness of his hallowed predecessor Thomas of Lancaster or of his brother Thomas in 1387. But by licensing his son Bolingbroke to make accusations against Mowbray he effectively challenged royal policy and sharpened the king's awareness that Lancastrian power was the greatest potential threat to the exercise of royal prerogative. Throughout his nephew's reign Gaunt had sought to avoid confrontations with the Crown, continuing the policy of Henry of Grosmont, duke of Lancaster, chief executor of Edward III's designs. He continued to appease Richard until his death, but in 1398 allowed Bolingbroke to embark on a policy, or spurred him to embark on it, which set the Crown and House of Lancaster on a collision course.

Notes and References

1 *C.P.R. 1396–9*, p.575; *W.C.*, pp.406–9; *H.A.*, Vol.2, pp.193–5; *R.P.*, Vol.3, p.313; Sparrow Simpson W 1887, p.502. For the gift of wine, P.R.O. E101/402/3 f11. I owe thanks for this reference to Dr C Given-Wilson. Gaunt refers in his will to Gloucester's gift.

2 *W.C.*, pp.406–9: Nicolas NH 1834, Vol.1, p.18.

3 *W.C.*, pp.408–9. Gaunt witnessed a royal charter dated Westminster 15 Dec. 1389 (P.R.O. C53/162/14). He appeared regularly as a witness to royal charters till his departure for Gascony in 1394 (ibid., *passim*).

4 *H.A.*, Vol.2, p.195. Robert Whitby, clerk of the wardrobe, gave the receiver of Hertford 100s. to prepare for Gaunt's Christmas sojourn (P.R.O. DL29/58/1081). Gaunt was party to an indenture dated Hertford 1 Jan. 1390 (Lewis NB 1964, nos 99, 100).

5 *W.C.*, p.1vi and n.6.

6 *R.P.*, Vol.3, p.258. Gaunt witnessed royal charters on 7 and 25 Feb. 1390 (P.R.O. C53/162/4).

7 *R.P.*, Vol.3, pp.263–4; *W.C.*, pp.414–15.

8 Boucicaut 1819, p.430; *St Denys*, Vol.1, pp.672ff; Froissart J 1872, Vol.14, pp.55–8, 105ff; Kirby JL 1970, pp.28–9.

9 *W.C.*, pp.432–5; P.R.O. DL28/3/2; Froissart J 1872, Vol.14, p.156; Kirby JL 1970, pp.29–30. Letters patent of Gaunt were dated Calais, 18 May 1390 (B.L.Add. Ch.7487), suggesting that he had accompanied or joined Bolingbroke there. Gaunt's name appears on the witness list to a royal charter dated Westminster 28 May (C53/112/5). John Beaufort was permitted by the French to go on the Tunis crusade.

10 *W.C.*, pp.440–3; *C.H.K.*, Vol.2, pp.313–14. Gaunt witnessed a royal charter dated Westminster 15 July (P.R.O. C53/163/1).

11 *W.C.*, pp.440–3, 442n, 454–5, 454n; Barron CM 1971, p.174 and n. The pardon granted to Northampton's associate Richard Northbury on 20 Oct. was made at Gaunt's request (*W.C.*, pp.442, 454–5).

12 Ibid., pp.442–3.

13 Palmer JJN 1971: 86ff.
14 *W.C.*, pp.450–1; Froissart J 1872, Vol.14, p.263. Gaunt probably went
    to Windsor Castle after the tournament for Ostrevant's induction as
    knight of the Garter; he was at the parliament at Westminster on 12
    Nov. (*W.C.*, pp.452ff; *R.P.*, Vol.3, p.277). He appears on witness
    lists of royal charters dated Westminster, 12, 16, 25 Nov. and 6 Dec.
    (P.R.O. C53/163/1, 2, 3).
15 Edinburgh University Library MS 183 f135v; part of text in *D.C.*,
    p.116n.
16 *W.C.*, pp.474–5.
17 Du Boulay FRH 1971, p.165.
18 Gaunt witnessed royal charters dated Westminster, 27 April and 1 and
    2 May (P.R.O. C53/163/1 and 2).
19 *W.C.*, pp.458ff. Gaunt witnessed royal charters dated at Westminster 9
    June and 20 July (P.R.O. C53/163/2 and 3).
20 *W.C.*, pp.476–7.
21 Ibid., pp.478–9; *C.P.R. 1396–9*, pp.478, 497, 499.
22 Goodman A 1971, p.57; *W.C.*, pp.474–5, 478–9. Gaunt granted a
    privilege dated Hertford Castle 4 Sept. (*L.B.* pp.293–4).
23 *W.C.*, pp.480–5.
24 Ibid. pp.480–3.
25 *R.P.*, Vol.3, p.286. Gaunt witnessed royal charters dated 7 Oct., 10,
    25 and 29 Nov. and 9 and 14 Dec. (P.R.O. C53/163/3; ibid.,
    164/2). He issued warrants dated London 17 Nov. and 12 Dec.
    (P.R.O. PL3/1/24, 32).
26 P.R.O. DL28/1/3.
27 Baldwin JF 1913, pp.489ff.
28 P.R.O. DL28/3/2.
29 Baldwin JF 1913, p.498.
30 *C.C.R. 1389–92*, p.434.
31 *C.H.K.*, Vol.2, p.318; *St Denys*, Vol.1, pp.734ff; Armitage-Smith S
    1904, pp.346ff and 346n.
32 Froissart J 1872, Vol.14, pp.378ff; *St Denys*, Vol.2, pp.736–9. Froissart
    only says that Gaunt bowed to the king.
33 *C.H.K.*, Vol.2, p.318.
34 *St Denys*, Vol.2, pp.734–41; Froissart J 1872, Vol.14, pp.376ff.
35 Armitage-Smith S 1904, p.346n.
36 *W.C.*, pp.488–91. Gaunt had sent a messenger to the north with letters
    summoning his knights and esquires to the council (P.R.O. DL28/3/2).
37 *W.C.*, pp.492ff; Barron CM 1971, pp.173–201.
38 *C.P.R. 1396–9*, pp.122, 468, 501. Bolingbroke prepared his expedition
    at King's Lynn (Norfolk) and embarked on 24 July at Heacham nearby
    (P.R.O. DL28/3/2; Du Boulay FRH 1971, pp.165, 167). Gaunt dated
    a warrant at Leicester Castle on 16 June (P.R.O. PL3/1/25).
39 Barron CM 1971, pp.185–8, 190–2. Ducal warrants were dated London
    5 and 21 July (P.R.O. PL3/1/21, 26).
40 Bateson M 1901, Vol.2, pp.204–5.
41 Barron CM 1971, p.194; Legge MD 1941, no.127. The letter was
    addressed to a bishop. Gaunt may have moved in Aug. from Yorks.
    to Lancs.; ducal warrants were dated Manchester 7 Sept. and Ightenhill
    manor 10th (P.R.O. PL3/1/20, 23). Gaunt dated grants London 26
    and 28 Oct. (*C.P.R. 1396–9*, p.74; *L.B.*, pp.291–2).

42 *W.C.*, pp.500–1; Froissart J 1871, Vol.15, pp.52–3.
43 *C.H.K.*, Vol.2, p.321; *Annales*, p.155; *W.C.*, pp.514–15; *C.P.R. 1396–9*, pp.500–1, 547. Gaunt was to have basic expenses of £20 *per diem* (Nicolas NH 1834, Vol.1, p.503). He witnessed royal charters at Winchester 30 Jan. and 9, 11, 12 Feb. (P.R.O. C53/164/3, 4) and issued letters patent there dated 24 Jan. (*L.B.*, pp.289–90).
44 *W.C.*, pp.514–15 and 514 n3; Palmer JJN 1971, pp.146ff.
45 *W.C.*, pp.514–15 and 515n; Toulmin Smith L 1894, p.lxxix.
46 *Annales*, pp.159ff; P.R.O. C47/14/6/44; *Foedera*, 1709, Vol.7, p.746; *R.P.*, Vol.3, pp.316–17; Bellamy JG 1964–5 : 261–7. The instructions to Huntingdon are summarised by Morgan P 1987, p.195. Gaunt dated warrants at Lancaster Castle on 10 and 14 Aug. (P.R.O. PL3/1/18, 19, 170) and a letter at Beverley, Yorks., on 28th (B.L. Cotton Cleo D 111 ff199). In accordance with a royal writ, he directed a writ under the duchy seal to Sir Robert Urswick and Thomas Radcliffe, dated 22 Aug., ordering the arrest of John Massy of Tatton and Sir Thomas Talbot (Bodleian MS Dodsworth 87 f77).
47 *W.C.*, p.515n; Palmer JJN 1972, pp.148ff.
48 *C.P.R. 1396–9*, p.478; P.R.O. DL28/1/4. Derby dated letters patent at Hertford 12 Jan. 1394 (*C.P.R. 1396–9*, p.469).
49 *Annales*, p.166; *R.P.*, Vol.3, pp.313–14 Armitage-Smith S 1904, pp.353ff; Aston M 1967, pp.358–9.
50 *W.C.*, pp.516–19; *Annales*, p.168; Palmer JJN 1972, p.149.
51 *R.P.*, Vol.3, p.338; Bellamy JG 1964–5 : 267–9, 271, 273n.
52 See p.369, n.54 below.
53 *Annales*, p.168; *W.C.*, pp.520–1; *C.H.K.*, Vol.2, p.321. For some of the heavy funeral costs for Constance, P.R.O. DL28/32/21.
54 Legge MD 1941, No.29.
55 Taunton, Somerset R.O., Trevelyan of Nettlecombe Papers, 25/1 : indenture for service between Sir Matthew Gournay and Simon Raly. I owe thanks for this reference to Professor Ralph Griffiths.
56 Bellamy JG 1964–5: 266–8.
57 Gournay–Raly indenture (see n.55); *C.P.R. 1391–6*, pp.521–2; B.L. Add. Ch. 8125. Gaunt may have moved to Kingston Lacy between 12 Aug. and 27 Sept. (P.R.O. DL28/1/9 f 12d). Gaunt's departure was probably delayed because the king's expedition to Ireland had taken up shipping.
58 Legge MD 1941, no.19; Otterbourne T 1732, p.184 Armitage-Smith S 1904, p.374.
59 *Annales*, pp.187–8; P.R.O. DL28/1/5.
60 *Annales*, p.188; *C.H.K.*, Vol.2, p.322. Gaunt witnessed royal charters dated Westminster, 3 and 18 Jan. and Nottingham Castle, 16 Feb. (P.R.O. C53/165/3, 4).
61 *C.P.R. 1396–9*, pp.496, 513. A ducal warrant was dated Rothwell manor, 31 March (P.R.O. PL3/1/8).
62 Froissart J 1871, Vol.15, pp.238–40.
63 Ibid., pp.196ff, 238; ibid., 1872, Vol.16, pp. 1ff.
64 *C.P.R. 1396–9*, p.496.
65 Legge MD 1941, nos 272, 275.
66 A.N., J.643, no.11; text in Chaplais P 1971, pp.39–40.
67 *D.C.*, no.229A. At the same time the marriage of Edmund of Langley's son Rutland to Charles's daughter Jeanne was proposed.

68 Froissart J 1871, Vol.15, pp.228–9, 269–71.
69 Aston M 1967, pp.361–2. The royal party was back in England soon after 22 Aug. Before 15 Sept., when the aged Abbot Thomas de la Mare of St Albans died, Gaunt and the duchess visited him on his sickbed – he was one of their last close personal links with Edward III and the Black Prince (*G.A.*, Vol.3, p.412).
70 Froissart J 1871, Vol.15, pp.298ff; Aston M 1967, pp.361–2; Legge MD 1941, No.89.
71 *R.P.*, Vol.3, p.388. Haxey was soon pardoned (Aston M 1967, pp.363–4).
72 *R.P.*, Vol.3, p.343; *Annales*, p.195.
73 *Foedera*, 1709, Vol.8 p.6.
74 Norwich. Norfolk R.O. MS 15, 171, 37 B 6 (account of duke's receiver in Norfolk 1397–8); cf P.R.O. DL28/1/6, f 30d. Gaunt dated warrants Pontefract, 17 March and London, 15 April (P.R.O. PL3/1/7, 10). At the king's command Gaunt, Bolingbroke and Langley assembled their retinues, which were mustered before the king on 10 Aug. (*C.P.R. 1396–9*, pp.190–1). This was five days after the appeal of treason was made before Richard in Nottingham Castle.
75 Froissart J 1872, Vol.16, pp.18–23.
76 Williams B 1846, pp.124–7; Palmer JJN 1978 : 145–81; Tuck A 1973, p.186.
77 *Foedera*, 1709, Vol.8, p.14.
78 *R.P.*, Vol.3, pp.337ff; *Annales*, p.220; Usk A de 1904, pp.156ff.
79 Walsingham (*Annales*, p.219) implies that the episode took place on 1 Oct.; Gaunt issued letters patent dated London that day (*C.P.R. 1396–9*, p.580).
80 Ibid., p.216 (hundreds of South Greenhoe and Launditch).
81 *Eulogium*, Vol.3, p.376. The archbishop left England by the end of Oct. (Aston M 1967, p.373).
82 Gaunt dated letters patent at Hertford Castle on 1 Nov., Bolingbroke on 6th (*C.P.R. 1396–9*, p.553); Gaunt at Leicester on 18 and 25 Dec. (Norwich, Norfolk R.O., MS 15171, 37, B6; *C.P.R.1396–9*, p.513).
83 Goodman A 1971, pp.68–9.
84 Froissart J 1872, Vol.16, pp.79–82.
85 *R.P.*, Vol.3, p.360; P.R.O. DL 28/1/6, ff8–9. This account runs from 1 Feb. 1397; the dinner was held during a parliamentary session. I owe thanks to Dr Anthony Luttrell for information from a forthcoming article about the return of John Mowbray's remains.
86 Usk A de 1904, p.169.
87 *C.C.R. 1396–9*, pp.291–2 Tuck A 1973, pp.208–9.
88 *R.P.*, Vol.3, pp.382–3.
89 *R.S.*, Vol.2, p.138; Bain J 1888, Vol.4, p.492.
90 *R.S.*, Vol.2, pp.139–40.
91 P.R.O. PL3/1/5; ibid., E403/557/29.
92 *R.S.*, Vol.2, pp.142–3.
93 *R.P.*, Vol.3, p.383.
94 Legge MD 1941, no.56.
95 *C.P.R. 1396–9*, p.547; *R.P.*, Vol.3, p.383; Williams B 1846, pp.146–7.
96 *C.P.R. 1396–9*, pp.499, 582, 593; *C.P.R. 1399–1401*, p.472.
97 *R.S.*, Vol.2, p.142.
98 *C.P.R. 1396–8*, pp.499, 582, 593; *R.S.*, Vol.2, pp.142–3.

99 Froissart J 1872, Vol.16, pp.110–11.

100 Ibid., pp.109–10, 132–3, 136–7; Kirby JL 1970, pp.49–50.

101 *R.S.*, Vol.2, pp.143–4. For the Lilleshall Abbey source for the sojourn of Gaunt and the duchess at the abbey, James MR ed. 1912, pp.170–72. I owe thanks for this reference to Dr Philip Morgan.

102 Wyntoun A 1879, Vol.3, pp.68–9.

103 Passage from Gascoigne cited in Armitage-Smith S 1904, pp.463–4. For the St Cuthbert window, Fowler JT 1875–6 : 249ff, 263; Baker M 1978 : 22–3. I owe thanks for these references to Dr Jeremy Goldberg and Dr P Lindley.

104 Contractions in the inscriptions have been expanded. The translation of Psalm 38 is from the King James Version.

105 *C.P.R. 1396–9*, p.478; Post JB 1981 : 3–4. Gaunt dated documents at Leicester Castle on 24 Oct. and 4 Nov. 1398 and 2 Jan. 1399 (*C.P.R. 1396–9*, pp.489, 494, 496). Otterbourne (1732, p.197) and John Strecche (B.L. Add. MS 35,295 f 260v) were chroniclers who noted Gaunt's death at Leicester.

106 *C.P.R. 1396–9*, pp.478, 489, 500. According to a near contemporary source, the dying Gaunt was 'graviter desolatus' because of his son's exile (Clarke MV and Denholm-Young N 1931, p.131).

107 *Eulogium*, Vol.3, p.381.

108 Stockton EW 1962, p.315. Writing some years later, John Strecche, canon of Kenilworth (a house in Gaunt's patronage) also casually noted the duke's death and burial in his chronicle (B.L. Add.MS 35, 295 f 260v).

109 Froissart J 1872, Vol.16, pp.137–9.

110 Ibid., pp.138–9.

111 Post JB 1981, pp.3–4.

112 *G.A.*, Vol.3, pp.438–40.

113 Usk A de 1904, p.171; Clarke MV and Denholm-Young N 1931, pp.131–2; *Annales*, p.232.

Chapter Nine

Gaunt and Christendom

To what extent did fourteenth-century princes define their activities and interests in terms of Christendom, and to what extent in terms of nationality? For Froissart, the Black Prince was a figure of universal significance, not notably English in his personality and culture. The chivalrous way of life which, for the chronicler, he for the most part worthily exemplified was an international code related to religious ideals and canon law, systems uninhibited by a sense of nationality. One of these ideals was that of the crusade, which, as Dr A. Luttrell has shown, revived strongly in English noble circles in the 1360s, embracing some of Gaunt's acquaintance and age group, notably his close friend the earl of Hereford.[1]

In the 1390s crusading fervour revived again in England, encouraged by the propaganda of Philippe de Mézières and one of his 'evangelists' in particular, Robert the Hermit.[2] But Froissart, well apprised of this movement, and sympathetic to it, emphasised an adverse factor in England – a strong current of opinion among gentlefolk there preferring war with France to the peace which the crusading propagandists promoted as a necessary prerequisite to the restoration of Christian unity, itself a necessity if the Turkish advances in the Balkans were to be rolled back and the Holy Sepulchre freed. One of the leaders in the 1390s of what might be termed the 'war party' was, according to Froissart, Thomas of Woodstock, for whom he concocted diatribes insisting on 'hard line' demands and spiced with a nationalistic distrust of the French.[3] Here we find a perceptive foreign commentator attributing to an English noble (and, by implication, his supporters) a sense of nationality fired by warfare and motivating views of how foreign policy should be conducted.

Such attitudes had presumably been hardened by decades of conflict and by Edward III's war propaganda, which had emphasised not only his just claims in France, but the malicious intent of his 'adversary of France' – and his adversary's allies – towards his English subjects as well as the English Crown.[4] Yet Froissart never attributed anti-French sentiments to Gaunt, and contrasted his pacific aims at the Anglo-French peace conferences of the early 1390s with the belligerent and suspicious attitudes of Woodstock.[5] The Westminster Chronicler's accounts of the hostile reception widely accorded to the peace proposals which Gaunt advocated, and the chronicler's own growing suspicions of his motives, reveal a gap between the duke's outlook and that of public opinion, as expressed by knightly representatives, in general.[6]

Nevertheless, in his character and preoccupations Gaunt did have a strong, specifically English ambience. His first wife was not, as was originally intended, and might have been expected, a foreign princess, but an Englishwoman, whose inheritance in England and Wales remained the basis of his magnate power, funding a household which was always primarily that of an English prince. Nearly all his councillors, as well as his principal administrative officials, were English. The envoys whom he used principally to negotiate with Juan I of Castile in 1386–8 were Sir Thomas Percy and Sir John Trailly, his fellow countrymen. Though warrants and letters under Gaunt's privy seal were drafted in French (presumably sometimes at his dictation), he is the first English prince of Norman-Angevin descent known to have been one of the subjects of a courtly poem written in English, and probably written for him.

Gaunt's sense of Englishness and his universalism were not, in his eyes, irreconcilable: they were both related to his dynastic status. He sometimes included among his titles that of 'son of the king of England' and on occasion publicly alluded to the naturalness of his allegiance to the English Crown and the seriousness with which he took its obligations. (see p. 72). He saw himself as a leading member of a royal family whose sovereign status and power were rooted in England, but which had historic roles to play in Christendom at large. This background impelled him, too, to take on a European role as its protagonist and to develop personal ambitions abroad tied up with its aggrandisement. Indeed, many English nobles in Edward III's reign sought the fulfilment of material aspirations abroad. But Gaunt's birth and his place in his father's policies in important respects differentiated his ambitions from theirs: the latter were mostly concerned with securing the financial profits of war, his primarily with dynastic claims and alliances and with territorial acquisitions. There were some English nobles who acquired estates abroad, who lived on them or sought to make good claims to them. The Bohun earls of Hereford tried to hang on to Annandale in Scotland and the Percies to Jedburgh. There was a considerable English settlement in Brittany;[7] Englishmen acquired estates too in Normandy, Poitou and Gascony. Sir Hugh Calveley received grants in Aragon and Castile.[8] But most magnates who campaigned abroad expected to rule there, if at all, only temporarily, as lieutenants of the king of England or the duke of Brittany. Otherwise they generally sought profits of war through royal wages, loot and ransoms. By contrast, in the 1360s Gaunt, like his brothers, wished for territorial aggrandisement abroad, partly as a means of implementing royal policy. As Professor A.A.M. Duncan has shown, his hopes of becoming a king had been nourished from boyhood by the scheme first proposed as part of a peace settlement by David II in 1350–1, that Gaunt should succeed to the Crown of Scotland in the event of his dying childless. In November 1363 David held peace talks with Edward at Westminster. As a result, two memoranda were drafted: one of these laid down stringent terms on which Edward himself might succeed the childless David. The other proposed that one of Edward's sons succeed him. These drafts were debated in the Scottish parliament at Scone in March 1364. It was agreed that Gaunt would be the best candidate to succeed David, particularly in view of his possession of the duchy of Lancaster. Since Gaunt held so much property in England, as king of Scots he would prefer to maintain peace rather than risk its forfeiture. In fact the Scottish parliament rejected this and all other arguments in favour of an English succession, upholding the rights of David's heir presumptive, Robert the Steward (the future Robert II).[9] Gaunt turned his attention to the promotion of the Lancastrian claim to Provence. In the spring of 1366 he demanded of Pope Urban V the surrender of his inheritance of Provence; his claims there were endorsed by Edward III in October. J.J.N. Palmer has connected this revived claim to Edward's attempts to put pressure on the pope, who was opposing the marriage of Gaunt's brother Langley to the heiress of Flanders. Provence was ruled by the papal vassal Queen Joanna of Naples, and Urban's residence at Avignon was an enclave there. He appears to have been alarmed at the possibility of English invasion – perhaps the threat of Gaunt's appearance at the head of *routier* companies, such as those which were, indeed, to appear there in 1367.[10]

But it was Gaunt's marriage in 1371 to Constance of Castile which made him the English noble with the most ambitious foreign aspirations in the later fourteenth century. Moreover, his lieutenancies in Aquitaine (1370–1, 1373–4, 1388–9) led him to develop, besides and interwoven with his Iberian contacts, a skein of regional and international relationships. His Iberian diplomacy of 1386–8 resulted in his making close family ties with the ruling houses of Portugal and Castile. From 1389 onwards he pursued territorial ambitions in France and intensified his relations with French royal princes to promote this interest and those of an Anglo-French and general peace, the ending of the Schism and the launching of crusades.

The nature and extent of Gaunt's foreign involvements, together with his unique ability to put large military retinues speedily into the field, gave him a powerful influence in the making of English foreign policy. This reached a peak in the period 1375–81, as a consequence of his father's and elder brother's illnesses and then of his nephew's minority. From 1382 to 1386, though often playing a leading role in diplomacy, he had to struggle to have his policies adopted by Crown and parliaments, and sometimes failed in the attempt. The restoration of his influence over policy after his return from Gascony in 1389 was precariously based on Richard's perception of the Crown's immediate interest. Richard's reliance on his uncle in part reflected a recognition of his mastery of diplomacy – evident earlier in his resolution of the crisis after the failure of Despenser's crusade and in the subtlety and boldness of his settlement with Juan I in 1387. It was to Gaunt's personal diplomacy that Richard turned to resolve problems with the Scots in 1398.

In reply to his contemporary critics, Gaunt may well have insisted that he used his power to further the interests abroad of his father's and nephew's house. In the Anglo-French war of 1369–75 he certainly subordinated his own dynastic ambitions in Spain to more pressing English priorities in France. In Richard's minority his strenuous Iberian diplomacy was largely negated up to 1381 by his absorption in defence against the French and Scots. But in the altered political climate of 1382–3 his attempts to drum up support for Iberian schemes ran into widespread opposition, and were decried as a means solely to personal aggrandisement. His peace policy of 1392–4 was widely suspect. In the long run, Gaunt's role as aspiring European prince appeared in the eyes of the more nationalistically minded among his compatriots as irreconcilable with that of a loyal English magnate.

The following survey of some of Gaunt's involvements abroad – with the rulers of the Low Countries, with John IV of Brittany and with the French royal princes; as lieutenant and duke in Aquitaine; – and as promoter of Mézières's movement for Christian unity – deals with aspects of his development as a prince of European importance. It is not a complete survey, as his dealings with the Iberian powers (covered in Chapter Seven) are omitted, and so are the important subjects of his relations with the papacy, and with the Scottish kings and magnates, which are touched on in other chapters.

Relations with the Low Countries

By descent Gaunt was an Hainaulter as well as an Englishman; he was a scion of the House of Avesnes, a distinguished family in the Holy Roman Empire. By place of birth he was a Fleming, as his contemporary soubriquet 'of Gaunt' indicated.[11] His principal godfather was probably John duke of Brabant (see p. 29). Such personal connections are likely to have enhanced his appreciation of the importance of the Low Countries in English policy. His ties with Hainault were to be reinforced. His first wife's sister, Maud (d. 1362) married in 1352 William V, count of Hainault, Holland and Zealand.[12] Two of his wives' *domicellae*, Philippa and Catherine (the latter of whom was to become his third wife) were daughters of a knightly Hainaulter, Payn de Roet. One of his leading retainers, Sir John Dabridgecourt, was the nephew of a renowned Hainault knight who served Edward III and the Black Prince, Eustace d'Aubréticourt.[13]

Royal policy as well as personal connections drew Gaunt into Netherlandish affairs – there were long-standing traditions in English foreign policy of trying to gain the alliance of imperial princes in the region against the rulers of France. Their support had been important to Edward III in the early stages of the Hundred Years War, so it is likely that Gaunt appreciated the significance of gaining it or at least securing their neutrality. The Netherlandish princes with whom English diplomacy was mainly concerned in the later fourteenth century were the rulers of Flanders, Brabant, Hainault (with Holland and Zealand), Guelders and Juliers. The most powerful of these were the counts of Flanders and the dukes of Brabant. In 1364, as we have seen (see pp. 43–5), Gaunt was deeply involved in the making of the Treaty of Dover. by whose terms his brother Edmund of Langley was to marry the count of Flanders' daughter Margaret – a marriage intended to create a great Plantagenet principality in the Low Countries. The aim was assiduously opposed by Charles V and frustrated by Urban V.[14] It was uncongenial too to the insecure rulers of Hainault and Brabant and to the Emperor Charles IV. Edward III had a claim to the succession of Hainault and its associated counties, in right of his wife, which in whole or part he promised to Langley and his heirs: this claim was opposed by William V's brother, Albert of Bavaria, who was ruling William's possessions on account of his insanity, and aimed to secure the succession for himself. Brabant was ruled by the emperor's brother Wenzel in right of his wife Jeanne: the clause in the Treaty of Dover by which Edward promised to support Margaret of Flanders' succession rights in Brabant and Limbourg was inimical to Wenzel's interest, as it was to his brother's imperial rights. Consequently, in the 1360s, the rulers of Hainault, Brabant and the Empire inclined towards Charles V of France.[15] However, Edward's relations with the imperial powers did not reach a critical stage, since the Treaty of Dover remained unfulfilled, and he negotiated with Albert of Bavaria over his claim to Hainault in a moderate spirit; there were plans for Albert to visit the English court, which materialised in 1367; he was received amicably.[16] But when war broke out between England and France in 1369, Edward had only two firm allies in the region – his nephew Edward duke of Guelders, and William duke of Juliers, who in 1367 did homage to the king in London and received arrears of his pension of 1,000 marks *p.a.*[17] In September Gaunt's army at Calais was joined by William of Juliers and 1,000 troops, from Brabant and Limbourg as well as from Juliers.[18] According to Froissart, Gaunt planned to persuade the dukes of Guelders and Juliers to join him on campaign in 1370, but his energies that year were to be concentrated in another sphere, Aquitaine, and in 1371 the duke of Guelders was killed in battle at Baestweiler, fighting against Wenzel of Brabant.[19] There were lesser Netherlandish lords who supported the English. Among Gaunt's captains in 1369, and influential in his counsels, was Robert of Namur, who had been married to Queen Philippa's sister Isabella. This distinguished veteran and crusader, who had done homage to Edward in 1347, had the annuity of 1,200 florins granted then to him and his heirs confirmed in 1376.[20] Jean de Janche, lord of Gommegnies, was appointed captain of Ardres in the March of Calais by Gaunt in 1369 and contracted to serve, leading a retinue of 120, on his 1373 expedition.[21] In Richard II's first parliament he was convicted of treason, for having negotiated the surrender of Ardres to the duke of Burgundy, but his execution was respited, possibly because he was regarded as a useful Hainaulter contact, and enjoyed Gaunt's patronage.[22] In 1381 the duke gave him a New Year's present, and he long continued to receive a royal annuity.[23]

Edward strenuously sought Albert of Bavaria's alliance against Charles V or, at least, his goodwill in their conflict. In June 1372 envoys were appointed to renew with Albert the alliance which Edward had had with his brother and to renounce on behalf of the king and his sons the claim on Hainault through Philippa. Albert, though concerned to maintain good relations with England, tended to remain neutral, usually with a pro-French bias: Louis de Male, count of Flanders and Wenzel of Brabant followed similar policies in the early 1370s.[24]

Gaunt played a part in cultivating good relations with the Netherlandish princes in the period 1375–81. It is likely that in his father's last years and the first years of Richard's minority, Gaunt, as a senior member of the king's family and as the Crown's most important military contractor, exerted an important influence on foreign policy. But it was not a dictatorial one. In the minority he had to take account of the opinions of the community of the realm, particularly as articulated by the earls who frequently attended the council. With them and their families Gaunt had and was cultivating close links; apart from Walsingham's anti-Gaunt invectives, there is little evidence of disagreements about foreign policy in this period – they were certainly negligible compared to those that surfaced in the 1380s. Gaunt and his fellow councillors were heavily influenced by some of Edward III's expedients and objectives. They flexibly pursued a 'grand design', attempting to secure alliances in the Empire (particularly among Netherlandish dynasties), Brittany and the Iberian Peninsula as the principal means of putting pressure on the French Crown. Gaunt's Spanish ambitions were not given primacy, but they were not neglected: they were interlocked with the aims of securing support along the western continental seaboard. Together, such alliances would, it was hoped, divert the French Crown from attacking English-held territories and make it amenable to seek an honourable peace. The preference for diplomatic rather than military pressure reflected a realistic appraisal of French military and naval superiority. It accorded well with Gaunt's disappointing experience in 1373 of trying to impose a military solution. But the 'grand design' did not produce quick results either: it placed too much faith on the ability of English diplomacy to secure effective and lasting allies.

In 1375, when Gaunt was in Bruges, he gave a golden goblet to Albert of Bavaria's wife, and in 1376 he was at Ghent with Albert, Louis de Male and Wenzel of Brabant for a series of jousts.[25] In 1377 Albert sent him a gift of horses.[26] Faced with the prospect of the renewal of war with France in 1377, Gaunt probably pushed for alliances with the Low Countries. In March, when he was highly influential in his father's government, his supporter Bishop Gilbert of Hereford was empowered to negotiate an alliance with the count of Flanders.[27] In September an embassy went in Richard's name to renew Edward's Flemish alliances.[28] In fact circumstances were more propitious in the Low Countries, as tension had arisen between Albert and Charles V over the former's friendly reception of his cousin, the anglophile duke of Brittany.[29] In 1378 Albert's subjects were helping the English war effort in spheres where Gaunt was promoting it. In the summer twelve Zealand ships helped to transport to Aquitaine the force commanded by Sir Thomas Trivet, destined to support Carlos of Navarre against the Castilians.[30] Two of Albert's leading officials, Jacques de Werchin, *sénéchal* of Hainault, and Gérard d'Obies, *prévôt* of Binche, took part in Gaunt's invasion of Brittany. The Sieur de Gommegnies, resurrected from his recent disgrace, was used as an intermediary with Albert.[31] It may be that Gaunt schemed to win over the Netherlandish princes by the ransom and marriage treaty made with their kinsman Waleran of Luxembourg, count of St Pol. On 1 April 1380 he married at Windsor Princess Joan's daughter Maud Courtenay. Gaunt was present and gave her as a wedding present a three-legged vessel, a 'hanap' and ewer.[32] St Pol received permission to leave England for a year: he intended to visit Charles V and his brothers, Louis de Male, Wenzel of Brabant and Albert of Bavaria. Charles had him arrested, accused of planning to hand over a castle to the English.[33]

Albert and Wenzel gave assistance to English negotiations for a much more significant alliance with the imperial Luxembourg family; the project for the marriage of Richard II and Anne of Bohemia, sister of Wenzel King of the Romans (i.e. ruler of the Holy Roman Empire) and niece of Wenzel of Brabant, an alliance promoted by Pope Urban VI as a coalition against supporters of the antipope Clement VII. An embassy which visited King Wenzel to discuss the marriage proposals, headed by Sir Michael de la Pole, was captured by brigands on its way back through Germany and had to be ransomed. Albert of Bavaria and Gaunt cooperated in helping to arrange for their release. In January 1380 Gaunt made an obligation to pay him 7,000 florins at Dordrecht for the ransom.[34] Perroy argued that the imperial marriage and alliance were promoted by a court party and that Gaunt and his brothers were kept out of the negotiations. Indeed, the match precluded the hope of a Spanish marriage for Richard, but Gaunt is likely to have appreciated that an imperial marriage was highly honourable for his nephew, and one which could bring both the king of the Romans and Netherlandish princes into a firm alliance with him. Such a threat to the French Crown might facilitate the end of the Schism and stimulate Castilian preparedness to settle Gaunt's claim honourably.[35] It is not clear that Gaunt was the moving spirit behind the marriage diplomacy. His influence was certainly not so rigidly excluded from the negotiations as Perroy argued.[36] Leading 'civil service' clerics at various times associated with him took part in them. The king's secretary Robert Braybrooke was appointed on an embassy in June 1380, to propose the conditions of marriage and alliance, and Bishop Gilbert of Hereford was on that appointed in December to conclude the terms: they both had Lancastrian connections.[37] In June Gaunt had rewarded munificently a knight of Wenzel who was being entertained at The Savoy.[38] In May 1383 he rewarded a valet of Sir Henry Poto, probably Wenzel's knight, who had presented to him his master's gift of a *destrier* (war-horse).[39] By then it was clear that the perpetual alliance with Wenzel had not borne the hoped-for fruit. But the attitude of the Netherlandish princes during its negotiations suggests that, if it had been effective, their orientation would have become more anglophile. The English embassy which set out in June 1380 for Wenzel's court was entertained at Cortenberghe by his uncle Wenzel of Brabant; Albert of Bavaria and Robert of Namur were among those there who jousted. When Anne of Bohemia passed through the Low Countries on her way to England in 1381, she was entertained by Albert and Louis de Male; Wenzel of Brabant obtained from the French Crown a safe-conduct for her sea passage.[40]

Thus from 1377 the English Crown followed a policy of seeking allies – the duke of Brittany, the count of St Pol, the king of the Romans – who, besides their own potential worth against France, might be able to persuade the Netherlandish princes to join a coalition. Though it cannot be proved that Gaunt was the architect of these policies, he and his associates were certainly involved in their implementation, and it is a fair assumption that he approved of and promoted them. Indeed, the three allies all proved broken reeds, and the Netherlandish princes, habitually reluctant to move against the Valois, became absorbed by new domestic concerns. In 1379 Ghent revolted against Louis de Male: Albert and Wenzel, faced too with urban discontent, though not on such a formidable scale, sympathised with and aided the count of Flanders.[41] It is likely that Gaunt (especially after his quarrels with the Londoners) was on Louis de Male's side, which would have put him at odds with a growing body of English opinion favouring alliance with Ghent. It was only in 1382 that the English Crown proffered help to Ghent, reversing the basis of its Netherlandish policy in the previous decade, whose aim had been to embrace the rulers of Flanders, Hainault and Brabant. The political scene in the Low Countries was, indeed, changing: besides the prolonged revolt of Ghent, there was the death of Wenzel of Brabant in 1383 and of Louis de Male in 1384, and the succession of Philip of Burgundy to Flanders. Flanders thus came firmly within the French political sphere; it looked as though Brabant might too.[42] In the autumn of 1383, when Gaunt recovered influence over foreign policy, he initiated a proposal to Albert for the marriage of his daughter Philippa to the latter's son and heir William count of Ostrevant – as a means of checking Philip of Burgundy's influence. However, according to Froissart, Albert was strongly influenced by Jeanne duchess of Brabant in favour of a Valois marriage alliance. When, early in 1385, envoys of Richard II took up the Lancastrian proposal with Albert, he brusquely rejected it, to Gaunt's annoyance (see p. 62).

In April Ostrevant married Philip of Burgundy's daughter Margaret, and Philip's son John married Ostrevant's sister Margaret – a great boost to Valois influence in the Low Countries.[43] This débâcle may have convinced Gaunt that there was no immediate hope of reviving traditional policies in the Low Countries (except in the cases of more marginal Guelders and Juliers) and that concentration on Iberian affairs was now the sole hope of defeating the French Crown. Conversely, Netherlandish courts may have concluded from Gaunt's disappearance to Spain that English influence in their affairs would be further enfeebled. The duke of Juliers allegedly tried to dissuade his son William duke of Guelders from implementing his 1387 alliance with England against Charles VI on the grounds that Gaunt was pressing for reinforcements to be sent to him in Gascony.[44]

In the 1390s Richard maintained the alliance with Guelders as part of the network of alliances in the Empire which, J.J.N. Palmer has shown, he built up in an attempt to counter the spread of Philip of Burgundy's influence. This was a version of traditional English policy there, a development which may not have seemed incompatible with Gaunt's own efforts from 1392 onwards to cultivate good relations with Burgundy, in order to assist the making of peace with France, the consolidation of his rule in Aquitaine and the launching of a crusade. In 1390 Richard had invited the count of Ostrevant, who had quarrelled with his father, to England, and invested him, together with the duke of Guelders, with the Order of the Garter. In 1391 Ostrevant did homage to Richard and received a retaining fee.[45] There is evidence once more in 1396 of close relations between the House of Bavaria and their Lancastrian kinsfolk – Bolingbroke's intention to support Albert and his son on a projected expedition against the recalcitrant Frieslanders.

It is probable that Gaunt, in the periods in the 1370s and 1380s when he had influence over foreign policy, promoted his father's aim of gaining the alliance of the Netherlandish rulers, sometimes as part of a larger coalition, embracing the duke of Brittany or the king of the Romans. But he failed to prevent the spread of Valois influence. This resulted fundamentally from Philip of Burgundy's marriage to Margaret of Flanders in 1369. Gaunt's attempts to counter this by cultivating his own family links with the Netherlandish princes were insufficient – as was the policy of marrying the king into one of the principal Netherlandish families. The revolt of Ghent threw the pursuit of such policies into turmoil. It is likely that Gaunt disapproved of this revolt and of growing

English support for it. In the early 1380s he may have felt at odds with a substantial part of the English political community over the issue. A crisis in English relations with the Low Countries (part of the larger failure of a grand design) first distanced Gaunt from foreign-policy aims widely canvassed in the community of the realm. In the wake of these failures, large sections of the community turned to Despenser's crusade as a remedy; Gaunt advocated the 'way of Spain'. In the circumstances the latter was a sensible option for the English Crown, threatening a sensitive French interest. But to many Englishmen it looked like Lancastrian self-interest. The crisis of 1381–3 over the Low Countries helped to form the opinion that Gaunt pursued foreign aims for his own aggrandisement rather than in the national interest.

Relations with Brittany

In the early years of Richard's reign, as in the Low Countries, Gaunt failed in Brittany to recreate the 'interest' once enjoyed by his father. Gaunt had close personal ties with the duchy. His first titled endowment was the earldom of Richmond, an appanage of the dukes of Brittany, which he held till the age of thirty-two. From boyhood he knew the Montfort claimant to the duchy, Duke John IV, who was about the same age as himself (born 1339–41) and who was brought up from 1345 under Edward III's guardianship. In 1361 John married Gaunt's younger sister Mary, who died within a few months. In maturity Gaunt probably derived knowledge of Breton affairs from one of the English noblemen who became best acquainted with them, William Lord Latimer (see p. 289). Gaunt first visited the duchy in 1366, on his way to Gascony, to support the Black Prince's Iberian intervention. He stayed then at John IV's court; not long before, the latter had married his kinswoman, the Black Prince's stepdaughter Joan Holand (d. 1384).[46] However much Gaunt and Duke John had in common, their relations were governed by a sense of self-interest: from their infancy Gaunt's possession of Richmond probably induced mutual wariness. In 1372 Duke John, driving a hard diplomatic bargain with Edward III, forced Gaunt to relinquish Richmond to him as part of the price of an Anglo-Breton alliance.[47] Yet the following year Duke John set out under Gaunt's command on an expedition one of whose objectives was to relieve French pressure on Montfort supporters in Brittany (see p. 232). In *Le libvre du bon Jehan, duc de Bretaigne*, generally hostile to Gaunt, the brotherhood in arms of the two dukes early on in the campaign is stressed:

185

Come deux compaignons et frères
De deux pères et de deux meres,
Et éussent tres bien promis
A touz jours mais estre amys.

But the idyll was broken: Gaunt became so enraged by and insulting about his companion's inability to help in the payment of his troops that the latter withdrew from the expedition.[48] Gaunt may have felt furious that his companion's contribution to the campaign was so negligible when he had been compelled to relinquish the honour of Richmond as the price of it. Relations between the two dukes probably remained frozen for several years. In 1375 Gaunt neglected John's interests in Brittany in favour of the wider one of implementing general truces. The terms which he agreed with the French at Bruges prevented the anticipated success of John's current campaign.[49] But, with the failure to make peace with France, Gaunt's attitude to the duke changed. In May 1377, when Gaunt was the dominant figure in his declining father's government, a mission was sent to John IV in Flanders: he contracted to serve with a retinue of 600 in the proposed expedition under the command of Richard prince of Wales, assembling in June; in the autumn John participated in an English naval expedition, and on 1 December Gaunt was among the witnesses and guarantors of his agreement with Richard, leasing Brest to the Crown for the duration of the war.[50] Gaunt's leadership of an army to besiege St Malo in 1378 showed his commitment to the duke's cause and to the strategy of controlling the major Breton ports (see pp. 226–7).

Duke John was re-established in his duchy in the summer of 1379 with the support of an English army and he was accompanied there by English ambassadors who had instructions to negotiate a treaty with him and his subjects.[51] In December another expedition set out for Brittany, commanded by Sir John Arundel; it included the Lancastrian retainers Sir Thomas Banastre and Sir Roger Trumpington.[52] Next year Duke John sent envoys to negotiate an alliance with Richard; they also received powers to negotiate with Gaunt, who in March appointed Bishop Gutiérrez, Lord Latimer and the Lancastrian councillors Sir John Ypres and Sir Robert Swillington to negotiate an alliance with the envoys. The text of this, if it was made, is not known, but a perpetual alliance with the English Crown was concluded against its French adversary, John agreeing to receive expeditions led by Richard in his duchy.[53] It is hard to see why Duke John should have contemplated a separate negotiation with Gaunt, unless it was in the latter's capacity as king of Castile, and had a bearing on his aspirations as such. Therefore Gaunt probably regarded John's entry into Charles VI's allegiance in January 1381 as a betrayal of obligations to himself as well as to Richard and Thomas of Woodstock (the latter then being in the duchy with an army). Duke John had been designated in English policy to provide ports which were both barbicans for the defence of England and sallyports for the invasion of France, and to be a link with both Netherlandish and Iberian interests. Not surprisingly, the English council now performed a volte-face, opening negotiations with the prisoners Jean de Bretagne, count of Penthièvre, rival claimant to the duchy, and his brother Guy, both then in the custody of Gaunt's retainer Sir John Dabridgecourt. Gaunt was heavily involved in this move, perhaps its instigator. In 1381–2 the agent of a Florentine banker came to England to discuss terms for Jean de Bretagne's ransom and left after ascertaining Gaunt's intentions. The royal council offered Jean de Bretagne marriage to Gaunt's daughter Philippa in return for his and his brother's acceptance of Richard's allegiance, according to Froissart.[54] The possibility of such an English-backed threat, as well as the desire to recover Richmond and Brest, probably inclined John IV in favour of an Anglo-French accord. In 1383 he helped to mediate the Anglo-French truce negotiated by Gaunt after the débâcle of Despenser's crusade.[55] But the failure of the 1384 peace negotiations once more made John a belligerent on the French side. In 1386 his forces were heavily besieging the English garrison at Brest, which Gaunt relieved on his way to Spain (see p. 227). That summer part of the fleet with which Charles VI intended to invade England was raised in Brittany and based at Lantréguier.[56] However, in 1387 Duke John's long-standing tensions with his vassal Olivier de Clisson reached a crisis; the following year the duke negotiated an alliance with the English government which resulted in the earl of Arundel's expedition. But Arundel did not receive the agreed Breton support; Jean de Montfort had changed his mind, submitting his dispute to the French royal council. Gaunt, as lieutenant in Aquitaine, likewise failed to cooperate with Arundel.[57] The two dukes may now have recognised their mutual interest in promoting peace. In the 1390s Gaunt looked to John to secure communications to his duchy of Aquitaine, and John looked to Gaunt to work for the return of his lordships in the English Crown's hands. In the years 1393–5 plans were discussed for a Lancastrian marriage for the duke's daughter Marie: in 1395 Gaunt visited the ducal court and on 25 November the dukes made an alliance for mutual support and dynastic alliance. This was the high point in their relationship; but no marriage took place.[58] The decline of Gaunt's rule in Aquitaine made him less concerned about Breton goodwill, and the decline of his influence on English foreign policy, and the making of a long Anglo-French truce, lessened John's dependence on Gaunt's goodwill.

Gaunt played a leading part in shaping Anglo-Breton relations. His policies were determined by a variety of personal and political factors – his lengthy and in some respects difficult personal relationship with John IV, the conviction of English policy-makers (which he shared) that Brittany was crucial to the control of the western seaboards of France and Spain, and John's own tortuous policies, determined by the strength of his domestic enemies as well as of the rival Crowns. Gaunt's most notable part in Anglo-Breton relations was his participation in the attempts to bring Duke John and his duchy firmly into the English camp (1377–81). Since they failed, it is easy with hindsight to condemn them. But, useful as access to the Breton ports was in English strategy and communications, it may be that English policy-makers (including Gaunt) placed too high a value on the Breton alliance. The French Crown could never, indeed, regard English influence in Brittany with indifference, but it had powerful supporters there who could be used to put pressure on the duke. Perhaps it would have been more profitable for the English if the forces sent to Brittany in 1378–80 had instead been used to support Gaunt's claim in Spain, where the French Crown was highly sensitive to threats to its allies. But the domestic political situation in England after Richard's accession prevented Gaunt from promoting Iberian intervention except as part of wider designs.

Gaunt's roles in Aquitaine and in relations with the Valois princes

Gaunt's long-standing acquaintance with the duke of Brittany is paralleled by his relations with the brothers of Charles V, the dukes of Anjou (d. 1384), Berry and Burgundy, whom he first got to know when they were hostages in England for their father John II's ransom in the early 1360s, and with whom he was frequently to negotiate, as well as fight, over several decades.[59] His friendships with them and with other French nobles were to be important in getting the peace process rolling in the 1390s. It is perhaps not too fanciful to surmise that Gaunt had a particular empathy with the magnificent Burgundy and Berry (reflected in Froissart's accounts of their amicable exchanges at conferences) and that his ambition to rule the duchy of Aquitaine was partly inspired by the desire to be a princely holder of an appanage like them. Gaunt was at home in the French courtly world, as Froissart's references to him frequently imply, and as does the presence in his household of knights and esquires with a French background.

He first became a landowner in France in the 1360s through his marriage to Blanche. who inherited lordships in Champagne, including Beaufort (now Montmorency) and Nogent-sur-Marne.[60] He acquired properties in Aquitaine in October 1370, during his first extended stay of fifteen months in the duchy; they were rewards from the Black Prince for undertaking the lieutenancy in Aquitaine, intended too to strengthen Gaunt's control of its defences. Three days after the prince's grants, by an agreement between them made at Cognac, Gaunt undertook to hold the lieutenancy until 24 June 1371, or to terminate his tenure before then, if his and his soldiers' pay fell into a month's arrears.[61] The prince had given him and his heirs male the lordships of La Roche sur Yon in Poitou and Bergerac in Gascony.[62] La Roche, on the northern frontier of maritime Poitou, had been rapidly lost and then recovered when war commenced in 1369.[63] Bergerac was the key to the control of the Dordogne valley: its grant to Gaunt was especially appropriate as it had been captured by Duke Henry of Lancaster in 1345 and granted to him in tail male by Edward III in 1347.[64] Both lordships were potentially lucrative. In 1363 the annual rents accruing to La Roche were estimated at 2,000 florins and, when the war started again, its garrison collected 'ransoms' from the lands of neighbouring lords in the Valois allegiance. Just before Gaunt left Gascony, at La Rochelle on 25 September 1371, he witnessed an agreement with Sir Thomas Percy, *sénéchal* of Poitou, Sir John Harpeden, *sénéchal* of Saintonge and the Poitevin Sir Reynaud Vivonne that they would hold La Roche during the present war for a rent of 500 marks sterling.[65] It fell to the duke of Anjou in 1373.[66]

In January 1371 Gaunt had entrusted the castle at Bergerac to Heliot Buada.[67] The prince's grant of Bergerac to Gaunt was confirmed by Edward III in 1376 and Richard II in 1377.[68] With the renewal of the war, the lieutenant in Aquitaine, Sir Thomas Felton, strengthened the town's defences and garrison, captained by Bertrand Buada. Felton anticipated an attack by the duke of Anjou: Bertonquat Dalbret was retained with a retinue to strengthen the local defences. That summer the siege was joined by the duke of Anjou and by Bertrand du Guesclin and Louis de Sancerre, the constable and marshal of France. Felton's attempts to disrupt the siege led to his defeat at Eymet (1 September): Bergerac promptly capitulated, though Dalbret and his retinue evaded surrender.[69] In May 1381 Gaunt had heard that Piers and Niot Buade were able to return Bergerac to the English allegiance; he ordered them to deliver it to Dalbret, whom he appointed guardian.[70] These measures show his continuing interest in Bergerac, as does his retaining till his death of Arnold Buade, presumably a member of the same family.[71]

During Gaunt's lieutenancy in Aquitaine in 1370–1, he had attempted to strengthen the crumbling defences of the great appanage

189

which his father had gained in 1360. He undertook one major military operation in person, the siege of Montpon in Périgord, whose capture by the Breton garrison which the duke of Anjou had placed in Périgueux threatened Bergerac's communications with Libourne and Bordeaux. Gaunt was investing the castle in January 1371; despite the determination of Anjou and Burgundy to relieve it, they were too slow to prevent its capitulation the following month. Gaunt, having garrisoned Montpon, disbanded his army and returned to Bordeaux. He turned a blind eye to the depredations of the free companies, whose services he needed.[72] In the spring he was much concerned with strengthening the defences of the parts of Aquitaine to the north of Bordeaux, Saintonge and the large and vulnerable province of Poitou. He dated a warrant at Niort in central Poitou on 6 April; then it was that he probably ordered purveyors to provision the town and castle.[73] In May he was further south, in Saintonge, securing communications between Poitou and the Bordelais. He dated warrants at Pons on 7 May and at Saintes, farther north, on the 13th; he doubtless went to Pons to secure and garrison it, for its lord had gone over to the French; however, his wife remained stoutly faithful to the English allegiance.[74] Gaunt's gift to 'la dame de Pontz' of a golden goblet on whose lid was a white hart reflects his admiration for the lady.[75] His subordinates had mixed fortunes after he gave up the lieutenancy. In August Sir Thomas Percy led a force including Sir Mauburney de Linières (whom Gaunt retained that year) and some of the mercenary free companies; this force captured Moncontour in Percy's *sénéchausée* of Poitou. But in Rouergue, in south-east Aquitaine, Bertrand du Guesclin, constable of France, captured English-held places.[76] Gaunt had only the resources to shore up temporarily the precarious English control over Aquitaine, which was to crumble away, leaving not much more than Gascony itself, in 1372–3.

Gaunt's awareness of the problems helps to account for his receptivity to papal diplomacy. On 19 January 1371 Pope Gregory XI had written to Charles V, urging him to avoid hindrance to the peace which Gregory was negotiating between him and Edward III, by forbidding his brothers to attempt in person the relief of Montpon, then being besieged by Gaunt. In April Gregory wrote to Gaunt saying that he had received the duke's letters from Jean de Reveillon, bishop of Sarlat (one of the nuncios he had sent to Bordeaux) on the subject of peace: the pope commended what Gaunt had done to that end.[77] Gregory was keenly aware of the ills the Church was suffering in Aquitaine as a result of Gaunt's struggles with the French there. In June Gregory replied to letters from Gaunt in which the latter had argued against the citation to the papal court of Thomas Percy and the marshal of Aquitaine, Guichard Dangle, among others, to answer for the seizure and death of the abbot of St Cyprien (Périgord). This and other outrages of which Gregory complained probably resulted from Gaunt's policy of allowing latitude to the free companies.[78] He had pressing motives for wishing to give up the lieutenancy and return to England. On 21 July he discharged himself from it, declaring that the king and Black Prince had not sent him any pay for six months. He had borrowed money to pay wages rather than exact impositions: if he held office any longer, he would have to live off the country at great charge, which would not be honourable to the king and Black Prince or profitable to the country. He was ready to defend the land as long as he remained there.[79] According to Froissart, Gaunt was anxious to report on the state of Aquitaine to Edward and his nobles, and hoped to return there in 1372 with a force sufficient to reconquer what had been lost. His marriage in September to Constance of Castile gave him another incentive to return: he wished to be publicly accepted in England as king of Castile. He returned in November 1371.[80]

Gaunt next visited Aquitaine about two years later, staying in Gascony, exercising the lieutenancy again, for five months or so. He arrived at Bordeaux in December 1373, at the end of his epic ride with an army from Calais. Even before he reached English-held territory, when he was at Brive la Gaillarde (Limousin) early in December, he set up a mission to Gregory XI to encourage him to revive the languishing peace process.[81] The precariousness of the English hold on Gascony, as well as Gaunt's failure to achieve victory, probably reinforced his conviction of the need for a compromise peace. He was shocked by the situation there: in his own words, he 'found the country in great mischief everywhere'.[82] During his stay, mainly at Bordeaux, he faced the same problems over supporting his troops as in 1371, magnified by the shrinkage of the area of ducal rule and the current dearth and dearness of food in the Bordelais.[83] The Anonimalle Chronicler says that his soldiers could not find enough victuals and fodder, and that Gaunt forbade them to take victuals without payment. Since wages were lacking, men and horses perished. The common soldiers petitioned either to be led into enemy territory or to be allowed home. But Gaunt refused them licence, 'to the great confusion and mischief of many'. Some of the common soldiers paid for their own shipping home; others, and knights and squires besides, were reduced to begging, 'poorly arrayed and attired'.[84] Gaunt raised loans, for example, from the cathedral chapter at St André at Bordeaux and from Aquitaine King of Arms.[85]

As well as trying to keep himself and his forces afloat in Gascony, Gaunt conducted vigorous diplomacy. A truce was negotiated with

Du Guesclin to last into May 1374.[86] In January a Lancastrian embassy arrived in Barcelona with the objective of promoting an alliance with Pere III of Aragon.[87] Gaunt scored one considerable diplomatic success, which at least relieved his financial position: he lured Gaston Fébus, count of Foix, from his neutrality. Two instruments were drawn up, dated Dax, 19–20 March 1374. One was a marriage contract for the count to marry Gaunt's daughter Philippa; the other an undertaking by the count to lend Gaunt and his retinue captains 12,000 florins of Aragon, receiving the château of Lourdes in pledge.[88]

In view of Gaunt's diplomatic offensive, it is not surprising that Charles V of France was reluctant to confirm the truce made by Du Guesclin. Gregory XI still strove to mediate. In his instructions to the patriarch of Jerusalem and the archbishop of Bordeaux, for their mission to Gaunt to promote negotiations, he said that the latter and Anjou were reported to be preparing to renew hostilities.[89]

But in April 1374 Gaunt returned to England – not much more than a month before the truce was due to expire. An indenture he made at Bordeaux on 4 April with the noted English mercenary John Cresswell and Geoffrey St Quinteyn shows his determination to support remaining isolated English garrisons in provinces which had been lost since 1369. These captains had long held Lusignan, an important strategic position on the route from Niort to Poitiers; they now undertook to continue to hold it till 1 September, in return for 6,000 florins (Avignon).[90] It was a measure of the critical situation, needing resolution by the Crown, that Gaunt abandoned Aquitaine and the hopes of intervention in Spain.[91] But Gascon defences did not collapse after the truce ended, though Gaunt's attempts to strengthen English enclaves elsewhere in Aquitaine proved a failure. In June Charles V's ally Enrique of Castile invested Bayonne, but its stout defence, the deficiencies of the Castilian forces and the inability of the duke of Anjou to cooperate as planned saved Gascony from a serious threat of conquest. However, the duke of Bourbon easily recovered the places which Gaunt had taken and garrisoned in Bas Limousin. Lusignan fell to the French at the latest by the end of September 1374.[92] The count of Foix reverted to neutrality, though Gaunt still had hopes of him; in 1375 the duke sent him a New Year's present of a golden goblet, the pommel of whose cover was enamelled with ostrich plumes – the badge of the Black Prince, who had given it to his brother. English envoys sought the count's alliance with Edward III.[93]

It was to be over thirteen years before Gaunt set foot in Gascony again; his experiences as lieutenant in 1370–1 and 1373–4 had probably convinced him that it was impossible to defend Gascony and recover control of other parts of Aquitaine without the acquiescence of the French Crown, which would involve major concessions. One might have expected that his experience of grappling with adverse circumstances in Aquitaine would have led him to eschew further personal involvement there. This does not seem to have been the case; the proposals discussed at Bruges in 1375–6 for his tenure of whole or part of the duchy indicate his predilections. Dr Palmer has argued that his tenure of Aquitaine (on one set of terms or another) was to be a constant proposal in negotiations for a final settlement up to 1394.[94] His concern for the duchy's security (at a time when he was preoccupied with Iberian intervention) is suggested by his remarks about the desirability of neutralising threats from 'frontier lords', the count of Armagnac and the lord of Albret, in the 1385 parliament (see p. 115). In October 1387, after his Iberian adventures, it was to Bayonne that Gaunt sailed. His decision to go to Gascony rather than England was, indeed, convenient for his negotiations with Castile. But his readiness to take over the lieutenancy again shows that the English Crown's problems in Gascony (which success in Spain might have helped to solve) were a constant preoccupation. Charles VI's councillors reacted with alarm to his reappearance in the duchy. On 19 December 1387 Charles ordered the levy of an *aide* in order to oppose his enterprises, alleging that he had recently arrived at Bordeaux and was raising soldiers there for the purpose of ravaging the realm.[95] There were indeed to be plans for an Anglo-Gascon force to take part in a multi-pronged invasion of France in 1388. On 2 June an Exchequer payment was recorded, made to Gaunt's clerk William Chisulden, for Sir Thomas Percy, in respect of wages and regard for 207 men-at-arms and archers sent with him to Gascony on the orders of the king and council, to accompany Gaunt on the king's service in war.[96] But on 18 August Gaunt's commissioners concluded local truces with those of his counterpart as lieutenant in Aquitaine, his old acquaintance the duke of Berry. Gaunt's pacific attitude contributed, as we have seen, to the failure of his brother Woodstock and the earl of Arundel (then dominant in English government) to maintain the offensive they planned in 1388, in which they intended that Gaunt and the duke of Brittany should cooperate with a force under Arundel's command.[97]

Symptomatic of Gaunt's francophile diplomatic leanings when in Gascony is the story Froissart tells of his sympathetic reception of the duke of Berry's proposal to marry Gaunt's daughter – clearly Catherine is meant. But her marriage into the Castilian House of Trastamara was the lynchpin of Gaunt's Iberian diplomacy. In this instance Froissart's apparent mistakenness is particularly surprising, for he was within a year or so in courtly circles well placed to inform him – he was at Orthez visiting the count of Foix from November 1388 to the beginning of 1389, when he went to Bordeaux in company with knights and esquires from Béarn and from the count's household, to watch a tournament held in Gaunt's presence. Various explanations are possible. Berry may indeed have made his proposal, in order to sow distrust between Gaunt and Juan I of Castile; alternatively, the story may have been spread by Lancastrian knights in order to persuade the Castilians that the French were nearer to *rapprochement* with the English than French envoys to Juan implied.[98]

Froissart's testimony to the presence of Lancastrian knights at Orthez and of Béarnais knights at Bordeaux reflects the close relations which Gaunt once again struck up with Gaston Fébus. By an indenture dated Orthez, 6 April 1389, Gaunt undertook on Richard's behalf and on his own as lieutenant to aid the count's wars against the francophile count of Armagnac and lord of Albret with 300 men-at-arms (at Foix's costs), if there was war or truce between England and France. Gaston-Fébus reciprocally agreed to help Richard against these lords with 200 men-at-arms. It may have been indicative of Gaunt's expectations that provision was made in case of an Anglo-French peace and the transfer under its terms of Armagnac and Albret to the English allegiance.[99]

Thus as lieutenant in Aquitaine in 1388–9, Gaunt was more successful than on previous occasions in stabilising the English Crown's position. He secured the alliance of a powerful southern neighbour against potential local threats, after taking measures which reduced the threats from Castile and France. Particularly in the days before he left for England, he was concerned with tidying up internal matters – reassuring the mayor and jurats of Bordeaux about their liberties, granting them the right to a levy for bridge repairs (23 October) and some minor building and trading permissions (given 'on board our ship', 25 October). Four days later he promulgated an *ordonnance* which categorised restrictions on benefit of clergy enjoyed by clerks who did not live in accordance with canonical rules.[100]

The contrasts between Gaunt's successes in Gascony and his recent vicissitudes in Spain and Portugal, together with his abandonment of his claim to the Castilian throne, may have rekindled his ambitions to become duke of Aquitaine. There is no evidence that he was anxious, as in 1371 and 1374, to return from Gascony to England. The initiative for his return appears to have come from Richard himself. According to a report to the royal council, the king sent a messenger to Gaunt, commanded to tell him that the king greatly desired his presence in England 'for the profit and honour of the King and his realm'. The duke responded by arranging to sail before 1 November

1389. But if he was unable to do so conveniently (*bonement*) he would do so before Candlemas (2 February 1390). If the king wished him to come in haste, he requested letters patent permitting him to travel overland through France, to avoid suspicion being cast on him in future by the people – an indication of his sensitivity to popular attitudes to his foreign involvements. The council approved the grant of such a patent: in July 1389 the Crown paid £100 and 200 marks to his officials to defray the costs of his voyage, the latter sum for the hire of six ships and a barge.[101] Gaunt returned in November. Once in England, he was not slow to promote his Gascon ambitions; on 2 March 1390 Richard granted him the duchy for life, to hold of the king and his heirs in their capacity as kings of France, suspending but not revoking the privileges conferred by Richard's predecessors that the duchy should not be separated from the English Crown or placed in other hands than the king's. Richard reserved to himself and his heirs (as kings of France) 'the direct lordship, sovereignty and resort'.[102] It is probable that Richard made such a radical change in the duchy's status in order to demonstrate to the French Crown the seriousness of his intent to negotiate a final settlement in which French sovereignty over the duchy and Gaunt's life-tenure of it would be key elements.

But Richard, Gaunt and the other royal councillors apparently failed to anticipate that the separation of the duchy from the English Crown would arouse protracted opposition from Gascon communities – especially Bordeaux – as they perceived it as a threat to their liberties. The attempts of Gaunt's lieutenant Sir William Scrope to reassure the Gascons were unavailing. A delegation petitioned the king against the terms of the grant. But he would not revoke it; by letters patent (23 November 1390) he reiterated that the grant only suspended the duchy's connection with the English Crown and did not affect their other liberties.[103] The delegation gained one important concession – but one which in the long run probably exacerbated relations between Gaunt's lieutenants and the Gascons. The king revoked the resumption of grants of ducal lands and revenues, thus depriving the Lancastrian regime of some of the patronage necessary to build up its interest in the duchy. Gaunt was keen to give his retainers and favourers a stake in Gascon lands and offices. In January 1390 his secretary William Kettering received a royal grant of property in Bordeaux;[104] in March, newly created duke, he granted Mauléon and Soule (Béarn) to Carlos II of Navarre's *alferiz* Charlot de Beaumont, on condition that Beaumont entered his fealty.[105]

Soon after Christmas 1390 the king sent his secretary with the Gascon delegates to Gaunt to inform him of the decision on resumptions. The duke was furious at having his hands tied:

195

on seeing and examining the documents and learning the king's decision, the duke addressed the Aquitanians at great length and with scant courtesy and then read out to them and forthwith tore up the king's patent granting him the duchy of Aquitaine.[106]

There may have been some calculation in this angry display: in March 1391 the Three Estates of Gascony responded prudently to Richard's assurances, accepting Gaunt as duke, subject to his and Scrope's recognition of their rights.[107] In September Gaunt, addressing the barons of Gascony and jurats of Bordeaux, ratified Scrope's confirmation of these rights in his name on first taking possession of the duchy.[108]

However, opposition to the authority of his lieutenants continued; their attempts to win support backfired. In 1392 the appointment of Pèlerin du Vilar (who later claimed to have been Gaunt's servant and loyal subject) as mayor of Bayonne aroused opposition. An appeal was made to the king, who by signet letter again confirmed the continuance of the link with the English Crown. Vilar was relieved of office.[109] When Gaunt appointed Sir Henry Percy as lieutenant in succession to Scrope in 1393, he was admitted to Bordeaux, according to Walsingham, only as king's lieutenant.[110] The following year the Three Estates, meeting in Bordeaux, entered into a union by which they refused to recognise Gaunt's authority as duke. Richard would have no truck with defiance. In September 1394 he confirmed the terms of Gaunt's 1390 grant and annulled adherence to oaths rejecting it.[111] In November Gaunt set sail with an army of 1,500 for the duchy.[112]

Uncertain of his reception at Bordeaux, he prudently landed further down the Gironde estuary: he was at Libourne, to the east of the city, on 1 December.[113] According to Froissart, the Gascon lord Jean de Grailly told him that the duke 'became very thoughtful and foresaw that the business he was come upon would not be so soon settled as he had first imagined or had been made to understand'.[114] He skirted round Bordeaux and refrained from attempting to exercise ducal authority there. By letters patent dated 9 January 1395 at Lormont (just outside Bordeaux), he declared his intention to go and live at St Sever, passing through Bordeaux on the way there, but without prejudice to civic rights.[115] Three days later, at St Sever, he confirmed rights and privileges to all who recognised his authority or would do so by 2 February.[116] But this failed to undermine the union, and he lived in deteriorating conditions at St Sever 'at great discomfort' to himself and his men, as he declared on 13 March, setting forth his intention to reside in Bordeaux and his agreement, at the prayer of the jurats and commune, not to exercise ducal authority while he

was there.[117] On the 22nd he confirmed his agreement to the terms
under which the estates would recognise his authority. There were to
be no condemnations or punishments for offences against the king
and Gaunt; reparation was to be made for their officials' violations of
franchises, and future restrictions on their activities were categorised.
The parties to this agreement were to seek approval for it from the
king.[118] In fact the Gascon communities were to make one more
effort through a delegation to the king to overturn Gaunt's authority
– and this time they came near to success. The official record of the
great council held at Eltham on 22 July 1395 to consider the case,
and the information about its proceedings ferreted out by Froissart
(who was present at court), show that expert legal opinion asserted
that Bordeaux was inalienable from the English Crown, and that the
nobles present were inclined to accept this opinion.[119] In fact Richard
did not in consequence revoke the 1390 grant. During the remaining
months of his stay in Gascony, Gaunt for the first time exercised
ducal authority in person. In a series of privileges and mandates
issued in October at Bordeaux, he dealt in a conciliatory manner
with the affairs of Dax. On petition, the number of its jurats was
decreased. A levy exercised by the mayor and jurats, of which Percy
as lieutenant had deprived them, was restored. The *sénéchal* of Landes
was ordered to allow the commune its ancient rights of imprisonment
and to settle the complaints of mayor, jurats and community about
the cathedral chapter's feudal rights.[120] For the rest of his life Gaunt
continued to be styled duke of Aquitaine (or Guienne). He is found
exercising authority as such in February 1397, when he granted a
privilege regarding tavern-keeping to Bordeaux, and ordered his
lieutenant in Guienne to stop *seigneurs* from making new impositions
on merchandise.[121] The lieutenants appointed successively in 1397 and
1398 were closely associated with Gaunt – his son John Beaufort,
marquis of Dorset and his leading retainer Thomas Percy, earl of
Worcester. Yet it appears that Gaunt's authority in practice had sunk
to a mostly nominal one. despite occasional Gascon fears that it might
be revived.[122] The success of the union in extracting concessions from
him and persuading a Great Council to query the validity of his grant
undermined the basis of his rule.

Gaunt has not been given sufficient credit for the skill with which
he defused the Gascon crisis which came to a head in 1394 – perhaps
because it has been perceived that his ambitions originated the crisis
and because he relied for too long on lieutenants to resolve it, rather
than returning to Gascony himself during its long gestation. Despite
long familiarity with Gascon matters, Gaunt had failed to appreciate
the Gascons' constitutional concerns, or the depth of feeling among
the English aristocracy – involved heavily for several generations in

the defence of Gascony – in favour of the sovereign claims of the English Crown there. Gaunt paid a heavy price in lost prestige for his display of political arrogance and ineptitude.

During his rule over Gascony as its duke Gaunt was more successful in dealing with specifically Aquitanian diplomatic affairs and, besides, during his visit of 1394–5, with a variety of diplomatic issues: officially the reason for his expedition was the conservation of the truces with the French Crown.[123] He had been concerned since the making of the regional truces with Berry in 1388 about the problems of their enforcement. Probably his eagerness to exercise direct influence over the duchy sprang in part from his desire to obviate threats to the Anglo-French peace process. He had had experience of similar frontier problems. There were parallels with the situation in the Anglo-Scottish borders which he had dealt with as lieutenant in the Marches in 1379–83. Kenneth Fowler has analysed the efforts of the English and French Crowns to deal with mutual infractions in the 1390s, and the involvement of Gaunt, Sir William Scrope, his lieutenant in Gascony, and of the mayor of Bordeaux Sir John Trailly, his retainer.[124] There were two aspects of the problem: infractions along the Gascon frontiers in Aquitaine, and the need to pacify *routiers* (mercenary bands) who held castles in other parts of Aquitaine, many of whom had at some time been in the English allegiance. The first aspect is illustrated by the activities of a Gascon frontier lord, the *seigneur* of Mussidan (himself, as Fowler points out, a conservator of truces). According to notes in a Périgueux communal register, in 1390 he seized the château of la Rolfie in Richard II's name. Twenty of his men made a *chevauchée* (mounted raid) up to the drawbridge of the pont d'Aguilterie at Périgueux, where they took four or five prisoners, and cattle. When the mayor and consuls complained to Mussidan, he alleged that he had only seized pledges for a sum owed to him by the city; far from promising restitution, he said that he would take more until he was quit.[125] However, the English government cooperated wholeheartedly with the French in trying to deal with infractions that year.[126] It may have been more ambivalent in attitude to the matter of the *routier* Mérigot Marchès in Auvergne: he had entered a truce and surrendered his castle there on promise of compensation and employment on the count of Armagnac's expedition to Italy; other *routiers* did likewise. Disappointed in the fulfilment of these promises, Marchès seized the castle of La Roche Vendeux and levied the borders of Auvergne and Limousin. The French royal council sent a force to besiege him; he appealed to Richard II and Gaunt, claiming that he was a subject of Richard, and asking them to have the siege lifted. Gaunt and the royal council were sympathetic; a mission was dispatched in the king's name and his uncle's, and for a time the duke of Berry responded to their requests. But he was unable to effect a composition; the castle fell and Marchès was captured, tried and executed in 1391. At his trial he claimed that at the age of sixteen he had paid homage to Gaunt in person 'and swore to serve the Duke and the King of England well and loyally for ever'; and that in August 1390 (during the siege), an envoy from Richard had arrived there, ordering him to leave the castle, but privately urging him to maintain the defence. About the same time he received an envoy with letters from Gaunt urging him to defend the castle and saying that he intended to mount an expedition against France.[127]

Froissart's and Marchès' own assertions about English backing for his actions are suspect. But it is credible that Gaunt tried to extricate Marchès because of his personal homage. Moreover, in 1389 Gaunt had allied with the count of Foix against Armagnac, and it is likely that the English government viewed with alarm in 1390 Armagnac's plans to invade Italy with the support of the *routier* captains (see p. 147). In these circumstances Richard and Gaunt, eager as they were to maintain the truces, may not have been displeased with Marchès' actions or inclined to treat him as expendable. In the early 1390s they were certainly eager for inducements to bring the count of Armagnac into the English allegiance. In 1392 the Crown appointed envoys to treat with the count on the matter, including prominent Lancastrian servants – Sir William Scrope, Sir John Trailly and Raymond Guillem.[128]

Another leading mercenary captain, Perrot le Béarnais, kept to the truce in 1390, but was infringing it in 1394. The French royal council was concerned lest Gaunt was prepared to countenance Perrot's seizure of castles and sent Marshal Boucicaut to complain to the duke. Froissart, who thought that Boucicaut's mission was prompted by French royal alarm at Gaunt's reappearance in Gascony, says that the latter went from Bordeaux to meet the envoys at Bergerac, where he entertained them in his château. The biographer of Boucicaut says that Gaunt received him 'with great honour and good cheer' and condemned Perrot's actions, carried out without his consent. He promised restitution and, indeed, compelled it, to the satisfaction of the French.[129] The cordiality between Gaunt and the French court is reflected in the warm tone of a letter from him to Charles VI (dated 20 August 1395), thanking the king for his favours to Gaunt's servants travelling through France and requesting future royal benevolence for them.[130]

While in Gascony, Gaunt carried on a variety of business with his princely Iberian neighbours (see pp. 134–5), as well as, presumably, concerting arrangements for his alliance with the duke of Brittany and his visit to the Breton court in November 1395 (see p. 187).

With an entourage of 300 horsemen and four carts he travelled from Brittany under Charles VI's safe-conduct through Normandy, arriving at Rouen on 9 December; there he was escorted to lodge in the archiepiscopal palace by the archbishop's brother, Jean de Vienne, admiral of France. Thence he journeyed to Calais for the voyage to England.[131] After his return he was kept informed about the negotiations which led to the Anglo-French treaties agreed on in Paris in July 1396 and took a prominent part in the conferences at Calais later that year.[132] For the remainder of his life Gaunt kept up his close links both with Gascony and the French princes. His receiver-general's account for 1397–8 records his payment of wages to Sir Richard Aston as his captain at the castle of Fronsac, and rewards to esquires of Charles VI and the dukes of Bourbon and Berry.[133]

Peace, the unity of Christendom and crusading

Gaunt's preoccupation in the 1390s with solving the Anglo-French problem over Aquitaine was not just a matter of Lancastrian aggrandisement, as the Westminster Chronicler came to believe, but part of his wider concern with the problems afflicting Christian society. Gaunt became convinced (along the lines argued by Philippe de Mézières) that the Schism could not be ended and the crusade commenced on a decisive scale until there was an Anglo-French peace. The renewal of crusading activity in the West in the 1390s aroused echoes from Gaunt's youth. He had attained his majority in 1361 soon after the restoration of peace, when, as we have seen, nobles' thoughts had turned to crusading. Urban V had preached the rescue of Jerusalem in 1363. The leader of the crusade, Pierre de Lusignan, king of Cyprus, visited England that year to gain Edward III's support and in 1364 met the Black Prince in Aquitaine. Among those whom Edward III sent to greet Pierre at Dover were nobles who were to be closely associated with Gaunt (if they were not so already) – the earl of Hereford, Lord Manny, Edward Lord Despenser and Sir Ralph Ferrers.[134] John Grey, lord of Codnor, subsequently in Gaunt's military retinues, was standard-bearer to the papal legate, Pierre Thomas, on the crusade and took part in the capture of Alexandria in 1365; in the indenture which Gaunt entered into with Sir Hugh Hastings in 1366, stipulations were made for the latter's service 'in case the said duke sets out against the enemies of God'.[135] Passages in *The Boke of the Duchesse* suggest a current crusading interest in the 1360s in ducal circles. The poet, dreaming about a May morning, hears birds singing so sweetly

That certes, for the toun of Tewnes [Tunis],
I nolde but I had herd hem synge.

In his elegy on Blanche, the Knight in Black declares that she did not
send lovers off frivolously on distant and hazardous feats,

> Ne sende men in-to Walakye [Wallachia],
> To Pruyse [Prussia] and in-to Tartarye,
> To Alisaundre, ne in-to Turkye . . . .[136]

Crusading, the tone of Chaucer's remarks imply, was a matter of
high seriousness in Gaunt's familiar circle. The duke was certainly to
contemplate going on crusade not long after this was written, though
circumstances had become unpropitious: a clause in Lord Neville's
indenture of service (November 1370) starts, 'Et si tallent preigne
le dit duc de travailler sur les enemy Deux'.[137] But when Leo of
Armenia, former king of Cyprus, came to the English court in 1385
to promote Anglo-French peace and a crusade against the Turks, he is
unlikely to have received more than polite evasions from Gaunt, then
planning his crusade against Castilian schismatics. The French royal
councillor Philippe de Mézières, writing *c*. 1389, pictured Gaunt at
Bayonne as 'an old Black Boar, duke of the Leopards', the scourge of
Castile, representing the disruptive behaviour of the princely family of
the Leopards (the Plantagenets), whose savagery disturbed the peace
of Christendom.[138] The Chronicler of St Denys also emphasised
Gaunt's brutality and destructiveness in Castile.[139] His subsequent
pacific efforts did not alleviate suspicions of him in Paris. The Treaties
of Trancoso and Bayonne (1387–8) show that Gaunt (perhaps inspired
particularly by the Virgin's miracles – see p. 246) had made the ending
of the Schism by negotiation a principal aim, now that he had failed
in 'the way of force'. But to the French council his attempt to arrange
a conference may have seemed like another ploy to isolate 'their'
pope, 'Clement VII'. It may not be coincidental that, according to
the Westminster Chronicler,

> there were reports at this time about a French knight who, while
> he was in the Holy Land, was bidden in a vision to visit all the
> Christian inhabitants of Europe, urging them to abandon their
> wars altogether and return to the unity of peace. This mission
> brought him to Bordeaux, where the duke of Lancaster (with
> whom, in pursuit of his purpose, the knight wished to travel
> to England) spent his Christmas [1388]).[140]

This knight is likely to have been an emissary of Mézières,

in fact, it sounds like Mézières himself. He probably received a sympathetic reception from Gaunt, but went away disappointed: the duke, absorbed in his Iberian diplomacy (potentially damaging to Valois and Clementist interests), was not prepared to accompany him forthwith to England. Hence perhaps the unflattering reference to Gaunt in *Le Songe du Vieil Pèlerin*. But in the following years French royal councillors were to recognise a convergence of Gaunt's views and their own on these questions. As J.J.N. Palmer has pointed out, French reports about his conversations on international affairs in the 1390s record his conviction that it was imperative to end the Schism – and that peace between England and France was a necessary precondition. His remark to a Clementist legate in 1393 that, once an Anglo-French peace was made, the former adversaries would be forced to put an end to the Schism or be exterminated, seems to allude to the Turkish menace.[141] Froissart reported how at the Amiens conference the previous year Charles VI himself supplemented Leo titular king of Armenia's discourse to Gaunt about the Turkish problem. Charles said that, if peace could be made between himself and Richard, he intended to attack Turkey in order to succour the king of Hungary and the emperor of Constantinople, and recover Armenia from the Turks. He urged Gaunt to promote his expedition when he returned to England.[142] Gaunt's family had, indeed, recently re-established the Lancastrian name for crusading against the infidels: his sons John Beaufort and Bolingbroke had respectively campaigned in North Africa and Prussia in 1390, the former under the command of the duke of Bourbon, who had been opposing Gaunt in Spain three years before then. Mézières (who promoted the Feast of the Presentation of the Virgin, reverenced by Gaunt's Carmelite friends) was to find him sympathetic to his aims.[143] When Mézières compiled a list of patrons of his proposed crusading Order of the Passion in 1395, Gaunt's name was among them. The duke's chamberlain Sir Richard Abberbury was listed among those who promised to join the order; so was the bishop of St David's, John Gilbert (d. 1397), who had at one time preached Gaunt's anti-schismatic crusade. Mézières' four 'evangelists' included Gaunt's retainer Othon de Graunson, who had often attended the duke.[144]

John Palmer has shown how in 1394–5 Gaunt cooperated closely with the dukes of Burgundy and Orleans in planning a joint crusade, eventually concerted with Sigismund of Hungary, and has argued that the army Gaunt took to Gascony was intended as his crusading contingent, whose leadership he was planning to hand over to his son John Beaufort.[145] But the military subcontract which Sir Matthew Gournay made in London in August 1394 for the service under him of Simon Raly esquire, accompanied by an archer, stipulated only military service with Gaunt in the duchy of Guienne for a year – about the time that Gaunt was there.[146] Beaufort did go on the crusade against the Turks in 1396 – and survived. The crusading army – which can be accounted the last notable western European force to go east on crusade – was commanded by a young man of about Beaufort's age, John de Nevers, son of Philip the Bold, duke of Burgundy. This army linked up with King Sigismund and his forces at Buda, the capital of Hungary, and crossed south of the Danube into Turkish-held Bulgaria. While the crusaders were besieging the town of Nicopolis, the Sultan Bayazid arrived with a relieving force. The impetuous tactics of the Westerners and Bayazid's sound generalship led to the capture or death of most of them – a disastrous end to the hopes of recent years. Gaunt was to die in the knowledge that the three causes he had espoused – peace, unity and the crusade – were not yet attained. In his opinion a final peace between England and France remained crucial for the wider objectives. He remarked in 1398 to Aymard Broutin, 'nothing substantial can be accomplished for the welfare of Christendom, unless the two kings make a final peace together'.[147]

Gaunt's diplomacy

Gaunt was unusual among later medieval English nobles in conducting his own foreign policy: he made treaties with the duke of Brittany in 1380 and 1395, with the kings of England and Portugal in 1386 and the king of Castile in 1388. Such treaties, made in his own name, resulted from his claim to Castile and his tenure of Aquitaine as duke. But, with the probable notable exception of the negotiations with Juan I in 1387–8, his foreign policy was usually decided and conducted in close concert with the king's council. Royal embassies to Iberian princes were sometimes partly composed of his retainers and had powers and sets of instructions from both king and duke. Iberian envoys to Richard, when not accredited to Gaunt as well, visited him informally.[148]

The diplomatic forms employed by Gaunt's English chancery were modelled on those of the Crown.[149] There is no evidence that his chancery compiled rolls or registers specifically of diplomatic documents. Gaunt relied for advice on questions of international law and right on experts such as the Gascon Master Raymond Guillem; occasionally he sought for advice from outside his habitual circles.[150] It is not clear whether he had one group of councillors to give advice on foreign policy. Doubtless he relied heavily on royal councillors and envoys, and he had his own servants and habitués who were expert on the affairs of particular regions. Juan Gutiérrez, from his entry into Gaunt's service in 1372 till his death in 1393, is likely to have been highly influential in advising him on Iberian affairs. Froissart attributes an influential role in the 1380s, up to the invasion of Castile, to the Duchess Constance. Sir Thomas Percy was a key figure in the making of the treaties with Castile (1386–8). He was one of several envoys used by Gaunt in the late 1380s and 1390s who probably influenced his policies in his foreign relations as duke of Aquitaine – others were Sir William Scrope and Sir John Trailly.

How successful was Gaunt in his conduct of foreign affairs? His diplomatic career, like his military one, can be seen largely as a series of failures, both to protect the interests of his paternal dynasty and to promote his more personal dynastic ambitions. When his influence over foreign relations was strong, during Richard's early years, he was unable to prevent the spread or consolidation of Valois influence in Spain, Brittany, Scotland and Flanders. Eventually he had to give up both his pretensions to the Castilian Crown and his subsequent attempt to rule Gascony as duke of Aquitaine. His efforts to make an Anglo-French peace in the 1390s failed.

Yet his achievements were more positive than this suggests. He played prominent roles in the making of Breton, Iberian, Netherlandish and imperial alliances in the 1370s and 1380s, some of which distracted French war efforts. In the same period he was frequently involved in truce and peace negotiations which provided some brief respites from and for long staved off Scottish attack. In the 1390s he made an outstanding contribution to bringing warfare with the French Crown to an end and to creating a climate of opinion in which peace might have been achieved.

In the previous decades Gaunt had constructed formidable alliances against Castile. Though these failed to win him its Crown, and though on occasion this conflict obstructed Anglo-French *rapprochement*, his policies helped to undermine Castile's effectiveness as a French ally. Relative Iberian neutrality in the fifteenth century owed a great deal to Gaunt.

From 1377 to 1389 the English 'empire' stretching from Roxburgh to Bayonne faced formidable threats; for much of this period an immature king provided uncertain leadership. Yet foreign threats were blunted and a general peace process was set in motion. A collapse of empire was averted, in contrast to what was to happen in the 1440s and 1450s. Gaunt's assiduity and expertise in diplomacy, as in war, were indispensable to this achievement. His policies helped to maintain England, in face of the resurgence of the French Crown and its allies, as the menacing imperialist power of the western seaboards of Christendom. In working for his family's and his own honour, he paradoxically sustained that nationalist English ethos which on occasion cast suspicion on him and which contributed to the decline of the ideal of Christendom, so beguilingly recast by Philippe de Mézières.

Notes and References

1 Luttrell A 1988: 143–53.
2 Mézières P de 1969; Iorga N 1896, pp. 490–2; Palmer JJN 1972, ch. 11.
3 Froissart J 1872, Vol. 14, pp. 314–15, 384–5; ibid. 1871, Vol. 15, p. 80. Woodstock was sympathetic to Mézières's plans for an international crusading Order of the Passion, promising to aid the order (Clarke M V 1937, p. 288 and n.).
4 Barnie J 1974, p. 102.
5 Froissart J 1872, Vol. 14, pp. 384–5; ibid. 1871, Vol. 15, pp. 80–1, 196–202.
6 *W.C.*, pp. 490–1, 516–19.
7 Jones M 1970, pp. 48–50.
8 Russell PE 1955, pp. 42, 50, 189.
9 Duncan AAM 1988; Ormrod WM 1987: 415; Nicholson R 1974, pp. 170–2.
10 Palmer JJN 1976: 356–7; Reading J de 1914, p. 186. For Urban V's protest in 1367 to Edward III about the claim, P.R.O. SC7/34/16, printed in *Foedera*, 1830, Vol. 3, pt 2, p. 830. Payment in connection with a bull concerning Gaunt's right in Provence is recorded in *J.G.R. 1372–6*, no. 935.
11 For examples of this usage (1364), *C.E.P.R. Papal Letters*, Vol. 3, pp. 10–11.
12 *Foedera*, 1825, Vol. 3, pt 1, p. 235; *C.P*, Vol. 12, pt 2, p. 177.
13 *J.G.R. 1379–83*, nos 39, 81; Lewis N B 1964, no. 25; Froissart J 1870, Vol. 11, p. 390.
14 Palmer JJN 1976: 339ff; Ormrod WM 1987: 415.
15 *Foedera*, 1830, Vol. 3, pt 2, pp. 750–1; Quicke F 1947, pp. 77–9, 83, 95.
16 *Foedera*, 1830, Vol. 3, pt 2, pp. 779, 830; Quicke F 1947, pp. 80–3.
17 Ibid p. 181n.
18 Sherborne J 1964: 720–1.
19 Froissart J 1869, Vol. 7, p. 443; Quicke F 1947, p. 86. In 1370 an English embassy was sent to Wenzel to try to revive the alliance with Brabant (*Foedera*, 1830, Vol. 3, pt 2, p. 892; Quicke F 1947, pp. 170–1).
20 Sherborne J 1964: 720–1; Froissart J 1869, Vol. 7, pp. 430ff; *Foedera*, 1709, Vol. 8, pp. 102–3; Quicke F 1947, p. 88.
21 P.R.O. E30/256; Sherborne J 1964: 728. Gommegnies had been Albert of Bavaria's lieutenant-general (Quicke F 1947, p. 92). In 1372 he was a member of an embassy from Edward to Holland, Zealand and Hainault (Mirot L and Déprez E 1899, p. 158).
22 *R.P.*, Vol. 3, pp. 10–12; Froissart J 1869, Vol. 8, pp. 404–8, 411–12; *H.A.*, Vol. 2, p. 342.
23 *J.G.R. 1379–83*, no. 557. For payment of Gommegnies' royal annuity, see, for example, P.R.O. E403/559/4.

24 *Foedera*, 1830, Vol. 3, pt 2, p. 947; Quicke F 1947, p. 173. For a series of English embassies to the Low Countries in 1369–73, principally to Holland, Zealand and Hainault, Mirot L and Déprez E 1899, pp. 186–9.
25 *J.G.R. 1379–83*, no. 1689; Vaughan R 1962, p. 18. For a gift from Gaunt to the count of Flanders' minstrels, *J.G.R. 1372–6*, no. 1661.
26 Ibid., no. 1807.
27 *Foedera*, 1709, Vol. 8, pp. 140–1.
28 *Foedera*, 1869, Vol. 4, p. 20.
29 Froissart J 1870, Vol. 11, pp. 282–5.
30 Mirot L and Déprez E 1899, p. 199.
31 Froissart J 1870, Vol. 1, pt 1, p. 285.
32 Ibid., 1869, Vol. 9, pp. 131–2; *J.G.R. 1379–83*, nos 83, 463.
33 Froissart J 1869, Vol. 9, pp. 132–3.
34 Perroy E 1933, p. 140; *J.G.R. 1379–83*, nos 925–6.
35 Perroy E 1933, pp. 147, 149–50; Russell P E 1955, p. 290 n.5.
36 Perroy E 1933, p. 147.
37 Butler LH 1952, pp. 64–6.
38 Perroy E 1933, pp. 145–51; *J.G.R. 1379–83*, no. 463.
39 Ibid., no. 803. Poto apparently accompanied Anne of Bohemia to England (Perroy E 1933, p. 155 n.7).
40 Quicke F 1947, pp. 402–5.
41 Ibid., pp. 307ff; Vaughan R 1962, p. 73.
42 For the background, Palmer JJN 1972, ch. 3.
43 Ibid., p. 58.
44 Froissart J 1869, Vol. 9, pp. 462–3.
45 Palmer JJN 1971, pp. 83–5.
46 Jones M 1970, p. 17 and n.5; Reading J de 1914, pp. 150, 292. I owe thanks to Professor Jones for information about Duke John's marriage to Gaunt's sister.
47 Jones M 1970, pp. 67–8, 176.
48 Charrière E 1839, pp. 490–3.
49 Holmes G 1975, pp. 45–6; Jones M 1970, pp. 78–9.
50 Alexander AF 1933, pp. 41–5; Jones M 1970, pp. 82–4 and 84n.
51 Mirot L and Déprez E 1899, pp. 203–4.
52 *A.C.*, p. 131. For their letters of protection and letters for another Lancastrian retainer intending to serve, Sir Hugh Hastings, *Foedera*, 1869, Vol. 4, pp. 69–70.
53 *Foedera*, 1709, Vol. 7, pp. 236–9; Jones M 1970, pp. 86–9. Richard's procurators included Latimer and Gaunt's retainer Richard Lord Scrope.
54 Brucker G 1967, p. 37.
55 Jones M 1970, p. 94.
56 Froissart J 1870, Vol. 11, pp. 359, 457.
57 Jones M 1970, pp. 107–12; Palmer JJN 1972, pp. 126ff.
58 Jones M 1983, Vol. 1 nos 930, 1033–5; Jones M 1970, pp. 135–6. Proposals for the 1395 alliance were probably negotiated on Gaunt's behalf by his envoys Sir William Par and Thomas Plays (P.R.O. DL28/32/21).
59 The duke of Berry was staying with John II at The Savoy in 1364 (Lehoux F 1966, Vol. 1 pp. 172–3). In Jan. 1366 Berry and Gaunt appeared in the White Chamber at Westminster to witness the duke of Bourbon's pledge to be a loyal hostage (ibid., pp. 191–2 and 192n; *Foedera*, 1830, Vol. 3, pt 2, pp. 782–3).

60 Armitage-Smith S 1904, p. 198; Somerville R 1953, p. 55. For Gaunt's grant of the keeping of Champagne lordships to John Wyn, dated The Savoy, 4 June 1365, C.C.C., 495 f16. Wyn surrendered Beaufort in 1369, entering Charles V's allegiance (Froissart J 1869, Vol. 7, pp. 324–5).

61 *J.G.R. 1372–6*, no. 9.

62 P.R.O. E101/178/19; *J.G.R. 1372–6*, nos 773–4; Delpit J 1847, nos ccxviii, ccxix.

63 Delachenal R 1928, Vol. 4, p. 43.

64 Fowler K 1969, pp. 56–7, 226.

65 *Foedera*, 1830, Vol. 3, pt 2, pp. 699, 701; *J.G.R. 1372–6*, no. 5. A petition from Gaunt to his father outlines the misdeeds of his first keeper of La Roche, to whom he had granted the castle, town and lordship after the capture of Limoges (P.R.O. C47/28/9/15). For his instructions to Percy about the vendage, *J.G.R. 1372–6*, nos 229–30, 966.

66 Froissart J 1869, Vol. 8, pp. 268–9; cf Delachenal R 1928, Vol. 4, p. 439.

67 *J.G.R. 1372–6*, no. 6. For payment for a certain Alvard de Guyane going to Bergerac, ibid., no. 1661.

68 Carte T 1743, p. 162; Armitage-Smith S 1904, p. 200.

69 Armitage-Smith S 1904, pp. 200–1; Alexander AF 1933, pp. 148–57. On 28 April 1377 a ducal warrant authorised payment of £16. 13s. 4d. to Eliote Buade, captain of Bergerac, a sum which his brother received (P.R.O. DL28/3/1 m4).

70 *J.G.R. 1379–83*, nos 522, 1095. Gaunt's confidence in the recapture of the town is reflected in his grant of revenue there (ibid., nos 523, 981).

71 Lewis NB 1964, no. 22; *C.C.R. 1396–9*, p. 450.

72 Froissart J 1869, Vol. 8, pp. 63–75; Delachenal R 1928, Vol. 4, pp. 351–3. Gaunt was party to an indenture dated 15 Jan. 'au siege devant Montpaon'; Gregory XI referred on 19 Jan. to his presence there (*J.G.R. 1372–6*, no. 6; *C.E.P.R. Papal Letters*, Vol. 4, p. 92). Gaunt dated a warrant at Bordeaux on 20 March (*J.G.R. 1372–6* no. 919).

73 Froissart J 1869, Vol. 8, pp. 77–8; *J.G.R. 1372–6*, nos 3, 777. Niort fell to Du Guesclin in 1373 (Delachenal R 1928, Vol. 4, pp. 439–40).

74 *C.E.P.R. Papal Letters*, Vol. 4, p. 94; Froissart J 1869, Vol. 8, p. 77.

75 *J.G.R. 1372–6*, no. 1090.

76 Froissart J 1869, Vol. 8, pp. 86–90; Delachenal R 1928, Vol. 4, p. 391. Montcontour was retaken by the French in 1372 (ibid., p. 424).

77 *C.E.P.R. Papal Letters*. Vol. 4, p. 92; Perroy E 1952, p. ix.

78 *C.E.P.R. Papal Letters*. Vol. 4, pp. 94–6.

79 *J.G.R. 1372–6*, no. 9.

80 Froissart J 1869, Vol. 8, pp. 107–8. Gaunt was at Bordeaux on 10 Aug.; after his marriage in the south at Roquefort early in Sept., he arrived at his embarkation port, La Rochelle, by 25th (*J.G.R. 1372–6*, nos 5, 778–80, 784, 786). For his departure see above, p. 48.

81 Perroy E 1952, p. xiv.

82 *J.G.R. 1372–6*, no. 42.

83 Boutruche R 1947, p. 210.

84 *A.C.*, pp. 74–5. Lord Basset left for England with his retinue without licence (Sherborne J 1964: 730n).

85 *J.G.R. 1372–6*, nos 1401, 1609. In 1374 Gaunt as lieutenant issued a *vidimus* confirming grants of privileges to the chapter of St André (A.N., *Inventaire Sommaire des Archives, Gironde, Inventaire des fonds de*

l'archevêché et du chapitre metropolitain de Bordeaux, sér. G.337).
86 Delachenal R 1928, Vol. 4, pp. 501–2.
87 Russell PE 1955, pp. 209–13.
88 A.N., *Arch. dép. Pyrénées–Atlantiques*, E410 (marriage settlement); Tucoo-Chala P 1959, pp. 306 and n., 353 (loan agreement). I owe thanks to Professor Michael Jones for the first reference.
89 Delachenal R 1928, Vol. 4, pp. 501–2; *C.E.P.L. Papal Letters*, Vol. 4, pp. 102, 131.
90 *J.G.R. 1372–6*, no. 42.
91 Russell PE 1955, pp. 212ff.
92 Delachenal R 1928, Vol. 4, pp. 440, 505–7.
93 Tucoo-Chala P 1959, pp. 306, 307 and n; *J.G.R. 1372–6*, no. 604; Carte T 1743, pp. 162–3.
94 Palmer JJN 1972, ch. 2.
95 A.N., Cartons des rois K73, no. 75; Douët-D'Arcq L 1863, Vol. 1, pp. 83–6 (no. xlii). On 29 March 1388 a royal exemption from subsidy referred to an intended expedition against Gaunt (A.N., Cartons des rois K73, no. 75).
96 P.R.O. E403/520/11.
97 Carte T 1743, p. 175;*Foedera*, 1709, Vol. 8, pp. 596–8; Palmer JJN 1972, pp. 126ff. Gaunt granted powers to his envoys to negotiate truces covering Aquitaine at Bayonne on 28 July (*Foedera*, 1709, Vol. 8, pp. 595–6). For the prolongation of the truces, A.N., Cartons des rois K53, nos 83, 85; Fowler K 1971, p. 197 and n.56.
98 Froissart J 1871, Vol. 12, pp. 22ff; Ibid., Vol. 13, pp. 110–16, 126–8, 132–4, 301–2. Lehoux F 1966, Vol. 2, pp. 232–3 is sceptical about Berry's alleged proposal; Palmer JJN 1972, pp. 128–9, 234–5 is prepared to accept it with corrections to Froissart's chronology.
99 P.R.O. E30/314; Tucoo-Chala P 1959, pp. 366–7. For the involvement of Gaunt's servants Sir William Scrope and Raymond Guillem in negotiating with the count of Foix, Baldwin JF 1913, p. 498. In Jan. and Feb. 1391 the Crown made payments to Gaunt towards reimbursing him for the 10,000 francs which he had paid to the count of Foix on the king's behalf (P.R.O. E403/532/13, 19).
100 *L.B.*, pp. 295–7, 300–1; A.N., *Archives de Landes. Inventaire des Archives de la ville de Dax*, Vol. 1, sér. E. suppl. 3, AA3.
101 P.R.O. E403/524/m12, 17; Nicolas NH 1834, Vol. 1, p. 14c.
102 *L.B.*, pp. 224–7 (no. lxv), 230–2 (no. lxvii).
103 Ibid., pp. 233–4 (no. lxviii).
104 Carte T 1743, pp. 176–7; *C.P.R. 1399–1401*, p. 74.
105 *D.C.*, pp. 221–2. Richard confirmed the grant in 1394. Beaumont was involved in the negotiations terminating the English lease of Carlos's port of Cherbourg. In 1392 Gaunt had granted a Gascon lordship to his knight William Par (*C.P.R. 1399–1401*, p. 74).
106 *W.C.*, p. 484–5; Vale MGA 1970, p. 5. Before Christmas 1390 a royal valet was sent to Eltham with memoranda and muniments concerning the duchy of Aquitaine which he was to deliver to Gaunt (P.R.O. E403/532/9).
107 Palmer JJN 1972, pp. 154–7.
108 *L.B.*, pp. 293–4 (no. xcvi).
109 Vale MGA 1970, pp. 32–4 and p. 32, n.4.
110 Carte T 1743, p. 179; *Annales*, p. 158.

111 *L.B.*, pp. 228–9 (no. xvi).
112 Palmer JJN 1972, pp. 92–3. The Crown undertook to pay 9,000 *m.* to the costs of the expedition, of which £4,000 were paid in Aug. 1394 (P.R.O. E403/558/20).
113 Armitage-Smith S 1904, p. 374 and n. Gaunt was at Libourne on 26 Dec. (*C.P.R. 1396–9*, p. 499).
114 Froissart J 1871, Vol. 15, pp. 148ff.
115 *L.B.*, pp. 253–4 (no. lxxx).
116 Armitage-Smith S 1904, p. 375.
117 *L.B.*, no. lxxxiii.
118 Ibid., pp. 259–67; Armitage-Smith S 1904, pp. 374ff. Gaunt dated documents at Bordeaux on 20 March (*C.P.R. 1396–9* p. 547) on 18 July and on 5, 12 and 15 Oct; at Dax on 7 Sept. (P.R.O. PL3/1/9; A.N., *Archives de Landes. Inventaire des Archives de la ville de Dax*, Vol. 1, sér. E. suppl. 1).
119 Baldwin JF 1913, pp. 504–5; Froissart J 1871, Vol. 15, pp. 165–6.
120 A.N., *Archives de Landes . . . Dax*, Vol. 1, sér. E. suppl. 1, A.A. 1.3.
121 *L.B.*, pp. 255–6, 268 (nos lxxxi, lxxxiv); cf ibid., pp. 214–15 (no. lx). On 6 July the king confirmed Gaunt's title as duke of Aquitaine for life (P.R.O. C61/105).
122 Ibid., (Dorset); Vale MGA 1970, p. 32 (Worcester).
123 P.R.O. E403/558/20.
124 Fowler K 1971, pp. 198ff.
125 A.N., *Départment de la Dordogne. Ville de Périgueux Inventaire Sommaire des Archives Communales*, p. 247 (F.F.92); Fowler K 1971, p. 201.
126 Ibid., p. 199.
127 Froissart J 1872, Vol. 14, pp. 159ff; Keen MH 1965, pp. 97–10; Fowler K 1971, p. 203.
128 Carte T 1743, p. 177.
129 Froissart J 1871, Vol. 13, pp. 151–3; Boucicaut 1819, p. 442.
130 A.N., J644/35/10; printed (wrongly dated) in Froissart J 1874, Vol. 19, pp. 581–2.
131 Cochon P de 1870, p. 196.
132 Legge MD 1941, pp. 137–8, 331–4.
133 P.R.O. DL28/3/5, f10v, 11r.
134 Froissart J 1868, Vol. 6, pp. 384–6.
135 Boehlke FJ 1966, pp. 267–8; Norwich, Norfolk R.O., Hastings MSS, MR 314/242x5.
136 Ll. 310, 1025–7.
137 Lewis NB 1964, no. 3.
138 Mézières P de 1969, Vol. 1, pp. 393–4.
139 *St Denys*, Vol. 1, pp. 444–5.
140 *W.C.*, pp. 374–5.
141 Palmer JJN 1968: 516–19.
142 Froissart J 1872, Vol. 14, pp. 386–7.
143 P.R.O. DL28/3/2. Pfaff RW 1970, p. 104.
144 Clarke MV 1937, pp. 286–8, 288n.
145 Palmer JJN 1972, pp. 197ff. On the orders of the dukes of Orleans and Burgundy, the former's chamberlain and secretary accompanied the envoys of Sigismund of Hungary to Gaunt in Gascony; they had arrived at the French court with letters inviting princes to aid the crusade which Sigismund intended to undertake (B.L., Add. Ch. 3373–4; Iorga N

1896, p. 488). Add. Ch. 3374 is a receipt for expenses incurred on the mission to Gaunt by Orleans' chamberlain Renier Pot.

146 Taunton, Somerset R.O., DD/WO, Trevelyan of Nettlecombe Papers 25/1. I owe thanks to Professor Ralph Griffiths for a transcript of the Gournay-Raly indenture. The Crown had financed Gaunt's service in Gascony for a year (P.R.O. E403/558/20).

147 Valois N 1901, Vol. 3, p. 623; Palmer JJN 1968: 519.

148 For a mission to Enrique III of Castile by Gaunt's knights Walter Blount and William Par on both his own and Richard's behalf, *D.C.*, no. 181.

149 The best examples are to be found in Palmer JJN and Powell B 1988.

150 For a letter from Gaunt to the chancellor of Oxford University requesting him to send two doctors of canon and civil laws to advise him in negotiating with France, Lawrence CH 1984, p. 149 n.6.

Chapter Ten

Gaunt and Warfare

The fact that Gaunt played a leading part in European warfare was determined by his princely birth, inclinations and abilities and by his first two marriages: the nature of his participation was determined by the successful development of the contract army and the strategy of the *chevauchée* in the campaigns in France under his father. It was inevitable that much of his military experience would be concerned with defending Edward III's territorial gains in France. But his service was to be extended into other regions, where different military problems loomed large – into the Iberian principalities, as a result of the Black Prince's and his own commitments there from the late 1360s onwards, and into Scotland as a result of the deterioration of Anglo-Scottish relations in Robert II's reign (1371–90). As a policy-maker, Gaunt had to wrestle with the problem of strategic priorities in a period when England faced war simultaneously on different fronts with limited resources.

By his marriage to Blanche of Lancaster Gaunt became heir to a tradition of acting as 'king's lieutenant' in France and the possessor of an inheritance which had been geared to recruiting and equipping contract retinues for Edward III's wars since the 1330s. Gaunt was eager to maintain and improve this military machine, in order to fulfil worthily the roles of retinue leader and royal lieutenant. But, as a campaigner, from the renewal of war with the French Crown in 1369 he was faced with a major change in French strategy, which negated some of the effectiveness of *chevauchées*. With regard to Scotland, he was to encounter the strategic problems in the defence of the remote and inhospitable English borders and in launching invasions across the frontier, which had bedevilled the English since the Scottish Wars of Independence. In Spain in 1386–7 he was to face a variety of problems, some of them new – unfamiliar geographical conditions, a version of the revised French strategy and eventual reliance on an ally with different objectives. Thus, in the period in which Gaunt entered on the highest military responsibilities, like other English policy-makers and field commanders he had to grapple with more complex and less favourable sets of strategic circumstances, which showed up the limitations of English military resources and methods.

Gaunt was one of the Crown's principal military contractors in the later Middle Ages: he led retinues and sometimes armies out of the realm in 1355, 1356, 1359, 1366, 1369, 1370, 1372, 1373, 1378, 1384, 1385, 1386 and 1394. On other occasions he planned to take forces on expeditions which failed to materialise.[1] He was first appointed to campaign abroad as king's lieutenant in 1369 and was often again to exercise supreme military command. By the time he invaded Spain in 1386, he had gained great experience in warfare, mainly in northern and south-west France and in south-east Scotland. He had previously fought in Spain only in 1367, but that experience is certain to have taught him some of the logistical problems of campaigning in the peninsula, and probably gave him his distinctive impressions of Spanish fighting methods and equipment.[2] Gaunt, typically of English magnates of his generation, became a seasoned soldier, with a professional's interest in modes of warfare; in fact he became one of the most experienced commanders among them. He led his first military retinues abroad in 1355–6 and 1359–60, learning the trade of war when he was the young earl of Richmond. With the awesome resources of the duchy of Lancaster at his disposal, he was able to muster much larger retinues in 1366–7, 1369 and 1373. In 1385 he contracted to take a contingent of 800 men-at-arms and 1,200 archers on Richard's Scottish expedition, but these totals were increased to 1,000 and 2,000 respectively – possibly to incorporate northern shire levies in his retinue. This was the size of the army which Edmund of Langley took to Portugal in 1381 and comprised nearly one-third of the 1385 expedition, being nearly half as large again as the king's retinue and five times the size of the next largest retinue, the earl of Northumberland's.[3]

Retinues constituted for service abroad were customarily made up largely of mounted knights, men-at-arms and archers hired for the duration. But the contractor had to compete with others for the best soldiers: he might end up with a group unused to working together or containing men prone to indiscipline and desertion. Such a one may have been Thomas de Evese de Wysewell, whom Sir John Marmion utterly refused to have in his company for the Spanish expedition of 1386.[4] The military potential of particular companies was doubtless a matter of keen debate. Walsingham noted the good quality of the retinue which Gaunt took to Gascony in 1366 before the first Spanish campaign.[5] The captain who wished to contract frequently with the Crown needed a reputation for constituting efficient retinues. He had an incentive to guarantee a reliable core for his retinues by retaining permanently knights and esquires obliged to serve whenever and wherever summoned. Sometimes the life indentures for service in war and peace, which both parties sealed, stipulated that the retainer was to contribute additional personnel to the military retinue.[6] Gaunt's expectation that he would need to constitute large military retinues, particularly after the start of war in 1369, and his assumption of the Castilian Crown in 1372, gave him incentives to expand this kind of military nucleus. The surviving portions of the duke's chancery registers for 1372–6 and 1379–83 contain the texts of 88 life contracts. N.B. Lewis printed the texts of another 42 contracts made during the period 1367–99 from their enrolment on the Patent Rolls in 1399–1401, when Henry IV confirmed his father's grants.[7] Retainers' halves of a few other indentures made by Gaunt for similar service have been found in private archives.[8] But the random survival of the texts of contracts is unlikely to give an accurate tally of the permanent military retinue. For Gaunt's registers record the payment of instalments of annuities to many other knights and esquires: some of these are likely to have been life retainers too. The best indication of the scale of Gaunt's retinue in a period when it was probably at its maximum is provided by a list headed 'Nomina militum et scutiferorum' in the 1379–83 register (ff8a–9a). This roll totals 222 names, including two earls (Bolingbroke and John Mowbray), three barons (Ros, Dacre and Neville), 96 knights and 121 esquires.[9] If all of them had been called out at once, the force would have been considerably larger, taking into consideration the one or more soldiers whom retainers were often under obligation to provide: Neville's 1370 life contract was exceptional in the stipulation that he would provide 20 men-at-arms and 20 archers.[10] More typically, Sir John Dabridgecourt (see p. 179) contracted in 1381 that, when he went to war in the duke's company, he would be accompanied by his esquire and as many other men-at-arms as the duke commanded.[11] The size of the committed portion of the duke's military retinues was probably increased by the making of contracts for service for a limited number of years. This is suggested by Lord Greystoke's letter to the earl of Nottingham (probably written in 1385), declining the earl's request for him to join his military retinue, on the grounds that Greystoke had agreed with Gaunt 'to stay in his retinue for two years', if he could receive royal licence to do so. Some knightly ducal annuitants were probably retained on similar terms.[12]

The huge Lancastrian military retinue of the second half of the fourteenth century seems to have been of recent expansion, a creation of the Hundred Years War, intended to sustain Duke Henry's role in war and diplomacy as the king's lieutenant. Dr J. Maddicott has calculated that Thomas of Lancaster's retinue in 1318–19 consisted of about 50 to 55 knights. According to Professor Holmes, his brother and successor, Earl Henry, was paying annuities to seven knights and at least 11 others in the period 1330–2.[13] But only a few texts of indentures for life service in peace and war to which Duke Henry was party survive. One was a contract with the Yorkshire landowner Sir Ralph Hastings, who had served Earl Henry too. He was retained for life by Gaunt, in whose military retinues he served in Spain in 1367, in France in 1369, in the Channel in 1372 and in Scotland in 1385.[14] Professor K. Fowler has, however, identified 46 of Duke Henry's leading retainers. Others were probably among 53 men who received lands or annuities from him. Fowler has noted 50 families which provided members of both Duke Henry's and Gaunt's retinues.[15]

A distinguished example of continuity in Lancastrian service was Sir John Ypres, appointed sheriff of Lancashire by Duke Henry, and chief of Gaunt's council in 1383.[16] In December 1367 Gaunt retained him for life, partly 'for the good and agreeable service which he did for the said duke in the parts of Spain and elsewhere, and at the same time the better to maintain the order of knighthood which he received from him the day of the battle of Nazare [Najera]'.[17] A distinguished Lancastrian knight who fought there in the vanguard (under Gaunt's command) was Hugh Hastings of Elsing (Norfolk) who had been retained by him to serve in peace and war for life the previous year, and who had soldiered with Duke Henry. The family were feudal tenants of Lancaster and had long-standing personal connections with their overlords. Earl Henry had named Sir Hugh's father as an executor; the earl is depicted on the father's brass in Elsing church. The son of Gaunt's retainer Sir Hugh, of the same name, was probably also his retainer: the son died in 1386 when serving the duke in the Galician campaign.[18] Thus feudal connections and loyalties helped to create and maintain neo-feudal ones: Gaunt's military retinues became a focus for family traditions of staunch service to the House of Lancaster.

Gaunt began to develop a network of knightly relationships which was to serve him well in war and peace when he was earl of Richmond. It was then that he appointed Sir Walter Urswick his master of game: in 1367 he granted Urswick £40 *p.a.* for life for his good service in Spain and elsewhere, and to help him sustain the order of knighthood, which he had received from Gaunt on the day of Najera.[19] In 1359 Gaunt's future life retainers Sir William Bracebridge, Sir Thomas Banastre and Sir Richard Scrope had been intending to serve in his retinue in France.[20] Military needs were among the incentives for expanding the permanent retinue in the 1370s and 1380s. The *Register* for 1372–6 records new contracts with 30 knights and 31 esquires; some of these had already been retained for life, but were now receiving improved financial terms. In the 1379–83 *Register* there are contracts with 10 knights and 17 esquires, made when Gaunt held lieutenancies in the northern Marches and was strenuously promoting his intended invasion of Castile. The expedition of 1386–7 produced new contracts; the Patent Rolls record ones made in Spain and Portugal with two knights and seven esquires.[21] Spain was a death-trap for some of his distinguished and long-serving knightly companions, such as Mauberney de Linières, retained in 1371 to serve in peace and war, and mortally wounded in a skirmish in León in 1387.[22] There also died in Spain Sir Richard Burley, Gaunt's 'very dear and well beloved bachelor', granted by him for life the constableship of Kidwelly Castle in 1373 and 50 marks *p.a.* in 1375. Burley, marshal of the army in 1386–7, was according to Froissart, among the most renowned in the army.[23]

In the period 1388–99 Gaunt appears not to have retained anew any knights, but he did make twenty contracts with esquires – six of them, indeed, within twelve months of his death. He is unlikely to have considered in the 1390s that the great semi-permanent retinue which he had inherited and augmented was now a redundant burden, to be run down once the wars in Spain and France had ceased. Peaceful service had its warlike aspects. Diplomatic missions to Scotland and France sometimes required a disciplined show of strength, and so might progresses to ducal estates and to court. In 1380 Gaunt took a force of 2,000 to Berwick, on his way to negotiate with the Scots.[24] The duke's prestige was enhanced when his retainers acquitted themselves honourably in jousts. Sir Thomas FitzSimond, whose huge annuity of 100 marks may have in part reflected his office as the duke's standard-bearer, was doubtless required to bear the standard in peace as well as war.[25] Bolingbroke, interested in the early 1390s in recruiting support for his crusading expeditions, and with an eye to his future estate as duke, was probably concerned that his father should not run down the retinue. Moreover, Gaunt still needed the assurance of available military service. War with Charles VI threatened in 1391. Gaunt probably relied on retainers to help suppress the Cheshire rebellion in 1393. Sir Matthew Gournay, a retainer who was a renowned military veteran, constituted a retinue for the Gascon expedition of 1394 (see p. 156); Gaunt probably hoped

215

that retainers would serve on his proposed crusade. Richard called for Lancastrian military aid after the arrests of his former opponents in 1397; he licensed Gaunt to bring 300 men-at-arms and 600 archers to parliament (Bolingbroke – 200 and 400).[26] The continued existence of this formidable potential force was a stabilising influence on English politics for much of the 1390s, deterring Richard's critics from rebellion, and Richard himself from attacking them until, that is, he was assured of independent support. When Henry of Bolingbroke landed to challenge Richard in 1399, prominent retainers of his father joined him.[27] Elements of Gaunt's former retinue were an important component in effecting the dynastic revolution and in maintaining the rule of the usurper in its early precarious years.

The annual fee which Gaunt most commonly granted to a knightly retainer was £20, and to an esquire, 10 marks.[28] But fees varied considerably according to the rank, age, military experience and reputation of the recipient and according to his readiness to provide the services of one or more additional soldiers. Sometimes the contract stipulated that the annuity would be paid at a higher rate in time of war. Gaunt usually undertook to provide then wages at Crown war rates and, sometimes, victuals. Generally, the size of annuities which he granted and the terms of military service which were laid down did not differ markedly from those in similar life contracts made by his fellow magnates. But there were particular incentives to join and remain in the Lancastrian service. Gaunt could offer an exceptional number of very large annuities. He could provide a *cursus honorum* of offices second only to the king's.

It is uncertain in the case of most ducal grants whether they were, at least in part, rewards for military achievement. The 1367 grant of an annuity to Ypres, as we have seen, specified that it was so. At Coimbra in July 1387 Gaunt granted the shrievalty of Lancashire to his bachelor Sir Robert Standish because he 'had acquitted himself well and loyally towards us in our last expedition to Spain and done good service for us then and at other times'.[29] Foreign retainers may have been valued for their diplomatic skills or, in the case of Sir Othon de Graunson, their courtly accomplishments. But it is likely that high payments to such men as the Poitevin Sir Mauburney de Linières were principally in recognition of their military abilities. His skill and bravery in the joust, and the heroism which led to his death, were commented on by Fernão Lopes.[30]

One foreigner whose military achievements probably earned him additional favour from Gaunt was the Scot John Swinton, whom the duke exceptionally 'wished and granted that he will not be obliged to take his [the duke's] part against his allegiance'. Swinton had distinguished himself by a feat of arms in 1370 on Sir Robert Knolles's expedition to France. In 1372 Gaunt retained him as an esquire with the high fee of £20. The following year Swinton took part in the duke's French expedition: soon after Gaunt returned, he retained Swinton as a knight, doubling his fee.[31]

Swinton's pride in being a ducal knight appears in his quixotic behaviour on the day in 1377 when a London mob set out to lynch the duke. Swinton, rash borderer, rode about the city sporting his Lancastrian livery collar (presumably that of the linked esses), in order to win his lord's favour, says Walsingham. The commons attacked him, dragging him from his horse and pulling off his collar: he was saved by the mayor. Walsingham notes that the right to wear the collar had hitherto been greatly prized.[32] This suggests that high *esprit de corps* had characterised ducal retainers. Thoses who contracted to serve Gaunt in peace and war in normal circumstances gained prestige from patronage by an eminent, generous and warlike prince. They had opportunities to rub shoulders with distinguished veterans in his service such as Richard Lord Scrope, who had fought at Crécy and taken part in the subsequent siege of Calais (see p. 289).

The efficiency, cohesion and comradeship of the duke's military retinues were founded on the existence of the permanently retained core of knights and esquires, and their personal recruitment and control over individual esquires and archers. The frequent summons of the life retainers, especially in the 1370s and 1380s, probably enhanced their value as the nucleus of a force, expected to encamp, muster and either embark or ride off at short notice. Thus on 10 July 1372 Gaunt wrote requesting the addressee 'with no default or excuse' to be at Sandwich on 8 August equipped to embark (without a horse) in his company on the king's expedition.[33] The ducal estate administration was used as the agency through which many of the retainers were summoned. By ducal warrants dated Leicester Castle, 26 August 1380, the receivers of Yorkshire, Lancashire and Tutbury were ordered to dispatch letters sent to them which were addressed to the duke's knights and esquires. These were summonses to them to be at Newcastle arrayed for war on 28 September, for his intended expedition to Scotland. The receiver in Lancashire and the receiver's deputy in the honour of Pontefract were ordered on 3 May 1381 to send out letters to certain knights and esquires 'with all possible haste' and in November 1382 a number of receivers were told to forward letters to members of the retinue and others. These letters concerned the duke's intended voyage to Spain and required an answer.[34] Receivers paid out wages to ducal tenants and other local men to deliver such letters: the receiver for Lincolnshire accounted for payments for men from Bolingbroke, Lincoln and Theddlethorpe for taking letters to knights and esquires of the retinue, and others who were not, to summon them to go in his company to Scotland in 1384.[35]

Gaunt thus also used the receivers to help to recruit knights and esquires in his lordships not retained by him, whom he hoped to persuade to give service on particular campaigns. In November 1383 he sent a batch of twenty-four letters to the Lancashire receiver 'without endorsement . . . which letters we order that you have endorsed [addressed] and sent to those persons who appear to you to be able and suitable for our service on the said expedition to those parts' (presumably France or Flanders). The receiver was to inform Gaunt's chamberlain Sir Robert Swillington as to whom he had sent the letters. Gaunt's military retinues were not entirely composed of soldiers raised under contract. The Crown commissioned sheriffs and others to raise archers for his service, for example, in 1366, 1369 and 1373. Gaunt's retainers were prominent on these commissions; thus in April 1369 Richard Scrope and Walter Urswick were appointed with John Seyvill to array 200 archers in Yorkshire and to lead them to Southampton, to travel in the duke's company to reinforce the prince in Aquitaine.[36]

The service of foresters was specially prized, because of their professional archery skills. In a ducal warrant of 1373 ordering the Yorkshire receiver to pay prests to archers, three of the duke's parkers, Smalwode, Hipperon and Tarletton, were singled out among them by name, possibly because of reputations for shooting and woodcraft.[37] Gaunt tried to exploit the personnel of his large forest and park administration generally for the 1373 expedition: it seems that his keepers were ordered to recruit among them. He was prepared to use up some of his forest resources as a private inducement to recruits. The keeper of Leicester Forest was to offer the handsome prize of two oaks apiece to five recruits 'if they will go with us on this next expedition, but if any of them does not come with us on the same expedition, we order you not to deliver any oak to him'.[38] Gaunt's recruitment of archers went well in 1373: 220 joined up from Lancashire and 100 from Yorkshire, in addition to archers in companies brought in under captains' contracts.[39] For the 1369 campaign the borough of Leicester had paid a tallage to raise a company of archers and for the manufacture of arrowheads for them. The duke's retainer, Simon Pakeman, coming to Leicester to negotiate about the matter, was given dinner, and the troops, setting out to join the duke at Calais, were piped from the town as far as Oadby (Leics.).[40] Shire, forest and borough contingents were probably used to make up the number of archers which the duke had contracted to bring in his retinue. To the same end, his permanent retainers were probably on occasion requested by the duke to bring a larger number of archers than was stipulated in their long-term contracts. Thus in 1372 Gaunt ordered certain Lancashire retainers to bring companies of archers with them for service in his retinue on the king's voyage.[41]

The organisation of Gaunt's retinues for war – and of the armies he commanded – was heavily dependent on Lancastrian officials and resources. In the duchy itself the sheriff of Lancashire (the duke's appointee) might be given important responsibilities for producing the local contingents. In February 1384 the duke's chancellor was ordered to issue letters commissioning the sheriff to have proclamations read in the duchy commanding those who were to participate in the Scottish campaign to assemble with the duke at the time and place notified.[42] The following month the sheriff, Sir Nicholas Harington, or his lieutenant, was ordered to assemble the duchy contingents and lead them to the rendezvous at Newcastle-upon-Tyne.[43] The receivers of lordships (as the examples above in part illustrate) were key figures in recruiting, activating, supplying and equipping the ducal forces. They might be responsible for transporting or safeguarding war material.[44] They helped to recruit specialist workmen for campaigns. In April 1373 the receiver of Tutbury was ordered to procure four carpenters, two masons and two iron workers 'to make and work engines and trepgeutes [trebuchet, a siege engine casting heavy missiles] and other such things needed by us for the same expedition [to France]'. Specialists were recruited for the same purpose in Lancashire and Leicestershire by ducal retainers, with the cooperation of the local receivers.[45] They played a crucial role in procuring a commodity usually essential to expeditions – horses. For the 1373 expedition, Gaunt wrote 'we greatly need horses'; he authorised his avener, Adam Pope, clerk, and his receivers to purchase them. The Lancashire receiver was to forward letters to the bishop of Lichfield, the abbots of Furness and Whalley and the priors of Lancaster and Cartmel, requesting them to send one or two horses each.[46] Pontefract was one centre to which horses were brought for the expedition, to be kept there by the Yorkshire receiver, who was later ordered to deliver them to a ducal servant to be taken to Plymouth (the original embarkation port).[47] Receivers were responsible on occasion for transporting or safeguarding war material.[48] Tenants might be involved *per se* in the ducal war effort. In 1372 those at Bassingburn and Badburgham (Cambs.) and Waltham Cross (Middx.) procured victuals and other supplies and conveyed them to the embarkation port, Sandwich, for the duke's retinue.[49]

The nerve-centre for the launching of the ducal army abroad was constituted by the household and leading officials in its organisation or frequently resident in it. Clerks in the secretariat activated local preparation. Wardrobe officials might be called on by the duke to take emergency measures. Possibly in 1369, John Yerdburgh, clerk of the wardrobe, was ordered to purvey as quickly as possible 50 bows and their appurtenances from Robert Waukere, 'bowyer' dwelling in Fleet Street, London.[50] Heads of the household's service departments were involved in purveying victuals, an important task because of the duke's contractual obligations to provide free victuals for some of his permanent retainers and their men.[51]

Central ducal officials played an important role in the crucial area of financing expeditions. Before one went, Gaunt formally appointed one of his leading clerks as treasurer of war; the treasurer was paid the sums which ducal officials received for payment of royal wages at the Exchequer,[52] and disbursed to retainers for their companies' wages, or issued them with warrants for payment by the clerk of the wardrobe, the receiver-general, or the receiver of a lordship. Payment by bills of credit was so routine that the duke's letters appointing treasurers of war stipulated that they should be prepared to issue such bills instead of wages.[53] The need for promissory notes sprang from the Crown's difficulties in paying its military contractors, such as Gaunt. The first instalment of wages due to them was often not paid in full before an expedition set off and later instalments tended to fall into arrears, further delays being increased by the hazards of transporting bullion in mid-campaign to an army whose whereabouts might not be precisely known by royal officials.

There are indications that, as the Crown's principal contractor in the war of 1369–75, Gaunt had to dig deeply into his own resources and credit to launch and sustain his retinues, and that the Crown became indebted to him on a large scale. This situation seems to have developed as a result of his service in Aquitaine in 1370–1 (see p. 191). According to his account for his retinue on the expedition, his total expenses, including payment of mariners, compensation for lost horses and the costs of the return voyage, were over £30,965. Before he and his retinue assembled at the embarkation port, his officials had received over £14,520 for wages and regard at the Exchequer.[54] He ran up debts for his service (as lieutenant as well as retinue captain) in Aquitaine: the earl of Arundel lent him 1,000 marks on the security of jewels – 'to our very great ease and refreshment'.[55] After his return to England, Gaunt received £4,000 arrears in 1372 for the expedition. But he was still owed £12,455 in 1377, when he was paid £4,979 of this debt.[56]

These arrears in fact represent a staggering amount owed to Gaunt's retainers on the 1370–1 expedition. In order to induce them to serve again under him in 1373, it was necessary for Gaunt to have them paid their arrears from his resources in hand. In 1372 Thomas Amcotes (former treasurer of war) was ordered to give the names of all creditors from the 1370–1 campaign in haste to the ducal chancellor Ralph Erghum.[57]

Consequently, Gaunt was urgently in need of cash before the 1373 expedition, though his receiver-general William Bugbrigge collected a total of over £15,762 at the Exchequer to defray the costs of his retinue, in a series of payments between 6 March (five days after Gaunt sealed his indenture with the Crown) and 16 July (the day before he and his men assembled at Dover).[58] In April the ducal receivers in Lincolnshire, Yorkshire, Norfolk and Suffolk were ordered to pay all the cash they had received in loans to John Yerdburgh, clerk of the great wardrobe, and cash from estate issues to the receiver-general.[59] So it may be that Gaunt customarily sought loans from his vassals and tenants before expeditions. The largest loan which he received in 1373 was apparently 2,000 marks from the earl of Arundel, which in May Bugbrigge was ordered to pay the treasurer at war, Thomas Swaby, clerk, towards the costs of the expedition.[60]

According to Gaunt's account for his retinue's service, made soon after his return to England, the only sums he received towards costs in France were £3,185 (16 August 1373), and the equivalent in francs of £109 from John de Humbleton, a ransom collector. Gaunt was still owed £9,642 for his total costs, a figure which must conceal a mass of obligations to knights and esquires who served under him.[61] In 1376–7, according to his receiver-general's account, Gaunt was paid £6,254 for arrears of war wages.[62] But when, in 1378, he was paid £2,000 at the Exchequer, it was said to be part of the debt of £9,642 for the 1373–4 service.[63] The 1378 expedition is likely to have increased debts for war service. In 1380 the grant to Gaunt of the marriage of Mary de Bohun, valued at 5,000 marks, was made in part satisfaction of a larger sum due to him for war wages.[64]

The interest which Gaunt showed in a negotiated settlement with the French Crown during the 1369–75 war is to be related to his experience of the English Crown's inability to pay for it and its consequent indebtedness to him, as well as to military failures and reverses. His view of war as a means of pursuing the Crown's claims in France may have been permanently soured. One wonders how knights and esquires who were owed wages for years after a campaign sustained any enthusiasm for war. Perhaps many did not: Froissart's picture of English gentlefolk in the 1390s, opposed to peace with France because they thirsted after the profits of war, may be overdone and influenced strongly by his acquaintance with the *routiers*, professional soldiers. Gaunt's bills of credit suggest that, as far as the war of 1369–75 was concerned, many knights must have experienced long-term financial loss as a result of serving in one of his military retinues. Why then did gentlefolk continue to serve? Incentives may have been the honour and good fame which accrued from serving in their lord the king's honourable war, under the command of a generous prince, alongside famous knights. As mentioned, there was the inducement, for those who had served once and were owed for part of their service, of recouping their losses if they re-enlisted – though at the risk of incurring new losses. This inducement was specifically one to serve in the same lord's retinue again. So the financial hazards of service in contract armies stimulated the formation of recurrent military-patronage relations in the aristocracy and the drawing of knights into the social orbit of a particular magnate.

This examination of Gaunt's military organisation suggests a number of conclusions about the interrelations of the waging of the Hundred Years War and the development of magnate power. It suggests that the later medieval army was heavily dependent for its functioning on the domestic and regional institutions of magnate power. It suggests, too, that magnates' participation in the war increased the activity of their private government in society and added to the power and influence of the higher nobility.

Here, then, is a summary of certain aspects of the ducal role in military organisation, and an elaboration of some of them. The run-up to the launching of an expedition placed heavy burdens on Gaunt's land resources and tested the efficiency and skill of both his central and local officials. The network of ducal castles became nerve-centres for the collection of funds, supplies and war material. The evidence for the 1373 expedition suggests that the castles were customarily staging posts for the tasks of mounting the duke and providing horse transports for the military retinue. Warrants in 1373 ordered the receivers to purchase horses, pay for their stabling and that of their grooms and, in some cases, for the cost of moving them to assembly points.[65] Moreover, the recruitment of a motley crowd of archers in scattered lordships placed another financial burden on these resources: their receivers had to provide an advance to each archer, to cover his expenses on the way to join the army. In July 1372 Gaunt ordered the Lancashire receiver to pay a month's wages to locally recruited companies of archers for the royal expedition; the rest of the money in hand he was to dispatch to the duke with the greatest haste possible.[66] In 1373 archers were to be provided by receivers with a prest of 40s. a head: the duke's warrants suggest acute nervousness that the receivers would not distribute this 'conduct money' and that the potentially impressive body of archers would melt away even before the army had assembled. To Robert Morton, Yorkshire receiver, he wrote: 'and make sure that this is done and in such a way that they [the archers] have no cause nor reason to excuse their non-appearance on the coast for default of payment . . . And so get this done without any slip-up as we have full confidence in you.'[67] He wrote to William Hornby, the Lancashire receiver, on the same subject in an even more hectoring tone:

> And make sure that this is done and in such a manner that the expedition is in no way disrupted, understanding that if it is disrupted we would not wish to impute the blame to you in this case, and therefore do not neglect this, on account of the hazard involved, and as you wish to avoid upsetting us.[68]

Gaunt's harsh and crude pressure on his officials shows that he possessed a professional soldier's realism about the 'other ranks': he knew what was essential to keep them together as a force. This was a period in which difficulties in providing pay threatened some English armies with disintegration. But, for the most part, Gaunt's retinue held together, though his army seems to have come near to collapse in Gascony in 1373–4 and it may have been to avoid a humiliating total collapse that the campaign in León was abruptly curtailed in 1387 (see p. 124–5). But in both these cases pay was not the only factor involved; both armies had endured a variety of privations. It is likely that the *esprit de corps* of Gaunt's retinue, his concern to keep up pay when possible and the credit of his treasurers' promissory notes were important factors in maintaining the integrity of English armies in the period.

References in Gaunt's *Registers* to the recruitment of his foresters as archers, to the purchase of bows and the movement of horses and victuals give us tantalising glimpses of the involvement in preparation for campaigns of ordinary folk in lordships of a participating magnate. It is clear that Gaunt's servants and many of his tenants had extra work and expenses (and, sometimes, reward). English kings' involvement of their subjects in pursuit of their claims abroad led to success in war being an important criterion in judging them in the fourteenth century. But, as Gaunt's example shows, to a significant extent kings delegated organisation as well as leadership in war to their magnates. They too were judged according to results by men who had committed labour and resources to launching their retinues – none more so than Gaunt. The fact that Lancastrian institutions and resources for so long underpinned the English war effort helped to produce a public opinion quick to judge his prowess and results in the field. How successful was he there, and what determined his fortunes in war?

He had his first experience of warfare at the age of ten (see p. 31). In his teens he learnt the trade of war from some of the most renowned captains of the age. In the 1359–60 campaign in France he was in the Black Prince's 'battle'[69] and at Reims fought alongside the distinguished veteran Sir Thomas Holand, learning the techniques of raiding in forays in the neighbourhood with Duke Henry of Lancaster.[70] When in command of the vanguard in Spain in 1367, he numbered among his captains some of the most famous of Edward III's knights – Sir John Chandos, Sir Hugh Calveley, Sir Robert Knolles and the Gascon Jean de Grailly, Captal de Buch.[71]

Gaunt certainly possessed some military virtues. According to Froissart, he was philosophical about the fortunes of war, a keen student of weaponry and fighting methods, and an admirer of individual deeds of arms.[72] The chronicler also represents him as amenable to the recommendations of military advisers and councils of war. At the siege of Montpon (1371), the advice of Sir Guichard Dangle modified his harsh attitudes towards the garrison, securing its surrender.[73] But he may have been too easily swayed on occasion by arguments of caution and appeals to his sense of honour. In 1369, in the March of Calais, he rejected Lord Manny's advice to launch a night attack, which his council of war opposed. Gaunt allegedly remarked that he always followed the advice of such councils. On this occasion Manny's counsel turned out to have been sounder.[74] Arguably, the decision of the council at Brest in 1386 to make Galicia the objective of Gaunt's Iberian expedition cost him a chance of gaining the Crown, for which he needed to concentrate his resources at their peak in an attack on the Castilian heartlands (see p. 121).

Gaunt's conduct of the brief winter campaign in Scotland in 1384 illustrates the positive side of his generalship, as well as his limitations as a politico-military strategist. He had encountered when young the hazards of campaigning there, in the 'Burnt Candlemas' campaign of 1356. His recent border forays to conclude truces and his Edinburgh visit in 1381 had given him opportunities to survey terrain and defences in the Scottish East March and Lothian. In February 1384 the truce expired and Lochmaben Castle in Annandale, the last English-held enclave in the West March, was promptly captured by the Scots.[75] As lieutenant in the Marches Gaunt had responsibility for the safeguard of Lochmaben, which he had tried to ensure. The objectives of his invasion were, presumably, to procure a new truce and to deter similar attacks on the enclaves held by the English in Roxburghshire. He wished to demonstrate English power and his own determination to Robert II and the Scottish magnates, but not to alienate a king and nobles with whom he had cultivated friendly relations, by unleashing unrestrained destruction. His brothers accompanied him on the expedition, which was probably strongly northern in composition: the earl of Northumberland led a retinue and the sheriff of Yorkshire, Sir Robert Hilton, led 600 archers arrayed at the expense of the county and sixteen men-at-arms ánd 100 archers at his own expense.[76] There was probably a strong contingent of men-at-arms and archers from Lancashire. The assembly of the army took place on schedule at Newcastle on 24 March.[77] A fleet was probably concurrently assembled there to shadow and supply the army; a ducal wardrobe account recorded the payment of James Hunt, tailor, for the expedition: he accompanied by sea Gaunt's pavillion, armour and *arteleria*.[78]

The army crossed the border early in April. Dwellings and woods were burnt by the invaders on their advance, but the Westminster Chronicler says that Gaunt limited the amount of destruction. He gave protection to Melrose Abbey (and, presumably, its extensive regality): the abbey had given Gaunt shelter as a fugitive in 1381. He had also been made welcome then in Edinburgh: in 1384 he ransomed the town instead of burning it.[79] The Scottish chronicler Wyntoun says that he 'skaythyd bot litill the cuntre'. The Scots, sticking to a well-tried strategy in face of English invasions, kept their forces out of the way. But Wyntoun noted an encounter which damaged Gaunt's supply lines, perhaps determining the timing of his withdrawal. When he was approaching Edinburgh, his victualling ships were anchored in the Firth of Forth. They launched boats to offload at South Queensferry, but Scottish knights routed a landing-party; as a result, the English did not attempt to use the port again.[80]

Supplies, as usual, were a major problem for the English invaders in Scotland. Many Scots had fled with their stocks and valuables north of the Firth of Forth. The weather turned freezing and it snowed. Famished Englishmen and their mounts collapsed: the Scots attacked stragglers. The army leaders in consultation decided to withdraw; back in Northumberland, the army fell eagerly on the inhabitants' food supplies.[81] By 23 April Gaunt was in Durham. He had returned, as Walsingham wrote, 'without the fruit of victory'.[82] He had failed to secure a truce or to deter the Scots from planning further attacks, spurred on by the prospect of French cooperation. Gaunt miscalculated the amount of pressure required as a deterrent. But the meagre evidence suggests that he conducted the expedition soundly: he held his army together in difficult campaigning circumstances, as Wyntoun acknowledged:

> But he his folk led sa wysly
> That hym befell na gret tynsale.[83]

Gaunt showed inability to read his opponents' minds in 1384. He lacked the gift of meshing together strategic and political aims successfully. But he did show himself a prudent field commander who made the best of difficult circumstances and denied the enemy major opportunities. He had demonstrated these qualities as lieutenant in Aquitaine in 1370–1 and 1374, when he managed to achieve a temporary stability in defence with inadequate funds and manpower. In 1387 he maintained control of much of Galicia and invaded León with pitifully stretched forces.

Gaunt's positive qualities as a commander made him adept at siege warfare, whose skills became especially needful when the French adopted a more passive strategy. Froissart indicated this predilection in his description of how the duke enjoyed watching the English assaults on Orense in 1387, calling one off when he considered the men were too tired.[84] He had learnt the methods in his youth at the investment of Berwick (1355) and of Reims and Chartres (1359). At the Black Prince's siege of Limoges in 1370, Gaunt, because of his brother's illness, supervised the mining operations. When the defenders succeeded in counter-mining, Gaunt joined in the mêlée in the pit. Eventually his miners brought down part of the city wall, making the breach through which the city was stormed.[85] In 1371 Gaunt vigorously conducted the siege of Montpon. The neighbourhood was scoured for victuals, the castle moat filled in and siege engines were deployed. Covering fire facilitated the undermining of the walls. The threat of assault induced surrender.[86]

Gaunt's most ambitious siege was a failure, though it is not clear that this was the result of his faulty strategy or dispositions. In 1378 Gaunt was commander of the naval forces constituted to counter the Franco-Castilian threat at sea and also, it appears, to seize and occupy French coastal ports in accordance with the strategy enunciated by Gaunt's friend Richard Scrope in the parliament of October 1377.[87] The naval force was an impressive one, with more than 5,000 soldiers and at least 5,000 sailors, in over 150 vessels; Gaunt's brothers and the earls of Arundel, Stafford, Suffolk and Warwick were among the retinue commanders.[88] Part of the fleet embarked in April and commenced operations to secure Carlos II of Navarre's Norman ports. Gaunt himself only embarked at Southampton in July.[89] Possibly he hoped to attack the Franco-Castilian fleet blockading some of his ships in Cherbourg: he was unable to prevent their defeat when they tried to break out.[90] A factor in the decision to attack St Malo may have been the hope of surprising the Castilians: they had docked there in June.[91]

St Malo was described by Walsingham as 'a town of Brittany among all the other towns of Britanny well defended'.[92] The present reconstructed ramparts may have been recently built then. St Malo is almost entirely surrounded by the sea; land access from the north-east is blocked by the castle. The siege commenced in August.[93] The French were able to strengthen the local defence forces by diverting troops concentrated in Lower Normandy to occupy Carlos II's possessions: some of these joined the garrison, and an army was eventually concentrated in the vicinity. Gaunt's initial attempts to take the port by assault were beaten back. A war of nerves ensued, in some respects reminiscent of that in the neighbourhood of Calais in 1369. Gaunt's plans were hamstrung. He risked defeat if he committed his forces to assault the walls when an enemy force was in the vicinity. On the other hand, as his was a naval expedition, unlike his opponents in the field he probably lacked the mounts which might enable him to manoeuvre the French army into a fight. So he stayed put in the encampment and relied on bombardment by his impressive siege train and on mining to breach the walls. But the defenders were able to destroy the mine, according to Froissart, as a result of the negligence of the captain of the guard, the young earl of Arundel. They then attacked the English camp. The astounded Gaunt and his brother Langley reprimanded the earl. A council of war agreed that it was too late in the season to start another mine and that the army should re-embark. Without mounts it would have been impossible to launch a *chevauchée*, as Gaunt had done in Normandy in 1369, and probably difficult to scour for victuals to maintain the army and its fleet at St Malo. The siege ended in September, probably by the 17th, when the able Du Guesclin (who is likely to have played a key role in the defence) left. If, as is likely, the English companies were on a six months' contract, there was another pressing reason for withdrawal: pay had just about run out.[94]

Gaunt had better success in a less important Breton siege in 1386. The English garrison of Brest was then being blockaded by a force acting on the duke of Brittany's behalf, which had erected a formidable siege-castle called by the English (perhaps ironically) 'le Dufhous'. It had walls ten feet thick, seven towers and a garrison of 300, well supplied with arms, guns, siege machines and victuals. Gaunt landed at Brest with his army on his way to the Iberian Peninsula and laid siege to le Dufhous. Assaults carried out over at least two days were unavailing. Surrender was negotiated after mining had made the garrison's position untenable.[95] Gaunt may have considered this siege useful as a means of testing techniques which would probably be needful in Spain. His troops were to be notably successful in taking fortified positions in Galicia – though often the fortifications were feeble and the defending forces inadequate and unprofessional. In Léon the siege weapons of the Anglo-Portuguese army overawed some defenders, but circumstances generally militated against mounting the siege of any formidably defended city.[96]

Gaunt's reputation as a commander among his contemporaries rested mainly on his conduct in five major expeditions – to Spain in 1367, to France in 1369, 1373 and 1378 and again to Spain in 1386–7. The 1378 land campaign has been described; the others will now be examined in turn, except that of 1386–7, which is dealt with in Chapter Seven.

The 1367 expedition is the only one which Gaunt did not command – and the only one from which he emerged with an untarnished and, indeed, enhanced reputation. The Black Prince honoured him from the start of the campaign by entrusting him with the command of the vanguard, though there were two kings in the army, either of whom, in consideration of their superior rank, might have more appropriately been given the honour. But the prince probably had military considerations uppermost in mind: by giving his brother the command, he was able to concentrate in the van some of his best English troops, effectively under the control of the renowned Sir John Chandos. In February the Black Prince advanced from Pamplona westwards into Castile, moving into the mountainous region of Alava, where he encountered little resistance to Pedro's claims.[97] The invaders easily captured Salvatierra and Vitoria; Enrique II then blocked any advance through the mountain passes. The English thought that Enrique would seek battle on the plain of Vitoria; their forces drew up in readiness. But he did not respond. He was to allow his brother Don Tello to probe the English positions; the latter achieved notable successes in attacks on detached English forces. His attempt on Gaunt's camp was driven off. But it was shortage of victuals and bad weather which led the Black Prince to abandon his positions towards the end of March; the army made a gruelling retreat through the mountains, back into Navarre. It is a measure of the prince's ability and his forces' quality that, soon after this defeat in Alava, they crossed back into Castile at Logroño and on 3 April won a great victory over Enrique at Najera, where Enrique rashly exposed his army to attack. Battle was joined there by the two vanguards, the Black Prince's commanded by Gaunt and Sir John Chandos;[98] in the Castilian vanguard, the French free companies were concentrated under the command of Bertrand du Guesclin and the Marshal d'Audrehem. The sources agree that the struggle between the vanguards was fierce; Froissart says that the eventual defeat of du Guesclin and D'Audrehem broke the Trastamaran resistance in general.[99] A number of chroniclers' accounts, such as those of Froissart and Knighton, were complimentary about Gaunt's brave leadership in the battle.[100] A monk of Revesby Abbey (Leics.), Walter of Peterborough, dispatched a well-informed poem celebrating the campaign to the ducal treasurer, John Marthon, in which the deeds of Gaunt and his men in Alava and at Najera were cast in a heroic light: clearly the campaign was a matter of rejoicing and congratulation in the Lancastrian household.[101] Memories of this expedition as a triumph for Gaunt were long-lasting. Dr J.J.N. Palmer has argued that the poem on the life of the Black Prince written *c.* 1385 by Chandos Herald was a propaganda piece intended to drum up support for Gaunt's Castilian ambitions. As Palmer points out, the duke's prowess at Vitoria and Najera is emphasised. A remark he made to Sir William Beauchamp at Najera is recalled, as are the exploits of his retainer Sir Ralph Hastings, 'who cared not two cherries for death' in Alava, and the knighting of his retainer John Ypres 'of the proud heart' at Najera.[102]

Therefore the Spanish campaign and victory may have become a part of Lancastrian military mythology, recalled as a special bond with their lord by some of his leading retainers who participated.[103] Walter of Peterborough singles out Richard Burley and Ralph Hastings, mentioning their respective injury and capture in Alava.[104] The Spanish campaign afforded Gaunt his greatest chivalrous renown and enhanced the military spirit of his retinue. Perhaps his famous livery collar commemorates the campaign; it first appears on the tomb effigy of Sir Hugh Swynford (d. 1372) at Spratton (Northants). Swynford was a Lancastrian retainer who had taken part in the campaign. In another way this laid sure foundations for Gaunt's later military enterprises. In Spain he strengthened links with some of the most famous leaders of the free companies, notably Sir John Chandos, Sir Robert Knolles, Sir Hugh Calveley, Sir Bertonquat Dalbret and Sir Matthew Gournay, who fought alongside him or under his command at Najera: some of these were later conspicuous in his service.

Gaunt's first exercise of command over a major expedition to France, in 1369, was not originally planned. When he contracted to serve there for six months with a very large retinue on 11 June, and was appointed captain and lieutenant in the lordships of Merck, Guines and Calais, and in the whole realm of France, the following day, it was intended that he should take there a substantial advance guard of the army which his father would command and lead – presumably, on an invasion of the Ile-de-France similar to that of 1359.[105] Gaunt's anticipation of the eventual arrival of Edward and the remainder of his force is the key to understanding his manoeuvres in and around the March. Gaunt was in Calais by 26 July: the threat of his presence there had – unintentionally, James Sherborne has argued – a decisive and limiting effect on overall French strategy. In August Charles V abandoned his aim of invading England and directed the forces which he had concentrated for this purpose in

Normandy against Gaunt, under the command of his brother Philip duke of Burgundy. Gaunt did not allow his forces to lie idle until his father's anticipated arrival. He relieved Ardres and pursued the besieging force south-eastwards from the March. Plundering the countryside, well served by his intelligence services, he forced the count of St Pol out of the towns of Thérouanne and St Pol. The count sought refuge in the castle of the town of 'Perle' (probably Pernes). Gaunt took the town by assault and stayed there for two days, but refrained from attacking the castle, because of its strength. The English withdrew towards the valley of Guines and Ardres.[106] When bivouacking on 23 August, they sighted Burgundy's force. The English hastily formed up on high ground, but, instead of attacking, Burgundy withdrew to a strong position two miles away, where he encamped and entrenched. It seems likely that both commands were taken by surprise by the encounter. For over a fortnight the armies stayed in their fixed positions. There were skirmishes, and negotiations were held to determine a field of battle. Such passivity provoked discontent in both camps. Gaunt presumably hoped that Philip of Burgundy would be goaded into attacking or that his father would soon arrive and force the issue with an augmented army. Froissart claims that Gaunt's force was heavily outnumbered, but Sherborne advanced the proposition that the armies 'may have been broadly well matched'. The chronicler also claims that Charles V forbade his brother to attack.[107]

Edward's retinue forces arrived at Calais early in September without the king, but including the earls of Warwick, March, Salisbury and Oxford with their companies. The veteran Warwick rode on ahead to Gaunt's camp, where he upbraided the duke and his subordinate the earl of Hereford for their caution. The news of the arrival of the fire-eating Warwick and of the reinforcements at Calais precipitated a French night withdrawal (12–13 Sept.). Acting again with caution, Gaunt refused to sanction an attack till daybreak. The abandoned French position was then occupied and captured supplies were taken to Calais. At St Omer Burgundy disbanded his army: he had failed to bar the way to an English invasion.[108] Gaunt now seized the initiative, but his objectives were somewhat limited, considering that he had a substantial army, much of which was fresh, with contracts which had several months to run. After three days 'refreshment' at Calais, he set off down the coast to invade Normandy, with the objectives, it seems, of attacking Charles V's base for the invasion of England, Harfleur, and of pillaging the countryside. Edward and his councillors were so thoroughly alarmed by the invasion preparations, which had caught them unawares, that they wanted Gaunt to give priority to disrupting them (which he had in effect already done), in cooperation with a fleet, rather than more ambitiously striking towards the Ile-de-France.

Froissart and the Anonimalle Chronicler give different routes for the advance, perhaps reflecting the divergence of separate 'battles'. The English spent twelve days in the Pays de Caux: the attack on Harfleur, which had strong defences, failed. The count of St Pol, organising resistance along the line of Gaunt's march, led reinforcements into the port before the English arrived. Gaunt withdrew from Harfleur, perhaps in the first fortnight of October, and returned to Calais: that was the premature end of the expedition. He stayed for some time in Calais, presumably to organise the March's defences; on 1 December an indenture was sealed by him with the Sieur de Gommegnies, attesting that he had received charge of Ardres in the presence of the duke, the earl of Hereford and other barons and lords of the duke's council, by whose advice and assent the appointment had been made.[109]

Gaunt's conduct of his first independent command aroused controversy in the army and in England. Walsingham thought that his passivity in the face of the French army was cowardly and bad for the English reputation. His and the Anonimalle Chronicler's accounts of Warwick's strictures probably reflect the crystallisation around the belligerent earl of discontent in Gaunt's forces.[110] But Froissart was conspicuously uncritical of his defensive stand.[111] Sherborne considered that he 'showed no bravado of a kind to fire the imagination and stir pride, but his generalship and the counsel of those who advised him were in no way despicable'.[112] He was perhaps exhibiting the caution of one of a younger generation of commanders in awe of the achievements of his elders and of the supreme responsibility suddenly thrust upon him. Philip of Burgundy was exhibiting apparently similar symptoms – perhaps more culpably: his conduct has been censured by Professor Richard Vaughan.[113] Duke Philip passed up an opportunity to defeat the English before their forces were concentrated, and he abandoned northern parts of France to their ravages. But at least he gave the towns, in particular the naval base of Harfleur, a breathing-space in which to organise their defences.

What did Gaunt achieve? At vast cost he strengthened the defences of the March of Calais and – possibly unintentionally – ended an invasion threat to England. He carried out fearful destruction on his *chevauchée*, testified to, for instance, by allegations of damage to the *ville* of Ste Genevieve (1374) and the saltpans at Bouteilles (1396).[114] The failure at Harfleur appears predictable, in so far as surprise was impossible and Gaunt does not appear to have made preparations for a regular siege. But such enterprises, probing for unexpected weaknesses, can sometimes succeed. Gaunt emerges from the campaign, as far as we can judge its circumstances, as a sound commander prepared to gamble for lesser objectives, but not for the supreme prizes.

In 1373 Gaunt received command of another army intended to invade France – the biggest English army dispatched in the 1369–75 war. Its precise objectives are unclear, though, in a general sense, its principal one was to reverse the tide of defeats endured by the English in 1370–2, which had left them with only fragments of the duchy of Aquitaine conceded by the French Crown in 1360.[115] In 1370–1 Gaunt himself had played a leading and worthy part in trying to hold back the French in Aquitaine, postponing pursuit of his Castilian claim. Professor Peter Russell argues that the 1373 expedition was ultimately aimed to prosecute this claim.[116] But Professor George Holmes asserts that there is no evidence connecting the expedition with the Iberian Peninsula. Whereas the indenture which Gaunt made for military service with the Crown in 1372 envisaged that he might switch his objective from France to Castile, the indenture which he sealed on 1 March 1373 stipulated service in France alone, for one year, commencing on 1 May. Recent opinion is that the intention was for him to sail from Plymouth (named as the embarkation port) to Brittany to aid Duke John. But in May the latter fled to England. A change of plan by 11 June is indicated by the substitution of Dover and Sandwich as embarkation ports. Whereas the original intention may have been to strike into the interior of France after securing Brittany, Holmes surmised that it was now to invade through Calais, putting pressure on the Ile de France, then turning westwards to secure Brittany.[117]

The army, which included the duke of Brittany as a retinue captain, crossed to Calais during July and set out thence on 4 August. Froissart says that the columns passed near St Omer, Thérouanne and Montreuil, then moved towards Arras, near where, at the abbey of Mont-Saint-Eloy, the two dukes lodged. The army crossed the Somme and Oise valleys by way of Ham, St Quentin and Ribemont, and encamped in and pillaged the Laonnais. Thence the English moved southwards, crossing the Aisne at Vailly and threatening Paris and other cities in the heartlands of the French monarchy. Gaunt's aim may have been to capture one of these cities, as his father's had been in 1359–60. He had with him miners and specialists to maintain siege-engines (*trepgettes*).[118] Probably he hoped to provoke the French into giving battle: he was a more experienced and confident commander than he had been in 1369, and doubtless keen to banish the slurs he had earned then. But, according to Froissart, Charles V 'who doubted the fortunes [of war], was utterly opposed to giving assent that his forces give battle'.[119]

Turning away from Paris, Gaunt moved south-east to threaten Troyes. There the French commanders, the dukes of Berry and Burgundy and Bertrand du Guesclin, concentrated their forces. They were joined by the duke of Anjou, who had withdrawn from the duchy of Brittany. At Plancy on the River Aube, north of Troyes, the duke of Bourbon fought a delaying action. Charles V was himself in Troyes when Gaunt drew his forces up outside it. But the king refused his challenge to do battle. When Gaunt ordered his men to cross the undefended ditches around the suburbs, they were driven out again with heavy loss by a large-scale sortie from within the city walls. Next morning the English decamped. Charles ordered a detachment to shadow and harass them. He wished to guard against any English attempt to recover Poitou or Limousin. Gaunt moved westwards, towards Sens, whose suburbs he occupied. There, allegedly, he suffered the heaviest losses yet, as a result of an ambush laid by Olivier de Clisson. After this, the English refrained from pursuing the French. In fact the invaders were not seriously attacked again after leaving Sens. Gaunt resumed his south-eastern movement: on 1 October the *bailli* of Auxerre reported that the English were in the Avallon region. From there they veered south-west, passing through Moulins as they went down the Allier valley. They were admitted to Tulle and Brive la Gaillarde. Passing through his own town of Bergerac, Gaunt reached Bordeaux about Christmas.[120]

The 1373 expedition, the principal English military effort of the war of 1369–75, has proved difficult to evaluate, particularly in the absence of firm evidence about Gaunt's objectives. English chroniclers tended to write it off as a failure, costly in men and horses.[121] Juan 1 in 1386–7 considered the French defence a model to be followed in face of Gaunt's invasion of Castile. A Norman chronicler considered that 'in this chevauchée nothing of note happened of which one should take account', but that it was 'the greatest raid and the greatest occupation made in France since the start of the wars'.[122] Bourbon's biographer claimed that only half the English who had set out from Calais mustered at Brive, and that half this remnant had lost their horses.[123]

Historians have mostly seen the expedition as a failure and a demonstration of Gaunt's lack of military ability. Professor Russell writes that 'the Great March of 1373 has been rightly regarded by all those who have described it as one of the outstanding failures of Lancaster's chequered career as a military commander'.[124] Professor Holmes has suggested that French pressure thwarted Gaunt's probable aims of first attacking the Paris region and then the French forces invading Brittany, and forced him to take a circuitous and difficult route to Gascony.[125] But Dr Palmer has described the march from

Calais to Bordeaux as 'a prodigious military achievement which has been unjustly denigrated'.[126]

Gaunt's challenge to Charles V suggests that he hoped for victory in battle and his threats to Troyes and Sens that he hoped to capture a city. If so, he failed in both aims. His army suffered heavy losses through harassment and privations, the latter probably intensified by the difficult passage across the Massif Central. Gaunt may have taken this rugged route in order to discourage the pursuit of increasingly straggling columns. The question of the extent to which his army's disintegration took place on campaign remains open. According to the Anonimalle Chronicler, his soldiers were 'in health and prosperity' till their arrival in Gascony, and they and their mounts starved after their arrival.[127]

Gaunt did have some successes in 1373. He relieved pressure on Duke John's supporters in Brittany. He temporarily revived English allegiances in Limousin: the submission of Brive particularly incensed his princely opponents.[128] He left a heavy toll of devastation, reflected in many French sources.[129] It was probably not coincidental that after the campaign both sides became seriously inclined to initiate peace talks and that Gaunt himself was to remain a prime mover behind them. Though there was to be heavy fighting on the peripheries of France and at sea in 1374–5, there was nothing on the scale of 1373. Gaunt's expedition produced a military stalemate. From the English point of view, this was an improvement, but it compared badly with the famous victories of Edward III and the Black Prince.

In 1373 (as again in 1387) Gaunt eagerly sought a pitched battle. He and his retainers had first won renown at the battle of Najera in 1367. Ironically, he passed up the one chance he had, in 1369, of fighting a decisive battle in France. Thereafter, French strategy denied him another opportunity. Froissart's verdict on his French campaigns was just:

> he had many times invaded France and overrun the country with small gain. He had undergone great bodily fatigue; and though he burnt and destroyed the flat country, it was as almost soon recovered again from the damages it had suffered.[130]

Gaunt had good qualities as a commander. He could adapt to a new strategy – the 'barbican' strategy pursued on the renewal of the war in 1377. He was capable of bold strokes and swift advances, such as his Norman *chevauchée* of 1369, the decision to invade Galicia in 1386 and the invasion of León with a depleted force in 1387. Allegedly, he had advocated an adventurous strategy in Scotland in 1385. His doggedness and practicality as a commander were best seen in difficult circumstances, holding his forces together in southern France in 1373, in Scotland in 1384 and in León in 1387. He was most in his element when participating in or conducting sieges – with notable success at Limoges (1370), Montpon (1371), Brest (1386) and Orense (1387). But siege warfare was not an English military speciality; English forces were more at ease on *chevauchée*, unencumbered by elaborate siege-trains. Such deficiencies may have been partly responsible for the failures at Harfleur (1369), Troyes and Sens (1373), St Malo (1378) and Benavente (1387).

Under Gaunt the military organisation based on the Lancastrian inheritance which Duke Henry had developed was maintained and improved, and became an important component of the defence of the Crown's possessions in a period when they were under increased threat (1369–89). The Crown's problems in paying wages to Gaunt's military retinues in the field, and his own pretensions abroad, gave him incentives to increase the size of his permanent retinue, as a means of guaranteeing a stable nucleus for the forces he might need. The financial burden on Gaunt's resources was considerable, and this was increased in the 1370s when he took a major part in the war, and the Crown started to pile up huge debts to him for military expenditure. From a financial viewpoint, peace became highly desirable for Gaunt. But he saw that further military action was necessary in order to force opponents at least to compromise. Two of his campaigns – in 1373–4 and 1386–7 – helped to stimulate negotiations. These and some of his other campaigns, despite the lack of the hoped for decisive victories, can be seen as contributing to the ending of the first phase of the Hundred Years War, in 1389, in a stalemate, on terms which did not bring disaster or dishonour to the English Crown. But the Crown had failed to fulfil the high expectations it had raised. Despite Gaunt's doggedness in war, much the same can be said of his campaigns. He was never able to regain the glory which he and his knights had won at Najera.

Notes and References

1 Abortive expeditions were planned for 1370 (northern France), 1377 (naval expedition?), 1382 (Spain), 1383 (France, Spain), 1391 (France), 1395 (against the Turks). In 1379 and 1380 Gaunt led military retinues to the Scottish border, in 1383 to the Kent coast and in 1393 against the Cheshire rebels. In 1381 and 1397 he brought armed retinues to parliament.
2 Froissart J 1871, Vol. 12, pp. 290–1.
3 Lewis NB 1964, pp. 17, 21n. For comparisons between the size of

Gaunt's and other magnates' retinues on expeditions abroad, Sherborne JW 1964: 720ff.

4 P.R.O. PL3/1/59.

5 *C.A.*, p. 58.

6 For the appearance of Duke Henry's donees in his *comitiva*, forming 'a nucleus around which other less stable elements could collect', Fowler K 1961, pp. 707–9. For military subcontracts in general, Sherborne JW 1964: 742–4.

7 Lewis NB 1964, pp. 77–112.

8 For Gaunt's indenture with Sir Hugh Hastings (1366), see below, p. 376.

9 *J.G.R. 1379–83*, pp. 6–13. The names of some knights are cancelled.

10 Lewis NB 1964, pp. 88–90.

11 *J.G.R. 1379–83*, no. 39.

12 B.L. Harley MS 3988 f42r.

13 Maddicott JR 1970, p. 45; Holmes G 1957, pp. 67–8, 72–3; Fowler K 1961, pp. 723–4.

14 Fowler K 1969, pp. 181–2. As earl of Lancaster, on 31 March 1362 Gaunt confirmed the life-rent of 50*m*. granted to Hastings by Duke Henry for attendance in peace and war (Huntington Library, San Marino, California, Hastings Charters, HAD 3200). On 22 Oct. 1391 Hastings acknowledged receipt from Gaunt's receiver Robert Morton of a half-year instalment (ibid., HAF Box 1, 23).

15 Fowler K 1969, pp. 182, 185–6.

16 *C.P.R. 1370–4*, p. 31; *J.G.R. 1379–83*, no. 899.

17 Lewis NB 1964, no. 1.

18 Froissart J 1869, Vol. 7, p. 201; Goodman A 1980: 114–15 and 114n.

19 *J.G.R. 1372–6*, no. 260; *C.P.R. 1367–70*, p. 78.

20 *Foedera*, 1830, Vol. 3, pt 2, pp. 442–3. Bracebridge had undertaken service for life as an esquire of Duke Henry in 1345 (Fowler K 1961, p. 676).

21 Lewis NB 1964, pp. 94–5, 97.

22 *J.G.R. 1372–6*, no. 786; Lopes F 1988, pp. 260–5.

23 *C.R.C.*, Vol. 2, p. 110; *J.G.R. 1372–6*, nos 565, 690; Froissart J 1871, Vol. 12, pp. 301, 324.

24 Storey RL 1957: 595.

25 Lopes F 1988, pp. 64–7; *J.G.R. 1372–6*, nos 70, 579, 838–40, 1592; *J.G.R. 1379–83*, p. 8, nos 499, 709, 822.

26 *Foedera*, 1709, Vol. 8, p. 14.

27 Kirby JL 1970, pp. 54–5. Among the Lancastrian retainers who joined Bolingbroke on his return from France in 1399 was Sir John Dabridgecourt (Wylie JH 1898, Vol. 4, p. 186).

28 Lewis NB 1964, p. 80.

29 *J.G.R. 1379–83*, no. 1237.

30 *J.G.R. 1372–6*, no. 786; Lopes F 1988, pp. 246–51, 260–3.

31 *J.G.R. 1372–6*, nos 789, 868; Swinton GSC 1919, pp. 263–5. Swinton was attendant on Gaunt in the household in 1381 (East Sussex R.O., Waleys cartulary B10, A7, B5). He was retained by the Scottish Crown by 1383–4, when he was paid £20 'pro feodo suo' (Burnett G 1880, Vol. 3, p. 124).

32 *C.A.*, p. 125.

33 *J.G.R. 1372–6*, no. 63. In April 1370 a messenger was sent from London to Lancs. with letters for 'gentz de nostre retenue celles

parties', presumably to request service for the forthcoming expedition to Aquitaine (C.C.C, 495 f15).

34 *J.G.R. 1379–83*, nos 357–9, 377, 526–7.

35 P.R.O. DL29/262/4070; cf ibid., 4069 for delivery of summonses for the 1369 expedition.

36 *J.G.R. 1379–83*, nos 500–1, 775–80; *Foedera*, 1830, Vol. 3, pt 2, p. 864. Similarly composed commissions were appointed in 1369 for Lancs., and for Derbys. and Staffs. combined. For the dispatch of ducal summonses in Aug. 1383, *J.G.R. 1379–83*, no. 909.

37 *J.G.R. 1372–6*, no. 1232. John Smallwood was parker of Cowick in 1373 (ibid., no. 576); John Hiperon was parker of Pontefract in 1379 (*J.G.R. 1379–83*, no. 87).

38 Ibid., nos 1222, 1226–7.

39 Ibid., nos 1232, 1237, 1239.

40 Bateson M 1901, Vol. 2, p. 144 (mayor's account 1368–9).

41 *J.G.R. 1372–6*, no. 1005.

42 P.R.O. PL3/1/77.

43 Ibid., 76.

44 C.C.C, 495 f 15.

45 *J.G.R. 1272–6*, nos 1244, 1246, 1248.

46 Ibid., nos 1194, 1200, 1222–4, 1228. A separate warrant ordered Pope to purchase 200 packhorses 'pur nostre cariage et somayl' (ibid., no. 230).

47 Ibid., nos 1195, 1224. For an order to the receiver of the south parts to provide fodder and litter for the horses which another servant was taking to Kingston Lacy, ibid., no. 1296.

48 Ibid., nos 250–2, 291, 996 (1372 and 1373 expeditions).

49 Ibid., nos 221–4.

50 C.C.C. 495 f15. In 1372 the Yorks. receiver was responsible for receiving 40 sheaves of arrows with peacock feather (*J.G.R. 1372–6*, no. 64). In Dec. 1382 the receiver of Kenilworth was ordered to supply a cart for the carriage of armour thence to London, needed for the proposed expedition to France (*J.G.R. 1379–83*, no. 786).

51 *J.G.R. 1372–6*, nos 1018, 1042, 1217–18.

52 P.R.O. E364/10; B.L. Add. MS 37, 494, account book of William Airmin, f 2v, 3v, 4v, 5r–v, 6v, 7r. For Gaunt's orders to Bugbrigge to transfer sums received (not corresponding to those listed by Airmin) to the treasurer of war Thomas Swaby, *J.G.R. 1372–6*, nos 1217–18, 1336.

53 See the terms of Thomas Ampcotes's appointment in 1369 and of Adam Pope's in 1373 (ibid., nos 294, 317). Richard Beverle was war treasurer in 1378 and John Norfolk in 1386–7 (*J.G.R. 1379–83*, nos 258, 1235). For promissory payments, see also Somerville R 1953, p. 103 and n.

54 P.R.O. E364/5.

55 *J.G.R. 1372–6*, no. 1336; cf ibid., nos 169, 1241.

56 P.R.O. E364/5; ibid., E403/461/1.

57 *J.G.R. 1372–6*, no. 1118. An example of payment ordered on a bill of credit is the £100 Sir Thomas Poynings was to receive in part payment for his service and that of his men in Aquitaine in 1370–1 (ibid., no. 1179).

58 P.R.O. E364/10; B.L. Add. MS 37, 494.

59 *J.G.R. 1372–6*, nos 1223–4, 1228.

60 Ibid., no. 1336.

61 P.R.O. E364/10.
62 Ibid., DL28/3/1, m3.
63 Ibid., E403/468/13.
64 *C.P.R. 1377–81*, p. 537.
65 *J.G.R. 1372–6*, nos 1195, 1224, 1228.
66 Ibid., no. 1005.
67 Ibid., no. 1232.
68 Ibid., no. 1237.
69 *A.C.*, p. 44; Froissart J 1868, Vol. 6, p. 223.
70 *C.Q.P.V.*, p. 105; *C.A.*, p. 59.
71 In 1371 Gaunt retained Calveley to serve him in Aquitaine for six months with 60 men-at-arms and 60 archers. In 1372 Gaunt referred to his payment of *regard* for six months' service for Calveley's retinue of 100 + 100, then in London; Calveley had undertaken to serve with them for a year in Gaunt's company in Spain (*J.G.R. 1372–6*, nos 981, 1000). Gaunt had given 'nostre tres cher et bien ame' Calveley a New Year's present (ibid., no. 915). Calveley was Gaunt's marshal in Aquitaine in 1374 (*C.E.P.R. Papal Letters*, Vol. 4, p. 131).
72 Froissart J 1870, Vol. 11, pp. 265–72.
73 Ibid., 1869, Vol. 8, pp. 69–70.
74 Ibid., Vol. 7, pp. 433–4. For Gaunt's appointment during the expedition of a captain to Ardres 'by common advice and assent' of the earl of Hereford and other barons and lords of his council, P.R.O. E30/256.
75 Nicholson R 1974, pp. 195–6.
76 P.R.O. E101/40/5; ibid., E403/504/7. For the muster of contingents led by Sir John Roos (banneret), Sir William Hilton, Lord Welles, Sir William Fulthorpe, Sir Richard Tempest, Sir John Felton, Sir Thomas Ughtred and Sir John Calveley, P.R.O. E101/40/5. Chroniclers do not mention the presence of Edmund of Langley on the expedition, but he was summoned to go on it (P.R.O. E403/504/1).
77 *W.C.*, pp. 66–7; *C.H.K.*, Vol. 2, p. 203. For the summons in March see also P.R.O. DL29/262/4070, account of receiver in Lincs. and Hunts.
78 James MR 1899, p. 61.
79 *W.C.*, pp. 66–7. Allowances were made in Scottish customs accounts for the year up to 12/18 March 1384 for the destruction of Edinburgh tron by the English and their burning of skins and hides at Leith (Burnett G 1880, Vol. 3, pp. 116–17, 124).
80 Wyntoun A 1879, Vol. 3, pp. 20–2.
81 Otterbourne T 1732, p. 158; *C.H.K.*, Vol. 2, p. 203; *C.A.*, pp. 358–9.
82 Armitage-Smith S 1904, p. 279 and n; *C.A.*, pp. 358–9.
83 Wyntoun A 1879, Vol. 3, p. 20.
84 Froissart J 1871, Vol. 12, pp. 186–99.
85 *C.Q.P.V.*, pp. 209–10.
86 Froissart J 1869, Vol. 8, pp. 64–71. In Feb. 1372 'nostre bien ame' William Calowe, miner, was to receive payment on a bill of credit for 75s. 4d., wages owed for his service in Gascony (*J.G.R. 1372–6*, no. 903). The same year six miners and a smith were to be selected by royal commission from the Forest of Dean for service on Gaunt's next expedition (ibid., no. 71).
87 *R.P.*, Vol. 3, p. 36.
88 Sherborne J 1967: 172.

89 Ibid., 172; Delachenal R 1931, Vol. 5, pp. 227–8; Russell PE 1955, p. 241; Pocquet de Haut-Jussé BA 1967: 157–8.

90 Delachenal R 1931, Vol. 5, p. 231.

91 Russell PE 1955, p. 242.

92 *C.A.*, p. 204.

93 Delachenal R 1931, Vol. 5, p. 231.

94 Froissart J 1869, Vol. 9, pp. 66–7, 70–1, 79–83, 89–93; Delachenal R 1931, Vol. 5, p. 231; Pocquet du Haut-Jussé BA 1967: 159–60. For payment to Gaunt of wages for his retinue on the expedition totalling over £6,491 by the war treasurers William Walworth and John Philpot, Easter term 1378, P.R.O. E403/468/15, 18, 19.

95 *C.H.K.*, Vol. 2, pp. 208–10; *St Denys*, Vol. 1, pp. 434–7; *C.A.*, pp. 368–9; Froissart J 1870, Vol. 11, pp. 331–7; Lopes F 1988, p. 192. Knighton's account, probably based on the eyewitness testimony of a Lancastrian retainer, has been preferred. The French accounts qualify Gaunt's success. For the siege see also Jones M 1970, pp. 102–3.

96 Lopes F 1988, pp. 264–5.

97 This account of the campaign and battle is based on *C.R.C.*, Vol. 2, pp. 551ff; Russell PE 1955, ch. 4.

98 Froissart J 1869, Vol. 7, p. 200.

99 Ibid., pp. 201ff.

100 Ibid., pp. 200–1; *C.H.K.*, Vol. 2, p. 122; *C.A.*, p. 59.

101 Peterborough W of 1859, pp. 97ff.

102 Pope MK and Lodge EC 1910, pp. 84, 98–9, 158, 162; Palmer JJN 1982; 271ff.

103 Among those granted protections Nov. 1366, intending to serve in Gaunt's company, were John Herle, Edmund Appleby, Robert Hauley, John Neville of Raby, Walter Urswick, Henry Grey, Richard Scrope, Thomas Metham, Thomas Banastre, John Plays, Hugh Swynford and Nicholas Langeford (*Foedera*, 1830, Vol. 3, pt 2, p. 812).

104 Peterborough W of 1859, pp. 109–10.

105 This account relies heavily on Sherborne JW 1986, pp. 41–61.

106 A detailed account of the frontier fighting is in *A.C.*, pp. 59–60.

107 The Anonimalle Chronicler says that the English formed up on 'le mountayn de Baligate'; Froissart that Burgundy occupied 'the hill of Tournehem' and Walsingham that he occupied 'montem Morianum qui vocatur le Chalkhull'.

108 Cf Sherborne's discussion of Burgundy's failure to attack (1986, pp. 50–1). Gaunt dated a warrant at 'ffreanes' (Fiennes?) on 16 Sept. (C.C.C, 495 f15).

109 P.R.O. E30/256. Privy Seal letters were taken to Calais by a valet paid 20 Nov.; they were directed to Gaunt, the earls of Warwick, Hereford and Salisbury, the governor of Guines and the treasurer of Calais (P.R.O. E403/439/15).

110 *C.A.*, pp. 63–4; *A.C.*, p. 61.

111 Froissart J 1869, Vol. 8, pp. 429ff.

112 Sherborne JW 1986, p. 51.

113 Vaughan R 1962, pp. 8–9.

114 Delisle L 1874, nos 657, 1076. The destruction is emphasised in Dickson W 1844, p. 43.

115 The best modern account of the 1373 expedition is in Delachenal R 1928, Vol. 4, pp. 453ff.

116 Russell PE 1955, p. 204.
117 Holmes G 1975, p. 29; *J.G.R. 1372–6*, no. 52; Sherborne JW 1964: 727; Jones M 1970, pp. 72ff.
118 Froissart J 1869, Vol. 8, pp. 280, 296, 303ff; Chazand A–M 1876, p. 50; Holmes G 1975, p. 28; Sherborne J 1964, p. 727. For 'trepgettes' see above, p. 219. Some places mentioned by Froissart were probably on parallel routes taken by English columns (Delachenal R 1928, Vol. 4, p. 489n; cf ibid., p. 484n.). Roye was occupied 21–8 Aug. (ibid., p. 490 and n.).
119 Froissart J 1869, Vol. 8, p. 292.
120 Ibid., pp. 310–14; Chazand A–M 1876, pp. 53–4; *C.Q.P.V.*, p. 246; Delachenal R 1928, Vol. 4, p. 494 and n.
121 *H.A.*, Vol. 1, pp. 315–16; *Eulogium*, Vol. 3, p. 336. According to a chronicler from the Franciscan house at King's Lynn, 'modicum . . . profecerunt, quia fame magna pars exercitus interiit, propter defectum capitaneorum, ut dicebatur a multis' (Gransden A 1957: 272). The monk of Alnwick Abbey was more complimentary about the damage inflicted by the army, its good order and high repute – doubtless with Lord Percy's participation in mind (Dickson W 1844, p. 143).
122 *C.Q.P.V.*, pp. 246–7.
123 Chazand A–M 1876, p. 55.
124 Russell PE 1955, p. 204.
125 Holmes G 1975, pp. 26–8.
126 Palmer JJN 1972, p. 6.
127 *A.C.*, p. 74.
128 Delachenal R 1928, Vol. 4, p. 507.
129 Ibid., pp. 502–3.
130 Froissart J 1871, Vol. 15, p. 81.

Chapter Eleven

Gaunt and the Church

As the political opponent at one time or another of Bishops Wykeham, Courtenay and Despenser, the advocate in 1377 of higher taxation of the clergy and the patron and protector of John Wycliffe, Gaunt acquired, especially in the 1370s, a reputation for anticlericalism and for at least a tolerant attitude towards unorthodox religious opinions, a reputation malignly reflected in Walsingham's works.[1] Gaunt's patronage of Wycliffe in the 1370s can be explained in terms of political expediency, but this is not the whole explanation. The most telling contemporary comment on his attitude to the Lollards is to be found in the chronicle of Henry Knighton:

> He believed them [the Lollards] to be holy, because of their appealing speech and appearance, but he was deceived, as were many others.[2]

This can be regarded as an authoritative comment, as Gaunt was the patron of Knighton's house, Leicester Abbey, and Knighton was sympathetic to the duke, received much information about his activities from members of the ducal household when they visited Leicester and knew the Lollard Swinderby, whom the duke patronised. The duke appears as a sincere but eventually disabused patron of Wycliffe and his followers in the work known as *Fasciculi Zizaniorum,* a file of documents partly about the heresy, with a connecting commentary compiled, Dr Crompton has argued, by successive priors provincial of the Carmelite Order and for their use

– a compilation of the later fourteenth and early fifteenth centuries. The order developed a strong tradition in this period of anti-Wycliffite polemic. Crompton surmises that the collection was kept in London at the Whitefriars in Fleet Street,[3] a house with which Gaunt had connections (see below, p. 245). In view of Gaunt's close links with the Carmelites – and the important part they probably played in weaning him away from Wycliffe – the attitudes attributed to him in their files are not to be lightly dismissed.

The *Fasciculi* provides striking instances of Gaunt's rapport with Wycliffe and his followers, and bears witness to its decline. In 1381 Wycliffe is alleged to have appealed to the king against the sentence of the chancellor of his university, and Gaunt to have travelled to Oxford and ordered him to be silent on the issues (a prohibition which Wycliffe ignored).[4] His supporter Philip Repingdon (a canon of Leicester Abbey) claimed in a sermon at Oxford that Gaunt favoured his master's followers and their opinions.[5] Repingdon and his fellow Wycliffite Nicholas Hereford travelled to protest to the duke against the condemnation by the Blackfriars council (May–June 1382) of twenty-four of Wycliffe's theses. They convinced the duke that the condemnation would lead to the 'destruction and weakening of the temporal dominion and of temporal kings'. He was harsh in countenance and words to a group of orthodox doctors, but having heard their arguments, he denounced Repingdon and Hereford as laymen or devils. He called them odious for their opinion on the Eucharist and himself expounded conventional beliefs, forbidding any doctor to answer them, and did this so eloquently himself that the orthodox doctors had nothing to add. He ordered the reprobates to accept Archbishop Courtenay's commands.[6] It was probably symptomatic of Gaunt's shift of sympathies away from Lollardy (and not just a change of political expediency) that in 1383 he received crusading privileges from Urban VI for his projected expedition to Castile. Urban appointed him as captain and standard-bearer of the cross and papacy against the schismatic Juan, with complementary crusading bulls.[7] The wills of some of Gaunt's leading knights do not hint at Wycliffite sympathies – unlike those of some of Princess Joan's and Richard II's knights – and they display a conventional devotion to the cult of the Virgin similar to Gaunt's. Sir Roger Trumpington (1379) commended his soul to God, the Virgin and All Souls; so, in almost identical terms, did Sir Robert Swillington the nephew (1379) and Sir Ralph Hastings (1397). Sir Richard Burley (1386) invoked the Trinity, the Virgin and the Company of Heaven. Trumpington and Swillington willed to be buried in Lady Chapels; the former made a bequest to Gaunt's Carmelite confessor Walter Diss.[8] One Wycliffite sympathiser highly favoured by Gaunt was

Thomas Brightwell, fellow of Merton College, Oxford and canon of Newarke College, Leicester; in February 1382 Gaunt presented him to the deanery of the college, the most prestigious benefice in his gift. This was several months before the Blackfriars council, at which Brightwell was accused of partiality to Wycliffe's followers at Oxford. Brightwell, after a show of defiance, submitted and joined in the condemnation of Wycliffe's views. Thereafter he had an orthodox career: in 1388 he was appointed on a royal commission to seize heretical writings and to have proclamation made forbidding the maintenance and distribution of heretical doctrines. He died in 1390, dean of Newarke College and canon of Lincoln.[9] A wilder and more intransigent heretic who had received Gaunt's patronage was the unbeneficed priest William Swinderby, whose piety and moralising had earned him the help of the Leicester canons as well as the duke, before he joined an unorthodox community living outside the towns walls. When, as a result of Bishop Buckingham's determined process against Swinderby in 1382, he was compelled early in July to repudiate before the bishop the unorthodox opinions attributed to him, Gaunt and his young son Bolingbroke were (according to Swinderby) among those present on the occasion at Lincoln.[10] It may be that Gaunt's attitude to Swinderby was now equivocal – Bolingbroke's future attitudes displayed nothing but contempt and horror for the likes of Swinderby. Perhaps Wycliffe, though, living in enforced retirement at Lutterworth, within easy reach of the ducal residences at Leicester and Kenilworth, fondly interpreted Gaunt's view of Swinderby as well as of himself as more favourable than it actually was. In 1384 he opined that the Carmelite friar's recent accusation against the duke at Salisbury was made 'because he was unwilling to punish faithful priests'.[11] Indeed, this opinion ought not to be lightly dismissed. It may well be that the favour shown by the Carmelites' patron to heretics caused controversy within the order, and lay behind the accusations at Salisbury against Gaunt (see p. 100). Wycliffe's explanation of this episode is as plausible as any other. For the eclecticism of Gaunt's religious patronage is likely to have aroused irritations as well as sharpened rivalries among the clerics he favoured. Orthodox as well heretical clergy hoped for his support in controversy. In February 1382 the heads of the four mendicant houses at Oxford wrote to him defending themselves against the charge that they had fomented the Peasants' Revolt: their principal accuser was Wycliffe's disciple Nicholas Hereford.[12]

As Armitage-Smith pointed out, Gaunt upheld the rights of established ecclesiastical institutions; he appears in the guises of a conventional patron and an upholder of orthodox worship.[13] Professor Holmes has demonstrated in *The Good Parliament* how he promoted a pro-papal policy in 1375–6; for much of the 1380s he presented himself as the executor of crusading bulls against schismatics and in the 1390s he earnestly supported Christian unity and crusades against infidels. Whatever appeal Wycliffe's doctrines had for Gaunt, he decisively rejected them, according to *Fasciculi Zizaniorum,* when the Oxford Wycliffites appealed for his support in 1382. Orthodox condemnations drove him irreversibly into the conformist laager, as indeed they drove most of Wycliffe's followers, including Brightwell and Repingdon.

An important influence on Gaunt's personal piety and his critique of ecclesiastical institutions is likely to have been exercised by his confessors. A series of papal privileges in the 1360s had marked the development of the Lancastrian household's religious institutions. In 1359 he, his wife Blanche and his household were permitted to have a portable altar and he was licensed to choose his own confessor; in 1363 the couple's chaplain was permitted to hear their confessions and those of the household and to administer the sacraments to all of them. In 1366 he and Blanche were allowed to change as well as choose their confessors.[14] These, as far as is known, were impeccably orthodox, but were drawn from an order possessing a distinctive religious ethos and brand of asceticism – the 'Order of the Brothers of the Blessed Mary of Mount Carmel'. The Carmelites were founded by a Latin monk in the kingdom of Jerusalem *c.* 1154–5 and received their first rule from the patriarch of Jerusalem *c.* 1220. The early Carmelites formed a community of hermits living under strict rule on Mount Carmel. Richard Grey, lord of Codnor (Derbyshire), returning from the Holy Land in 1242, brought Carmelites to England and founded a house for them at Aylesford (Kent), a few years before changes in the rule altered the character of the order from an eremitical to a mendicant one. Richard Grey's descendant and heir John Grey (d. 1392) cherished the family link with the Carmelites, in 1355 petitioning for an indulgence for those who visited Aylesford Friary. In this petition he was described as a companion of Duke Henry; four years later he was intending to serve in France in Gaunt's retinue. He may have developed the duke's interest in the order: he and Sir Miles Stapleton brought back from the Middle East Jean Carmesson's life of the Carmelite crusading saint Pierre Thomas soon after its composition in 1366.[15] In that year the pope granted a petition made by Gaunt on behalf of a Camalite, John Wauncy, and in 1368 the Carmelite John Swaffham, bishop of Cloyne, a distinguished preacher and future controversialist against the Wycliffites, was present in the Duchess Blanche's funeral cortège.[16]

The duke's goodwill to the order is reflected in his petition to Pope Urban VI denouncing certain slanderous and malicious insinuations against the spiritual and historical claims of the order and requesting that these false articles should receive papal condemnation, and the brothers' claim to a special relationship with the Virgin receive papal confirmation.[17] In 1382 the provincial chapter of the English Carmelites asked Gaunt to assume the position of founder of the Doncaster friary, a request which he accepted

> to the honour of God and Our Lady and of holy religion and at the same time for the great and special affection which we have for the said order.[18]

This affection (which was to be shared by some of his children) remained so great that he willed in 1398 that, if he died outside London, his corpse should be taken to lie overnight for a requiem mass at the Whitefriars in Fleet Street, before interment in St Paul's Cathedral. What did he intend if he was mortally ill in London? Perhaps to receive the last rites at Whitefriars. In any case, he probably intended to wear on his deathbed and to be buried wearing the brown Carmelite scapular, whose origin lay in the vision of Simon Stock in 1251. Little is known about Stock, whose holiness is celebrated by Carmelites. He was born at Aylesford in Kent and died in 1265. In 1254 he was elected superior general of the order, and it was under his guidance that the Carmelites turned from the eremitical to the mendicant way of life, and that notable new houses were founded. The Virgin, according to Carmelite legend, appeared to Stock and handed him a scapular, saying

> This is the privilege granted to you and all Carmelites; he who shall piously die wearing this habit shall be preserved from eternal flames.

Members of the confraternity of the order wore the scapular; the first notice of the Feast of the Commemoration of the Virgin, celebrated by the confraternity in memory of Stock's vision (17 July) occurs in the *Kalendarium* presented by Nicolas of Lynn to Gaunt in 1386. The implication is that Gaunt celebrated the feast as a Carmelite *confrater* – a feast which was regarded as specially significant at Whitefriars in the late 1390s, if that is indeed the provenance of the 'Reconstructed Carmelite Missal'.[19]

Gaunt's respect for exponents of the eremitical life, even when exemplified by so troublesome and doctrinally erratic a personality as Swinderby, was probably enhanced by his attachment to the Carmelites, with their eremitical traditions. But they also pushed him towards the mainstream of purely orthodox values, particularly as expressed in the cult of the Virgin Mary. In 1399, shortly before his death, he alluded to 'a certain devotion' which he had to Lincoln Cathedral, of which the Virgin was patroness – the same who was dubbed by Lollards the 'wyche of Lincolne'.[20] In this devotion Gaunt was responding to and promoting Marian trends which were developing strongly in the fourteenth century and whose appeal came to outweigh that of the Wycliffites in elite circles. In 1389 Pope Boniface IX completed a project of Urban VI's by instituting the Feast of the Visitation (2 July), with the purpose of imploring the Virgin to end the Schism – an objective central to Gaunt's policies. Walsingham recorded the new feast in 1392, and in 1393 the Carmelites recognised it, earlier than most other orders.[21]

Gaunt's special attachment to the Virgin was not new in the 1380s – his connection with the Carmelites was also long-standing – but it may have intensified then and have acquired a centrality in his religious life which gave new direction to some of his ecclesiastical and secular policies. For there is no suggestion that he interceded with the Virgin in the versions given by Knighton and Walsingham of his repentance for adultery during the Peasant's Revolt in 1381. According to Knighton, he promised 'amendment of his way of life to God'; according to Walsingham, his penances 'it is believed turned away the wrath of God'.[22] Soon after the revolt (23 July), a grant of land was made by him to facilitate the foundation of a chapel in Roecliffe (Yorks.) to be built in honour of the Virgin and St Catherine.[23] On the assumption that his gift was already intended before the repentance (which involved his repudiation of Catherine Swynford), it would appear that he then saw nothing amiss in such a blatant association of the Virgin, Catherine's name-saint and himself. A further stage in what Walsingham describes as his 'conversion to religion' in 1381 may have been his purchase and the delivery into his own hands (recorded in May 1383) of a rosary and a prayerbook containing the matins of Our Lady, the Seven Psalms and *Dirige* – a volume which may have been intended for his private devotions.[24] Two crises in which he was involved in the Iberian Peninsular in 1387, as recorded by Walsingham and Fernão Lopes, were given by them a Marian context which is likely to reflect the interpretation of events in the duke's familiar circles. According to Walsingham, Gaunt's invocations to the Virgin from the depth of despair in Spain led her to supplicate for him and procure from her Son his restoration to prosperity.[25] In fact soon afterwards in Portugal, according to Lopes, the Virgin saved Gaunt and his family from another disaster. Philippa of Lancaster's husband João I fell desperately ill: she and her father hurried to his side. The king's life was despaired of; Philippa prayed especially to the Virgin as the Mother of Mercy:

Out of compassion, the Mother of God was pleased to ask her Blessed Son for such a great favour, so that the King began to get better and to improve in health. This caused as much astonishment as if he had risen from the dead.[26]

The centrality of the Virgin in Gaunt's later religious life is perhaps reflected in the Marian imagery on many of the chapel furnishings which he was to bequeath to one of her greatest shrines, Lincoln Cathedral. On some of the altar cloths she is associated with representations of the deity; on others, with Gaunt's name saints. One, which he probably donated, depicts the Crucifixion with the Virgin and St John; in another, she and her Son are decoratively encircled. Most pointed is the 'cloth' in which the Virgin stands between St John the Baptist and St John the Evangelist.[27] It seems likely, then, that Gaunt's devotion to the Virgin progressively intensified after he escaped from the disaster of 1381, rejected Wycliffite views, and was saved by her from further disasters in 1387; this sequence is paralleled by the beginnings of a further intensification of her cult in princely circles, which the Carmelites are likely to have encouraged.

Gaunt's Carmelite confessors included distinguished members of the order. In 1372 he granted his confessor William Badby an annuity of £10, referring to his 'great affection' for him. Badby (d.1380/1) was a famous preacher, to whose sermons people flocked 'as to a show'; Bale mentions works written by him.[28] In 1375 Gaunt granted another Carmelite, Walter Diss, £10 *p.a.* for as long as he remained ducal confessor, with a similar expression of affection: this annuity was doubled in 1380. In 1382 Diss attended the council which condemned Wycliffe, as the Cambridge representative of his order.[29] Diss was heavily involved in Gaunt's plans for a crusade against the Castilian schismatics, receiving a papal faculty to grant indulgences, to preach the cross and license its preaching. He probably acted as Gaunt's agent in organising members of his order to preach the crusade: a fragment of the text of a Carmelite sermon in its favour survives, which indicates that the crusade ran into opposition on the grounds that it was directed against Christian Spaniards, and that the crusading bulls were invalidated by the fact that they were purchased. This was not the end of the controversies caused by the bulls; in 1389 the pope forbade their continued use, which had been prolonged as a means of collecting contributions after Gaunt had made peace with the king of Castile.[30] Diss had a long-standing association with Gaunt, whom he visited in 1396.[31] Probably Gaunt's Carmelite confessors in the 1370s and early 1380s, Badby and Diss, were a decisive factor in his rejection of Wycliffite doctrines. In 1392–3 and 1397–8 Gaunt's confessor was the Carmelite John Kynyngham (d. 1399), who the following year became prior provincial. He had distinguished himself as an opponent of Wycliffe as early as 1370: his 'Three Determinations against Wycliffe', dating from then, was to be copied into *Fasciculi Zizaniorum*. He had appeared on the order's behalf at the Blackfriars council in 1382.[32]

Confessors were among the members of the duke's *familia* most intimate with him, habitués of his chamber, which occupied the private suites of apartments where he lived when staying at his various castles, manor houses and hunting lodges. Some of his castles had endowed chaplaincies to serve their chapels, where, presumably, the permanent staff and other residents worshipped. The duke also needed to provide for the worship of his household in a fittingly impressive manner.[33] He was concerned that the principal chapels in his habitual residences should be appropriately maintained: in 1380 he contracted with William Wintringham of Southwark, carpenter, to have work done on the chapel at Hertford Castle (among other buildings there).[34] The household had costly sets of instruments of worship and other chapel goods among its furnishings, such as those that the duke ordered the dean of the chapel to deliver for his use at Bruges in 1375.[35] Gaunt was to bequeath impressive collections of altar furnishings and vestments to St Paul's Cathedral, St Edmund's Abbey, Lincoln Cathedral and Newarke College, Leicester. Among the gifts to Lincoln was a gold chalice made at Bordeaux with a crucifix engraved on the foot and a 'vernicle' (picture of the face of Christ) on the dish. The cathedral was also to receive an altar (*table*) purchased at Amiens, 'in my chapel, which altar I call Domesday', his largest gold candelabra 'made for my chapel', a new 'vestment' set of cloth of gold, whose red ground was worked with falcons, and its altar cloth embroidered in gold and depicting Christ, His mother and the twelve apostles 'which I purchased at Amiens'. The Domesday altarpiece was to be valued at over £387. Some idea of its magnificence can be gathered from a contemporary description of part of its decorations:

> One great sapphire within a circle on the foot of a Majesty [God The Father or Christ in Majesty], worth £40; within the circle are twelve clusters, each of four pearls, with a diamond in the middle, each cluster worth 100s, and the whole £60; above the circle, the figure of a pope, having a small ruby and sapphire on his feet, worth 20s.

The cathedral clergy had a foretaste of these treasures when the dying duke sent them to be exhibited on their high altar on the Feast of the Epiphany (6 January) 1399.[36] The two elaborate, imposing candelabra and other ducal gifts were to figure in the cathedral's later inventories.[37]

The ducal chapel was staffed in 1372 by at least four clerks who formed a distinct group in the household, under the authority of a dean.[38] Three 'little clerks' (choristers) are mentioned in 1379–80.[39] The clerks of the ducal chapel were a curious assortment of secular clerks, monks, friars and at least one married layman – there Chaucer is likely to have been familiar with examples of the 'monk out of his cloistre'. In 1380 the duke gave 'two silver pairs of Pater Noster' (rosaries) to the secular clerk John Grantham, dean of the chapel, and to Henry, 'monk of Canterbury, singing in our . . . chapel'. In order to enhance the quality of chant in his public chapel, Gaunt probably encouraged a few musically talented monks and friars to seek dispensations from their vows. The number of clerks of the chapel does not seem to have increased in the 1390s, but Gaunt by then recruited foreigners heavily, particularly Frenchmen.[40]

But this was minor lay exploitation compared to Gaunt's use of secular benefices in order to reward primarily clerics who were among his leading administrators. Like Duke Henry,[41] he used his advowsons of parochial livings and of chaplaincies to provide them with rewards throughout his career, but after 1366 he does not appear to have resorted as well to petitioning for papal provision of benefices on the scale to which Duke Henry had been accustomed, perhaps as a consequence of a decline in the number of clerical officials in Lancastrian service. In the divisions of Henry's former properties in 1361 are listed 27 parochial benefices, 12 prebends besides in the collegiate church of St Mary Newarke, Leicester, and the deanery and three prebends in Pontefract Castle's chapel.[42] Letters of presentation to Gaunt's livings, addressed by him to bishops, were copied into his chancery registers, collected under the heading 'presentaciones'. Presentations between February 1371 and August 1375 were consolidated in such a list; 28 were made, involving 19½ parochial advowsons (two of them in Gaunt's gift through his exercise of wardship) and a chaplaincy. But 16 of the parochial presentations were related to exchanges of livings by Gaunt's clerks. So over five years or so he made presentations to only 8 parish churches in his gift.[43]

In the early 1380s Gaunt's chancery clerks compiled lists of presentations annually. In the regnal year 1380–1 presentations were made to 9 churches, 2 chaplaincies and a prebend of Newarke College; those to 5 of the churches and to the chapels were not the result of exchanges.[44] A ducal benefice expected to become vacant was doubtless the subject of intense lobbying. In unusual circumstances (and probably not only then), assignations were promised in advance.

In 1373, for the duration of Gaunt's imminent expedition abroad, he delegated the right to bestow his ecclesiastical patronage 'for our clerks' to his councillors Sir Robert Swillington and Sir William Croyser. Just before leaving, he wrote instructions on how they were to bestow vacancies. The first prebend in the chapel of Pontefract Castle was to go to John de Segenaux, dean of the duke's household chapel. The deanery of the castle chapel was assigned to John Bosoun, chaplain; the first vacant prebend in Newarke College to John Cowyk, parson of Little Steeping (Lincs.). Ralph Erghum, the duke's chancellor, was to receive the first other vacant benefice, to hold

> without hindrance and he can enjoy each benefice of our patronage given to him or to which he is presented by us;[45]

Preston rectory (Lancs.), to which Gaunt presented Erghum after his return from Gascony in 1374, was singled out.[46] Thus, in order to reward outstanding officials, the duke abetted the practice of pluralism. Another ducal pluralist was the keeper of the wardrobe John Yerdburgh. Two warrants issued on the same day in 1375 facilitated his exchange of the duke's church of Ribchester for another and his acquisition of the duke's church of Stoke (Staffs.).[47]

Gaunt's ecclesiastical patronage was insufficient for him to satisfy the aspirations of his more ambitious and able clerks; part of the attraction of his service was that it might lead to the acquisition of canonries and bishoprics. In 1359 the pope, at his petition, granted his treasurer Walter Campden, rector of Somercotes (Lincs.), a canonry of York, with expectation of a prebend.[48] Other papal provisions to canonries were granted to three of his servants in 1363: William Hornby, receiver of the duchy, was granted a canonry at Lincoln; John Lincoln, treasurer, one at York; and William Sutton, chancellor, one at Salisbury.[49] It was at Gaunt's instance that Gregory XI bestowed the bishopric of Salisbury on Ralph Erghum in 1375, and in 1380 Gaunt secured Juan Gutiérrez's provision to the Gascon see of Dax.[50] Besides using influence to secure ecclesiastical plums at the curia, Gaunt sought to exploit the rights of advowson possessed by fellow patrons. In a letter to the abbot of Selby (Yorks.), dated Bordeaux, 30 June (1389), he said that the ducal chancellor William Assheton had resigned at his request the parish church of Stanford of which the abbot was patron, so that Thomas Tutbury, treasurer of the duke's household, could have it. Gaunt asked the abbot to present Tutbury to the living, showing goodwill in the matter, as he hoped for the duke's goodwill; this would greatly please the duke and incline him to show 'good lordship to our power in your dealings with us'. The abbot and convent duly requested Bishop Buckingham of Lincoln to bestow the benefice on Tutbury.[51] One should not conclude that this was simply a case of ducal bullying; Selby Abbey (and other monastic and ecclessiastical institutions) may have been happy to bestow benefices on the clerks of great men (or even, as in this case, allow a benefice to be reserved for the use of their clerks) as a means of securing influence in their counsels.

Professor Storey has shown how the first steps to a distinguished fifteenth-century episcopal career were taken in Gaunt's service. Thomas Langley, future bishop of Durham (born *c.* 1360) said in 1407 that he had served Gaunt since his youth. This had given him access to Richard II's patronage: in 1394 Gaunt sent him to speak to the king in Wales about his affairs. The following year Langley's estate as prebendary in the royal free chapel of St Martin-le-Grand, London, was confirmed and in 1396 he received a London rectory, St Alphege's, in the gift of the dean of the chapel. In 1398 Gaunt presented Langley to the church of Castleford in the honour of Pontefract.[52] Gaunt's influence in obtaining higher offices in the Church was an attraction for his secular as well as his clerical servants. His councillor Sir Godfrey Foljambe's sons Adred and Thomas were studying civil law in 1366; Gaunt procured for them respectively provision to canonries at York and Beverley.[53] The links thus formed with canons help to account for Gaunt's close relations with some cathedral chapters.

Gaunt did not use his property rights over benefices merely as a means of rewarding servants. He was concerned to protect the rights of individual churches and to ensure maintenance of worship. In 1372, after an enquiry by his retainers Sir Godfrey Foljambe and Thomas atte More, he ordered the restoration of a pension to the chaplain at Tutbury Castle, said to have been unjustly withheld since Duke Henry's time.[54] The same year he ordered Sir Robert Swillington as steward of the honour of Pontefract to receive the fruits pertaining to the castle chapel, as its dean had ignored ducal admonitions to repair the buildings attached to it and to sustain its rights – he was under summons to appear before the duke's council concerning the matter. Gaunt wished to provide a remedy 'sicome nons seumes tenuz come patron et avowe'.[55] He was concerned too with the maintenance of the fabric of parish churches in his gift. On the same day as Erghum was admitted to Preston rectorship, Gaunt wrote that its rectory (*maisons*) was utterly cast down as a result of the previous parson's neglect. Gaunt ordered his goods to be seized since he was accountable to us for the rights of the said church, which we wish to maintain as is our obligation as patron and holder of its advowson.[56]

By discharging his duties as a patron, Gaunt might both win merit in God's eyes and protect his property rights. Others, too, hoped for his intervention to protect parochial rights which were not his direct concern. At some time in the 1390s, his 'poor tenants of the soke of Snaith' (Yorks.) petitioned for his help against the scheme of the inhabitants of Carlton to gain parochial rights for their chapel of ease, to the detriment of Snaith parish. They asked Gaunt to put pressure over the matter on the abbot of Selby (the appropriator of Snaith) and to speak to the archbishop of York about it, when he came to Beverley, in order to enlist him in the same cause. Gaunt's response was favourable; he wrote from Pontefract to the abbot and monks of Selby in support of his Snaith tenants.[57]

Thus the duke displayed a legalistic concern with the minutiae of parochial duties and rights. A conscientious and prudent prince concerned himself too with the minutiae of holiness, the devout worship and living of clerics and laymen who might be obscure or of only local fame in the world's eyes, especially those within his lordship and having formal claims on his patronage. He maintained in Lancastrian lordships traditions of presenting incumbents to established *reclusoria* and of patronising a variety of solitaries, such as William de Byngham, hermit, to whom he gave permission in 1372 to live as a solitary and serve God in ruinous huts near St Thomas's Hill, just outside Pontefract. The town had strong eremitical traditions[58] and the hill was named in honour of Thomas of Lancaster, beheaded there in 1322, and was the site of a chapel which attracted devotees of his cult. In this eremitical context, Gaunt's patronage of Swinderby is unexceptional – 'he sought to occupy the hermitage in the lord duke's wood [Leicester Forest] . . . the lord duke helped with his sustenance'.[59]

In 1394 Gaunt received royal licence to grant the advowson of Thorner (Yorks.) to the Trinitarian house of St Robert of Knaresborough (near his castle) of which he was patron. Robert (d. 1218) had set up a hermitage on the bank of the River Nidd: within two decades of his death his tomb was a centre of pilgrimage and he seems to have been formally canonised by 1252. In 1255 the Friars of the Holy Trinity and of the Redemption of Captives in the Holy Land (an order more akin to Augustinian canons than to mendicants) settled there. The house remained a local cult centre in the fourteenth century.[60] Gaunt, who acquired the lordship of Knaresborough in 1372, presumably went on pilgrimage to St Robert, and wished to associate himself with this Yorkshire cult. In his admiration for hermits and anchorites he may have been influenced by distinctive regional traditions (he liked to visit Yorkshire in summer), fostered by local noble families with whom he was familiar, such as the Scropes of Bolton.[61]

Gaunt showed fitting princely charity to the poor and the sick. In 1372 his household almoner accounted for 12*s*. 6*d*. which the duke was accustomed to distribute to the needy every Friday, and 10*s*. on Saturdays.[62] Concerning the infirm, Gaunt was not content to rely on the services provided by the hospital which was part of the Lancastrian foundation of Newarke College, Leicester: he did occasional favours for other hospitals, probably when he passed them on his journeys. At his request in 1359 the warden of St John and St James at Royston (Herts.), a centre for sick men and women and for wayfarers on the road from London to Cambridge, was licensed to acquire property in mortmain.[63] Other hospitals which he patronised were Our Lady of Rouncivall near Charing Cross and The Savoy, and one at Winchelsea (Sussex), a port well known to military men such as himself. It is curious that Gaunt supported the licence for the house of Rouncivall to seek alms in England, when it was a Rouncivall pardoner whom Chaucer later satirised so bitingly.[64]

Gaunt also had a charitable concern for education, reflected in his exercise of patronal rights. In 1372 he appointed Master Henry Barton to keep the grammar school at his manor of Higham Ferrers (Northants.) 'for the good exploit and profit which he will do daily to scholars and infants wishing to learn the faculty of grammar under his discipline'.[65] He granted Landbeach manor (Cambs.) *c*. 1390 to the master and scholars of Corpus Christi College, Cambridge, whose patronage he acquired through marriage to Blanche.[66] Gaunt maintained poor scholars at the university. In 1383 he informed the clerk of his great wardrobe that, for alms, he had undertaken to provide for 'un petit clerc' (a young scholar) at the schools in the University of Cambridge, one Thomas de Asshebourne, and had written to John Kynne, warden of St Benet (Corpus Christi) asking for the boy to be received at college and set to study in the schools. He had explained to Kynne that the ducal wardrobe would be responsible for paying for Asshebourne's upkeep there and for his clothes and other necessities.[67]

Gaunt's particular kindness to poor clerks and ascetics is consonant with his political assaults on clerical wealth and pretensions in 1376–8, which brought him into sympathy with Wycliffe's criticisms of 'possessioner' clergy and into conflict with bishops. Before then some of his attentions to bishops may not have been welcome. In March 1373 a ducal letter was dispatched to Bishop Hatfield of Durham asking for a loan of £200 till Michaelmas, and in May Gaunt's councillors entered into an obligation with Bishop Harewell of Bath and Sir Thomas Hungerford, acknowledging a loan of £300.[68] But habitually Gaunt's episcopal relationships were cordial; as royal councillor, diplomat and soldier he rubbed shoulders with careerist bishops (including those whom he had helped to promote), and became firm friends with some, possibly including Thomas Appleby, bishop of Carlisle from 1363 to 1397, whom he addressed as 'faithful friend' in a request for the people of Holy Church to say masses and pray devoutly for the salvation of the deceased Duchess Blanche.[69] Appleby, an Augustinian canon of Carlisle who had worked in the papal curia, was a man of unusual delicacy and boldness of character: soon after his third appointment to the wardenship of the West March, he wrote to Edward III that he could not execute some of the duties in his commission without harm to his conscience and episcopal office. Edward respected his feelings releasing him from the tasks concerned, but requesting him to carry out the other duties of office diligently.[70] Gaunt probably knew Appleby well before he became lieutenant of the Marches, since the bishop's London residence was next to The Savoy.[71]

One of Gaunt's closest episcopal friends was his 'grant amy' the secular Adam Houghton, bishop of St David's from 1361 to 1389. He was appointed chancellor in January 1377, during Gaunt's political ascendancy. The duke's support of the attack on the Church in the Gloucester parliament, before which Wycliffe was brought to preach, must have caused Houghton great embarrassment. He resigned the chancellorship during the parliament, not wishing to shoulder responsibility for attacks on ecclesiastical immunities.[72] Other 'civil service' clerics who rose to bishoprics and had links with Gaunt were the secular Robert Braybrooke, the Dominican John Gilbert and the secular John Fordham. Braybrooke, a royal kinsman who was bishop of London from 1381 to 1404, gave Gaunt hospitality on occasion at his Fulham residence in the early 1380s, after the destruction of The Savoy – a courageous action at times, in view of the continued explosions of anti-Gaunt feeling in London (see p. 90). Gilbert, bishop of Hereford from 1375 to 1389, was a confessor of the Black Prince, a negotiator with the papacy in 1373–4 and head of the English delegation to the Bruges conference in 1376. Like Houghton, he was to be on the 'intercommuning' committee in Gaunt's 'Bad Parliament' of 1377. Gilbert advocated Gaunt's Iberian strategy in parliament in 1382 and was to receive papal faculties for preaching the crusade which the duke was to execute against Castilian schismatics, together with another Dominican, Bishop William Bottlesham of Llandaff, Bishop Gutiérrez of Dax, and Diss.[73]

John Fordham, like Gilbert, served the Black Prince – he was his secretary and one of his executors, keeper of the Privy Seal for the first four years of Richard's reign, and bishop of Durham from 1381 to 1388,[74] when he was succeeded by Walter Skirlaw, who at some time in the 1390s, Gaunt anticipated, would help to determine a dispute involving the parishioners of Whalley (Lancs.) in his presence at Pontefract Castle.[75] Fordham had been translated to the see of Ely in 1388; in the 1390s his episcopal residence in London, the capacious and magnificent Ely Place in Holborn, was used by Gaunt, who may have leased it for several years; it was ideally situated, not far from St Paul's or Westminster. A fragment of Ely Place survives – the chapel with its crypt, now St Etheldreda's church, whose fine late thirteenth-century east and west windows, imposing in scale, must have been familiar to Gaunt and his household, a fitting setting for princely worship.[76]

Gaunt's friendships and business dealings with bishops, besides his exploitation of ecclessiastical patronage, suggest that he took Wycliffe's strictures on the possessioner clergy as the moralising of a holy man and as a convenient political weapon, not as a platform for practical reform. Indeed, the ageing Gaunt was inclined to set dynastic advancement before even the conventional ecclesiastical proprieties, by assisting the promotion of his son Henry Beaufort, despite his youthfulness. In January and February 1390 Beaufort (then aged about fifteen) had collation by royal grant of two Lincoln prebends, the second the wealthiest in the cathedral church, and in August received a prebend in York Minister. In January 1397 the king granted him the deanery of Wells, confirming a papal provision, and in February 1398 Boniface IX provided him to the see of Lincoln, from which the aged Bishop Buckingham was pressed into resigning – an appointment which Walsingham disapprovingly attributed to Gaunt. At least the duke saw to it that his son was fittingly educated for high ecclesiastical office: Henry had lodgings in Peterhouse, Cambridge in 1388–9 and in Queen's College, Oxford in 1390–1 and 1392–3.[77] However unprincipled Gaunt's promotion of his son may have been, he did promote a boy who was to be one of the outstanding prelates of the fifteenth century.

Gaunt's propulsion of his son into the rich and prestigious see of Lincoln was a conventional example of medieval exploitation of the Church by princely laymen. Gaunt was entirely conventional, too, in his beneficent patronage of secular cathedral chapters and their churches, notably at Lincoln, to whose cathedral he bequeathed such magnificent furnishings from his chapel. Gaunt may have been drawn in sympathy to this chapter for secular as well as devout reasons: he and they had parallel long-running disputes with the citizens of Lincoln over the jurisdictions of their respective liberties, the Bail (appurtenant to the castle, of which the duke was constable) and the adjacent Close (appurtenant to the dean and chapter). Grievances of the bishop and canons against the citizens were considered in the 1390 parliament, soon after Gaunt's return from Gascony and at a time when he was politically ascendant. He was appointed as arbitrator concerning the immunities claimed by the dean and chapter, and made an award largely favourable to their jurisdiction.[78] The dean and chapter's expenses for the year 1389–90 include £19, a gift for Gaunt to enlist his help against the city, payments to the judges sent to hear the plea in Lincoln Castle and the travelling expenses of canons who visited the duke at London and Hertford. In 1390–1 the gift of £6 13s 4d. was made to Sir William Par (a leading ducal retainer) for his help concerning Gaunt and the agreement with the citizens.[79] Gaunt's widow Catherine had good relations with the dean and chapter. She gave the cathedral many fine ecclesiastical vestments, some embroidered with her device of a Catherine wheel, and she died at Lincoln in 1403 in a house rented from the dean and chapter. Duchess Catherine had the privilege of burial within the presbytery of the cathedral, close to the high altar, where her tomb remains, together with a mutilated fragment of the arched canopy which covered it and her chantry, which Harvey tentatively dates to the early fifteenth century.[80]

The most impressive secular community of which Gaunt was hereditary patron was the College of the Annunciation of the Blessed Virgin in The Newarke, the outer ward of Leicester Castle. In 1330–1 Henry earl of Lancaster founded the Hospital of the Annunciation for poor and infirm folk. In 1350 John II of France gave Duke Henry a thorn from the Holy Crown, the supposed crown of thorns: this possession probably inspired the duke to extend the foundation of the Annunciation as a collegiate church in which the Holy Crown could be fittingly housed. In 1353–4 the hospital was erected into a college, with an establishment of a dean, 12 canons, 13 vicars, 3 clerks and a verger. The hospital was expanded to accommodate a hundred poor folk and ten female attendants.[81] Duke Henry willed to be buried in the new collegiate church, near his father's tomb in the choir, before the high altar. At the duke's death the endowment and building works were incomplete: Gaunt tended to the foundation, granting 100 marks *p.a.* for the costs of the works. The church was the principal Lancastrian mausoleum: Duchess Constance, Mary countess of Derby and Bolingbroke's infant brothers were buried there.[82] With its notable relic and its charitable institutions the church stimulated the piety of some members of Gaunt's household, often resident in the adjacent castle: the cult centre formed another link between the lord and the circles of some of his retainers. The aged Simon Symeon of Gosberton (Lincs.) (d. 1387). doyen of Lancastrian esquires (and a witness to Duke Henry's foundation charter for the college) set up a chantry there in 1381 for the souls of the two dukes, for his wife Elizabeth's soul and his own. He willed to be buried in the church before the image of the Blessed Virgin on the south side.[83] By 1389 his widow had married John lord de la Warr (d. 1398), whose paternal kin had Lancastrian connections, and whose brother Master Thomas, canon of Lincoln and formerly clerk of Princess Joan, was doubtless well known to Gaunt. In her will of 1393, Elizabeth made bequests to the canons and vicars of the New Work and the poor of the Maison Dieu.[84] In 1391 Gaunt's councillor Sir Robert Swillington bequeathed his new missal 'a le Esglise cathedral de la novel college nostre dame de leycestre'; he granted an old missal as well. One of his executors (to whom he devised £20) was William Chisulden (d. 1396), Gaunt's receiver-general in 1388–9, who was appointed dean of the college in 1390.[85] Swillington's desire to improve the church's liturgical collection was shared by his master, who bequeathed to it all the chapel books not disposed of in his lifetime. Another Lancastrian servant attracted by the Newarke was the former *domicella* Mary Hervy, who in 1405–6 founded a chantry in its church.[86] The church and college were pulled down soon after the dissolution of the college in 1547; a few arches are preserved in the College of Art and Technology which occupies the site. But the aisled hall and chapel of the hospital survive as part of Trinity Hospital Almshouses.[87]

This recent foundation, in scale and probably in appearance one of the most magnificent set up in fourteenth-century England, made it unnecessary for Gaunt to devise a major college for the repose of his soul and those of his kinsfolk, as his brothers Edmund and Thomas did respectively at Fotheringhay and Pleshey. Gaunt made some chantry foundations closely connected with his wives. He and Blanche were accounted among the founders of St Mary's College which stood beside St David's Cathedral, a chantry set up by their friend Bishop Houghton.[88] Gaunt's best-known foundation was the chantry originally erected for Blanche at her tomb in St Paul's Cathedral, directly to the north-east of the high altar. Payment was ordered in 1372 (backdated to Michaelmas the previous year) to two chaplains whom Gaunt had appointed to celebrate there, and to a joiner for an altar he had erected next to the tomb. A missal, a chalice and vestments were provided for the altar.[89] In June 1374 Gaunt ordered the receiver of Tutbury to send six cartloads of alabaster to London for an 'ymage' for the tomb.[90] A copy of the roll of expenses for the solemn commemoration of Blanche's anniversary that September survives: eight canons of St Paul's participated, one of them saying high mass. This remained an important annual event in the Lancastrian year.[91] The tomb, chantry and its furnishings were elaborated with appropriate magnificence.

In 1376–7 Henry Yevele and a London mason received £108 in part payment for their work in making the tomb, and by 1379 an elaborate enclosure (*ferment*) had been set up around it, on which £80 had been spent.[92] Next year two London painters, Richard Burgate and Robert Davy, contracted to paint the stages (*aysshelers*), and the statues within them, surrounding the tomb.[93] These stages are likely to have comprised the storied canopy depicted in the seventeenth-century drawing. Gaunt's executors were charged with converting the chantry into a permanent one for himself as well as for Blanche. They were also to endow a chantry for Constance and himself in Newarke College, Leicester.[94] But he took more immediate steps for the welfare of the current Duchess Catherine's soul. In September 1398 royal licence was issued for his foundation of a chantry of two chaplains for Catherine and himself in Lincoln Cathedral and his grant to it in appropriation of the advowson of St Peter's (South), Somercotes (Lincs.). But John Harvey has shown that his intention was only implemented by a new foundation by their daughter Joan countess of Westmorland in 1437.[95]

Chantries served by secular priests were the only new religious institutions which Gaunt is known to have had the intention of founding. This does not necessarily imply that he had a coolness towards monastic devotion. The expensive business of founding a new monastery was otiose. The lists of Duke Henry's properties in 1361 included the patronage of two abbeys and seven priories – a very incomplete tally of the monastic patronage which Gaunt inherited from him. There is no evidence that Gaunt shared with Wycliffe a contempt for monasticism or, with some of the Lollard knights, an interest in secularising alien monastic property. On the contrary, evidence suggests that he had a warm and appreciative relationship with some religious communities. Generally he was respectful of monastic property rights, but was careful to safeguard his own either as patron or neighbouring landowner. His orders to his stewards, on receiving conventual complaints about allegedly unjustified ducal demands for aid or relief, or about encroachments on property rights, demonstrate his determination that justice should be done by his officers or council. In 1372 the prior of Penwortham, Lancs. (a Benedictine house dependent on Evesham Abbey) complained that a ducal tenant had encroached on the priory's fishing rights in the River Ribble, and had set a bad example by failing to pay tithes owed for fishing to the priory. Gaunt's response was that 'we wish to do to holy church whatever right we ought to do'.[96] He was concerned in the 1370s about settling disputes at the alien convent of Nuneaton (Warwicks.), a cell of Fontevrault Abbey of which he was patron, 'because we are obliged to succour and aid the said nuns and their goods and possessions'. So he appointed guardians and surveyors over the convent, choice of whom included the abbot of Leicester and two ducal councillors, Sir Robert Swillington and Sir William Croyser.[97]

The abbot in question was William Clown, who ruled the rich house of Augustinian canons at Leicester (Lancastrian in patronage) from 1345 to 1378. He was a close friend of Edward III and the Black Prince:

> He yaf nat of that text a pulled hen,
> That seith that hunters been nat holy men,

for he was reputed 'the most notable and distinguished among all the lords of the realm in hunting the hare', a skill likely to have impressed Gaunt.[98] But documentary evidence about Gaunt's relations with the Leicester canons is lacking. One of them, Henry Knighton (d. *c*.1396) explicitly derived material for his history of the times from members of the ducal household (presumably staying in and around Leicester Castle) and was anxious to put the sometimes controversial and sometimes questionable activities of the 'pius dux' in the best possible light.[99]

More evidence about Gaunt's relations with houses in his patronage survives in the case of those which needed his help because of internal conflicts, difficulties caused by status as alien priories, or by economic problems. St John's Priory in the town of Pontefract, just below Gaunt's castle, was an alien house, the only Cluniac one in the north of England. It appears to have been well-off and flourishing, and pilgrims were attracted there to the tomb of Thomas of Lancaster, who was buried beside the high altar.[100] In 1369 the prior was granted the custody of the house's lands by the Crown, after Gaunt had testified before the royal council that it housed sixteen monks, who served divine offices there well and laudably. In 1393 the Cluniacs of Pontefract were granted the status of denizens at his supplication.[101] He helped to prop up the finances of a Cistercian house of his patronage, Kirkstall Abbey (Yorks.). In a charter of 1 October 1395, Charles VI of France alluded to Aumale Abbey's grant of its cell, Birstall Priory (West Riding), to Gaunt, and in 1396 Gaunt supplicated the curia to permit the annexation of Birstall's advowsons to Kirstall.[102]

In 1371 Gaunt had received a papal indult to enter monasteries of men and women once a year with thirty persons of good repute.[103] Doubtless, he had pious reasons for wishing to do so. But, like other nobles, he used monastic guesthouses as a convenience on his travels. Monasteries were particularly attractive as residences when he was abroad or in the remoter parts of the north, in places where secular buildings provided limited accommodation and amenities, or had been ravaged by war. Prior Robert Berrington of Durham excused himself in 1381 from attendance at his order's provincial chapter at Northampton on the grounds that the visit of Gaunt and other lords to negotiate with the Scots required his presence. Gaunt found it convenient to stay at Durham Priory on his journeys to and from the Scottish border.[104] Doubtless the monks were prepared to endure these secular invasions because of the opportunities they provided to win the duke's goodwill. Moreover, he had spiritual relationships with the house. Probably long before his 1381 visit, his name had been inscribed in the *Liber Vitae,* recording those to be prayed for, and kept in the cathedral. In or by 1383–4 he gave a gold necklace (a collar of esses?) to adorn St Cuthbert's shrine: he shared with his friend John Lord Neville, one of the cathedral's most famous benefactors, a devotion to the saint.[105] Instances of his presence in other monasteries are found in warrants dated Wardon Abbey (Beds.) in 1375 and a charter dated at Kirkstall Abbey (Yorks.) in 1392, both Cistercian houses.[106] But the relatively small number of documents dated at religious houses suggests that he did not generally abuse monastic hospitality.

However, on occasion he was not averse to tapping monastic resources for secular convenience. To aid the expedition to France in 1373, he wrote to the heads of some abbeys and priories in the duchy – Furness, Whalley, Lancaster and Cartmel – requesting them to send him one or two horses each (see p. 219). He exploited some monasteries in his patronage in ways not calculated to enhance the quality of their spiritual life. In 1373 he had an arrangement for five Spanish *damoiselles* to stay with his friend the prioress of Nuneaton at the priory, but they found life there unsatisfactory.[107] Gaunt flagrantly exploited the subservience of the Augustinian canons of Kenilworth, whose house was a brief canter from his castle. In November 1379 he ordered spars to be provided for relaying a floor in a great chamber in the priory, for dancing, to be ready for his intended Christmas celebrations – presumably because building works at the castle hampered its use as a residence. A priory was no fit setting for the revels of a secular household. How could the observance of the rule have proceeded unperturbed by the proximity of boisterous and amorous Christmas games? The prior was expected by the duke to put service to him first in other ways: in 1380 he was master of works at the castle.[108] But it was not because of this sort of exploitation that Gaunt was treated sourly by two of the most forceful contemporary monastic chroniclers, Thomas Walsingham of St Albans Abbey and the 'Monk of Westminster'. Walsingham, who started to write history *c.* 1380, villified Gaunt in his original account of events from 1376 to 1381 as immoral, unscrupulous, anti-clerical, consumed by pride and ambition. After his description of Gaunt's repentance in 1381, Walsingham refers to him in a neutral or even favourable way, reserving his venom for Richard and his friends.[109] The Westminster Chronicler also portrays Gaunt as suffering from court machinations in the early 1380s. The chronicler thought that the duke was wilful and overbearing at times, but what gradually turned him against Gaunt in the early 1390s was his ambition to rule Gascony and his readiness to make concessions to the French.[110] Gaunt does not seem to have been notable as a benefactor of Westminster Abbey, unlike his brother Thomas or Richard II himself, though he sometimes stayed at the abbot's Middlesex house, La Neyte.[111] His lack of sympathy with the monks over the violation by royal officers of the abbey's sanctuary in 1378 may have led to a mutual coldness. But Gaunt was a considerable patron of St Albans Abbey. His love of the house and its outstandingly able abbot Thomas de la Mare (d. 1396), his many gifts of wine to the monks, his help with business affairs and frequent donations for the abbey church are recorded in the *Liber Benefactorum*.[112] Moreover, Walsingham knew that Gaunt had long been a benefactor of Benedictine monks in general: he records in the *Gesta Abbatum* how Gaunt attended the provincial chapter of the order at Northampton in 1366 and mediated between its president, Abbot de la Mare, and delegates from Christ Church Priory, Canterbury, in the long-running dispute over whether their prior was obliged to attend such chapters. In view of Walsingham's appreciation of Gaunt's benevolence towards his order and house it is hard to explain his extremist denunciation of the duke's character and policies. One explanation is that Walsingham was reflecting the widespread intensity of feeling against Gaunt in 1376 and the following years. Dr John Thomson suggests that Walsingham's hostile feelings were connected with his hatred for Wycliffe and Wycliffe's sympathisers.[113]

Gaunt showed generosity in aiding the building works of some leading Benedictine houses. In 1392 he granted Christ Church Priory, Canterbury, £66 13*s.* 4*d.* towards the rebuilding of the cathedral, and an identical amount to the fabric fund for the nave of Westminster Abbey in 1393–4.[114] The monastic house to which Gaunt showed most favour was a Benedictine foundation, St Edmunds (Suffolk), which had features in common with St Albans Abbey. In his will, Gaunt left this ancient, rich and privileged house (whose monks, like himself, had suffered badly during the Peasants' Revolt) £1,000 and sets of vestments. A tract by the almoner of the abbey, John Gosford, on the abbatial election of 1379, disputed between the subprior John Timworth and a papal provisor, gave a sympathetic view of Gaunt's role in the affair. Gosford described Gaunt as advising the king about this cause célèbre of papal provision, and as being present with the king and queen in the abbey church when Timworth was finally consecrated in 1383.[115] Gaunt's devotion to St Edmund was shared not only by Richard, but by the most pious of Gaunt's sons, Thomas Beaufort, duke of Exeter (d. 1426), who willed to be buried in the Lady Chapel of the abbey church.[116]

Gaunt made many random gifts to monasteries, especially of timber; he had a kindly regard for nuns.[117] There are doubtless many gaps in the surviving evidence of his monastic patronage and benefactions. A stray document from the house of Premonstratensian canons at Barlings (Lincs.) shows that he was regarded by them as a benefactor and arranged for them to celebrate for his temporal welfare and to commemorate his obit.[118] But it is reasonably certain that, as was the case with most other landowners in the period, Gaunt's favours to monasteries were in the form either of support for their supplications or of gifts of money or chattels – rarely of grants of properties. In 1394 he received a licence to alienate Owston manor (Leics.) in mortmain to Premonstratensian Welbeck Abbey (Notts.) and in 1396, with his son Bolingbroke, one to alienate property in Thetford (Norfolk) to the Cluniac priory of St Mary's there.[119] It is difficult to ascertain how Gaunt rated the way that houses fulfilled the *Opus Dei* and their level of spirituality. He valued highly masses and prayers offered in monastic houses for his soul, and was concerned as patron of a variety of houses to ensure that the spiritual offerings carried out there for the founder and his kin were made with due reverence. He wrote, apropos Nuneaton Priory in 1373, that he wanted to have tranquillity and peace there, so that the nuns and brethren

> might in charity perform divine service and pray for us, our progenitors and ancestors.[120]

His patronage of St Edmunds, St Albans and other houses may, indeed, have been inspired more by reverence for their patronal saints and the other saints whose images and relics they housed than by admiration for the way in which monks and canons discharged their holy offices. Significantly, the only monastic order to which he bequeathed money in general was the Carthusian – £5 to each Charterhouse in England. The Carthusians had an outstanding reputation for asceticism in courtly circles, reflected in the foundation of new houses by Lord Manny, the De la Poles, Lord Zouche, Thomas Mowbray, earl of Nottingham and Thomas Holand, duke of Surrey.[121]

Gaunt spread minor benefits widely among the mendicants, many of them granted to houses of which he was patron. Typical was his grant in 1373 to the Dominicans of Pontefract, of his patronage, of oaks to repair their ruinous church and houses, and of the right to take peat in the nearby ducal park.[122] In 1394–5 Gaunt paid £20 for a new window for the Dominican house at Dunstable (Beds.). Perhaps he noticed the need for it as he passed by on the way between London and Kenilworth or Leicester, and felt benevolently disposed towards the friars, who maintained a chantry for his brother Clarence.[123] But his gift was more a reflection of his own status than an encouragement to the austerity which ought to characterise friars.

Franciscans too benefited from his charity. In 1372, the year in which he relinquished possession of the borough of Richmond, he gave the Franciscans there the right to receive fuel from the forest for two years. The house was a well-regarded one: it received benefactions from his friends Lords Neville and Scrope of Bolton.[124] In the same year he gave the Augustinian friars of Leicester £10 for the expenses of the general chapter which had recently been held there.[125] However, the order of friars with which Gaunt formed a close personal connection was, as we have seen, that of the Carmelites. Their houses, too, were recipients of minor favours. In August 1372, shortly before his departure on his father's naval expedition, he ordered the gift of 40s. for charity to the Carmelites at Sandwich, the embarkation port, hoping doubtless in the efficacy of their prayers. He felt benevolently disposed towards the order soon after his return from his gruelling French expedition in 1374, granting it 40s. in London in the summer in aid of the chapter and in alms and, when he had moved on to Yorkshire, making provision of oaks from his parks for its houses at Nottingham and Doncaster.[126]

The English magnate of the later fourteenth century inherited complex ideas about the discharge of his religious responsibilities. As patron of monasteries, friaries, hospitals and secular benefices he had obligations to ensure the maintenance of their canonical and statutory functions, as well as a spiritual interest in doing so. His discharge of his individual Christian duties and the development of his spiritual relationships were not matters simply concerning his confessors, patron saints, the Virgin Mary and God. He was supposed to be the exemplar of his *familia,* his household, for whose individual and communal piety and morality he was deemed to have a responsibility. In the eyes of the Church, princes received their privileges in return for faithfully carrying out such tasks, and generally upholding the Christian way of life by protecting the rights of the Church and defending the Christian people.

Magnates more or less accepted such role-models – for instance, in their continued adherence to crusading ideals. But in adhering to them they were influenced by fundamentalist religious critiques and by secular attitudes. To take the first of these influences: the mendicant orders maintained a tradition of questioning the validity of the wealthiness of other ecclesiastical bodies, especially monasteries. As patrons of both monks and friars, magnates were confronted by a conflict in concepts of the ideal Christian life whose theological dimensions some of them (probably including Gaunt) were well equipped to appreciate. Since the later thirteenth century, there had been an emphasis in the education of the nobility on the importance of acquiring Latin, in order to follow the liturgical hours and to read devout works, so better ensuring salvation. The conscientious noble, encouraged by confessors to practise austerity, reward holiness and observe the canonical hours, might well grow uneasy at the inadequacies and abuses in ecclesiastical institutions which he was pledged by ancestral right or by custom to maintain. Yet secular attitudes, stemming from self-interest and tradition, impelled nobles to perpetuate rather than eradicate questionable traits, by making service and aid to their secular interests a principal obligation for clergy in their patronage. Gaunt's sympathy with friars who despised the benefice system and with its more extreme critics, Wycliffe and Swinderby, suggests that he was aware of its deficiencies, though he vigorously exploited it in the Lancastrian interest. But there may have been times when, at least theoretically, he contemplated the reform of the system with equanimity. For, valuable though his own ecclesiastical patronage and that of others was to him as a means of attracting clerical administrators to his service, and keeping their goodwill if they became leading servants of the Crown and bishops, it was far outweighed by his incomes from secular sources as a means of patronage. For in this period there was a growing pool of laymen who could be engaged to provide expert conciliar and literate services. Moreover, in a period when knights and esquires were playing important roles in parliament, in shire administration and in overseas warfare, it was their patronage rather than that of the clergy which was crucial to Gaunt's worldly interests.

Tensions arose between the type of secular culture evolving in princely households, aimed to attract gentlefolk's service, and the pious fundamentalism making such a powerful appeal to individual aristocrats. These tensions probably inclined Gaunt to encourage and associate himself with holiness, even when it had a dangerously radical edge. In princely households of the period a culture of conspicuous consumption was being elaborated, partly, indeed, poured into religious ceremony, but partly into the pursuit of hedonistic pleasures.

Duchess Blanche, according to Chaucer, rejected the *courtoisie* which made the crusade part of the game of courtly love. Duchess Constance enjoyed the conceits of worldly romance, but she too established a pious reputation. Gaunt and his wives were doubtless acutely aware of the contrast between their earthly splendour and the Gospel standards to which the Carmelites and anchorites whom they patronised strove to adhere. In Gaunt's case his realisation of how his liaison with Catherine Swynford offended the canons of familiar decency enjoined on princely householders was another psychological pressure which probably helped impel him to connections with radical holiness of one sort or another. Gaunt did not patronise Wycliffe just for political expediency, though that was an important factor in his patronage. Gaunt's Wycliffism – and his Mariology – are to be seen as responses to the pressures of contrary ideals and conventions on the noble society of his day, to which his temperament and status made him peculiarly susceptible. Like other layfolk in a period when spiritual dilemmas were to become a characteristic phenomenon of secular European spirituality, he experienced periods both of despair and of spiritual illumination. The middle-aged Gaunt emerged as a complacently exploitative lay patron who was also a passionate Marian and intending crusader. But the routes by which he reaches these conclusions make him of more general interest than many other such figures.

Notes and References

1 *C.A.*, p. 117. For a discussion of Gaunt's attitude to Wycliffe, Dahmus JH 1952, pp. 14–18.
2 *C.H.K.*, Vol. 2, p. 193.
3 Crompton J 1961 : 35ff, 158ff.
4 *F.Z.*, pp. 3, 114; McFarlane KB 1966, pp. 97–8.
5 *F.Z.*, pp. 299–300.
6 Ibid., p. 318; commentary on passage in Dahmus JH 1952, pp. 113–14.
7 *R.P.*, Vol. 3, p. 184; *C.E.P.R. Papal Letters*, Vol. 4, pp. 264–5. Texts of bulls in Raynaldus O 1752, Vol. 7, pp. 471–2.
8 Lincoln R.O., D and C archives, Reg Buckingham ff190v–191r (Trumpington); *Test. Ebor.*, Vol. 1, p. 107 (Swillington), p. 217 (Hastings); Parry JH 1915, p. 109 (Burley).
9 *B.R.U.O.*, Vol. 1, pp. 266–7; Crompton J 1968–9 : 22; Dahmus JH 1952, p. 110. In his will (1389), Brightwell said that he was about to make a pilgrimage to Rome (Gibbons A 1888, p. 37).
10 Lincoln R.O., D and C archives, Reg Buckingham f 242r–243r; McFarlane KB 1966, pp. 121–4; *F.Z.*, pp. 334–40; *C.H.K.*, Vol. 2, pp. 193–7; Crompton J 1968–9: 18–21.
11 McFarlane KB 1966; p. 116.

12 *F.Z.*, pp. 292–5.

13 Armitage-Smith S 1904, pp. 166ff.

14 *C.E.P.R. Petitions*, Vol. 1, pp. 337, 401, 422, 528.

15 Boehlke FJ 1966, pp. 35–7, 267–8; *C.P.*, Vol. 6, pp. 125–7 and 126n; *V.C.H. Kent*, Vol. 2, pp. 201–2; Luttrell A 1988 : 148–9.

16 *G.A.*, Vol. 3, pp. 274, 277; Owst GR 1926, p. 66; *B.R.U.C.*, p. 569. Swaffham became bishop of Cloyne (1363) and was translated to Bangor (bull 2 July 1376), holding the see till his death in 1398. Bale credited him with *Contra Wiclevistas* and *Conciones*.

17 Text in MS Bodley 73 f185; printed Zimmerman B 1905–7, fasc. 1–5, pp. 354–5.

18 *J.G.R. 1379–83*, no. 1198. In the 1370s Gaunt granted timber for fuel to the Carmelites of Doncaster (*J.G.R. 1372–6*, nos 1504, 1528). For his offering for the Sandwich Carmelites in 1372, shortly before embarkation for war, and a gift of fuel to the Nottingham Carmelites in 1374, *ibid.*, nos 1043, 1476.

19 Sheppard LC 1943, p. 14; MacEoin G and Eisner S 1980, p. 138; Rickert M 1952, pp. 39–40.

20 Wickenden JF 1875: 318, 322; *C.H.K.*, Vol. 2, pp. 182–3.

21 Pfaff RW 1970, pp. 40, 42–3.

22 *C.H.K.*, Vol. 2, pp. 147–8; *H.A.*, Vol. 2, p. 43; cf *A.C.*, pp. 152–3. In 1356–9 payments were made for a window in the Lady Chapel of Ely Cathedral donated by Gaunt (Alexander J and Binski P 1987, p. 743). Cf New Year's gifts representing cult scenes of the Virgin purchased by Gaunt in 1381 (*J.G.R. 1379–83*, no. 557).

23 Ibid., no. 553.

24 Ibid., no. 803.

25 *H.A.*, Vol. 2, p. 193; *V.R.S.*, p. 129.

26 Lopes F 1988, pp. 288–9.

27 Wordsworth C 1892 : 25ff (treasurer's inventory, 1536).

28 *J.G.R. 1372–6*, nos 423, 1089, 1142; Owst GR 1926, pp. 66, 221; *B.R.U.O.*, Vol. 1, p. 90.

29 *J.G.R. 1372–6*, no. 686; *J.G.R. 1379–83*, nos 123, 686, 1063; *F.Z.*, p. 272. Diss was attendant in the ducal household in 1381 (East Sussex R.O. Waleys cartulary B10, A7, B5).

30 *F.Z.*, pp. 506–11; *C.E.P.L. Papal Letters*, Vol. 4, pp. 270–1. A certain John Elys of Stowmarket (Cambs.) hindered the crusade by preaching widespread sermons in which he cast doubt on the validity of the crusading bulls (*C.P.R. 1385–9*, p. 319).

31 Norwich, Norfolk R.O., receiver's account 1397–8, MS 15171, 37 B6.

32 P.R.O. DL28/3/2; DL28/3/5; *F.Z.*, pp. 4–104, 272, 357, 453–80; *B.R.U.O.*, Vol. 2, p. 1077; Crompton J 1961 : 158, 163. At various times in 1392 and probably at other times in the early 1390s, Kynyngham was resident in the ducal household (East Sussex R.O., Waleys cartulary AI, A2, A6, A9, B4, B9).

33 For worship in noble households and the vogue for private chapels, Mertes K 1988; pp. 139ff; Catto J 1981, p. 46.

34 *J.G.R. 1379–83*, no. 921.

35 *J.G.R. 1372–6*, no. 1786; cf ibid., nos 1334, 1341. That year 10 *m.* were paid for a missal for the ducal chapel.

36 Wickenden J 1875 : 317ff. Gaunt bequeathed sets of vestments to Newarke College, Leicester, to his son Henry Beaufort and to

Whitefriars (the Carmelites), London. Newarke College received his
chapel's liturgical books.

37 Wordsworth C 1892 : 50. For the expenses of clerks sent to London
to fetch *jocalia* donated by Gaunt, Lincoln R.O., D and C, archives
Bj/2/10 (1399–1400) 12r; Wickenden J 1875 : 319. See also Sparrow
Simpson W 1887 : 502, 519–20 for other bequests.

38 *J.G.R. 1372–6,* no. 1041 (frere Henry de Bruton, daune Richard de
Stanley, frere Henry Wapplod and John Crowe). William de Burgh
was retained by indenture (1372) 'ministrer les divines services en sa
chapelle' (*ibid.,* no. 818; cf no. 828 for retaining of Crowe). For the
dean (John Seggenaux) and clerks of the chapel in 1376–7, P.R.O.
DL28/3/1 m 6, 9. For the chapel's personnel, see also Harrison F L1
1958, pp. 24–5.

39 *J.G.R. 1379–83,* nos 96, 425.

40 Ibid., no. 327; P.R.O. DL28/3/2; DL28/3/5. John Grantham was dean
in 1381 (ibid., no. 557); Henry was probably Henry de Croydon (ibid.,
no. 206).

41 Fowler K 1969, pp. 666–72.

42 *C.C.R. 1360–4,* pp. 201–5, 338–9.

43 *J.G.R. 1372–6,* nos 182–209.

44 *J.G.R. 1379–83,* nos 1–21.

45 *J.G.R. 1372–6,* no. 1750.

46 Ibid., no. 199; *J.G.R. 1379–83,* no. 222; *B.R.U.O.,* Vol. 1, pp. 644–5.
Erghum did in fact vacate the rectory of Winstead (Yorks.) on receiving
Preston.

47 *J.G.R. 1372–6,* nos 202, 204, 354. Yerdburgh was in ducal service
in 1373 and was keeper of the duke's seal in 1379 (*C.P.R. 1377–81,*
pp. 262, 350).

48 *C.E.P.R. Petitions,* Vol. 1, p. 337. Campden was intending to serve
overseas in Gaunt's company in 1359 and 1369 (*Foedera,* 1825, Vol. 3,
pt 1, pp. 443, 871). For some of his benefices, *V.C.H. Lancs.,* Vol. 2,
p. 164 and n. He died in 1370.

49 *C.E.P.R. Petitions,* Vol. 1, p. 423.

50 *J.G.R. 1379–83,* no. 7; Russell PE 1955, pp. 167–8, 176–7, 183–4.

51 B.L. Cotton Cleo D 111 Cartae Monasterii de Selby, Ebor. f196r–197v.
I owe thanks to Dr Michael Bennett for bringing Gaunt's letters in this
register to my attention and to Dr David Smith for allowing me to use
a microfilm of it in the Borthwick Institute, York.

52 Storey RL 1961, pp. 2–4; Swanson RN 1981, no. 88.

53 *C.E.P.R. Petitions,* Vol. 1, p. 259.

54 *J.G.R. 1372–6,* no. 415.

55 Ibid., no. 1537.

56 Ibid., no. 1542.

57 B.L. Cotton Cleo D 111 Selby Cartulary f199r, 201v–202r. The copy
of the tenants' letter is undated; Gaunt's is dated 7 Aug. In both he is
styled duke of Guienne as well as duke of Lancaster. Snaith Priory was
a cell of Selby; in 1393 the abbot and Gaunt were in dispute over the
jurisdiction of Snaith church and manor (*V.C.H. Yorks,* Vol. 3, p. 100).

58 *J.G.R. 1372–6,* no. 949; *V.C.H. Yorks.,* vol. 3, p. 186n. For Lancastrian
patronage of anchorites, Clay RM 1914, pp. 69–70, 224–7, 240–1, 254–5,
258–9; Warren AK 1985, pp. 171–5.

59 *C.H.K.,* Vol. 2, p. 190. Gaunt granted timber to the recluse of Snaith
and to 'Johan Ermet' in 1374, and to a Pontefract recluse in 1382 (*J.G.R.*

1372–6, nos 1497, 1512; *J.G.R. 1379–83,* no. 722). For a receipt from Robert Riell, recluse living in Beverley, for the payment of a quarter's ducal annuity by the Yorks. receiver (1396), B.L. Stowe Ch. 432. Gaunt bequeathed money to every poor hermit and recluse living in London or within five leagues.

60 *V.C.H. Yorks.,* Vol. 3, pp. 296–9.

61 For bequests to anchorites by Gaunt's friend Richard Lord Scrope, Clay RM 1914; p. 77. For a grant of timber by Gaunt to the brothers of Knaresborough, possibly in 1374, *J.G.R. 1372–6,* no. 1496.

62 Ibid., no. 932. Also 15*d.* was to be distributed on Saturdays among five poor women.

63 *C.P.R. 1358–61,* p. 256.

64 In 1372 Gaunt wrote to leading ecclesiastics in favour of three 'freres et procureurs' of Rouncivall, seeking alms for the house in various parts of England (*J.G.R. 1372–6,* nos 60, 73). For Gaunt's letter (1382) in favour of the Winchelsea hospital, burnt by the French, *J.G.R. 1379–83,* no. 1183. In 1381 Gaunt was paying for the new kitchen he had undertaken to provide for the poor in his Maison Dieu at Leicester and in 1382 he provided timber to repair the hospital at Castleton (Yorks.) (ibid., nos 493, 683). He bequeathed money to every leperhouse with at least five lepers within five leagues of London.

65 *J.G.R. 1372–6,* no. 244; cf ibid., no. 259 for a similar appointment in 1372 of John de Bradley at Crofton.

66 *C.P.R. 1388–92,* p. 205. For the licence they received to acquire property from Gaunt and others in 1373, *C.P.R. 1370–4,* pp. 357–8.

67 *J.G.R. 1379–83,* no. 856. A wardrobe account records the payment to Kynne, authorised by warrant April 1384, of £11 4*s.* 1*d.* for Ashbourne's expenses (James MR 1899, p. 62). In 1382 Gaunt was maintaining another scholar at Cambridge (*J.G.R. 1379–83,* no. 856).

68 *J.G.R. 1372–6,* nos 169, 1182. In Nov. 1379 Gaunt ordered repayment of 400 *m.* received as a loan from Archbishop Sudbury and £100 from John Harewell, bishop of Bath and Wells (*J.G.R. 1379–83,* no. 76). In Oct. 1380 Sudbury was to be repaid £200 and Bishop Braybrooke £100 (ibid., no. 481).

69 Cumbria R.O., Carlisle, Reg Appleby f 192r.

70 Ibid., f 210r; Rose RK 1984, pp. 15–16, 98–9.

71 Cumbria R.O., Carlisle, Reg Appleby f12r. I owe thanks to Dr Rose for his transcript of a letter from Edward III to Appleby apropos his and the duke's adjacent properties; see below, p. 322, n.20.

72 *B.R.U.O.,* Vol. 1, pp. 972–3; Tout TF 1928, Vol. 3, pp. 278, 332, 342. Houghton was appointed on the 'intercommuning' committees in both the 1376 and Jan. 1377 parliaments (ibid., pp. 294, 315).

73 Ibid., p. 315; Perroy E 1952, pp. 44, 52; *C.E.P.L. Papal Letters,* Vol. 4, pp. 270–1. He was translated to Hereford from Bangor, and from Hereford to St David's.

74 Tout TF 1928, pp. 330, 399–400.

75 P.R.O. PL3/1/12; warrant dated Pontefract Castle, 6 March; Gaunt styled duke of Guyenne and Lancaster.

76 Aston M 1967, pp. 271–6; cf *C.C.R. 1389–92,* pp. 409, 521.

77 *B.R.U.O.,* Vol. 1, pp. 139–40; Hamilton Thompson A 1947, p. 72n; Harriss GL 1988, pp. 2, 8.

78 Hill JWF 1948, pp. 262–8.

79 Lincoln R.O., D and C archives, treasurer's accounts, Bj/2/8 (Simon de Luffenham from Sept. 1389 and Sept. 1390), f 8v, 9r, 10v, 29r. The 1390–1 account records payment of a fine in chancery for an agreement with Gaunt (ibid., f 28v). This settlement did not end the dispute (Hill JWF 1948, pp. 267–8).

80 Wordsworth C 1892, pp. 23–4; Harvey JH nd, pp. 1, 9, 11–15.

81 Somerville R 1953, pp. 46–7; Fowler K 1969, pp. 188ff; *V.C.H. Leics.*, Vol. 2, pp. 45–9.

82 Gibbons A 1888, pp. 17–18; *J.G.R. 1379–83*, nos 145–6, 960. For Gaunt's aid to the college's endowment, *C.P.R. 1361–4*, p. 387; with its works, *J.G.R. 1372–6*, no. 1017; *C.P.R. 1396–9*, p. 74; P.R.O. DL28/32/21. For his other favours to the college, *J.G.R. 1372–6*, no. 1414; *C.E.P.L. Papal Letters*, Vol. 4; p. 544. In 1370 he granted one of the canons, William Chisulden (who rose high in his service) oaks with which to construct a new chamber in his lodgings (C.C.C.495 f15). In 1394–5 Gaunt's receiver-general accounted for an extra 100 marks donated for repairs to the college buildings and walls (P.R.O. DL28/32/21). For Gaunt's presentations to the deanery and canonries in 1381–3, *J.G.R. 1379–83*, nos 17–19, 21.

83 Gibbons A 1888, p. 78.

84 *C.P.*, Vol. 4, pp. 144–50; Gibbons A 1888, pp. 84–5.

85 Lincoln R.O., D and C achives, Reg Buckingham f 383r–384r; *J.G.R. 1379–83*, p. xix and n; *V.C.H. Leics.*, Vol. 2, p. 51.

86 Hamilton Thompson A 1937, p. 92.

87 *V.C.H. Leics.*, Vol. 4, p. 346. Pevsner N 1984, pp. 219–20. A remnant from the collegiate church is a female alabaster effigy, poorly preserved.

88 Yardley E 1927, pp. 57, 372ff; Emery A 1970, p. 115n. The duke and duchess granted the advowson of St Ishmaels in Kidwelly to Houghton, apparently as an endowment for St Mary's College (*C.P.R. 1388–92*, p. 34).

89 *J.G.R. 1372–6*, nos 915, 918, 944, 1091. Payments were made to two chaplains celebrating in St Paul's for Blanche in 1376–7 (P.R.O. DL28/3/1; cf P.R.O. DL28/3/2; DL28/3/5). For the location of the tomb and chantry see plan of cathedral opposite p. 16 in Benham W 1902.

90 *J.G.R. 1372–6*, nos 1394, 1417.

91 Ibid., no. 1585; Lewis NB 1937 : pp. 176–82. In 1376 Sir William Croyser, steward of the household, was paid for staying for three days in London for Blanches's anniversary (P.R.O. DL28/3/1); in 1397 Robert Whitby stayed two days at Hertford for it. That year, as in 1392, the expenses at St Paul's were £10; this included in 1397 payments to the canons and alms for the poor and those held in Newgate, Ludgate and the Fleet prisons. New furnishings were then provided for the chapel (P.R.O. DL28/3/2; DL28/3/5).

92 P.R.O. DL28/3/1; *J.G.R. 1379–83*, no. 92.

93 Ibid., no. 213.

94 Gaunt purchased reversions of London properties with which to endow the chantry, which was set up in 1403 in the new chapel at his tomb. Bishop Braybrooke granted land for a house for the chantry priests, which became known as Lancaster College (*V.C.H. London*, Vol. 1, p. 427). For a file of documents mostly relating to the chantry, London, Guildhall Library, St Paul's D and C archives, nos 1941–6.

95 *C.P.R. 1396–9*, pp. 398, 412; Harvey JH nd, pp. 11–12.

96 *J.G.R. 1372–6,* no. 1116.
97 Ibid., no. 330. For Gaunt as patron (1380) of the Augustinian canonesses of Lacock (Wilts.) *J.G.R. 1379–83,* nos 20, 924.
98 For parallels between Clown and Chaucer's Monk, Hamilton Thompson A 1949, pp. 28ff; Knowles D 1955, Vol. 2, pp. 185–6, 365–6. Duke Henry named Clown as executor in 1360 (Gibbons A 1888, p. 24). The abbot had connections with leading Lancastrian retainers:' in 1365–6 he witnessed indentures between Simon Pakeman and Sir Ralph Hastings, and in 1373 one between Pakeman and Sir Robert Swillington, which Gaunt's clerk William Chisulden, canon of Newarke College, also witnessed (Huntington Library, San Marino, Hastings Charters, HAD 879, nos 2869–70). Clown was in Duchess Blanche's funeral cortège in 1368 (*G.A.,* Vol. 3, p. 274).
99 Gransden A 1982, Vol. 2, pp. 159, 180–1.
100 Bellamy CV 1965, pp. xiii–xvi, 99, 127–8. The cult of Earl Thomas flourished locally, as instanced in the will of William de Northfolk of Pontefract (1401): 'Lego ad sustentacionem luminis Gildae B. Thomae Lancastr' xii d.' (*Test. Ebor.,* Vol. 1, p. 281).
101 *C.F.R. 1369–77,* pp. 38–9; *C.P.R. 1391–6,* pp. 215–16. Gaunt appointed attorneys to deliver property to Pontefract Priory in 1373 (*J.G.R. 1372–6,* no. 296).
102 Bodleian, MS Dodsworth 7, f 239a–b; Matthew D 1962, p. 118; *C.E.P.R. Papal Letters,* Vol. 4, pp. 16–17. The abbot of Kirkstall granted powers to his proctors concerning the purchase of Birstall from Aumale, 21 Feb. 1396 (Bodleian, MS Dodsworth 7, f 238a). Gaunt had granted a fee of £20 to Kirkstall in 1392 (Bateson M 1901, Vol. 2, pp. 204–5).
103 *C.E.P.R. Papal Letters,* Vol. 4, p. 167.
104 Pantin WA 1937, Vol. 3, pp. 208–9. The bursars' rolls record rewards by the prior to Gaunt's steward and cook in 1378; to his butler in 1380–1 (purchase of a cask of red wine from ducal ministers also recorded); to his minstrel accompanying a dancer performing in the prior's chamber, 1381–2; to his huntsman, 1384–5; to his minstrel(s), 1391 (*Accounts . . . Durham,* 1900, Vol. 3, pp. 588, 590, 592, 594, 598–9). On his way back from the 1384 invasion of Scotland Gaunt purchased from the prior oats, straw and hay for his and his retinue's use (ibid., 1898, Vol. 1, p. 133).
105 Hamilton Thompson A 1923, f68; Nilson B 1989, p. 94.
106 *J.G.R. 1372–6,* nos 1711–12; Bateson M 1901, Vol. 2, pp. 204–5.
107 *J.G.R. 1372–6,* nos 1171, 1478; Russell PE 1955, pp. 178–9. Gaunt gave a New Year's gift to the prioress in 1381 (*J.G.R. 1379–83,* no. 557).
108 Ibid., nos 132, 1083. In June 1372 Gaunt ordered wine to be stored in the priory in anticipation of this arrival and in Jan. 1380 ordered payment for works on his great chamber there, probably the chamber with the dance floor (*J.G.R. 1372–6,* no. 983; *J.G.R. 1379–83,* no. 206).
109 Gransden A 1982, Vol. 2, pp. 129–30, 138–9.
110 *W.C.,* pp. lxiii, 491, 519.
111 Gaunt stayed at La Neyte in 1383, 1384 and 1390 (*W.C.,* p. lvi). It was the manor house of Eye (Harvey B 1977, p. 87); the manor was later called Ebury, a name presently commemorated by street names.
112 B.L. MS Cotton Nero D vii, f7r.
113 *G.A.,* Vol. 3, pp. 403–4; Pantin WA 1933, Vol. 2, pp. 56ff. In 1368 Duchess Blanche's body lay in the abbey church for a Requiem Mass at which the monastic community was present (*G.A.,* Vol. 3, pp. 274ff).

For a favour secured by Gaunt for the house from the Crown (1380), *ibid.*, pp. 135ff; for favours for the abbey and its cell, Tynemouth Priory, for which he petitioned, *ibid.*, pp. 146ff, 157; *H.A.*, Vol. 2, p. 199; *C.P.R. 1388–92*, p. 194. For a discussion of Walsingham's attitudes to Gaunt, Gransden A 1982, Vol. 2, pp. 138–9. I owe thanks to Dr Thomson for his remarks about the problem.

114 P.R.O. DL28/3/2; Westminster Abbey Muniments 23463, account of the warden of the new work for 1393–4. I owe thanks for the latter reference to Dr N. Saul.

115 Arnold T 1896, Vol. 3. pp. 132–3; cf *W.C.*, pp. 42–3; Gransden A 1982, Vol. 2, p. 403.

116 Nicolas NH 1826, Vol. 1, pp. 207–8.

117 For ducal gifts of timber and windfalls to Tutbury Priory (Benedictine) and Darley Abbey, Derbyshire (Augustinian) in 1374, *J.G.R. 1374–6*, nos 1478–80. In 1373 the prioress of Handale, N.R., Yorks. (Benedictine) and the nuns of Gokewell, Lincs. (Cistercian) received timber, as did the nuns of Arthington, W.R., Yorks. (Cluniac) in 1374 (ibid., nos 1305, 1307, 1492). Gaunt bequeathed 5 marks to each nunnery in London and £5 to the nuns of St Mary de Fonte, Clerkenwell (Augustinian).

118 Guildhall Library, London, St Paul's D and C archives, A74 no. 1944; cf *V.C.H. Lincs.*, Vol. 2, p. 204. In 1345 Henry earl of Lancaster had appointed the abbot of Barlings as an executor (Gibbons A 1888, pp. 17–18).

119 *C.P.R. 1391–6*, pp. 381, 666–7; *V.C.H. Notts.*, Vol. 2, pp. 129–38; *V.C.H. Norfolk*, Vol. 2, pp. 364–9. For the involvement of Gaunt's officials at the Roman curia over the appropriation of Owston in 1396, P.R.O. DL28/3/5.

120 *J.G.R. 1372–6*, no. 330.

121 Knowles D 1955, Vol. 2, pp. 129ff; Catto J 1981, pp. 51–2. Gaunt responded favourably to a petition from the prior and convent of the London Charterhouse (*J.G.R. 1372–6*, no. 990). For his gift of £20 in alms to the prior, ibid., no. 1661.

122 *V.C.H. Yorks*, Vol. 3, pp. 271–2; *J.G.R. 1372–6*, nos 1249, 1525. Ducal favours were granted to the Dominicans of Ilchester (Somerset) in 1372, and of Derby in 1374 (ibid., nos 927, 1477) and Lancaster in 1380 (*J.G.R. 1379–83*, no. 218).

123 P.R.O. DL28/32/21; Gibbons A 1888, pp. 51–2.

124 *J.G.R. 1372–6*, no. 963; *V.C.H. Yorks.*, Vol. 3, pp. 273–4.

125 *J.G.R. 1372–6*, no. 1033. In 1373 Gaunt gave the friary two oaks (ibid., no. 1734).

126 Ibid., nos 1043, 1441, 1476, 1503, 1528.

Chapter Twelve

Gaunt and the Secular Peerage

The concept of hereditary nobility underwent considerable modification in fourteenth-century England.[1] There gradually developed a corporate group with distinctive legal rights and social privileges, the 'peerage of parliament', consisting of some sixty or seventy lords who had individual summonses to parliament. At the end of Edward III's reign ten of these were dukes and earls; the rest were 'barons of parliament' whose titles derived from their receipt of individual summonses to parliament, but were coming to be regarded (like the ancient dignity of earl) as creating a hereditary right. The sense that the parliamentary peerage constituted a separate and hierarchically graded nobility was enhanced by the introduction of the title of duke, expressive of royal blood and favour, and of outstanding wealth and power. Edward III conferred the new duchy of Cornwall on his son and heir Edward in 1337. In 1351 he raised the earldom of Lancaster to a duchy for Henry, and in 1362 made Lionel, his second surviving son, duke of Clarence. From Richard II's accession to the grant of dukedoms to Langley and Woodstock in 1385, Gaunt was the only subject who was a duke – besides holding three earldoms and claiming a kingdom. These solitary eminences neatly corresponded to his domestic and diplomatic roles; then from 1390 he uniquely possessed two duchies. His special social and political stature was more than adequately registered in the hierarchy of peerage. But was he able to fit in comfortably with his fellow peers, when so distanced from them? Chroniclers give prominence to tensions between him and heads or members of comital families – the earls of March, Northumberland,

Arundel and kinsmen of the earl of Devon. They also show him on occasion taking a strong and successful political lead in the Lords in parliament. At both national and regional levels, he was faced, as his Lancastrian predecessors had been in the fourteenth century, with the problem of reconciling growing Lancastrian influence with the interests of fellow peers. The problem was exacerbated for him by his royal birth and the particular circumstances of domestic politics in the 1370s and early 1380s. The maintenance of a *modus vivendi* was crucial for Gaunt: the benevolence of fellow peers, especially the most eminent among them, was as necessary for the wellbeing of his interests as was that of kings.

Conflict was hard to avoid; in order to ameliorate it he depended on the devices which an aristocratic society lacking strong rules of clan behaviour, and possessing a patronage system tinged by careerist ethics, uncertainly relied on. These were its kinship ties, the creation of new ones and of informal and formal obligations, through the practice of gift exchange, hospitality, chivalrous companionship and the grant of fees, offices and properties. The bonds of kinship gave Gaunt a hoard of capital which might be used to soothe the strains imposed by his eminence. Since by this period magnates were commonly closely related to the king's family, as a king's son he had a central position in the peerage's kinship networks, and this was enhanced by his marriage to his kinswoman Blanche of Lancaster, since her father had busily cultivated kinship and a variety of other links with fellow peers.

Gaunt's relations with his brothers turned out to be crucial elements in his career and, indeed, especially in Richard's reign, in politics. His rise in his father's favour and assumption of a role in international affairs were greatly assisted by the favour which he received from the Black Prince, who, granting him lordships in Aquitaine in 1371, referred to 'the very great affection and love' he had for him;[2] in his will of June 1376, the prince appointed 'our very dear and beloved brother of Spain' to head his executors.[3] Gaunt's forbearance with Richard in the early 1380s probably owed a good deal to his devotion to the prince's memory – and to his friendship with the prince's widow, Princess Joan (d. 1385), with whom he had a separate kinship tie – she was a grand-daughter of Edward I. In 1380 she received from the duke. besides the conventional New Year's gift of a covered gold cup, a crucifix garnished with precious stones and pearls and adorned with figures of the Blessed Virgin and St John, sacred persons of special significance to Gaunt.[4] His kindly feelings towards the princess doubtless prompted his patronage of her sons by her marriage to Sir Thomas Holand (d. 1360). The elder son, also Sir Thomas (d. 1397), fought at Najera in 1367 and was in receipt of fees from Gaunt in 1373, when he served on his French expedition and was apparently a member of his council as lieutenant in Aquitaine.[5] This Thomas Holand had a kinship tie with Gaunt through their respective marriages: in the 1360s Holand married Alice, daughter of the earl of Arundel and grand-daughter of Earl Henry of Lancaster. Styled earl of Kent from 1380 onwards, he played little part in public affairs, being eclipsed by his forceful and wayward younger brother John (earl of Huntingdon 1388; duke of Exeter 1397). The latter's marriage to Gaunt's daughter Elizabeth rescued him from the depths of disgrace in 1385 (see p. 98) and his appointment as constable of Gaunt's army in the Iberian Peninsula in 1386–7 enabled him to establish a military reputation. In 1397 Huntingdon was in receipt of a life annuity of 200 marks from Gaunt.[6]

Besides the Black Prince, the brother with whom Gaunt had particularly cordial relations was Edmund of Langley, near to him in age. In 1372 they linked their political fortunes through Edmund's marriage to Gaunt's vivacious sister-in-law Isabel. This marriage gave Edmund and his descendants a reversionary interest in the legitimist claim to the Castlian Crown: Gaunt apparently granted him the lordships of Vizcaya and Lara.[7] Edmund was poorly endowed with English lands, but was prepared to accept a Spanish bride who brought him only prospects of landed wealth. Froissart repeatedly represented the brothers as acting together over Iberian affairs in the early 1380s; Edmund's Portuguese expedition in 1381 and his son Edward's Portuguese betrothal were part of a Lancastrian plan (see p. 113–14). There is no clear evidence that Gaunt blamed his brother for the débâcle in Portugal: there was a dispute between them over the debts that Edmund incurred on the expedition, which Gaunt refused his requests to pay. and repudiated in his will. The dispute may have been the reason why neither Edmund nor his sons took part in Gaunt's 1386 expedition. In the 1390s Edmund's family had good relations with Gaunt. Isabel (d. 1392) in her last will bequeathed to him 'a tablet of jasper which the King of Armenia gave me',[8] a bequest whose crusading associations are likely to have appealed to him. Correspondence between Gaunt and her son Edward (earl of Rutland 1390; duke of Aumale 1397) in 1396 suggests that they had a friendly relationship: Rutland wrote that he was delighted that his uncle had made use of his staghounds.[9]

Langley's Iberian involvement had been of use to Gaunt in the 1370s and early 1380s, but of restricted use, because of Langley's moderate landed resources; moreover, Froissart (with unaccustomed and gratuitous bluntness) says that he was of limited understanding.[10] In the Treaty of Bayonne the claims of Edmund, Isabel and their children in the Castilian succession were not alluded to, but were cut out by the concessions of Gaunt and Constance to Juan I, though a version of the treaty circulating in England alleged that the Yorkist reversionary right was specifically mentioned in it. Gaunt did not secure compensation for his brother's family for a cession of their rights: his brother had contributed nothing to the arduous expedition which procured the settlement. Edward's later attempt to assert a claim to the Castilian throne shows that the Yorkist family did not give up their right or accept the terms of the Treaty of Bayonne.[11] Relations between the brothers in the 1390s were not as close as they had once been: it may be significant that Gaunt's bequest to Edmund, a gold cup, was among the less lavish ones to his close kinsfolk.

In domestic and, indeed, eventually in international politics, Gaunt's relationship with his youngest brother Thomas of Woodstock was to matter more than that with Edmund. For Thomas became the possessor of half the inheritance of a leading comital family and emerged as one of the most forceful and ambitious personalities in the peerage. The age difference between Gaunt and Thomas (fifteen years) may have put a distance between them. Gaunt apparently failed to act as his brother's boyhood mentor in the way that the Black Prince had acted towards him. However, he probably approved and promoted Thomas's marriage into the related family circles of Arundel and Bohun, circles he was close to in the 1370s, as a means of joining Thomas's interests more firmly to his own.[12] Gaunt was particularly friendly with the young Humphrey de Bohun, earl of Hereford, a notable crusader, who campaigned in Prussia in 1363 and with Pierre de Lusignan in the Middle East in 1365. Four years later Gaunt appointed him as a feoffee and campaigned with him in France. Hereford gave Gaunt an intriguingly elaborate present of plate, perhaps a reflection of the Bohun family's notable artistic and literary tastes and of a shared appreciation of them by Gaunt: 'a *triper* [three-legged stand] made in the shape of a *dragon volant* with a crowned damsel sitting on a green ground; a chased silver ewer shaped like a shepherd with two oaks on a green ground; a silver chased cup for the *triper*, with a lid crowned and enamelled but otherwise plain.'[13] Hereford died in 1373 and the following year Thomas of Woodstock married his daughter and co-heir Eleanor, whose widowed mother Joan was the earl of Arundel's daughter. Woodstock was granted custody of parts of the Bohun inheritance, to hold till Eleanor came of age.[14] It is likely that he emerged into the political limelight as his elder brother's supporter: he was associated with the latter's ally Lord Percy in the attempt in the first 1377 parliament to reduce the privileges of London (see p. 61). Thomas may have owed his chance in 1380 to lead an invasion of France to Gaunt's advocacy: before his departure he appointed Gaunt as his deputy in the constableship of the realm.[15]

But, according to Froissart, during Thomas's absence on campaign Gaunt treacherously destroyed his brother's further territorial ambitions. As a result, Thomas 'never after loved the duke . . . as he had hitherto done'. Froissart's story deserves to be taken seriously as it is one of the few which he tells against Gaunt. He says that Thomas was bringing up his sister-in-law Mary de Bohun and had been attempting to persuade her to become a Poor Clare, so that her half of the Bohun inheritance would devolve on his wife. But while he was in France, the girl's aunt, the countess of Arundel, visited his castle at Pleshey (Essex) and took Mary back with her to Arundel. There she was immediately married to Gaunt's son Henry of Bolingbroke. The marriage had been plotted with Gaunt.[16]

The royal grant (28 July 1380) of Mary de Bohun's marriage to Gaunt for the purpose of wedding her to Bolingbroke – at about the same time as Thomas sailed for France – gives credence to Froissart's tale of surreptitious haste.[17] But this is only one side of the story and not completely accurate. Documentary evidence shows that the wedding took place not at Arundel, as Froissart says, but at Rochford (Essex). Gaunt, his daughters Philippa and Elizabeth and, most significantly, the bride's mother Joan countess of Hereford were probably present, since officers and valets of Joan's chamber were; so were royal minstrels and those of Edmund of Langley, whose presence suggests their masters' approval. Gaunt entrusted Mary to her mother's care, to remain in it at his costs till she was fourteen.[18]

Therefore the marriage had the cooperation of the doyenne of the Bohun family, Countess Joan, and probably the general approval of the king's family. Perhaps there had been a previous intention of the Bohuns and Arundels as well as Gaunt to promote the marriage; the former royal grant of it to Gaunt and swift wedding may have been precipitated by apprehension that the headstrong Thomas's devout and devious persuasions would upset the plan. Whether this was the case or not, Froissart's account of Thomas's anger on his return from Brittany is credible. His hopes of gaining a whole comital inheritance were dashed; its division between him and Bolingbroke was to present complicated and long-lasting problems.[19] Nevertheless, formally cordial relations between Gaunt and his brother were soon restored. They exchanged presents on New Year's Day 1382, and Thomas sent an esquire to Gaunt to announce the birth of his son Humphrey. Gaunt was probably present at Thomas's residence, Pleshey Castle, for the baptism of one of his daughters, which took place before 6 May 1383.[20] In the tension between Richard and Gaunt in 1384–5, Thomas of Woodstock appears to have sympathised with and on occasion publicly supported his brother. Thus during the crisis over the Carmelite friar's accusations at Salisbury in 1384, Thomas rushed into the king's presence, and swore a terrible oath that he would fight or kill anyone who accused his brother of treason, not excluding the king; early in 1385, together with Edmund of Langley, he supported Gaunt's protest in the royal council against the failure to agree on an expedition to France.[21] Thomas's political relations with Gaunt in the 1390s were less straightforward, but there are indications of private cordiality. In 1392 Thomas's son Humphrey was staying in Gaunt's household, and his daughter Anne, the widowed countess of Stafford, received royal licence to marry whenever she pleased, without paying for the privilege, at Gaunt's supplication.[22] Probably early in 1397 Gaunt's grandson Henry (the future Henry V) was staying in Thomas's household at Pleshey.[23]

Nevertheless, the furore over Bolingbroke's marriage in 1380 suggests that Woodstock was already proving difficult to fit into Gaunt's scheme of things. His political activities during the latter's absence abroad (1386–9) showed disregard for his brother's domestic policies, though he may have helped to facilitate conciliar acceptance of the Castilian settlement. But Woodstock's violent proceedings against royal *familiares* recalled Thomas of Lancaster's extremism, not Gaunt's respect for the king's prerogatives. Moreover, there was a contemporary report that among some of the lords appellants' supporters Woodstock was being canvassed as a rival to Richard, irrespective of Lancastrian reversionary claims on the throne. The story was that the commons wished to make Woodstock king and that his fellow appellant Bolingbroke protested that his own right to the succession was superior.[24]

One consequence of Thomas's assertion of political leadership was that he formed bonds with a number of comital families hitherto linked to the Lancastrian interest. This was notably so in the case of the Arundels. Gaunt had benefited from the financial backing of his father's friend Richard earl of Arundel (d. 1376) (see p. 220). They were linked through the earl's marriage to Duke Henry of Lancaster's sister. In 1378 the earl's son, another Earl Richard, served on Gaunt's Breton expedition and in 1379 there was Lancastrian backing for the Breton expedition led by Earl Richard's younger brother Sir John Arundel (see p. 186). The earl's offer to command the crusade in Flanders in 1383 as Bishop Despenser's lieutenant (an offer rebuffed by the bishop) does not necessarily imply that he was an opponent of Lancastrian advocacy of the Iberian option. Gaunt may well have thought that, with Arundel in command, there was a better chance of the crusading army eventually joining him for the invasion of Castile. In this period Gaunt was friendly with the earl's brother Thomas

Arundel, bishop of Ely. On 14 and 24 December 1382 Gaunt dated warrants at Hatfield (Herts.), which indicates that he was staying at the episcopal manor there, though at the time the bishop was at Downham (Cambs.).[25] Ducal warrants were again dated at Hatfield early in 1383.[26] In the Salisbury parliament of 1384 Gaunt composed the clash between the earl of Arundel and the king. Gaunt and Arundel appear at implacable odds after the latter had become Woodstock's political ally in 1386–8. In 1388 Gaunt's unhelpful attitude as lieutenant in Aquitaine constrained Arundel's attempts to invade France (see p. 187). Their mutual rancour erupted in public in parliament in 1394 and 1397. It was probably fuelled by differences over the peace policy and by rivalry for Woodstock's alliance.

The New Year's and other gifts recorded in Gaunt's registers in the 1370s and 1380s give some indication of his relations with his brothers, their families and with other nobles. For instance, in 1372 recipients of New Year's gifts from him included Princess Joan, his brother Edmund and Edmund's Spanish wife Isabel.[27] In April 1373 Gaunt gave presents to all of them, to the Black Prince and to his niece Philippa, wife of Edmund Mortimer, earl of March.[28] Philippa was the daughter of Gaunt's vigorous and able elder brother Lionel duke of Clarence (d. 1368), who through his marriage to Elizabeth de Burgh had acquired an impressive inheritance, comprising a large part of the Clare earldom of Gloucester in England, the earldom of Ulster and the lordship of Connacht.[29] The young earl of March therefore rivalled Gaunt as a property-holder, and represented too a rival claim to the succession to Richard. March and Gaunt were certainly at odds during and after the Good Parliament of 1376, at least over the conduct of the former's steward Sir Peter de la Mare, if nothing else. Walsingham (perhaps reflecting contemporary fears and rumours rather than hard fact) considered the rift more sinister. He alleged that the duke agitated in the Good Parliament to have the royal succession settled in his favour instead of March's – an anticipation of the main dynastic issue to disrupt domestic peace in the fifteenth century.[30] According to Walsingham, March gave up the marshalship of the realm – which Gaunt procured for his ally Lord Percy before December 1376 – because he feared that its possession exposed him to machinations springing from the duke's 'inveterate hatred'. Gaunt even succeeded in forcing March to go to Ireland.[31] But Walsingham's assertions are suspect. Percy is likely to have been highly acceptable to March as his successor in the marshalship, for March married his daughter Elizabeth to Percy's son Henry, and in his will of 1380 referred to Percy as 'our dear brother'.[32] March was needed in Ireland because of the deteriorating political situation there; both his family's and the Crown's control were threatened by rebellion. Even so, he only went several years after giving up the marshalship, in the meantime cooperating with Gaunt in government. He was appointed lieutenant in Ireland in October 1379 and went there in May 1380.[33] The Mortimer interest remained ineffective in English politics for most of the rest of Richard's reign. Earl Edmund died in Ireland in 1381; his son and heir Roger, who did not come of age till 1395, was given livery of his lands in 1393. He left for Ireland at lieutenant in 1394 and was killed by rebels there in 1398. Even without these premature deaths, it is likely that Irish preoccupations would have prevented the Clarence/March interest from becoming a rival to that of Lancaster. There is no sound evidence that Gaunt ever agitated to secure recognition of Lancastrian rights in the succession, exploiting Mortimer weakness. If he indeed showed restraint, this was good political sense and a sign of kin solidarity.

Had Gaunt been unremittingly hostile to the Mortimers, especially during Roger's minority, he would have offended his royal kinsfolk and the network of magnate families connected with the Mortimers. But he was keen to maintain the alliances which he had inherited from the House of Lancaster and to make new ones. In the latter aim he was assisted in the 1370s and early 1380s by one of those long-lived heiresses and dowagers who were often influential behind the scenes in medieval English politics. This was his older kinswoman Margaret countess of Norfolk (*c*.1320–99), grand-daughter of Edward I and widow of a distinguished soldier who had fought alongside Gaunt, Walter Lord Manny (d.1372).[34] Their daughter Anne married John Hastings, earl of Pembroke, a choleric young man emerging as a promising soldier in Anglo-French warfare after 1369; he was with Gaunt at the siege of Montpon (1371). He was a close companion and presumably brother-in-arms of his kinsman Sir William Beauchamp, the earl of Warwick's brother.[35] Beauchamp was with Gaunt in the vanguard of the Black Prince's army in 1367; he was a leading ducal retainer in the early 1370s, serving on the 1373–4 expedition. On 20 March 1374 he was one of a group of captains who acknowledged receipt with Gaunt of a loan from the count of Foix, but on 20 September Gaunt ordered the receiver of Tutbury not to pay any of Beauchamp's fees; he apparently left the ducal service abruptly. Perhaps he was involved in the tensions in Gascony over the duke's treatment of his army.[36]

Pembroke was appointed lieutenant in Aquitaine in 1372 in succession to Gaunt, but had the misfortune to be captured on the way there by the Castilians in the naval battle off La Rochelle. That year his wife gave birth to a son and heir, John. Gaunt gave the baby an enamelled silver cup and matching ewer.[37] Pembroke died in 1375 on his way back from harsh imprisonment in Spain. The following year the wardship of his son was granted to his widow Anne and her mother the countess of Norfolk, and the marriage was granted to Gaunt.[38] Probably there were already plans to marry the infant John Hastings into the House of Lancaster. In 1380 he was espoused to the duke's daughter Elizabeth; in 1381–2 the boy was being educated in the ducal household. In June 1384, soon after the death of John's mother, Gaunt and his leading retainer Sir Richard Burley received the wardship of the lands which she had held in dower and jointure of her son's inheritance. This grant, according to a petition by the countess of Norfolk, the young earl and Sir William Beauchamp, was appropriate, as by reason of the earl's marriage Gaunt was 'nearest' to him, and he displayed 'great solicitude for the said inheritance'. However, Elizabeth of Lancaster 'disagreed' with the marriage and married another. The vivacious adolescent bride was seduced by the dashing Sir John Holand and married him instead. The rebuffed John Hastings was placed in the custody of his grandmother the countess of Norfolk. Still under age, he died in a jousting accident in 1389 and his inheritance was split between co-heirs, including Sir William Beauchamp.[39]

The countess of Norfolk also helped in an attempt to ally Gaunt with the Mowbray family. By her first marriage she had a daughter, Elizabeth Segrave, who married the head of a leading northern baronial family, John Mowbray, lord of Thirsk (Yorks.) and Axholme (Lincs.). Born in the same year as Gaunt, Mowbray was one of the boys knighted like him by Edward III in the fleet crossing the Channel in 1355. He was killed when on crusade or pilgrimage by Muslims in 1368, leaving two infants, John and Thomas. Favours were to be showered on them: John was granted the earldom of Nottingham soon after Richard's accession,[40] and Thomas was long treated indulgently by Richard. The favour they received may have been partly due to their royal descent, but also in part to the high regard in which their father, considered a martyr for the faith, was held in royal and noble circles where there was eagerness to revive crusading. Gaunt had planned John earl of Nottingham's future with his grandmother the countess and with the earl of Northumberland. By July 1378 he purchased John's marriage from her,[41] and he acquired the wardship from Northumberland.[42] The young earl of Nottingham was being educated in the ducal household in 1380–2, but died unmarried early in 1383 and was buried in Whitefriars.[43] Developments after his death suggest that Gaunt may have intended to marry him to Elizabeth, daughter and heir of John Lord Strange of Blackmere (d. 1375), a leading Shropshire landowner. The duke received grants of her wardship and marriage on generous terms from Edward III during the last months of the king's life.[44] Immediately after Nottingham's death Richard II determined to procure Elizabeth Strange's marriage for the earl's brother and heir Thomas Mowbray, a royal boon companion. By May 1383 the king prevailed on Gaunt to surrender the marriage grant to Mowbray, with the promise of compensation to Gaunt of the wardship of the next female heir to a tenant-in-chief whose lands were worth between 600 and 1,000 marks, a promise which apparently failed to materialise. In fact, Elizabeth died later that year.[45] The new earl of Nottingham did not feel in the least beholden to Gaunt, emerging in 1384–5 as one of his bitter opponents at court.

Gaunt's acquisition of Elizabeth Strange's wardship and marriage, and the advantageous match which he probably planned for her, were, it seems, intended to strengthen his ties with a group of related comital families – Ufford, Beauchamp and Stafford – with whom he had associations through kinship and war, and who were powerful in East Anglia and the midlands. Elizabeth Strange's widowed mother Isabel married William Ufford, earl of Suffolk by June 1376; he had been previously married to the countess of Norfolk's niece Joan. Elizabeth Strange, while in Gaunt's wardship, was apparently brought up in the Suffolk household. The earl had Lancastrian links. His uncle Ralph Ufford had married a sister of Duke Henry; another uncle, Edmund Ufford, was a ducal retainer.[46] Suffolk himself served in 1373 on Gaunt's expedition to France and he probably went on his Breton expedition in 1378.[47] His closeness to Gaunt is reflected in his appointment of two leading Lancastrian retainers as his executors in 1381 – Richard Lord Scrope and Sir Robert Swillington. The earl's unexpected death the following year deprived Gaunt of a useful ally and contact among the magnates – he was one of the few magnates whose character was unreservedly praised by Walsingham, who says that his death caused consternation among the nobles and others in the realm. His death snapped a tie between Gaunt and another magnate family, for Suffolk left no issue. His title went into abeyance and his entailed estates fell to the Crown. His heirs general, three nephews and a niece, may well have looked on askance when Richard II revived the earldom for Sir Michael de la Pole in 1385, his title maintained by royal grants of former Ufford estates. De la Pole was no longer a Lancastrian retainer.[48]

Suffolk's death, and the loss of Gaunt's connection with the Strange inheritance, may have weakened his personal ties with two closely connected comital families who had concentrations of estates near some of his own in the midlands – the Beauchamps (earldom of Warwick) and the Staffords (earldom of Stafford). Suffolk's wife (Elizabeth Strange's mother) was sister of the earl of Warwick

(d. 1401): Warwick married a wife of Ufford descent. Like Suffolk, he had military retinues under Gaunt's command in 1373 and 1380: his brother Sir William Beauchamp was, as we have seen, for a time Gaunt's retainer.[49] Warwick and his Stafford kinsfolk were further distanced from Gaunt after 1385 by his conspicuous patronage of Sir John Holand, who ignominiously killed Warwick's nephew Ralph, son and heir of the earl of Stafford. In 1386, a few months after Gaunt and Holand disappeared abroad, Warwick emerged as a leading political ally of Thomas of Woodstock and the Arundels in opposition to Richard II, and he was never again to appear associated with Gaunt in any significant capacity.

Hugh earl of Stafford was a contemporary of Gaunt's (he was born *c*. 1342): he succeeded to the earldom in 1372, and was married to a sister of the earl of Warwick and the countess of Suffolk. He too served on Gaunt's 1373 expedition.[50] He had family connections with two of Gaunt's northern baronial retainers: his sister Beatrice married Thomas Lord Ros (d. 1384)[51] and his daughter Margaret married Lord Neville's son Ralph. In 1386 Stafford went on pilgrimage to Jerusalem and died on the way back: three of his executors, Warwick, Neville and Sir William Beauchamp, secured the wardship of his son and heir Thomas in 1387, probably with the help of Warwick's political allies, Woodstock and the Arundel brothers.[52] The Staffords (and through them the Beauchamps) were to forge close family ties with Woodstock: in 1391 Thomas Stafford (d. 1392) married his daughter Ann, and Thomas's younger brother Edmund was later to marry her.[53]

Thus Gaunt's ties with the leading midlands magnates slackened. But, surprisingly, he renewed his links with the family of the northern magnate whom he had humiliated in 1381 – Henry Percy, earl of Northumberland. The Percies seem to have decided that it was politic to swallow their pride where the duke was concerned, in view of his long-standing interest in Anglo-Scottish relations, the proximity of Lancastrian properties to their own in Northumberland and Yorkshire and their wide-ranging ambitions. Henry Percy – in Walsingham's view an impetuously rough-tongued northerner – and his persuasive younger brother Thomas were Gaunt's contemporaries, the former born in 1341, the latter in 1343. They were Duke Henry's nephews: Henry Percy received his courtly education partly in the duke's household; he grew very fond of his nephew. In 1366 Percy received a papal privilege to have a portable altar at the supplication of Gaunt and his wife, and he led retinues in France under Gaunt's command in 1369 and 1373.[54] In 1372 Gaunt licensed Percy to take two or three deer in each of his forests (a particularly generous provision),

because of the very great and entire affection and perfect love
which we have towards the person of our very dear and
well-beloved cousin.[55]

Thomas Percy served at the siege of Limoges with Gaunt in 1370
and, as *sénéchal* of Poitou, was among the duke's right-hand men
when he took over as lieutenant in Aquitaine soon afterwards (see
p. 189–90).[56] The Percies were the only members of a magnate family
who participated in the 1386 expedition, apart from the ill-reputed Sir
John Holand. Sir Thomas Percy was admiral of the fleet and Gaunt's
principal negotiator with Castile. Even before Percy had negotiated
the Peace of Bayonne and gained English royal support for it, Gaunt
showed high regard for his services by granting him the very large
life annuity of £100 when in Portugal in 1387.[57] Sir Thomas Percy the
younger (the earl's second son) was among the knights who sickened
and died in Galicia in 1386.[58]

Gaunt's close association with the veteran Thomas Percy continued
after they had returned to England. In 1390 they together received
from the Crown the keeping of the English and Welsh lands of the
countess of Norfolk's recently deceased daughter, the countess of
Pembroke.[59] Percy assisted in the endowment of Gaunt's Beaufort
children. In 1391 Gaunt, Percy and the ducal receiver-general Robert
Whitby were licensed to alienate the manor of Overstone (Northants.)
to Sir John Beaufort, with remainders to his brother Thomas and his
sister Joan.[60] In 1398 Gaunt appointed Percy one of his executors.
The earl of Northumberland's son and heir Henry Percy (Hotspur)
had been appointed by Gaunt as his lieutenant in Aquitaine in 1393.[61]
The maintenance of links between Gaunt and the Percies, despite the
quarrel of 1381, smoothed the way for Gaunt's lieutenancy in the
Marches in 1398 and for their support of the Lancastrian cause when
Bolingbroke returned from exile in 1399.

Another comital family with whom Gaunt had kinship ties and at
times bitter relations was that of Courtenay (earls of Devon). The
friendship of the Courtenays may have seemed unimportant to Gaunt,
as they were not wealthy and he did not possess important territorial
interests in their 'country'.[62] Their influence in the west country was
to be largely eclipsed, when challenged by Gaunt's son-in-law John
Holand in the 1390s.[63] By then Edward Courtenay, earl of Devon's
political effectiveness may have been impaired by the onset of
blindness. He had succeeded his aged grandfather Earl Hugh in 1377:
the Courtenays were connected in blood to Gaunt by Hugh's marriage
to Margaret de Bohun (d. 1391), a grand-daughter of Edward I.[64] In
1377, according to Walsingham (then hostile to Gaunt), the latter
publicly threatened the Courtenays, in a moment of anger spurning

the 'natural' ties by which he on another occasion claimed he set such store. At Wycliffe's trial in St Paul's he told Earl Hugh's son William Courtenay, bishop of London, 'Do not rely on your parents, for they can do nothing useful for you: they will have enough to do to protect themselves.'[65] When Courtenay succeeded Simon Sudbury as archbishop of Canterbury, Gaunt made a friendly gesture towards him: he ordered twelve live does to be sent from Ashdown Chace (Sussex) to restock the archbishop's park.[66] But next year Gaunt publicly voiced his anger with the archbishop's brothers Philip and Peter (the king's knights) for their advocacy of Despenser's crusade. However, in 1385 the fearless and upright archbishop incurred royal wrath by standing up for Gaunt, publicly voicing the complaints of leading churchmen and some secular lords against the evil advice of those councillors who had induced the king to countenance plotting against the duke.[67] This must have reconciled the latter with some of the Courtenays, if he was not reconciled already. Before Gaunt's departure abroad in 1386, he appointed the earl of Devon lieutenant of his fees in Devonshire, addressing the earl as 'our very dear and well-beloved Cousin' and 'trusting entirely in his great goodness and special love'.[68]

Three earls were accused by chroniclers of instigating the plot about which the archbishop complained – Robert de Vere, earl of Oxford, Thomas Mowbray, earl of Nottingham (and earl marshal) and William Montague, earl of Salisbury. Their animus against the duke may have been essentially derived from Richard's. Mowbray may also have resented the influence Gaunt had in the counsels of his grandmother the countess of Norfolk (whose heir he was), and in the regional politics of Yorkshire and Lincolnshire, where he had lordships. Vere may have hoped that, if the king repudiated Gaunt's influence, he would be better placed to assert his territorial power in Essex against that of Gaunt's kinsfolk, his brother Thomas and Thomas's mother-in-law the countess of Hereford.[69] Rivalry with Vere may have increased the importance to Gaunt of his grant of an annual rent of 100 marks to James Butler, earl of Ormond, an annuity which his father, Earl James, had held (27 November 1385).[70] The father, who had died in 1382, was a descendant of Edward I and of the Bohun family, and had married into the Darcy of Knaith family, which had Lancastrian connections. The father of Earl James the younger's bride, Lord Welles, had been Gaunt's retainer. Earl James the younger, whose main territorial interests were in Ireland, was in England in 1385 to do homage and fealty for his lands.[71] In October Robert de Vere had received royal grants in anticipation of his creation as marquis of Dublin, together with the lordship of Ireland. With this in mind, Gaunt may have been keen to have some influence in Ireland through his patronage of Ormond, whom he retained in part 'for the good and agreeable service which he will do to us in time to come'.[72]

The ageing earl of Salisbury (1328–97) was an improbable bedfellow for the impulsive young courtiers such as Mowbray and Vere. The son of one of the young Edward III's best friends, he was a veteran of Crécy, 'Les Espagnols sur Mer' (1350) and Gaunt's 1369 expedition.[73] In 1365 Gaunt secured from him by suit of law considerable Dorset property – a decision which may have rankled with the Montagues.[74] In 1372 Gaunt ordered delivery to be made to a member of Salisbury's household of two oaks from the forest of Wimborne Holt (Dorset), and in 1375 he granted a favour to the tenants of 'our very dear and well-beloved companion' the earl in his lordship of Canford in the same shire.[75] Salisbury had, in his teens, in the 1340s, been married to Gaunt's friend Princess Joan in strange circumstances, within two years or so after her marriage (when she was aged about eleven) to Sir Thomas Holand (*c*.1339). The marriage to young Montague took place when Holand was in Prussia, doubtless on crusade. The probable explanation of this bigamy was that he was presumed dead. But he returned and eventually regained his wife; in 1349 the pope ordered the re-establishment of Joan's first marriage. In 1384 Salisbury was married to a daughter of another friend of Gaunt, Lady Mohun. Indeed, Salisbury might have found it congenial if Gaunt's Dorset influence was reduced. But it seems more likely that, rather than he, his brother Sir John Montague (d.1390), steward of the household (and his prospective heir), or the latter's son Sir John, a king's knight who succeeded his uncle in the earldom in 1397, participated in the court plotting against Gaunt.

There is not much evidence that after his return to England in 1389 Gaunt had many habitually close associations with fellow magnates in government and politics, apart from his brothers and the Percies. His son-in-law John Holand, his nephew Edward earl of Rutland and, indeed, his own son John Beaufort (created marquis of Dorset in 1397) were drawn particularly into Richard's orbit. But Lancastrian power could still be plausibly represented as an objective which magnates plotted to overthrow. A Ricardian apologist alleged that the noble plot against the king in 1397 was aimed against Gaunt too, and Thomas Mowbray allegedly described to Bolingbroke the plotting of young nobles to overthrow Lancastrian power (see pp. 159, 162). The earl of Arundel had emerged in the 1390s as a bitter opponent of the duke's influence and policies, and the quarrel between Mowbray and Bolingbroke in 1398 seems to have involved Gaunt as well (see p. 162–4).

How, then, can we characterise and judge Gaunt's relations with his powerful close kinsmen and with the magnates in general? His youthful devotion to the Black Prince helped to establish military and political roles for him, and his close relations with the prince's widow helped to alleviate some of the difficulties he faced (especially in relations with Richard) till her death in 1385. Up to then Gaunt won, too, in the royal minority a good deal of support from his younger brothers, whose marriages were intended to strengthen their ties with him. But from his return to England in 1389, when his relations with Richard became closer, he no longer appears to have acted as a focus for leadership and alliance among the king's close kin. His brothers, though still cordial, did not follow his political leads so readily. Younger nobles looked primarily to the king to enhance or establish their fortunes as magnates.

A similar retreat to relative isolation is found in Gaunt's relations with other magnate families (most of whom were also related to him, but more distantly). During his father's reign and during Richard's minority, Gaunt looked for support for his military endeavours and eventual political ascendancy particularly to the circle of kinship links cultivated by Duke Henry of Lancaster. Notable among these were Duke Henry's brother-in-law the earl of Arundel, Henry's nephews the Percies, his nephew John Mowbray's mother-in-law the countess of Norfolk, and the earl of Suffolk, whose uncles had had close ties with him. In the 1370s Arundel and his sons, the Percies, Suffolk and his kinsmen the earls of Warwick and Stafford cooperated with Gaunt in government, diplomacy and war. They came to regard him as the principal exponent of royal policy – his lonely defence of his father's government probably increased their respect for his zeal as the guardian of royal interests. Probably to enhance his ascendancy, as well as Lancastrian interests, Gaunt set out to strengthen kinship ties with these and other comital families. He planned the marriage of the earl of Pembroke to one of his daughters, and of the newly created John Mowbray, earl of Nottingham to his ward, who was closely connected with the earl of Suffolk. But these plans went awry – accidents cut his ties with the Pembroke, Nottingham and Suffolk interests – and, through the breach with the last, with those of Warwick and Stafford. Surprisingly, he retained links with the Percies (a comital family since 1377), despite his well-publicised disputes with Henry Percy in 1381. Gaunt's tendency to an overbearing assertion of his honour and high estate, and of the policies he promoted as a royal councillor, undoubtedly alienated some magnates families, such as the Courtenays, though in this case, too, the breaches were not permanent. His characteristic attitudes may have been a factor in the deterioration of his relations with the youthful earl of Oxford and

Thomas Mowbray, earl of Nottingham, and with the Montagues. But this deterioration was basically a reflection of Richard's growing antagonism.

After his return to England in 1389, Gaunt failed to make close ties with fellow magnates. By October 1397 his son John Beaufort was married to Huntingdon's niece Alice Holand, daughter of the earl of Kent, but John's sister Joan was married into a baronial family, and proposals for Bolingbroke's remarriage were with foreign princesses. Gaunt set great store by his new relationship with Richard, and perhaps feared that if he tried for a reconciliation with Arundel, cultivated Warwick and patronised younger nobles, he would arouse the king's suspicious nature. Consequently, when Richard arrested Woodstock in 1397, when Woodstock was (almost certainly) assassinated at Richard's command, and when Bolingbroke was exiled, Gaunt was in no position to rally fellow magnates in protest. This Lancastrian isolation is likely to have been an important factor in Richard's political calculations in 1397–8. Gaunt's Ricardian policies after his return in 1389, intended to defuse the recent domestic crises, left the Lancastrian interest exposed when there was a return to crisis.

Gaunt also maintained relations with families whose heads were accustomed to receiving, or were starting to receive, individual summonses as 'barons of parliament'. A survey of such ties will emphasise regional factors and the connections between baronial territorial power-bases and Lancastrian interests, starting with the English Marches and the regions 'north of the river Trent', and moving southwards. In the Marches up to 1381 Gaunt relied heavily on the Percies, whose magnate rather than baronial standing was recognised by the grant of the earldom of Northumberland in 1377, a grant which Gaunt is sure to have promoted. But the Percies were not Gaunt's only noble connections in the region. In 1372 Sir Hugh Dacre, member of a leading baronial family in Cumberland, was his bachelor. Dacre was suspected of procuring the family inheritance in 1375 by engineering his brother's death. But, as a border fighter and lord of the strategically crucial frontier barony of Gilsland (Cumberland), his help was indispensable in defending the West March: Gaunt as lieutenant probably procured Dacre's appointments as its warden in 1379 and 1383.[76] The duke was to patronise another bellicose Cumberland landowner, Ralph Lord Greystoke. His castle and estate of Greystoke near Penrith (Cumberland) were almost as vulnerable as Gilsland to Scottish raids, and he had acquired great expertise in border affairs when holding wardenships in the 1370s. His mother Joan was the sister of the Yorkshire landowner Lord FitzHugh, who had served in Gaunt's military retinues, and she was probably holding as jointure the lordship of Morpeth in Northumberland (of her son's inheritance) when Gaunt dated warrants there in June 1383, on his way to Roxburgh.[77] Probably in 1384 or 1385, Gaunt offered to retain Greystoke for two years, an offer he was inclined to accept.[78]

The family involved in border affairs with which Gaunt had the most durable and eventually the closest ties were the Nevilles. They were accustomed to hold border wardenships, but the centre of their power was just outside the Marches, in the bishopric of Durham, and they were lords of Middleham in Yorkshire, to the south of Gaunt's lordship of Richmond.[79] John Neville was in receipt of a fee from Gaunt in 1366, the year before he received livery of his father's lands.[80] He intended to go on overseas service with Gaunt then and in 1369;[81] he was captured in Spain (presumably when serving Gaunt on the 1367 expedition). The duke contributed substantially to his ransom.[82] In 1370 Neville indented with Gaunt to serve him in peace and war, bringing a larger retinue than any of the duke's other retainers whose indentures survive were habitually obliged to do – an index of the duke's high regard for his military capability.[83] In 1372 Gaunt ordered the delivery of twenty-four deer from his park and chase of Pickering Lythe to his 'very dear and very well-beloved, the lord of Nevill' in order to stock one of his places. Loans from Neville and his mother helped to finance Gaunt's participation in the 1372 and 1373 expeditions.[84] After the duke's quarrel with Henry Percy in 1381, he appointed Neville to the wardenship of the East March in order to reduce Percy influence.[85] Neville died in 1388; his son and heir Ralph (born *c*.1364) married Gaunt's daughter Joan Beaufort in 1396 and as earl of Westmorland was to be the most steadfast magnate supporter of Henry IV's rule in the north.[86]

The concentration of Lancastrian lordships in Yorkshire and other parts of the north drew other baronial families there into contact with Lancastrian circles – by retaining, by association with Lancastrian retainers, and service on expeditions led by Gaunt. Henry FitzHugh (1338–6), lord of Ravensworth, five miles from Gaunt's castle of Richmond, apparently served in his retinues on the 1359 and 1369 expeditions.[87] In 1364 he is found in association with two knights who were to be among Gaunt's most trusted retainers: FitzHugh and Sir John Marmion witnessed a grant to Sir Richard Scrope.[88] Another North Riding landowner who served on Gaunt's campaigns, Thomas Lord Ros of Helmsley, made lasting contractual links with Gaunt by 1366.[89] He served abroad in Gaunt's company in 1369, 1370–1 and 1373–4.[90] The duke permitted Lady Ros (Beatrice Stafford) to go hunting in Pickering Lythe in the summer of 1372. Ros was still receiving his ducal annuity in 1380.[91] He was well connected in northern Lancastrian circles: he named Lord Neville as an executor in

1373.[92] The royal grant in 1384 of his son John's wardship to Robert de Vere seems like a snub to Gaunt and the northern baronage. But the Ros family gravitated to traditional connections: by 20 August 1385 Lord Ros's widow Beatrice married Sir Richard Burley, a leading retainer of Gaunt who possessed a connection with Richard's familiar circles through his uncle Sir Simon Burley. The supervisors of the heir's 1392 will included the earl of Northumberland and two close associates of Gaunt, Ralph Lord Neville and Richard Lord Scrope.[93]

Gaunt's relationship with William Lord Latimer (1330–81) of Danby (North Riding) was very different from that with Thomas Lord Ros. Though Latimer's paternal grandfather had been a retainer of Thomas of Lancaster, he does not seem to have been Gaunt's retainer: he was a colleague and friend whose talents and achievements were probably regarded by the duke with considerable respect. Latimer had had a distinguished career going back to his youthful service under an equally youthful Black Prince at Crécy. From 1360 to 1362 he had been Edward III's lieutenant in Brittany. He was a particular friend of John Lord Neville, who married his daughter and to whom he willed his inheritance. Latimer contracted to serve on Gaunt's 1373 expedition, but in June of that year was appointed to treat with Fernando I of Portugal, a closer involvement in Gaunt's affairs. In 1376 the duke tried to shield Latimer from the onslaughts in parliament.[94] In 1380 he appointed Latimer as one of his commissioners to treat with the duke of Brittany's envoys.[95] Gaunt found Latimer a congenial companion as well as a valuable diplomat. In 1373 he presented him with an enamelled silver 'hanap' (cup) and ewer, and in 1374 lost 66s. 8d. dicing at his house. When they were together the following year at the Bruges conference, Gaunt gave him a barrel of wine.[96]

But Gaunt had more formal ties with another Yorkshire baron of Latimer's generation who, like him, made his mark as a soldier and royal administrator – Sir Richard Scrope, of Bolton, also in the North Riding (c. 1327–1403). He had fought at Crécy, Neville's Cross, the siege of Calais, 'Les Espagnols sur Mer' and in Edward's French and Scottish campaigns of 1355–6. He was one of the young Gaunt's military mentors, serving abroad in his retinues in 1359–60, at Najera in 1367, and in 1369. In November 1367 Scrope had been retained by Gaunt with the large annuity of £40 (which he was still receiving at the time of the duke's death) and in 1371 he first received an individual summons as a peer of parliament.[97] Scrope was closely associated with other 'Lancastrians'. In 1371 Lord Neville was his feoffee in an estate (Henry Percy witnessing one of the deeds) and in 1372 Sir Ralph Hastings and Sir John Marmion witnessed a grant to him.[98] The personal friendship between Scrope and Gaunt is attested by the purchase by the former's servant George of a black courser as a present to Gaunt from his master.[99] They shared pious as well as equine interests (see pp. 253, 263). Scrope was in Gaunt's military retinues in 1373–4, 1384 and 1385; his distinguished career in royal government probably owed something to Gaunt's patronage. He was appointed as warden of the West March in February 1381.[100] Scrope was a good friend to have, not only because of his technical abilities, but because he was widely trusted and liked among the nobility. The earl of March appointed him as a supervisor of his will in 1380, the earl of Suffolk as executor in 1381.[101]

Scrope's son and heir William (born *c.* 1350) was an able man too, but widely disliked. He carried on the family tradition of Lancastrian service, campaigning with Gaunt in France in 1369 and 1373, and acting as his lieutenant in Gascony in 1390–3. From 1393 to 1398 he was vice-chamberlain of the royal household; perhaps Gaunt's influence helped him to gain this office. In September 1397 he was created earl of Wiltshire. But, in contrast to Sir Michael de la Pole in the early 1380s (when relations between the king and Gaunt were very different), Scrope did not sever Lancastrian links when he ascended in royal favour.[102] In 1398, Gaunt appointed him and Thomas Percy as executors, describing them as 'my very dear and well-beloved . . . companions'. But Walsingham gave Scrope a bad character as one of Richard's councillors at the end of the reign. He was captured in 1399 when Bristol Castle fell to Bolingbroke. Despite his closeness to Bolingbroke's father, he was excepted from pardon and executed. Bolingbroke did, however, exempt Scrope's aged father from forfeiture, declaring that he had always accounted him a loyal knight.[103]

Gaunt's earldom of Lincoln provided him with links with the shire's nobility, such as the Darcys of Knaith: Lord Darcy gave Bolingbroke a courser in 1391 or 1392.[104] Another Lincolnshire landowner, John Lord Welles (1352–1421), was retained by Gaunt to serve for life in peace and war in February 1372 and was preparing in August to go abroad in the ducal retinue.[105] According to the Scottish chronicler Wyntoun:

> This Wellis wes a commendit man,
> Manfull, stoute, and off gud pythe,
> And hey off harte he wes tharewyth.[106]

He drifted from Gaunt's circle to that of Thomas Mowbray, who was probably keen to enhance his standing at Gaunt's expense in Lincolnshire, by forging ties with Welles. Before May 1386 the latter married Mowbray's sister, and in 1389 probably led a retinue as part of Mowbray's forces as warden of the East March, and took part with him in the obscure border campaign that year against the earl of Fife's army. In 1390 Welles fought the Scot Sir David Lindsay on London Bridge by prior agreement, as a result of Lindsay's slander on Welles, which probably related to the war of words between opposing captains on the campaign.[107] In 1398 Welles was present at Lowestoft to take leave of Mowbray when he went into exile.[108]

The Willoughbys of Eresby (Lincs.) do not seem to have had formal life contracts with Gaunt as did Lord Welles, but their links of military service were more enduring. John Lord Willoughby (1329–72), who had served on the Black Prince's expeditions, was with Gaunt in France in 1369. He married Cecily, sister of Gaunt's friend the earl of Suffolk, whose co-heir was his son Robert (d. 1396). Robert Willoughby took part in Gaunt's expeditions in France in 1373–4 and in Spain in 1386–7. He may have felt aggrieved by Richard's grant of the earldom of Suffolk to Michael de la Pole in 1385; in his will he emphasised his own family's connection with the earldom by mentioning that a diamond he was bequeathing to his son William had belonged to the earl of Suffolk. After the death of Robert's first wife in 1391, he strengthened Lancastrian ties by marrying Lord Latimer's daughter, the widow of Lord Neville (d. 1388). His son William was one of the first to join Bolingbroke when he landed in Yorkshire in 1399 and was one of those present in the Tower of London when Richard allegedly abdicated.[109]

The military service to Gaunt of the Greys of Codnor, landowners in his earldom of Derby, seems, like that of the Willoughbys, to have become a family tradition, again without the making of lasting formal contracts. In 1359 John lord Grey (d. 1392), who had given service in war to Duke Henry of Lancaster, intended to go to France in Gaunt's company. His son Sir Henry was preparing in 1366 and 1369 to go on expeditions in Gaunt's retinues.[110] In April 1373 the duke presented him with three deer from High Peak.[111] Henry predeceased his father: his son and heir Richard, who came of age in the 1390s, may have stayed as a young man in Gaunt's household.[112]

Few baronial families whose principal estates were in the midlands and south had close or lengthy connections with Gaunt; some families and individuals were attracted to serve on his military expeditions. The Shropshire landowner Hugh Lord Burnell (d. 1420) served in Gaunt's French expeditions of 1369 and 1373, when in his twenties, and took part in his 1384 expedition to Scotland.[113] The Ferrers family of Groby (Leics.) had a tradition of military service to the House of Lancaster. William Lord Ferrers (1331–71) served in France under Duke Henry in 1359–60 and under Gaunt in 1369. His two wives were, respectively, the sisters of Gaunt's friends William Ufford, earl of Suffolk and Henry Lord Percy. His daughter Margaret (by his first wife) married the earl of Warwick (d. 1401). Ferrers' son and heir Henry (1356–88) served under Gaunt in 1378.[114] A number of barons, some of whom had few or no Lancastrian connections, joined his army in 1386 – perhaps attracted by its crusading privileges. But the high mortality among them in Spain militated against Gaunt making more permanent connections with their families. The Herefordshire landowner Gilbert Lord Talbot (born *c.* 1332) died of pestilence in Spain in 1387: he had had a distinguished military career, including service with the Black Prince in the 1350s. He was married to a daughter of the earl of Stafford.[115] A much younger man who succumbed in Galicia in 1386 was the Norfolk landowner Roger Lord Scales, one of the nephews of William Ufford, earl of Suffolk.[116] The Essex landowner Walter Lord FitzWalter (born 1345) also died on the expedition. He had been an ally of the Londoners against Gaunt in 1377 and had considerable military experience. He needed patronage and profit to recover his lordship of Egremont in Cumberland, mortgaged to pay a ransom in 1375. He may also have sought Gaunt's patronage because of annoyance at court favour enjoyed by the earl of Oxford, who aspired to exercise dominant influence in Essex. FitzWalter probably gravitated to Lancastrian circles through his marriage to Philippa, a daughter of Gaunt's friend Lady Mohun. In March 1382 Gaunt ordered payment for a large covered cup, silver and enamelled, with a ewer, a present to Philippa on her wedding day.[117] Yet another southern baron who died on the Spanish expedition was the Sussex landowner Richard Lord Poynings (born *c.* 1355). The wardship of his elder brother Thomas had been granted in 1369 to Gaunt, who married him to Blanche, daughter of John Lord Mowbray (d. 1361), a grand-daughter of Henry earl of Lancaster and one of the countess of Norfolk's family circle.[118] Thomas Poynings probably served in Gaunt's retinues in France in 1369 and 1370–1. He contracted to do so for the proposed expedition there in March 1373, as did his cousin Thomas Lord Poynings of Basing (Hants.).[119] Gaunt seems to have been particularly attached to his ward Thomas and Thomas's wife. From France in 1369 he wrote that his 'treschere cousine de Ponynges' was to be requested to attend the Duchess Blanche's anniversary; in 1372 he ordered her to be a sent barrel of Gascon wine, and in 1374 she and her husband accompanied Gaunt to attend the anniversary.[120] Thomas died the following year. His brother and heir Richard married into the Grey of Codnor family, and made a will at Plymouth on 10 June 1386, when waiting to embark for Spain. The duke was to send him from Galicia on a mission to João of Portugal.[121]

Gaunt had few properties and fees in south-west England, and few baronial links there. A landowner in Devon and Pembrokeshire, Guy

Lord Brian (c. 1319–90) was appointed one of the feoffees of the duchy in 1369. He had long been eminent in Edward III's service as a soldier, diplomat and household official. His services were valued by magnates too – in 1372 the earl of Hereford appointed him an executor. It was for his administrative talents, not his military abilities or territorial influence, that Gaunt became connected with him. In 1377 he was to be ranged among Gaunt's political opponents.[122]

The reasons for Gaunt's friendship with Joan Lady Mohun of Dunster (Somerset) (d. 1404) were quite different. She was the daughter of a distinguished soldier, Barthelomew Lord Burghersh (d. 1369). Her husband, John Lord Mohun, KG (d. 1375) was in 1354 a member of the Black Prince's household, and distinguished himself in war in the service of both the prince and Duke Henry.[123] Probably in 1373 he was intending to go on campaign in Gaunt's retinue.[124] Lady Mohun, as a mature widow, had qualities of birth and character which led Gaunt to commit the prospective heiress of Spain, his daughter Catherine, to her care in 1380.[125] Lady Mohun's high connections and sterling reputation are reflected in the permission she obtained for her burial and foundation of a chantry near one of the most sacred places in England, at the altar of Our Lady Undercroft in the crypt of Canterbury Cathedral, where her battered effigy remains.[126]

So members of at least twenty baronial families (including three families which received comital titles in Gaunt's lifetime) performed military and other kinds of services for him. But not many of these families had continuous, concurrent, or formal links with Gaunt. Some probably had only one member in a temporary relationship with him. Only six individuals of baronial status are known to have been retained for long-term service by the duke. It is clear that he never pursued a general policy of extending patronage among the baronage; he is unlikely to have seen them in collective terms as a political group, or, indeed, as a social group worth cultivating for its own sake. However, his possession when young of the earldom of Richmond and his early leadership of military retinues attracted the services of the baronial families of the North Riding – FitzHugh, Ros, Latimer, Neville and Scrope – and led him to encourage their aid and amity. His role on expeditions abroad also brought the military service of barons from his other earldoms – Welles, Willoughby and Darcy (Lincoln), Grey of Codnor (Derby) and Ferrers of Groby (Leicester). In the 1370s and early 1380s he relied particularly on baronial families with expertise in frontier affairs to support his authority, especially as lieutenant in the Marches – the Dacres, Greystokes and, above all, the Nevilles.

Some connections made on campaign and business had enduring consequences (for example, with the Willoughbys); some were to prove of great importance for Lancastrian affairs (for example, with the Nevilles and Scropes). Other connections weakened, sometimes when a baron came under the influence of another magnate (Welles), often as a result of deaths and family discontinuities. A number of barons who had been involved in one way or another in Gaunt's affairs died in the 1380s – William Latimer (d. 1381), Thomas Dacre (d. 1383), Thomas Ros (d. 1384) and Henry FitzHugh (d. 1386).

When he went to Spain in 1386 Gaunt enrolled the services of some barons whose main territorial interests lay south of the River Trent, mostly not in close proximity to Gaunt's. They may have been attracted to his service because of the lack of opportunities to go campaigning in France in recent years – whereas northern baronial families were preoccupied with the Scottish threat. Some of the southerners may have served in Gaunt's huge retinue in Scotland the previous year. In 1386 Lords Scales (Norfolk), Talbot (Herefordshire) and FitzWalter (Essex) went to Spain. So did Lord Poynings (Sussex), whose family had close Lancastrian links. All these peers died on the expedition – a setback to possible new extensions of Lancastrian influence in the peerage.

Thus, in summary, as a young man Gaunt valued baronial links he forged with neighbours and tenants in the honour of Richmond, and he was to value those with baronial frontiersmen in his government of the Marches. He cultivated the friendship and sought the service of barons who were veterans in war, diplomacy and administration, notably Lords Scrope and Latimer, and of younger men adept in warfare such as John Neville and Thomas Ros (the latter in his own age group). He was to remain intimately connected with only a few baronial families, above all with the Nevilles and Scropes. If he had sought the alliance of barons generally, the political losses would probably have outweighed the gains. The baronage did not form a solid political bloc in or out of parliament. The extension of Lancastrian influence over them would have drawn Gaunt into the settlement of disputes and fulfilment of ambitions, and would have been likely to impair his relations with the king and his fellow magnates.

Gaunt was particularly concerned to keep the goodwill of princely kinsfolk and other magnates, to which purpose as a young man he exploited the interwoven royal and Lancastrian family networks. In his father's reign and his nephew's minority he used these connections to sustain his growing roles in warfare, diplomacy and government. But, by the time he set out for Spain, accidental factors, chiefly mortality, and the fraying of relationships resulting from his ten years of dominance in national affairs, had torn holes in the threads of his kinship networks. Nevertheless, he had not aroused a national or regional anti-Lancastrian movement among the nobility. There was no move among them to destroy his standing and the Lancastrian interest when he was forced into exile in 1381, when the king withheld protection from him in 1385, or when he was abroad from 1386 to 1389.

During the last period, the central political crisis of the reign occurred, throwing up new key issues and inducing new magnate alliances and antagonisms. After his return to England, Gaunt seems to have remained more politically isolated than hitherto from his fellow magnates. His foreign ambitions may have induced this; so may have his unswerving support for the king, in part springing from these ambitions, and in part, perhaps, from fears that the king might suspect him if he built close relationships with fellow magnates. Gaunt's political isolation eventually facilitated Richard's 'tyranny'.

Gaunt had only a qualified success in harmonising his own interests with those of his fellow peers, but his relations with them neither provoked the Crown to turn against him nor stirred up a baronial movement aimed to reduce the Lancastrian interest. In the often fraught political circumstances of Richard's reign, it was perhaps no mean feat to have avoided polarising the peerage into 'pro' and 'anti' Lancastrian factions. However, it was during his career that Lancastrian power, perhaps inevitably, became a controversial issue among his fellow nobles as well as for the king, one for which they acquiesced in drastic solutions as soon as he died.

Notes and References

1 McFarlane KB 1973; Given-Wilson C 1987.
2 P.R.O. E101/178/9.
3 Nicolas NH 1826, Vol. 1, pp. 12–13. For the prince's grant of 100 marks *p.a.* to Gaunt from the earldom of Chester, *J.G.R. 1372–6*, nos 1642, 1775. For Gaunt's gifts to the prince and princess in 1373, ibid., no. 1342. Gaunt bequeathed a missal and prayer book which had been the prince's.
4 *J.G.R. 1379–83*, no. 327. For other gift exchanges between Gaunt and the princess, *J.G.R. 1372–6*, nos 915, 1342–3, 1431; *J.G.R. 1379–83*, nos 557, 714–15. In 1376 Gaunt received her oath to refrain from remarrying without royal licence (*C.P.R. 1374–7*, pp. 374ff). Like Gaunt, she patronised Wycliffe (McFarlane KB 1966, pp. 58, 81).
5 *C.P.*, Vol. 8, p. 154; *J.G.R. 1372–6*, nos 50, 1784.
6 *C.P.*, Vol. 7, pp. 155–6; Norwich, Norfolk R.O., MS 15171, 37B6, receiver's account 1396–7 for Huntingdon's annuity.

7   Zurita G 1579, pp. 92–3. The claim to the throne was made many years later by Langley's son and heir Edward duke of York (ibid.).

8   Nicolas NH 1826, Vol. 1, pp. 134–5. For loans made by Gaunt to the duke and duchess of York in the early 1390s, P.R.O. DL28/3/2 m12.

9   Legge MD 1941, nos 272, 275. Langley and Rutland stayed with Gaunt at Pontefract in 1394 (ibid. no. 29).

10 Given-Wilson C 1987, pp. 43–4. Froissart says that Woodstock made critical remarks about Richard's peace policy to Langley in 1396 'et le attraioit ce qu'il povoit à ses oppinions, pour tant que il le sentoit mol et simple et paisible' (Froissart J 1871, Vol. 15, p. 238).

11 Goodman A and Morgan D 1985 : 63; *H.A.*, Vol. 2, p. 194; *V.R.S.*, pp. 129–30.

12 Holmes G 1957, pp. 20ff. For the reciprocal marriages between the Bohun and Arundel families, McFarlane KB 1973, p. 86.

13 *J.G.R. 1372–6*, no. 1124.

14 Holmes G 1957, p. 24; Goodman A 1971, pp. 88–9. For Gaunt's presents to the Lady of Woodstock on her wedding day, *J.G.R. 1372–6*, no. 1431.

15 *J.G.R. 1379–83*, no. 1088.

16 Holmes G 1957, p. 24 and n.

17 *C.P.R. 1377–81*, p. 537.

18 *J.G.R. 1379–83*, nos 556, 646–7, 679, 688. A receiver's account for Lincs. and Hunts., 1383–4 records a payment to the countess (P.R.O. DL29/262/4070). The Crown also contributed to the countess's costs for Eleanor's upbringing (P.R.O. E403/508/18).

19 Holmes G 1957, pp. 24–5.

20 *J.G.R. 1379–83*, nos 714–15, 803, 905.

21 *H.A.*, Vol. 2, pp. 114–15; *W.C.*, pp. 110–13.

22 East Sussex R.O., Waleys cartulary B9; *C.P.R. 1391–6*, p. 133.

23 P.R.O. DL28/3/6. For Bolingbroke's participation in jousts at Hertford, ibid., DL28/1/5 f12d.

24 Clarke MV 1937, pp. 91–5.

25 *J.G.R. 1379–83*, nos 790, 851, 1003; Aston M 1967, p. 384.

26 *J.G.R. 1379–83*, nos 833–8, 853–4, 1009–12, 1039 (12–14, 16 March, 16 April). Bishop Arundel was in London on 7 March, at Ely on 21, 24 and 28 April (Aston M 1967, p. 385). So he and the duke may have been together at Hatfield.

27 *J.G.R. 1372–6*, no. 915.

28 Ibid., no. 1342.

29 Holmes G 1957, pp. 17–18; Otway-Ruthven AJ 1968, p. 313.

30 *C.A.*, pp. 92–3.

31 Ibid., pp. 107–8.

32 Nicolas NH 1826, Vol. 1, pp. 110–13.

33 Otway-Ruthven AJ 1968, ch. 10, pp. 309–15.

34 *C.P.*, Vol. 9, pp. 599–60; Archer RE 1987 : 264ff. For mention of a gift from the countess of Norfolk to Gaunt in 1372, *J.G.R. 1372–6*, no. 1343; for their New Year gift exchanges, 1380–2, *J.G.R. 1379–83*, nos 327, 556–8, 715.

35 *C.P.*, Vol. 10, pp. 391–5. For Pembroke's character and career, Jack RI 1965 : 6–9. In 1381 Gaunt gave a New Year's gift to his 'cousin' the countess of Pembroke (*J.G.R. 1379–83*, no. 557).

36 Tucoo-Chala P 1959, p. 353; *J.G.R. 1372–6*, nos 1086, 1548. Beauchamp entered royal service (*B.R.U.O.*, Vol. 1, p. 138).

37 *J.G.R. 1372–6*, no. 1343.

38 Archer RE 1987 : 269; *C.P.R. 1374–7*, p. 396–7, 437.

39 *C.P.*, Vol. 10, pp. 394–7; P.R.O. SC8/224/11176. The petitioners asked for the wardship to be granted to them as 'pluis proscheins' to the earl. The petition is endorsed with a note that the matter should be settled in Chancery.

40 *C.P.*, Vol. 9, pp. 383–4, 599–600, 780–1.

41 *C.P.R. 1377–81*, p. 456.

42 Goodman A 1971, p. 157; *J.G.R. 1379–83*, p. 941. For payments by Gaunt to the countess for the marriage, ibid., nos 68, 88, 175–6, 297, 310, 452.

43 *C.P.R. 1377–81*, p. 393; *J.G.R. 1379–83*, no. 556; *W.C.*, pp. 34–5, 62–3.

44 *C.P.*, Vol. 12, pt 1, pp. 344–5; *C.P.R. 1374–7*, pp. 340, 437.

45 *C.P.R. 1381–5*, pp. 269–70.

46 *C.P.*, Vol. 12, pt 1, p. 433; Nicolas NH 1826, Vol. 1, pp. 73–4; Holmes G 1957, pp. 66–7.

47 *Foedera*, 1869, Vol. 4, p. 45. In Sept. 1380 Suffolk and Warwick were among those appointed with Gaunt to correct infractions of the truce with Scotland (see above, p. 76).

48 *C.P.*, Vol. 12, pt 1, pp. 432–4; Nicolas NH 1826, Vol. 1, pp. 114–15; *H.A.*, Vol. 2, pp. 48–9; Tuck A 1973 pp. 76–7.

49 *C.P.*, Vol. 12, pt 2, pp. 375–8.

50 Ibid., Vol. 1, pp. 177–9. Stafford was appointed as Gaunt's fellow envoy to negotiate with the Scots in 1381 (see above, p. 78).

51 Ibid., Vol. 11, p. 101.

52 Nicolas NH 1826, Vol. 1, pp. 118–19.

53 Goodman A 1971, pp. 93–4.

54 *C.P.*, Vol. 9, pp. 708–9; *ibid.*, Vol. 12, pt 2, pp. 638–40; *H.A.*, Vol. 2, p. 44; Dickson W 1844, p. 42; *C.E.P.R. Petitions*, Vol. 1, p. 528.

55 *J.G.R. 1372–6*, no. 414. In 1373 Percy received a gift from Gaunt of six oaks from Bowland Forest (ibid., no. 1293).

56 Ibid., nos 5, 42, 230, 966. Thomas Percy may have taken part in the 1378 siege of St Malo (*J.G.R. 1379–83*, no. 258).

57 *C.P.R. 1399–1401*, p. 110.

58 *Foedera*, 1709, Vol. 8, p. 501; *C.R.C.*, Vol. 2, p. 110. In Feb. 1386, a few days before Bolingbroke was received into the confraternity of Lincoln Cathedral, in his father's presence, the earl of Northumberland's son Sir Henry was similarly received. Percy's name was originally recorded as 'Thomas' and it is tempting to believe that this was in fact Sir Thomas Percy the younger, in Lincoln to meet Gaunt, and not his elder brother Sir Henry (Lincoln R.O., D and C archives, Chapter Acts A.2.27 f12v–13r).

59 *C.F.R. 1383–91*, pp. 312, 353.

60 *C.P.R. 1391–6*, p. 15; *ibid., 1388–92*, p. 461.

61 Carte T 1743, p. 179.

62 Holmes G 1957, pp. 32–5.

63 Cherry M 1979 : 90–2.

64 *C.P.*, Vol. 4, pp. 324–6.

65 *C.A.*, p. 120.

66 *J.G.R. 1379–83*, p. 676.

67 *W.C.*, pp. 116–17.

68 B.L. Add. Ch. 13,190 (letters patent under duke's seal, Plymouth 25 June).

69 Cf Tuck A 1973, p. 102.

70 P.R.O. PL3/1/58.

71 *C.P.*, Vol. 10, pp. 116–23. Earl James the younger married Ann Welles before 17 June 1386, the month in which he returned to Ireland. He had contracted to take a military retinue as part of a force commanded by Vere (Otway-Ruthven AJ 1968, p. 319).

72 Ibid., pp. 318–19.

73 *C.P.*, Vol. 11, pp. 388–90.

74 Holmes G 1957, p. 29; Given-Wilson C 1987, pp. 39–40. For Gaunt's letters appointing a steward for Trowbridge and Aldbourne (Wilts.), two of the properties he gained, dated 14 June 1365, C.C.C., 495 f16.

75 *J.G.R. 1372–6*, nos 375, 1069. For a present of a 'hanap' from Gaunt to his 'chere cousine' the countess of Salisbury, given to her at his manor of Kingston Lacy (Dorset) at Christmas 1372, *ibid.*, no. 1090.

76 *J.G.R. 1372–6*, no. 934; *C.P.*, Vol. 4, pp. 5–6.

77 Ibid., Vol. 4, pp. 419–20; *ibid.*, Vol. 6, pp. 193, 195; *J.G.R. 1379–83*, nos 891, 893, 1043. For the Greystokes and Morpeth, Newcastle, Northumberland R.O., Morpeth Corporation Records, BMO/D2 (reversionary grant by Lord Greystoke of properties in Morpeth to abbot and convent of Newminster, 13 Jan. 1388).

78 B.L. Harley MS 3988 f41v–42r. Greystoke was an executor of Gaunt's leading Yorks. retainer Sir Ralph Hastings (Huntington Library, San Marino, Hastings Charters HAD 3392).

79 For the careers of John Lord Neville and his son and heir Ralph, *C.P.*, Vol. 9, pp. 502–3; *ibid.*, Vol. 12, pt 2, pp. 544ff.

80 Receipt by Neville for his fee of 20*m.* from Gaunt, dated Brancepeth 3 June 1366 (*Bibliotheca Phillippica*, Sale, Sotheby's 13/4/1981). I owe thanks for this reference to Professor Michael Jones.

81 *Foedera*, 1825, Vol. 3, pt 1, pp. 812, 871.

82 Ducal warrant 28 April 1370 (C.C.C., 495 f15).

83 Lewis NB 1964, no. 3.

84 *J.G.R. 1372–6*, nos 163, 170, 891, 1091, 1182, 1332, 1337. In 1381 Gaunt possessed a 'hanap' which Neville had given him (*J.G.R. 1379–83*, no. 564).

85 Tuck A 1968 : 41.

86 *C.P.*, Vol. 12, pt 2, pp. 544, 549. Gaunt granted Ralph and Joan an annuity of £206 13*s.* 4*d.* for their lives (*C.C.R. 1396–7*, p. 463).

87 *C.P.*, Vol. 5, pp. 420–1.

88 Vale B 1987, Vol. 2, no. 285.

89 *C.P.*, Vol. 11, pp. 100–1; *J.G.R. 1372–6*, no. 945.

90 Ibid., no. 1185; C.C.C., 495 f15 (ducal warrant dated 28 April 1370); P.R.O. DL28/3/1.

91 *J.G.R. 1372–6*, no. 989; *J.G.R. 1379–83*, no. 236.

92 Gibbons A 1888, p. 70.

93 Ibid., pp. 70–1; *C.P.*, Vol. 11, pp. 101–2.

94 Ibid., Vol. 7, pp. 470–5; Holmes G 1975, pp. 65–8.

95 *J.G.R. 1379–83*, no. 953. The previous month the king appointed Latimer to head royal commissioners to treat with the Breton envoys,

whose commission was also copied into the ducal register (ibid., no. 201).

96 *J.G.R. 1372–6*, nos 1342, 1664, 1689.
97 *C.P.*, Vol. 11, pp. 539–41; *Foedera*, 1825, Vol. 3, pt 1, p. 442; *J.G.R. 1372–6*, nos 600, 1136; *C.P.R. 1399–1401*, p. 155.
98 Vale B 1987, Vol. 2, nos 222, 719–22.
99 *J.G.R. 1372–6*, no. 1242.
100 Tuck A 1968 :41. Scrope had previously held the wardenship jointly with Lords Clifford and Dacre, and Bishop Appleby of Carlisle.
101 Nicolas NH 1826, Vol. 1, pp. 112–13, 115.
102 *C.P.*, Vol. 12, pt 2, pp. 441–2; Carte T 1743, pp. 177, 179.
103 *Annales*, pp. 220, 240, 243, 246–7, 252; *C.P.*, Vol. 11, p. 541.
104 P.R.O. DL28/1/3 f20d. Philip Lord Darcy (d. 1399) had had livery of his lands in 1374 and served under Gaunt in France in 1369 and in Scotland in 1384 (*C.P.*, Vol. 4, pp. 61–2).
105 Ibid., Vol. 12, pt 2, pp. 502–3; *J.G.R. 1372–6*, nos 49, 788, 1125. Reference was made in 1373 to a 'hanap' and its cover which Lady Welles had given to Gaunt's daughter Elizabeth (ibid., no. 1343).
106 Wyntoun A 1879, Vol. 3, p. 48.
107 Ibid., pp. 40–1, 47–8; *R.S.*, Vol. 2, pp. 103–11.
108 *C.P.*, Vol. 12, pt 2, p. 442.
109 Ibid., Vol. 12, pt 2, pp. 659–62; *C.E.P.R. Papal Letters*, Vol. 4, pp. 131–2; Froissart J 1870, Vol. 11, pp. 326–7; Gibbons A 1888, pp. 90–1. For Robert Willoughby and the Ufford inheritance, Tuck A 1973, pp. 76–7.
110 *C.P.*, Vol. 6, pp. 125–9; *Foedera*, 1825, Vol. 3, pt 1, pp. 442, 812, 871; *J.G.R. 1372–6*, no. 1245.
111 Ibid., no. 1247.
112 *C.P.*, Vol. 6, pp. 125–9; East Sussex R.O., Waleys cartulary A2, A6, B4, B9.
113 Nicolas NH 1832, Vol. 2, pp. 456–9; *C.P.*, Vol. 2, p. 435. Burnell's first wife was Philippe, daughter of Sir Michael de la Pole, at one time Gaunt's retainer.
114 *C.P.*, Vol. 5, pp. 348–53; *Foedera*, 1830, Vol. 3, pt 2, p. 871. Ayala (*C.R.C.*, Vol. 2, p. 110) lists 'el Señor de Ferres' among those who fell sick and died in Spain, 1386–7.
115 Ibid., Froissart J 1870, Vol. 11, p. 326; *C.P.*, Vol. 12, pt 1, pp. 614–16.
116 *C.R.C.*, Vol. 2, p. 110; *C.P.*, Vol. 11, pp. 502–3.
117 *C.R.C.*, Vol. 2, p. 110; *C.P.*, Vol. 5, pp. 477–9; Maxwell Lyte HC 1909, Vol. 1, pp. 51–2; *J.G.R. 1379–83*, p. 714.
118 *C.P.*, Vol. 10, pp. 661–3; Saul N 1986, p. 37.
119 *J.G.R. 1372–6*, nos 49, 50, 969, 1675, 1776; *Foedera*, 1830, Vol. 3, pt 2, p. 871; *C.P.*, Vol. 10, p. 667.
120 C.C.C., 495 f15; *J.G.R. 1372–6*, nos 982, 1585.
121 *C.P.*, Vol. 10, pp. 662–3; Nicolas NH 1826, Vol. 1, pp. 122–3; *Foedera*, 1709, Vol. 8, p. 497; Froissart J 1870, Vol. 11, p. 389. Ayala (*C.R.C.*, Vol. 2, p. 110) mentions the death through sickness of 'el Señor de Polingas'.
122 *C.P.*, Vol. 2, pp. 361–2.
123 Maxwell Lyte HC 1909, Vol. 1, pp. 44–5, 51–3; *C.P.*, Vol. 9, pp. 23–4.
124 *J.G.R. 1372–6*, no. 50.
125 *J.G.R. 1379–83*, no. 319; cf ibid., nos 490, 699, 803.

126 For New Year gift exchanges by Gaunt and Lady Mohun, 1380–2, ibid., nos 327, 556, 714–15. Her daughter Philippe married Gaunt's nephew Edward earl of Rutland (*C.P.,* Vol. 12, pt 2, pp. 904–5). In 1392 Gaunt purchased the marriage of Matilda daughter and heir of Sir John Burghersh from Lady Mohun (P.R.O. DL28/3/2). Her 1404 will reveals her closeness to Archbishop Arundel, 'ever my spiritual father in my lifetime'; she was then living in the cathedral close at Canterbury (Weaver FW 1903; pp. 302–4).

Chapter Thirteen

Lancastrian Residences and Governmental Institutions

Residences and building works

Like other magnates, Gaunt needed apartments in his principal residences where he and his *familiares* could be housed and where administrative and domestic departments which travelled with him could be accommodated. Moreover, he needed horses to be stabled, hawks to be mewed and goods to be stored in places where he was not necessarily staying. In 1381, while he was in the Anglo-Scottish borders, the valuables kept in his wardrobe and military stores were at The Savoy and other valuables were at Leicester Castle. The treasury of Leicester, where large amounts of coin were being stored in 1392–3,[1] and other 'receipts' (such as the exchequer of Lancaster) were probably in the castles which were the heads of the honours the respective receivers served. It is likely, too, that the chancery and courts of the duchy functioned in Lancaster Castle and that the stewards of the various honours customarily held their courts in the honorial castle. The steward was often the constable of the castle and, as such, he or his lieutenant had accommodation there. The ducal castles might be convenient domiciles for itinerating councillors and auditors.

Thus these castles were essential to the duke's governing and estate-owning roles in different regions, as well as to his domestic life. It was necessary to maintain the fabric of castles which the duke might not visit often, so that they provided sound accommodation for his officials and horses, and secure premises for keeping his coin and documents. Moreover, there were psychological reasons for good maintenance, even when a castle was inhabited only by a few ministers, chaplains and grooms: dilapidations had a bad effect on the owner's standing. The description of the impressive façade of Sir Bertilak's castle in the poem *Sir Gawain and the Green Knight* shows how the aesthetic projection of lordship was an important facet of military architecture. One must not forget the military function of castles – less pressing, indeed, in late fourteenth-century England than in most other parts of Europe. However, the defences of Lancastrian castles near the borders of the realm and in Wales and France needed to be maintained.

When Gaunt was a young man his principal castle was in the north – the old and imposing Richmond Castle (Yorks.), in aid of whose repair his father made him a grant in 1358.[2] But this was remote from the usual habitats of the royal court; when residing there, presumably with a restricted entourage, Gaunt needed a southern residence for his household, particularly within easy reach of London. In 1360 the king granted him Hertford Castle, on the grounds that he did not yet possess 'castles, houses or other buildings wherein he can lodge or stay as befits his estate'.[3] Hertford was to remain his favourite suburban residence. Building works went on there throughout his tenure. In 1372 the bailiff of Hertford was ordered to repair houses and do other necessary works within the castle, as the houses were ruinous and greatly in need of repair.[4] In 1375 the parker at nearby Hertingfordbury – which was to be used as an assembly point on future occasions for the collection of timber for the castle repairs – was ordered to deliver timber from the park for the works. The castle's pallisade (*la palice*) and walls were in need of repair.[5] In 1376–7 over £66 was paid for various works within the castle.[6] In 1380 reference was made to the agreement of the duke's chief carpenter William Wintringham to make new houses and other buildings within the castle, according to a pattern drawn up. The large scale of the new works is reflected in the assignment to Wintringham for them of £440, and the grant to him of 100 marks *p.a.* for the works.[7] It is also reflected in the huge amounts of timber which Gaunt cajoled ecclesiastics to let him have from their parks – his own main timber resources were too far away for economic use. For instance, the Hertford receiver's account for 1381–2 lists 66 oaks procured from the parks of Bishop Braybrooke of London, the parson of Hatfield, Bishop Despenser of Norwich, the abbot of Waltham, Abbot Thomas de la Mare of St Albans and the prior of Bermondsey. Robert Hales, prior of the Order of St John, and Bishop Arundel of Ely also contributed trees.[8] Thomas Walsingham thoroughly disapproved of the duke's pressure on ecclesiastics to give him timber for the works, and the denuding of his abbey's woods at Northaw for them.[9] Though the castle was ransacked by the rebels in 1381, the continuing procurement of timber shows that the works went on. In March 1382 the bailiff was ordered to have the kitchen repaired and a new storehouse built for the duke's present stay.[10] Gaunt's liking for the castle is shown by his choice of it for his Christmas festivities in 1389, in the month following his return after his long absence from England (see p.145). The tempo of the works there, if it had slackened, picked up in the 1390s in response to his frequent visits. In the spring of 1391 William Shurlok, master carpenter, and his colleagues were at work on *le parlour*, among other works;[11] in the year 1391–2 the cost of works included the new almshouse outside the castle gate.[12] In the following financial year the treasurer of the household paid £60 for repairs;[13] carpenters and other workmen were at work on the new chamber next to the outer gates of the castle in 1394–5. The major item of expenditure (over £29) was the cost of a new lodge in the old park.[14] By warrant dated Hertford, 2 March 1397, the controller of the household was assigned £180 for repairs at the castle.[15] It seems that Gaunt transformed Hertford Castle into a major country house, but, because his domestic additions were timber-framed, they proved relatively ephemeral, and his achievement has not been recognised. His extensive use of timber-framing as the main component does, indeed, seem unusual for a magnate of the period. The works at Hertford facilitated his decision not to rebuild The Savoy: with such a well-equipped base easily accessible from London, he could rely during visits to the court and city on hospitality and property-leasing.

Through his succession to the duchy of Lancaster Gaunt acquired the largest and finest collection of castles, manor houses and hunting lodges possessed by any subject in England, with some too in Wales. Their upkeep was a major charge on ducal finance. In 1362, when he became duke, repairs were in progress at three principal castles, Kenilworth (Warwicks.), Tutbury (Staffs.) and Pontefract (Yorks.).[16] Central direction of building works is reflected in a warrant of 1374, referring to William Wintringham's appointment as master and surveyor of the works.[17] The *Register* for 1372–6 records payments for works at a great variety of properties, most of which were said to be in need of repair. Works had notably been carried out at The Savoy and at the castles of Hertford, Higham Ferrers (Northants.), Kenilworth, Melbourne (Derbys.), Bolingbroke (Lincs.), Tutbury and Newcastle-under-Lyme (Staffs.), Pontefract, Tickhill and Pickering (Yorks.).[18] This is a surprising amount of works, considering that Gaunt was abroad a great deal in the period and maintaining a high level of military expenditure. These undertakings suggest that Gaunt saw his future in England rather than Castile. However, as a king he now needed to live in royal estate, and his queen had to be fittingly housed. The *Register* for 1379–83 suggests that work in hand was concentrated at fewer properties, partly, perhaps, because so much work had been done at the end of the previous reign.

Gaunt often travelled widely in England and had the almost unique privilege of being able to choose to stay in his own residences both in the north and south, a preference he inclined to exercise whenever their accommodation was of an acceptable standard. A characteristic pattern of his movements between the south-east and Yorkshire is found in his itinerary for 1382. From January at least until late in May he was mostly in or not far from London and Westminster. When not on business there he retired to Hertford Castle. In the summer he and his household set off northwards. Late in July he stayed briefly at Higham Ferrers Castle en route for Leicester Castle. In August he left there for Yorkshire, where he stayed in his castles of Pontefract and Pickering and at York – since he did not have property in the city, he may have lodged in the guesthouse of St Mary's Abbey, of which he was *confrater* (see p.30), or in one of the houses of the cathedral canons. In the autumn he returned to the vicinity of London. By late October he was again warranting letters at Westminster and continued to do so, with a few suburban exceptions, till the end of the year.[19]

From the 1360s till 1381 he lived a great deal, when south of the Trent, at The Savoy, just outside London, near Charing Cross, a house with a frontage on the Strand, the main thoroughfare from the city to Westminster, and with a garden running down to the Thames, in the maintenance of whose plants, fruit and fishpond Gaunt took an interest.[20] As rebuilt by Duke Henry, The Savoy was reputedly the most beautiful house in England: it has been considered a fitting residence for John II of France. Chroniclers agree that it was pretty thoroughly destroyed in the Great Revolt of 1381; it was probably gutted by a fire started by the explosion of the gunpowder stored there. Gaunt appears to have made no effort to rebuild the house. Instead, when visiting court and attending councils and parliaments, if not lodging in the royal household he did so in ecclesiastics' suburban residences. In the 1390s he appears to have leased the bishop of Ely's fine and capacious London house, in Holborn (see p.255); this was probably the 'hostel' where on one occasion he and the Duchess Catherine entertained Richard's bride Isabella, the duke then presenting her with a great golden cup and bowl and the duchess with a smaller cup, as befitted a child.[2]

Gaunt's governmental roles drew him towards London and its hinterlands, where the only large residences he possessed were The

Savoy and Hertford Castle; his other 'great houses' and country retreats were concentrated particularly in the midlands and north of the Trent, and to some of these he was drawn by his interests as a landowner, his love of hunting and his involvement in Anglo-Scottish affairs and the defence of the north. There follows a brief survey of some of his principal castles and other residences.

Leicester was the Lancastrian 'capital' south of the Trent. Fragments of the castle remain, principally two of its main buildings in Castle Yard, the inner bailey, both of which would have been used by Gaunt's household and are still in use. The great hall, a very substantial aisled hall of the twelfth century, much altered, retains most of its original arcade posts.[22] The church of St Mary de Castro, a fine building mainly of the twelfth century too, was the castle's collegiate chapel.[23] Leicester Castle was one of Gaunt's favourite residences: one of its attractions was the proximity of his Leicester Forest, where he sometimes stayed in his commodious lodge, Birds Nest.[24]

A convenient stopping place on the way southwards from Leicester was the castle at Higham Ferrers (Northants.). The historian of this vanished castle, W.J.B. Kerr, gave an impression of its large extent and variety of buildings, and showed how Gaunt took care to maintain it as a fitting residence.[25] A reeve's account for Higham for 1375–6 shows expenditure on the exchequer, kitchen, chapel and the lord's and treasurer's chambers, including some new doors and windows; a similar account for 1382–3 records works on the lord's great chamber and on Bolingbroke's chamber and its oratory.[26]

Kenilworth Castle was a favourite midlands residence of the duke, within easy reach of Leicester. At Kenilworth one can gain a good impression of how Gaunt ideally wished to be housed, for substantial ruins remain of his reconstruction of the principal apartments. These probably date mainly from the 1370s. In September 1373 the clerk of the wardrobe was ordered to pay Henry Spenser, chief mason at Kenilworth, 400 marks for works to be done in the castle in the following year.[27] The receiver of Leicester had been ordered to purchase 24 oaks for the works at the castle, and the following year the receiver of Tutbury was to have a lodge dismantled and lead from it sent for repairs to Kenilworth.[28] In the receiver-general's account for 1376–7, payment is recorded to Spenser, styled supervisor of the new work within Kenilworth Castle, of over £266 for the wages of carpenters and masons, and over £276 for timber for the ceiling of the new hall.[29] The large amount spent on timber makes it likely that this marked the final stages in the building of the still existing (but roofless) great hall. Large-scale works were going on from the autumn of 1379 to the summer of 1380.[30] In April 1380 payment was ordered to the surveyor of works at Kenilworth of over £13 for hinges, latches and iron catches for the windows and one of the doors of a new chamber.[31] The considerable expenditure on these standard fittings, and the fact that the chamber had more than one door, make it probable that this entry signals the completion of a principal part of the domestic ranges Gaunt built. However, there was to be high expenditure in the 1390s too. In 1392 Robert Skillyngton, mason, received part payment of 750 marks owed to him for works completed within the castle.[32]

Gaunt's new buildings are ranged around three sides of the inner bailey, in three blocs on the site of the previous domestic ranges dating from the twelfth century onwards. The new buildings were mainly of two storeys. The domestic block was to the north, abutting on the twelfth-century keep, the block's principal chamber being the kitchen. These offices stretched into the three-storied Strong Tower, whence screened passages gave entry for the servers to the first-floor great hall, which with the Strong Tower and, at the southern end of the hall, the Saintlowe Tower, formed the western range of the bailey. The great hall, with its undercroft, is magnificent, 90 × 45 feet in dimensions. It was rebuilt unaisled, and a huge hammer-beam roof probably complemented the effects of spaciousness and the grandeur of the main architectural features, mostly ranged along the eastern, inner wall – the lobbied and highly arched main doorway, at the north end (to which stairs led from the bailey); one of a pair of facing fireplaces; four tracered windows soaring from stone alcove seats to the roof; an oriel chamber with its own fireplace at the southern end, projecting into the bailey from the line of the dais. Diners at high table entered the great hall from a door opposite the oriel chamber, a door which led from the south-western angle tower, the Saintlowe Tower. This tower in the other direction gave access to the 'Chamber' (as opposed to the 'Hall'), the southern range occupied by the duke, his family, knights and esquires. The first room reached on the first floor of this was the rectangular great chamber, the White Hall; this is presumably where Gaunt held audience and received guests. Beyond it, projecting into the moat, was the four-storied Gaunt's Tower, which had comfortable paired latrines at ground and first-floor level. Beyond was the lesser chamber, which was entered separately from the inner bailey up a circular stairway and through a lobby; this chamber comprised the private apartments of the duke and those close to him. Though these building works were probably carried out over two or more decades, their effect, in dazzling sandstone, is a unitary one. Even in their ruined state they convey an impression of pomp and luxury appropriate to one who bore a regal title. Perhaps the fame of Gaunt's new great hall was one of the incentives for Richard to have the even larger Westminster Hall remodelled, a decision taken in 1393.[33]

Two other ducal houses south of the Trent are worth a mention. One was Pevensey Castle in Sussex, which Gaunt was criticised in 1377 for failing to garrison in face of the Franco-Castilian attacks on the county. In the year September 1376 to September 1377, payment was made for the delivery of a letter under the seals of Sir John Ypres, Sir William Croyser and William Bugbrigge (his councillors), ordering the constable of the castle, John Colepepir, to safeguard it; attempts were made too to keep the castle in repair.[34] There is no record of a visit by Gaunt to Pevensey – it probably lacked suitable accommodation. He did stay on a number of occasions at his manor of Kingston Lacy (Dorset), a convenient stopping place on the way to and from Plymouth (see pp.45, 48).

Among the most notable of Gaunt's northern castles was Tutbury (Staffs.). The duke frequently stayed there: it was convenient for the game in Needwood Forest and Duffield Frith. The amenities available at Tutbury were also probably among the factors which led Gaunt to prefer it to his other castles in the region.[35] These were at Melbourne (Derbys.), where the repair of his chamber was ordered in 1375;[36] Newcastle-under-Lyme, where a refit was undertaken in 1374–5 to remedy neglect by the lessee, Gaunt's retainer Sir Godfrey Foljambe,[37] and The Peak or Peveril Castle (Derbys.), of which there are substantial remains, showing it to have been largely antiquated by the later fourteenth century. In 1374 Gaunt ordered the lead to be stripped from its chamber (in the twelfth-century keep?), for eventual carriage to Pontefract Castle, probably for use in the reconstruction of the donjon (great tower) there.[38]

Tutbury Castle, basically a motte and bailey, occupies an imposing promontory north-west of the borough and south of the River Dove; most of the surviving buildings date from the fifteenth century and later. Just below the castle is an impressive Romanesque fragment of the church of the Benedictine priory of St Mary; the priory was of ducal patronage.

Gaunt did make brief visits to Lincoln, the *caput* of his earldom, a centre for his devotion to the Virgin and near to his mistress Catherine Swynford's country house at Kettlethorpe (see pp.363–4). Lincoln Castle, of which Gaunt was hereditary constable, was constructed from the eleventh to the thirteenth century. What remains visible of its medieval parts suggests that it may have been antiquated by the later fourteenth century, apart from the main gatehouse, the only relatively unchanged medieval building.[39] The large area enclosed by the castle walls would have been convenient for stabling and storage, but it was probably more convenient for Gaunt to stay nearby in the bishop's palace, one of the canons' houses, or in a commodious merchant's house down in the city.[40]

To the south-east of Lincoln, not far from the port of Boston (of which Gaunt was lord till he relinquished the earldom of Richmond in 1372), he possessed Bolingbroke Castle, the centre of his rather remote group of manors in the shire. The castle is on a low-lying site: its enceinte, enclosing a small courtyard, was constructed in the thirteenth century; the domestic buildings were probably of timber. Gaunt dated warrants there occasionally in the early 1360s and the Duchess Blanche gave birth to the future Henry IV there. In 1372–3 ducal warrants alluded to the need to repair the castle and its bridge: timber was ordered to repair 'maisons' and construct new ones in 1373 in anticipation of a visit by Duchess Constance.[41] After this the castle seems to have been neglected: the vicinity of Lincoln held greater attractions for the duke.

North of the Trent Gaunt's favourite castle was Pontefract, one of the strongest and stategically most important northern castles, and the *caput* of one of his West Riding honours. Castle, borough and other Lancastrian appurtenances made Pontefract the northern ducal 'capital' – there was the priory where the miracle-working Thomas of Lancaster was buried, and the chapel on the nearby hill on which he had been executed. Castle and borough lie on an escarpment commanding the valley of the River Aire, the motte and bailey at the apex. The imposing trefoil-shaped donjon was the castle's main feature, the lower part of which dates from the thirteenth century. In 1374 Gaunt made arrangements for this 'old tower called le Doungeon' to be heightened, so that it should be higher than any other tower in the castle. The seventeenth-century painting of the castle by Joos de Mompers shows that this addition, with corbelled turrets elaborating the donjon, gave the castle a stylish grandeur which would have made it worthy of depiction among the châteaux of Gaunt's friend the duke of Berry in the *Très Riches Heures*.[42] In 1381 Gaunt urgently wanted the castle's defences to be improved; Duchess Constance had not felt safe there during the Peasants' Revolt.[43] In January 1386 he ordered the Yorkshire receiver to pay for the costs of a horse-mill, newly made 'on our advice' in the castle in the manner he had told Thomas Carpenter, and for the repairs to one of the castle entrances, *la derneyate*.[44] Only fragments of the keep and walls remain; recent excavations of chambers in and adjacent to the wall-towers have revealed a high standard of workmanship. Some ten miles north-west of Pontefract was Gaunt's hunting lodge at Rothwell, a favourite residence, near his manor of Leeds. Sport probably drew him too to Pickering Castle (North Riding), with its adjacent forest and deerpark of Pickering Lythe: the castle was not far from Helmsley, the home of the Ros family, his friends. There are substantial remains of the stone defences at Pickering, which Thomas of Lancaster and Edward II had brought up to date: the New Hall constructed by Thomas probably provided reasonable lodgings for Gaunt and his company.[45]

In 1372, when Gaunt had to give up the castle and honour of Richmond, he was granted in compensation by the Crown those of Knaresborough and Tickhill, both also in Yorkshire. The remaining buildings of Tickhill Castle date essentially from the twelfth century. In 1374 Gaunt wrote to the receiver of Yorkshire that he had heard that the walls and tower of the castle, the chambers and houses within and the castle bridge were very ruinous and greatly in need of repair. He ordered that the tower, the chamber called 'le garret' and the chamber over the gate should be repaired and the defects to the walls and other buildings be amended. He stayed at the castle later that year, but it never became a favourite residence – it was probably too antiquated.[46] Gaunt may have been more attracted to Knaresborough because of its forest and the shrine of St Robert (see p.252). Castle and borough rear up dramatically over a bend in the River Nidd, the castle at the nub, part of the forest still dense on the opposite bank. The scanty remains of the castle, principally its keep, have early medieval features. In 1373 Gaunt ordered the bridge, towers and walls of the castle to be repaired.[47] In June 1381, probably while staying there, he ordered the provision of lead, urgently needed to repair the roofs of the keep and other buildings. His chamber (*sale*) and the bridge were also to be repaired.[48] The Duchess Constance was soon afterwards to endure in misery the castle's defects on her enforced stay there during the Peasants' Revolt.

Gaunt was disinclined to visit his north-western properties, for the most part. There is no evidence that he stayed at Halton Castle (Cheshire) or at Liverpool Castle.[49] He made infrequent visits to Lancaster Castle. The present imposing gatehouse was built by Henry IV. Gaunt had carried out extensive works there: in 1378 the keeper of Quernmore Forest was ordered to provide 260 oaks to reconstruct and repair houses and other buildings within the castle which were particularly dilapidated.[50] The reconstruction may have been intended to improve facilities for the duchy offices.[51] Gaunt stayed occasionally in his lodge at Ightenhill, probably for the hunting in Blackburnshire. The lodge was in his honour of Clitheroe; there are remains of the keep and walls of its castle.[52]

Gaunt possessed a castle near the Scottish border – Dunstanburgh, in his barony of Embleton (Northumberland). This is on a formidable coastal cliff and has a large outer ward whose purpose was probably to provide shelter for the inhabitants and stock of the barony during raids. In 1380, the leading mason John Lewyn undertook to add a stone 'mantellet' around the 'great tower' – the imposing gatehouse, the castle's strongest defence work built by Thomas of Lancaster, which substantially remains.[53] When Gaunt examined Lewyn's work (in 1380 or 1381), he was dissatisfied with the result and commissioned another mason, Henry Holme, to build a new masonry work to abut on to the 'mantellet', probably the barbican covering the gateway to the outer ward.[54] Though little of Gaunt's work is standing to any great height, ruins and foundations show that extensive additional defences were built, probably the product, to some extent, of his considerable experience of siege warfare in France. The main entrance gateway between Earl Thomas's great drum towers, which led directly to the inner ward, was blocked and a new entrance was made to one side of them. If besiegers forced that, they would have to brave an alleyway of fire 74 feet long between the wall along the inner ward and the new mantlet, then force the barbican to a new main gateway, which only gave access to the outer ward.

Thus Gaunt maintained castles at the vulnerable coastal extremities of the realm, at Dunstanburgh as well as Pevensey. Especially in view of the threats to invade Wales in the 1370s, as a Marcher lord Gaunt had an obligation to maintain the defences of his castles there, though there is no evidence that he stayed in any of them or visited his Welsh lordships. There are extensive remains of the earlier fortifications and domestic buildings at Kidwelly Castle and at Carreg Cennen Castle on its precipice (both in Carmarthenshire); Ogmore Castle (Glamorganshire) was also Lancastrian. There are considerable remains of the earlier fortifications of the strategically important 'Three Castles' (Monmouthshire) – Skenfrith, Grosmont and White Castle. Only Grosmont exhibits a recently built set of apartments worthy of accommodating the duke.[55] Little remains of Monmouth Castle – just fragments of the early keep and of the great hall, the latter, probably, late thirteenth century in date. There are indications that upper apartments in the keep were modernised in the mid-fourteenth century; the castle was granted by Gaunt to Bolingbroke, and was considered fit for his wife Mary's lying-in in 1387, when she gave birth to the future Henry V.[56] Occasionally, in emergencies, Gaunt activated or strengthened the defences of his Welsh castles. In June 1372 he ordered the receiver of the lordship of Kidwelly to victual its castle and those at Carreg Cennen and Ogmore, in response to the threat of Owain Lawgoch's plans to invade Wales with French help.[57] Owain's fleet was recalled by Charles V in 1372, but he continued to attempt to enlist French and Castilian support for his claim to the principality. It was probably with Owain's activities in mind that Gaunt ordered the receiver of Kidwelly to have Carreg

Cennen and Ogmore, both 'en feble estat', repaired (1374?) and in 1375, saying that he had heard that Ogmore, Grosmont, Skenfrith and White Castle badly needed repairing, and ordering his receiver in Wales to see to it.[58] By virtue of a warrant dated 12 June 1376 payments were made to three individuals for going from London to, respectively, the castles of Kidwelly, Carreg Cennen and White Castle to safeguard them, at Gaunt's command.[59] In 1381 Gaunt garrisoned his Monmouthshire castles to meet an emergency of a different kind. On 19 June, before he took refuge with the Scots during the Peasants' Revolt, he issued orders at Berwick for the garrisoning of Monmouth, White Castle, Skenfrith and Grosmont; a key role was assigned to John Serjeant, lieutenant of the steward of Monmouth Castle, Sir Richard Burley. Serjeant was to stay in Monmouth Castle with six archers and to bar any unauthorised entry. He was to provide victuals and pay for the specially appointed governors of the other castles and their comparable garrisons. If need be, he was to arrange for the defence of the castles. Whence did Gaunt anticipate attacks? Perhaps he feared that discontented tenants would take advantage of 'rumour' to challenge his lordship, or that men of neighbouring lordships would ransack his properties.[60]

Gaunt spent heavily on many of his castles, in particular on modernising Hertford and Kenilworth. He was, indeed, concerned to maintain defences, especially when frontier castles – in Wales, at Pevensey, but, above all, at Dunstanburgh – were threatened. The resources of his northern chases and the proximity of quarries assisted his maintenance of some of his castles and lodges in the region: building materials and fittings were sometimes parsimoniously removed from surplus residences to help repair or extend those in common use. His customary itineraries were an important factor in the maintenance of particular castles and hunting lodges.

For, as the surviving remains at Kenilworth and the receivers' accounts for Hertford and Higham Ferrers bear witness, much of the new works were to improve domestic accommodation for Gaunt and his household – a characteristic trend among magnates of the period. He required appropriately luxurious accommodation for himself and catering facilities for what was probably customarily the largest household in England after the king's. Competitive consumption was a notable feature of English aristocratic politics – and so was competitive architectural magnificence. In the light of our dim perception of the state of the Lancastrian castles, this concept must not be applied too rigidly to Gaunt's building works, but it is worth speculating about. One reason for the apparent lack of attention to Leicester Castle may have been that no magnate challenged Gaunt's influence in the shire or built on a grand scale there. In Hertfordshire and Northamptonshire, where Gaunt often stayed, he had little territorial influence, so may have particularly marked his presence by the maintenance of a splendid castle. Tutbury needed to be maintained, for Stafford Castle had been rebuilt by the earls of Stafford as one of the finest in the midlands. The ducal castles in Yorkshire had to compete with both comital and baronial building works – such as Richard Lord Scrope's rebuilding of Bolton Castle imposingly in the modern manner. Gaunt's heightening of the donjon at Pontefract, with its pleasing decorative additions, asserted his ducal status. Most strikingly, such assertiveness is seen in the new work at Kenilworth, in the 'country' of the earls of Warwick. It is likely that their extensive building works at Warwick Castle, a few miles away, had put Kenilworth in the shade: work was continuing in the 1390s on Guy's Tower, matching the equally awesome Caesar's Tower.[61] However, the new great hall at Kenilworth was fit for a king.

Lancastrian government

As earl of Richmond, Gaunt became heir to 'a well-defined series of local courts in individual lordships of the honour. These were administered by local bailiffs and provosts chosen by the community under the supervision of seigneurial stewards.' The lordships each had a receiver who paid over monies to a receiver-general.[62] Professor Jones has adduced evidence of the decay of the Richmond inheritance in the early fourteenth century, which Gaunt's officials were trying to remedy after 1355.[63]

When Gaunt took over the Lancastrian inheritance in 1361–2 he gained control of a well established and well oiled administrative system designed to coordinate control of lordships throughout and beyond the realm. He took some of his existing leading officials into Lancastrian administration. Walter Campden (d. 1370), Gaunt's receiver in 1354, and guardian of his lands in 1356, was his chancellor in 1368.[64] John Lincoln, clerk of the kitchen in 1358, was appointed treasurer of the household in 1372.[65]

The chancellor was the lynchpin of Gaunt's secretariat as duke. He was in charge of the principal authenticating seal, the privy seal, under which and by his direction clerks prepared and issued charters and warrants. (For Gaunt's seals and secretariat as king of Castile and in the palatinate county of Lancaster, see pp. 135, 315). When work occasionally threatened to overwhelm the ducal privy seal office, royal clerks were paid for writing documents.[66] The chancellor, who was frequently resident in the household,[67] was in charge of some sorts of records, such as the registers recording warrants and indentures.[68] The earliest example of a Gaunt register is a fragment (Corpus Christi College, Oxford, MS 495) containing copies of 25 warrants, chronologically arranged, from the years 1365 to 1370. The two registers surviving in full (1372-6, 1379–83) record warrants more fully and with some efforts to group them into categories under particular years. The duke had a secretary who waited on him to receive orders for the drafting of his correspondence and warrants. His letters were sealed with the ducal signet which, Gaunt said in his will, 'I always keep with me'. In January 1390 William Kettering was the duke's secretary: in the early 1390s he was frequently resident in the household.[69]

The essential coordinating institution in ducal administration was the council, sometimes referred to as the great council. This held frequent meetings in London or Westminster, and also met in ducal lordships. It may have kept regular terms, meeting daily; then service as a councillor would have been quite arduous.[70] Sir John Bussy was paid for his service with other councillors in London in Easter term 1396 and again for 26 days in November and December.[71] Some leading ducal officers were *ex officio* councillors; others might be specifically appointed. The composition and degree of formality of council meetings probably varied considerably according to availability and the nature of the business to be dealt with. When questions of judicial right were to be considered, there was probably a strong showing of lawyers retained by the duke to be of his counsel in his palatine courts or the king's courts. Magnates appointed as the duke's general attorneys during his absences abroad may have on occasion attended the council. There is no evidence that the duke ever formally presided: his instructions frequently imply that the council was to consider cases in his absence. Sir John Ypres was termed chief of the council in 1383 and as such may have conducted business.[72] A file of privy seal warrants includes four petitions on which the names of the three (and in one case four) councillors present to consider them are listed. Their conclusion as to the action to be taken on the bills by the leading palatine officials was also endorsed together, in some cases, with a privy seal warrant for the action proposed for these officials. The council considered petitions addressed solely to Gaunt and remitted to them; petitions addressed to Gaunt and the council, and petitions addressed to the council alone.[73] The duke did determine some petitions in person: an example is a relatively unimportant question of assigning a sum of money held by his 'simple subject' John de Esslak of Lancaster. The endorsement for authorisation starts 'to be remembered that my lord ordered me in his own words in the presence of master William de Assheton his chancellor to make a warrant out to the said Johan Esslak . . . .'.[74]

As Somerville has shown, the council exercised essential advisory, administrative and judicial functions. It was concerned with finance, appointments to offices, patronage and the determination of judicial rights. Its business, as far as documentary evidence shows, was concentrated on the affairs of household and estates: in the latter context, within ducal lordships, the arrival of the council to hold a session and determine pleas was probably often as momentous an event as the arrival in a shire of justices of the King's Bench to hold a session.

The council thus exercised judgement and expertise over a wide spectrum of the duke's affairs. In 1380 household plate and other goods were to be sold on the council's advice;[75] the sourcing of the great wardrobe's finances on particular receiverships was implemented on its advice the following year. In 1380 local ducal officials had been ordered to facilitate the judgement by the council on cases brought by petition, when it met in London and when it visited Gloucestershire and Wales.[76] Some councillors were acting in 1380–1 as pledges for sums which Gaunt owed to the countess of Norfolk.[77] The council sometimes considered Gaunt's family affairs: it was by the advice and assent of 'our great council' that Gaunt ordered that his daughter Catherine was to be sent to live with Lady Mohun.[78]

What is not apparent from the duchy records is whether 'the great council' was habitually asked to give advice or to take decisions on national and international affairs in which Gaunt was immersed. He probably relied heavily in these and other matters on the 'official' councillors, kinsfolk, *familiares* and friends who happened to be in his company. His bachelors in attendance (fifteen of them on some occasions, eight on others) formed a pool of varied expertise. In foreign affairs Gaunt doubtless set great store by the advice of Duchess Constance, Juan Gutiérrez, Lord Latimer, Sir Thomas Percy and Sir John Trailly, among others. Before going on campaign in 1373, Gaunt empowered Constance to pardon, restore and reward all rebels from his Spanish realms who submitted to him, using the authority of her own seal. At the same time he confered upon his councillors Sir Robert Swillington, Sir William Croyser, William Bugbrigge and Juan Gutiérrez powers to make alliances on his behalf as king of Castile.[79]

The chief officers in Lancastrian government – besides those of the secretariats, the household and county palatine – were the receiver-general and the chief stewards; during Gaunt's tenure there came to be two instead of one chief steward, with jurisdiction respectively over estates north and south of the River Trent.[80] The receiver-general was the principal financial official. He received much of the net profits from the receiver of each lordship and from other accounting officers, and he paid out on the authority of ducal warrants for a huge variety of charges and costs, for example, annuities, wages, household and building expenses.[81] The chief stewards had jurisdiction over the officers in their region; they travelled round its lordships to enforce ducal rights and to enquire into complaints.[82] Below the chief steward and receiver-general stood the stewards and receivers, who mostly paired responsibility for the administration of an honour or a scatter of manors (or both). The steward within his jurisdiction was like the chief steward within his: he was there to keep officers up to the mark.[83] The receiver was responsible for the funding of local administration (such as the cost of building repairs) and for remitting the net profits paid to him by bailiffs and keepers of fees and franchises to the receiver-general or others as directed by ducal warrants.[84]

The administration of the earldom of Lancaster came to stand apart from that of the rest of the Lancastrian inheritance. Gaunt inherited the right as earl to appoint the sheriff of Lancashire. By his father's grant of 28 February 1377, he received the regalian rights in the county for life which Duke Henry had held on the same terms since 1351. In April 1377 Gaunt set up governmental institutions for the county palatine modelled on the central ones of the Crown – a chancellor, justices to hear all manner of pleas, law officers, a chief baron of the exchequer and an escheator. Royal letters patent of November 1378 specified his right to have an exchequer with barons and other ministers and his authority to appoint justices for pleas of the forest. Royal writs were passed on by Gaunt to the chancellor.[85]

The good government and sustenance of the household were particular concerns of the duke and his councillors.[86] A lord's household not only immediately provided for his needs and many of his pleasures, but was a principal source of his power and prestige. Its chief officers were among his most trusted and responsible servants. In the duke's household they were the chamberlain, steward, controller, treasurer and keeper of the great wardrobe, who all probably frequently resided there. The chamberlain was in charge of the chamber, the suites of private apartments where the duke and his guests lived, attended on by his, and their, chamber knights and esquires and more menial servants. The importance of the duke's chamberlain lay both in his access to the duke and in the authority he exercised over the serving denizens of the chamber. On analogy to the royal chamberlain (or his deputy), he may have exercised the influential right of controlling access to the duke's person by those seeking favours.

The steward had general oversight of household management; he was responsible for the smooth functioning of the service departments, those which were part of the hall and kitchen, as opposed to the chamber. The treasurer was responsible for payment of the living costs of the household and the wages of its officers. The scope of his duties is reflected in ducal letters patent appointing John Norfolk, clerk, to the office in 1380. He was granted full power to receive

all the monies assigned by us or to be assigned for the expenses of the same our household from our receiver general for the time being and from our other receivers, assigned by us to the same our household, and to pay for all the purveyances and purchases and all other things needful for the same our household.[87]

In default of ready cash, the treasurer frequently issued debentures under his seal.[88]

Another important household official was the clerk of the great wardrobe. He had overall responsibility for the storage and safe-guarding of the lord's precious possessions such as jewels, expensive plate and furnishings, both those kept in the privy wardrobe of the lord's chamber for his personal use, and chattels stored elsewhere. Like the treasurer, the clerk of the great wardrobe received lump sums for his expenses from the receiver-general and from particular receivers. Warrants were drawn up listing a variety of payments to be made by him, for example, for debts to craftsmen and merchants supplying the duke's purchases for his personal use and for gifts, and to servants of the chamber for the discharge of the duke's privy expenses and alms.[89] The 1381 revolt was a disaster for the wardrobe, which its clerk, William Oke, probably bewailed to the chronicler Henry Knighton or one of his fellow canons of Leicester. Up to 1381 The Savoy was the principal wardrobe – there were kept the duke's bed-hangings, tapestries, and other precious possessions, his chattels in daily use, his charters and muniments. The rebels, when they broke down the doors, headed first for the wardrobe; everything there was destroyed.[90] Oke had only been able to remove a bed and a few small items beforehand. He lamented the loss of what he swore was a finer wardrobe than any other Christian king possessed, for, he said, there were so many vessels and *jocalia*, of silver, gilt and gold, that five carts would hardly suffice to transport them. Oke was also responsible for a wardrobe in Leicester Castle: fearing that that would be destroyed too, he conscientiously set out from London to try to save it.[91]

The treasurer's clerks, besides receiving obligations and acquittances for payments for supplies from the departmental clerks, and issuing advances for further payments, compiled checkrolls of the household and stables, and journals of the household. There are random survivals of sometimes mutilated checkrolls for weeks in 1381 and the early 1390s. They list, grouped according to wage rates, the names of the members of the household in residence and tabulate their daily attendances. Horses are listed, in some cases under the name of guests and household members. In one period in 1391 or 1392, Bolingbroke was stabling four horses, Humphrey of Gloucester and Sir John Beaufort six each, and Catherine Swynford twelve. Three rolls tabulating the daily expenses of household departments survive, forming a journal covering the period 5 July to 6 September; K.B. McFarlane identified the year as 1383.[92]

The size of the household doubtless fluctuated according to circumstances, reaching maximum numbers when the lord celebrated the principal feasts in one of his residences. In 1366 Gaunt received a papal indult enabling him, the duchess and thirty companions to enter monasteries.[93] In 1381 and the early 1390s totals of around 130 appear. Daily expenditure by the service departments and on wages fluctuated markedly according to where the household was staying, according to the 1383 journal. Total daily expenditure at Kenilworth amounted only to a few pounds or less, and went down notably after Constance's departure for Tutbury. On the move from Kenilworth to Westminster, daily expenditure rose from between about £17 and £32, and more steeply at Westminster, rising to over £129 on the third day there. Presumably purchases were few at Kenilworth because ducal stocks were laid in there.[94] The high cost of attendance at court is surprising. The Black Book of Edward IV's household (allegedly founded on the precedents of Edward III's household organisation) provided a diet of essential commodities at royal expense for twelve resident attendants of a duke, including one knight, a chaplain, three esquires and four yeomen.[95] Such a provision hardly seems sufficiently honourable for someone of Gaunt's royal status. He is likely to have had to pay for the board and lodging of most of his retinue at London prices – a retinue probably augmented since the household's departure from Kenilworth.

Notable among the service departments were the pantry, buttery, kitchen, poultery, scullery, saltery, hall and stable. Some of their officers had to show considerable administrative as well as specialist skill. The valet Rand de Tynneslowe, usher of the hall, was ordered in September 1380 to oversee delivery of wood from Leicester Chace for the hall, chamber, cupboard and kitchen for the stay of Gaunt and the household at Leicester.[96] In the same year John Reynald, the master cook (who ranked as an esquire), had charge of certain utensils and in 1383 of plate. Reynald then contracted loans for the expenses of the household's stay at Kenilworth.[97] Some servants combined offices in separate but closely related departments. John de Sprotteburgh was both naperer and ewerer in 1380.[98] That year William Overbury, esquire, was appointed as chief baker (or panterer) and chief butler.[99] Chamber servants who performed intimate duties for the duke might be entrusted with important tasks (see p.355, for the case of Lewis Recouchez, physician). A presumption of personal closeness with the duke probably lay behind the rebels' determination to make a terrible example of his physician Appleton in 1381 (see p.79). In 1373 Gaunt granted his barber, Godfrey, a life rent of 100*s. p.a.* Godfrey Barbour was entrusted with large sums of money – in 1379–80 he received cash from the clerk of the wardrobe for privy expenses in the chamber and for ducal alms.[100]

Other specialist household servants, some of whom are likely to have had close personal rapport with their master, were his confessor, the dean and clerks of the chapel, Leicester and Lancaster Heralds,[101] and his professional entertainers. As befitted the patron of the traditional annual gathering of minstrels at Tutbury, Gaunt retained his own company, often, their names suggest, of Netherlandish origin. In 1368 five of his pipers were going overseas, presumably to entertain a princely court; among them were Hankin, Werens, Durlens and Spalteneys.[102] In June 1373, shortly before setting off on campaign in France, Gaunt retained three other foreign pipers and a clarion player for service in peace and war.[103] In the period 1377–9, Gaunt's minstrels were rewarded by the mayor of Leicester when they played as he feasted the duke's steward Sir Thomas Hungerford. The mayor also rewarded the duke's minstrel Henry Piper who played, with others, when the mayor met Gaunt at Oadby and escorted him to Leicester.[104] In 1380 warrants were issued for payment of arrears of annuities to John Tyes and Piers Cook 'our trumpeters' and to John de Bukyngham, 'clarioner'.[105] The text of Bukyngham's life contract for service as clarioner in peace and war survives. In peace he was expected to serve in the household at the four great feasts of the year, and when sent for by the duke; 'And the said John will preside over (*comencera*) the minstrels' table'. He was also expected to serve in peace out of court and in war arrayed as a man at arms; in addition to wages and peacetime allowances, he was to receive an annuity of £5 in peace and £10 in war.[106] This suggests that Gaunt put a higher value on skilful clarion-playing than on any other form of minstrelsy. The duke provided uniforms and instruments for his musicians; in 1381 the treasurer of the household was ordered to deliver to 'our well-beloved minstrel' John Cliff of Coventry 'a silver escutcheon with a collar for a minstrel and a pair of nakers [kettle drums] with two collars and a belt and two silver sticks made for the same nakers'.[107]

The stable was an important service department: the duke's prestige and the success of his ventures required a stock of well-groomed warhorses, hunters, palfreys, carriage horses and packhorses, and suitable stabling as well for those of his guests and leading servants. The stables must have been a notable feature of his residences. In 1372, prior to his embarkation on a naval expedition, he notified the receiver at Higham Ferrers that he had dispatched nine servants thither with nineteen of his coursers, whose expenses the receiver was to provide for.[108] In 1382 he arranged for the stabling at Hertford of warhorses (*destreres*), coursers, palfreys and other horses, which were to be looked after by seven valets of the stable.[109] A *destrere* was thought a fit present for him by a German knight in 1383.[110] Presumably *destreres* were kept for display or for use in tournaments, and coursers were for hunting; for travelling and on *chevauchée* workhorses distinguished by stamina would be ridden. In September 1380, when Gaunt was preparing to go the Scottish border, he sent his *destrere* south from Knaresborough to Pontefract; while he was in the Marches, his 'great horses' were to be stabled at Tutbury Castle.[111] Presumably, he did not wish to risk disabling his 'great horses' in parts of the borders where the going was rough and fodder scarce; such impractical ostentation would not have impressed Scottish lords. Rare horseflesh was part of household display; the serious English campaigner of the period, like Chaucer's Knight, required a horse that was not 'gay'. In 1381 reference was made to the purchase by the ducal avener and a local bailiff of one good ambling palfrey at Pontefract Fair and of another by the duke's palfreyman from a Smithfield coper.[112] The duke had his own stud at Bowland (Lancs.).[113]

Gaunt possessed carriages for the convenience of ladies, infants, the sick and elderly; payments were made for the repair of Duchess Constance's carriage in 1380.[114] There were carts for the transport of household stuff, such as those on which the panicky William Oke had had chattels loaded at Leicester Castle during the Peasants' Revolt. Carts and carters were hired to help with household supply and movement. In 1382 the duke pardoned a carter of Tadcaster for the loss of a barrel of wine on the way between York and Pontefract; he pardoned the loss of another by William the carter between Knaresborough and Pontefract.[115] Perhaps these losses resulted from robberies during the Peasants' Revolt. The duke had his own barge for use on the Thames, staffed by a keeper and company of bargemen.[116]

The purchase or procurement of commodities for household consumption was a responsibility laid on the heads of service departments by their terms of appointment. This was a continuous activity in which other household officers were involved too, some as specialists. Expert buyers included poulterers who purveyed fowls, and purveyors of meat and fish (*acatours*). In 1383 Gaunt appointed his valet Adam de Welle as *acatour*, to purchase 'both cartloads and fish and carriage [for them] and other things needful and duly appurtenant to the office of our *acatour*'.[117] Payment for goods purchased was made by purveyors with prests received from the treasurer or with loans which they had individually secured. They received letters of acquittance from vendors for presentation to the treasurer. They also purchased on credit, payment eventually being made by the treasurer, clerk of the wardrobe, receiver-general or receiver of a lordship – in the last case, often for purchases within the lordship. In 1383 the receiver of Leicester was ordered to pay from his issues for the purchase of 30 cattle and 300 sheep by the *acatour* Adam de (Welle).[118] Because of the lord's frequent visits to London and Hertford, the lordship of Hertford was especially useful as a source of supplies and payment. In 1380 its receiver was ordered to pay for 40 quarters of wheat and 100 quarters of charcoal, which ducal valets were coming to purchase for the arrival of the duke and his household in London and their stay there during parliament.[119] The duke apparently exercised a right of pre-empting tenants' produce: in 1379 he ordered *acatours*, purveyors and other officers to take corn, cattle, and so on, from Erdbury Priory only by reasonable bargain.[120]

Most of the food supplies which Gaunt purchased in his lordships appear to have come from tenants and neighbours rather than from his demesne production. His Tweed fishery was at farm in the 1380s, but under the terms of the lease the farmer was obliged to supply good, large and seasonable salmon which the receiver of Dunstanburgh shipped south for the duke's table.[121] Some ducal resources not leased out were maintained to provide a guaranteed source of delicacies for the table. In 1380 the constable of Pevensey Castle was ordered to be present when the duke's servant Richard Skargulle fished in Maresfield stank, and to deliver to the duke's cook or his deputy 40 of the biggest luces and 60 of the biggest bream taken.[122] Aldbourne chase (Wilts.) had a fine warren. In October 1380 its parker was ordered to deliver to the poulterer twelve dozen rabbits for the household's stay at La Neyte (Middlesex) during parliament and six dozen rabbits every week from 1 December till 2 February.[123]

However, for bulk commodities, especially of fish and wine, the household was heavily reliant on merchants of London and east-coast ports. In 1381, for instance, receivers were ordered to pay the Londoners John atte Noke and John Trygg for supplying, respectively, poultry and fish.[124] The officers of the eastern lordships made bulk purchases of dried fish in their regional ports. In November 1379 the receiver of Lincolnshire was ordered to pay from his issues for 2,000 stockfish (*Halnewaxenfisshe*) which the local feodary, William Spaigne, had purveyed. The following April Spaigne was ordered to purchase a further 2,000 stockfish. These he secured at Boston in the autumn, to be conveyed to Leicester Castle, into the custody of the duke's larderer.[125] John Chyvyngton, valet of the buttery, purchased wine at Hull and York.[126]

Gaunt's duchesses had their own establishments of male and female servants: they received a fixed annual grant to fund a wardrobe and chamber. In 1372 Gaunt assigned Constance 1,000 marks *p.a.* for the expenses of her wardrobe and chamber, funded from the receipts of the lordships of Tutbury and Pontefract. Orders to receivers of other lordships to pay her in 1380–1 suggest that these arrangements had not been working well.[127] From infancy the duke's children, individually or severally, had their own servants and establishment, though they were likely to reside in a ducal castle away from the household or in another noble household. Philippa, Gaunt's eldest child, aged eight when her mother died in 1368, was then taken care of admirably by Alyne Gerberge, wife of a ducal esquire, who was rewarded with a life annuity in 1370.[128] In 1372 Philippa, her sister Elizabeth and her brother Henry had a common chamber for whose upkeep their father granted 300 marks *p.a.*[129] In 1375 Henry had a governor, Thomas de Burton, and a tutor, chaplain and keeper of his wardrobe; £50 was assigned for the expenses of his chamber in 1376.[130] In that year Philippa and Elizabeth shared a chamber and wardrobe, under the control of their mistress Catherine Swynford (see p.363). Elizabeth received a separate establishment on her marriage to the earl of Pembroke; in 1380 Gaunt granted them £100 *p.a.* for their joint expenses.[131]

Constance's daughter Catherine (the future Queen Catalina of Castile), who was considerably younger than Gaunt's children by Blanche, was apparently brought up separately from them and, notably, not under the governance of Catherine Swynford. The infanta had her own chamber in 1375, when she was living at the ducal castle of Melbourne (Derbys.); in 1380 she was placed in the household of Lady Mohun, who was to receive from the duke £100 for the costs of her wardrobe and chamber and for the living expenses of her servants.[132]

Notes and References

1 P.R.O. DL 28/3/2. Financial totals in this chapter, where shillings and pounds are not given, have been rounded to the nearest pound.
2 *C.P.R. 1358–61*, p.61.

3 Ibid., p.375.
4 *J.G.R. 1372–6*, no. 925.
5 Ibid., nos 926, 1398.
6 P.R.O. DL 28/3/1.
7 *J.G.R. 1379–83*, nos 278, 521; P.R.O. DL 29/58/1080.
8 Ibid.; *J.G.R. 1379–83*, nos 339, 448, 466, 519.
9 *C.A.*, pp.163–4.
10 *J.G.R. 1379–83*, no. 707.
11 P.R.O. DL 29/58/1082.
12 Ibid., 1083.
13 P.R.O. DL 28/3/2.
14 P.R.O. DL 29/58/1084.
15 P.R.O. DL 28/3/5 m13.
16 *C.P.R. 1361–4*, p.232.
17 *J.G.R. 1372–6*, no. 154; cf no. 854. For some references to Win-
    tringham's employment, *J.G.R. 1379–83*, nos 339, 448, 519, 521.
18 *J.G.R. 1379–83*, nos 997–9 (The Savoy), 925–6, 1398 (Hertford),
    1447 (Higham Ferrers), 1319, 1323, 1475 (Kenilworth), 1474, 1737
    (Melbourne), 965, 1213, 1368 (Bolingbroke), 1161–3, 1236, 1475,
    1550 (Tutbury), 1538, 1547, 1630, 1721, 1724–5 (Newcastle), 1508–10
    (Pontefract), 1524 (Tickhill), 1514 (Pickering).
19 Itinerary based on the dating of warrants, etc., in *J.G.R. 1379–83*.
20 P.R.O. DL 28/3/1, m3; *J.G.R. 1372–6*, nos 998–9. By warrant dated
    27 Nov. 1377, Master Henry Yevele and William Wintringham were
    paid for works at The Savoy; £20 was spent in 1376, £40 in 1377
    (P.R.O. DL 28/3/1, m3). Edward III had written in some exasperation
    to Bishop Appleby of Carlisle in response to his son's complaint that the
    bishop's neglect of his adjacent property was exposing The Savoy to
    flooding from the Thames (Cumbria R.O., Carlisle, Appleby's Register,
    f107, Privy Seal letter dated Westminster 3 May). I owe thanks to Dr
    Richard Rose for his transcript.
21 Douët-D'Arcq L 1864, Vol. 2, p.276. In 1383 John de Norton, bailiff
    of The Savoy, was ordered to sell lead from it to the value of 100*s*.
    and to pay for the carriage of 12 fothers of it thence to Hertford Castle
    for the works there (*J.G.R. 1379–83*, no. 837). In 1383–4 Gaunt was
    renting London properties from Thomas Faringdon and Henry Yevele
    for the use of the clerk of the wardrobe and storage of ducal possessions,
    including ones for the duke's personal use (James MD 1899, p.61).
22 Alcock NW and Buckley RJ 1987; 73–4. Some repairs to the castle
    were accounted for by the receiver of the honour in the same year from
    Michaelmas 1377 (P.R.O. DL 29/3247/212).
23 Gaunt had an obligation to pay its canons for the maintenance of lights
    in the church (Huntington Library, San Marino, HAM 49/1).
24 The lodge of Bird's Nest was rebuilt 1377–8 (Fox L and Russell P 1948,
    pp.32–4).
25 Kerr WJB 1925, pp.98ff.
26 P.R.O. DL 29/321/5302; ibid., 324/5308. For further expenditure on
    Bolingbroke's chapel in 1391–2, DL 29/324/5314.
27 *J.G.R. 1372–6*, no. 1156.
28 Ibid., nos 1319, 1323.
29 P.R.O. DL 28/3/1 m4.
30 *J.G.R. 1379–83*, nos 92, 206, 422, 486.

31 Ibid., no. 279.
32 P.R.O. DL 28/3/2.
33 Thompson MW 1958: Wood M 1981, pp.29–31, 104; Emery A 1970, pp.198–9, 236n. Emery p.236 dates the great hall at Kenilworth to 1389–93.
34 P.R.O. DL 28/3/1 m8. In 1375 Gaunt had written to the chief steward of Pevensey saying that he had heard the castle was in great need of repair and ordering the necessary works to be carried out (*J.G.R. 1372–6*, nos 76, 1639).
35 Orders were made for the repair of Tutbury in April 1373, so that it could be a suitable residence for the duchess, the duke's children and others of his affinity (ibid., no. 1236). The castle had suffered storm damage (ibid., no. 1550).
36 Ibid., no. 1737.
37 Ibid., nos 1547, 1630, 1721, 1724–5.
38 Ibid., no. 1509.
39 Hill JWF 1948, pp.82–106.
40 A letter written by Gaunt probably in 1391 is dated Lincoln Castle (Edinburgh University Library, MS 183, f135v–d).
41 *J.G.R. 1372–6*, nos 965, 1213, 1368. In 1379 the garret on the castle bridge was panelled with 'waynescotbord' (*J.G.R. 1379–83*, no. 109; cf ibid., no. 555).
42 *J.G.R. 1372–6*, nos 1508, 1510; Brown RA 1963, Vol. 2, p.782 (painting of castle, plate 51).
43 Two bridges were to be renovated in 'la horsebaille', the walls repaired in freestone and 'buldres' brought to make spurs to strengthen towers. A new well was to be dug and existing ones repaired (*J.G.R. 1379–83*, no. 579).
44 Nottingham R.O., Foljambe of Osberton deeds, IX i 787, dated Leicester Castle 4 Jan. 1386.
45 Thompson MW 1958, pp.9, 11–12.
46 *J.G.R. 1372–6*, no. 1524; cf ibid., nos 1519–21, 1523. The original of the privy seal warrant, whose text is enrolled in the ducal register, is Nottingham R.O., Foljambe of Osberton deeds, IX i 694. Gaunt ordered repairs to the buildings and chambers of Gringley manor house at the same time.
47 *J.G.R. 1372–6*, nos 1280, 1287.
48 *J.G.R. 1379–83*, no. 542. The collector of rents in Knaresborough forest accounted for sums spent on repairs to the castle and other properties in the lordship in the year from Michaelmas 1384 (P.R.O. DL 29/465/7604).
49 Liverpool Castle was apparently being used as a prison in 1380 (*J.G.R. 1379–83*, no. 214).
50 P.R.O. DL 37/3 m1.
51 *J.G.R. 1379–83*, pp. xxv–xxvi.
52 There was a prisoner in Clitheroe Castle in 1380 (ibid., no. 216).
53 Ibid., nos 410, 566, 922; Blair CHH and Honeyman HL 1971, pp.8, 14ff. Gaunt had ordered the repair of the castle and the making of a new wall in 1372 (*J.G.R. 1372–6*, no. 954).
54 *J.G.R. 1379–83*, no. 624. In 1383 Holme contracted to make a new gatehouse, with portcullis, barbican and postern, using the old gatehouse for the works (ibid., no. 923).

55 Radford CAR 1952; Craster OE 1970; Knight JK 1980; Radford CAR 1972.

56 Taylor AJ 1972, pp.11, 16–17.

57 *J.G.R. 1372–6*, no. 1797.

58 Ibid., nos 1467, 1797; cf nos 253, 1011.

59 P.R.O. DL 28/3/1 m8.

60 *J.G.R. 1379–83*, nos 532, 534; cf nos 530–1, 536. In 1374 William Tutbury, receiver of Kidwelly, was in fear of being attacked on his travels in those parts on ducal business (*J.G.R. 1372–6*, no. 1586).

61 Morris RK 1986 pp.161–74.

62 Jones M 1970, pp.177–81.

63 Ibid., pp.175–6.

64 *C.P.R. 1354–8*, p.105; *V.C.H. Lancs.*, Vol. 2, p.164 and n; Somerville R 1953, p.366.

65 B.L. Add. MS 18632, f101 printed in Crow MM and Olson CC 1966, p.15; *J.G.R. 1379–83*, p.xxviii.

66 P.R.O. DL 28/3/5.

67 For the residence of the chancellor in the household in the early 1390s, East Sussex R.O., Waleys cartulary no. 3469, A2, B4, B9.

68 *J.G.R. 1379–83*, p.xxviii; Somerville R 1953, pp.115–17.

69 Ibid., p.115; Carte T 1743, p.176; East Sussex R.O., Waleys cartulary no. 3469, A1. For a reference by Gaunt to the dispatch of letters 'desouz le signet de nostre anel', *J.G.R. 1379–83*, no. 747.

70 For the council, Somerville R 1953, pp.120–30; *J.G.R. 1379–83*, pp.xlvii–l.

71 P.R.O. DL 28/3/5. For a warrant to the treasurer of the household to pay wages for councillors' attendance in 1373, *J.G.R. 1372–6*, no. 1382.

72 *J.G.R. 1379–83*, no. 899; cf ibid., nos 256, 280.

73 P.R.O. PL 3/39, 44, 65, 149.

74 Ibid., 107.

75 *J.G.R. 1379–83*, nos 253–4, 256.

76 Ibid., nos 185, 187, 190–1, 431.

77 Ibid., nos 297–8, 452.

78 Ibid., no. 319.

79 *J.G.R. 1372–6*, nos 321–2.

80 For the evolution of the two stewardships, Somerville R 1953, pp.113–15.

81 For the evolution of the office under Gaunt, ibid., pp.100–2; *J.G.R. 1379–83*, pp.xxviii–xxx.

82 Somerville R 1953, pp.114–15; *J.G.R. 1379–83*, p.xxxi.

83 Somerville R 1953, pp.111–13; *J.G.R. 1379–83*, pp.xxi–xii.

84 Somerville R 1953, pp.98–101; *J.G.R. 1379–83*, pp.xxxii–xxxiii.

85 Somerville R 1953, pp.120–1. For the chancery *J.G.R. 1379–83*, pp.xxiv.

86 For household administration, Somerville R 1953, pp.102–4.

87 *J.G.R. 1379–83*, no. 1082. For examples of ducal warrants authorising payments from the receiver-general, ibid., nos 92, 106. The controller sometimes handled money assigned to pay household debts (ibid., nos 128, 411).

88 For examples of ducal warrants ordering the receiver-general to make payments on treasurer's bills, *J.G.R. 1372–6*. nos 1087, 1176, 1179–80.

89 A warrant of 1375 ordered the clerk of the great wardrobe to pay a sum to the duke himself for his privy expenses and for gambling (*pur juer*) and a sum to a servant for chamber expenses (ibid., no. 1674). The duke gambled at dice (*a les detz*) (ibid., no. 1705).

90 *A.C.*, p.141.
91 *C.H.K.*, vol. 2, pp.134–5. 143. For some goods, including plate, destroyed at The Savoy, *J.G.R. 1379–83*, no. 743. For Oke's activities at Leicester, see above p.79.
92 East Sussex R.O., Waleys cartulary, no. 3469, Al. For McFarlane's analysis of the household rolls, Dell RF 1964, pp.260–2.
93 *C.E.P.R. Papal Letters*, Vol. 4, p.167.
94 East Sussex R.O., Waleys cartulary, no. 3469, B2. Notices of Gaunt's itinerary over this period in 1383 in other sources are sparse, but McFarlane's dating of the journal to 1383 receives some support from a ducal warrant dated Banbury, 1 Sept. 1383 (P.R.O. PL 3/1/80).
95 Myers A R 1959, pp.94–5.
96 *J.G.R. 1379–83*, no. 372. Tynneslowe had been given the same task in Oct. 1379 for a sojourn at Kenilworth (ibid., no. 121).
97 Ibid., nos 179, 257, 881, 913.
98 Ibid., nos 254, 257, 911.
99 Ibid., nos 332, 1072.
100 *J.G.R. 1372–6*, no. 399; *J.G.R. 1379–83*, nos 128, 327. Barbour is found residing in the ducal household in the early 1380s, for example, Waleys cartulary, no. 3469, A7.
101 For the two heralds residing in the household in the early 1390s, ibid., A9.
102 *C.P.R. 1367–70*, p.74.
103 *J.G.R. 1372–6*, nos 859–62, 1416.
104 Bateson M 1901, Vol. 2, pp.170–1. Hankyn and seven other minstrels of the duke were rewarded by him at Kenilworth in Jan. 1380 (*J.G.R. 1379–83*, nos 73, 327). For the grant of annuities to Jacob Bumepiper in 1380 and Hankyn Fryssh in 1382, ibid., nos 790, 959, 1003.
105 Ibid., nos 127, 272.
106 Ibid., no. 272.
107 Ibid., no. 783.
108 *J.G.R. 1372–6*, no. 1027.
109 *J.G.R. 1379–83*, no. 783.
110 Ibid., no. 803.
111 Ibid., nos 366, 399.
112 Ibid., no. 783.
113 His storer was ordered to sell nine colts from the stud in 1380 (ibid., no. 571).
114 Ibid., no. 204.
115 Ibid., no. 688.
116 Ibid., nos 262, 771–2. Payments to the bargemen are recorded in P.R.O. DL 28/3/1 m5 and DL 28/3/5 f10d. A new barge had been purchased from William Brid of Mortlake in 1373 (*J.G.R. 1372–6*, no. 1242).
117 *J.G.R. 1379–83*, no. 1137; cf ibid., nos 229, 811, 866.
118 Ibid., no. 811.
119 Ibid., no. 134; cf ibid., nos 226, 311–12; *J.G.R. 1372–6*, nos 1148–9.
120 *J.G.R. 1379–83*, no. 1170; cf ibid., nos 1171, 1182.
121 Ibid., nos 538, 893, 1096. In 1383 the farmer of Rodley (Gloucs.) was allowed 44*s.* in his account for lamphreys purchased from him (ibid., no. 810).
122 Ibid., no. 179.

123 Ibid., nos 441, 739. In 1371 the keeper of Aldbourne was ordered to deliver deer and rabbits to the duke at Kingston Lacy for the Christmas celebrations; the parker of Hungerford was to deliver deer (*J.G.R. 1372–6*, nos 876–7, 889). Game from Ashdown Forest was delivered to Hertford Castle for the following Christmas (ibid., no. 1103).

124 *J.G.R. 1379–83*, nos 518, 638. Noke was owed over £38, Trygg over £154; the latter was owed over £92 for fish in 1383 (ibid., no. 836). For ducal debts of £66 10s. to London fishmongers that year, ibid., no. 835. For a debt to Richard Kent of London in 1372 for purchase of fish, *J.G.R. 1372–6*, no. 1088.

125 *J.G.R. 1379–83*, nos 266, 394. For payment by the Norfolk receiver in 1381 for 'pesson sale et hareng sore' purchased at Blakeney and Great Yarmouth, ibid., no. 602; cf ibid., no. 851; *J.G.R. 1372–6*, no. 1028.

126 *J.G.R. 1379–83*, no. 370. Chyvyngton was ordered to transport the wine to Newcastle – presumably for the use of the duke and his retinue in the borders. One of the duke's wine merchants was Walter Derby of Bristol, owed sums for wine in 1383 (ibid., nos 834, 852).

127 *J.G.R. 1372–6*, no. 408; *J.G.R. 1379–83*, nos 206, 479, 482–3. For an assignment to Duchess Blanche's, C.C.C. 495 f15r; for payment by the receiver-general of 1,000 *m.* assigned for Constance's wardrobe and privy chamber expenses for the year 1376–7, P.R.O. DL 28/3/I. For an assignment of £600 for Catherine's wardrobe expenses, 1396–7, P.R.O. DL 28/3/5.

128 *J.G.R. 1372–6*, nos 473–4. Edward Gerberge was retained for life in war and peace in 1372 (ibid., no. 509).

129 Ibid., no. 524. These costs were assigned on the honour of Tutbury. For the children's treasurer John Cheyne, ibid., no. 525 and for a ducal grant (1375) to Amye de Melbourne for her care of them, ibid., nos 694–5.

130 Ibid., no. 1614; Kirby JL 1970; p.15; P.R.O. DL 28/3/1 m5. Blanche Lady Wake, daughter of Henry earl of Lancaster, was paid 100m. for accommodating Henry and his servants (ibid., p.14; see above, p.48).

131 *J.G.R. 1379–83*, nos 397, 426.

132 *J.G.R. 1372–6*, nos 670, 1611; *J.G.R. 1379–83*, nos 319, 490. Catherine was living with Lady Mohun in 1383 (ibid., no. 803). For the latter, see above, p.293.

Chapter Fourteen

Gaunt's Regional Interests, Estate Administration and Finances

Regional interests

As the holder of the earldoms of Derby, Leicester and Lincoln, Gaunt received titles which reflected concentrations of properties in their particular shires, but minimal public rights.[1] However, as an earl he had the expectation of appointment as first-named on a variety of occasional important commissions in 'his' shires as well as the normal ones, notably the peace commissions. Magnates seldom participated personally in the work of all but the most exceptional commissions, such as the one over which Gaunt presided at York in the autumn of 1382, to investigate 'treasons, felonies, uprisings and other misdeeds' in the aftermath of the Peasants' Revolt.[2] However, their nominal headships carried the implication that working commissioners – royal justices and local knights and esquires – ought to treat their interests with respect.

Magnates sought to ensure such protection for their interests by securing the appointment of gentry who held offices and fees from them as sheriffs, escheators and justices of the peace. The evidence that Gaunt influenced such appointments in favour of his retainers is inferential: the retainers who secured them were in any case well qualified for selection. Dr Astill has shown that in his earldom of Leicester Gaunt did not pursue a policy of domination over the gentry through office-holding. Very few of the Leicestershire gentry were his retainers. Only three sheriffs (John Peche, 1369–70), William Breton (1375–6) and William Bagot (1383–4) are known to have had

Lancastrian service links; of these, only Bagot seems to have been a retainer when appointed sheriff. The proportion of Lancastrian retainers appointed in Gaunt's time to the commission of peace was at most a third, and these were men well qualified for the office.[3] There are various possible explanations for Gaunt's moderation over the shire's government. Attempts at domination might have been counter-productive if they had gone against the traditional grain of regional politics. Moreover, as earl of Leicester Gaunt could expect a residue of traditional respect, which he augmented by his frequent visits to the shire. There was, perhaps, no need for him to strive for domination. There were no other locally predominant magnate families with whom he had to compete and, as Astill points out, there was no gentry caucus which controlled shire affairs. Elsewhere, according to the particular circumstances, Gaunt felt more pressure to push his men into shire offices or to retain those who often held them; there were periods (especially in the 1370s) when royal administration in a large number of shires took on a decidedly Lancastrian colouring, especially the peace commissions.[4] His retainers did not necessarily form a Lancastrian caucus on such commissions nor a dominant force in local affairs. Gaunt, as a prudent lord, in many regions, even in Yorkshire, Lincolnshire and Staffordshire, where he was a considerable landowner, recognised and accommodated the interests of other magnates.

In exercising influence over lesser landowners Gaunt had advantages unrivalled by fellow magnates – the deep, but not bottomless, well of Lancastrian patronage, comprising not only a lucrative *cursus honorum* (see p.216), but a great range of benefits and favours, such as the recreational facilities of his chaces and their resources of game and timber. Feudal ties provided ways of binding gentlefolk to Lancastrian service and rewarding them for good service. His retainers Sir Hugh Hastings (d. 1369), his son Sir Hugh and Sir Thomas Banastre were among the prominent retainers who were nudged towards his service by their tenures. In 1392–3 the chief steward of Lancashire, Thomas Pinchbeck, was holding the marriage and wardship of a prominent local heir, John Harington, granted to him by Gaunt.[5]

In Lancashire Gaunt's concentration of baronies gave him intermediate control of many fees, and his control of government developed to a higher point than in any other of his lordships with the grant of palatine powers in 1377. For instance, he gained a commanding influence over the return of shire knights to parliament. He and his officials controlled the process of election; the writs of summons were drafted in his name. Professor J.S. Roskell's analysis of Lancashire representation in Richard's reign has shown that, with few exceptions, present and former Lancastrian retainers, or duchy estate officials, were returned.[6] However, one must not exaggerate Gaunt's influence over the Lancashire gentry: Dr Simon Walker concludes that he maintained links with slightly more than a third of the influential gentry and more haphazard connections among the mass of esquires.[7] Gaunt's resources were finite: K.B. McFarlane calculated that, in the years 1394 and 1395, when his gross income from estates was about £11,750, £3,000 was spent on the annuities of retainers.[8] This widespread retaining had to serve curial, military and diplomatic as well as regional purposes. Gaunt simply could not afford to buy up the gentry of the shires where his estates were concentrated.

In Lancashire, Walker suggests, the combination of a Lancastrian interest among the gentry and of a judicial and governmental machine which often favoured its members helped to create recurring disaffection with the regime.[9] This was encouraged by the existence of the neighbouring royal palatinate, the earldom of Chester, whose gentry were interlinked with those of Lancashire (not least in unruly habits) and whose royal lieutenants were perhaps encouraged into competitiveness with Gaunt by his possession of the honour of Halton, which made him second only to the royal earl as a landowner in Cheshire.[10] In 1385 Gaunt complained to the king and lords in parliament that the Cheshireman Sir John Stanley had, in right of his wife, entered Lathom manor (Lancs.) – in ducal wardship because of the minority of the previous heir – without sueing out his right in the duke's palatine chancery, to his 'grave contempt'. After deliberation by the royal justices and sergeants-at-law, it was declared in parliament that Stanley's entry was illegal and manifestly against Gaunt's liberty and that he ought to proceed, as Gaunt had suggested, in his chancery.[11] The following year Stanley was appointed to deputise as lieutenant in Ireland for the king's favourite, Robert de Vere, who was justiciar of Chester.[12] It is likely that Stanley was already enjoying Vere's patronage in 1385, and that an element in the tension between Gaunt and the court was the maintenance by Vere of Stanley's possession of Lathom. In 1387 Sir Thomas Molyneux recruited Lancashire gentry for the army which Vere led to rescue the king, which was defeated by the lords appellant at Radcot Bridge (recruits whom Gaunt sorely needed a few months before when he invaded León).[13] This intrusion into Gaunt's sphere of influence by Vere may have been one of the factors which induced Bolingbroke to join the lords appellant.[14] In 1393 prominent Lancashiremen took part in the 'Cheshire Revolt', which appears to have been in part a protest against government in the ducal palatine. The following year the new justiciar of Chester Thomas Mowbray showed his lack of sympathy with its government by pardoning the Lancashireman Richard Crofts, who had slain Gaunt's justice

of oyer and terminer Robert Blakeburn.[15] Yet, as we have seen, Gaunt
was on the whole remarkably successful in avoiding regional conflicts
with other magnates, especially ones based on competing territorial
influence. Some of his most notable disputes and clashes were with
gentlefolk and others who were his neighbours and tenants, including
groups whose stings the attractions of his *cursus honorum* was designed
to draw. Illustrative of such clashes was the wave of violence against
his Yorkshire possessions and some others in the years after Duke
Henry of Lancaster's death. In 1362 a commission of oyer and terminer
was appointed, composed of Lancastrian retainers and well-wishers,
on Gaunt's complaint that unnamed trespassers had broken into his
parks and closes at thirty places in the West and North Ridings
(including at Richmond, long held by him). They had hunted his
deer and felled his trees, carrying away their spoils; likewise, they
had fished in his ponds and taken away the catch, and had taken hares,
conies, pheasants and partridges from his warrens. They had assaulted
his servants, presumably when they tried to interrupt this bonanza.[16]
Such mayhem was recurrent, perpetrated by the well-to-do as well as
the commons, though apparently never on the same scale (not even
in 1381) as in Yorkshire in the early 1360s. Two more examples will
suffice. In 1370 a commission of oyer and terminer was appointed
(its composition biassed in Gaunt's favour) on his complaint that
Sir William de Wareyn's son John and others had trespassed in
Cowick Park and in his warrens at Snaith (Yorks.); in 1376 he
accused Thomas Mundvill and others of breaking into his property
at Pontefract, Tickhill, Knaresborough and Sledburn.[17]

Recent work by Dr David Crook, Dr Simon Walker and Professor
John G. Bellamy has provided instructive examples of regional
opposition to Lancastrian government, in Derbyshire, Sussex and
Yorkshire as well as in Lancashire. The origin of the Derbyshire
troubles, according to Crook, lay in a dispute over property between
Gaunt and Ralph Stathum (d. 1380); in 1371 a verdict against
Stathum was given in Gaunt's hundredal court, whose jurisdiction
he disputed. In subsequent years Stathum bickered with beneficiaries
of this judgement and in 1380 Gaunt obtained commissions of oyer
and terminer directed against members of his family, composed
of Lancastrian well-wishers. The Stathums took advantage of the
Peasants' Revolt to lead an attack (18 June 1381) on Horston Castle,
held of the Crown by one of Gaunt's most eminent retainers, his
councillor the elder Sir Robert Swillington.[18]

In Sussex Gaunt held properties as part of the earldom of Richmond,
which he surrendered in 1372; in exchange he received from the
Crown former properties of his mother – Willingdon, Grinstead and
Maresfield, the forest of Ashdown and the Rape and castle of

Pevensey. Lancastrian officials tightened up the administration of these properties, causing resentment among customary tenants and neighbouring gentry. This was vented in attacks on Gaunt's property and officials, particularly during the Peasants' Revolt, though they did not cease thereafter – a subforester was murdered in 1384. Some of these attacks were orchestrated by a leading landowner, Sir Edward Dallingridge, with his accomplices Sir Thomas Sackville and Sir Philip Medsted (all clients of the earl of Arundel). Dallingridge particularly resented the threat posed to his franchisal profits by the operations of the ducal court at Hungry Hatch, near Fletching. In 1384 Gaunt secured commissions for Dallingridge's prosecution; he was convicted on almost all the charges. Walker shows that, once his rights were vindicated, Gaunt behaved in a conciliatory manner, preferring the goodwill of the gentry to the perpetuation of the opposition among them provoked by his 'intrusive lordship'.[19]

Much worse and more prolonged troubles were to flare up during Gaunt's absence abroad in 1386–9, in the lordship of Knaresborough, which he had received from the Crown in 1372 as part compensation for his surrender of Richmond. In the next few years Gaunt had set about reforming what he clearly considered to be a lax administration of seigneurial rights there. In 1373, by the advice of the council, he ordered the making of a new extent of the vills.[20] On a visit to Knaresborough in September 1374 he displayed his lack of confidence in its officials, from the master forester downwards. The bailiff of the lordship was ordered to seize their wages, and its receiver to pay them on a former scale.[21] A few days later, when at Tickhill, he ordered that unauthorised taking of profits in the forest should be stopped.[22] These measures provoked local discontent. In November Gaunt wrote that he had heard that there were those in the lordship who were not obedient (*de bon port*) to his authority, and ordered that sureties be taken from anyone who damaged his ministers, tenants, vert or venison.[23] However, he did make a few remissions of tallage and rent to the tenants of impoverished vills.[24] In February 1375 Gaunt issued ordinances for the lordship and forest to William Nesfeld, the steward of Knaresborough. New assarts were to be let at farm; tenants who refused to pay a reasonable rent were to be evicted and replaced by those who would. Demesnes and other lands in seigneurial hands in the vills of Knaresborough, Aldborough and Roecliffe were to be put at farm for greater profit, at their true value. 'Foreigners' who exercised common rights of wood and turbary in the forest as a result of the laxity of the late queen's ministers were to be ousted, and tenants' rights of this sort were to be narrowly enforced.[25]

Opposition in the late 1380s to the duke's officials acquired a local leader whose exploits achieved widespread fame – William Beckwith, member of a ministerial family whose revolt, the Westminster Chronicler had heard, was precipitated by his failure to be appointed to an office in the lordship of Knaresborough which had been held by a forebear. Beckwith's known associates were nearly all from villages around Knaresborough, and were mostly drawn from the ranks of peasant landowners, labourers and servants. The extent of his support and the ferocity and recurrence over several years of his attacks show that this was more than a personal feud: it was too a protest movement against ducal administration, whose persistence suggests that it benefited from the protection or neutrality of more elevated locals. Repeated objectives of these malcontents were to kill Sir Robert Rokeley, steward of the lordship and constable of Knaresborough Castle, and Robert Doufbyggyng, chief forester of the forest and chace; the latter was a 'stranger' (from Lancashire) with a reputation for violence and for protecting criminals.[26]

By October 1387 Beckwith was waging war against officials in the lordship with a score of kinsfolk and inhabitants. About twelve months later, his band shot at Knaresborough Castle, hoping to hit Rokeley, but instead injuring Doufbyggyng's son. Five weeks later they congregated at the ducal lodge in Haverah Park, eight miles from Knaresborough, with the intention of killing the father; Haverah was to be attacked again in August 1389 and June 1390. No commissions were procured to deal with the problem until those issued in March and July 1390, after Gaunt's return to England. They were used to undercut Beckwith's support; he was killed in 1391 or 1392, and seven of his closest henchmen were killed by Rokeley and his men. This was not the end of disturbances in the lordship, but it took the heart out of them.

The local opposition to Gaunt suggests that, just as kings faced recurrent problems of defiance and revolt by magnates, so magnates had to contend with unruliness by gentlefolk and other neighbours. Traditional gentry ties with lords did not automatically gain them gentry respect. The trespasses committed soon after Gaunt's succession to the Lancastrian inheritance seem like a testing of the new and untried lord's will and competence. He was disadvantaged in that he was not the natural heir to the earldom of Richmond or the Lancaster inheritance and that the vast extent of his lands and his frequent foreign commitments necessitated his absenteeism. His drives to develop efficient judicial and estate organisation sometimes appeared to tenants and neighbours as unjustified and expensive novelties. Palatine government was not the customary form in Lancashire; in the comital lordships of Richmond, and in the rape of Pevensey and honour of Knaresborough, where Gaunt's rule was a novelty, attempts to tighten up administration were unwelcome.

In these situations gentlefolk might incite or sympathise with the opposition of lesser folk. Moreover, landowners great and small were habitually inclined to evade or postpone the payment of tenurial dues, just as they were inclined to drive hounds and fly hawks in carelessly guarded chaces. Gaunt and his council were well aware that their insistence on ministerial efficiency in the enforcement of ducal rights stimulated excesses by overzealous and corrupt officers; they had to deal with a stream of accusations alleging unreasonable behaviour, an undercurrent of discontent threatening to undermine the goodwill of those on whose benevolence or service ducal interests in other respects depended. In 1373 officials in the honour of Tickhill (recently acquired) were ordered to suspend distraint against Sir Ralph Cromwell (vociferous in complaint), and Sir John Crescy;[27] likewise, in 1381 they were to cease distraining Gaunt's leading retainer Richard Lord Scrope.[28] The good governance of a magnate and his councillors depended on their sensitivity to these issues. One objective of Gaunt's regular northern perambulations was probably to scrutinise his administration and receive petitions. Other strategies for protecting his interests were to dazzle gentlefolk with the patronage, his own and the Crown's, at his disposal and to procure key local government offices for his retainers.

In this period there was a particular danger that Gaunt's measures to win over potential critics and opponents and to ensure good ministerial service might backfire. For public opinion, as expressed in the Commons, was agitated in the 1370s and 1380s about the misdeeds of retainers and ministers, encouraged by the protection they looked to from their patrons. Gaunt was pre-eminently vulnerable to such accusations, especially since he had expanded the Lancastrian retaining net so widely. For instance, as Dr Nigel Saul has shown, by his retaining in Gloucestershire 'in the 1380s and 1390s . . . [he] drove the biggest inroad into the dominance of local magnates like the Berkeleys, Talbots or Despensers'.[29] Moreover, some of those patronised by Gaunt were doubtless violent and ambitious men, like William Par, the Lancashireman of humble origins for whom Gaunt secured a pardon for murder in 1371 in order that he should join his military retinue. Par had secured a pardon for another murder the previous year. He was to marry an heiress, to become one of Gaunt's bachelors and enjoy a distinguished career in his service – surprisingly, as a diplomat.[30]

Though there are a few petitions to the Crown complaining about intimidation and perversion of justice by Lancastrian retainers, there is an apparent dearth of complaints about maintenance by Gaunt or of complaints to him about the ill-doings of his retainers. Why is there no evidence of bills about this being considered by the duke's council? The cynical explanation is that opponents and victims were too overawed to complain, or feared that they would not receive justice in cases to which the duke or his retainers were party. There may be other reasons: perhaps Gaunt set his face against encouraging illegal maintenance, and regarded complaints against his retainers with such severity that he summoned the parties to deal with them in person, as he did in the case of a variety of disputes. The Westminster Chronicler says that, in response to the complaints of the Commons generally about the abuses of maintenance, in the Salisbury parliament of 1384, Gaunt promised that he and his brothers would inflict exemplary punishments on any of their own retainers who committed outrages by colour of their liveries.[31] Some confirmation of his sincerity may be gleaned from an undated letter probably written by a Northumberland knight, William Swinburne, concerning also a fellow countryman, Sir John Fenwyk.[32] Both of them were Gaunt's bachelors; the letter-writer, addressing Bolingbroke, requested him to intercede with the earl of Northumberland and his son Sir Henry Percy, in order to persuade them not to take the part of another Northumberland knight with whom the bachelors were disputing the possession of property. It may be that the supplicants addressed Bolingbroke rather than Gaunt because the latter was abroad. Another possible explanation is that they were wary of involving Gaunt because he might be disapproving and unhelpful to their cause, especially in view of the Northumbrian gentry's reputation for quarrelsomeness and violence. In the past Swinburne had been prepared to annoy the earl of Northumberland; on this occasion he and his colleague displayed a prim correctness which may have reflected the tone Gaunt tried to inculcate in his retainers. The conduct of a retinue certainly reflected significantly the attitude of its master: the many illegalities committed by the rapidly expanding retinue of the earl of Huntingdon in the late 1390s stemmed from his scandalous tolerance and encouragement of their misdeeds. These were denounced after the earl was killed and his interest dissolved in 1400; no comparable opportunity presented itself to those aggrieved by any Lancastrian interest. Yet there had been periods when Gaunt's standing at court was low and when his opponents comprehensively denounced his works. However, the conduct of his affinity was not a matter of general complaint. It is feasible that the principal reason was Gaunt's well-publicised abhorrence of the abuses of maintenance and a prudent discouragement by him of the formation of caucuses by his retainers and ministers designed to exploit royal and ducal offices for their mutual benefit at the expense of their neighbours.

Estate administration

The practice of leasing particular agrarian resources was well established in Lancastrian administration in the fourteenth century
and was widespread at the end of it. The auditors' valuations for
the year to Michaelmas 1400 show, for instance, that at Melbourne
(Derbys.), the demesne meadows and pastures, the fishery in the
River Trent, the mill and grazing were let at farm.[33] At Kingston
Lacy (Dorset) the demesnes, mills, meadows, pastures and dovecot
were farmed.[34] So, in 1392–3, was the lead mine at Wirksworth
(Derbys.) and the market toll at Tutbury, according to another such
valuation.[35] Many leases made by stewards were probably of short
duration (for example, for one year), but longer leases, of whole
manorial properties as well as of particular tenements and resources,
were usual. Thus, on the one hand, the whole manor of Redmore
(Norfolk), with its fishery, was leased for nine years in 1382;[36] in
1392 it was in the hands of another lessee, John Feltwell, clerk of
the duke's chapel.[37] On the other hand, the duke's valet and falconer
Antoyn had in 1379 been granted parcels of land formerly held by
a villein of Higham Ferrers. The following year another valet, John
de Ascheford, received a house with appurtenances in the lordship
of Peak.[38] Lancastrian servants eagerly sought long-term leases from
their master since they provided more assured sources of revenue than
did annuities.

In the early 1380s the chancellor regarded the making of leases as
of such routine occurrence that he had the texts of indentures entered
in one section in the ducal register under the appropriate year. Two
farms of ducal properties were recorded for 1379–80, six for 1380–1,
five for 1381–2, nine for 1382–3. Most of these farms were of small
pieces of property in the north and were mainly for a short term
of years, twelve or less.[39] A twelve-year term was frequently fixed.
Grants for life of substantial properties were often made as a means
of rewarding knightly retainers. Sir Walter Urswick was granted the
manor and lordship of North Thoresby and Skarthowe (Lincs.) in
1380; Sir Nicholas Sharnesfield received the manor of Berwick St
James (Wilts.) in 1382 in place of an annuity.[40]

In the unstable market conditions of the later fourteenth century,
ducal stewards often sought to make leases on favourable terms for
their master as a more assured source of income than the sometimes
uncertain returns from sale of crops and stock. On many of the
northern estates, often emparked, stock-raising was predominant and
agistment (lease of grazing rights) was an important source of revenue
as well as the keeping of herds. In this period agistment and the lease
of whole pastures appear to have increased. A schedule of 1379 for

agistment at Shottle Park in Duffield Frith (Derbys.) lists the names
of at least 175 graziers who had 858 cattle and horses in the park.
However, by 1376–7 the ducal herd in Duffield Frith had been run
down; the remnant was to be customarily leased for periods of eight
years or more.[41] In Lancashire a system of vaccaries (dairy farms) had
been developed in the twelfth and thirteenth centuries as an important
domainal resource. In 1399–1400 the vaccaries of Wyresdale, Calder,
Grisdale, Blesdale, Mirescough and Hore Appleton were at farm.[42]

Gaunt's large number of northern retainers kept up pressure
for farms in the region. For instance, in 1373 the steward of
Knaresborough was told that the esquire Thomas Haselden had asked
Gaunt for a farm of Boroughbridge for ten years; the steward was
ordered to make a lease for that period on the usual terms.[43] In 1383
Richard Brennand, appointed bailiff of franchises in Knaresborough
and Boroughbridge in 1379, and the protector of Duchess Constance
in 1381 (see p.79), secured the farm of a large number of Yorkshire
mills and, besides, the tolls and court profits of Knaresborough and
of the borough court at Boroughbridge.[44]

Overall, the most common pattern on ducal manors at the time
of Gaunt's death was one where many of the domainal resources
– pasture, meadows, grazing, mills, fishponds – were leased, but
other sources of profit (perhaps, in total, the major part) were
not. A characteristic case is Cowick (Yorks.) in 1383–4; the reeve's
account shows over £15 profit from farms, but profits also from
assized rents (£32), sales (nearly £5) and perquisites of court (over
£6).[45] In the same year, out of eleven properties in Lincolnshire and
Huntingdonshire, only two, Wainfleet and Wodcroft in Wrangle (both
in Lincs.) were completely leased.[46] The Norfolk receiver's account
for 1396–7 mentions four farms: the manor of Redmore was farmed
and so were the demesnes of Methwold and Snettisham and various
lands and a mill at Thetford.[47] Three of the 23 manors accounted for
by the receiver of Leicester in 1399 were wholly farmed.[48] One of
these, Daventry (Northants.) was customarily farmed: it had been by
Duke Henry and then by Gaunt in 1372,[49] though he was arranging
to keep it in his hands in 1382.[50]

In the Marches of Wales land rents and renders formed the most
important item in seigneurial revenue. There direct farming ended
on Duke Henry's death in 1361 (see p.344). This was not generally
the case on English estates, which, in whole or part, continued to go
in and out of direct farming. There, when leases fell in, if a decision
to put property to farm was not determined by the pressures of
ducal patronage, the steward weighed the interrelated factors of the
strength of manorial resources and the movements of market prices
and of rent. Methwold was in the lord's hands in 1388, though

leased the previous year. Profits were down, the stock of sheep had been ravaged by murrain and tenements were badly maintained. At Fakenham and Aylsham (Norfolk) the mills, in the lord's hands, had produced lower profits than usual because of a fall in grain prices. Maybe the retention of some Norfolk properties in demesne in 1388 resulted from stewards' inability to make profitable farms, consequent on a conjunction of unfavourable economic circumstances.[51]

On the other hand, resources were sometimes directly farmed because of buoyant market conditions. The timber in northern parks was well maintained to meet local demands for this diminishing resource as well as ducal needs. Some vaccaries were still managed there: in 1399–1400 the receiver of Lancashire paid for 120 cows and nine bulls to be pastured in Bowland Forest, and the receiver of Tutbury for 40 cows with which to stock a vaccary.[52] Warrens were kept in hand and, in southern regions where the demand for high-quality wool could be met from ducal estates, the administration was responsive to the demand. In the year 1399–1400 the receiver of the south purchased 4,000 sheep; there were ducal flocks on some manors in Dorset, Wiltshire and Gloucestershire.[53] In 1392–3, in Norfolk, rabbits, sheep and fleeces had been sold from Snettisham, grain, beasts and rabbits from Gimingham (where 303 sheep were bought for stock in 1399–1400), grain and beasts from Methwold, and faggots from Tansted. The market for rabbits was voracious; 9,460 were sold in 1392–3 from Methwold warrens, at a clear profit of £75 1s.[54]

The duke communicated to his councillors and ministers a determination to maintain the value of his properties, whether in hand or leased out; and to maximise profits, except in cases of preferential grants to members of his family and favoured servants. For instance, a ducal order was made in 1375 for the sale of wood from the lordship of Knaresborough and the application of its profits to the repair of mills in the lordship.[55] The watermill at Maresfield (Sussex) and the sluice and bridge there were to be repaired in 1380.[56] Isabelle de Stabille was to receive timber from Knaresborough Forest in 1381 to repair the houses given to her by the duke;[57] the executors of Edmund Cockayne, life tenant of the bercheries at Ashbourne (Derbyshire), were to be compelled to pay to remedy the ruinous state in which he had left them.[58]

The council, at Gaunt's prompting, was probably mainly responsible for putting pressure, directly or indirectly, on lessees and ministers in his interest. Officials were expected to be vigilant in opposing attempts by farmers and customary tenants to evade obligations. The duke and/or his council were sometimes deaf to pleas for remission. The tenants of Dunstanburgh alleged in 1375 that they were impoverished and could not pay their farms without great hardship, because of the low yield (*feblesse*) of their lands and the low value of Scottish money (on whose circulation they had to depend). Gaunt's response was to draft in his Yorkshire steward William Nesfeld, to ensure that the rents were fully levied.[59] Another ducal warrant addressed to Nesfeld in October of that year anticipated trouble over gathering rent in Yorkshire, because of the recent pestilence. Farmers were to be made to give surety for payment or face eviction.[60] The rights of manor courts had to be maintained. On 6 May 1381 Gaunt wrote to his Norfolk ministers, Edmund Gournay and Adam Pope, saying that he had been informed that bond tenants in his lordship of Gimingham were settling suits between themselves in an ecclesiastical court and not, as customarily, within the ducal court in the lordship. The ministers were to forbid Thomas Smyth and all other bond tenants from practising any such novelty.[61]

On the other hand, Gaunt and his council were well aware that their regime encouraged ministers to overstep the mark, and responded scrupulously to tenants' petitions alleging ministerial oppressions, attempting to secure restorations of their rights and property and a fair hearing for them. In 1380 Gaunt sent the chief steward of lands north of the Trent and officials of the lordship of High Peak a bill from its tenants, ordering them to examine both bill and tenants in order to provide a remedy, in the meantime returning their distrained beasts and taking equivalent sureties in case judgement went against them.[62] A warrant to John Holt, steward of Higham Ferrers, ordered the return to the tenants of Sutton of their sheep, distrained without the command of Holt or any of his ministers, 'at which we are very unpleasantly surprised [*merveillous durement*]'. If Holt found that the sheep had been arrested with good cause, their owners were to provide surety to give answer to Gaunt and his councillors during the Northampton parliament.[63] In March 1381 the chief steward of Lancashire was ordered to stop the bailiffs of Salfordshire from summoning or constraining the tenants of Rochdale to answer outside their own franchise. The ducal warrant vigorously expressed anger that the franchise had been flouted, to the tenants' material loss.[64]

However, good administration was menaced by inefficiency as well as oppressiveness. A report by the auditors in 1388 analysing falls in profit, besides outlining economic problems, emphasises the bad effects of the laxity and recalcitrance of local ministers in allowing the duke's revenues to go by default – in particular, the inefficiency of stewards, such as those who failed to hold court in person. When this report was made, Gaunt had been abroad for about two years: it may be that the councillors had been less successful in keeping local ministers up to the mark, losing conciliar drive without his insistence on an often harsh enforcement of rights. On occasion that had, indeed, been tempered by mercy, in cases which the duke and his council adjudged to be ones of unjust exploitation or of genuine hardship, such as that of Knaresborough vills in 1374–5 (see p.331). During the Northampton parliament of 1380, Gaunt remitted three bills to his officials there, one of them from 'our poor and servile [*neif*] tenants' of the lordship of Skenfrith. His auditor and steward in Wales, having examined the evidence, were to do 'right and reason' to these and the other supplicants and to make allowances to them in accordance with their findings.[65] The same year oaks suitable for fuel from Needwood Forest were to be delivered to the 'well-beloved' tenants of Uttoxeter (Staffs.) 'of our special grace and as a charitable work'.[66] Another charitable work was his assent to the petition of his bondwoman, Agneys Snelle of Knowsthorp near Leeds, to discharge her and members of her family from the office of reeve during her intended pilgrimage to Rome and elsewhere to pray for him and her other benefactors.[67] After the Peasants' Revolt Gaunt showed sensitivity to the tax burden of his tenants at Methwold, many of whom had been convicted of destroying his property during the revolt. In 1383 he wrote to the farmer there, ordering him to pay the fifteenth on his goods in the vill 'in ease of the poor tenants'; an allowance in the farm was promised.[68]

Gaunt's properties suffered relatively lightly from the malice of his tenants during the revolt. Much of the destruction of his property, at The Savoy and Hertford, was carried out by men not in his lordship. In some places tenants acted hostilely. At Methwold, 49 of them were fined for destruction of his corn and hay, and eleven for damage to his property at Thornholm.[69] The court profits at Higham Ferrers were reduced in 1381 because of the 'great rumour'; they were small that year at Pevensey and Maresfield – no courts could be held in the honour of Pevensey.[70] The worst and most lasting damage to his estate administration was the destruction of records. The accounts of many bailiffs of southern franchises were burnt at The Savoy, where they usually accounted: the process of account was still disrupted in 1388. At Methwold manorial administration was handicapped then by the destruction by the rebels of rentals and customary extents.[71]

One probable reason why Gaunt's estates did not fare worse in 1381 was that many of his resources were at farm, in many places presumably to the tenants themselves. For instance, part of Methwold was leased in 1381. Gaunt was then in dispute with the farmer, Thomas Schragger – who may indeed have winked at the destruction of Gaunt's crops.[72] Moreover, many ducal properties lay north of the Trent, where rural society was less generally affected by the revolt,

and where Gaunt may have been widely respected by the commons
because of the protection he afforded against the Scots. The movement
against his Derbyshire officials was prompted by a property dispute
(see p.330). Gaunt apparently regarded his tenants' offences in 1381
as minor compared to the destruction of The Savoy and the mayhem
of other major riots. As Professor Tuck has pointed out, he wanted
the offences of his Norfolk tenants to be treated leniently.[73]

Indeed, according to the confession of John Cote, mason, of Loose
in Maidstone (Kent) about a new rising in Kent in September 1381,

> pilgrims who had come out of the north country to the town
> of Canterbury, related in the county of Kent that John, duke of
> Lancaster had made all his natives free, in the different counties
> of England; whereupon the foresaid malefactors wished to have
> sent messengers to the foresaid duke, if it were so or not; and if
> it were so, then the said malefactors consented one and all, to
> have sent to the said duke, and him, by their own real power
> to have made their lord and king of England.[74]

The conspirators' caution about believing the pilgrims' tale was
amply justified! The section headed 'Manumissiones' at the end of
the 1379–83 register unimpressively contains only one manumission of
a serf, a customary kind of manumission – once Andrew son of Simon
Grayne of Steeping (Lincs.) had fulfilled his intention of entering holy
orders, he was to be free.[75] Gaunt occasionally altered the status of
land from bond to free – in the case, for instance, of a grant of land
in Cheshunt (Herts.) to his servant Edmund Fauconer and Fauconer's
heirs in 1370.[76] A grant in Wirksworth (Derbys.) in 1380 makes a
similar change of tenure, but the tenement was to remain freehold
only during the duke's lifetime.[77] It was often concomitant on leases
of demesnes that work obligations were sold – in 1392–3 at Raunds
(Northants.), Hertingfordbury and Bayford (Herts.), Gimingham,
Tansted and Methwold (Norfolk). Then, however, servile status of
folk and tenements was widespread on ducal estates; the payment of
their characteristic levies – tallage, chevage, or aid – was vigorously
enforced, for example, at Tutbury, Duffield, Gimingham, Tansted,
Pevensey and at Willingdon (Sussex).[78]

One tribute to Gaunt's success as a landowner was that he
significantly augmented the Lancastrian inheritance, principally
through the royal favours which he received because of his
birth and as rewards for his outstanding services to the Crown
in peace and war. There were, indeed, some losses and alienations.
The French successes deprived him – permanently, as it turned out
– of the Lancastrian lordships in Champagne and of the estates in

Gascony and Poitou granted him in 1370 (see p.189). Remarkably few properties were detached by him to endow chantry and other religious foundations – the Lancastrian family, already outstanding ecclesiastical patrons, did not need to make great new endowments. In the late 1390s Gaunt succeeded in making his Beaufort sons landed nobles mainly through new purchases and royal grants. By then he had made massive permanent augmentations in Lancastrian resources and privileges – the royal grants of lordships in Hertfordshire, Yorkshire, Sussex and Norfolk;[79] the interest in half of one of the largest comital inheritances, through his son Henry's marriage to Mary de Bohun, and the establishment of the hereditary palatinate.

Finances

In the year to Michaelmas 1331, Henry earl of Lancaster had a net income of £6,877 from his estates (£8,074 gross); Professor K. Fowler arrives at a tentative total of over £8,380 gross for Duke Henry's income from his English and Welsh estates.[80] Gaunt's estate income, according to the valuations drawn up by his auditors for the years ending Michaelmas 1394 and Michaelmas 1395, was about £10,000 net (£11,750 gross).[81] Part of this increase is accounted for by Gaunt's acquisitions: the lordships of Knaresborough, Hertford and Pevensey brought in over £765 clear in the year to Michaelmas 1400.[82]

The bulk of these profits came from assized rents and farms; there were also profits from rights over boroughs, from franchises and feudal rights. The administrative and financial responsibilities of the feodary, the keeper of franchises and fees, have been described by Somerville.[83] There were various sources of feudal revenue which, like fines and amercements (unfixed penalties) made in franchisal courts, produced a fluctuating revenue. In 1374 orders were given to stewards, keepers of fees and franchises, and feodaries to enquire into wardships and marriages recently escheated and due to escheat, and to certify them to the council.[84] Wardships and marriages were often sold by the duke (sometimes to members of the family concerned) for payment in instalments: in 1380 the council was scrutinising and probably making these bargains. The sums involved (for example, £120, £100, £40, 20*m*.)[85] were worthwhile windfalls. Lancastrian, like royal wardships, were used as a means of rewarding distinguished servants. In 1392–3 Thomas Pinchbeck, chief steward of Lancashire, held the marriage and wardship of a local heir, John Harington.[86] In the year to Michaelmas 1377, the receiver-general William Bugbrigge had received £34 from the keepers of fees in various shires and £858 in payments for wardships, marriages and other obligations.[87] In that year Gaunt's feudal revenues started to be boosted by the grant to him of palatine rights in Lancashire: by virtue of these, his exercise of the right to wardship and marriage was not restricted by the Crown's prerogative of enjoying it in the case of any estate a fraction of which was held in chief.

A more occasional expedient, intended to bring in large profits speedily, was the levy of a feudal aid. In February and April 1372 Gaunt notified the officials in his lordships that he had appointed sets of commissioners to make assemblies of his tenants; the commissioners were to request freemen, and command bondmen, to grant him an aid in his great necessity. This was presumably to assist his intended expedition to France, for which preparations were in train.[88] In the same year Gaunt raised an aid from his free tenants in order to marry his eldest daughter, at the rate of 20s. on the knight's fee and on £20 worth of rent held in socage.[89] In 1378–9 the sheriff of Lancashire was ordered by ducal warrant to levy an aid for the knighting of Bolingbroke, as Gaunt's eldest son – the ceremony had been performed by Edward III in 1377. Feodaries received similar orders elsewhere.[90]

What range of incomes did Gaunt receive from particular lordships? They might be affected by various factors besides the general economic ones depressing the profits of noble landowners in the second half of the fourteenth century. These economic trends, Professor Holmes has argued, were principal causes of 'the beginning of a slow but perceptible decline in the lord's profits' evident in the last decades of the century on the Lancastrian estates.[91] Perennial factors – the degree of continuity in effective lordship and of efficiency in conciliar and ministerial management – accounted for considerable fluctuations in income. The honour of Richmond, granted to Queen Philippa for the upkeep of her children in 1341, seems then to have been indifferently managed and to have made poor returns. The valuation put on the rental value of the earldom of Richmond was £1,333 6s. 8d, the same amount, indeed, as in 1269. In 1381, nine years after Gaunt had relinquished possession of it, its rental was valued at £1,796: Professor Jones calculates the income in 1383–4 as over £1,455. It seems likely that by the 1370s Gaunt's administration in the earldom had raised its income near to the late thirteenth-century level of expectation; his officials certainly made strenuous efforts to repair its properties and protect the lord's rights.[92]

The remotest Lancastrian lordship in the realm was Dunstanburgh, on the coast of Northumberland not far from the Scottish border. This was a valuable lordship, assessed as worth £220 *p.a.* in 1361.[93] In 1373 Gaunt anticipated that its receiver would be able to produce (on top of his income earmarked for fees) 100 marks for the repayment of a loan; in 1376–7 the receiver was able to contribute £133 to the receiver-general's income and in 1392–3 £40.[94] The lordship had suffered from the Anglo-Scottish hostilities of 1384–9.[95] In 1399–1400 its clear value was £130 8*s.* 10*d.* Large arrears (£41 6*s.* 1*d.*) were debited to the reeve of the manor of Dunstanburgh and the value of the Tweed fishery was reduced.[96]

The lordship of Knaresborough in Yorkshire, granted to Gaunt in part compensation for the loss of the honour of Richmond in 1372, was valued at £668 13*s.* 4*d.* in 1364.[97] Gaunt considered that its previous administration under his mother's officials had been lax. His attempts at reform (see p.331) encountered resistance, and he does not seem to have succeeded in restoring it to its earlier nominal value. The collector of rents in Knaresborough accounted for receipts of £233 in 1382–3; in 1391–2, after a long period of disturbances in the forest, the collector accounted for £194.[98] By 1399–1400 the revenue from Knaresborough had somewhat recovered; it stood at £390.[99] Pontefract, bringing in £789, was the most valuable of the Yorkshire lordships, and Pickering produced £260 – £138 less than the combined total for these two lordships in 1361.[100] Lancashire was Gaunt's most buoyant northern source of income, assessed at £982 in 1361 and producing £1,668 in 1399–1400, a remarkable increase resulting doubtless from Gaunt's exploitation of its renewed palatine status. In neighbouring Cheshire, the income from the lordship of Halton declined over this period from £312 to £272. The Staffordshire and Derbyshire properties were of far greater value.[101] In 1380 the great council decided that the receiver of the lordship of Tutbury (Staffs.) should contribute 1,000 marks *p.a.* to the expenses of the wardrobe, in addition to 500 marks *p.a.* for the duchess's chamber and wardrobe and the other annuities charged on the lordship.[102] In 1392–3 the clear income from the lordship was £1,763, but this had fallen to £1,391 in 1399–1400.[103] The Derbyshire income in 1392–3 was £696.[104]

Gaunt's most valuable lordship in the south parts was the honour of Bolingbroke in Lincolnshire and Huntingdonshire. Its income seems to have shrunk considerably, from £1,481 in 1383–4 to £1,049 in 1399–1400.[105] The first plague pandemic had produced a sharp decline in income from the honour of Leicester. The gross income accounted for by the receiver in the year to Michaelmas 1348 was £786, but this was down to £635 in the year to Michaelmas 1352.[106] However, by the 1370s there had been a remarkable recovery – in 1376–7 the receiver-general received £809 from the lordship.[107] By the 1390s income had drifted downwards – to £688 clear in 1392–3, £708 in 1399–1400.[108] The Norfolk lordship was more lucrative, nearly as much so as the honour of Bolingbroke. In 1376–7 the receiver for Norfolk and Suffolk contributed £671 to the receiver-general, in 1392–3 £889.[109] In 1379 the receiver had the obligation to provide £500 *p.a.* for the expenses of the wardrobe, but, because of the weight of other assignments on the receivership, he was unable to oblige the wardrobe and was relieved of the burden the following year.[110] The Norfolk revenue was holding up well in the 1390s – £973 in 1392–3, £920 in 1396–7, £997 in 1399–1400.[111] Other important revenue sources in the south parts were the receivership of the south (estates in Dorset, Wiltshire and Gloucestershire), which produced £974 clear in 1399–1400, Northamptonshire (£482), Sussex (£263) and Hertford (£111).[112]

The valuations of 1399–1400 show that Gaunt's properties in the northern parts were slightly more valuable than those in the south (£4,807 to £4,584). As might be expected, no clear national pattern of trends in income appears. Income seems to have remained particularly buoyant on some of the Lancashire, Yorkshire, Staffordshire and Norfolk estates, but there is also widespread evidence to support Professor Holmes's contention that profits were tending to fall in the 1380s and 1390s.

A more uniform and positive trend has been discerned in the Lancastrian lordships in the Marches of Wales. According to Professor Rees Davies, 'The fourteenth century was, on the whole, an era of high and even increasing profits for most Marcher lords'; their relative lack of dependence on demesne profits insulated them from the danger of financial deterioration resulting from the decline of arable demesne farming which was so notable a feature of the English economy in the later fourteenth century. Gaunt's Marcher lordships were of great value to him. Davies has calculated that they produced some 15 per cent of his territorial revenue.[113] Their single most important item of seignorial revenue (as in the majority of Marcher lordships) consisted of land rents and renders; in the three years 1386–8 these accounted for £1,351 out of £1,839 gross revenue in the receivership of Monmouth.[114] In the Marches extraordinary levies were much more lucrative – and burdensome to the tenantry – than in England. Mises (fines on the entry of a new lord) were established and fixed in the Lancastrian lordships by 1400 – £242 for Kidwelly and £67 for Monmouth.[115] The exercise of the lord's judicial authority was another source of profit: a tourn (judicial visitation) would be held by one of the chief officers in a lordship. In 1395 the tourn of Kidwelly produced £155 in communal subsidies, £153 in fines and £8 in confiscated goods.[116]

The Lancastrian estates in England and Wales were to remain Gaunt's principal customary source of income; potentially lucrative French lordships which he inherited or was granted proved a disappointment. The landed endowments he received as the king's son were not financially commensurate with his status. Edward III anticipated that these would be supplemented through the profits of marriage; indeed, by his first marriage, Gaunt soon won the jackpot of English noble inheritances. Consequently, he was less driven by the desire for land acquisition in England and Wales than was common among magnates; he preferred to pursue dynastic aggrandisement by seeking from the Crown palatine rights, wardships and marriages and, in the 1390s, offices and endowments for his younger sons. Nevertheless, his father's failure to provide him with a princely endowment may have justified, in his eyes, his later possession of a large slice of the Crown's patrimony, the duchy of Aquitaine.

Gaunt's greatest augmentation of revenues after his first marriage resulted from his settlement with Juan I of Castile in 1388: he was to receive from Castile a capital payment of 600,000 francs (£100,000) and an annual pension for life of 40,000 francs (£6,600).[117] Despite a penalty clause, the pension probably always remained in arrears, but the large sums in Iberian and other foreign coin accounted for by the receiver-general in 1393 and 1395 leave no doubt that the pension transformed Gaunt's finances.[118]

To what extent did Gaunt set an example of princely prudence by living within his means? Receivers-general's accounts provide much information, but not the whole picture, since local receivers paid out on authority of ducal warrants for a variety of costs, debts and obligations. Above all, retainers' fees normally accounted for a large slice of the latter's receipts. In 1392–3 the receipt of Tutbury (clear income £1,762 13s.) paid out £600 9s. 2d. on annuities; Leicester (£708 16d.) £236 13s. 4d; Norfolk (£973 15d.) £245 18s 4d.[119] Bearing these charges in mind, it is instructive to review the evidence of the receivers-general's accounts. For the year 1376–7 the receiver-general accounted for £12,803: he was comfortably able to meet expenses of £8,752. However, his expenses would have greatly exceeded his receipt if he had not received £6,255 arrears of wages for war from the Exchequer.[120] Payments by Gaunt's receivers on debentures for war services in the 1370s (see pp.220–1) suggest that his estates had borne much of the burden of war debt, besides that of the new annuities he had granted (see p.215); it is likely that receivers-general in the early 1370s were starved of funds and unable, like Bugbrigge in 1376–7, to pay many instalments of annuities. It is significant that he did not record any loans made by the duke, but the repayment of two substantial loans, £767 to the London financier John Philpot and £667 to the earl of Arundel's brother Sir John Arundel.

In the year to February 1392, £9,786 was accounted for in English money, £7,032 from the estates, not much more than in 1376–7; discharges were markedly more (£11,724). Payments at the Exchequer (£2,754) were down; they were for the expenses of Gaunt's diplomatic missions to France, his payment of a royal subsidy to the count of Foix and the costs of the government of Aquitaine. However, the receiver-general was put into surplus by the large sums in foreign specie at his disposal from the Castilian pension. Much of the increase in expenditure which this facilitated stemmed from Gaunt's lavishness in making loans and gifts to his kinsfolk and friends; above all there was £1,333 paid to Bolingbroke as part of his father's finance for his crusades and pilgrimage to Jerusalem.[121]

The account for the year to February 1395 shows expenses whose total had risen steeply from those of 1392–3, to £16,594. Nevertheless, the receiver-general balanced his account. The contributions of the regional receivers were, in total, puny – only £2,626; they had to absorb the costs of the retinue's annuities. The Exchequer was once more a major contributor, with a total of £6,698 owed for Gaunt's costs in negotiating the Anglo-French treaty at Leulighen in 1394 and for the government of Aquitaine (the latter swollen by the costs of his expedition there). The largest contribution was the Castilian resource – £7,266. The treasurer's role in handling payments for the Gascon expedition doubtless accounts for his heavy expenditure (£5,146 15s.) in the period from 12 August 1394 to 2 February 1395. Other expensive items were the purchase of the reversion of properties from the earl of Salisbury (£2,667), expenses connected with Constance's exequies (£584) and the settlement of her debts (£410).[122] The receiver-general's account for the year to 29 September 1397 presents an entirely different picture. Receipts at £5,589 (£3,127 from the receivers) and expenses at £5,530 (£3,432 on the household, wardrobe and privy wardrobe) were at conspicuously lower levels than in 1376–7, 1392–3 and 1394–5. The Spanish income made a smaller, but significant contribution to the receiver-general's account, but the Crown did not contribute through payment of debts. There was no expenditure on diplomatic missions or 'one-off' expensive items.[123] As demonstrated by the events of the last sixteen months of his life (those after the period of this account), Gaunt had by no means withdrawn from the national and international political scene. However, the year of this account was an abnormally quiet one for him: his expenditure was largely domestic and private, a pattern presaging a more retired way of life, which the pressure of events was soon to negate.

A conspicuous sign of a noble's ability to manage his affairs prudently was his ability to fund adequately a household establishment whose magnificence was commensurate with his rank. However, it was not unusual for nobles to fail to cover running expenses and to accumulate bills. Gaunt's treasurers – whose funds were vulnerable to raids to pay for extra-curricular expenses – were customarily in debt for victuals and other necessities, which they listed in bills headed *Nomina creditorum*. In 1372 the receiver-general was ordered to pay a loan of 1,000 marks from the earl of Arundel to the treasurer Matthew Assheton to reimburse creditors of the household.[124] Between March 1380 and March 1383 the treasurer, the receiver-general and the keepers of Hertford, Kidwelly and Monmouth were ordered to pay off debts incurred for commodities by previous treasurers, sums ranging from £220 down to £13 10s. for wine for Gaunt's consumption and £50 worth for the household's, purchased from Walter Derby of Bristol, a wine importer often used by the household. The biggest single creditor was John Trygg, London fishmonger. These debts (excluding the unstated amount charged to the receiver of Hertford) totalled £633.[125] In September 1383 the treasurer was ordered to use £212 from a sum received from the earl of Nottingham in order to settle debts in the city of London owed from the time of five of his predecessors, going back to Thomas Amcotes (in office in 1371) and the clerk of the wardrobe John Yerdburgh (out of office by 1376).[126] Such payments may, indeed, reflect only a fraction of household debt, but they certainly do not give the impression that the Lancastrian household was massively in debt for commodities in this period.

One of the main problems of household finance for a noble such as Gaunt, with his high retaining, diplomatic and military costs, was to make certain that sufficient funds were available from landed and other resources, which might be sucked out by other pressing assignments. The warrants for payments of sums to the treasurer recorded in the chancery register for the period 5 January to 30 August 1373 show that a total of £3,376 was paid out for household expenses by the receiver-general. He also provided two lump sums of £1,000 in January and April 1373, before finances were put on a war footing for Gaunt's summer campaigning in France. For Easter term 1374, after his return from Gascony, the clerk of the wardrobe was in funds to supply household expenses, in haphazard amounts, but to the sizeable total of £1,465.[127] The receiver-general's account for the year ending Michaelmas 1377 show that he then had the prime role in financing the household; the treasurer's expenses appear to have been high that year. This may be accounted for by Gaunt's frequent residence in London and his attendance at the coronation. Warrants for the year to Michaelmas 1380 (mainly on the receiver-general) totalled £2,626, nearly all of this for the current year.[128] However, the funds the receiver-general had produced or was likely to produce in order to fund the year from Easter 1380 were adjudged inadequate; on the great council's advice, the constable of Dunstanburgh was ordered to pay all his issues for that term and the next for the costs of the household (11 May); so was the receiver of Lancashire and Cheshire, whose letters of assignment for the wardrobe were cancelled.[129]

Like the treasurer, the clerk of the wardrobe was responsible for a large outlay; his funds, too, were vulnerable to 'raiding', for example, to supplement those of the treasurer or to pay instalments of annuities and fees. The relatively few payments by the receiver-general to the clerk of the wardrobe in the years 1371–2 and 1372–3 (compared to his payments to the treasurer)[130] suggest that the clerk was usually more heavily dependent on regular biannual assignments from particular lordships. This produced problems, since the duke and his councillors often overestimated the sums which receivers had in hand, pressing too many warrants for payment on them. In November 1379 Gaunt wrote testily to Adam Pope, the Norfolk receiver, ordering him to pay the clerk of the wardrobe, William Oke, the sums due for Michaelmas and Easter terms to the wardrobe, for which Oke had waited in vain at Kenilworth.[131] The great council considered the problem that had arisen and decided to shift the assignment from the Norfolk receivership: on the council's advice, John Cheyne, receiver of Tutbury, was ordered to make biannual payments of 500 marks to the clerk of the wardrobe.[132] This did not solve Oke's problem; Cheyne paid him nothing at Michaelmas. It was perhaps because Oke was so desperate for cash that the treasurer, John Norfolk, gave the duke £80 for the private expenses of his chamber.[133] Cheyne's explanation for his failure was that his disposable income over the past twelve months had been spent on paying out as ordered by ducal warrants. On 30 November Gaunt told him to levy sums due from before and after Michaelmas and deliver them to Oke as quickly as possible; once he had shown Gaunt that all annuities and fees for that term were fully paid, he was to cease all other payments till Oke was paid in full.[134] The letter gives an inkling of the pressure which bailiffs felt from on high to produce rents and farms; it is notable for its reasonable tone, in contrast to the anger Gaunt often expressed in his communications with defaulting ministers. This suggests a good understanding on his part of the financial problem. One of its causes was that the receiver of Tutbury was also charged with 500 marks *p.a.* for Duchess Constance's chamber and wardrobe; in March 1381 he was relieved of this burden, though his annual contribution to the duke's wardrobe was increased from 1,000 marks to £1,000.[135] It is likely that Cheyne failed to meet his Easter payment fully, for within a month of Easter, on the great council's advice, the receivers of the south, of Pevensey and Leicester were ordered to put aside a total of 500 marks for wardrobe expenses.[136]

The total expenditure on household, great wardrobe and privy wardrobe in the receivers-general's accounts amounted to £5,525 in 1376–7, £4,192 in 1392–3, £7,122 in 1394–5 and £4,432 in 1396–7; it is likely that these figures were supplemented by annual assignments from receiverships of either 1,000 marks or £1,000 for the wardrobes, and possibly by other assignments for the treasurer.[137] These figures are to be contrasted with the annual estate income of £10,000 clear for 1394 and 1395. The level of expenditure on household, affinity, and so on, tended to rise up to and over the level of estate income, producing the problems evident in the 1379–83 register in financing wardrobe and household when estate income was not supplemented from other sources. Gaunt maintained a household notable for its size and distinction; he was assiduous in his building works; he purchased fine jewels and plate, used often for gift exchange. Yet, according to contemporary standards. he was hardly extravagant – except, perhaps, in the size of his fee'd retinue. That, however, could be partly justified by the need for exceptional regional cooperation to keep the Lancastrian inheritance in good order and partly by Gaunt's need for elaborate services to sustain the princely roles to which he aspired. Above all, it was the expenditure necessitated by his dominance in war and diplomacy which at times drove his expenses beyond the resources of the Lancastrian estates.

Notes and References

1 As an earl Gaunt was entitled to the fee farm from the revenues of the shire of the earldom, e.g. £20 *p.a.* from Derbyshire (P.R.O. DL 43/15/4).
2 Dobson RB 1984, p.113n.
3 Astill GG 1977, pp.147ff.
4 Goodman A 1987a.
5 Somerville R 1953, p.373; P.R.O. DL 28/3/2. In 1380 Gaunt ordered gifts of venison from the chase of Peak to be made to local folk, explicitly so that they would respect his game (*J.G.R. 1379–83*, no. 378).
6 Roskell JS 1937, p.6; cf Astill GG 1977, p.151 for a comparison of Lancastrian influences in the composition of parliamentary representation for Lancs., Staffs., Lincs. and Leics.
7 Walker SK 1989: 333.
8 McFarlane KB 1973, pp.134–5.
9 Walker SK 1989.
10 Morgan P 1987, pp.72–3. For Gaunt's retaining of Cheshiremen, ibid., pp.161–2, 169.
11 *R.P.*, Vol. 3, pp.204–5.

12 For Stanley's career, Morgan P 1987, pp.171ff; Bennett MJ 1983, pp.215ff.
13 Walker SK 1989: 340–2.
14 Goodman A 1971, p.29.
15 Walker SK 1989: 333, 342–3.
16 *C.P.R. 1361–4*, p.286; for similar commissions in Yorks., 1363–4, ibid., pp.367, 454, and Norfolk, 1363, ibid., no. 373.
17 *C.P.R. 1367–70*, p.472; *C.P.R. 1374–6*, p.321.
18 Crook D 1987.
19 Walker SK 1983: 87–94; Saul N 1986, pp.28–9, 75, 191.
20 *J.G.R. 1372–6*, no. 326.
21 Ibid., nos 1487–8.
22 Ibid., no. 1523.
23 Ibid., no. 1554.
24 Ibid., nos 1555, 1649.
25 Ibid., no. 1650.
26 For the Yorks. troubles in the 1390s, Bellamy JG 1964–5.
27 *J.G.R. 1372–6*, nos 1275, 1375.
28 *J.G.R. 1379–83*, no. 454.
29 Saul N 1981, pp.80–1, 92–3.
30 Rowling MA 1957: 87ff; James SE 1981: 15. Par was listed among the esquires of the household in Jan. 1381 (East Sussex R.O., Waleys cartulary, no. 3469, B10).
31 *W.C.*, pp.80–3.
32 Northumberland R.O., Swinburne (Capheaton) MSS, ZSW/1/105.
33 P.R.O. DL 29/728/11987.
34 Ibid., 11991.
35 P.R.O. DL 43/15/4.
36 *J.G.R. 1379–83*, nos 757, 1032.
37 DL 43/15/4.
38 *J.G.R. 1379–83*, nos 205, 271. Anton ffauconer had rent remitted for life at Higham Ferrers in 1392–3 (P.R.O. DL 43/15/4).
39 *J.G.R. 1379–83*, nos 1016–43.
40 Ibid., nos 1017, 1030.
41 Birrell JR 1962: 120–4.
42 P.R.O. DL 29/728/11987; cf Shaw RC 1956. p.375.
43 *J.G.R. 1372–6*, no. 1326.
44 *J.G.R. 1379–83*, no. 1038; Somerville R 1953, p.372.
45 P.R.O. DL 29/507/8228.
46 Ibid., 262/4070.
47 Norfolk R.O., MS 15171, 37 B6.
48 Huntington Library, San Marino, HAM Box 1 (19).
49 *J.G.R. 1372–6*, nos 339, 831, 1172.
50 *J.G.R. 1379–83*, nos 695, 1112. In 1381 the farmer of Daventry was ordered to repair a shop there (ibid., no. 520).
51 P.R.O. DL 29/728/11975: text in Holmes G 1957, pp.127–8.
52 P.R.O. DL 29/728/11987.
53 Ibid.
54 Ibid., 11191; P.R.O. DL 43/15/4.
55 *J.G.R. 1372–6*, no. 1652.
56 *J.G.R. 1379–83*, no. 241.
57 Ibid., no. 545.

58 Ibid., no. 600.
59 *J.G.R. 1372–6*, no. 1653.
60 Ibid., no. 1696.
61 *J.G.R. 1379–83*, no. 514.
62 Ibid., no. 213.
63 Ibid., no. 382.
64 Ibid., no. 477.
65 Ibid., nos 436–8.
66 Ibid., no. 365.
67 Ibid., no. 381.
68 Ibid., no. 808.
69 Tuck A 1984, pp.201–2.
70 *J.G.R. 1379–83*, p.xv.
71 P.R.O. DL 29/728/11975; Holmes G 1957, pp.127–8.
72 *J.G.R. 1379–83*, no. 697.
73 Tuck A 1984, pp.201–2.
74 Dobson RB 1970, pp.322–4.
75 *J.G.R. 1379–83*, no. 1242.
76 *J.G.R. 1372–6*, no. 413.
77 *J.G.R. 1379–83*, no. 1018.
78 P.R.O. DL 43/15/4.
79 *Foedera*, 1830, Vol. 3. pt 2, p.949. These estates included Gringley and Wheatley (Notts.), Glatton and Holm (Hunts.) and Soham (Cambs.).
80 Fowler K 1969, p.226.
81 McFarlane KB 1973, p.134.
82 P.R.O. DL 29/728/11987.
83 Somerville R 1953, p.98.
84 *J.G.R. 1372–6*, no. 1584.
85 Cases (1380) of Robert Bayhous (for whose wardship and marriage an annuity of 6 *m.* was also to be paid), William de Bradeshagh, Hugh de Totehill and Thomas Woderofe (*J.G.R. 1379–83*, nos 1046–7, 1049–50).
86 P.R.O. DL 28/3/2; Somerville R 1953, p.373.
87 P.R.O. DL 28/3/1. In 1392–3 the following casualties were accounted for: from Derbys. £12. 16s. 9d., Staffs. £15 11s. 2d., Leics. £15 7s. 4d., Northants. £16 14s. 10d., Sussex £34 12s. 8d., Norfolk £115 6s. 8d. (P.R.O. DL 34/15/4).
88 *J.G.R. 1372–6*, nos 231–43.
89 Ibid., nos 245, 1147, 1263. For a receipt from the Somerset feodary for payment of a contribution, Dunning RW 1968, p.11 (no. 26).
90 Baines E 1836, Vol. 1, p.374. In 1379 the former keeper of fees in Yorks. was ordered to pay the clerk of the great wardrobe £72 levied for the aid (*J.G.R. 1379–83*, no. 320).
91 Holmes G 1957, pp.117–19.
92 Jones M 1970, pp.181–2. Incomes from Norfolk estates (£308 17s 1d. in 1392–3) and from Knaresborough and Sussex (£390 10s. 10d. and £263 6s 9d. respectively in 1399–1400) suggest that Gaunt may have been undercompensated by his father for the loss of the earldom in 1372 (P.R.O. DL 43/15/4; P.R.O. DL 29/78/11987). But this does not cover all the landed compensation.
93 Fowler K 1969, p.226.
94 *J.G.R. 1372–6*, no. 1332; P.R.O. DL 28/3/1; ibid., 2.
95 Bateson E 1895, p.30.

96 P.R.O. DL 29/728/11987. The demesne and mills at the manor were then farmed. So were three coble boats for sea-fishing – a type still found on that coast.
97 *Foedera*, 1830, Vol. 3, pt 2, p.750.
98 P.R.O. DL 29/465/7604; ibid., 7605. Arrears were £13 7s. 9d. in 1382–3 and £37 7s. in 1391–2.
99 P.R.O. DL 29/728/11987.
100 Ibid.; Fowler K 1969, p.226.
101 Ibid., P.R.O. DL 29/728/11987. The receiver-general in 1376–7 received £1,407 from Lancs. and Cheshire combined (P.R.O. DL 28/3/1).
102 *J.G.R. 1379–83*, no. 308.
103 P.R.O. DL 43/15/4; DL 29/728/11987. In 1348 the revenue from the lordship had been only £970 (Fowler K 1969, p.225). The various charges on Tutbury account for the fact that its receiver contributed relatively little to the receiver-general's costs – £353 in 1376–7 (P.R.O. DL 28/3/1), £216 in 1392–3 (ibid., 2) and £250 in 1396–7 (ibid., 5).
104 P.R.O. DL 43/15/4.
105 P.R.O. DL 29/262/4070; DL 29 728/11987. In 1368–9 the income from the receivership had been £2,283; it then included the lands there of the honour of Richmond (P.R.O. DL 29/262/4069). The receiver contributed to the receiver-general £983 in 1376–7 (P.R.O. DL 28/3/1), £52 in 1392–3 (ibid., 2) and £404 in 1396–7 (ibid., 5).
106 Fowler K 1969, p.225. In 1348 there was also £308 income from casuals.
107 P.R.O. DL 28/3/1.
108 Ibid., DL 43/15/4; ibid., DL 29/728/11987; Huntington Library, San Marino, HAM Box 49 (1).
109 P.R.O. DL 28/3/1; DL 28/3/2.
110 *J.G.R. 1379–83*, no. 397; cf above, p.348.
111 P.R.O. DL 43/15/4; Norfolk R.O., MS 15171, 37 B6; P.R.O. DL 29/728/1991.
112 P.R.O.; DL 29/728/11987.
113 Davies RR 1978, p.189.
114 Ibid., p.178.
115 Ibid., p.186 and n.
116 Ibid., p.167.
117 Russell PE 1955; p.506 and n.
118 P.R.O. DL 28/3/2; DL28 32/21. Gaunt's envoys to Castile in 1393 complained of arrears (Russell PE 1955, p.538) and he referred to arrears in his will.
119 P.R.O. DL 43/15/4.
120 P.R.O. DL 28/3/1.
121 DL28/3/2.
122 DL28/32/21. I have relied heavily on the analysis of this summary of account in Armitage-Smith S 1904, pp.447–50.
123 P.R.O. DL 28/3/5.
124 *J.G.R. 1372–6*, no. 1002.
125 *J.G.R. 1379–83*, nos 226, 232, 546, 638, 745. 834.
126 Ibid., no. 914.
127 *J.G.R. 1372–6*, nos 885–6, 906, 921, 971, 1059, 1402, 1441, 1458, 1546, 1665, 1671.
128 *J.G.R. 1379–83*, nos 92, 175, 206, 228, 423, 463.

129 Ibid., nos 303–4.
130 *J.G.R. 1372–6*, nos 894, 909, 1091, 1159.
131 *J.G.R. 1379–83*, no. 93.
132 Ibid., nos. 308, 397.
133 Ibid., no. 423.
134 Ibid., nos 421, 432.
135 Ibid., nos 308, 482–3.
136 Ibid., nos 322–4.
137 Gaunt made an assignment on the receiver-general's account of £5,000 *p.a.* to the treasurer commencing 21 May 1391 (P.R.O. DL 28/3/1).

Chapter Fifteen

Gaunt Characterised

The lack of reliable and revealing biographical detail makes it difficult to reach sure conclusions about many aspects of Gaunt's personality. We do not even know what he looked like. The wall paintings completed by 1363, representing him and other members of Edward III's family, which once existed in St Stephen's Chapel in Westminster Palace, depicted a conventional mailed figure.[1] So apparently did the armoured effigy which was on his tomb in St Paul's.[2] The fifteenth-century portraits in stained glass in the St Cuthbert window in York Minister and in the chapel of All Souls College, Oxford, give no certain guide to his appearance.[3] In 1380 Alan Strayler executed a miniature portrait of the duke in the *Liber Benefactorum* of St Albans Abbey.[4] This shows him with curly, light-coloured hair, a forked beard, full lips and a somewhat florid complexion for a man of forty. Fernão Lopes, writing many years later, gave a description of Gaunt in 1386 which may have been based on the reminiscences of his daughter Queen Philippa, her husband João I, or elderly Portuguese courtiers. Gaunt 'was a well-built man, tall and upright, carrying less weight than one would expect from the size of his frame. He would be about sixty years old, with fewer white hairs than is normal for one of his age. He spoke well and without haste, being self-controlled and good-humoured'.[5] He was in fact then forty-six; strain and illness on the León campaign may have caused him loss of weight.

Gaunt was certainly robust. Between the ages of ten and forty-seven he took part in twelve major military and naval expeditions. He apparently suffered no lasting ill effects from the injury he received from a falling pit prop at the siege of Limoges in 1370.[6] He coped well physically too in the 1367 campaign which undermined the Black Prince's health and on the 1369 campaign in northern France from which Lord Percy was invalided home and on which the earl of Warwick died of plague. Though many barons and knights died in the epidemics which ravaged his forces in Spain in 1386–7, Gaunt survived what Froissart alleged was a serious illness.[7] 'Maestre Loys de Luca, fisigo del señor duque', one of the witnesses to Gaunt's and Constance's confirmation at Bayonne in July 1388 of the treaty with Juan I, may have been in close attendance on the duke because the latter was sick – his appearance as a ducal witness is unique.[8] At the age of fifty-four Gaunt was to consider seriously crusading in distant places. But not long after, in 1395, he declined to commit himself to attend Bolingbroke's proposed marriage in Brittany, as its duchess wished: 'as to this consider that it will be very hard going and very uncomfortable for him to sail'.[9] His health may have suddenly deteriorated. In a letter to Richard probably dating from the late 1390s he alluded to a recurrent illness which frequently incapacitated him.[10] Hard living on campaign and in the hunting field (combined with a rich and unbalanced diet) probably frequently undermined the health of medieval nobles who survived into middle age. Edmund of Langley's presumed skeleton, that of a powerful man, has a crippled spine consistent with wounds.[11] Some time during the three months or so between Bolingbroke's exile and Gaunt's death, the former's envoy was told by ducal physicians that his father was mortally ill, according to Froissart.[12] Ill-health may have prompted Gaunt to make a new will in February 1398 and to procure a licence, granted the following September, for the setting up and endowment of a chantry for Catherine and himself.[13] Nevertheless, in March 1398 he led a diplomatic mission to the Scottish border east of Jedburgh and was expected in October to return to the border in 1399 (see pp. 164, 166).

Though Gaunt appeared attired and accompanied with suitable magnificence on public occasions, he was remembered as an example of moderation in dress.[14] Chaucer did not feel it necessary to flatter his appearance in *The Boke of the Duchesse*. He had, according to various sources, an imposing presence and was an eloquent, if sometimes prolix public speaker. Like his Plantagenet forbears, he gave vent to a blazing temper. Circumspection and courtesy then went by the board: it was easy to accuse him of being a bully. He addressed a Gascon delegation in 1390 'at great length and with scant courtesy'.[15] The earl of Arundel asserted in 1394 that he used 'great and harsh words' in council and parliament, so that the earl and others often dared not fully declare their intent.[16] It was easy to hate and fear a prince who combined these traits with such power and ability, and who was determined to uphold his dynastic status by an unrelenting pursuit of land and office and to exact his property rights to the full.

But Gaunt could be likeable. He loyally served his father and the Black Prince; though some of his actions towards Richard were more questionable, he was suitably deferential and remarkably forbearing. His relations with his children were apparently on the whole cordial: he was tireless in promoting his sons' interests. He had a gift for friendship. Froissart says that in 1392 there was a loving reunion between him and the count-dauphin of Auvergne, who had been a good companion in England when a hostage for John II of France in the 1360s.[17] Gaunt was reputed a merciful man: Knighton tells how he forbade his officers to prosecute members of his household who had stolen his silver vessels, saying that he did not wish any man to die for his goods. The poet Hoccleve says that he was merciful.[18] He continued to give protection to those in his patronage, John Wycliffe, William Swinderby, John Northampton, when it was no longer patently meritorious or politic to do so. His determination to punish intimidation by his followers seems to have been genuine. He was receptive to complaints that his estate officials had overstepped the mark and exhorted them, sometimes in harsh phrases, to exact his rights to the full and no more. Those with a variety of grievances hoped for his mercy in helping to have them redressed.

Gaunt could be adept at winning over lesser folk by his charm when he was in an affable mood or when he recognised the advantage in doing so. The courtesy and delicate condescension which Chaucer attributed to him in *The Boke of the Duchesse* is confirmed by Froissart and French chroniclers. It is seen in the delightful story of his encounter in the Limoges mine in 1370. His opponent in combat there excused himself as a poor and undistinguished knight: Gaunt hastened to reassure him: 'I am indeed very happy to prove myself against such a good knight as yourself.'[19] His ability to set the awed at ease made him a formidably manipulative diplomat. In 1384 he interrupted the duke of Brittany's envoy Robert Brocherel, asking him to write down his master's requests, because he (Gaunt) 'cannot remember nor hear half of what the said Procurator said, because he had a head and memory feeble at remembering, he said'.[20] According to Froissart, the following year he extracted information from João I of Portugal's envoy, the chancellor Lourenço Anes Fogaça, by his garrulous ramblings, frank avowals of his shortcomings and high good humour. When Fogaça listed the Castilian casualties at the battle of Aljubarrota,

he was interrupted by a burst of laughter from the duke, and Laurence asked, 'My lord, what makes you laugh so heartily?' 'Why, have I not sufficient cause? For I never in my life heard such a catalogue of strange names as you are repeating.'[21]

This anecdote may, indeed, be an invention of Froissart's – the duke had been used to grappling with Spanish names for nearly twenty years. But Froissart considered that he was painting a recognisable portrait. A habitual admirer of Gaunt – 'qui sage et vaillant prince estoit'[22] – he on occasion drew attention to his acts of duplicity. Gaunt's political skills led the unenthusiastic Westminster Chronicler to give him grudging praise, commending his prudence and ability.[23] One of Gaunt's harshest critics, Thomas Walsingham, unintentionally paid tribute to a princely quality which probably often saved Gaunt from the disasters which his ambitions courted – the ability to accept unpalatable advice. In 1376, Walsingham says, one of his councillors strongly criticised his dismissiveness about the Commons. Gaunt consequently modified his opposition to them, though, the chronicler says, his more amenable behaviour was insincere (see p.56).[24] It is a revealing vignette, displaying both a princely hauteur and politic flexibility. This latter quality was most significantly displayed in his renunciation of the right to a Crown (following his father's precedent). It was a statesmanlike act which his descendants the Lancastrian kings would have benefited Christendom by emulating, with respect to their claim to the French Crown.

Moralists found one aspect of Gaunt's character reprehensible – they regarded him as inclined to lechery, a reputation which was alive in Henry VI's reign, as an anecdote told by Thomas Gascoigne reveals (see p.167). Walsingham denounced him for dishonouring the Duchess Constance by cohabiting openly with Catherine Swynford.[25] The chronicler Knighton, favourably inclined to the duke, was embarrassed by this behaviour. Both writers – and the Anonimalle Chronicler – gave prominence to the duke's expressions of repentance for his immorality when he was humiliated during the Peasants' Revolt (see p.246). The diffusion of these accounts suggests that the duke publicly humbled himself – and did so in part to counteract unfavourable reactions to his behaviour. His long-lasting relationship with Catherine (which survived this crisis) was not his only liaison. He had an affair with one of his mother's *domicellae*, Marie de Saint Hilaire, by whom he had a daughter, Blanche. Marie was in receipt of a life annuity of 20 marks from him at the time of his death.[26] Either in 1380 or 1381, Gaunt married Blanche to a leading Norfolk landowner, Sir Thomas Morieux, presenting her with a table service on the day of her marriage and an annuity for their joint lives of £100.[27] The couple remained in Gaunt's favour: on New Years Day 1382 he gave both of them a 'hanap' (cup) and in 1383 a rent of over £25 for past service, from a Norfolk manor, and Morieux a lease of Fakenham (Norfolk).[28] Morieux had a good reputation as a soldier: Gaunt made him a marshal of his army in Galicia in 1386 and there he showed adeptness in conducting small-scale operations. Froissart's repetition of Morieux's verbal sallies suggests that he enjoyed a reputation as a wit in the Lancastrian household and beyond, expressed (if Froissart is to be believed) in a mocking humour, perhaps akin to his father-in-law's.[29]

Thus, despite the austere and reserved figure which Chaucer and Hoccleve gave to Gaunt, he had an addiction to *luxuria*. His lifestyle provided one of the most notable examples of that multi-faceted conspicuous consumption characteristic of princely European families in the fourteenth century. In his case the style was probably copied in part from that of his father and his father's companions such as Duke Henry, and in part probably reflected the tastes of John II of France and the French nobles who were hostages in England for him, and whom Gaunt came to know well at an impressionable age. Gaunt's lifestyle and court probably provided the closest English counterpart to those of Charles V's brothers, in the number of knights and esquires customarily in attendance on him, the splendour of his jewels, plate and furnishings, the elaboration of his banquets, the resources of his stable, kennels, mews and forests. Kenilworth, Tutbury and Pontefract Castles were fitting counterparts of French princely châteaux. Gaunt had a particular love of exquisite sets of French tapestries, *draps d'Arras*, reflected in his references to them and their purchase in his will.[30] It is likely that Richard II's francophile tastes were in part an emulation of his uncle's. The princely practice of discriminating consumption might bring public rewards as well as private pleasure. Froissart says that Gaunt entertained João of Portugal to dinner at Ponto do Mouro with the same magnificence he might easily have summoned up in London or Hertford.[31]

One of Gaunt's addictions was the hunt, a hereditary sort of addiction – Walsingham in his obituary of Edward III remarked on his love of hunting, and of falconry as well.[32] Gaunt's enthusiasm for such sport is reflected in the care he lavished on the maintenance of his forests and parks, the finest private collection of hunting preserves in England.[33] Folk memories of his hunts long survived (see p.24). It may be a tribute to these predilections that Chaucer set his dreamer in *The Boke of the Duchesse* in a forest. The king hunting there

> Gan [quikly] hoomward for to ryde
> Unto a place ther besyde,
> Which was from us but a lyte,
> A long castel with walles whyte,
> By seynt Johan! on a riche hil.
>   [i.e., Richmond]

Chaucer seems to be describing a prime Lancastrian forest, dwelling on the magnificence of the trees, how well proportioned and spaced, and how well stocked the woodlands were with wild life. This setting was likely to have a particular appeal to Gaunt as a reader. But the depth of his grief as the 'man in black' in the poem, isolated from his normal companionable pleasures, is emphasised by his indifference to the exciting hunting scene going on around him and to its exquisite sylvan setting, of which the dream-poet is keenly aware.

The hunt was an abiding enthusiasm which Gaunt shared with close kinsfolk such as his nephew Edward earl of Rutland.[34] A few years after Gaunt's death Edward translated into English (adding observations of his own) *Le Livre de la chasse* composed by Gaunt's friend Gaston Fébus, count of Foix.[35] One of Gaunt's best rewarded and most devoted servants was Walter Urswick, who became his master of game. As Gaunt's esquire, in February 1361 he was granted for life the keeping of the new forest in Richmondshire (perhaps the one Chaucer had in mind) and in October his annuity of £10 was doubled. The following year Gaunt appointed Urswick his master of game.[36] The Black Prince (in whose service he had been in 1353) granted him an annuity of £20 for bringing news that Blanche had borne a child.[37] In 1374 Gaunt gave Urswick an expensively decorated hunting horn, ornamented with gold and pearls; as a New Year's present in 1381 he gave Urswick a goblet.[38] This old companion of the hunting field and battlefield was soon to prove his outstanding loyalty. He was prepared to risk all by going into exile with the duke that summer (see p.82). Urswick was in receipt of a royal favour from the duke in 1393, not long before his death.[39]

Like his father, Gaunt was keen on falconry. An Italian observer noted that he entered Bruges with hawk on wrist in 1375.[40] In 1380 the Grand Master of the Teutonic Order thought that six falcons made an acceptable present for him, and in 1396–7 the falconer of Giangaleazzo Visconti, duke of Milan, presented him with falcons.[41] Gaunt often paid large sums for birds to stock his mews or to give as presents. Falconry was an enthusiasm which he shared with Richard's half-brothers Thomas and John Holand: in 1380 he presented a 'sore' falcon (young male) to each of them.[42] The ducal mews acquired an international reputation; according to Froissart, Gaunt sent João of Portugal two outstanding peregrine falcons (and six greyhounds).[43] Gaunt was served for many years as falconer by John Saffrey. In 1368 he was granted a life annuity of 40s., increased to £4 in 1372.[44] The master falconer in 1383 was Arnold Fauconer, who had the rank of esquire and a life annuity of £10 in return for service in war as well as peace.[45] Nobles enjoyed their hawking and hunting on campaign; licence to trespass on their opponents' game was a privilege of war.

359

The chronicler Jean le Bel describes Edward and his sons hunting their way through northern France in 1359: Froissart the English nobles trying out their packs after they landed at La Coruña in 1386.[46] At the mews in 1381, besides Arnold Fauconer, there were two other falconers, Antoyn and Haukyn, and three porters, William, Pool and Eylkyn. They had charge of thirteen falcons.[47]

As well as being a keen huntsman and falconer, Gaunt was a devotee of the combat, both in war and peace. Despite his disclaimer to Fogaça – 'I am no great knight myself' – when a young man he had won fame in single combat at the siege of Limoges. Allegedly he told Fogaça, 'My greatest delight is the hearing of gallant deeds of arms'. Then in his mid forties, he probably tended to watch rather than participate in jousts.[48] The lance and ornate shield which hung on his tomb in the seventeenth century may have been memorials of his delight in chivalrous sports. During the León campaign he insisted that the French knight Reginald de Roye should fulfil his challenge to Sir John Holand in his presence. The English spectators accused the Frenchman of fighting unfairly, since his helmet was not fastened securely:

> 'Hold your tongues', said the duke, 'and let them alone: in arms everyone takes what advantage he can: if Sir John thinks there is any disadvantage . . . he may do the same. But, for my part, were I in their situations, I would lace my helmet as tight as possible; and if one hundred were asked their opinions, there would be fourscore of my way of thinking.'[49]

In 1389 Froissart was present at Bordeaux among the knights and esquires of Béarn and of the count of Foix's household, when five members of Gaunt's household fought over three days five of Charles VI's allegiance in the square before the cathedral. The duke, the duchess and their daughter Catalina were spectators. Gaunt became very angry when a knight on the English side killed the Bastard of Chauvigny's horse: 'he blamed the knight much for having pointed his lance low, and presented the bastard with one of his own horses'.[50] Such vignettes suggest the middle-aged sports enthusiast, irascible and opiniated about the play in which he can no longer easily participate. Pride in the jousting career of Bolingbroke may have been a bond between a father and son with conflicting political opinions.

A little about the duke's temperament and familiar milieu is revealed by what is known of his family relationships. There is Chaucer's image in *The Boke of the Duchesse* of his grief at Blanche's death. One cannot be sure that Chaucer intended to reproduce actual emotions rather than apposite literary conventions. But it may be significant that the poet apotheosised the relationship of duke and duchess in the ideal world of *amour courtois*. Froissart as well as Chaucer was to lament Blanche's death; it is not improbable that she captivated the duke. The fame of the magnificent tomb which he provided for her spread abroad; she lay, according to the Monk of St Denys, 'in sepultura incomparabili'.[51] The celebration of her obit there was a principal event in the Lancastrian liturgical year: Gaunt chose to be buried next to her rather than with either of his other wives.

It is significant that the Monk of St Denys thought that it was Constance, not Blanche, whose tomb in St Paul's was so splendid. It may be a reflection of Gaunt's relationship with Constance that she was buried in relative obscurity at Leicester. After his marriage to Constance in 1371, Gaunt had her fittingly provided with gifts of jewels and clothes. Her separate wardrobe and household were adequately funded and she was lodged with due magnificence. The fact that Constance failed to provide a son who survived infancy was a blow to the pair's dynastic interests.

They had only one surviving child, whereas Gaunt's first wife and his long-term mistress were prolific. His continuing liaison with Catherine Swynford and the birth of their children in the 1370s confirmed the marriage to Constance as one of political convenience alone; they probably ceased to cohabit. He showed concern for Constance's danger during the Great Revolt of 1381, and after it they were publicly reconciled with a dramatic display of affection (see p.88). In the 1380s Gaunt relied heavily on her judgement in Iberian affairs, according to Froissart's anecdotes, though he attributes to her a fierce hatred of the House of Trastamara in 1387 which, if accurate, must have made acceptance of the Treaty of Bayonne difficult for her.[52] After 1388 she lost her political importance and was ignored by the chroniclers – and possibly by Gaunt too: she was an obstacle to his cherished legitimation of his Beaufort children. But Constance kept the good opinions she had won widely in England, especially at St Albans Abbey, into whose confraternity she had been received in 1386.[53] In 1393 she was a guest of Bishop Braybrooke at a hunting party at his country house, Much Hadham (Herts.).[54] Nuns from Stamford attended her funeral at Leicester.[55] But there was more to Constance than the face of a pious queen, fanatical in her filial devotion, wronged by her husband. She had in the late 1370s a jester called Yevan, perhaps a Welshman or Breton, perhaps comically nicknamed after the hero of romance.[56] In 1388 she had in her entourage a 'wild knight' – presumably mimicking for the entertainment of her and her ladies the 'wodewose', the savage forest denizen of contemporary Anglo-French courtly literature and art.[57]

It is likely that Gaunt's adultery in the late 1370s had a negative effect on his political standing. The condemnations of it by monastic chroniclers probably reflect lay opinion as well as religious bias. Walsingham tells, under the year 1378, how Gaunt flaunted his liaison, even in the duchess's presence, and how, during the Peasants' Revolt, he repented and rejected his mistress.[58] The Anonimalle Chronicler of St Mary's Abbey, York, considered Catherine 'a she-devil and enchantress'.[59] Knighton (close to sources in the ducal household), recounting the duke's repentant ruminations in Edinburgh in 1381, has him recalling how he had frequently been told of the ill effects of his adultery on his reputation by clerics and members of his household (*a suis domesticis*).[60] The liaison may have factionalised his retainers and dependents to some extent, since it provided an alternative means of approaching the duke to the proper one provided by his wife. The burgesses of Leicester decided to use Catherine, not Constance, as their means of access. The mayor's account for 1375–6 has an allowance for wine sent to her. In 1377–9 the mayor sent her presents, a horse and an iron pan, the latter a reward

> for expediting the business touching the tenement of Stretton, and other business for which a certain lord besought the aforesaid Catherine with good effect for the said business and besought so successfully that the aforesaid town was pardoned the lending of silver to the king in that year.[61]

Two passages in *The Canterbury Tales* may have a bearing on the issue of Gaunt's marital problems. One is the panegyric on Pedro I and lament for his cruel death in *The Monkes Tale*. It is unlikely that Gaunt thought well of Pedro; the information Chaucer had about his death is precise and accurate, and the animus against his betrayer notable. Chaucer may have been writing as a sympathiser with Constance.[62] A passage in *The Physicians Tale*, whose significance Professor Cowling noted, suggests scant sympathy with the poet's sister-in-law Catherine Swynford. In this passage Chaucer referred to the past peculations of governesses who formed liaisons with their master. Though what he says does not fit Catherine's case, it cannot but call her to mind.[63]

These references cannot be taken as clear testimony of the attitudes current in Gaunt's household in the 1370s. Chaucer was writing a decade or so later; there is no evidence that he had ever been a member of Gaunt's household, and he is not known to have had close associations with Gaunt's *familiares*. Gaunt retained Chaucer in 1374 with a standard annuity for esquires of £10, with no stipulation for war service or provision for *bouche de court* (daily fare) and household wages.[64] Chaucer was a member of the royal household, who had recently showed his worth on diplomatic missions. Nevertheless, Chaucer's attitudes may reflect, besides a family sense of shame at his sister-in-law's ambiguous role, devotion within the Lancastrian household to Constance. In August 1372 (less than a year after she arrived in England), Gaunt ordered the payment of an annuity of £10 to Chaucer's wife Philippa, granted to her for past and future service to Constance. None of her other *domicellae* received such a high reward.[65] It is likely that Philippa Chaucer was one of Constance's first English confidantes (despite the fact that her sister was the duke's mistress) and that Chaucer's remarks about Pedro and about errant mistresses reflect divided loyalties in the ducal household as well as the Chaucer family circle.

Catherine Swynford, who became the duke's third wife in 1396, was a daughter of Payn de Roet, a knight from Hainault in Queen Philippa's service. Catherine married Sir Hugh Swynford (d.1372), a Lincolnshire landowner and ducal retainer. On 24 January 1365 she was described as *ancille* (female servant) of the duchess of Lancaster; she then received episcopal permission to have divine service celebrated whenever she was staying within Leicester, up to Pentecost.[66] Her fellow countryman Froissart remarked (apropos her marriage in 1396) that she was well suited to assume the role of duchess, since she had been brought up in princely courts since her youth.[67] Only a lady with outstanding courtly accomplishments would have been appointed governess of Blanche's daughters Philippa and Elizabeth, a post she was holding in July 1376 (when Gaunt granted her a wardship especially for good service to the girls) and still held in 1380–1.[68] Her office may have seemed a good cover for the duke's visits to her. In the 1370s she gave birth to four of his children – John, Henry, Thomas and Joan, whose births Armitage-Smith dated tentatively in 1373, 1375, 1377 and 1379.[69] The surname they were given, Beaufort, may have been akin to the romantic ones found in chivalrous poetry; there is no obvious reason whey they should have been named after an obscure (and lost) Lancastrian lordship in France.

The scandal caused by their births was probably enhanced by Catherine's attachment as governess to the ducal household. During pregnancy and lying-in she probably retired to the Swynford manor of Kettlethorpe, not far from Lincoln. Childbirth may be connected with the appearances of Kettlethorpe in the ducal registers. In January 1375 Gaunt ordered wine to be sent to Kettlethorpe as soon as possible, and in July he ordered wood to be sent from his parks at Gringley and Wheatley (Notts.) to repair Catherine's houses there.[70] He dated warrants at Kettlethorpe for three successive days in 1379.[71] Catherine was lavishly rewarded. In February 1377 Gaunt received royal licence to grant her Gringley and Wheatley for life;[72] early in 1381 there are references to his grant of a wardship and marriage to her, and to the cosily domestic gift of a silver chafing-pan (*chaufour*).[73] But soon afterwards Gaunt's vicissitudes during the Peasants' Revolt led to his repentance and public undertaking to give her up. She ceased to be governess; on 7 September he granted her for good service to his daughters the huge annuity of 200 marks for life.[74] She may have retired to live more discreetly at Kettlethorpe – but perhaps in some style. In front of the post-medieval Kettlethorpe Hall is a reconstituted medieval arch, which hints at unexpected magnificence.[75] Gaunt's marriage to Catherine in 1396 was for the purpose of enabling their children to be legitimised.[76] The new duchess was duly honoured at court; she was prominent at the king's wedding festivities at Calais.[77] In 1398 Gaunt made lavish bequests to her, including all the jewels he kept in a little coffer, his best royal badge of the white hart, with a fine ruby, and his best collar with 'all the diamonds'.

Gaunt had four legitimate and five illegitimate children who survived infancy. The eldest of the former was Philippa (1360–1415). Since she was married only at the age of twenty-six, her father may have grown used to her adult company and have developed a particular affection for her. As queen of Portugal she won golden opinions; Lopes preserves details of her pious observances, which may have been based on practices in her father's household. Her role in Portugal is symbolised in her effigy on her tomb in the monastery at Batalha; she clasps her husband João I with one hand and a liturgical book with the other.[78] Philippa's younger sister Elizabeth (1364?–1425) was of a less serious temperament. She was married at Kenilworth in 1380 to the much younger earl of Pembroke; her father gave her a gold ring set with a ruby on her wedding day.[79] As we have seen, her seduction by Sir John Holand ended the marriage before her husband was old enough to consummate it and she married the dashing and ruthless Holand (see above, p.280). When in her mid-thirties she outshone the young ladies at court, winning the prize for dancing on one occasion in 1398.[80] Less than a year after her husband's lynching in 1400, she married another famous jouster, one of lower social status – Sir John Cornewall, who captivated her at a joust at York in which he worsted two foreign opponents. Dr Emery has characterised her as 'formidable' in her determination to restore the family estates after Holand's forfeiture. Her effigy – tall, slender-featured – can be seen on her tomb in Burford church (Salop).[81]

Their brother Henry (1366?–1413) was the apple of his father's eye. In his teens Henry was addressed by one of his father's titles, earl of Derby, and had his own household and estates. In 1380

Gaunt apparently risked jeopardising his relations with his brother Woodstock in order to provide Henry with a great marriage and another inheritance (see p. 276). In the early 1390s Gaunt gave financial and diplomatic support for his son's crusades and pilgrimages. His delight in Henry's prowess is reflected in his bequest to him of all his armours, swords and 'dags'. Gaunt's youngest legitimate child, Catherine (1372–1418), Constance's daughter, was described by Froissart as beautiful, but in Spain she was considered rather tall and unfeminine. Catherine, or Catalina, had a more difficult role to play than her sisters, for she had to adapt to a court which was indifferent or hostile to English ways. The premature death of her husband in 1406 and the minority of her son Juan II led to her emergence, as co-regent, as a figure of considerable political importance: she did not make the mistake of appearing anglophile.[82]

Gaunt's affection for his Beaufort children, remarked on by Froissart, was amply demonstrated by his care to secure their legitimation in 1396–7, as well as to advance their fortunes as they approached adulthood.[83] The eldest, Sir John Beaufort (1373–1410) had a chivalrous career rivalling that of his half-brother Bolingbroke. In 1390 he participated in the St Inglevert jousts and the Tunis crusade. His father's Holand connections probably helped to secure for him in 1394 the marriage of Margaret, daughter of Thomas Holand, earl of Kent. In 1396 he led his father's contingent on the disastrous crusade of Nicopolis, and rose spectacularly the following year in royal favour, being created first earl of Somerset and later marquis of Dorset.[84] Gaunt shamelessly promoted the clerical career of the next brother, Henry (1375–1447), the ablest of the Beauforts (see above, p. 255), whose father's fondness is reflected also in his bequests to Henry of the Black Prince's missal and prayer book. More attractive – and able as well – was the youngest Beaufort brother, Thomas (1377–1426). In July 1397 he was retained for life by the king with a grant of 100 marks *p.a.* and in September 1398 received a life grant of Thomas Mowbray's forfeited lordship of Castle Acre (Norfolk).[85] Thomas Beaufort was to have a successful military career, culminating in the important commands which he held during Henry V's conquests in France. Henry thought so well of him that he entrusted the guardianship of his infant son to

> Thomas Beauforde, his uncle dere and trewe
> Duke Excester, full of all worthyhode.[86]

The memories of his household governance recorded many years later by the antiquary William Worcestre help to explain his high reputation. According to Worcestre, he was notably charitable to the poor and wayfarers. He would not tolerate swearers, liars and tale-bearers, and would accept no gifts or rewards.[87]

The character of the one Beaufort girl, Joan (1379–1440), emerges as strong and pious too. She showed an interest in her thirties in devout exercises and mystical experiences of Christ, for she communed with the excitable and controversial Margery Kempe, the itinerant holy bourgeoise of Lynn.[88] In her mature widowhood, Joan appears in her surviving correspondence, as Professor R.B.Dobson has remarked, as a formidable dowager, often adopting a somewhat dictatorial tone with the prior of Durham, and with her son Robert Neville, after his elevation to the see of Durham in 1438. For the last two years of her life she stayed at his episcopal manor of Howden (Yorks.), where she interfered in the affairs of the collegiate church.[89] Joan's effigy can be seen with those of her husband and his first wife in Staindrop church (Co. Durham), near their great castle at Raby. But she was not content to share a tomb with a previous wife. She was buried in one beside her mother, Duchess Catherine in Lincoln Cathedral. Joan had received royal licence to found a chantry for her mother and other members of the Lancastrian family there. Possibly Joan was setting right the failure of her father's executors to found such a chantry.[90]

Gaunt's children were, on the whole, sturdy and vigorous. There are hints that some of them, at least, inherited Plantagenet good looks. The men tended to be competent, soldierly and conventionally devout. The women were not ciphers; we have some striking manifestations of their temperaments. The duke's offspring included both puritans and sensualists. Gaunt's treatment of them suggests that he was a generous and tolerant father, tireless in pushing their interests. Through his promotion of their marriages and careers, he developed a strong Lancastrian entrenched position in the English nobility and among European princes. His children, though some of them clashed bitterly on occasion, were often to display a strong sense of family solidarity, perhaps imbued by his character and precept. Gaunt reared a family well suited to take over as the English royal house.

The duke's surviving will of 1398 has been used in preceding chapters as evidence of his temperament and predilections. Wills must, indeed, be used cautiously for such a purpose, as they are often highly conventional in phraseology and sentiment, and they reflect drafting and suggestions by councillors and confessors. Gaunt's will is clearly not a hasty construction made *in extremis* by a highly suggestible testator. It is carefully organised and itemised and is probably one of a series of drafts made over three decades by a prince who was also an experienced and forceful administrator, likely to supervise punctiliously the drafting of such an important document. Some of the provisions (especially those concerning piety) are quite unlike anything in his father's or the Black Prince's will. There is the unusual proviso that his body should lie unburied and unembalmed for forty days. Possibly, this may indicate a fear of being buried alive (a medieval hazard), but is it likely that he believed the chances of revival lasted for such a period? Rather, he may have wanted his pitiful corpse to remain exposed out of humility and as an *exemplum*.

The provisions for his eventual burial exhibit an educated piety, the distillation in a blaze of lights around the decayed corpse of a lifetime of dilemmas over princely sinfulness and communings with confessors and holy men, and prayers before images and at shrines. Allegorical tapers were to be lit around the body on the day of interment to signify the deceased's contrition for the worldly life he had led, and his trust in the merits of Christ and mercy of God. There were to be ten great tapers representing the Commandments 'against which I have too badly offended', and above them were to be seven more for the Works of Mercy, 'of which I have been negligent' and for the seven mortal sins. Five tapers were to honour the Five Wounds of Christ and also were to denote 'my five senses which I have very negligently wasted'. Above all these, three tapers were to burn for the Holy Trinity, 'to whom I submit for all the evils I have done, supplicating for pardon and mercy and pity that of his benign grace he has made for the salvation of myself and other sinners'. Here perhaps we have the authentic voice of the seducer of Catherine Swynford, the wilful and choleric prince, patron of Wycliffe and Pontefract hermits, and crusader.

Notes and References

1 Alexander J and Binski P 1987, pp.499–500.
2 William Sedgewick's original drawing of Gaunt's tomb is in Sir William Dugdale's 'Book of Draughts', 1640–1 (B.L., Loan MS 38 f183). It was engraved with minor modifications by Wenceslas Hollar for Dugdale's *History of St Paul's Cathedral* (1658) (Wilson C 1980, p.103 n.31).
3 The St Cuthbert window is usually dated to the mid 1440s, but *c*.1430 has been suggested on stylistic grounds (Baker M 1978 : 22–3). For the All Souls College window, Hutchinson FE 1949, plate xxiv.
4 B.L. Nero D vii f 7r; Gransden A 1982, p.123 and n.
5 Lopes F 1988, pp.212–13.
6 'Et fut là blecié le duc de Lencastre d'une des estaies qui froissa' (*C.Q.P.V.*, p.210).
7 Froissart J 1871, Vol.12, p.324.
8 Palmer JJN and Powell B 1988, pp.62–3. This 'Loys de Luca' can be identified as Lewis Recouchez, long retained by the duke as his physician.
9 Jones M 1983, no.1033.
10 B.L., Harley MS 3988 ff 39r–40d.

11 Evans J 1881, p.322.
12 Froissart J 1872, Vol.16, pp.136–7.
13 Harvey JH nd, p.11.
14 Hoccleve J 1897, p.20.
15 *W.C.*, pp.484–5.
16 *R.P.*, Vol.3, p.313.
17 Froissart J 1872, Vol.14, p.379. For the dauphin of Auvergne's presence in England in 1361, *Foedera*, 1830, Vol.3, pt 2, p.618.
18 *C.H.K.*, Vol.2, pp.149–50; Hoccleve J 1897, p.121.
19 *C.Q.P.V.*, pp.209–10.
20 Morice H 1744, Vol.2, p.450; Jones M 1970, p.99 and n. I owe thanks to Professor Jones for discussing this episode.
21 Froissart 7 1870, Vol.11, pp.265–72. For P.E. Russell's views on Froissart's sources for this conversation, Palmer JJN 1981, pp.93–4.
22 Froissart J 1871, Vol.13, p.111.
23 *W.C.*, pp.112–3.
24 *C.A.*, pp.74–5.
25 Ibid., pp.196–7. Walsingham accused Gaunt of committing adultery against Duchess Blanche too (ibid., p.75).
26 Crow MM and Olson CC 1966, p.95; *C.C.R. 1396–9*, p.463.
27 *J.G.R. 1379–83*, nos 543, 558.
28 Ibid., nos 1009–10, 1039.
29 Froissart J 1870, Vol.11, pp.410ff.
30 In 1393 the duke of Burgundy gave a tapestry to Gaunt (Froissart J 1871, Vol.15, p.366).
31 Ibid., 1870, Vol.11, pp.406–8.
32 *H.A.*, Vol.1, pp.327–8.
33 For Lancastrian forests see Cox JC 1905; Shaw RC 1956; Fox L and Russell P 1948.
34 Legge MD 1941, no.272.
35 Foix G de 1904.
36 *J.G.R. 1372–6*, no.260; *C.P.R. 1367–70*, pp.77–8.
37 *C.P.R. 1377–81*, p.194.
38 *J.G.R. 1372–6*, no.1431; *J.G.R. 1379–83*, no.557.
39 *C.P.R. 1391–6*, p.538; Shaw RC 1956, pp.249–50; Roskell JS 1937, pp.61–7.
40 Holmes G 1975, p.60.
41 *J.G.R. 1379–83*, no.557, P.R.O. DL 28/3/5 f 11d.
42 *J.G.R. 1379–83*, no.463.
43 Froissart J 1870, Vol.II, p.390.
44 *J.G.R. 1372–6*, nos 483, 485. Saffrey was still in service in the early 1380s (*J.G.R. 1379–83*, nos 495, 877).
45 Ibid., no.887.
46 le Bel J 1863, Vol.2, p.256; Froissart J 1870, Vol.11, p.341.
47 *J.G.R. 1379–83*, no.492. For payment for wages to falconers in the year ending Michaelmas 1397, P.R.O. DL 28/3/5 m 9r. Purchases of hawks for Gaunt's use show that advancing years did not diminish his pleasure in the sport (ibid., m 11r).
48 Froissart J 1870, Vol.11, pp.298, 318. In 1383 reference was made to the duke's participation in jousts at Smithfield, Windsor and Hertford (*J.G.R. 1379–83*, no.803).
49 Froissart J 1871, Vol.12, pp.116–17, 120–1.

50   Ibid., Vol.13, pp.301–2.
51   *St Denys*, Vol.1, pp.448–9.
52   Froissart J 1871, Vol.12, pp.100, 123–4.
53   B.L. Nero D vii, Liber Benefactorum f 132d. Constance gave £10 for the fabric of the monastic kitchen and cloth of gold to Abbot de la Mare (ibid., f110d).
54   Account of Bishop Braybrooke's clerk, 1392–3, St Paul's Cathedral MSS, B, Box 95, unnumbered, cited in Butler LH 1952, pp.233, 490, 498, 502.
55   Power E 1922, p.370 and n.
56   Bateson M 1901, Vol.2, p.170.
57   Castro JR 1956, Vol.17, no.398.
58   *C.A.*, pp..196–7, 328.
59   *A.C.*, p.153.
60   *C.H.K.*, Vol.2, p.146.
61   Bateson M 1901, Vol.2, pp.155, 171.
62   It has been suggested that Chandos Herald's poem about the Black Prince was written *c.*1385 to encourage support for Gaunt's claim to the Castilian throne (Palmer JJN 1982). The poem is markedly hostile to Pedro.
63   Cowling GH 1926 : 410.
64   *J.G.R. 1372–6*, no.608.
65   Ibid., no.1056. The 1374 annuity to Geoffrey was partly in reward for Philippa's good service to Queen Philippa and Constance. For Philippa Chaucer's presence in the ducal household in 1381, East Sussex R.O., Waleys cartulary no.3469, A7, B10.
66   Lincoln R.O., Bishop Buckingham's Register, Memoranda 1363–98, Lincoln Cathedral, D and C archives, Reg. 12 f 26r. In 1375 Gaunt granted Catherine tenements for life for her good and agreeable service to Duchess Blanche (*J.G.R. 1372–6*, no.720).
67   Froissart J 1871, Vol.15, p.240.
68   *J.G.R. 1379–83*, nos 963, 984; cf P.R.O. DL 28/3/1 m5 (payments to Catherine for wardrobe and chamber expenses of Philippa and Elizabeth, 1376–7).
69   Armitage-Smith J 1904, p.389.
70   *J.G.R. 1372–6*, nos 1608, 1711.
71   14–16 Nov. (*J.G.R. 1379–83*, nos 108–15).
72   *C.P.R. 1374–7*, p.433; *C.P.R. 1377–81*, p.7.
73   *J.G.R. 1379–83*, nos 558, 979.
74   Ibid., nos 984, 1157
75   For Catherine's presence in the ducal household in the 1390s, East Sussex R.O., Waleys cartulary no.3469, A2, A9, B9.
76   Froissart J 1871, Vol.15, pp.238–40.
77   Ibid., pp.274, 299, 306.
78   Lopes F 1987, pp.236–7; Russell PE 1955, pp.541–8.
79   *J.G.R. 1379–83*, no.463. Elizabeth's future seducer, Sir John Holand, was also present at her wedding at Kenilworth (ibid.).
80   Williams B 1846, p.140.
81   *Annales*, p.333; *C.P.*, Vol.5, pp.253–4; Emery A 1970, p.56.
82   Froissart J 1871, Vol.15, p.306; Russell PE 1955, p.550. For Russell's characterisation of Catalina as queen, ibid., pp.550–3. Her effigy and tomb are in the Capilla Real of Toledo Cathedral.

83   In the early 1390s the Beauforts are found residing on occasion in the ducal household; so did their half-brother Sir Thomas Swynford and Joan Beaufort's first husband Sir Robert Ferrers (East Sussex R.O., Waleys cartulary no.3469 A1, A2, A9, B4, B9).

84   *C.P.*, Vol.12, pt 1, pp.40–4; Harriss GL 1988, pp.1ff. Gaunt helped to finance John Beaufort's 1390 crusade (P.R.O. DL 28/3/2 f24).

85   *C.P.*, Vo.5, pp.200–4.

86   Cited in *Dictionary of National Biography*.

87   Worcestre W 1969, pp.356–9.

88   Meech SB and Allen HE 1940, pp.133–4.

89   Dobson RB 1973, p.187.

90   Harvey JH nd, pp.11–12.

Conclusion

The accumulation of earldoms and lordships by the House of Lancaster, a process which Gaunt augmented, significantly changed the profile of landed wealth and power in fourteenth-century England, elevating the income of one magnate family of royal descent above all others. The authority of the Crown and the habitual prudence of nobles prevented this great change from destabilising the realm. Warned by the unquiet career of Thomas earl of Lancaster, his successors sought an honoured and profitable niche in the realm's affairs by placing their resources at the disposal of royal policies, particularly abroad. They laid in abeyance Earl Thomas's fantasies about the supposed constitutional rights attached to the stewardship of the realm.[1] They cold-shouldered his cult, one in a sequence of politically charged popular canonisations.[2]

Henry duke of Lancaster's lack of a male or of a solitary female heir presented solutions to two problems: Edward III's wish to provide a secure and splendid endowment for his son John, and the danger that Lancastrian power might again be harnessed to aspirations threatening to royal authority. However, accidents of inheritance gave John of Gaunt the Lancastrian inheritance intact in 1362. This turn of events is unlikely to have worried Edward. The youthful Gaunt was proving himself tireless and dutiful in serving his father. He sacrificed to the family interest glamorous opportunities to crusade in the early 1360s. He phlegmatically subordinated personal ambitions abroad to the policy needs of his revered father, as he was to do for Richard in the minority. He never forgot that he had more at stake than the ambiguous honour of the House of Lancaster: the first title he used in the 1360s, recurring in the 1390s, was 'son of the king of England'. A king himself, he reverenced kingship, and, Polonius-like, lectured Richard II and Wladyslav of Poland on their obligations. He first earned widespread unpopularity in 1376–7, by using his brief political ascendency, not to entrench a Lancastrian faction, but to defend royal authority harshly and maladroitly.

Walsingham was not alone in attributing the blackest motives to Gaunt in 1376–7. He also seriously distorted the duke's role in his account of Richard's difficult early years (1377–81). Then Gaunt's more circumspect behaviour betokened a sound reappraisal of political realities; he deserves credit for preserving royal authority intact at home and abroad. The tensions of the early 1380s suggest that his cardinal error was his failure to develop a harmonious personal relationship with Richard. By seeming to countenance plots against his uncle, Richard threatened the political consensus Gaunt had striven to maintain, and initiated the crisis of royal authority which reached its fullest intensity in 1386–8, when Gaunt's moderating influence was lacking.

During over three years absence abroad Gaunt characteristically served the interests of the English Crown as well as fostering his own ambitions. His statesmanlike settlement with Juan I facilitated the renewal of the Anglo-French peace process, which he had long been convinced was in the English interest. However, his prolonged absence crucially accentuated his differences of outlook and experience from those of his fellow countrymen. An ambition to rule the duchy of Aquitaine was fired, an aspiration which they regarded with suspicion. He became fervently committed to the pursuit of peace, the termination of the Schism and the union of Christendom to fight the Turks – to a European rather than an English vision of policy. This, however, endeared him for the first time to Richard, seeking peace as a means of reasserting his battered authority.

Gaunt had not experienced the national trauma of the invasion scare in 1386 and the bitter domestic conflicts which ensued between the king and a coalition of magnates and gentlefolk headed by Thomas of Woodstock. What role, if any, Gaunt had *in absentia* in this central drama of the reign is hard to determine. From his arrival in Portugal in June 1387 onwards he had the means, through good commercial shipping links, to keep in close touch with English affairs. Incentives to communicate were provided by his need to consult king and council about the negotiations with Castile, and his officials in England about his finances. The texts survive of a few warrants Gaunt dispatched from Coimbra in July to his councillors in England.[3] He is likely to have been kept well informed about Richard's attempts to have the law of treason redefined, about the appeal and rising of the lords appellant and the condemnations for treason of Richard's leading supporters in the Merciless Parliament of 1388. Gaunt, like many in England who remained on the sidelines in this conflict, may have had ambivalent feelings about both the king's and his opponents' proceedings. No enemy to royal prerogative, he was no friend of the appellants' *bête noire*, Robert de Vere, duke of Ireland. He is likely to have been shocked by the appellants' more extreme courses and to have regretted their assault on the Neville interest.

After the duke of Ireland (justiciar of Chester) raised an army in Cheshire and Lancashire to challenge the lords appellant in December 1387, Bolingbroke joined them in arms. His primary aim, probably, was to prevent Robert de Vere's interest in both national and local affairs from eclipsing the Lancastrian interest. Bolingbroke may also have wanted to exert influence on the king's opponents in the more unpredictable conditions of civil war which the duke of Ireland's call to arms threatened. It is probable that the youthful Bolingbroke's action was licensed by his father. If Gaunt was involved in this way, no hint of it reached chroniclers. After his return to England in 1389, it suited both the king and his former opponents to treat him as if he had clean hands; his presence facilitated a restoration of the political stability for which it was more widely recognised he stood. However, his international aims, in which self-interest was strongly intermixed with idealism, kept him out of tune with many, and his zealous support of royal prerogative, especially in 1397, probably alienated others. Isolated and beholden to Richard's support for family favours, he was unable then to moderate the king's extremism; apparently for a second time he licensed Bolingbroke to oppose a royal favourite, Thomas Mowbray. For Richard the implications were so serious that in 1398–9 he dismantled (at least temporarily) Lancastrian power. He fatally underestimated Bolingbroke's determination and miscalculated the relative support which the royal and Lancastrian affinities would rally to their respective masters. In 1399 Bolingbroke depended heavily on the cooperation of regional Lancastrian officials for the success of his invasion. The receivers of Lancashire, Pontefract, Bolingbroke and Higham Ferrers provided wages for his soldiers and the Norfolk receiver provided victuals. Receivers were concerned with the maintenance of garrisons at Dunstanburgh, Pontefract and Kenilworth Castles.[4]

In 1399 Bolingbroke resurrected political traditions which his father had preferred to keep interred – Thomas of Lancaster's claims for the stewardship, as James Sherborne argued,[5] as well as the precedent of Edward II's deposition. Indeed, as King Henry IV, Bolingbroke soon revived royal authority, and his rule gave it the bonus of the duchy of Lancaster's annexation to the Crown. But the Elizabethans were right in decrying the evil precedents set by his cunning and brutal actions in 1399. He swiftly unpicked his father's life's work.

Gaunt does not exemplify the political vices which modern historians have attributed to the 'overmighty subject'. He did not aspire to be a mayor of the palace or to monopolise royal patronage for the benefit of an affinity. His widespread retaining and the activities of his estate officers did on occasion provoke regional tensions, but he was apparently eager to placate local society.. Like other magnates, he needed to cultivate and manipulate gentry supporters to protect his regional interests, but he wanted royal patronage (unlike fellow magnates) particularly to support continental ambitions which dated back to his Plantagenet ancestors.

To use anachronistic but not wholly inappropriate terms, public opinion (as reflected by English chroniclers) did not fully appreciate the example which Gaunt habitually set of public service – service, indeed, which went hand-in-hand with self-aggrandisement, but not of the sort which led to civil war in France under Charles VI and in England under Henry VI. For much of his adult life Gaunt was preoccupied in giving military, conciliar, diplomatic and proconsular service to the Crown. The fact that he spent so much time in England at The Savoy and later in rented houses on the outskirts of London, or within easy reach of court and city at Hertford, rather than in his broad lordships, where the sport was superior, was probably due mainly to his frequent immersion in government business. He was often involved in the administrative as well as the formal and public aspects of conciliar and proconsular office. Such essentially bureaucratic service paralleled that given to the Crown by barons and knights whose expertise fitted them for offices and missions hitherto mainly clerical preserves. Gaunt was the very model of the working duke. In his dedication to the royal service he foreshadowed Tudor ideals of nobility, exemplified in the military and conciliar careers of such diverse characters as Thomas Howard, duke of Norfolk (d. 1554), Edward Seymour, duke of Somerset and Robert Dudley, earl of Leicester. These Tudor nobles shared an ethic of service to the sovereign and a conviction of the unlawfulness of rebellion against divinely constituted authority. Some of Gaunt's attitudes anticipate theirs. He too had a revulsion to rebellion, opposing a delinquent king only by a ritual demonstration of power and dissent at Sheen in 1385, and throwing down violent challenges to his policy in 1387 and 1398 by proxy, if at all.

So Gaunt's instincts helped to advance the embryonic authority of the state, as embodied in the sovereign power and exalted dignity of the king. He could have gazed with approval at the iconographical scheme of the Wilton Diptych, with its intensely religious projection of Richard's authority. He could have identified himself with its eremitical figure of John the Baptist, who presents Richard to Christ, and whose right arm protectively encircles the king and appears to touch him familiarly on the shoulder. Moreover, Gaunt conspicuously propped up and enhanced royal authority in practical ways. He harnessed his resources and the machinery of his private government more effectively and fully than most other fourteenth-century magnates to the fulfilment of both its domestic and international objectives. Take, for example, the composition and organisation of the imposing, semi-military expeditions which Gaunt led to the Anglo-Scottish borders to negotiate about peace and truce during his lieutenancies in the region. His private government largely organised these expeditions and provided many of the supporting personnel. Magnate power thus enhanced royal authority at the remote boundaries of the realm. There was, indeed, a contrary tendency in later medieval England – for 'overmighty subjects' to harness royal office and favour to build up their family authority, eroding the effective government of kings. The tendency exemplified by Gaunt's good service eventually triumphed under the Tudors. He was the later medieval noble who most notably upheld royal authority, an example likely to have been more influential if it had not been undercut by his son's usurpation.

Notes and References

1   Maddicott JR 1979, pp.208, 241–3, 289–92.
2   For the growth of Thomas of Lancaster's cult, ibid., pp.329–30.
3   *J.G.R. 1379–83*, nos 1236–7, 1239; cf ibid., 1235, 1240.
4   P.R.O. DL 29/728/11987; DL 29/728/991.
5   Sherborne JW 1988 : 221–3, 231–4.

Calendar of Documents

A selection is given of various sorts of documents connected with John of Gaunt, excluding those in the Public Record Office.

9 June 1362
Letters patent of John son of the king of England, earl of Lancaster, Richmond, Derby, Lincoln and Leicester, steward of England, confirming with his wife's assent the licence granted by his late sister (-in-law) Maud countess of Hainault to the abbot and convent of St Mary in the Meadows, Leicester for their purchase of the manor and advowson of Kirkby Mallory and other properties held of the honour of Leicester, from Simon Pakeman of Kirby, Thomas de Rippeley clerk and Richard de Leycestre.
Leicester Castle
French; seal attached
B.L. Add. Ch. 71913

1 April 1365   Bolingbroke Castle
John son of the king of England, duke of Lancaster, earl of Richmond, Derby, Lincoln and Leicester, steward of England orders the receiver of Pontefract to pay £50 *p.a.* by equal portions for Easter and Michaelmas terms to Sir Godfrey Foljambe, Sir Robert Swillington, Simon Symeon and William Fyncheden, or one of them. They are leasing to the duke's use from his mother the queen for her life the manor of Cowick and the Soke of Snaith. They are to pay the sum to the queen's receiver-general.
French; fragment of seal
Nottingham R.O., Foljambe of Osberton MSS, DDFJ i 650

16 May 1366   London
Indenture between John duke of Lancaster and Sir Hugh Hastings witnessing that Hastings is retained to serve Gaunt in peace and war for life.

376

French
Norfolk R.O., MR 314/242 x 5

3 June 1366   Brancepeth
John de Neville acknowledges receipt of his fee of 20*m*. from John duke of
Lancaster, received from Robert Morton.
French
Phillipps MS. 41017 (not seen) (see above, p.298, n.80)

(1372–7)
John king of Castile and León, duke of Lancaster to the receiver or his
lieutenant in Yorkshire, ordering repairs to Tickhill Castle and Gringley
manor house.
Privy seal
French; fragmentary
Nottingham R.O. Foljambe of Osberton MSS, DDFJ i 694

(1372–88)
John king of Castile and León, duke of Lancaster to the pope. Denounces
slanderers who seek to undermine the Carmelite Order by questioning its
holy origins and privileges. Requests papal backing for the order by silencing
the slanders.
Latin; sixteenth-century copy
Bodleian Library, Oxford, MS Bodley 73 f 185

4 Feb. (1372–86)   The Savoy
The king of Castile and León, duke of Lancaster concerning the addressee's
accounts for service with him on various expeditions; certain of the duke's
clerks and ministers will be at The Savoy from 1 March until his arrival at
the coast and for fifteen days afterwards to account with the addressee and
others for their service on these expeditions.
Privy seal
French
B.L. MS Harley 3988 f 39r

Michaelmas 1375 – Michaelmas 1376
Account roll of the bailiffs of Pontefract.
Latin
Archives Department, Leeds City Libraries, Gascoigne Collection GC/DL/4

Michaelmas 1375 – Michaelmas 1376
Roll of accounts of reeves of Tanshelf, Beal, Campsale, Owston, Kypax and
Ackworth, within the honour of Pontefract.
Latin
Archives Department, Leeds City Libraries, Gascoigne Collection GC/DL/5

Michaelmas 1375 – Michaelmas 1376
Account roll of Henry de Bubwyth, bailiff of fees within the honour of
Pontefract.
Latin
Archives Department, Leeds City Libraries, Gascoigne Collection GC/DL/6

1 Nov. 1378   Gloucester
Letters patent of John king of Castile and León, duke of Lancaster; of special
grace and for past and future services he has granted his well beloved valet
Godfrey Barbour the properties of Robert Tebbe in Leics., in the duke's
hands because of the nonage of Tebbe's son and heir Henry.
Privy seal
French; seal attached
Huntington Library, San Marino, California, HAD 2044

20 May 1382   Westminster
John king of Castile and León, duke of Lancaster to John de Lynstede,
Thomas Horne, clerks, John de Heigh and Thomas Claymond. Licence for
them, for 40*m.*, to grant the manor of Mendham (Suffolk) to Mendham
Priory.
Sixteenth-century(?) copy
Phillipps MS 40292 (not seen) (see p.298, n.80)

1 June 1384   Newbury
Instructions from John king of Castile and León, duke of Lancaster, to
his steward of Sombourne concerning an exchange of properties by two
tenants.
Privy seal
French
Magdalen College, Oxford MS 84

n.d. (1385?)
Reply by Ralph baron of Greystoke to a letter from Thomas earl of
N(ottingham) requesting Greystoke to join his military retinue, since the
king intends to go to Scotland to punish Scottish incursions. Greystoke,
apologising profusely, declines, on the grounds that he has agreed with the
duke of Lancaster to join his retinue for two years if the king will license
it, as he (the king?) has promised him the keepership of Berwick for the
whole of this year.
French
B.L. Harley MS 3988 f 42r
(The text of the earl's letter, to which this is a reply, is given at f 41d.)

4 Jan. 1386   Leicester Castle
John king of Castile and León, duke of Lancaster to Robert Morton, receiver
in Yorkshire, or his lieutenant, ordering him to pay for the making of a new
horsemill in Pontefract Castle in the manner in which the duke has instructed
his servant Thomas Carpenter; and for the repair of the castle gate called 'la
derneyate'.
French
Nottingham R.O., Foljambe of Osberton MSS, DDFJ i 787

14 March 1386   London
Indenture between Hugh de Sherley esquire on one part and William
Bevdele and Henry Bakere archers on the other, witnessing that the latter
are retained by Sherley to serve with him for half a year wherever he

pleases. They will receive from him such wages and regard as the king of Castile and León, duke of Lancaster gives to people of their estate, paid in the same manner as Sherley is paid by the said king. Other conditions of service.
French
Leicestershire R.O., Shirley MSS, 26D53/2543 (see Preface)

1 April 1386   Barlings Abbey
John abbot of Barlings and the convent acknowledge the favours received from their lord John king of Castile and León, duke of Lancaster, and pledge themselves and their successors to celebrate for his good estate during his lifetime and for his soul after death.
Latin; seal
Guildhall Library A Box 74, no.1944

18 June 1386   Plymouth
Letters patent of John king of Castile and León, duke of Lancaster witnessing an accord made in his presence by Sir Hugh Hastings and John Chercheman, citizen of London.
Privy seal
French
Norfolk R.O., MS NA 44 Le Strange

25 June 1386   Plymouth
Letters patent of John king of Castile and León, duke of Lancaster, appointing his cousin the earl of Devonshire as lieutenant of his fees and franchises within the shire during his absence abroad.
Privy seal
French
B.L. Add.Ch.13,190

(After 25 July 1386)   Zamora
Juan I of Castile to the *concejo* of Seville; gives an account of the expedition with which the duke of Lancaster has arrived at La Coruña and weighs up the significance of the invasion threat.
Spanish
Archivo Municipal, Carmona, Privilegios y cartas reales, siglo xiii y xiv (see Preface)

15 Feb. 1387
The *concejo* of Carmona to the archbishop of Seville: they give news of the preliminaries of the Anglo-Portuguese invasion of León and the defence measures adopted.
Spanish
Archivo Municipal, Carmona, Varios, siglo xiv (see Preface)

16 Feb. 1387 (or 1386)?   Westminster
John king of Castile and León, duke of Lancaster, orders Robert Morton, receiver in Yorks., to pay dame Catherine Swynford £100 in part payment of 500 *m.* which she lent the duke in his great necessity.
Privy seal

French
Nottingham R.O., Foljambe of Osberton MSS, DDFJ i 796

30 June (1389)   Bordeaux
John duke of Lancaster to (John Sherburn) abbot of Selby. At the duke's
request, his chancellor Master William Assheton has resigned the parish
church of Stanford, of the abbot's patronage, into the hands of the bishop of
Lincoln; with the intention that the duke's clerk Thomas Tutbury, treasurer
of his household, should have the church. The duke requests the abbot to
present Tutbury. By doing so he will ensure the duke's good lordship.
French
B.L. Cotton Cleo D 111 f 196r, register of Abbot Sherburn (see Preface)

18 May 1390   Calais
John, son of the king of England, duke of Aquitaine and Lancaster, earl of
Derby, Lincoln and Leicester, steward of England; letters patent in favour
of Nicholas de Luka of Florence, going to Italy, Germany and elsewhere
on his business.
Latin
B.L. Add. Ch. 7487

5 March (1391)   Lincoln
John son of the king of England, duke of Aquitaine and Lancaster, earl of
Derby, Lincoln and Leicester, steward of England to (Wladyslav) king of
Poland, requesting the release of his son Derby's knights Thomas Rempston
and John Clifton.
Latin
Edinburgh University Library MS 183; commented on and partly printed
in *D.C.*, p. xxiv n and no.116n.

7 April (1393?)   Pontefract Castle
John duke of Guienne and Lancaster to the abbot and monks of Selby in
support of a petition he has received from his tenants at Snaith, recounting
a threat to their parochial rights.
Signet
French
B.L. Cotton Cleo D 111 f 20ld–202r, register of Abbot Sherburn. The
petition from the Snaith tenants is enrolled at f 199r (n.d.) (see Preface)

28 Aug. 1393   Beverley
Letter from John duke of Guienne and Lancaster requesting support for the
same petition of the Snaith tenants.
Signet
French
B.L. Cotton Cleo D 111 f 199, register of Abbot Sherburn (see Preface)

20 Aug. 1394   London
Indenture made by Sir Matthew Gournay and Simon Raly esquire for the
latter's service with an archer for one year on the expedition which the
duke of Guienne and Lancaster is to make to Guienne.
French; seal

Somerset R.O., Trevelyan of Nettlecombe papers, DD/WO/25/1 (see Preface)

24 April 1395   Pontefract
Sir William Swinburne acknowledges receipt of £10 for last Easter term from William Kettering, the duke of Aquitaine and Lancaster's receiver in Yorkshire.
Northumberland R.O. Swinburne of Capheaton MSS, 25W/1/91.
A similar receipt dated 16 April 1396 makes clear that these payments were instalments of an annuity granted for life by the duke to Swinburne (ibid., 1/92; cf ibid., 1/106).

15 May 1395
Renier Pot knight, chamberlain of the duke of Orleans, acknowledges that he has received 150 fr. from the duke's treasurer Jean Poulain which the duke granted him for the daily wages which he and the duke of Burgundy granted Pot to accompany ambassadors from Hungary for their business with the duke of Lancaster, as appears by the duke of Orleans' warrant dated 12 May 1395.
French
B.L. Add. Ch. 3374; cf ibid., 3373

1 Oct. 1395   Paris
Charles VI says that he has heard that the abbot and convent of Aumale have granted Birstall Priory to his dear and beloved cousin the duke of Lancaster for 10,000 *l. tournois*; permission for them to have this sum and to acquire lands in France in recompense for Birstall.
French
Bodleian Library, Oxford, MS Dodsworth 7 f 239 a-b (cf *ib* f 237a–238a)

13 Oct. 19 Richard II (1395, year misdated?) manor of K.
Richard II to his uncle John duke of Guienne and Lancaster, requesting his counsel at Westminster concerning Scottish attacks by land and sea. Wishes him to enquire how the Irish are conducting themselves towards the Scottish incursions.
Privy seal
French
B.L. MS Harley 3988 f 39

n.d.
Reply by John duke of Guienne and Lancaster to the last letter, excusing himself from attendance at Westminster on account of illness, and reporting that the Irish have stood firm against the Scots and defeated them, but that they urgently require military assistance in order to resist renewed Scottish ravages.
French
B.L. MS Harley 3988, f 39d–40d

Michaelmas 1396 – Michaelmas 1397
Account of John Wynter, receiver of the duke of Aquitaine and Lancaster.
Latin
Norfolk R.O., MS 15171, 37 B 6

18 September 1397   London
John duke of Guienne and Lancaster to receiver of honour of Pontefract, ordering him to make payments of 10*m p.a.* to the duke's esquire William de Balderston, retained by him for life in peace and war by indenture.
French
Folger Library, Washington, MS X d 91 (see Preface)

(Before 29 Sept. 1397)
Anon. to the earl of Derby requesting his influence to persuade the earl of Northumberland and his son Sir Henry Percy not to take the part of the opponents of Sir William Swinburne and Sir John Fenwyk, bachelors of Derby's father, in a property dispute.
French
Northumberland R.O., Swinburne of Capheaton MSS, 25W/1/105

18 Dec. 1397   Leicester Castle
John son of the king of England, duke of Guienne and Lancaster, earl of Derby, Lincoln and Lancaster, steward of England to John Wynter, receiver in Norfolk and Suffolk, giving instructions about the carriage of wine which the duke's butler John Curteys will purchase there.
French
Norfolk R.O., MS 15171, 37 B 6

3 Feb. – 30 Sept. 1399
Account of Simon Bache, receiver of Henry duke of Lancaster in the honour of Leicester.
Latin
Huntington Library, San Marino, California, Hastings MSS, HAM Box 49(1)

Bibliography

Titles given in full in the List of Abbreviations are not repeated
here.

Manuscript Sources

Public Record Office, London
C47   Chancery Miscellanea
C49   Parliament and Council Proceedings
C53   Great Charter Rolls (see Preface)
C61   Gascon Rolls
DL28   Duchy of Lancaster, Various Accounts
DL29   Duchy of Lancaster, Ministers' Accounts
DL37   Duchy of Lancaster, Chancery Rolls
DL43   Duchy of Lancaster, Rentals and Surveys
E30   Exchequer, Diplomatic Documents
E36   Exchequer, Miscellaneous Books
E101   Exchequer, King's Remembrancer, Various Accounts
E364   Exchequer, Lord Treasurer's Remembrancer, Enrolled Accounts
E403   Exchequer Issue Rolls
PL3   Lancaster Palatinate Warrants
SC1   Ancient Correspondence
SC7   Diplomatic Documents
SC8   Ancient Petitions

British Library, London
Additional Charters
Additional Manuscripts
Cotton Manuscripts
Harley Manuscripts
Stowe Charters

383

National Library of Scotland, Edinburgh
Adv. MS 21.4.8   Dickson: treatise defending Elizabeth's right to the
                  English Crown

Archives Nationales, Paris
Trésor des Chartes:
J 291-2, 294, 639, 642-3, 654-7

Archivo de la Corona de Aragón, Barcelona
Cartas Reales y Diplomáticas – Pere III; Joan I
Chancery Registers, Joan I (see Preface)

Regional Repositories and Libraries (by place)

Cumbria R.O., Carlisle
DRCI/2   Register of Bishop Appleby of Carlisle (see Preface)

Archivo Municipal, Carmona
Privilegios y cartas reales, siglos xiii y xiv (see Preface)

Edinburgh University Library
MS 183   collection of diplomatic documents

Archives Department, Leeds City Libraries
GD/DL/4   accounts of honour of Pontefract, 1375-6

East Sussex R.O., Lewes
MS 3469   John of Gaunt's household rolls, Waleys cartulary,
                 Glynde Place Archives

Leicestershire R.O.
Shirley MSS

Lincoln R.O.
Reg. 12   Bishop Buckingham's register
Reg. 13   Bishop Beaufort's register
A.2/26-7   Dean and chapter archives: Chapter Acts 1348-55,
                 1384-94
Bj 2/7, 8, 10   Treasurer's accounts 1377-1406

Guildhall Library, London
A.74/1941-6   Dean and chapter of St Paul's: John of Gaunt's
                 chantry

Norfolk R.O., Norwich
MS 15171 37 B 6: receiver's account for duchy of Lancaster's Norfolk
                 properties, 1396-7
MSS NA: Le Strange collection

MSS MR: Hastings collection

Northumberland R.O., Newcastle-upon-Tyne
ZSW: Swinburne (Capheaton) MSS

Nottinghamshire R.O.
DDFJ: Foljambe of Osberton Collection

Bodleian Library, Oxford
MS Bodley 73:   John Bale's collection on Carmelite Order
MS Dodsworth 7: Kirkstall Abbey deeds
MS Dodsworth 87:roll of writs of duchy of Lancaster, 1377–90

Corpus Christi College (C.C.C.), Oxford
MS 495:   collection of Gaunt's warrants, 1365–70

Magdalen College, Oxford
MS 84:   privy seal warrant of Gaunt

Huntington Library, San Marino, California
HAM Box 49 (1): receiver's account for honour of Leicester, 1399–1400
HAD: Hastings charters
HM 48570:   chronicle of the History of Britain to end of Henry
              VI's reign. Latin

Somerset R.O., Taunton
DD/WO: Trevelyan of Nettlecombe Papers 25/1; indenture for
              service with Gaunt in Guienne, 1394 (see Preface)

Folger Library, Washington
MS X. d. 91:   order by Gaunt for payment of William Balderston, 1397
              (see Preface)

Unpublished dissertations
Alexander, A.F. (1933) The war with France in 1377. Unpublished Ph.D. dissertation, University of London.
Astill, G.G. (1977) The medieval gentry: a study of Leicestershire society 1350–1399. Unpublished Ph.D. dissertation, University of Birmingham.
Butler, L.H. (1952) Robert Braybrooke bishop of London (1381–1404) and his kinsmen. Unpublished D.Phil. dissertation, University of Oxford.
Fowler, K. (1961) Henry of Grosmont, First Duke of Lancaster, 1310–1361. Unpublished Ph.D. dissertation, University of Leeds.
Nilson, B. (1989) The shrine of St Cuthbert in the later Middle Ages. Unpublished M.A. dissertation, University of York.
Rose, R.K. (1984) The bishops and diocese of Carlisle: church and society on the Anglo-Scottish border, 1292–1395. Unpublished Ph.D. dissertation, University of Edinburgh.
Vale, B. (1987) The Scropes of Bolton and of Masham, c.1300–c.1450: a study of a northern noble family with a calendar of the Scrope of Bolton cartulary, 2 vols. Unpublished Ph.D. dissertation, University of York.

Published and Calendared Documents

Bain, J., ed. (1888) *Calendar of Documents Relating to Scotland*, Vol. 4, Register House, Edinburgh.

Bateson, M., ed. (1901) *Records of the Borough of Leicester*, Vol. 2, London.

Brucker, G., ed. (1967) The diary of Buonaccorso Pitti, in *Two Memoirs of Renaissance Florence*, Harper & Row., New York.

Burnett, G., ed. (1880) *The Exchequer Rolls of Scotland*, Vol. 3, Register House, Edinburgh.

Carte, T., ed. (1743) *Catalogue des rolles gascons*, London.

Castro, J.R. (1954–9) *Archivo General de Navarra. Catálogo de la Sección de Comptos Documentos*, Vols 7–23, Pamplona.

Chambers, R.W. and Daunt, M., ed. (1931) *A Book of London English 1384–1425,* Oxford University Press.

Champollion-Figeac, M., ed. (1847) *Lettres des rois, reines et autres personnages des cours de France et d'Angleterre*, Vol. 2, Paris.

Crow, M.M. and Olson, C.C., ed. (1966) *Chaucer Life-Records*, Oxford University Press.

Delisle, L., ed. (1874) *Mandements et Actes Divers de Charles V*, Paris.

Dell, R.F. (1964) *The Glynde Place Archives, A Catalogue*, East Sussex County Council, Lewes.

Delpit, J., ed. (1847) *Collection générale des documents français qui se trouvent en Angleterre*, Paris.

Devon, F. (1835) *Issue Roll of Thomas de Brantingham*, London.

Devon, F. (1837) *Issues of the Exchequer*, Vol. 1, London.

Douët-D'Arcq, L. (1863–4) *Choix de pièces inédites relative au règne de Charles VI*, 2 vols, Paris.

Dunning, R.W., ed. (1968) *The Hylle Cartulary*, Vol. 68, Somerset Record Society, Frome.

Extracts from the Account Rolls of the Abbey of Durham 1898–1900, Vols 1–3. Surtees Society.

Gibbons, A., ed. (1888) *Early Lincoln Wills*, Lincoln.

H.M.C. (1928) *Report on the Manuscripts of the Late Reginald Rawdon Hastings*, Vol. 1, London.

James, M.R., ed. (1899) *A Descriptive Catalogue of the Manuscripts in the Library of Peterhouse*, Cambridge University Press.

James, M.R. (1912) *A Descriptive Catalogue of the Manuscripts in the Library of Corpus Christi College, Cambridge*, Vol. 2, Cambridge University Press.

Jones, M., ed. (1983) *Recuiel des actes de Jean IV, duc de Bretagne*, 2 vols, Devonshire Press, Torquay.

Kirby, T.F. (1899) *Wykeham's Register*, Vol. 2, Hampshire Record Society, London.

Legge, M.D. (1941) *Anglo-Norman Letters and Petitions*, Basil Blackwell, Oxford.

Lewis, N.B. (1964) Indentures of retinue with John of Gaunt, duke of Lancaster, enrolled in Chancery 1367–1399, in *Camden Miscellany*, Vol. 22, Camden 4th series, Vol. 1, London.

Martin Fuertes, J.A. and Alvarez Alvarez C., ed. (1982) *Archivo histórico municipal de León. Catálogo de los documentos*, León.

Meech, S.B. and Allen, H.E., ed. (1940) *The Book of Margery Kempe*, Early English Texts Society.

Mirot L. and Déprez, E. (1899) *Les ambassades anglaises pendant la guerre de cent ans. Catalogue chronologique*, Bibliothèque de l'École des Chartes fasc 60, Paris.

Morice, H., ed. (1744) *Memoires pour servir de preuves à l'histoire ecclesiastique de Bretagne*, Vol. 2, Paris.

Nicolas, N.H. (1826) *Testamenta Vetusta*, 2 vols, London.

Nicolas, N.H., ed. (1832) *The Controversy between Sir Richard Scrope and Sir Robert Grosvenor in the Court of Chivalry*, 2 vols, London.

Nicolas, N.H., ed. (1834) *Proceedings and Ordinances of the Privy Council of England*, Vol. 1, London.

Palmer, J.J.N. and Powell, B., ed. (1988) *The Treaty of Bayonne (1388) with Preliminary Treaty of Trancoso (1387)*, University of Exeter Press.

Pantin, W.A., ed. (1933–37) *Documents Illustrating the Activities of the General and Provincial Chapters of the English Black Monks 1215–1540*, Vols 2 and 3, Camden 3rd series, London.

Parry, J.H., ed. (1915) *Registrum Johannis Gilbert, Episcopi Herefordensis* Canterbury and York Society, London.

Pascal Martínez, L. (1983) *Coleccion de Documentos para la Historia de Murcia*, Vol. 8: *Documentos de Enrique II*, Murcia.

Perroy, E., ed. (1952) Anglo-French negotiations at Bruges, 1374–1377, in *Camden Miscellany*, Vol. 19, London.

Raynaldus, O. (1752) *Annales Ecclesiastici*, Vol. 7, Lucca.

(1930–3) *Register of Edward the Black Prince, 1346–1365*, 4 vols, H.M.S.O., London.

Sparrow Simpson, W. (1887) Two inventories of the cathedral church of St Paul, London, dated respectively 1245 and 1402, *Archaeologia*, **50**.

Swanson, R.N., ed. (1981) *A Calendar of the Register of Richard Scrope Archbishop of York, 1398–1405*, Vol. 1, Borthwick Texts and Calendars, Borthwick Institute, York.

Toulmin Smith, L., ed. (1894) *Expeditions to Prussia and the Holy Land made by Henry Earl of Derby*, Camden Society, London.

Weaver, F.W., ed. (1903) *Somerset Medieval Wills*, Vol. 19, Somerset Record Society.

Wickenden, J.F. (1875) 'Joyalx' of John of Gaunt bequeathed to the cathedral church of Lincoln, Archaeological Journal, **32**.

Wickham Legg, L.G., ed. (1901) *English Coronation Records*, Westminster.

Wilkins, D., ed. (1737) *Concilia Magnae Britanniae et Hiberniae*, Vol. 3, London.

Wordsworth, C. (1892) Inventories of plate, vestments, etc., belonging to the cathedral church of . . . Lincoln, *Archaeologia*, 2nd series, **3**.

Zimmerman, B. (1905–7) *Monumenta Historica Carmelitana*, Lérins.

Chronicles, Treatises and Poems

Arnold, T., ed. (1896) *Memorials of St Edmund's Abbey*, Vol. 3, Rolls series, London.

Baker, G. Le., (1989) *Chronicon*, ed. E.M. Thompson, Oxford.

Boucicaut M (1819) Livre des faicts du bon messire Jean le Maingre dit

Boucicaut, in M. Petitot (ed.) *Collection complète des mémoires relatif à l'histoire de France*, Vols 6 and 7, Paris.

Brandon, J. (1870) Chronique, in K.de Kettenhove (ed.) *Chroniques des religieux des Dunes*, Brussels.

Capgrave, J. (1858) *Liber de Illustribus Henricis*, ed. F.C. Hingeston, Rolls series, London.

Charrière, E., ed. (1839) *Le Libvre du bon Jehan, duc de Bretaigne*, Paris.

Chaucer, G. (1951) *The Complete Works*, ed. W.W. Skeat, Oxford University Press.

Chazand, A-M., ed. (1876) *La Chronique du bon duc Loys de Bourbon*, Société de l'histoire de France, Paris.

Clarke, M.V. and Denholm-Young, N., ed. (1931) The Kirkstall Chronicle, 1355–1400, *B.J.R.L.*, **15**.

Cochon, P. de (1870) *Chronique Normande*, ed. C. Robillard de Beaurepaire, Rouen.

Dickson, W., ed. (1844) *Chronicles of Alnwick Abbey, Archaeologia Aeliana*, **3**.

Eisner, S. and MacEoin, G., eds (1980) Nicholas of Lynn's *Kalendarium*, University of Georgia Press, Athens.

Foix, G de (1904) *The Master of Game*, trans. Edward, second duke of York, ed. W.A. and F. Baillie-Grohman, London.

Fortescue, J. ed. C. Plummer, (1885) *The Governance of England*, Oxford.

Froissart, J. (1867–77) *Oeuvres*, ed. K. de Lettenhove, 25 vols, Brussels.

Froissart, J. (1975) *Le Joli Buisson de Jonece*, ed. A. Fourrier, Librairie Droz, Geneva.

Gairdner, J. ed. (1880) *Three Fifteenth-Century Chronicles*, Camden Society, London.

Gransden, A. (1957) A fourteenth-century chronicle from the Grey Friars at Lynn, *E.H.R.*, **72**.

Hamilton Thompson, A., ed. (1923) *Liber Vitae Ecclesiae Dunelmensis*, Vol. 1, Surtees Society, **136**.

Hoccleve, T. (1897) The Regement of Princes, in F.J. Furnivall (ed.) *Works*, Vol. 3, Early English Text Society.

le Bel, J. (1863) *Les Vrayes Chroniques*, ed. M.L. Polain, Brussels.

Lopes, F. (1988) *The English in Portugal 1367–87.* ed. D.W. Lomax and R.J. Oakley, Aris & Phillips, Warminster.

Mézières, P. de (1954) *The Life of Saint Peter Thomas*, ed. J. Smet, Institutum Carmelitanum, Rome.

Mézières, P. de (1969) *Le Songe du vieil pèlerin*, ed. G.W. Coopland, 2 vols, Cambridge University Press.

Mézières, P. de (1975) *Letter to King Richard II*, ed. G.W. Coopland, Liverpool University Press.

Otterbourne, T. (1732) Chronicon Regum Angliae, in T. Hearne (ed.) *Duo Rerum Anglicarum Scriptores Veterum*, Vol. 1, Oxford.

Peterborough, W. of (1859) Prince Edward's expedition into Spain, and the battle of Najara, in T. Wright (ed.) *Political Poems and Songs*, Vol. 1, Rolls series, London.

Pope, M.K. and Lodge, E.C., eds (1910) *Life of the Black Prince by the Herald of Sir John Chandos*, Clarendon Press, Oxford.

Reading, J. de (etc.) (1914) *Chronica*, ed. J. Tait, Manchester University Press.

Rossiter, A.P., ed. (1946) *Woodstock. A Moral History*, Chatto and Windus, London.

Stockton, E.W., ed. (1962) *The Major Latin Works of John Gower*, University of Washington Press, Seattle.

Usk, A. de (1904) *Chronicon*, ed. E.M. Thompson, Oxford University Press, London.

Williams, B., ed. (1846) *Chronique de la traison et mort de Richart Deux Roy Dengleterre*, London.

Worcestre, W. (1969) *Itineraries*, ed. J.H. Harvey, Clarendon Press, Oxford.

Wyntoun, A. (1879) *The Orygynale Cronykil of Scotland*, ed. D. Laing, Vol. 3, Edinburgh.

Secondary Works

Alcock, N.W. and Buckley, R.J. (1987) Leicester Castle, *Medieval Archaeology*, **31**.

Alexander, J. and Binski, P. (1987) *Age of Chivalry. Art in Plantagenet England 1200–1400*, Royal Academy of Arts and Weidenfeld & Nicolson, London.

Anglo, S. (1969) *Spectacle Pageantry and Early Tudor Policy*, Oxford University Press.

Archer, R.E. (1987) The estates and finances of Margaret of Brotherton, c. 1320–1399, *B.I.H.R.*, **60**.

Armitage-Smith, S. (1904) *John of Gaunt*, Constable, London.

Aston, M. (1967) *Thomas Arundel*, Oxford University Press.

Aston, M. (1965) The impeachment of Bishop Despenser, *B.I.H.R.*, **38**.

Baines, E. (1836) *History of the County Palatine and Duchy of Lancaster*, Vol. 1, London.

Baker, M. (1978) Medieval illustrations of Bede's *Life of St Cuthbert*, *Journal of the Warburg and Courtauld Institutes*, **44**.

Baldwin, J.F. (1913) *The King's Council in England during the Middle Ages*, Clarendon Press, Oxford.

Baquero Moreno, H. (1988) *Os Itinerários de El-Rei João I (1384–1433)*, Instituto de Cultura e Língua Portuguesa, Lisbon.

Barnes, J. (1688) *The History of that Most Victorious Monarch Edward III*, Cambridge.

Barnie, J. (1974) *War in Medieval Society. Social Values and the Hundred Years War 1337–99*, Weidenfeld & Nicolson, London.

Barron, C.M. (1971) The quarrel of Richard II with London 1392–7, in F.R.H. Du Boulay and C.M. Barron (eds) *The Reign of Richard II*, Athlone Press, London.

Bateson, E. (1895) *A History of Northumberland*, Vol. 2, Newcastle-upon-Tyne.

Beaumont, W.A. (1873) *A History of the Castle of Halton and the Priory or Abbey of Norton*, Warrington.

Bellamy, C.V., ed. (1965) *Pontefract Priory Excavations 1957–1961*, Thoresby Society, **49**, Leeds.

Bellamy, J.G. (1964–5) The northern rebellions in the later years of Richard II, *B.J.R.L*, **47**.

Benham, W. (1902) *Old St Paul's Cathedral*, London.

Bennett, M.J. (1983) *Community, Class and Careerism. Cheshire Society in the Age of 'Sir Gawain and the Green Knight'*, Cambridge University Press.

Bird, R. (1949) *The Turbulent London of Richard II*, Longman, London.

Birrell, J.R. (1962) The forest economy of the honour of Tutbury in the fourteenth and fifteenth centuries, *University of Birmingham Historical Journal*, **8**.

Blair, C.H.H. and Honeyman, H.L. (1978) *Dunstanburgh Castle, Northumberland*, H.M.S.O., London.

Boehlke, F.J. (1966) *Pierre de Thomas Scholar, Diplomat and Crusader*, University of Pennsylvania Press, Philadelphia.

Boutruche, R. (1947) *La crise d'une société. Seigneurs et paysans du Bordelais pendant la Guerre de Cent Ans*, Les Belles Lettres, Paris.

Braddy, H. (1947) *Chaucer and the French Poet Graunson*, Louisiana State University Press.

Brown, R.A. *et al.* (1963) *The History of the King's Works*, Vols 1 and 2, H.M.S.O., London.

Campbell, L.B. (1947) *Shakespeare's 'Histories'*, Huntington Library Publications, San Marino, California.

Catto, J. (1981) Religion and the English nobility in the later fourteenth century, in H. Lloyd-Jones and B. Worden (eds) *History and Imagination. Essays in Honour of H.R. Trevor-Roper*, London.

Chaplais, P. (1971) English diplomatic documents 1377–99, in F.R.H. Du Boulay, and C.M. Barron (eds) *The Reign of Richard II*, Athlone Press, London.

Cherry, M. (1979) The Courtenay earls of Devon: the formation and disintegration of a late medieval aristocratic affinity, *Southern History*.

Clarke, M.V. (1937) *Fourteenth Century Studies*, ed. L.S. Sutherland and M. McKisack, Oxford University Press.

Clay, R.M. (1914) *The Hermits and Anchorites of England*, Methuen, London.

Colman, J. (1981) *English Literature in History 1350–1400: Medieval Readers and Writers*, Hutchison, London.

Cowling, G.H. (1926) Chaucer's *Complaintes of Mars and of Venus*, *Review of English Studies*, **2**.

Cox, J.C. (1905) *The Royal Forests of England*, Methuen, London.

Craster, O.E. (1970) *Skenfrith Castle, Monmouthshire*, H.M.S.O., London.

Crompton, J. (1961) Fasciculi Zizaniorum I, *Journal of Ecclesiastical History*, **12**.

Crompton, J. (1968–9) Leicestershire Lollards, *Leicestershire Archaeological and Historical Society Transactions*, **44**.

Crook, D. (1987) Derbyshire and the English rising of 1381, *B.I.H.R.*, **60**.

Dahmus, J.H. (1952) *The Prosecution of John Wyclyf*, Yale University Press, New Haven, Conn.

Daniel, S. (1595) *The First Fowre Bookes of the ciuile wars between the two houses of Lancaster and Yorke*, London.

Daniel, S. (1621) *The Collection of the History of England*, London.

Daumet, G. (1898) *Étude sur l'alliance de la France et de la Castille au xive et au xve siècles*, Bibliothèque de l'école des hautes études fasc 118, Paris.

Davies, R.R. (1978) *Lordship and Society in the March of Wales 1282–1400*, Oxford University Press.

Delachenal, R. (1916–31) *Histoire de Charles V*, Vols 3–5, Paris.

Dobson, R.B. (1970) *The Peasants' Revolt of 1381*, Macmillan, London.

Dobson, R.B. (1973) *Durham Priory 1400–1450*, Cambridge University Press.

Dobson, R.B. (1984) The risings in York, Beverley and Scarborough, 1380–1381, in R.H. Hilton and T.J. Aston (eds) *The English Rising of 1381*, Cambridge University Press.

Du Boulay, F.R.H. (1971) Henry of Derby's expeditions to Prussia 1390–1 and 1392, in F.R.H. Du Boulay and C.M. Barron (eds) *The Reign of Richard II*, Athlone Press, London.

Duncan, A.A.M. (1988) *Honi soit qui mal y pense*: David II and Edward III, 1346–52, *Scottish Historical Review*, **67**.

Eisner, S. (1976) Chaucer's use of Nicholas of Lynn's calendar, in E. Talbot Donaldson (ed.) *Essays and Studies 1976*, London.

Emery, A. (1970) *Dartington Hall*, Oxford University Press.

Fisher, J.H. (1965) *John Gower*, Methuen, London.

Fowler, J.T. (1875–6) On the St. Cuthbert Window in York Minster, *Yorkshire Archaeological Journal*, **4**.

Fowler, K. (1969) *The King's Lieutenant*, Martin Elek, London.

Fowler, K. (1971) Truces, in K. Fowler (ed.) *The Hundred Years War*, Macmillan, London.

Fox, L. and Russell, P. (1948) *Leicester Forest*, Leicester University Press.

Given-Wilson, C. (1987) *The English Nobility in the Late Middle Ages: The Fourteenth-Century Political Community*, Routledge, London.

Goodman, A. (1971) *The Loyal Conspiracy*, Routledge & Kegan Paul, London.

Goodman, A. (1980) The military subcontracts of Sir Hugh Hastings, 1380, *E.H.R.*, **95**.

Goodman, A. (1987a) John of Gaunt: paradigm of the late fourteenth-century crisis, *Transactions of the Royal Historical Society*, 5th series, **37**.

Goodman, A. (1987b) Sentiment and policy: English attitudes to Spain in the later Middle Ages, in J.E. Lopez de Coca Castañer (ed.) *Estudios sobre Málaga y el Reino de Granada en el V Centenario de la Conquista*, Diputación Provincial de Málaga.

Goodman, A. (1989) Alfonso X and the English crown, in J.C. de Miguel Rodriguez *et al. Alfonso X El Sabio, Vida, Obra y Epoca I*, Sociedad Española de Estudios Medievales, Madrid.

Goodman, A. and Morgan, D. (1985) The Yorkist claim to the throne of Castile, *J.M.H.*, **11**.

Gransden, A. (1982) *Historical Writing in England*, Vol. 2, Routledge & Kegan Paul, London.

Green, J.R. (1875) *A Short History of the English People*, London.

Hamilton Thompson, A. (1935) *St Mary's Guildhall Lincoln*, Lincoln.

Hamilton Thompson, A. (1937) *The History of the Hospital and the New College of the Annunciation of St. Mary in the Newarke*, Leicester Archaeological Society.

Hamilton Thompson, A. (1947) *The English Clergy and their Organization in the later Middle Ages*, Oxford University Press.

Hamilton Thompson, A. (1949) *The Abbey of St Mary of the Meadows Leicester*, Leicester Archaeological Society.

Harrison, F.Ll. (1958) *Music in Medieval Britain*, Routledge & Kegan Paul, London.

Harriss, G.L. (1988) *Cardinal Beaufort*, Clarendon Press, Oxford.

Harvey, B.H. (1977) *Westminster Abbey and its Estates in the Middle Ages*, Clarendon Press, Oxford.

Harvey, J.H. (n.d.) *Catherine Swynford's Chantry*. Lincoln Minster Pamphlets,

2nd series, no. 6.

Hayward, J. (1599) *The First Part of the Life and Raigne of King Henrie the IIII*, London.

Hill, J.W.F. (1948) *Medieval Lincoln*, Cambridge University Press.

Holinshed, R. (1807) *Chronicles of England* (etc.), London.

Holmes, G. (1957) *The Estates of the Higher Nobility in XIVth Century England*, Cambridge University Press.

Holmes, G. (1975) *The Good Parliament*, Oxford University Press.

Hume, D. (1834) *The History of England*, Vol. 3, London.

Hutchinson, F.E. (1949) *Medieval Glass at All Souls College*, Faber & Faber, London.

Iorga, N. (1896) *Philippe de Mézières, 1327–1405, et la croisade au XIVᵉ siècle*, Bibliothèque de l'école des hautes études fasc 110, Paris.

Jack, R.I. (1965) Entail and descent: the Hastings inheritance, 1370–1436, *B.I.H.R.*, **38**.

James, S.E. (1981) Sir Thomas Parr (1407–1461), *Transactions of the Cumberland and Westmorland Antiquarian and Archaeological Society*, **81**.

Jones, M. (1970) *Ducal Brittany 1364–1399*, Oxford University Press.

Keen, M.H. (1965) *The Laws of War in the Late Middle Ages*, Routledge & Kegan Paul, London.

Kerr, W.J.B. (1925) *Higham Ferrers and its Ducal and Royal Castle and Park*, Northampton.

Kirby, J.L. (1970) *Henry IV of England*, Constable, London.

Knight, J.K. (1980) *Grosmont Castle, Gwent*, H.M.S.O., Cardiff.

Knowles, D. (1955) *The Religious Orders in England*, Vol. 2, Cambridge University Press.

Lawrence, C.H. (1984) The university in church and state, in T.H. Aston (ed.) *The History of the University of Oxford*, Vol. 1: Catto, J.I. (ed.) *The Early Schools*, Oxford University Press.

Lehoux, F. (1966) *Jean de France, duc de Berri. Sa vie, son action politique (1340–1416)*, Vols 1 and 2, A. & J. Picard, Paris.

Lewis, N.B. (1926) The 'Continual Council' in the early years of Richard II, *E.H.R.*, **41**.

Lewis, N.B. (1937) The anniversary service for Blanche, duchess of Lancaster, 12th September 1374, *B.J.R.L.* **21**.

Lewis, N.B. (1958) The last medieval summons of the English feudal levy, *E.H.R.*, **73**.

Liddell, W.H. and Wood, R.G.E. (1982) *Essex and the Great Revolt of 1381*, Essex Record Office Publications.

Lucas, H.S. (1929) *The Low Countries and the Hundred Years War, 1326–1347*, University of Michigan Press, Ann Arbor.

Luttrell, A. (1988) English Levantine crusaders, 1363–1367, *Renaissance Studies* **2**.

McFarlane, K.B. (1966) *John Wycliffe and the Beginnings of English Nonconformity*, English Universities Press, London.

McFarlane, K.B. (1972) *Lancastrian Kings and Lollard Knights*, Oxford University Press.

McFarlane, K.B. (1973) *The Nobility of Later Medieval England*, Oxford University Press.

McKisack, M. (1959) *The Fourteenth Century 1307–1399*, Oxford University Press.

Maddicott, J.R. (1970) *Thomas of Lancaster 1307–1322*, Oxford

University Press.

Matthew, D. (1962) *The Norman Monasteries and their English Possessions*, Oxford University Press.

Maxwell Lyte, H.C. (1909) *A History of Dunster*, Vol. 1, St Catherine Press, London.

Mertes, K. (1988) *The English Noble Household 1250–1600*, Basil Blackwell, Oxford.

Morgan, P. (1987) *War and Society in Medieval Cheshire 1277–1403*, Chetham Society, Manchester, 3rd series, **34**.

Morris, R.K. (1986) The architecture of the earls of Warwick in the fourteenth century, in W.M. Ormrod (ed.) *England in the Fourteenth Century*, Boydell Press, Woodbridge.

Mosley, O. (1832) *History of the Castle, Priory, and Town of Tutbury*.

Nicholson, R. (1974) *Scotland. The Later Middle Ages*, Oliver & Boyd, Edinburgh.

Myers, A.R. (1959) *The Household of Edward IV*, Manchester University Press.

Orme, N. (1983) The education of the courtier, in V.J. Scattergood and J.W. Sherborne (eds) *English Court Culture in the Later Middle Ages*, Duckworth, London.

Orme, N. (1984) *From Childhood to Chivalry*, Methuen, London and New York.

Ormrod, W.M. (1987) Edward III and his family, *J.B.S.*, **26**.

Otway-Ruthven, A.J. (1968) *A History of Medieval Ireland*, Ernest Benn, London.

Owst, G.R. (1926) *Preaching in Medieval England*, Cambridge University Press.

Palmer, J.J.N. (1966a) The Anglo-French peace negotiations, 1390–1396, *T.R.H.S.*, 5th series, **16**.

Palmer, J.J.N. (1966b) Articles for a final peace between England and France, 16 June 1393, *B.I.H.R.*, **39**.

Palmer, J.J.N. (1968) England and the great western Schism, 1388–1399, *E.H.R.*, **83**.

Palmer, J.J.N. (1971) English foreign policy 1388–99, in F.R.H. Du Boulay and C.M. Barron (eds) *The Reign of Richard II*, Athlone Press, London.

Palmer, J.J.N. (1971) The parliament of 1385 and the constitutional crisis of 1386, *Speculum*, **46**.

Palmer, J.J.N. (1972) *England, France and Christendom, 1377–99*, Routledge & Kegan Paul, London.

Palmer, J.J.N. (1973–4) The historical context of the 'Book of the Duchess': a revision, *Chaucer Review*, **8**.

Palmer, J.J.N. (1976) England, France, the papacy and the Flemish succession, 1361–9, *J.M.H.*, **2**.

Palmer, J.J.N. (1978) The authorship, date and historical value of the French chronicles on the Lancastrian revolution, *B.J.R.L.*, **61**.

Palmer, J.J.N. ed. (1981) *Froissart: Historian*, The Boydell Press, Woodbridge, Suffolk; Rowman and Littlefield, Totowa, New Jersey.

Palmer, J.J.N. (1982) Froissart et le héraut Chandos, *Le Moyen Age*, **88**.

Pape, T. (1928) *Medieval Newcastle-under-Lyme*, Manchester University Press.

Parsons, R. (1594) *A Conference about the next succession to the Crowne of Ingland*.

Perroy, E. (1933) *L'Angleterre et le grand Schisme d'Occident*, Librarie J. Monnier, Paris.

Pevsner, N. (1964) *The Buildings of England. Leicestershire and Rutland*, Penguin, Harmondsworth.

Pfaff, R.W. (1970) *New Liturgical Feasts in Later Medieval England*, Oxford University Press.

Phillips, H., ed. (1982) *The Book of the Duchess*, Durham and St Andrews Medieval Texts, **3**.

Phillpotts, C.J. (1990) John of Gaunt and English policy towards France 1389–1395, *J.M.H.*, **16**.

Pocquet du Haut-Jussé, B.A. (1967) La dernière phase de la vie de Du Guesclin, l'affaire de Bretagne, *Bibliothèque de l'École des Chartes*, **125**.

Post, J.B. (1981) The obsequies of John of Gaunt, *Guildhall Studies in London History*, **5**.

Power, E. (1922) *Medieval English Nunneries, c. 1275 to 1535*, Cambridge University Press.

Prestwich, M. (1988) *Edward I*, Methuen, London.

Quicke, F. (1947) *Les Pays-Bas à la veille de la période bourguignonne 1356–1384*, Les Presses de Belgique, Brussels.

Radford, C.A.R. (1952) *Kidwelly Castle, Carmathenshire*, H.M.S.O., London.

Radford, C.A.R. (1962) *White Castle, Monmouthshire*, H.M.S.O., London.

Ramsay, J.H. (1913) *Genesis of Lancaster*, Vol. 2, Clarendon Press, Oxford.

Rapin-Thoyras, P.de (1732) *The History of England*, Vol. 1, London.

Rickert, M. (1952) *The Reconstructed Carmelite Missal*, Faber & Faber, London.

Roskell, J.S. (1937) *The Knights of the Shire for the County Palatine of Lancaster (1377–1460)*, Chetham Society, Manchester, **96**.

Rowling, M.A. (1957) William de Parr. King's Knight to Henry IV (c.1350–1404), *Transactions of Cumberland and Westmorland Antiquarian and Archaeological Society*, **56**.

Russell, P.E. (1955) *The English Intervention in Spain and Portugal in the Time of Edward III and Richard II*, Clarendon Press, Oxford.

Saul, N. (1981) *Knights and Esquires: The Gloucestershire Gentry in the Fourteenth Century*, Oxford University Press.

Saul, N. (1986) *Scenes from Provincial Life*, Clarendon Press, Oxford.

Saul, N. (1990) The Commons and the abolition of badges, *Parliamentary History*, **9**.

Schofield, R.S. (1965) The geographical distribution of wealth in England, 1334–1649, *Economic History Review*, 2nd ser. 18.

Shaw, R.C. (1956) *The Royal Forest of Lancaster*, The Guardian Press, Preston.

Shaw, S. (1798) *The History and Antiquities of Staffordshire*, Vol. 1. London.

Sheppard, L.C. (1943) *The English Carmelites*, Burns Oates, London.

Sherborne, J.W. (1964) Indentured retinues and English expeditions to France, 1369–80, *E.H.R.*, **79**.

Sherborne, J. (1967) The Hundred Years War. The English navy: shipping and manpower 1369–1389, *Past and Present*, **37**.

Sherborne, J.W. (1986) Edward III's retinue and the French campaign of 1369, in R.A. Griffiths and J.W. Sherborne (eds) *Kings and Nobles in the Later Middle Ages*, Alan Sutton, Gloucester.

Sherborne, J.W. (1988) Perjury and the Lancastrian revolution of 1399, *Welsh Historical Review*, **14**.

Somerville, R. (1953) *History of the Duchy of Lancaster*, Vol. 1, Chancellor and Council of the Duchy of Lancaster, London.

Sparrow Simpson, W. (1889) *Gleanings from Old St Paul's*, London.

Steel, A. (1941) *Richard II*, Cambridge University Press.

Storey, R.L. (1957) The wardens of the Marches of England towards Scotland 1377–1489, *E.H.R.*, **72**.

Storey, R.L. (1961) *Thomas Langley and the Bishopric of Durham 1406–1437*, S.P.C.K., London.

Stubbs, W. (1875) *The Constitutional History of England*, Vol. 2, Oxford.

Suarez Fernandez, L. (1959) *Navegación y Comercio en el Golfo de Vizcaya*, Madrid.

Suarez Fernandez, L. (1977) *Historia de Reinado de Juan I de Castilla*, Vol. 1, Universidad Autonoma, Madrid.

Swinton, G.S.C. (1919) John of Swinton: a border fighter of the Middle Ages, *Scottish Historical Review* **16**.

Taylor, A.J. (1972) *Monmouth Castle and Great Castle House, Monmouthshire*, H.M.S.O., London.

Taylor, J. (1987) *English Historical Literature in the Fourteenth Century*, Oxford University Press.

Thompson, J. (1849) *History of Leicester*.

Thompson, M.W. (1958) *Pickering Castle, Yorkshire*, H.M.S.O., London.

Thompson, M.W. (1977) *Kenilworth Castle, Warwickshire*, H.M.S.O., London.

Tout, T.F. (1905) *The History of England from the Accession of Henry III to the Death of Edward III*, Longman, Green, London.

Tout, T.F. (1928) *Chapters in the Administrative History of Mediaeval England*, Vols 3 and 4, Manchester University Press.

Trevelyan, G.M. (1899) *England in the Age of Wycliffe*, London.

Tuck, A. (1968) Richard II and the border magnates, *Northern History*, **3**.

Tuck, A. (1973) *Richard II and the English Nobility*, Edward Arnold, London.

Tuck, A. (1984) Nobles, Commons and the Great Revolt of 1381, in R.H. Hilton and T.H. Aston (eds) *The English Rising of 1381*, Cambridge University Press.

Tucoo-Chala, P. (1959) *Gaston Fébus et la vicomté de Béarn (1343–1391)*, Imprimerie Bière, Bordeaux.

Vale, M.G.A. (1970) *English Gascony 1399–1453*, Oxford University Press.

Valois, N. (1901) *La France et le grand schisme d'Occident*, Vol. 3, A. Picard, Paris.

Vaughan, R. (1962) *Philip the Bold*, Longman, London.

Vergil, P. (1556) *Historia Anglicana*, Basel.

Vernon Harcourt, L.W. (1907) *His Grace the Steward and Trial of Peers*, London.

Walker, S.K. (1983) Lancaster v. Dallingridge. A franchisal dispute in fourteenth-century Sussex, *Sussex Archaeological Collections*, **121**.

Walker, S.K. (1989) Lordship and lawlessness in the palatinate of Lancaster, 1370–1400, *J.B.S.*, **28**.

Wallon, H. (1864) *Richard II*, Vol. 1, Paris.

Warren, A.K. (1985) *Anchorites and their Patrons in Medieval England*, University of California Press, Berkeley, Los Angeles and London.

Waugh, S.L. (1991) *England in the Reign of Edward III*, Cambridge University Press.

Wilson, C. (1980) The Neville screen, in *Medieval Art and Architecture at Durham, British Archaeological Association Conference Transactions*, **3**.

Wood, M. (1981) *The English Mediaeval House*, Ferndale, London.

Wylie, J.H. (1898) *History of England under Henry the Fourth*, Vol. 4, London.

Yardley, E. (1927) *Menevia Sacra*, ed. F. Green, London.

Zurita, G. (1579) *Los cinco libros primeros de la Segunda parte de los Anales de la Corona de Aragon*, Saragossa.

Maps

Map 1   England and Wales in the later fourteenth century

Map 2   Some lordships of John of Gaunt

Map 3   The Low Countries and Burgundy in the later fourteenth century

Map 4   *The Iberian Peninsula in the later fourteenth century*

Calais • St Omer

PICARDY

Cherbourg
• Amiens
Harfleur
Laon
Rouen •
NORMANDY   Paris   Reims

St Malo   *CHAMPAGNE*

Brest

BRITTANY   *MAINE*   Chartres   Troyes

Orléans

ANJOU   Avallon
Nantes   Dijon
BERRY
POITOU   Moulins
La Roche Sur Yon
Poitiers   *BURGUNDY*
Niort   *BOURBONNAIS*
La Rochelle   *MARCHE*
Limoges
Saintes   *LIMOUSIN*   Lyons
Tulle *AUVERGNE*

Perigueux
Bergerac
Bordeaux

GASCONY   Avignon
Agen   *PROVENCE*
Dax
Bayonne Orthez
BEARN Lourdes Toulouse
FOIX

N

Map 5   France in the later fourteenth century

404

Genealogical Tables

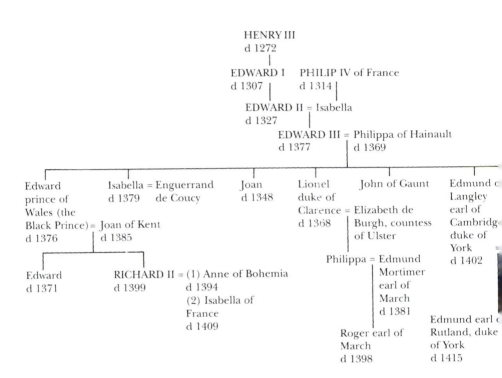

HENRY III
d 1272

EDWARD I   PHILIP IV of France
d 1307   d 1314

EDWARD II = Isabella
d 1327

EDWARD III = Philippa of Hainault
d 1377   d 1369

Edward   Isabella = Enguerrand   Joan   Lionel   John of Gaunt   Edmund c
prince of   d 1379   de Coucy   d 1348   duke of   Langley
Wales (the   Clarence = Elizabeth de   earl of
Black Prince) = Joan of Kent   d 1368   Burgh, countess   Cambridg
d 1376   d 1385   of Ulster   duke of
                                                                                          York
                                                       Philippa = Edmund   d 1402
Edward   RICHARD II = (1) Anne of Bohemia   Mortimer
d 1371   d 1399   d 1394   earl of
                             (2) Isabella of   March
                             France   d 1381
                             d 1409   Edmund earl c
                                                       Roger earl of   Rutland, duke
                                                       March   of York
                                                       d 1398   d 1415

Table 1   *The descent and family of Edward III*

Mary = John de Montfort   Margaret = John Hastings   Thomas of Woodstock
d 1361 duke of   d 1361   earl of Pembroke   earl of Buckingham,
        Brittany   d 1375   duke of Gloucester = Eleanor
                                                d 1397   de Bohun

abel of Castile   d 1399
1392

                                                      Humphrey
                                                      d 1399

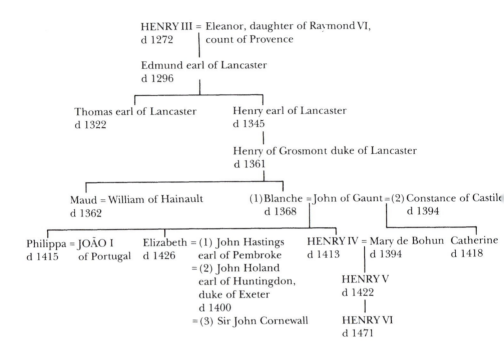

HENRY III = Eleanor, daughter of Raymond VI,
d 1272 | count of Provence

Edmund earl of Lancaster
d 1296

Thomas earl of Lancaster
d 1322

Henry earl of Lancaster
d 1345

Henry of Grosmont duke of Lancaster
d 1361

Maud = William of Hainault
d 1362

(1)Blanche = John of Gaunt = (2) Constance of Castile
d 1368   d 1394

Philippa = JOÃO I
d 1415   of Portugal

Elizabeth = (1) John Hastings
d 1426   earl of Pembroke
    = (2) John Holand
    earl of Huntingdon,
    duke of Exeter
    d 1400
    = (3) Sir John Cornewall

HENRY IV = Mary de Bohun
d 1413   d 1394

HENRY V
d 1422

HENRY VI
d 1471

Catherine
d 1418

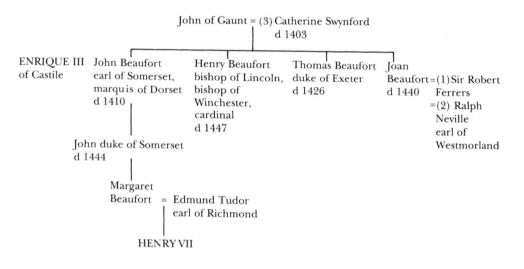

Table 2   *The House of Lancaster*

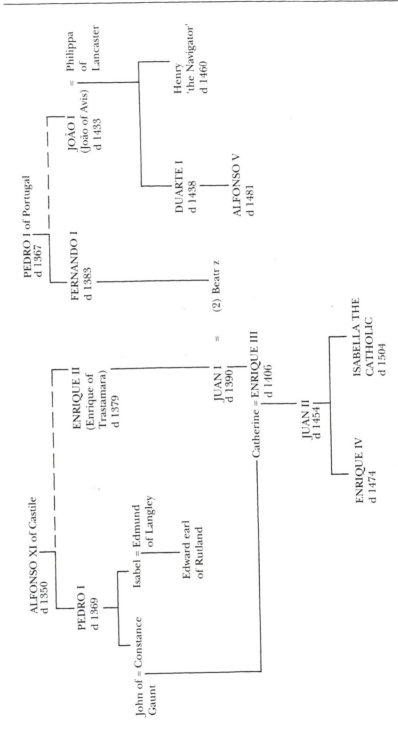

Table 3   The royal houses of Castile and Portugal

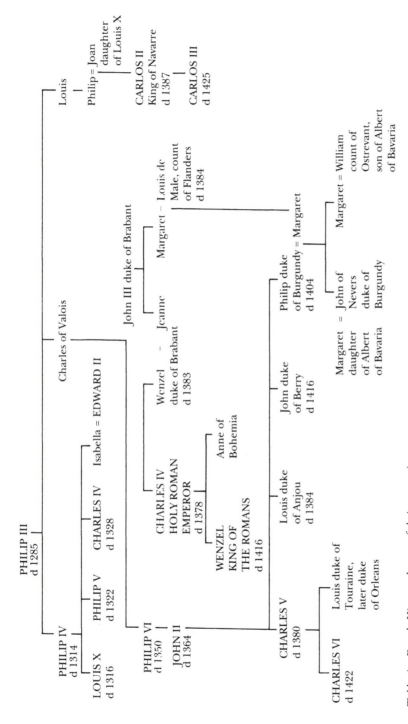

Table 4 French Kings and some of their connections

411

Index

Printed in the USA/Agawam, MA
December 26, 2013

583414.021